Reflecting the Mind

Reflecting the Mind

Indexicality and Quasi-Indexicality

EROS CORAZZA

CLARENDON PRESS · OXFORD

Great Clarendon Street, Oxford OX2 6DP

Oxford University Press is a department of the University of Oxford.
It furthers the University's objective of excellence in research, scholarship,
and education by publishing worldwide in

Oxford New York

Auckland Bangkok Buenos Aires Cape Town Chennai
Dar es Salaam Delhi Hong Kong Istanbul Karachi Kolkata
Kuala Lumpur Madrid Melbourne Mexico City Mumbai Nairobi
São Paulo Shanghai Taipei Tokyo Toronto

Oxford is a registered trade mark of Oxford University Press
in the UK and in certain other countries

Published in the United States
by Oxford University Press Inc., New York

© Eros Corazza 2004

The moral rights of the author have been asserted
Database right Oxford University Press (maker)

First published 2004

All rights reserved. No part of this publication may be reproduced,
stored in a retrieval system, or transmitted, in any form or by any means,
without the prior permission in writing of Oxford University Press,
or as expressly permitted by law, or under terms agreed with the appropriate
reprographics rights organization. Enquiries concerning reproduction
outside the scope of the above should be sent to the Rights Department,
Oxford University Press, at the address above

You must not circulate this book in any other binding or cover
and you must impose this same condition on any acquirer

British Library Cataloguing in Publication Data
Data available

Library of Congress Cataloging in Publication Data
Data available

ISBN 0–19–927018–X

1 3 5 7 9 10 8 6 4 2

Typeset by Newgen Imaging Systems (P) Ltd., Chennai, India
Printed in Great Britain
on acid-free paper by
Biddles Ltd, King's Lynn, Norfolk

TO MY FAMILY

Preface

I began thinking about indexicality and related issues in 1988 when, as a Fulbright student, I met Hector-Neri Castañeda. Castañeda has been a constant inspiration. He taught me that one cannot fully appreciate the phenomenon of indexicality if one does not also focus on quasi-indexicality. It took me a moment to appreciate this idea, but I am now convinced that he was right. I hope that I am capable of showing why in what follows. I like to remember the lively discussions I had with Castañeda and I often wonder what he would think about my direct-reference approach to indexicality and quasi-indexicality and what illuminating criticisms he would come out with.

My Wittgensteinian influence comes from my undergraduate studies at the University of Geneva, where I had the opportunity to be taught by Jacques Bouveresse. Whilst there, I benefited from being taught by (and having discussions with) Curzio Chiesa, Richard Glauser, Jean-Pierre Leyvraz, and Kevin Mulligan. Bouveresse and Mulligan also supervised my Ph.D. dissertation, which constituted the basis of my *Référence, contexte et attitude* book published in 1995 by Vrin-Bellarmin. I also began a long-term friendship with Jérôme Dokic in Geneva, with whom I have since spent a great deal of time discussing philosophy and other, more important things.

During my Ph.D. period I had the chance to meet John Perry. His influence and friendship crystallized between 1992 and 1995 when, as a post.-doc., I visited CSLI. My CSLI experience has been positive in many ways. As well as meeting some very bright people I found myself in a friendly atmosphere. I also owe the title of this book to Perry: it was his suggestion that I should write a monograph on quasi-indexicality and that I should call it *Reflecting the Mind*, which triggered the writing of this book. It will be obvious to anyone who knows Perry's work that his influence on me has been both profound and extensive.

During my stay in California, I also came to know Stefano Predelli and Howard Wettstein. The discussion and correspondence I have had with both of them on indexicality and related topics since then has been inspiring. Stefano Predelli, Jérôme Dokic, and Mark Whitsey read a penultimate version of this book and gave me many valuable comments. Discussion and correspondence with François Recanati has also been influential over the last few years. Pierre Jacob, Elisabeth Pacherie, and Joëlle Proust have been instrumental in directing me to relevant studies in the cognitive sciences. The friendly atmosphere and intellectual surroundings of the Jean-Nicod Institute, which I have had the chance to visit several times over the last few years, has always been refreshing and inspirational. I can hardly imagine a place where one's research can be conducted in such a friendly and intellectually challenging atmosphere.

Many other people have provided me with comments and suggestions during the preparation and writing of this book and I am sure I have forgotten many of them, but I will nonetheless supply the following list of people whom I wish to thank: F. Adams, J. Almog, K. Bach, S. Barker, J. Biro, R. Black, D. Bodrozic, E. Borg, B. Carr, R. Carston, R. Casati, M. Clark, F. Correia, G. Currie, K. Donnellan, F. Dretzke, W. Fish, J. Ganeri, J. Gorvett, N. Jones, D. Kaplan, P. Keller, J. Ketland, J. King, B. Kirk, E. LePore, B. Loar, D. Marconi, G. Marti, A. Mercier, S. Mumford, P. Noordhof, A. Palma, J. Pelletier, M. Popa, N. Salmon, G. Segal, G.-F. Soldati, C. Swain, R. Vallée, A. Voltolini, and T. Wilkerson.

I should also mention the audiences to whom previous versions of the papers which form the basis of several chapters were presented during the last six or seven years. Comments by referees for journals to which these papers were submitted have also been valuable. Some of the material has also been presented in my philosophy of language class at the University of Nottingham in 2001–2 and in a twenty-four-hour seminar I conducted at the University of Fribourg in Spring 2003—Gian Franco Soldati and Davor Bodrozic merit a special mention for their incisive and friendly comments during that seminar. During my teaching experience I have had the chance to encounter many bright students whose questions have helped in clarifying many points and ideas. Needless to say, the remaining mistakes are entirely my responsibility.

I would also like to thank the French Research Ministry for awarding me a fellowship (No. 303553L), which allowed me to spend June and July 2001 at the Institute Jean-Nicod in Paris. The AHRB (Arts and Humanities Research Board) Research Leave Scheme should also be thanked, for it permitted me to have a sabbatical during the Autumn Semester 2002–3, during which most of the manuscript was put together.

The people at Oxford University Press have been extremely encouraging, and I would particularly like to thank Peter Momtchiloff and Rebecca Bryant for their support during the preparation of this book. Rowena Anketell made a wonderful job of copy-editing the typescript. The comments from two Oxford UP referees (and from the four referees from the two other publishers to which this manuscript was also submitted) have also been useful.

Last, but not least, I should thank my family for their unconditional support and for constantly reminding me that indexicality, in particular, and philosophy, in general, are not the most important things in the world or in one's life. It is to them that I dedicate this book.

Let me add a methodological note. In writing this book, I did my best to avoid formal apparatus. This for two main reasons. First, I sometimes have the feeling that formalisms tend to mask the basic philosophical problems in philosophy of language and mind. This is not to deny, of course, that formal techniques have their place in philosophical inquiry and, in particular, when investigating linguistic phenomena. Formulas can be useful in helping us to clarify many issues, such as, for instance, binding, logical form, attitude ascriptions, etc. Secondly, I have tried to avoid formal apparatus in the hope that the book may be accessible to non-specialist readers.

Acknowledgments

Several of the following chapters are based on material which has been published previously. The material which appears here, however, does not fully and accurately reproduce what has been published elsewhere; many changes and many additions have been made. I thank the editors and the publishers concerned for their permission to reprint and reuse the relevant material.

Chapter 1, *Language and Context*. This chapter is based on a talk "Reference and Competence" presented at a conference in honor of David Kaplan, *David Kaplan's Contribution to Philosophy*, in San Marino, May 2001. The paper for the talk has been reviewed and expanded. It has been published under the title: 'Kinds of Contexts: A Wittgensteinian Approach to Proper Names and Indexicals', *Philosophical Investigation*, 27 (2004), 158–88. Reused with kind permission from the editor and from Blackwell Publications.

Chapter 2, *Thought and Context*. The first part is based on 'Thinking the Unthinkable: An Excursion into Z-land', in M. O'Rourke & C. Washington (eds.), *Situating Semantics: Essays on the Philosophy of John Perry* (Cambridge, Mass.: MIT Publications, forthcoming). Reused with kind permission from the editors and MIT press.

Chapter 3, *A Multiple-Propositions Approach*. The first part is based on 'Description-Names', *Journal of Philosophical Logic*. 31 (2002), 313–25. Reused with kind permission from the editor and from Kluwer Academic Publishers. The second part is based on ' "She" and "He": Politically Correct Pronouns', *Philosophical Studies*, 111 (2003), 173–96. Reused with kind permission from the editor and Kluwer Academic Publishers.

Chapter 4, *Demonstrative, Pure Indexicals, and Essential Indexicals*. The first part is based on 'Temporal Indexicals and Temporal Terms', *Synthese*, 130 (2002), 441–60. Reused with kind permission from Kluwer Academic Publishers. The second part is based on 'On the Alleged Ambiguity of "Now" and "Here" ' *Synthese*, 138 (2004), 289–313. Reused with kind permission from the editor and Kluwer Academic Publishers.

Chapter 5, *The First-Person Pronoun*. The first part is based on 'Understanding "I": A Wittgensteinian Perspective', *Wittgenstein Studies*, 2 (2001), 23–33. Reused with kind permission from the editor and Peter Lang Publishing Group. The second part is based on a paper co-written with William Fish and Jonathan Gorvett, 'Who is I?'. *Philosophical Studies*, 107 (2002), 1–21. I thank William Fish and Jonathan Gorvett for allowing me to use it. Reused with kind permission from the editor and Kluwer Academic Publishers.

Chapter 6, *Perspectival Thoughts and Psychological Explanation*. It is based on 'Perspectival Thoughts and Psychological Generalizations'. *Dialectica*, 48 (1994), 307–36. Reused with kind permission from the editor. The original paper has been considerably expanded.

Chapter 7, *Empathy, Imagination, and Reports*. It is based on 'Reports and Imagination', *Protosociology: Reported Speech and Radical Interpretation*, 17 (2002), 78–98. Reused with kind permission from the editor. The original paper has been considerably expanded and modified.

Chapter 8, *Anaphora, Logophoricity, and Quasi-Indexicality*. The first part is based on a talk, 'Essential Indexicals and Quasi-Indicators', presented at the *Semantics, Pragmatics, and Rhetoric Conference* in San Sebastián, November 2001. Forthcoming in *Journal of Semantics*.

Chapter 9, *Quasi-Indexicality and Puzzling Reports*. This chapter is a development of some material presented in chapter 5 of *Référence, contexte, et attitudes* (Paris/Montréal, 1995: Vrin-Bellarmin) and ' "She*": Pragmatically Imparted or Semantically Encoded?', in F. Orilia & W. Rapaport (eds.), *Thought, Language, and Ontology—Essays in Memory of Hector-Neri Castañeda* (Dordrecht: Kluwer Academic Publisher), 217–34. Major changes have been made: the views defended here bear only a slight resemblance to the ones defended here.

Contents

Introduction 1
   1. Context-Sensitivity 2
   2. The Semantics/Pragmatics Divide 7
   3. Situational Contextualism 14
   4. Structure of the Book 28

Chapter 1: Language and Context 31
   1. Words as Tools 32
   2. Anchored *vs.* Unanchored Information 33
   3. Pure Indexicals *vs.* Demonstratives 35
   4. Indexicals *vs.* Proper Names 38
   5. Types of Context 54
   6. Identity Statements 58
   7. Indexicals and Cognitive Significance 63

Chapter 2: Thought and Context 67
   1. Varieties of Implicitness 68
   2. Varieties of Context-Exploitation 74
   3. A Case Study: Meteorological Verbs 75
   4. Implicit Arguments and Representation 80
   5. Understanding Proper Names *vs.* Understanding Indexicals . 89
   6. Two Types of Singular Thoughts 92

Chapter 3: A Multiple-Proposition Approach 97
   1. A Case Study: Description-Names 98
   2. Definite Descriptions 100
   3. Description-Names 103
   4. Dname and Dthat 107
   5. Pronouns and Complex Demonstratives 110
   6. Complex Demonstratives *qua* Definite Descriptions 112
   7. The Character Approach to Complex Demonstratives 113
   8. Complex Demonstratives *qua* Articulated Terms 114
   9. A Naïve, Politically Correct, Theory of Pronouns 115

10.	Complex Demonstratives *qua* 'Dthat'-Terms and Anaphora	125
11.	Evading Some Objections	129

Chapter 4: Demonstratives, Pure Indexicals, and Essential Indexicals — 135

1.	The Background: Indexical Identification	136
2.	Demonstratives and Pure Indexicals	138
3.	Temporal Indexicals and Temporal Terms	140
4.	Temporal Indexicals *qua* Singular Terms	147
5.	The Data and the Multiple Characters Thesis	151
6.	The Data and the Fixed Character Thesis	156
7.	Some Advantages of the Fixed Character Thesis over the Multiple Characters Thesis	171

Chapter 5: The First-Person Pronoun — 174

1.	The (De)Construction of the Self	175
2.	The Meaning of 'I'	178
3.	Does 'I' Refer?	180
4.	Answering Machines and Other Devices	187
5.	On the Referent of 'I'	190
6.	An Intentionalist Proposal	192
7.	An Anti-Intentionalist Solution	195
8.	Issues Arising	198

Chapter 6: Perspectival Thoughts and Psychological Explanation — 203

1.	Some Desiderata	204
2.	Object-Dependent Thoughts	206
3.	Thoughts in Context	213
4.	Perspectival Thoughts	218
5.	Perceptual Thoughts	222
6.	Psychological Generalizations	230
7.	Answering an Objection	232

Chapter 7: Empathy, Imagination, and Reports — 237

1.	The Background: Imagination	238
2.	Empathy and the Attribution of Sensations	239
3.	Further Empirical Evidence: The Case from Autism	246

4. Sentences *qua* Thought Classifiers 256
  5. Reports and Mental Representations 262
  6. Reports and Types of Mental States 263
  7. Some Further Alleged Puzzles 271
  8. Bound to Unfaithfulness 273

Chapter 8: Anaphora, Logophoricity, and
           Quasi-Indexicality 275
  1. *De Se* Thoughts 276
  2. In Search of Quasi-Indicators 279
  3. Quasi-Indicators, Coindexation, and Dependence 286
  4. Quasi-Indicators, Logophoric Pronouns, and Anaphora 290
  5. Quasi-Indicators and the Unanalyzability Thesis 301
  6. Analyzing 'Herself' 302
  7. Quasi-Indicators *qua* Attributive Anaphors 304

Chapter 9: Quasi-Indexicality and Puzzling Reports 308
  1. Quasi-Indicators: Pragmatics or Semantics? 309
  2. *De Se* Reports 312
  3. The Dual Feature of 'That'-Clauses 315
  4. The Logical Form of Reports 316
  5. *n*-Acceptance, Translation, and Twin-Earth 321
  6. *De Re*, *De Dicto*, *De Se* 328
  7. Propositional Opacity and Propositional Transparency 330
  8. Getting the Inferences Right 335
  9. Logical Validity and Psychological Validity 339

Conclusion 347
Bibliography 351
Index of Names 363
Index of Subjects 366

The conservative lives life in the first person singular—I, ME, MINE—and that is the pronoun-centric language you must speak if you are to be heard.

(Michael Moore 2003: 187)

Introduction

> Every sign *by itself* seems dead. *What* gives it life?—In use it is *alive*. Is life breathed into it there?—Or is *use* its life?
>
> (Wittgenstein, *PI*: § 432)

> Even the most elementary notions, such as *nameable thing*, crucially involve such intricate notions as human agency. What we take as objects, how we refer to them and describe them, and the array of properties with which we invest them, depend on their place in a matrix of human actions, interests, and intent in respects that lie far outside the potential range of naturalistic inquiry.
>
> (Chomsky 2000: 21)

This is a book about small words. Amongst them, the smallest (and probably the most important) is 'I' and its attributive counterpart 's/he (her/himself)'. We also have 'she', 'this', 'today', 'here', and the like. These words designate something relative to the context in which they are used. If we change the context (the speaker, the time, and the location) in which they are uttered, we are likely to end up with a different referent. If two distinct people say 'I', for instance, they inevitably refer to two different people (i.e. themselves). These context-sensitive words have been termed *indexicals* (following Peirce) and the phenomenon involved with the use of indexicals is known as *indexicality*.

Indexicals caught the interest of those working within the boundaries of cognitive science for several reasons. They play crucial roles when dealing with such puzzling concepts as the nature of the self, the nature of perception, the nature of time, social interaction, psychological pathologies, psychological development, and other related issues. I believe that clear comprehension of these topics cannot be achieved without a good understanding of the way in which indexicals work, both in our linguistic interchanges and in our cognitive activities.

In this book, my first aim is to provide a plausible picture concerning the way in which indexicals work in linguistic interchanges and thoughtful episodes and to stress their linguistic and psychological importance. In so doing I shall also show how they differ from other linguistic expressions and why they are, to some extent, more basic and psychologically important.

My second aim is to provide a reasonable story to explain how, from a third-person perspective, we attribute the use of an indexical to another, i.e. how we are able to capture another's mental attitude. To be more precise, how we are able to capture another's indexical thought. To attribute indexical reference (or an indexical thought) to someone, we appeal to the phenomenon of *quasi-indexicality*, i.e. we employ expressions such as 'she (herself)', 'then', 'there'. To represent Jane saying, "I am prosperous", for example, we can use what Castañeda termed *quasi-indicators* and end up with a report of the form "Jane said that *she (herself)* is prosperous". Quasi-indicators play such an important role in such attributions that they have a *cognitive* primacy over other mechanisms of reference, or so I am going to argue.

The underlying idea and *fil rouge* of this book is that quasi-indexicality is amongst the most significant and extraordinary phenomena in the philosophy of language and mind. The phenomenon of quasi-indexicality will be examined against the basis of logophoricity. I show how the use of quasi-indicators mirrors the use of logophoric pronouns, i.e. those pronouns which in certain languages (mostly West African languages) are used to report and represent the attributee's perspective (e.g. her feelings, thoughts, or states of consciousness). This parallel helps to stress how predicates of propositional attitudes (e.g. to believe, wish, say, desire, and the like) have more structure in their arguments than has usually been thought. In particular, the structure of reportive predicates extends beyond the propositional content of their arguments. Moreover, a careful investigation of this phenomenon does not merely help us to understand how we attribute indexical references to other people. It also helps us to understand the intriguing and philosophically fundamental issues of self-knowledge, perception of others as conscious beings, successful communicative interaction, etc.

1. Context-Sensitivity

Amongst the expressions which may switch reference with a change in context, we have: personal pronouns ('my', 'you', 'she', 'his', 'we', . . .), demonstrative pronouns ('this', 'that'), complex demonstratives ('this table', 'that woman near the window', . . .), adverbs ('today', 'yesterday', 'now', 'here', 'near', . . .), possessive pronouns ('my pen', 'their house', 'your birthday', . . .), adjectives ('actual' in 'the *actual* president', 'present' in 'the *present* circumstance', 'local' in 'Jon's *local* pub', 'distant' in 'a *distant* town', ...), nouns ('foreigner', 'enemy', 'neighbor', ...). The reference of some noun phrases ('Monday', 'December', 'Aristotle', 'Janet', 'Rome', ...) also seems to depend on the context in which they occur. I shall show, however, how the latter differ from indexicals. In so doing, I shall claim that they cannot be reduced to indexicals. All these expressions are, in some way or another, context-sensitive. I shall mainly concentrate on context-sensitive expressions used to single out an object of discourse. That is to say, on the noun phrases (NPs) that are used to select a specific individual, a specific group of individuals, a specific place(s) or time(s) (e.g. "*This* is tasty", "*I* am happy", "Are *these men* rich?", "*Today* is sunny", "It is warm *here*", "*Now you* must leave", etc.). These NPs contribute the referent(s) in the proposition expressed. As such they are generally characterized as *singular* terms. Following the received, direct reference, view (see in particular Kaplan 1977 and Perry 1977) utterances containing indexicals express singular propositions, i.e. propositions whose constituents are the referents referred to by the indexicals. As such, indexicals are usually characterized as expressions whose interpretation requires the identification of some element of the utterance context, as stipulated by their linguistic meaning. Thus an utterance of "I am tired" expresses a proposition containing as constituents the referent of the first-person pronoun and one understands it insofar as one comes to know who the referent of 'I' is. The linguistic meaning governing the use of the indexical—such as "the agent of the utterance" *qua* meaning of 'I', "the day of the utterance" *qua* meaning of 'today'—does not enter as a constituent of the proposition expressed. The linguistic meaning (or *character*, to use Kaplan's famous label) merely helps in fixing the reference:

What is common to the words or usages in which I am interested in is that the referent is dependent on the context of use and that the meaning of the word provides a rule which determines the referent in terms of certain aspects of the context. The term I now favor for these words is 'indexicals'. (Kaplan [1977] 1989: 490)

If we were to characterize indexicals along this line, adjectives such as 'local', 'distant', 'actual'—not to mention count nouns like '(a) foreigner', '(an) enemy', '(an) outsider', '(a) colleague'—would not fall into the same category, for they do not contribute a referent to the proposition expressed. Yet they are, undeniably, context-sensitive expressions. 'Local', 'foreign', and 'native' in "A *local* bar is promoting *foreign* wine", "A *foreign* forward joined our *local* team", "A *native* speaker should correct your essay" do not contribute a specific individual or individuals to the proposition expressed. As such they are not singular terms. It should be evident that context-sensitivity does not merely concern singular terms. It may be worth distinguishing between indexicals *qua* singular terms contributing the

4 Introduction

referent(s) into the proposition expressed and *contextuals qua* expressions which, though context-sensitive, are not singular terms and, thus, do not contribute in expressing a singular proposition. The picture which seems to emerge turns out to be more complicated than we first thought.

Proper names also contribute individuals into the proposition expressed. As such they are singular terms as well. Yet they are not indexicals, or so I shall argue in Chapter 1.[1] Nouns like 'Monday', 'February', and the like also seem to contribute specific individuals in the proposition expressed. I shall claim, though, that they must be viewed as count nouns, i.e. as nouns like 'lemon', 'frog', and 'table'. As such they can be used to build singular terms. This happens when they are coupled with an indexical expression such as 'this', 'next', 'last' and contribute in forming *complex* demonstratives of the form 'next week', 'last Saturday', 'next Christmas'. This peculiarity parallels the way count nouns can participate in building complex demonstratives such as 'these lemons', 'that table', 'this pen'.

As a general criterion distinguishing indexical and contextual expressions, on the one side, from proper names on the other side, we can say that an indexical NP can, in principle, work as an anaphoric pronoun, while a proper name can never be anaphoric on another NP. Indexical and contextual expressions can be used either *deictically* or *anaphorically*. The distinction can be roughly spelled out as follows: in communication the speaker uses an expression in a deictic way in order to direct her audience's attention to an item to which no previous attention has been directed. That is, one uses an expression deictically in order to select a new item of discourse.[2] On the other hand, anaphoric uses tend to draw the audience's attention to an item previously mentioned in the discourse or previously raised to salience by a stretch of discourse.

Seen from a psychological perspective every anaphoric use of deictic words presupposes one thing: that the sender and the receiver *have the flow of speech in front of them* and can reach ahead and back to its parts. (Bühler 1934/1990: 122/138)

To stress this difference, consider the following:

(1) Do you know someone who could buy my car?
     She [pointing to Mary] could buy *it*.

In this discourse situation 'she' is used deictically, for it is used to direct the audience's attention to someone present in the context of the utterance, Mary.

---

[1] "Deictic words do not need the symbolic field of language to make their full and complete contribution; but they do need the deictic field and determination from case to case by the deictic field, or . . . determination by perceptual factors of a given speech situation" (Bühler 1934/1990: 119/135). For an account of Bühler's theory of language and how it compares with Wittgenstein's, see Mulligan (1997*a*).

[2] This characterization may not be accurate in the case of the first-person pronoun for in a stretch of discourse one can use 'I' several times without it being anaphoric on previous uses.

Mary has not previously been raised to salience or mentioned in the discourse. 'It', on the other hand, is used anaphorically insofar as it draws the audience's attention to an item previously mentioned by another NP, 'my car':

Anaphora presupposes that the referent should already have its place in the universe-of-discourse. Deixis does not; indeed, deixis is one of the principal means open to us of putting entities into the universe-of-discourse so that we can refer to them subsequently. (Lyons 1977: 673)

An expression used anaphorically inherits its value from another expression. It goes without saying, however, that in some cases anaphoric uses do not inherit their reference from another NP. This is particularly evident when a pronoun is anaphoric on a quantified NP.[3] In

(2) Every girl believes that, sooner or later, *she* will find *her* lover

'she' and 'her' are anaphoric on 'every girl'. Since they are anaphoric on a quantified expression they cannot be said to inherit their reference from it, for a quantified expression is not a referential expression, i.e. is not a noun phrase singling out a specific object of discourse and contributing an individual into the proposition expressed. In (2) 'she' and 'her' work like the bound variables of predicate logic (e.g. 'x' in "$\exists x(Fx)$" or "$\forall x(Fx \rightarrow Gx)$").[4] Contextuals as well can work both in an anaphoric way and as bound variables:

(3) a. Jon saw the *local* philosophers
 b. Jon has just returned from Paris where he met the *local* philosophers
 c. In every city where Jon spends more than a week he usually meets the *local* philosophers

In (3a) 'local' works like a free variable receiving a deictic interpretation, while in (3b) it works as an anaphoric pronoun suggesting that Jon meet the philosophers inhabiting Paris. In this interpretation 'local' gets interpreted somewhat along 'local relative to Paris'. In (3c) 'local' works like a bound variable, i.e. it is bound by the quantified NP 'in every city where Jon spends more than a week'. As we shall see in Chapter 2 the best way to understand contextuals like 'local' is to treat them as relational predicates with an implicit argument. The latter triggers the contextual interpretation. Descriptions can sometimes be used anaphorically as well:

(4) a. Jon promised to come but *the idiot* missed the train

---

[3] An anaphor can also inherit its value from a verb phrase, VP, such as 'so' in "Jane has been jogging and *so* did Ivan", where 'so' is anaphoric on the VP 'has been jogging'.

[4] Demonstratives can be used as bound variables as well: "Every student brought a can of beer to the party and drank *that* instead of the wine that Jane bought"; "Every professor read five essays and presented *these* to the faculty board". Complex demonstratives can be bound by a quantifier as well: "Every student brought a can of beer to the party and drank *that can of beer* instead of the cocktail prepared by Jane".

6   Introduction

To be precise, the description *per se* is not anaphoric. When a description like 'the idiot' in (4a) gets the anaphoric reading it suggests the presence of a hidden variable or anaphoric pronoun. Thus (4a) would get interpreted along:

(4) b. Jon promised to come but *he* (*the idiot*) missed the train[5]

where the anaphoric link is granted by 'he'.

Proper names do not and cannot work as anaphoric pronouns insofar as the reference of a proper name is always *in*dependent of another NP. In

(5) Jon has just bought a new car, but *Jon* wants to have a new bike as well

the reference of the second occurrence of 'Jon', though coreferential with the first occurrence, is not dependent on it. To be sure, an utterance like (5) is odd because we usually use an anaphor for coreference and a name for noncoreference. When we use a name for coreference as in (5) we do so against the default reading. This is further evidence in favor of the thesis that names cannot be use anaphorically.

One could think that indexicals such as 'now', 'here', and 'I' (the so-called pure indexicals) could not be anaphoric either. In Chapter 4, however, I shall show how they can work in an anaphoric way. To anticipate, the basic idea is that when 'now' and 'here' are not used as indexicals picking out the time and location of the utterance, they work in an anaphoric way. As such they inherit their reference from another NP. To illustrate this feature consider:

(6) a. In June 1942 Jane visited Paris, *now* under SS occupation
     b. Jon spent last year in Paris. *Here* he found a new mistress

In (6a) and (6b) 'now' and 'here' do not pick out the time of the utterance but refer respectively to June 1942 and Paris. In this situation their reference is inherited from another NP.[6] Even in the case of the first-person pronoun we can find utterances where it works as an anaphoric pronoun (to be precise as a quasi-indicator). It would be the case of the second occurrence of 'I' in

(7) a. I think that *I* am rich

---

[5] Furthermore, descriptions, like plural pronouns, can also be viewed as e-type pronouns (see Evans 1977):

(4) c. Jane bought some donkeys and Igor vaccinated *them*
     d. Some of the students promised to come but *the idiots* missed the train

In (4c) and (4d) 'them' and 'the idiots' are unbound. The bound reading would deliver the wrong truth-conditions insofar as it would suggest that Igor vaccinated some of the donkeys and that some of the students missed the train. The intuitive and natural reading suggests that Igor vaccinated all the donkeys that Jane bought and that all the students who promised to come missed the train. These plurals are best viewed as unbound anaphors. I shall discuss further unbound anaphora in Ch. 8, below.

[6] We shall also see how an indexical can be anaphoric on a tacit initiator. An example is 'there' in the following telephone exchange between A in Rome and B in Paris: A: "It is sunny", B: "I would like to be there". In this exchange, 'there' can be viewed as coreferential with Rome, even though A did not explicitly mention it. A tacitly referred to Rome, hence the notion of tacit initiator.

As we shall see in Chapter 8, a self-attribution like this should be understood similarly to an attribution like:

(7) b. Jane thinks that *she herself* is rich

where 'she herself' is a quasi-indicator anaphoric on 'Jane'. If we focus on the anaphoric/deictic distinction we can, in principle, have four possibilities (see Corblin 1995: 13–14): (i) terms which can be used both deictically and anaphorically, (ii) terms which can be used deictically but cannot be used anaphorically, (iii) terms which cannot be used deictically but can be used anaphorically, and (iv) terms which can be used neither deictically nor anaphorically. As a rough approximation we can propose the following classification:

	Deictic	Anaphoric
Indexicals	+	+
??[7]	+	−
Logophoric Pronouns, Quasi-Indicators, Contextuals, Descriptions	−	+
Proper Names	−	−

2. The Semantics/Pragmatics Divide

A few words may be appropriate to set out the background on which the picture I propose rests. The general framework I have in mind is Wittgenstein-inspired. At the beginning of analytic philosophy (at least if Dummett 1993 is right in suggesting that it began with Frege), philosophers were concerned with language *qua* formal system. Natural language was conceived at best as a trap for philosophers and logicians:

Instead of following grammar blindly, the logician ought rather to see his task as that of freeing us from the fetters of language. For however true it is that thinking, at least in its highest forms, was only made possible by means of language, we have nevertheless to take great care not to become dependent on language; for very many of the mistakes that occur in reasoning have their source in the logical imperfections of language. (Frege [1897] 1979: 143)

Among the "traps" or logical imperfections of natural language one can quote structural ambiguity (e.g. "Visiting relatives can be boring", meaning either that

---

[7] The French 'voici' may be a candidate. In "Jean a écrit un roman et voici son œuvre", 'voici' cannot be anaphoric on 'un roman'. 'Ceci', like 'this', on the other hand, can be anaphoric; in "Jean a écrit un roman et *ceci* est son œuvre"/"Jean wrote a novel and *this* is his masterpiece", 'ceci' and 'this' are anaphoric on 'un roman' and 'a novel'.

to visit relatives can be boring or that the visit of relatives can be boring; "Jane bought two dogs and cats" meaning either that Jane bought two dogs and two cats or that Jane bought two dogs and an unspecified number of cats; "Mary saw Jon with binoculars" meaning either that she used binoculars to look at Jon or that she saw Jon carrying binoculars), semantic ambiguity (e.g. 'bank' *qua* financial institution or riverside, 'mistress' *qua* teacher or lover), polysemy (e.g. 'heavy' in "Jane's luggage is heavy" *vs.* "Jane has a heavy teaching load"), homonymy (e.g. 'Socrates' the teacher of Plato *vs.* 'Socrates' the Brazilian football player), etc.[8]

Last, but not least, the context-sensitivity of natural language was also seen as a burden the philosopher and logician must overcome:

[I] can use the words 'this man' to designate now this man, now that man. . . . The sentences of our everyday language leave a good deal to guesswork. It is the surrounding circumstances that enable us to make the right guess. The sentence I utter does not always contain everything that is necessary; a great deal has to be supplied by the context, by the gestures I make and the direction of my eyes. But a language that is intended for scientific employment must not leave anything to guesswork. (Frege [1914] 1979: 213)

If—inspired by Wittgenstein (and the ordinary-language philosophers)—we ignore Frege's worries and concentrate instead on natural language, context becomes a key notion. Actually, as soon as one focuses on everyday language then its context-sensitivity should be conceived as one of its *intrinsic* and possibly more important features. Frege is right in claiming that "sentences of our everyday language leave a good deal to guesswork". Indexicals and contextuals, as we just saw, are context-sensitive. Thus an utterance containing an indexical and/or a contextual must be understood within a given context. Actually, if one reads a piece of graffiti saying "I love you" one does not understand the message if one does not know who wrote it and to whom it is addressed. Yet a competent speaker can infer that the one who produced the graffiti is in love with the addressee. A similar story can be told about (incomplete) definite descriptions (e.g. 'the book', 'the car', 'the cat', . . .), not to mention indefinite descriptions (e.g. 'a man', 'a book', 'a cat', . . .). If we follow Russell, a sentence like "Fido is under the table" must be analyzed as: "there is at least one table; there is at most one table; and Fido is under it". Yet, this is not what one communicates in using a sentence like this; if it were, such sentences would inevitably be false inasmuch as there is more than a single table in the world. Moreover, if one says "It is raining", one is not saying that it is raining somewhere or other. To understand utterances of sentences like these, one must rely on context as well. Thus a plausible study of language and communication,

---

[8] But: "Where is it written that only naming words [i.e. no deictic words], conceptual signs, language symbols can facilitate the sort of intersubjective communication about things which is necessary in human life? Such an axiom is the *proton pseudos* of the logicians whom I have in mind" (Bühler 1934/1990: 105/120).

i.e. a reasonable study of how natural language works, cannot avoid taking on board its context-sensitivity.

In order to deal with all the variegated aspects of context entering the scene, philosophers and linguists often appeal to the semantics/pragmatics distinction. As a first approximation one could say that what is explicitly expressed by the utterance of a given sentence concerns semantics, while what is implicitly conveyed or imparted concerns pragmatics. This is particularly evident in the case of irony when one says something and communicates something else. One can utter, in an ironic mood, "Jon is so intelligent that he does not need to study" to mean that Jon is lazy. One can further focus on the distinction between a sentence and an utterance and argue that a sentence's literal meaning concerns semantics while an utterance of this very sentence concerns pragmatics. The former is a type, while the latter is an event which enters into existence and disappears:

> This [semantics/pragmatics] distinction has been drawn in various ways, but no matter how it is drawn the term 'semantic' has something to do with meaning and 'pragmatic' has something to do with use.... A semantic-pragmatic distinction can be drawn with respect to various things, such as ambiguities, implications, presuppositions, interpretations, knowledge, processes, rules, and principles. For me, it applies fundamentally to types of information. Semantic information is information encoded in what is uttered—these are stable linguistic features of the sentence—together with any extralinguistic information that provides (semantic) values to context-sensitive expressions in what is uttered. Pragmatic information is (extralinguistic) information that arises from an actual act of utterance. Whereas semantic information is encoded in what is uttered, pragmatic information is generated by, or at least made relevant by, the act of uttering it. (Bach 2001: 22)

A key notion in a theory of language and communication has been considered to be *what is said*. If we concentrate on this notion, the semantics/pragmatics distinction could be cashed out as follows: what a sentence (in context c) says concerns semantics, while what a speaker using a sentence (in context c) says concerns pragmatics. This characterization, though, is not quite felicitous. For, strictly speaking, a sentence does not say something. Only speakers using sentences say something. While one can ask "What did Jane say?" one cannot ask "What did sentence S say?" Correspondingly, one can report "Jane said that we will meet next Monday" while one cannot report "Sentence S said that we will meet next Monday". To escape this difficulty one can focus on the distinction between what is said and what is communicated:

- *What is Said (Semantics)* vs. *What is Communicated (Pragmatics)*
  (i) A speaker using a sentence (in context c) expresses proposition p and communicates proposition q and p may differ from q.
  (ii) The proposition expressed (p) concerns *semantics*, while the proposition communicated (q) concerns *pragmatics*.

We seem thus in a position to capture the idea that only agents say something. We distinguish, though, between what is said (expressed) and what is communicated. A speaker using a sentence performs different acts: she says something, but may also communicate something completely different (e.g. cases of irony, sarcasm, metaphor). One can also communicate something richer than what is said, e.g. in uttering "Ivan is too small" one can say that Ivan is too small and communicate that Ivan is too small to play basketball. This feature of language can also be stated in terms of utterances:

- *What is Conveyed (Semantics)* vs. *What is Imparted (Pragmatics)*
  (i) With an utterance *u* one conveys proposition *p* and imparts proposition *q*.
  (ii) What is conveyed is what is said and concerns *semantics*, while what is imparted is what is communicated and concerns *pragmatics*.

Some (e.g. Searle, Travis, Recanati, and relevance theorists such as Sperber & Wilson, and Carston), hold the view that an utterance is essentially underdetermined. We can characterize this view *Radical Contextualism*. Carston, for instance, defends a radical form of underdeterminacy and, as such, can be characterized as a radical contextualist:

I shall argue against the 'underdeterminacy as convenience' view [the view that a fully context-insensitive, complete, proposition or thought could always be supplied] and in favor of the essentialist view . . . I think that public-language systems are intrinsically underdetermining of complete (semantic evaluable) thoughts because they evolved on the back, as it were, of an already well-developed cognitive capacity for forming hypotheses about the thoughts and intentions of others on the basis of their behavior. (Carston 2002: 30)

An utterance can be underdetermined in two main ways. First, a given utterance can be underdetermined insofar as its truth-value may vary according to different discourse situations. Secondly an utterance can be underdetermined insofar as it is intrinsically incomplete and could be completed in infinitely many ways.

As an example of the first kind of underdeterminacy, which we can label the *discourse situation underdeterminacy*, we can consider:

(8) There is some beer in the fridge

uttered when there are a few drops of beer in the corner of the fridge. Let us first imagine the situation in which Jon is thirsty and looking for some beer. If Jane utters (8), she says something false. In another scenario, however, the very same utterance can be true. If Jon has just finished cleaning the fridge and Jane utters (8), she says something true. Yet the state of affairs in both situations is exactly the same: the very same fridge with the very same drops of beer in its corner. The moral seems to be that an utterance like (8) is intrinsically or essentially context-sensitive.[9] To capture this fact, Travis introduces the notion of *speaker-use sensitivity* (S-use) and suggests that all utterances must be viewed as being speaker-use sensitive:

If 'weight 79 kilos' or 'contains milk' refers to a family of S-use insensitive properties, the question is what the members of this family might be. (Travis 1989: 23)

For an item to have a semantic property P is for it to be so that a reasonable (informed) judge would take it to have P. (Travis 1989: 48)

If the reasonable judge reacts differently to a sentence *S* on different occasions, then *S* has semantic *S*-use sensitivity. As Searle puts it:

[I]n general the meaning of a sentence only has application (it only, for example, determines a set of truth-conditions) against a background of assumptions and practices that are not representable as a part of meaning. (Searle 1980: 221)

The literal meaning of a sentence only determines a set of truth-conditions given a set of background practices and assumptions. Relative to one set of practices and assumptions, a sentence may determine one set of truth-conditions; relative to another set of practices and assumptions, another set; and if some sets of assumptions and practices are given, the literal meaning of a sentence may not determine a definite set of truth-conditions at all. (Searle 1980: 227)

In favor of the second kind of underdeterminacy—which we can label *utterance underdeterminacy*—i.e. the fact that utterances are intrinsically incomplete, we can quote utterances like:

(9) a. Igor is not tall enough
    b. Jane is late
    c. Jon is too old

In principle, these utterances can be completed in infinitely many ways. Yet nothing in the utterance itself seems to suggest how the completion, expansion, or enrichment should occur. In other words, no element in the utterance directs us toward one particular completion or another, i.e. nothing seems to direct us toward a particular aspect of context. One could claim that 'tall', 'late', and 'old' trigger a completion. One can also claim (e.g. Stanley 2000; Stanley and Szabo 2000) that comparative adjectives involve an implicit comparison class and, like contextuals in general, must be understood as involving an argument place at the level of logical form ('small *relative to x*', 'tall *relative to x*', 'local *relative to x*', 'enemy *relative to x*'). The truth-conditions of utterances involving these expressions would also depend on the value of this implicit argument working as a kind of hidden

---

[9] "What words mean plays a role in fixing when they would be true; but not an exhaustive one. Meaning leaves room for variation in truth-conditions from one speaking to another" (Travis 1996: 451).

indexical. If one rejects this move (e.g. Bach 2000; Carston 2002; Recanati 2002) one is likely to endorse the view that when contextual expressions are involved we have a case of *free enrichment*, i.e. an enrichment which is not triggered by a syntactic element present either at the surface or logical form level of the utterance. Be that as it may, the result is that the truth-evaluable propositions which are expressed by underdetermined utterances like (9a–c) contain the enriched content, i.e. they are fully fledged truth-evaluable propositions.

Bach (1994), focusing on the distinction between what is said and what is communicated, defends the view that one does not express a fully fledged proposition with an underdetermined utterance. Instead, one expresses a propositional radical, i.e. a kind of subproposition. This propositional radical lacks a truth-value; it must be completed before it gets evaluated and becomes a fully fledged proposition. It is only the fully fledged proposition, which is the result of an enrichment process (which Bach calls an impli*ci*ture), that is communicated.[10] So far, all parties seem to agree that context helps in understanding the message conveyed.

One can, however, recognize that context plays this role and yet maintain that it does not contribute to the expression of a fully fledged *determinate* proposition. In other words, one can defend the view that the understanding of an underdetermined utterance does not rest on the grasping of a specific proposition and that the success of communication does not require the transmission of specific propositions and/or thoughts. To put it in a nutshell, contextual exploitation need not result in the formation and/or grasping of a specific proposition. We may understand each other insofar as we grasp *similar* propositions. The proposition that one's audience grasps may remain indetermined insofar as one can recognize the existence of *some* (enriched) proposition or other, which one need not be able to specify. For example, if one says "Jon is too old", one expresses the (minimal) proposition *that Jon is too old*. What one communicates, though, is a richer proposition that features information concerning what Jon is too old for (say, the proposition *that Jon is too old to play in the tournament*). One could also maintain that we merely communicate that some way or other of completing the proposition exists (i.e. we communicate some kind of existential message). I am not sure, though, that in this case we can still maintain that successful communication occurs. For, if what one understands is *that Jon is too old for something or other* we are unlikely to claim that one grasps the relevant message. At least we would not attribute to her full

---

[10] Bach (1994) argues that underdetermined utterances express a propositional matrix or radical. A propositional radical is truth-conditionally incomplete and must be enriched by an impli*ci*ture process. Impli*ci*ture differs from impli*ca*ture insofar as in the latter case one says and communicates one thing and further communicates something else. In the former case, one says something but communicates something richer. With impli*ci*ture, what is said (the propositional radical) is part of what is communicated. As such what is communicated is only implicit in what is explicitly expressed.

understanding of the message. Be that as it may, the proposition communicated need not be specified and, I shall show, can*not* be specified: it remains intrinsically indetermined. Slightly different propositions could do the job: the propositions *that Jon is too old to participate in this year's tournament, that Jon is too old to play in our tournament,* ... would all be good candidates. One grasps the message transmitted when one comes to entertain one of these propositions (of which there are, potentially, infinitely many). The communicative act is successful insofar as the speaker and hearer come to entertain a *similar* proposition. Moreover, the specific proposition and the thought communicated may "remain in the dark", i.e. neither the speaker nor the hearer need to conceptualize it. If someone uses an underdetermined utterance and we ask her to be more explicit, she can end up using many different, more rich and complete sentences and thus express different, though similar, propositions and entertain different thoughts. Similarly, if someone is asked what she meant by saying "Jon is too old", the reply might be: "I mean that Jon is too old to play in this competition", "I mean that Jon is too old to play in our tournament", "I mean that Jon is too old to play in this year's tennis tournament", etc. It goes without saying that all these potential enriched propositions have the same minimal proposition in common.[11]

In the case of indexicals the story is a bit different, for context must contribute in the expression of a specific proposition. As we have seen, an indexical's linguistic meaning directs us to some specific aspect of context, which ends up in the proposition expressed. In the case of indexicals, context contributes to the expression of the proposition. In the case of contextuals, context does not affect the minimal proposition expressed, even if it is likely to contribute to the understanding of the message transmitted and thus to the enrichment of the minimal proposition.

One can thus defend a minimalist position, i.e. the view that the constituents of the proposition expressed must be triggered by syntactic elements present at the surface level of the utterance and directly conveyed by the meaning of the expressions appearing in the utterance. One can also recognize that in the case of contextuals there is a contextual variable present at the level of logical form without committing oneself to the view that this variable must be satisfied when the (minimal) proposition is expressed. In that case, what would be said (the minimal proposition) would be a propositional function. This variable would also help us to explain what is going on when contextuals are bound, as is the case with 'local' and 'enemy' in: "In all major cities, the local newspaper is widely read" and "In every army, every reasonable soldier is scared by the enemy". The fact that the

---

[11] Even in the case of non-sentential utterances like "On the top shelf" uttered when one observes one's audience searching for a given book, the situation should help in completing the message and, thus, expressing some relevant proposition.

variable associated with a contextual need not be satisfied when the minimal proposition is expressed also explains the difference between indexicals and contextuals both *vis-à-vis* context and *vis-à-vis* their contribution to the proposition expressed. The difference ultimately rests on the fact that indexicals and contextuals seem to be distinct linguistic tools. While the character of an indexical directs us toward a particular aspect of context, the meaning of a contextual does not direct us toward a specific, determinate contextual feature. If one looks in the dictionary, under the entry for an indexical expression one is likely to find a description or a rule suggesting how to use it. Under 'I', for instance, one reads (see the *Shorter Oxford English Dictionary*) that it is used to refer to "the speaker or writer", under 'here' that it is used to refer to "this place or position", under 'this' that it stands for "the thing or person present, close at hand, indicated, already mentioned, understood". Dictionary entries for contextuals do not contain rules of this kind, but instead contain a kind of definition. Under 'local' one reads "pertaining to a particular place in a system; belonging to or existing in a particular locality or neighborhood", while under 'enemy' one finds "a person who nurses hatred for or seeks to harm a person, group, or cause; a member of a hostile army or nation".

To summarize, the conceptual enrichment involved in the interpretation of underdetermined utterances does not seem to be grammatically triggered in the way it is with indexical reference. As such, it must be characterized as a pragmatic feature. The main fact seems to be that utterances like (9a–c) can be completed in many different ways. Even if we fix the discourse situation, an utterance like "Jon is too old" can still be completed in infinitely many ways, but an utterance involving an indexical must be understood in a specific way.

3. Situational Contextualism

I am sympathetic to the ordinary-language philosophers' view, which centers on the way in which language is used. In a nutshell, I endorse the famous Wittgensteinian motto that meaning is use. I am also happy to endorse views, like Perry's for instance, that focus on utterances and token-reflexivity instead of sentences.[12]

One of the main questions we face concerns the way context enters the picture in determining the truth-value of a given utterance. To begin with, we can adopt the classical Tarkian framework. Thus a sentence's truth-value can be represented,

[12] "I move the utterance to the center of things. The subject-matter content of an utterance is one of many content properties it has; semantics is the study of how these properties relate to one another and to other properties of utterances" (Perry 2001: p. xi).

adopting Tarski's T-sentences ('S' is true *iff* S), as follows:

(10) a. "Jane is not tall enough" is true *iff* Jane is not tall enough
b. "Jane is late" is true *iff* Jane is late
c. "Jon is too old" is true *iff* Jon is too old

We saw, though, that many sentences are context-sensitive. One way we can handle the context-sensitivity is to focus on utterances and quantify over them. Thus sentences containing context-sensitive elements can be represented, in terms of utterances, using the following T-schema:[13]

(11) a. If u is an utterance of "Jane is not tall enough", then [u is true *iff* Jane is not tall enough]
b. If u is an utterance of "Jane is late", then [u is true *iff* Jane is late]
c. If u is an utterance of "Jon is too old", then [u is true *iff* Jon is too old]

When an utterance contains context-sensitive expressions like indexicals, for instance, it should be evaluated following a T-schema of the form:

(11) d. If u is an utterance of "I am too old" and x is the agent of u, then [u is true *iff* x is too old]
e. If u is an utterance of "He is too old", and the agent of u refers to x with 'he', then [u is true *iff* x is too old]

This representation allows us to capture the context-sensitivity of an utterance. The T-schema appears in the consequent (it is represented within the square brackets). The T-schema, though, is contextualized inasmuch as it is conditional on the various contextual parameters appearing in the antecedent of the conditional.

If this is the right picture, i.e. if representations like (11d–e) capture the truth-conditions of utterances like "I am too old" and "He is too old", then the reason why the agent of u in (11d) and the referent of 'he' in (11e) are too old does not enter the T-schema. As such, they do not seem to affect the truth-conditions of underdetermined utterances. However, this does not seem to be the full story insofar as utterances like these do not state what the specified individual is too old for. As I understand it, we face a dilemma. Either we reject the view that (11e) can represent the truth-condition of an underdetermined utterance like "I am too old" *or* we accept the view that the truth-condition of an utterance is itself context-sensitive.

If one endorses the first horn of the dilemma, one is likely to agree with the view that further information must enter the scene in determining the truth-conditions of an underdetermined utterance. That is to say, one must hold the view that the utterance (or the proposition it expresses) undergoes a process of

---

[13] This formulation is borrowed from Higginbotham (1988). For a detailed discussion of it see Carston (2002: 50 ff).

completion or enrichment and that it is only once such a process is fulfilled that the utterance's truth-conditions can be established. This position seems to commit itself to the view that, in order for utterances like (9a–c) to be true or false, they must undergo an enrichment process. It is only thanks to the latter that these utterances succeed in expressing a truth-evaluable proposition. I believe that this strategy is bound to be unsatisfactory. Actually, if we were to open this door, i.e. to make the utterance's truth-conditions sensitive to these extra elements, we would inevitably find ourselves in a situation where we would be unable to determine how much extra information should enter the scene.

As I view it, the difference between the two approaches is best understood using the notion of a proposition. Thus we can assume, at least for the sake of argument, that both camps accept the view that an incomplete utterance expresses a proposition. The difference comes when characterizing the nature of such propositions. The friends of radical contextualism can take two routes. They can assume that either an enrichment process is involved in the expression of a proposition (we would thus have a case of pragmatic intrusion)—in that case one does not distinguish between what is said and what is communicated—or they can follow Bach and argue that a minimal proposition (or propositional radical) is semantically expressed and that pragmatic considerations enter the scene in determining the proposition communicated—in that case we would have two distinct propositions involved: the semantic proposition corresponding to what is said (to be precise, this is a kind of subpropositional content) and the communicated proposition. The proposition expressed, though, is incomplete in the sense that it lacks a truth-condition. Only the complete, i.e. the communicated, proposition can bear a truth-value and, thus, can enter truth-conditional semantics.

If one tries to resist the appeal of radical contextualism, one is likely to endorse the view that the proposition expressed is complete and truth-evaluable. To be sure, an utterance may express a proposition only relative to the context of the utterance; this is the case when the utterance contains indexical or context-sensitive expressions.[14] The proposition is either true or false but its truth or falsity must be determined in the context of the discourse or in the discourse situation. To stress this fact we can focus on a classical example (see Barwise and Etchemendy 1987: 121–2). Looking at a poker game, Jon says: "Claire has the three of clubs". Jon's utterance expresses the proposition *that Claire has the three of clubs*. This utterance concerns the situation of the game of poker being watched by Jon. For Jon's utterance to be true, it is not sufficient that the proposition or fact it expresses obtains. This proposition must obtain in the relevant situation, i.e. the poker game being watched by Jon. If Jon is mistaken in

---

[14] In that case we have what Recanati (1993) characterizes as *saturation*. The semantic completion is not free but triggered by indexical elements and/or grammatical ellipsis.

identifying Claire, and Claire is not among the players of the poker game, Jon's utterance is not true. And his utterance would not be true even if Claire were playing poker in another part of the city and happened to have the three of clubs. Jon's utterance is true only if Claire has the three of clubs in *that poker game*, i.e. the game being watched by Jon. The notion of a situation should capture the intuitive idea that our discourses and linguistic interchanges, not to mention our cognitive activity, concern given situations. If I say "Henry scored a wonderful goal" whilst watching the Manchester-Arsenal match, what I say is true if and only if Henry scored a wonderful goal *during that match*. The wonderful goal he scored the previous Wednesday when playing for France does not make my utterance true. In short, my talking concerns the Manchester-Arsenal game I am watching; it does not concern another game. My utterances, and my thoughts, are situated:

In *situation* theory, we take note of the fact that an agent's world divides up into a collection, a succession, of situations; situations encountered, situations referred to, situations about which information is received, and so on. That is to say, our theory reflects the fact that agents discriminate (by their behavior) situations . . . the behavior of people varies systematically according to the kind of situation they are faced with: threatening situations, spooky situations, pleasant situations, challenging situations, conversations, and what-have-you, all evoke quite different responses. (Devlin 1991: 30)

Following this suggestion, the proposition expressed is *situated*. In other words, a given proposition gets its truth-value in a context-sensitive way. I characterize this view *Situational Contextualism*. In terms of propositions, this view can also be characterized as *The Slim Propositions View*, with radical contextualism characterized as *The Obese Propositions View*. The following chart should summarize the differences between radical contextualism and situational contextualism. These differences rest on the dissimilar way in which context is claimed to enter the picture. While the friends of the obese propositions view argue that context enters in determining a proposition, i.e. in the enrichment process, the picture I favor, i.e. the slim propositions view, rests on the idea that context (a situation to be precise) enters the scene in determining the proposition's truth-value. According to this view the proposition need not be enriched.

- *Radical Contextualism, The Obese Propositions View*
Underdetermined utterance + Context of Utterance
↓
Minimal Proposition + *Contextual Enrichment*
↓
Complete Proposition
↓
Truth-value

18   Introduction

- *Situational Contextualism, The Slim Propositions View*
Underdetermined Utterance + Context of Utterance
↓
Minimal Proposition + *Situation*
↓
Truth-value

According to the slim propositions view, a proposition's (and derivatively an utterance's) truth-value is *relative* to a given situation. That truth-value may change from one situation to another.[15] The position I have in mind is reminiscent of Kaplan's two-step theory of evaluation, i.e. the distinction between the context of the utterance and the circumstance of evaluation. The latter is familiar from modal logic where propositions are evaluated relative to possible worlds. Though the possible worlds are necessary to truth-evaluation, they are not themselves represented in the propositions that we evaluate. The difference between situational contextualism and Kaplan's original position is that the circumstance of evaluation is not a possible world but a situation in a possible world (i.e. a partial possible world). It goes without saying, though, that utterances involving modal operators are evaluated *vis-à-vis* other possible worlds. In the example I mentioned earlier, the proposition *that there is some beer in the fridge* may be true in situations in which Jon asks for a drink and false in situations in which Jon has just finished cleaning the fridge. But the truth or falsity of the proposition does *not* rest on it undergoing some change. According to the obese propositions view, a proposition's (and derivatively an utterance's) truth-value is absolute. This is possible inasmuch as one allows post-semantic contextual features to participate in the determination of a complete proposition. In the example just mentioned we would have different propositions with a switch of the situation. The question which springs to mind is how we can define these propositions. To state it slightly differently, the position I have in mind distinguishes between the proposition expressed and the truth-maker, the latter being the situation which makes true the former.

If one accepts situational contextualism as I have defined it, one is likely to accept the view that (11a–c) should incorporate the fact that truth is relative to a

[15] Barwise and Etchemendy capture these intuitions in introducing the notion of Austinian propositions: "In terms of the Austinian account, our assertion is true about the situation we are talking about, but might be false about other situations" (Barwise and Etchemendy 1987: 122). Following their proposal, an utterance expresses an Austinian proposition. The latter is richer than what I characterized as the minimal proposition, for an Austinian proposition also involves the situation tacitly referred to by the utterance. The position I defend, though, need not appeal to Austinian propositions. For a discussion and a defense of Austinian semantics see also Recanati (2000: esp. ch. 5).

situation:

(11) f. If *u* is an utterance of "Jane is not tall enough" and *s* is the situation in which *u* occurs, then [*u* is true *iff* Jane is not tall enough relative to *s*]
g. If *u* is an utterance of "Jane is late" and *s* is the situation in which *u* occurs, then [*u* is true *iff* Jane is late relative to *s*]
h. If *u* is an utterance of "Jon is too old" and *s* is the situation in which *u* occurs, then [*u* is true *iff* Jon is too old relative to *s*]

The distinction between radical contextualism and situational contextualism can also be highlighted in distinguishing, following Perry (2001), between *pre-semantic*, *semantic*, and *post-semantic* uses of context. By pre-semantic uses, I mean contextual features entering the scene before an utterance can be said to express a proposition. This is, for instance, the case when we deal with ambiguity, homonymy, polysemy, and the like. Before deciding which of the possible propositions is expressed, we must decide which terms, which structure, etc. are involved. By semantic uses, I mean the contextual features (e.g. agent, time, and location of the utterance) in virtue of which indexicals and other context-sensitive elements appearing within a given utterance get their value. By post-semantic uses, I mean the features that may still be involved in determining a given proposition after pre-semantic and semantic uses of context have been operative. The notion of post-semantic uses of context is particularly evident when one appeals to the free enrichment involved in expressing an obese proposition. As we saw, if we grant that these post-semantic features enter the scene in determining a proposition, we face the difficulty of knowing precisely how much extra information enters the proposition, i.e. we end up being unable to determine how obese the proposition should be. The slim propositions view avoids this difficulty in admitting that a proposition's truth-value is context-sensitive, i.e. is situated. Situated contextualism avoids appealing to the notion of enrichment in determining what is said, i.e. the proposition expressed by an utterance. Enriched (obese) propositions, therefore, do not play a semantic role. For this reason, the notion of post-semantic uses of context need not enter the scene when characterizing what is expressed/said by an utterance. All we need know is the situation in which an utterance occurs and in which a (minimal) proposition is expressed. A situation can be understood as the background upon which a linguistic and/or thinking episode occurs. One can object that the position I propose faces a similar difficulty to the obese propositions view. While the latter is faced with the problem of determining how much extra information should enter the proposition, the former is faced with the problem of determining which components of the situation in which an utterance occurs are relevant. Furthermore, how does a hearer wanting to understand what is being communicated discern what the relevant situation is? All I can say is that this information is pragmatically furnished and constitutes the background upon which the communicative interchange or thinking episode occurs. It need not be specified or even conceptualized. As such, it does not enter the proposition expressed. Indeed, for one to understand the message conveyed, one must "grasp" the relevant situation. As I understand it, the difficulty I face can be summarized as follows. While the obese propositions view faces the problem of explaining how one grasps/selects an obese proposition, situational contextualism faces the problem of explaining how one grasps/selects a given situation. To be honest, I do not have a clear-cut answer to this question. All I can suggest is that the grasping of a situation seems to be a less cognitive activity than the grasping of an obese proposition. In other words, recognizing a situation may not involve any conscious selection or discrimination, while the grasping of a fully fledged proposition seems to require some cognitive effort. I take it that it is part of our cognitive makeup that we can discriminate a given situation without conscious effort. This is, I reckon, the background for language use. To state the same point slightly differently, one can act and react in an appropriate way insofar as one is properly situated, i.e. insofar as one's behavior rests on a given situation. One's behavior need not be triggered by one's grasping of an obese proposition. On the one hand, the obese propositions view seems to commit itself to the idea that one needs to entertain an obese proposition. On the other hand, situational contextualism does not need to appeal to the idea of entertaining a situation. Similarly, when it comes to psychological explanation, the obese propositions view is likely to explain one's behavior by claiming that it is triggered by entertaining an obese proposition/thought, while situational contextualism merely states that one's behavior is situated (more on this specific issue in Chapter 6).

The basic idea underlying situational contextualism is that the truth-condition of an utterance must be determined by the syntactic elements active in the utterance. These elements must be present either at the surface level or in the underlying logical form. In terms of propositions, this amounts to saying that all the propositional constituents must be represented in the logical form of the utterance.[16] What one says and communicates, however, often transcends what the utterance expresses. That is to say, the message communicated and understood is often richer than the

---

[16] Indeed, if one were to assume (like Stanley and Szabo e.g.) that comparative adjectives involve an implicit comparison class and, like contextuals in general, must be understood as involving an argument place at the level of logical form ('small *relative to* x', 'tall *relative to* x', 'local *relative to* x', 'enemy *relative to* x'), given my principle of syntactic determination of propositional content, the truth-conditions in (11f) and the like should be amended as follows:

If *u* is an utterance of "Jane is not tall enough [to x]" and *s* is the situation in which *u* occurs and *F* is the value of *x* in this situation, then [*u* is true *iff* Jane is not tall enough *to F* relative to *s*]

This, though, is not the position I defend (see Ch. 2).

proposition expressed by the utterance, yet it need not correspond to a specific proposition. A (slim) situated proposition may succeed in transmitting a message. The latter may be situated as well. To be sure, in order to understand what one aims to communicate, one must grasp the (slim) proposition expressed by the utterance. This very proposition *could* be expanded/enriched in many different ways. But one need *not* enrich a proposition in a specific way in order to understand the message. If I say "Jon is too old" in stressing that he cannot play for the junior team, do I communicate that he is too old to play in the Arsenal junior team, that he is too old to play in this year's junior football team, that he is too old to play in this year's junior Arsenal team, . . . ? Similarly, which alleged enriched proposition must my interlocutor entertain in order to understand the message I communicate? It is often the case that one understands a given message insofar as one grasps the basic (slim) proposition, without necessarily enriching it one way or another (or at least without conceptualizing the relevant enrichment). The simple fact that one finds oneself in a given discourse situation and in a given context often suffices for the success of the communication. Linguistic underdeterminacy easily expands to thought underdeterminacy (or so I am going to argue in Chapter 6). Furthermore, linguistic underdeterminacy must not be considered as a defect of natural language. It is the *sine qua non* of our linguistic interaction and our thinking activity. In short, it is because we are context-bound agents that we constantly use underdetermined utterances and exploit context both in our linguistic interchanges and cognitive episodes. We can*not* do otherwise, for Mother Nature (or God if you prefer) has programmed us to be context-bound. We cannot escape the boundaries of the context in which our thoughts and communicative exchanges appear; context seems to be an essential feature of our nature. If I am right, our thoughts are best understood as *situated* in a given context or discourse situation as well. It is often because a thought is entertained in a given context that it concerns a given item or event. The thought need not represent the latter and an utterance expressing a thought can be underdetermined. These issues will be taken up in Chapters 2 and 6.

From a methodological viewpoint I propose the following principle, which parallels the idea that both propositions and thoughts must be viewed as situated:

- *Economy of Saying Principle*
  One need not state what can be conveyed implicitly.

In particular, one should exploit context (broadly understood) as much as one can. In other words, what can be contextually transmitted should not be made explicit. For this very reason utterances turn out to be underdetermined. This methodological principle should be coupled with the following semantic principle, inspired by Grice:

- *Semantics of Saying Principle*
What is not triggered by meaning does not affect what is said, i.e. the proposition expressed by an utterance.

Before going further (and to avoid confusion) I should stress that I do not have a clear-cut notion of what is said. I also believe that we do not have clear-cut intuitions about such a notion and each definition is bound to be theoretically informed and *ad hoc*. If we focus, for instance, on what happens when we report what someone said, we certainly end up with conflicting intuitions. Actually, if someone (Jane, to give her a name) utters "Jon is so intelligent" in a sarcastic way, insinuating that he is stupid, the report is likely to be something like, "Jane said that Jon is stupid". The report does not capture what Jane actually said, nor the proposition literally expressed by the words she uttered. If we tell a young child that Jane said "I have been to the oculist", our report is likely to be "Jane said that she has been to the eye doctor" or simply "Jane said that she has been to the doctor". Our reports do not seem to help us to capture what is strictly said. Yet, from an intuitive viewpoint we can say that a report captures what is said even if the latter does not correspond exactly to the proposition expressed by the speaker with a given utterance.

The semantics of saying and the economy of saying principles are two sides of the same coin and are subsumed under the following principle:

- *Context Exploitation Principle*
The proposition expressed by an utterance, i.e. what is strictly said, is context-situated. One succeeds in transmitting a given message and one understands this very message insofar as one grasps the context in which the proposition expressed is situated.

As I have already stressed, one of the main difficulties consists in characterizing the notion of grasping the context in which the proposition is situated. I do not believe that one can propose a specific account of this kind of knowledge. I take it to be a kind of *knowing how*, i.e. a general pragmatic or procedural knowledge one comes to master insofar as one belongs, to borrow Wittgenstein's terminology, to a given form of life. It may also be that we are, at least partially, hard-wired in such a way to make the most out of the context in which an utterance occurs.

From a semantic viewpoint, the picture I am proposing is, indeed, a minimalist one inasmuch as the proposition expressed by an utterance is extremely slim. Yet it is truth-conditionally evaluable. Propositions must be viewed as context-situated; it is because they are situated that they acquire truth-conditions and that information can be transmitted. The picture I have in mind embraces a form of contextualism as well. To be sure, it embraces a full-blooded form of contextualism. The contextualism I favor is best viewed as situational contextualism, i.e. the view that both the proposition expressed and the thought entertained are situated.[17] If I am right, the capacity to understand a given message need not rest on any inferential activity. It is often automatic and carried out at a subconscious level. The fact that we are context-bound agents constitutes one of the main ingredients guaranteeing both the success of communication and our interaction with the external world. In other words, situational contextualism may be seen as the result of the fact that we are essentially embodied in context, both in our thinking episodes and our linguistic interchanges. This position can be characterized as *Contextual Embodiment*.

- *Contextual Embodiment*
  Our thinking and linguistic activity must be understood as context-situated. This idea contrasts with the view that context must determine a thought which can then be evaluated in a context-insensitive way, i.e. the view that context participates in enriching what one thinks/says, with the enriched version being true/false across situations. In different situations, one may well end up entertaining the very same thought, yet that thought may be true in one situation and false in another.

In Chapter 6 I shall develop this idea in arguing that thoughts are object-independent and in showing how context bridges the gap between a thought and what it is about.

Furthermore, since I do not believe that what is communicated can be extracted fully from the context of the speech act, I commit myself to the following underdeterminacy and inscrutability view concerning communication.

- *The Underdeterminacy and Inscrutability of Communication*
  What is communicated transcends what is (strictly speaking) said, i.e. what is communicated is richer than the (slim) proposition expressed. Yet (i) what is communicated is essentially underdetermined insofar as it can neither be encapsulated in an eternal sentence nor in a specific proposition and (ii) since what is communicated is intrinsically context-bound it cannot be characterized in a context-free way. For this very reason it is compelled to be inscrutable, for context potentially presents infinitely many facets.

This principle is the direct consequence of the view I proposed above, when I claimed that speakers must be conceived as context-bound agents, i.e. it is a consequence of what I characterized as contextual embodiment. Communication is inscrutable inasmuch as trying to encapsulate communication with a context-free sentence is like trying to encapsulate an analogue image with a digital discourse.

---

[17] For an accurate discussion on the way our thinking activity must be viewed as situated, see Dokic (2002).

To be sure, one can describe a given picture and the description can be extremely accurate, yet something will be missed. It is logically impossible, I think, to go from analogue to digital content without losing information. A discursive description and an image, say a photographic picture of a landscape, may represent the same scene. But they are bound to be irreducible to one another. In claiming that communication is inscrutable, though, I do not mean that we do not succeed in understanding each other. I simply mean that our understanding is context-bound and is so necessarily. That is to say, understanding rests on agents being context-embodied.

In distinguishing between the (slim) proposition expressed by an utterance—what is (strictly speaking) said, or what is literally said—and what is communicated, does one also distinguish between pragmatics and semantics? That is, can one draw the parallel between what is said and semantics, on the one hand, and what is communicated and pragmatics on the other (as many, inspired by Grice, would like to claim)? Basing the semantics/pragmatics divide on the distinction between what is said and what is communicated looks promising. I also believe that this is the best we can do in order to distinguish between semantics and pragmatics. However, I do not believe that a clear-cut distinction can be drawn, for in equating semantics with what is (strictly speaking) said, we automatically blur the semantics/pragmatics distinction insofar as what is said, even in its more austere conception, is often pragmatically informed. In other words, in order to compute what an utterance expresses, we often have to rely on pragmatic phenomena. Semantics is often pragmatically informed.[18] This is particularly evident if we consider the case of anaphora. To illustrate this point, let us consider the case of zero-anaphora, i.e. the use of gaps in selecting a referent. Gaps determine their reference in an anaphoric way, i.e. in virtue of being linked to (and coindexed with) an antecedent:

(12) Zidane$_1$ passed the ball to Henry and a_1 stopped running

In English, a zero-anaphora like 'a' in (12) is highly grammatically constrained. In other languages (e.g. Guugu Yimidhirr, an Australasian language), however, zero-anaphora may be grammatically unconstrained (see Levinson 1987). In such cases, pragmatic features enter in determining the relevant anaphoric relations and thus the value of the null-anaphora. To stress how pragmatic considerations enter the scene in the case of zero-anaphors, we can also consider utterances like:

(13) Jon went to the pub and got drunk

The default interpretation of (13) seems to be:

(13) a. Jon went to the pub and, *there and then, he* got drunk

---

[18] In saying that semantics is pragmatically informed I do not mean that one cannot propose a distinction between the two. I simply mean that the distinction may not be as useful as is often claimed in capturing and explaining such notions as what is said, what is communicated, and the like.

However, nothing in the original utterance suggests that Jon became drunk in the pub when he visited it. With further background information we could force another interpretation, i.e. that Jon performed two separate actions:

(13) b. Jon went to the pub and, *later that night, he* got drunk *elsewhere*

Only pragmatic considerations seem to force one interpretation over the other. Nothing at the grammatical level or at the logical form level triggers one interpretation instead of the other. Granted that in Guugu Yimidhirr there is no single solution to the problem of null-anaphora, Levinson proposes a pragmatic interpretation concerning anaphora. Consider:

(14) John$_1$ came into the room. He$_1$ sat down. The man$_2$ coughed

[T]he preferred interpretation is as indicated by indices: i.e. the reduced pronominal form tends to pick up reference from the last relevant NP (preferably a subject). Reversion to a full lexical NP (*The man*) tends to implicate disjoint reference. Since these are merely default implicatures, operative in the absence of information to the contrary, it will of course be possible to find many exceptions to these tendencies—but in these cases there should be specific reasons to prefer another interpretation. (Levinson 1987: 382)

The preferred pragmatic interpretation fits the economy of saying principle insofar as, if coreference is intended, one should use a semantically poor expression or a general one (see Levinson 2001: 181). To illustrate this phenomenon we can consider:

(15) a. As soon as Jane arrived *she* asked for you
 b. As soon as Jane arrived *the woman* asked for you
 c. As soon as Jane arrived *the woman with the blue hat* asked for you

The natural, default interpretation of 'she' in (15a) is the anaphoric one, i.e. 'she' is anaphoric and thus coindexed with 'Jane'. The interpretation of 'the woman' in (15b) presupposes further information insofar as 'the woman' does not force the anaphoric reading. In (15c) the default interpretation of 'the woman with the blue hat' is certainly not the anaphoric one. This is because the anaphoric interpretation rests on the economy of saying principle and, therefore, a speaker intending to convey the anaphoric reading should choose (15a) over (15b) or (15c). In short, everything being equal, one should choose the most economical (the semantically poorer) expression. One chooses to use the longer (richer) expression in order to avoid the default, anaphoric, interpretation. Further empirical evidence in favor of the thesis that semantics is pragmatically informed is furnished by Huang (2000) who convincingly argues that an exhaustive study of anaphora cannot be made in purely semantic or syntactic terms, insofar as an anaphor's antecedent cannot be selected uniquely on the basis of syntactic and semantic considerations. Pragmatics factors often operate in determining the antecedent of an anaphor. This is particularly evident when one concentrates on Asiatic languages. These languages rely more heavily on pragmatics than English, Italian, French, etc.:

(i) syntax, and pragmatics are interconnected to determine many of the processes of anaphora that are thought to fall within the province of grammar, and (ii) the extent to which syntax, semantics, and pragmatics interact varies typologically. (Huang 2000: 205)

There seems to exist a class of languages (such as Chinese, Japanese, and Korean) where pragmatics appears to play a central role which in familiar European languages (such as English, French, and German) has hitherto been alleged to be played by grammar. In these 'pragmatic' languages, many of the constraints on the alleged grammatical processes are in fact primarily due to principles of language use rather than rules of grammatical structure. (Huang 2000: 213)

Further evidence in favor of the view that semantics is pragmatically informed is given by comparatives of the form (see Wilson 1975):

(16) a. Driving home and drinking three beers is better than drinking three beers and driving home

Utterances of the form "u is better than v" would be contradictory if the proposition expressed by u is not distinct from the proposition expressed by v. If the propositions are distinct then the conjunction 'and' in u and v must convey temporality. If so, 'and' must differ from '&'. The semantic equivalence "$p \& q \leftrightarrow q \& p$" fails to capture the truth of (16a). Actually, if we apply the standard semantic interpretation of '&' to 'and', (16a), (16b), and (16c) would be equivalent:

(16) b. Driving home and drinking three beers is better than drinking three beers and driving home
c. Drinking three beers and driving home is better than drinking three beers and driving home

While (16b) is awkward, (16c) is contradictory. Thus 'and' and '&' cannot be treated on a par and pragmatic considerations must enter the picture when dealing with 'and', at least when it appears in comparatives. As further evidence in favor of the pragmatic intrusion idea, we can quote conditionals (see Levinson 2001: 205 ff):

(17) a. If you have a baby *and* get married, the baby is strictly speaking illegitimate
b. If Bill's book is good, he will get tenure
c. If Bill's book is good, he will never return it to the library

From a semantic viewpoint, (17a) would be equivalent to

(17) d. If you get married *and* have a baby, the baby is strictly speaking illegitimate

which generates a contradiction. Thus pragmatics forces the temporal reading of 'and' as meaning 'and then'. In (17b) and (17c), pragmatics suggests the relationship (author *vs.* borrower) between Bill and the book. Cohen (1971) noticed that Grice cannot simultaneously maintain the truth functionality of 'and' and 'if'. When conjunctions are embedded in the antecedent of a conditional, 'and' and '&' cannot be treated on a par. The temporal relation holding between the conjuncts should be an integral part of the antecedent. It is only in virtue of this temporal relation that conditionals whose antecedents are conjunctions can differ in truth-value, as is the case with (18a–b) and (19a–b):

(18) a. If Arsenal plays Chelsea *and* Arsenal wins the FA Cup, then Roman will have been deceived
b. If Arsenal wins the FA Cup *and* Arsenal plays Chelsea, then Roman will have been deceived

(19) a. If Mary gets married *and* gets pregnant, her father will be happy
b. If Mary gets pregnant *and* gets married, her father will be happy

The general moral seems to be that we should recognize pragmatic intrusion, i.e. pragmatic phenomena contributing to the expression of a given proposition. As Carston puts it:

These observations are at one with the view that pragmatic inference plays a fundamental role in determining the proposition expressed; however, they do not have to be taken as entailing that what is implicature (a propositional form distinct from the proposition expressed) of a simple sentence/utterance changes its status when that simple sentence is embedded, becoming then part of the proposition expressed (the truth-conditional content). Rather, we have a pragmatic contribution to the proposition expressed in both cases (unembedded and embedded) and an implicature in neither. (Carston 2002: 193)

It remains to be seen, though, whether Chomsky is right in suggesting that natural language has only syntax and pragmatics:

As for semantics, insofar as we understand language use, the argument for a reference-based semantics (apart from an internalist syntactic version) seems to me weak. It is possible that natural language has only syntax and pragmatics, it has a "semantics" only in the sense of "the study of how this instrument, whose formal structure and potentialities of expression are the subject of syntactic investigations, is actually put to use in a speech community", to quote the earlier formulation in generative grammar 40 years ago, influenced by Wittgenstein, Austin and others. . . . In this view, natural language consists of internalist computations and performance systems that access them along with much other information and belief, carrying out their instructions in particular ways to enable us to talk and communicate, among other things . . . it is not assumed that language is used to represent the world. (Chomsky 2000: 132)

If Chomsky is right, then it seems that a serious, scientific, semantic study is impossible. Be that as it may, the picture I am proposing may be in harmony with Chomsky's general program, insofar as it rejects a clear-cut distinction between semantics and pragmatics. Furthermore, the picture that will emerge in the course of this book rests on notions such as rules and conventions guiding our actions. It may be that these Wittgensteinian notions are more promising when trying to analyze the meanings of linguistic expressions. At least, they are more promising inasmuch as we work within the framework according to which meaning is use.

4. Structure of the Book

In Chapter 1, I further develop the issues discussed in the Introduction. In particular, I stress, in a Wittgenstein-inspired fashion, the semantic differences between proper names and indexicals (including demonstratives). The chapter refines and builds upon David Kaplan's semantics of indexicals. It also builds upon the direct reference work on proper names. It is argued that proper names are Millian 'tags' and that their cognitive role differs drastically from the cognitive role of indexicals (and demonstratives). Unlike proper names, the information associated with indexicals is anchored. Deference to conventions governs the use of names, but not of indexicals. Perceptual attention and intention play a special role in securing the reference of demonstratives, but not of pure indexicals. The chapter ends with a discussion of the puzzles of cognitive significance and shows how the Frege-inspired puzzles can be accommodated within a direct reference framework.

Chapter 2 develops certain aspects concerning underdeterminacy. In focusing on tacit reference, this chapter shifts the focus from language to thought. The starting point is Perry's seminal work on unarticulated constituents. I distinguish three kinds of incompleteness: syntactic, semantic, and conceptual incompleteness or underdetermination. I argue for the presence of variables at the level of logical form which take unarticulated semantic constituents as their value. This goes some way towards bridging the gap between the concept of unarticulated constituents and the exact methods of Chomsky's generative grammar. In particular, it is argued that tacit arguments are articulated at the level of logical form, yet they need not be mentally represented. The chapter ends by pursuing the distinction between the deferential role of proper names and the perspectival role of indexicals at the level of thought.

Chapter 3 begins by discussing what I call description-names (such as 'the Holy Roman Empire') and complex demonstratives ('that F'). From a Kaplanian starting point, I offer a multiple proposition approach. Description-names function both as

Millian tags and as descriptions. The descriptive content of a description-name makes a contribution to a subordinate proposition so that the utterance of a sentence containing a description-name and a predicate can be said to express two distinct propositions: the background proposition and the official (singular) proposition. The former is a tool helping to identify the referent of the official proposition. But the utterance is true iff the official proposition is true; thus, the background proposition does not play a truth-conditional role. This view should help to solve a number of puzzles involving description-names and complex demonstratives. I introduce the operator 'Dname', modelled on Kaplan's 'Dthat': the former does for names what the latter does for descriptions. Finally, it is shown that the multiple-proposition approach helps to explain how description-names and complex demonstratives can interact with anaphoric pronouns whose antecedents are encapsulated within description-names or complex demonstratives.

In Chapter 4, I pick up the general idea of the thesis, discussed in Chapters 1 and 2, that indexical thoughts are perspectival and their referents anchored. I begin by distinguishing between temporal indexicals and temporal terms (such as 'Monday', 'June') and argue that the latter are best understood as count nouns. I further claim that all indexicals are systematically ambiguous insofar as they can be used either as genuine indexicals or as anaphors (in which case they inherit their reference from some antecedent NP). I apply what I termed the Fixed Character thesis to temporal and locational indexicals such as 'now' and 'here' and argue that when they are used as pure indexicals, 'now' and 'here' always refer to the time/location of utterance. When these indexicals are not so used, they work as anaphoric pronouns whose antecedents are sometimes explicit in the discourse and sometimes merely supplied by the context. In the latter case, the indexical is linked to what I term a tacit antecedent or initiator.

Chapter 5 examines the semantic behavior of the first-person pronoun 'I'. This chapter is a defense of the neo-Wittgensteinian view that self-consciousness arises from one's mastery of 'I'. I directly argue against Anscombe's view that 'I' does not refer. I oppose Anscombe's view in claiming that 'I' is neither a demonstrative nor a proper name, and argue that Anscombe fails to appreciate that the first-person pronoun is a pure indexical. The chapter goes on to offer an anti-intentionalist solution to the puzzle of how a person can use a token of 'I' on a post-it note or on an answering machine to refer to somebody else. These uses, it is claimed, depend on conventions regimenting the way post-it notes and answering machines are exploited. A conventionalist interpretation will thus be proposed.

Chapter 6 focuses on issues concerning the role of thoughts expressible with indexicals in causal psychological explanations. It is shown that our thoughts and perceptions are intrinsically embedded in a situation which gives rise to perspectival, context-sensitive thoughts. I contrast this view with that of Evans and McDowell, who claim that object-dependent thoughts involve the object they are about. After rejecting their view I argue in favor of an object-independent view, according to which the content of a perspectival thought depends on context; the object is not part of the content of the thought. This position exploits the idea developed in the Introduction that we are context-bound agents. I thus defend a radical anti-Fregean line—that the very thought is context-dependent—and argue (along with Fodor) that psychological laws do not concern object-dependent thoughts. This chapter should show how an account of perspectival thoughts has interesting consequences for psychological theorizing.

Chapter 7 stresses the role of imagination in attributing feelings and propositional attitudes. This chapter offers an account of ascriptions of propositional attitudes (and of indirect quotation) based on the central concept of what I term "neutral acceptance". On this view, the attributor's and the attributee's mental representations are two tokens of the same type. I argue that the attributor of an attitude uses a sentence of her language which is such that, were she in the attributee's circumstances, her mental representation would cause her to utter that very sentence. On this view, an ascription relates a subject both to the proposition expressed by the 'that'-clause *and* to a sentence that the subject is disposed to *n*-accept. In referring to psychological studies of empathy, I show that my account of propositional attitude ascription is consonant with the psychological literature on autism. This is so because my account is rooted in simple empathetic identification with the distress, pains, and emotions of others. I also argue in favor of the role of types of mental representations and contrast my view with that proposed by Crimmins and Perry (1989) (which makes reference to token mental representations).

Chapter 8 picks up the general ideas of several earlier chapters (in particular Chapters 4 and 5) in dealing with first-person thoughts, *de se* attributions, and Castañeda's quasi-indicators. In appealing to cross-linguistic evidence I argue that natural languages contain quasi-indicators and show that they can be compared to logophoric pronouns. Using some linguistic tools, I analyze the behavior of quasi-indicators and argue that they function as a kind of attributive anaphor.

In Chapter 9 I pursue the enterprise of Chapters 7 and 8 to reinforce the triadic view of ascriptions, according to which an ascription of a propositional attitude relates a subject both to a proposition and to the sentence that the subject would *n*-accept. A detailed account of the logical form of ascriptions involving quasi-indicators is proposed. In using the technical apparatus introduced in the previous chapter (comparing quasi-indicators to logophoric pronouns), I show that the phenomenon of quasi-indexicality cannot be explained away merely as a pragmatic phenomenon of *de se* ascriptions.

1

Language and Context

> Let us begin with my name. We substitute 'B.R.' for 'I' or 'you' or 'he', as the case may be, because 'B.R.' is a public appellation, appearing on my passport and my identity card. If a policeman says "Who are you?" I might reply saying "Look! this is who I am", but this information is not what the policeman wants, so I produce my identity card and he is satisfied.
>
> (Russell 1948: 101)

> Nothing is more characteristic of a proper name A than we can use it in such a phrase as "This is A"; and it makes no sense to say "This is this" or "Now is now" or "Here is here".
>
> (Wittgenstein, *BB*: 108–9)

In this chapter, I mainly concentrate on indexicals and proper names and the different ways in which their use relies on context to fix their reference. This exercise will illustrate how our linguistic practice rests on context, broadly construed. As I stressed in the Introduction, it is difficult, if not impossible, to conceive of a linguistic interaction without considering the context, situation, setting, etc. in which it occurs. We are context-bound agents.

Here is the way in which I proceed. In Section 1, I argue that noun phrases are best conceived as linguistic tools designed to fulfill particular functions. In Section 2, I distinguish between two main kinds of information, namely anchored information, i.e. the information one gathers in using and entertaining indexical expressions, and unanchored information, i.e. the information one may gain in hearing a proper name. In Section 3, I show how indexicals divide into pure indexicals and demonstratives while in Section 4 I put forward what I believe to be some of the major features that distinguish indexical expressions from proper names. In Section 5, it is shown how these different features rely on the differing ways in which extra-linguistic context enters the scene. In Section 6, I take on Frege's challenge and show how identity statements of various kinds can differ in cognitive significance. Finally, in Section 7, I explain and distinguish between the bearer of cognitive significance and the bearer of truth-value and, using Perry's distinction between reflexive truth-conditions and incremental truth-conditions (or official content), I show how an utterance's reflexive truth-condition helps us handle the Fregean worries regarding cognitive value or significance.

My aim is twofold. On the one hand, I claim that proper names and indexicals are distinct and irreducible tools of reference. As such, this chapter can also be viewed as an anti-reductionist exercise. On the other hand, I show how the Kaplanian framework in particular, and the framework of direct reference in general, is best understood within the background of a Wittgensteinian conception of language. In particular, I appeal to Wittgenstein's notions of language-games, form of life, and practice:

Here the term 'language-*game*' is meant to bring into prominence the fact that the *speaking* of a language is part of an activity, or of a form of life. (Wittgenstein, *PI*: §23)

What has to be accepted, the given, is—so one could say—*forms of life*. (Wittgenstein, *PI*: p. 226)

I argue that Kaplan's consumerist semantics is Wittgensteinian in spirit. It goes without saying, however, that my use and understanding of Wittgenstein's writings does not necessarily reflect the whole of Wittgenstein's philosophy. It may be the case that my reading and understanding of Wittgenstein has been influenced by Kaplan's and Perry's work. My understanding of Wittgenstein—"the father of the revolution", to borrow Wettstein's words—and how his philosophy relates to direct reference has, without doubt, been influenced over the years by the writings of Wettstein (1988; 2004).

1. Words as Tools

It is a platitude to claim that one of the main goals in using language is to gather information about our surroundings and to share it with other members of our community. This information is what enables us to actively interact within our community and, thus, what contributes to guiding our social actions. Language, as I conceive it, is the most powerful and useful tool humans ended up developing. A carburetor is a tool for charging air with a fine spray of liquid fuel for combustion which contributes to the working of an engine. The kidneys are (natural) tools for filtering blood. A word is a tool with a specific function as well. As such, it contributes to the functioning of the language to which it belongs. We have lots of different linguistic tools with different functions.

The *proper* function of a screwdriver is to turn screws, while the proper function of a hammer is to beat and drive nails. To be sure, a hammer and a screwdriver can be used to do other jobs. They can both be used as weapons, for instance—this is why we cannot bring them on board when we fly with commercial airlines: they can become weapons of mass destruction, or so we are told. The latter, though, is not their proper function, for they were not designed as tools for injuring people, nor to become weapons of mass destruction. The same applies in the case of biological organs. The proper function of the heart is to pump blood, while the proper function of the stomach is to digest food. In pumping blood the heart makes some noise. As such, it may scare the mosquito landing on our chest. It is not the proper function of the heart, though, to scare mosquitoes. A similar story can be told about language:

> Think of words as instruments characterized by their use, and then think of the use of a hammer, the use of a chisel, the use of a square, of a glue pot, and of the glue. (Wittgenstein, *BB*: 67)

As I said, in this chapter I concentrate on two linguistic tools: proper names and indexicals. Proper names such as 'David Kaplan', 'Paris', 'San Francisco', etc. can be viewed as tools enabling us to label people, objects, places, etc. and to collect and pass information about the individuals so named. Their proper function is to enable the speaker and audience to collect information about individuals and to keep track of them. Since we are not omniscient beings, we are precluded from knowing individuals and keeping track of them under all their properties across time. We are thus in need of a tool of reference differing from a descriptive method of identification. In other words, we need linguistic tools that allow us to pick out objects and keep track of them, not by virtue of their contingent and ephemeral properties, but simply by working as tags for these objects. Proper names play this specific role. On the other hand, indexicals such as 'now', 'here', 'today', 'this', 'she', 'I', etc. can be viewed as tools enabling us to single out objects, periods, locations, persons, etc. relative to our surroundings. Their proper function is to enable the speaker to single out an object in relation to her enclosing.[1] Because of this peculiarity, Russell (1940; 1948) characterized these expressions *egocentric particulars*:

> I give the name 'egocentric particular' to words of which the meaning varies with the speaker and his position in time and space. The four fundamental words of this sort are 'I', 'this', 'here' and 'now'. (Russell 1940: 100)

2. Anchored *vs.* Unanchored Information

To begin with, consider the following scenario. At a party, Jane, a long-term admirer of Kaplan's theory of demonstratives, knowing that Kaplan is among the guests, approaches Jon, the party organizer, and asks him:

(1) Do you know which person *David Kaplan* is?

Jon's answer is:

(2) *That man* [indicating Kaplan] is David Kaplan.[2]

---

[1] I can refer to Saturday, 12 May 2001 using 'tomorrow' because today is Friday, 11 May 2001. The reference depends on the time I utter 'tomorrow'. It is in this sense that I mean that reference depends on one's enclosing or surrounding broadly understood.

[2] Jon's answer could also have been: "*He* [pointing to Kaplan] is Kaplan". For in using 'he' instead of 'that man' Jon would have reached the same goal.

A minute later Sue, fascinated by the charisma of a man who is drinking martini and is entertaining a few ladies, approaches Jon and asks him:

(3) Do you know who *that man* [indicating Kaplan] is?

Jon's answer is:

(4) That man is *David Kaplan*.

Without doubt, both Jane and Sue are interested in Kaplan. Their interest, though, is guided by different goals.

Jane has some information about David Kaplan. She knows that someone named 'David Kaplan', the author of "Demonstratives", is attending the party. She may also know that Kaplan is professor at UCLA, that he is a garden expert with special interest in orchids, etc. Jane may have a lot of information about David Kaplan. She could also possess some information applying only to Kaplan such as, for instance, Kaplan's date of birth and genealogical tree, his social security number, etc. She may even be in possession of a blueprint of Kaplan's DNA. Nonetheless, she is unable to single out Kaplan among the party attendants. In a sense, Jane *does not know who* Kaplan is; hence her question. To recognize Kaplan, Jane relies on Jon. She *knows that* Kaplan is such and such but this kind of knowledge may not suffice in enabling her to single out Kaplan and thus to know *who* he is. Knowing *that* Kaplan has such-and-such properties may not lead someone to know *who* Kaplan is or, at least, to know which person Kaplan is.[3]

Sue, on the other hand, may have no idea about Kaplan's existence. She may have never heard about him. Like Jane, Sue is interested in Kaplan. But she is interested in Kaplan *qua* man she is currently perceiving. In a sense she does not know who Kaplan is as well, hence her question. To know who the man she is perceiving is, she must rely on Jon as well.

Jane's and Sue's difference in attitude toward Kaplan, as manifested by the different questions they ask, can be captured in distinguishing between two kinds of information one can have about a given object. On the one hand, we have the information one associates with proper names. On the other hand, we have the information one associates with demonstrative expressions. I characterize the latter *anchored information* and the former *unanchored information*. To know *who* Kaplan is, both Jane and Sue need to entertain the thought that *that man is Kaplan*. They need to relate their anchored information to their unanchored information about Kaplan.

These distinct types of information rest, or so I claim, on the difference between proper names and indexicals, i.e. on the different way indexicals and proper names

---

[3] It is worth mentioning that the fact that one knows who someone is does not eliminate the cognitive puzzles (e.g. Frege's puzzle). Lois knows who Clark Kent is and who Superman is. She does not know though, that Clark Kent is Superman.

contribute in bridging the gap between language, thought, and reality. In short, I subscribe to the following thesis:

[I]t must be stressed that deixis and naming are two different acts and must be distinguished from each other, that deictic words and naming words are two different word classes that must be clearly separated; there is no justification for assuming that in Indo-European, say, the one emerged from the other. (Bühler 1934/1990: 86/101)

In the next section I spell out how proper names and indexicals differ and, in particular, the different competencies one manifests when using them. I argue, *pace* Burge (1973), Almog (1981), Recanati (1993), Voltolini (1995), Pelczar and Rainsbury (1998), to name just a few, in favor of the thesis that proper names cannot be reduced to, or explained away in terms of, indexicals.[4] As Jespersen noticed some time ago:

[I]t is very unnatural to the unsophisticated mind to say that "I see you" stands instead of "Otto Jespersen sees Mary Brown". . . . We may also say "I, Otto Jespersen, hereby declare . . .", which would be preposterous if "I" were simply a substitute for the name. (Jespersen 1924: 82)

3. Pure Indexicals *vs.* Demonstratives

Thanks to the seminal works of Castañeda, Kaplan, Kamp, and Perry, it is nowadays a triviality to claim that indexical expressions are context-sensitive; that is, their reference depends on the context in which they are used. If you change the context of use (the speaker, the time, the location) you may end up with different referents. It is also common knowledge that the best way to capture this platitude is *via* Kaplan's content/character distinction.[5] Character *qua* linguistic meaning of an indexical expression is represented by a function from context to content. The character of 'I', for instance, is represented by a function of the form "The utterer of this token" which takes as its argument the context and gives as its value the

---

[4] "Indexical reference is personal, ephemeral, confrontational, and executive. Hence it is not reducible to nonindexical reference to what is not confronted. Conversely, nonindexical reference is not reducible to indexical reference" (Castañeda 1989: 70). As for proper names, Barcan Marcus summarizes my position as follows: "Proper names have a logically irreducible use. They permit us to entertain a separation in language of the object under discussion from its properties" (Barcan Marcus [1975] (1993): 107).

[5] See Kaplan (1977). To be precise, in Kaplan's logical framework the content is a function from circumstances of evaluation to extensions. Henceforth I shall forget these subtleties for Kaplan's distinctions between context of utterance and circumstance of evaluation and between content and extension do not affect my argument, i.e. they do not concern the difference between proper names and indexicals. These distinctions are relevant when one deals with modal (and temporal) operators.

referent, usually the speaker or writer.[6] The relevant contextual parameters needed to fix an indexical reference are *the agent*, *the time*, and *the location*.

Not all indexical expressions, though, work the way 'I', 'now', 'here', 'today', etc. do. The character of so-called demonstrative expressions like 'this', 'that', 'she', etc. is incomplete. To be sure, 'this', unlike 'that', suggests proximity, just as 'she' suggests that the referent is a female. Nonetheless, it is often the case that, when using a demonstrative expression, something extra is needed to fix the reference:

[A] sign consisting of the word 'this' and a gesture has a different meaning from a sign consisting of the word 'this' and another gesture. . . . 'This is beautiful and this is not beautiful' is not a complete sentence, because these words have to have gestures going with them. (Wittgenstein, *RPPI* i: §39)

When facing several women, we may appeal to a pointing gesture to single out the referent of 'she'. If the pointing gesture is not appropriate, because it is impolite to single someone out by pointing at her, we may end up using a complex demonstrative of the form 'that brunette with a red shirt near the window', etc.

To capture the difference between expressions whose character is complete and those that have an incomplete one we can, once again, follow Kaplan in distinguishing between *pure indexicals* and *demonstratives*. Roughly, a demonstrative without an associated demonstration is incomplete, for the linguistic rule which governs its use is not sufficient to determine its referent in each context of use. A pure indexical, on the other hand, does not rest on an associated demonstration; any demonstration supplied is either for emphasis or irrelevant.[7] If, pointing toward a group of people, one says, "He/She/That woman/ . . . is in my class" the pointing gesture is needed to fix the reference. The pointing gesture *per se*, though, is neither a necessary nor a sufficient condition. One can successfully use a demonstrative expression without pointing. Besides, one's pointing gesture can be off target.[8] Kaplan (1989) circumvents these difficulties in arguing that with demonstrative expressions reference is fixed by the *directing intention*:

The directing intention is the element that differentiates the 'meaning' of one syntactic occurrence of a demonstrative from another, creating the *potential* for distinct referents, and creating the *actuality* of equivocation. (Kaplan 1989: 588)

---

[6] As we shall see when dealing with essential indexicals (Ch. 4), in some cases the agent *qua* referent of the first-person pronouns differs from the writer and/or speaker.

[7] "The mouth which says 'I' or the hand which is raised to indicate that it is I who wish to speak, or I who have toothache, does not thereby point to anything. . . . The man who cries out with pain, or says that he is in pain, *doesn't choose the mouth which says it*. . . . If, in saying 'I' I point to my own body, I model the use of 'I' on that of the demonstrative 'this person' or 'he' " (Wittgenstein, *BB*: 71).

[8] "And what does 'pointing to the shape', 'pointing to the color' consist in? Point to a piece of paper.— And now point to its shape—now its color—now its number (that sounds queer)—How did you do it?" (Wittgenstein, *PI*: §33).

As I understand it, the directing intention does not coincide, though, with the individual one intends to talk about, i.e. the individual one has in mind. If, believing that the man in front of me is Marcello Lippi, I claim "That man is the famous Juventus manager" I have Lippi in mind and I intend to say something about Lippi. If, unbeknownst to me, though, the man in front of me is not Lippi but, say, Sir Alex Ferguson, I do refer to Sir Alex Ferguson, regardless of my having Lippi in mind. For my *primary* intention is to refer to the man in front of me, not to the man I have in mind. It is this *communicative* intention that I take to be the directing intention. For this reason it may be better to label it *directing attention*.

A word of clarification may be useful. One could argue that in introducing the notion of directing intention, Kaplan fundamentally changed his original (1977) view insofar as people's intentions enter the scene. One can go on to argue that reference is not fixed by the "pointing gesture" but by the speaker's intention. The difference can be stressed in focusing on Kaplan's original Carnap-Agnew example where one points backwards toward a picture and says "That man is the greatest philosopher of this century" intending that Carnap is the greatest philosopher of the century. Unbeknownst to the speaker, Carnap's picture has been replaced by a picture of Agnew. If reference is fixed by the pointing gesture then one refers to Agnew while if reference is fixed by the speaker's intention then one refers to Carnap.[9] Kaplan seems to suggest this interpretation when he argues that "the demonstration . . . is there only to help *convey* an intention and plays no *semantical* role at all . . . the referent is properly determined by the perceptual intention" (1989; 583–4). Though I subscribe to Kaplan's view that the demonstration does not play a semantic role I do not subscribe to the view that reference is fixed by the speaker's intention. For this reason I introduced the more neutral notion of directing attention. This seems to fit the data in a more elegant way insofar as it does not blur the distinction between the object one has in mind *and* the object one refers to. And in some cases, like in the Carnap-Agnew example, the two objects differ. From the audience's viewpoint the distinction between the object one intends to refer to (the object one has in mind) and the actual object one ends up referring to is also relevant when it comes to detecting whether one succeeds in transmitting the message one intended.

The directing attention can be viewed as resting on the communal practice of using demonstrative expressions. One masters the use of a demonstrative expression when one is able to exploit both the linguistic features and the features available from one's surroundings in order to single out an object of discourse. In using 'she', for instance,

---

[9] Kaplan's notion of directing intention could be understood as follows. The speaker's intention fixes what is selected, not what is referred to. Hence, in our example the intention is to point to a picture, so the picture is selected, even if the pointing gesture does not point exactly at the picture, or points somewhere between a picture and a window. Either way, Agnew is referred to. I do not know, though, whether Kaplan would be keen on this interpretation (I suspect not) which comes close to the picture I am putting forward.

a speaker expects to refer to a female (this is given by the meaning of the demonstrative, i.e. by the fact that 'she' is gender-sensitive). To single out the relevant object the speaker must also know how to exploit features available from the context in which the linguistic interchange occurs, such as a physical gesture, a glimpse, a previous remark. In a word, when using a demonstrative expression the speaker is *responsible*, with this very use, for fixing the reference; our competent speaker makes the best use of the traits available from the context. We can thus propose the following thesis:

- *Demonstrative Reference vs. Pure Indexical Reference*
  Demonstrative reference rests on the directing attention, which is not required in the case of pure indexicals.

With pure indexicals, the story is more straightforward insofar as what is relevant in fixing the reference is given by the utterance itself. That is to say, the utterance gives us the relevant contextual parameters such as the agent, time, and place. The latter are what indexical expressions direct us to. In their paradigmatic uses (i.e. if we forget answering machines, post-it notes, fictional uses, and the like), when one uses a pure indexical one *automatically* refers to the relevant item. If one uses 'today', one refers to the relevant day regardless of one's intention. The simple act of uttering that word suffices to fix the reference. In other words, in the paradigmatic cases of pure indexical use, the utterance itself suffices in directing attention to the relevant referents and the producer of the utterance need not appeal to contextual clues in order to help the audience in their interpretation. The understanding of a pure indexical rests on the grasping of the contextual parameters and the latter are furnished by the utterance itself. One does not understand a use of 'I', for instance, if one does not understand *who* the agent of the utterance is. In short, the understanding of a specific use of 'I' rests on the grasping of the relevant contextual parameter to which the very utterance of 'I' directs us. The contextual parameters are constantly exploited, they are *part of what is said and communicated* and have to be grasped for the message to be successful, while directing attentions are not part of what one says and primarily aims to communicate.[10]

4. Indexicals *vs.* Proper Names

It has been claimed that proper names, like indexicals, are context-sensitive and, therefore, that the Kaplanian picture can be expanded and stretched to accommodate proper names as well:

The reference of the name thus depends on a contextual factor, as the reference of an indexical expression does. . . . proper names are very much like indexicals. (Recanati 1993: 140)

[10] For a more detailed discussion of indexicals *vs.* demonstratives, see Ch. 4, Sect. 2, below.

The reference of a proper name is contextually dependent: the same proper name may refer to different objects in different contexts. . . . What is referred to by a particular use of the name depends on which convention happens to be invoked, and which convention happens to be invoked depends on the context of utterance. . . . Therefore a proper name is referentially context-dependent, exactly as an ordinary indexical. (Recanati 1993: 143).[11]

If a proper name is like an indexical then 'Aristotle' in the context of a philosophical discussion and 'Aristotle' in the context of a financial discussion is the *same* name type referring to different individuals because it appears in different contexts of utterance. Would one be keen to tell the same story about ambiguous expressions? Would one say that 'bank' is a single noun which, according to the context of use, may pick out either the financial institution or the riverside?

I guess that I would not find many opponents if I claim that 'bank' is not an indexical changing meaning with a change in the context of utterance and that ambiguity ought to be distinguished from indexicality. By the same token, I would argue that, insofar as context is concerned, the case of homonyms is closer to the phenomenon of ambiguity than indexicality. There are, though, many differences between so-called ambiguous expressions and homonyms: (i) the former, unlike the latter, appear in dictionaries, (ii) there are only a few terms which look and sound alike while there are many distinct proper names which happen to share the same generic name, (iii) competent speakers happen to know and master so-called ambiguous expressions, while it is practically impossible for a single speaker to know all the referents of all the single proper names which look and sound alike, i.e. which share the same generic name. In what follows I try to spell out some details to justify these claims.

Unlike indexicals (either demonstratives or pure indexicals), proper names can be used to refer to an object even if the speaker and hearer are not and have never been "in contact" with the referent. When you and I use 'Aristotle' we both refer to the same individual and we may understand each other even if Aristotle is not, and has never been, in our perceptual field:

We said that the sentence "Excalibur has a sharp blade" made sense even when Excalibur was broken in pieces. Now this is so because in this language-game a name is also used in the absence of its bearer. But we can imagine a language-game with names (that is, with signs which we should certainly include among names) in which they are used only in the presence of the bearer; and so could *always* be replaced by a demonstrative pronoun and the gesture of pointing. (Wittgenstein, *PI*: §44)

Since proper names are usually used in the absence of their bearer, they do not rely on the context of use to fix their reference. The context of reference-fixing and the

---

[11] Pelczar and Rainsbury (1988: 296) make a similar point.

context of utterance are often different. It goes without saying that during a baptism or dubbing, the context of utterance and the context of reference-fixing are the same. This, though, is not the paradigmatic use of a proper name—usually an individual gets baptized only once in her life (for argument's sake we can also ignore the fact that some people change their name when they get married). We do not perform an act of baptism each time we utter a proper name:

> Proper names serve as a long finger of ostension over time and place. On this account 'proper name' is a semantical, not a merely syntactical notion. Reference is supposed. We may mistakenly believe of some syntactically proper name, say 'Homer', that it has an actual singular referent and is a genuine proper name, but if its use does not finally link it to a singular object, it is not a genuine name at all. . . . Proper names have fixed values in our language as a historical institution and are part of the public vocabulary. In this way they allow reference to an object despite the vicissitudes the objects undergo and despite the absence of direct acquaintance with many and perhaps most of the objects that the language user correctly names. (Barcan Marcus [1985/6] 1993: 203–4)

One of the reasons we need proper names is that we want to be able to keep track and speak of objects that are not in our perceptual field.[12]

The general point I would like to make is that the use of a proper name does not appeal to context in the same way that the use of an indexical does. To be sure, the context may affect the referent of a given label: in the context of gossiping about Jackie Kennedy's lovers 'Aristotle' refers to Aristotle Onassis, while in a philosophical discussion, it refers to the philosopher. To evade confusion it is worth stressing that I am not claiming that Aristotle Onassis and Aristotle the philosopher share the same name, for I take proper names to be private. They are like private properties one cannot transfer to someone else:

> There is a traditional distinction between 'proper' names and 'class' names, which is explained as consisting in the fact that a proper name applies, essentially, to only one object, whereas a class name applies to all objects of a certain kind, however numerous they may be. Thus 'Napoleon' is a proper name, while 'man' is a class name. (Russell 1948: 87)

Indexicals, on the other hand, are not private. It does not make sense to claim that 'you', for instance, is the private label of a given addressee or 'today' the private name of a given day. The picture I have in mind bears some similarities to Kaplan's (1990) distinction between proper names and generic names. A generic name is what parents look at when they choose how to name their baby: it is what we find in books such as *A Thousand Ways of Naming Your Kid* and attached to some keyrings.

---

[12] "And there is also the language-game of inventing a name for something, and hence of saying, 'This is . . .' and then using the new name. (Thus, for example, children give names to their dolls and then talk about them and to them. Think in this connection how singular is the use of a person's name to *call* him!)" (Wittgenstein, *PI*: §27).

A proper name, on the other hand, is intrinsically linked to the object it names. So Aristotle Onassis and Aristotle the philosopher, like David Kaplan, David Ginola, and David Beckham, bear *distinct*, though homophonically and syntactically indistinguishable, proper names.[13] The words 'Aristotle' and 'David', by means of which both the philosopher and the magnate on the one hand and the philosopher and the football players on the other, are called are not, properly speaking, proper names. They are *generic* names from which infinitely many distinct proper names can be drawn and created.[14] The latter are best understood in naturalistic terms, as natural objects usually created with an act of dubbing or baptism, i.e. as objects which come into existence, stay around for a while, and then may disappear:

One might think of them [proper names] as trees. Stemming out from their creation, with physical and mental segments; the mental segment able to produce many physical branches and able to merge many physical branches. . . . At any rate, they are objects of the created realm, created by language makers. (Kaplan 1990: 117)

The reference of a proper name is not fixed in the same way in which the reference of an indexical is fixed. Reference is a *social* matter: it is a social convention that brings the name to its bearer, a convention that began with some sort of baptism or dubbing.[15] The utterance itself may suggest which convention we are relying on. If one says "Campbell is a gorgeous model", the utterance itself suggests that the utterer uses the name of Naomi Campbell and not the name of, say, Sol Campbell or Kevin Campbell, the football players. The context of the utterance (i.e. the agent, time, and place) does not affect, though, the use of the name; it does not help in fixing the reference. There is simply no need to fix the reference. Once a name enters the physical realm it cannot easily be dismissed. A proper name can die out, just as a secular tree can vanish. It is possible, though, at least in principle, to track that name just as it is possible to track the existence of a secular tree. Think, for instance, of the many Nazi war criminals that, with the help of some anti-Communist movements (mainly based in the USA and GB) and the Vatican, changed their names and found refuge around the American continent. Most of

[13] The same story applies to ambiguous words as well: two or more distinct terms can look and sound alike (e.g. 'bank', 'mistress', . . .). On the other hand, it may also be that the very same name or term will look and sound differently as it is the case of proper names which undergo translation (e.g. 'London', 'Londra', and 'Londres') or terms spelled differently and/or pronounced differently within various dialects (e.g. 'behavior' and 'behaviour', 'amazing' and 'amasing', 'color' and 'colour', . . .).
[14] Generic names help us to understand the predicative use of proper names: e.g. "There are lots of Johns in my class", "A Mary Smith was looking for you".
[15] Notice that I am not arguing that the only way a name can come into existence is via a baptism. A proper name may be introduced in many different ways. For a different way in which a proper name may be generated, see e.g. Ch. 3, Sect. 1, below, where I discuss description-names.

them, sooner or later, were discovered nonetheless and their original name (the one they tried to hide) became current again.[16]

A rather similar story can be told about names, such as 'Madagascar', that switched reference. As the story goes, Marco Polo, in picking up the name 'Madagascar' from the natives, thought that it referred to the island while the natives used it to refer to the mainland. My analysis goes like this. The mistake, i.e. the switch of reference, occurred when Polo *incorporated* the name within his own language (Italian) and transmitted it to the other members of his linguistic community. In incorporating the name into his own linguistic practice Polo *associated* the name with the island. He somewhat rebaptized the island: he entertained the thought *this (island) is Madagascar* or *this island is called 'Madagascar'*. The practice of using 'Madagascar' as the name for the island took over the native practice of using 'Madagascar' to refer to the mainland. Actually, what happened is that Polo, unbeknownst to him, *created* a new name. This is similar to what may happen in translation. I have been told that 'lama' was introduced into Spanish by some conquistadors who, inquiring about the name of a lama, asked the native: "¿Cómo se llama?" The native, puzzled and unable to understand the question, simply repeated 'lama'. The conquistadors, believing that 'lama' was the noun the native used for the lama, introduced it into their linguistic practice. Once again a new noun has been created. This can happen in different ways: one can create a new name or nouns from scratch, one can create a new name or nouns in translation from an unknown language (as in Quine's 'gavagai' example), etc. The 'Madagascar' and 'lama' cases fall into the last category. In these kinds of cases there is an interpretation and/or translation going on. To claim, though, that an interpretation and/or translation happens each time one uses or hears a name or noun amounts to a misunderstanding of our general, consumerist, practice of using and transmitting names and nouns.[17]

---

[16] A historical note: The change of name and personality of major war criminals has been a common practice after the Second World War: "One aspect of suppressing the anti-fascist resistance was the recruitment of war criminals like Klaus Barbie [the butcher of Lyon], an SS officer who had been the Gestapo chief of Lyon, France. . . . Although he was responsible for many hideous crimes, the US Army put him in charge of spying on the French. When Barbie was finally brought back to France in 1982 to be tried as a war criminal his use as agent was explained by Colonel (ret.) Eugene Kolb of the US Army counterintelligence Corps: Barbie's 'skills were badly needed. . . . His activities had been directed against the underground French Communist party and the resistance', who were now targeted for repression by the American liberators. . . . Later on when it became difficult or impossible to protect these useful folks in Europe, many of them (including Barbie) were spirited off to the United States or to Latin America, often with the help of the Vatican and fascist priests" (Chomsky 1992: 18).

[17] My story can thus accommodate Mercier's worries and criticisms of the consumerist picture: "But the appeal to the social character of language will not explain how Polo's speaker-referent (or anyone else's) becomes the semantic-referent. The social character of language could possibly play a part in such an explanation only if there existed at some point a social language in which the semantic-referent of 'Madagascar' were Madagascar-the-island. . . . To begin to explain how Polo's speaker-referent can become his semantic-referent, I claim, we have to look at *individualistic* aspects of Polo's interaction with the *word* 'Madagascar' as it gets transmitted to him" (Mercier 1999: 104).

The way context affects the use of a proper name mirrors the way it influences the use of ambiguous expressions. Before using 'bank', for instance, we have to decide whether we use it exploiting the convention which brings us to the river or to the financial institution.[18] The contextual features we appeal to in these cases are better understood as helping us decide *which* particular term/name is used rather than determining which referent is picked out by a single context-sensitive word. Take, for example, 'bank'. The contextual features may help the audience to decide whether the speaker is using *the* term of the financial institution or whether she is using *the* (distinct though homophonic) term standing for the embankment. Hence, 'bank' is not a single term that, like an indexical, may pick out different referents in different contexts. Actually, proper names, like nouns, are cultural artifacts with a genealogical history. 'Bank' as the noun for the riverside derives from the old German 'banke' which is related to what in English we call 'bench', while 'bank' *qua* noun for the financial institution derives from the Latin words 'bancus' and 'banca'. We thus have two homophonic names with very different histories. These names cannot be dissociated from their histories. We cannot, though, tell the same story with indexicals: 'today' uttered today and 'today' uttered yesterday are not two distinct homophonic words with different histories.[19]

We can follow Perry and capture these intuitions in distinguishing between *pre-semantic* and *semantic* use of context:

Sometimes we use context to figure out with which meaning a word is being used, or which of several words that look or sound alike is being used, or even which language is being spoken. These are *pre-semantic* uses of context. In the case of indexicals, however, context is used *semantically*. It remains relevant after the language, words and meaning are all known; the meaning directs us to certain aspects of context. (Perry 1997a: 593)

If one (e.g. Burge 1973) is inclined to think that proper names are disguised complex demonstratives, then one commits oneself to the thesis that the reference of a proper name, like the reference of a demonstrative, is fixed by the agent's directing attention. One way to understand this proposal would be to argue that the latter singles

---

[18] As I already said, I am not suggesting, however, that proper names are ambiguous. For a discussion on how proper names differ from ambiguous expression see Napoli (1997). Proper names, unlike ambiguous expressions or synonymous expressions, do not usually occur in dictionaries. So one can argue that a speaker who does not know that 'bank' is ambiguous, like one who does not know that 'unmarried man' and 'bachelor' are synonymous, is not fully competent in English. On the other hand, we cannot say that one who does not know the meanings of the thousands of 'Jane Black', i.e. all the individuals who happen to share the same *generic* name, is linguistically incompetent. Notice that from the fact that from "NN is F" a competent speaker may be able to infer "Someone called 'NN' is F" or "The bearer of 'NN' is F", we cannot say that our speaker must know the bearer of 'NN' to be competent with 'NN'. In order to make this inference the speaker merely needs to know that 'NN' is a proper name.

[19] A similar story can be told in the case of syntactic ambiguity. An utterance of "Visiting relatives can be boring" could be the utterance of two distinct sentences which merely happen to look alike. The two sentences have different logical forms. I shall discuss the notion of logical form in Ch. 2, below.

out the convention that supposedly bridges the gap between the name type and its referent. I cannot see, though, how this can be possible. In particular, I cannot see how an agent can direct her attention to a given convention. Roughly, one can demonstrate/point toward/ . . . an individual while one cannot point toward/ demonstrate/ . . . an individual who is not present, nor to a given convention. In my picture, homonyms are individuated by the convention governing their use, the very convention one exploits when using a name.[20] To be honest, though, Burge's proposal is that a proper name works like a complex demonstrative. A proper name, 'Aristotle' for instance, expresses the property of being an Aristotle. Aristotle has this property insofar as he acquired the name 'Aristotle'. The name *qua* complex demonstrative, '*that* Aristotle', singles out a salient Aristotle. This is pretty much like an utterance of 'that apple' singling out the relevant apple. The problem I foresee can be summarized as follows. While 'this apple' may single out a relevant apple insofar as the referent is in the perceptual field of the speaker and the audience, 'that Aristotle' cannot pick out the relevant Aristotle insofar as Aristotle is not present. As I suggested earlier, indexicals, unlike proper names, are usually used to make reference *in praesentia*. Hence if 'Aristotle' goes proxy for '*that* Aristotle' Aristotle should be present for the reference to succeed. If the referent is not present, the proper name *qua* complex demonstrative should select the relevant convention.[21]

A word of clarification may be appropriate. I argued that a name standing for its bearer is a matter of convention and that the convention helps individuate the name. So, a speaker exploiting a given convention automatically refers to the bearer of the name. This way of speaking, though, suggests that there is a relation between the name and its bearer and, therefore, that the name can be dissociated from its bearer, i.e. that there is a gap between the name and its bearer. In that case one needs to tell a story of how the gap gets bridged. While Frege introduced senses, others ended up arguing that names are like indexicals and that it is the context in which the name is uttered that bridges the gap. This is not the picture I have in mind. If one likes to speak about a relation between a name and its bearer then I would claim that this relation is, to borrow Wittgenstein's terminology, *internal*. That is, a relation which cannot fail to obtain inasmuch as it is given, is constituted, by the terms it relates. In his later development Wittgenstein speaks of grammatical or logical relations suggesting that

[20] For simplicity's sake I ignore cases when demonstrative expressions are used in a deferential way, such as 'she' in "She is not in today" while pointing to someone's office door, or 'it' in "It must be a male" indicating a bear's footprint. In such cases indexicals are used in another language-game. I shall discuss deferred reference further in Ch. 6, Sect. 4, below.

[21] If one (e.g. King 2001) assumes that complex demonstratives are not singular terms but quantified noun phrases, then Burge's proposal would become a version of the Russellian picture according to which proper names are disguised definite descriptions. This position would then face the well-known problems put forward by Kripke (1980) and Donnellan (1966). This is not, though, Burge's aim. I discuss and criticize King's quantificational account of complex demonstratives in some detail in Corazza (2003).

the relata are not connected by a relation of matching or fitting. So the name and its bearer do not stand in a relation of satisfaction and/or fitting as the Fregean picture and the indexical theory of names suggest.[22] The name and its bearer are simply two aspects of the same convention. As two sides of the same coin cannot be dissociated, so the name cannot be dissociated from its bearer. The identity condition of the name depends on the bearer. In other words, if we take the name–bearer relation to be internal, then no intermediary condition can interfere between the relata. When one exploits the relevant convention, i.e. when one uses a proper name, one manifests one's competence simply by using the name in appropriate ways.[23] One does not need to grasp senses, ideas, concepts, descriptions, or whatever in order to competently exploit the convention, i.e. use the name. This mirrors the case when one follows a given rule. One follows it blindly, i.e. without interpreting it. One knows exactly what to do and manifests that knowledge by acting in an appropriate way.[24]

'How am I able to obey a rule?'—if this is not a question about causes, then it is about the justification for my following the rule in the way I do.
If I have exhausted the justification I have reached bedrock, and my spade is turned. Then I am inclined to say: 'This is simply what I do'. (Wittgenstein, *PI*: §217)

When I obey a rule I do not choose. I obey the rule *blindly*. (Wittgenstein, *PI*: §219)

The moral I would like to draw so far is that we seem to have strong reasons to resist the assimilation and/or reduction of proper names to indexicals. They are distinct tools of reference involving different competencies.[25] When one uses an indexical one directs one's attention toward a given object while when one uses a name one uses it with its fixed meaning and semantic value. Bühler seems to have anticipated this point:

The proper name is a linguistic structure that is suited by virtue of its *form* to function as an individual sign within the circle of those who know it and use it. (Bühler 1934/1990: 114/130)

---

[22] "But this is a bad picture. It is as if one were to say 'The king in chess is *the* piece that one can check'. But this can mean no more that in our language game of chess we only check the king" (Wittgenstein, *PI*: §136).

[23] The position I am here defending also bears similarities with Barcan Marcus insofar as she claims: "Proper names have fixed values in our language as a historical institution and are part of the public vocabulary. In this way they allow reference to an object despite the vicissitudes the objects undergo and despite the absence of direct acquaintance with many and perhaps most of the objects that the language user correctly names" (Barcan Marcus [1985/6] 1993: 204).

[24] For the simplicity of argument I do not address the case of empty proper names. Are they proper names or, as Frege suggested, simply mock proper names? In other words, since one of the relata is missing the name *qua* internal relation cannot exist. A way out of this problem would be to claim, following Donnellan (1974), that an empty name is still a relation with one of its relata corresponding with a block. An empty name could thus be viewed as a convention ending in a block.

[25] "If you do not want to produce confusion you will do best not to call these words ['this' and 'that'] names at all.—Yet, strange to say, the word 'this' has been called the only *genuine* name; so that anything else we call a name was one only in an inexact, approximate sense" (Wittgenstein, *PI*: §38).

As Kaplan suggests:

> Words come to us prepackaged with a semantic value. If we are to use *those words*, the words we have received, the words of our linguistic community, then we must defer to *their* meaning. Otherwise we play the role of language creators. (Kaplan 1989: 602)

Here Kaplan and Bühler join the Wittgensteinian picture I proposed above. Actually, as I already suggested, proper names, like nouns, are cultural artifacts with a genealogical history. Names cannot be dissociated from their history. In the case of indexicals the situation is rather different: 'today' uttered today and 'today' uttered yesterday are not two distinct homophonic words with different histories. If this were the case we could use 'today' to refer to a previously fixed day. But, as Frege told us:

> If someone wants to say the same today as he expressed yesterday using 'today', he must replace this word with 'yesterday'. (Frege [1918] 1988: 40)

So far I have argued that the difference between an indexical and a proper name rests on the fact that in the first case we need context to *determine the referent*, while in the second we need context to *determine which name* is being used.[26] Once again, the same point can be made in a slightly different way in exploiting Kaplan's notion of consumerist semantics:

> In our culture the role of language creators is largely reserved to parents, scientists, and headline writers for *Variety*; it is by no means the typical use of language as the subjectivist semanticist believes. To use language as language, to express something, requires an intentional act. But the intention that is required involves the typical consumer's attitude of compliance, not the producer's assertiveness. (Kaplan 1989: 602)

As I said, when one uses a proper name one is *exploiting* and relying on an already existing convention while when one is using an indexical one is *creating*, by this very use, the link between the linguistic expression and the referent. This link is created by the very utterance or speech act. It is for these reasons that proper names, like other nouns, but unlike indexicals, can be used in a deferential way. As Kripke and Putnam told us, one can competently use 'Gellman' and 'Feynman' without knowing who Gellman and Feynman are—without even knowing that they are famous scientists—as one can use 'elm' and 'beech' without being able to distinguish an elm from a beech.[27] On the other hand, it does not make sense to claim

---

[26] As Perry aptly points out: "The conventions of English do not associate particular individuals with the words 'I' and 'you', but conditions that individuals must satisfy to be the designata of uses of those words" (Perry 1997b: 346).

[27] "On my view, acquisition of a name does not, in general, put us *en rapport* (in the language of 'Quantifying in') with the referent. But this is not required for us to use the name in the standard way as a device of direct reference" (Kaplan 1989: 605).

that one can competently use an indexical, say 'I' or 'she', in a deferential way, i.e. without being able to tell apart oneself from, say, the female one directs one's attention toward. In simply uttering 'I' one picks out oneself as referent and the 'I'-thought expressed is cognitively grounded to oneself. Someone's use of the first-person pronoun does not rest on some principles of differentiation selecting oneself from others. Indexicals by their very nature put us *en rapport* with their referent, i.e. our thoughts get (automatically, cognitively) anchored to reality. One could object that indexicals do not automatically put us *en rapport* with their referents. One can lose track of the time and say 'today' without knowing which day one refers to. Moreover, one can say 'this' whilst holding a box containing a surprise and refer to the item in the box without knowing what it is. I do not believe, though, that one needs to identify the relevant day, i.e. be able to replace 'today' with a specific date, in order to refer to the relevant day. When one refers to the content of a box with 'this' without knowing what is inside, one is nonetheless "in contact" with the referent. One can easily refer to the relevant object using 'the content of *this* box', 'the content of the box *I* hold', etc. This is similar to the case when one perceives an object never previously encountered or when one is unable to characterize the referent. In these cases, our subject is also cognitively linked to the object inasmuch as one is in a position to acquire perceptual information from the perceived object. In all these cases there is a channel of information going from the referent to the agent and this suffices, I believe, to put one in cognitive contact with a referent. As the scenario that I discussed at the beginning shows, the information we associate with indexical thoughts is anchored to reality.[28] We can, once again, capture the relevant difference in terms of different competencies involved. Actually, if one argues that proper names reduce to indexicals one commits oneself to a rather implausible theory of reference, i.e. that the user is *responsible* for bridging the gap between the name and its bearer:

This is connected with a conception of naming as, so to speak, an occult process. Naming appears as a *queer* connection of a word with an object.—And you really get such a queer connection when the philosopher tries to bring out *the* relation between name and thing by staring at an object in front of him and repeating the name or even the word 'this' innumerable times. For philosophical problems arise when language *goes on holiday*. And *here* we may indeed fancy naming to be some remarkable act of mind, as it were a baptism of an object. And we can also say the word 'this' *to* the object, as it were *address* the object as 'this'—a queer use of this word, which doubtless only occurs in doing philosophy. (Wittgenstein, *PI*: §38)

---

[28] "On my view, our connection with a linguistic community in which names and other meaning-bearing elements are passed down to us enables us to entertain thoughts *through the language* that would not otherwise be accessible to us. Call this the *Instrumental Thesis*" (Kaplan 1989: 603).

I suspect that one of the motivations lying behind the reduction of proper names to indexicals is Fregean in spirit. Actually, if one is looking for something which bridges this alleged gap, a natural place to search would be the representations associated with the linguistic expressions. Following this picture an expression is used successfully if the speaker and hearer grasp the relevant representation associated with the expression. This picture is, if not in the letter, at least in the spirit, Cartesian:

> There is for Frege a realm of intrinsically significant representations, distinct from the things represented and accessible to (even if not resident of) the mind, and linguistic expressions come alive by association with these representations. It is the Fregean senses, not their linguistic embodiments, Frege tells us, that refer in the primary instance. (Wettstein 1998: 432)

The Fregean picture ultimately rests, to borrow Wettstein's happy expression, on *the cognitive fix requirement*. In order to think and talk about a given item one must be in a substantial cognitive relation with the latter. One ultimately needs to possess a discriminative cognitive fix on the referent.[29] It is because of the search for the cognitive fix that Russell at some point argued that the only genuine proper names are 'this' and 'that' insofar as they put us in direct contact with reality. Following this trend some have been tempted to reduce, or at least explain, proper names in terms of indexicals.[30] For the latter do indeed put us in a direct relation with the object we refer to. It is part of our linguistic practice that we usually use indexicals

---

[29] To be sure Frege stresses that senses are not residents of the mind and postulates a third, objective, realm of senses. Frege (and the neo-Fregeans), though, maintains that an expression refers *via* the mediation of a sense and that the speaker's and hearer's understanding of and competence with the relevant expression depends on the grasping of the expression's sense. As Dummett puts it: "The extrusion of thoughts from the mind initiated by Bolzano led to what is often termed 'Platonism', as exemplified by Frege's mythology of the 'third realm': for, if thoughts are not contents of the mind, they must be located in a compartment of reality distinct both from physical world and the inner world of private experience. This mythology served Frege and Husserl as a bulwark against the psychologism which they opposed. If, now, our capacity for thought is equated with, or at least explained in terms of, our ability to use language, no such bulwark is required: for language is a social phenomenon, in no way private to the individual, and its use is publicly observable. It is for this reason that the linguistic turn may be seen as a device for continuing to treat thoughts as objective and utterly disparate from inner mental events, without having recourse to the platonistic mythology" (Dummett 1993: 131).

[30] Evans's appeal to what he terms 'Russell Principle' in explaining the use and understanding of singular terms (e.g. proper names) is symptomatic of this tendency. Frege's senses are supposed to play the very same role, i.e. to be what puts us in contact with the world of referents. So Evans claims: "I think it will be universally acknowledged that understanding a use of a proper name requires one to go beyond the thought that the speaker is referring to *some person known as NN*, and to arrive at a thought in the thinking of which one actually thinks of the object in question. The reason for this is not the one that is usually given, namely that the property of being known as NN is semantical in character, but rather, a consideration of the same sort as I brought to bear in the case of, say, 'you'. One does not understand a remark of the form 'You are F', addressed to oneself, just by knowing that the speaker is saying that the person he is addressing is F; one must go beyond the referential feature and identify the person as oneself. Similarly,

to pick out objects in our surroundings. It is for this reason that Sue asks about *that man*, the man she is perceiving and is interested in. In other words, it is because indexicals, unlike proper names and other terms, are intrinsically perspectival, i.e. they are tied to an agent's (egocentric) setting, that they put us in "direct contact" with the referent.[31] The understanding of an indexical requires the grasp of the context in which it is uttered. One does not understand a use of 'I', for instance, if one does not grasp the contextual parameter, in that case, the agent. On the other hand, one can understand a proper name, say 'Plato', even if one does not know when or by whom it has been uttered and/or written. If one reads a piece of graffiti saying "Plato is a Greek philosopher" one may understand what is said even if one does not know when it has been produced or by whom, while if one reads a piece of graffiti stating "I was here yesterday" one does not understand what is said inasmuch as one does not grasp the contextual parameters. Indexical identification, unlike identification using proper names, is perspectival. Without a perspectival identification indexicals are silent.[32]

In the scenario I described at the beginning, it is because Jane starts from a publicly identified individual, Kaplan, that she asks (1) [Do you know which person David Kaplan is?]. On the other hand it is because Sue starts from a perspectival identification that she asks (3) [Do you know who that man is?]. While Sue's thought about Kaplan is cognitively grounded to Kaplan (she perceives him and refers to him as 'that man'), Jane's thought about Kaplan is deferential (she relies on Jon to identify Kaplan). Once again, this remark is inspired by Wittgenstein:

Our difficulty could be put this way: We think about things,—but how do these things enter into our thoughts? We think about Mr. Smith; but Mr. Smith need not be present. A picture of him won't do; for how are we to know whom it represents? In fact no substitute for him will do. Then how can he himself be an object of our thoughts? . . .

We said the connection between our thinking, or speaking, about a man and the man himself was made when, in order to explain the meaning of the word 'Mr. Smith' we pointed to him, saying "this is Mr. Smith". And there is nothing mysterious about this connection. I mean, there is no queer mental act which somehow conjures up Mr. Smith in our minds when he really isn't here. What makes it difficult to see that this is the connection is a peculiar form of expression of ordinary language, which makes it appear that the connection between our thought (or the expression of our thought) and the thing we think about must have subsisted *during* the act of thinking. . . .

if one has a dossier of information associated with the name 'NN', and fails to bring it to bear in understanding 'NN is F', going no further than the thought 'Someone named "NN" is F, one has surely failed to do what it was the point of utterance that one should do" (Evans 1982: 399).

[31] I discuss in more detail the notion of perspectival thoughts in Ch. 4 and 7, below.
[32] "In perspectival identification, we use an agent's first-hand cognitive relations to persons, objects, places, etc. as the identificatory framework" (Hintikka 1998: 205).

Someone says, "Mr. N. will come to see me this afternoon"; I ask "Do you mean him?" pointing to someone present, and he answers "Yes". In this conversation a connection was established between the word 'Mr. N.' and Mr. N. But we are tempted to think that while my friend said, "Mr. N. will come to see me", and meant what he said, his mind must have made the connection....

This is partly what makes us think of meaning or thinking as a peculiar *mental activity*; the word 'mental' indicating that we mustn't expect to understand how these things work. What we said of thinking can also be applied to imagining. Someone says he imagines King's College on fire. We ask him: "How do you know that it's *King's College* you imagine on fire? Couldn't it be a different building, very much like it? In fact is your imagination so absolutely exact that there might not be a dozen buildings whose representation your imagination could be?"—And still you say: "There is no doubt I imagined King's College and no other building". But can saying this be making the very connection we want? For saying it is like writing the words "Portrait of Mr. So-and-so" under a picture....

The fault which in all our reasoning about these matters we are inclined to make is to think that images and experiences of all sorts, which are in some sense closely connected with each other, must be present in our mind at the same time. (Wittgenstein, *BB*: 38–9)

As Bühler aptly points out:

Words like *I* and *you* are time and again accused of incurable subjectivity, and the accusation can be consistently extended from them to all other deictic words; but it is based on a misunderstanding, because what can be legitimately expected of naming words is improperly expected of deictic words. They are subjective in the same sense that every signpost only gives 'subjective' information, that is, information that is valid and can be given without mistake only from the position of the post. (Bühler 1934/1990: 106/122)

In a similar spirit Kaplan claims:

Contrary to Russell, I think we succeed in thinking about things in the world not only through the mental residues of that which we ourselves experience, but also vicariously, through the symbolic resources that come to us through our language. It is the latter—*vocabulary power*—that gives us our apprehensive advantage over the nonlinguistic animals. My dog, being color-blind, cannot entertain the thought that I am wearing a red shirt. But my color-blind colleague can entertain even the thought that Aristotle wore a red shirt. (Kaplan 1989: 604)

So far the general moral seems to be that proper names and indexicals are distinct tools enabling us to pick up objects of discourse and to think about them. Their semantic difference parallels the different competencies involved in using them.

For these reasons, if proper names have a linguistic meaning, the latter cannot be represented as a non-trivial function taking as its argument the context of utterance and giving as its value the referent. To put it slightly differently, if proper names have linguistic meaning, the latter does not work like the meaning of an indexical insofar as if names had a character represented by a function, the latter would yield, in every context, the same value. That is to say, the character of a proper name, if any, would not be context-sensitive, i.e. it would not take as its argument the context of utterance and change value with a change in that context. For the reason I gave above when I claimed that proper names are individuated by the conventions governing their use and argued that name–bearer relation should be an internal relation, I believe that the Kaplanian notion of character is an unhappy notion to appeal to when discussing proper names. I would thus suggest that only indexicals have characters.[33]

What I just said is not, though, a knockdown argument against the indexical view of proper names.[34] For, the friends of the indexical view of proper names can argue that an extended notion of context of utterance would furnish a context-dependent semantics for proper names. In that case the context of utterance does not merely contain as parameters the agent, the time, and place of the utterance. It also contains what Pelczar and Reinsbury (1998) call "the dubbing-in-force" or what Voltolini (1995) calls the "context of acquisition".[35] In that case the character of a proper name is a function from the context of acquisition or from the dubbing-in-force to the referent. Following this suggestion the context of utterance acquires new parameters. This way a given name type can acquire different values in different contexts of utterance. The introduction of new contextual parameters such as the dubbing-in-force or the context of acquisition, seems to be, at least to me, an *ad hoc* move proposed in order to accommodate proper names along with indexicals. As I show in the next section, a more plausible picture distinguishes between the context of utterance (in a narrow sense) and a broad notion of context in which during a linguistic interchange and a speech act all relevant features may appear and may be invoked in order to guarantee and explain the success of the communication. As I argue, following Perry and Kaplan, the former is semantical in nature while the latter is pre-semantical or meta-semantical.

[33] For a recent discussion on why the character of a name cannot be represented by a description like "the bearer of 'N' " see Predelli (2001).

[34] To be honest, I do not believe that there are knockdown arguments on this issue. Ultimately, whether the indexical theory of proper names should be preferred to the picture I am proposing rests on economical and esthetical reasons. I do believe, though, that the picture I propose is more intuitive and economical than the indexical theory of proper names. But this is not for me to judge.

[35] "The indexicals 'I', 'here', 'now' and 'Madagascar' can be distinguished from one another by the contextual factors to which they are sensitive. 'I' is sensitive to the 'utterer'-feature of a context of utterance, 'here' and 'now' to a context's place and time, and 'Madagascar' to the dubbing-in-force of a context" (Pelczar and Rainsbury 1998: 298).

52   Language and Context

Along this line we can quote another feature pointing to a difference between proper names and indexicals, which is that the latter, unlike the former, do not occur as rules in dictionaries. Actually, there is a *rule* each competent speaker applies when using the first-person pronoun. If one looks in the dictionary one can read that 'I' is "a pronoun used by the speaker or writer referring to him or herself". This is all one needs to know. To be sure, to be a competent speaker one does not need to be able to spell out the rule in the same way that the dictionary or the semanticist does. As Wittgenstein would say, one manifests one's competence with the rule in following it. In our particular case one manifests one's competence with the relevant rule in using 'I' in an appropriate way:

The grammar of the word 'know' is evidently closely related to that of 'can', 'is able to'. But also closely related to that of 'understands'. ('Mastery' of a technique) (Wittgenstein, *PI*: §150)

Try not to think of understanding as a 'mental process' at all.—For *that* is the expression which confuses you. But ask yourself: in what sort of case, in what kind of circumstances, do we say, 'Now I know how to go on', when, that is, the formula *has* occurred to me?— (Wittgenstein, *PI*: §155)

The rule, or character (which, as we saw, can be represented by a function from context to content or referent), is not more mysterious than the other rules we follow in our everyday linguistic practice. When using 'I' we all follow and apply the same rule. On the other hand, we do not usually find proper names in the dictionary as we find them in the telephone books. A person has to be rather famous to get her name into the dictionary. The same for a place: it has to be rather famous to get the same honor. Besides, if we get lucky and find a proper name, say 'Rome', as an entry in the dictionary we do not read that 'Rome' means the same as "the place called 'Rome'", we rather find some information such as that Rome is the capital of Italy, the city where the Pope resides, etc. So, one can argue that a speaker who does not know that 'I' is a pronoun referring to the speaker or writer (i.e. one who does not master its character), like one who does not know that vixens are female foxes and bachelors unmarried men, is not fully competent in English. On the other hand, we cannot say that one who does not know the meanings of the thousands who happen to share the same generic name, say 'Mary Smith', is linguistically incompetent. It is instructive to mention that one of the reasons proposed in favor of excluding proper names from dictionaries is that proper names are used as pure labels, "only for the distinction of one person from another".[36] Did the lexicographers who decided to exclude proper names from the dictionary because they merely function as labels anticipate one of the

---

[36] See T. Dyche and W. Pardon's preface to their 1735 dictionary, *A New General English Dictionary*. See also J. Serranus who in 1539 (*Dictionarium Latinogermanicum*) claimed that proper names have been left out "as they stand in no need of interpretation". Quoted by Marconi (1990: 81).

main, if not the chief, lessons of direct reference? For I take proper names *qua* tags to be the paradigm of direct reference.[37]

Besides, if we pause to think of how we come to learn the use of a proper name and the use of an indexical we gain further evidence in favor of the thesis that they are distinct tools, distinct instruments, in our language. Actually one can come to learn a proper name, say 'Jane', by being told "She/this woman/ . . . is Jane" while one does not come to learn the use of 'I', 'you', 'she', 'today', and the like by being told "This is *I*", "This is *today*", etc. In learning how to use indexicals and proper names one comes to learn how to manipulate distinct tools of reference; one comes to master different techniques of reference. When one correctly uses these different tools one manifests different competencies. While on the one hand one *exploits a pre-existing convention*, on the other hand *one applies a given rule* to fix the reference.[38] That is, while in the former case one *defers* to the linguistic community to fix the meaning of the words one uses (names come to us prepackaged with their semantic value), in the latter case one *creates* the link between the word (indexical) and the referent. Indexicals and proper names are very different tools with very different purposes. To underrate this difference amounts to underestimating the linguistic richness and varieties of natural language:

> One has been tempted to say that 'now' is the name of an instance of time, and this of course, would be like saying that 'here' is the name of a place, 'this' the name of a thing, and 'I' the name of a man. . . . But nothing is more unlike than the use of the word 'this' and the use of a proper name—I mean *the games* played with these words, not the phrase in which they are used. For we do say "This is short" and "Jack is short"; but remember that "This is short" without the pointing gesture and without the thing we are pointing to would be meaningless.— What can be compared with a name is not the word 'this' but, if you like, the symbol consisting of this word, the gesture, and the sample. We might say: Nothing is more characteristic of a proper name A than we can use it in such a phrase as "This is A"; and it makes no sense to say "This is this" or "Now is now" or "Here is here". (Wittgenstein, *BB*: 108–9)

This distinction between proper names and indexicals ultimately rests on the different way in which the use of proper names and indexicals exploits context. I now turn to the discussion of the different ways in which context enters my picture.

---

[37] I can but agree with Barcan Marcus when she writes: "A feature of genuine directly referring names, in contrast to many descriptions, is that the values of such names remain fixed . . . When proper names and such essential descriptions were conflated in a category of rigid designators, a crucial distinction was obscured. Object must *be there* to be *named*. Descriptions are prescriptions for finding an object. The *relation* between a name and its referent and between a description and its satisfier are different" (Barcan Marcus [1985/6] 1993: 212).

[38] As Barcan Marcus aptly points out: "Proper names have fixed values in our language as a historical institution and are part of the public vocabulary. In this way they allow reference to an object despite the vicissitudes the objects undergo and despite the absence of direct acquaintance with many and perhaps most of the objects that the language user correctly names" (Barcan Marcus [1985/6] 1993: 204).

5. Types of Context

To deal with the complexity of how context affects our linguistic interchanges I distinguish between *the setting, narrow context,* and *broad context.* The following chart should summarize these distinctions:

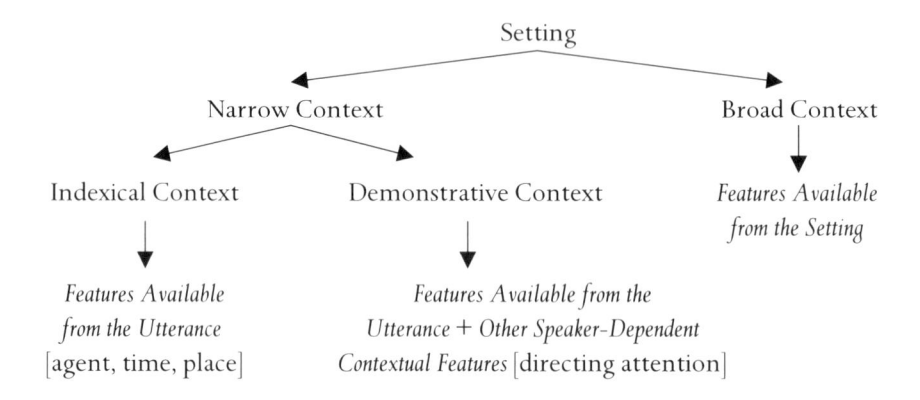

```
                        Setting
          ┌───────────────┼───────────────┐
          ▼                               ▼
    Narrow Context                  Broad Context
    ┌─────┴─────┐                         │
    ▼           ▼                         ▼
Indexical    Demonstrative          Features Available
 Context       Context                from the Setting
    │             │
    ▼             ▼
Features Available    Features Available from the
from the Utterance    Utterance + Other Speaker-Dependent
[agent, time, place]  Contextual Features [directing attention]
```

As I understand it, the *setting* is the scene or scenario underlying a linguistic interchange. As such it is the *sine qua non* of each speech act and can be viewed as the background upon which a linguistic episode takes place. Think, for instance, of the differences involved when we speak to acquaintances and when we speak with foreigners. In the former case much more information can be presupposed. If you and I happen to know and interact with only one John Smith, we do not have to specify which particular name we are using. If the members of a given family or community happen to have no philosophical knowledge at all, when they use 'Aristotle' they do not have to stress that they use the name of the magnate. If someone joins our discussion she may be puzzled and may ask us whether we are speaking about the philosopher or the magnate. If members of a given linguistic community never travel, they never have to specify the time zone when they state the time. An example may clarify this point. In a philosophy lecture the proper names used by the teacher are likely to refer to philosophers (or students). So if our teacher utters the names 'Aristotle' and 'Russell' they quite certainly stand for the famous philosophers who bear these names. The teacher does not need to stress that she is not referring to, say, Aristotle Onassis or the former British prime minister. The fact that the names she uses stand for philosophers can be understood as some basic assumption or background knowledge underlying the linguistic interchange. If, on the other hand, our teacher were lecturing in political and economic studies the setting would differ. In that case other background assumptions and presuppositions would be involved and these names would, by default, be the names of Onassis and the former British prime minister. It goes without saying that misunderstandings occur. We sometimes get confused. When joining a discussion and hearing someone uttering a given name, say 'Mary', we may not know whom among our acquaintances they are talking about. In that case we just ask: it is as simple as that. This should show that when one comes to the utterance of a proper name, a lot of information is taken for granted and can be viewed as background knowledge upon which the linguistic interchange occurs. The assumption that 'Aristotle' refers to the Greek philosopher is safer to make in a philosophy class than it is when reading about Jackie Kennedy.

The notion of setting, as I conceive it, is inspired by Wittgenstein. As such it bears some resemblance to Wittgenstein's notions of form of life and language-games. Like any game, a language-game presupposes a setting.[39] The latter is the background upon which a language-game rests. If a given setting undergoes considerable changes the game would not be played or it would become a different game. There are thus elements of the setting which, even if they are not primarily or directly involved in the explanation of the meaning of some expressions, are nonetheless relevant for their meaning; they are the condition upon which expressions came to possess the meaning that they actually possess. For:

Commanding, questioning, recounting, chatting, are as much part of our natural history as walking, eating, drinking, playing. (Wittgenstein, *PI*: §25)

To stress the relevance of the notion of setting in the overall explanation of a given linguistic activity, I invite you to think of the way we use recording devices such as answering machines or post-its. One cannot successfully use and/or understand a recorded message on an answering machine or on a post-it stating "I'm not in, leave a message" if one is not familiar with the way these tools are used in everyday life, i.e. with the language-game involved when these devices are at work. Post-its, for instance, are conceived, among other things, as gadgets enabling one to leave messages. So if one reads a post-it on someone's office door stating "I'm not in today" one takes it to mean that the occupier of the office is not in his/her office the day the message is read. If the post-it ends in the dustbin, one does not take it to mean that the agent is not in the dustbin on the relevant day. This rests on the general practice of using post-its, i.e. it rests on patterns of the communal

---

[39] Actually, Wittgenstein claims that to imagine a language is to imagine a form of life (*PI*: §§7, 19) and that to imagine a language means to imagine a culture (*BB*: 134). "We could easily imagine a language (and that means again a culture) in which there existed no common expression for light blue and dark blue, in which the former, say, was called 'Cambridge', the latter 'Oxford'. If you ask a man of this tribe what Cambridge and Oxford have in common, he'd be inclined to say 'Nothing' " (Wittgenstein, *BB*: 134–5). Forms of life thus provide the foundation of language; they are the cultural activities on which language-games are embedded.

activities of using them. A similar story can be told about the way we use and manipulate other communication-conceived devices. Moreover, the same story can also be told when people engage in a communicative exchange. If, chatting to a colleague, one says "Let's meet at 3.15 p.m., on 12 April 2001" one is likely to refer to 3.15 p.m. relative to the time zone in which the conversation takes place, while if someone from London is talking on the phone to someone in Rome, further information is required to see whether the 3.15 p.m. stands for 3.15 p.m. CET or 3.15 p.m. GMT. A change of setting may involve a change in the language-game and, thus, a change in what is said, not to mention a change in what is communicated. Homophonic words and/or sentences can be used to express very different things in different settings. To put it in a nutshell, the setting enables us to determine which are the relevant aspects that concur in determining what is said by a given utterance. The setting also helps in fixing the meaning of the words used or, more precisely, in determining *which* words are used. As I have already claimed, it is the setting which helps to determine whether one is using 'Aristotle', the name of the philosopher, or 'Aristotle', the name of the magnate. Similarly, whether one is using 'mistress' the noun for the governess, 'mistress' the name for the teacher, 'mistress' the noun for the female head of the household, 'mistress' the noun for the lover, . . . In short, the setting *qua* presupposition of the existence of a (language-) game, is the *sine qua non* upon which an activity, linguistic or not, rests.

One may wonder about the difference between the notion of setting and the notion of situation I introduced in the Introduction when arguing in favor of the view that both the (minimal) proposition and the thought expressed should be understood as situated and that a given utterance is true/false relative to a given situation. To be honest I do not have a clear-cut distinction between the two in mind. I nonetheless prefer to keep the two notions separate for the following reason. When speaking of a setting I mainly intend to focus on the external features surrounding a linguistic interchange or thinking episode. Thus the external components of the context, broadly understood, are put on the front line. When talking about situations, on the other hand, the focus switches to the intentional features surrounding our linguistic activity. In that case the speakers' intentions, aims, discourse situation, etc. come to the fore. We can understand the distinction between setting and situation as two distinct ways of characterizing context, broadly understood, by focusing on its different aspects.

The notion of *narrow context*, on the other hand, is what we need to understand indexical expressions: it furnishes the relevant contextual parameters that help fix the reference. In order to deal with the distinction between pure indexicals and demonstratives, though, we have to recognize two subcategories of narrow context: (i) the context created/exploited by the utterance, i.e. the agent, time, and place, and (ii) the features created by the speech act such as pointing gestures, glimpses, etc.

On the other hand, the features which pertain to the setting, such as speaking English, being a member of a given community, attending such and such a party, being dressed in such and such a way, etc. are not part of what one says and usually aims to communicate. The fact that one speaks German when one says 'Ich' is not what one says. Our German speaker merely refers to herself using the first-person pronoun 'Ich': if she were to speak English she would have used 'I', for if she had uttered 'Ich' she would probably have expressed disgust.[40]

Finally, the notion of *broad context* should capture the fact that the understanding of a given expression and utterance often rests on the setting in which it is produced. The audience often needs to appeal to features of the setting to understand a given expression. The way the speaker is dressed, for instance, may help the audience to infer whether she is using 'bank' as the name for the financial institution or not—one does not need, though, to dress as a fisherman to use 'bank' as the name for the embankment.

A couple of examples may help to elucidate and reinforce the distinction between narrow and broad context. When indexicals are at work, reference is fixed by the utterance produced. If one reads the token "I'm not in now, but I'll be back soon" on someone's office door or hears the token "I am not in now, please leave a message after the tone" recorded on someone's answering machine, the reference of 'I' and 'now' is fixed the very moment one reads/hears the token, i.e. by the utterances produced by these tokens. One can read/hear the very same token at different times and/or places. In that case different utterances would be produced and different references fixed. In the case of proper names, though, we do not have to rely on the utterance for reference to be fixed. If one reads "Tony Blair is not in London on 25 May 2003" one may understand this very message without relying on the utterance. The time and place one reads this note is irrelevant in fixing the reference, i.e. the utterance produced by the reading of the note does not affect who/what the referents are. For these very reasons proper names do not exploit context in the same way indexical expressions do. Context, if relevant in understanding the use of a proper name, is not the context of utterance or narrow context, it is a broad notion of context.

These different notions of context nicely fall into Kaplan's semantics/metasemantics taxonomy:

The fact that a word or phrase *has* a certain meaning clearly belongs to semantics. On the other hand, a claim about the *basis* for ascribing a certain meaning to a word or phrase does not belongs to semantics. "Ohsnay" means *snow* in Pig-Latin. That's a semantic fact about Pig-Latin. The *reason* why "ohsnay" means *snow* is not a semantic fact; it is some kind of

---

[40] This example comes from Perry (1997).

historical or sociological fact about Pig-Latin. Perhaps because it relates to how language is *used*, it should be categorized as part of the *pragmatics* of Pig-Latin (though I am not really comfortable with this nomenclature), or perhaps, because it is a fact *about* semantics, as part of the *Metasemantics* of Pig-Latin (or perhaps, for those who prefer working from below to working from above, as part of the *Foundations of semantics* of Pig-Latin). . . . For present purposes let us settle on *metasemantics*. (Kaplan 1989: 573–4)

The notion of narrow context clearly belongs to semantics, while the notion of broad context belongs to meta-semantics. The fact that Aristotle came to bear 'Aristotle' is a historical fact that, as such, belongs to meta-semantics while the fact that 'I' refers to the agent of the context is a semantic fact. The rationale why 'Aristotle' names Aristotle is not reported in the dictionary while the fact that 'I' refers to the writer or speaker (the agent) is reported, is symptomatic of the semantics/meta-semantics distinction and, as I have been arguing, of the fact that indexicals and proper names are different linguistic tools.

6. Identity Statements

I argued against the reduction of proper names to indexicals, claiming that they were different tools of reference involving different competencies. Among the main differences the following deserves special attention. While indexical identification is perspectival, identification by proper names is public. In particular, the information one attaches to one's use and/or understanding of an indexical expression is cognitively anchored to reality while the information one attaches to a proper name may not, and need not, be so anchored. As a consequence identity sentences like:

(5) Tully is Tully
(6) Tully is Cicero
(7) He is Tully [demonstrating Tully]

play different roles in our cognitive architecture. While (6), unlike (5), may convey the information that there are two distinct naming conventions for a single individual—roughly that a single man carries two names—, (7) conveys the information that the demonstrated individual is named 'Tully', i.e. that the demonstrated individual and the 'Tully'-convention converge.[41] When one comes to accept (6) as true one, as Frege claims, expands one's knowledge:

$a = a$ and $a = b$ are obviously statements of different cognitive value; $a = a$ holds *a priori* and, according to Kant, is to be labeled analytic, while statements of the form $a = b$ often contain

---

[41] For the time being I ignore the Kripke's inspired puzzles such as the Pierre 'London'-'Londres' and the Peter 'Paderewsky'-'Paderewsky' case (see Kripke 1979). I discuss in some detail these cases in Ch. 7, Sect. 6 and Ch. 9, Sects. 5 and 8, below.

very valuable extension of our knowledge and cannot always be established *a priori*. The discovery that the rising sun is not new every morning, but always the same, was one of the most fertile astronomical discoveries. (Frege [1892] 1952: 56)

When one accepts (7) as true, one also expands one's knowledge.[42] The expansion of the knowledge is, though, different. In the former case one comes to be aware that the information one associated with the name 'Tully' can also be associated with the name 'Cicero' and *vice versa*. In the latter case, one comes to entertain anchored information. That is to say, one is now able to anchor the information one associates with the name 'Tully' to a specific individual one is able to single out in an indexical way. One comes to entertain a perspectival thought. Actually, the aim of uttering (7), like an utterance of (2) [That man [indicating Kaplan] is David Kaplan] in the scenario I described at the beginning, is to allow someone to anchor her information to reality. To put it in a nutshell, in one case one comes to relate two sets of information associated with two distinct conventions, while in the other case one comes to relate one set of information with an individual one is cognitively related to; an individual with whom one entertains a perspectival identification. In the latter case, unlike the former, the referent is in the cognitive field of the thinker.

It is well known that to deal with identity statement and the problem of cognitive significance Frege introduced the distinction between sense (*Sinn*) and reference (*Bedeutung*):

Now if we were to regard equality as a relation between that which the names 'a' and 'b' designate, it would seem that $a = b$ could not differ from $a = a$ (i.e. provided that $a = b$ is true). A relation would thereby be expressed of a thing to itself, and indeed one in which each thing stands to itself but to no other thing. What we apparently want to state by $a = b$ is that the signs or names 'a' and 'b' designate the same thing, so that those signs themselves would be under discussion; a relation between them would be asserted. But this relation would hold between the names or sign only in so far as they named or designated something. It would be mediated by the connexion of each of the two signs with the same designated thing. But this is arbitrary. Nobody can be forbidden to use an arbitrary producible event or object as a sign for something. In that case the sentence $a = b$ would no longer refer to the subject matter, but only to its mode of designation; we would express no proper knowledge by its means. But in many cases this is just what we want to do. If the sign 'a' is distinguished from the sign 'b' only as an object (here, by means of its shape), not as a sign (i.e. not by the manner in which it designate something), the cognitive value of $a = a$ becomes essentially equal to that of $a = b$, provided $a = b$ is true. A difference can arise only if the difference between the signs corresponds to a difference in the mode of presentation of the signs designated....

It is natural, now, to think of there being connected with a sign (name, combination of words, written mark), besides that which the sign designates, which may be called the

---

[42] For a discussion of why various solutions to Frege's puzzle are unsatisfactory see Corazza and Dokic (1995). For a recent historical account of the puzzle see Thau and Caplan (2001).

meaning of the sign, also what I should like to call the *sense* of the sign, wherein the mode of presentation is contained. (Frege [1892] 1952: 56–7)

Frege's picture has been criticized lately. The criticisms are sound. First of all, Frege never told us exactly what a sense is. Fregean senses are often explained in a functional way: they are *whatever* satisfies Frege's constraint, i.e. what one comes to grasp when one comes to understand a term, what determines reference (if any), what is referred to by terms appearing in *oratio obliqua* constructions, etc. Whether one accepts Frege's notion of sense or not, one must tell a story about the cognitive significance we associate with proper names and why some statements involving coreferential terms are not to be taken on a par. One may, for instance, accept as true "Tully is Roman" while rejecting or suspending one's judgement on "Cicero is Roman" even if Tully is Cicero.

Without entering into this debate, I assume the anti-Fregean or Millian theory of proper names. Mill told us that names denote but do not connote; a name is just a tag, in other words. According to Millianism, the semantic contribution of a proper name is exhausted by its reference (where by 'semantic contribution', I simply mean the name's contribution to the truth-value of the utterance containing it). Thus, the semantic contribution of 'Tully' and 'Cicero' is the same. One of the main tenets of Millianism is that the semantic contribution of a proper name differs drastically from the contribution of a definite description. Following the widely accepted view inaugurated by Russell, the semantic contribution of a definite description, say 'the tallest Californian philosopher', is a descriptive condition which the referent must satisfy. The latter is whatever object happens to satisfy the description: in our case, the individual who happens to be the tallest Californian philosopher. In other words, while names give us objects, descriptions give us conditions that must be satisfied. Descriptions describe while names name. However, in saying that a name's semantic contribution is exhausted by the object it refers to we do *not* say that this is its only contribution. As we shall soon see, a name may contribute plenty of interesting information; the *semantic* contribution may not even be the most interesting or important.

It has often been suggested that Millianism faces two major, but related, problems. First, since coreferential names contribute the very same value, the cognitive significance associated with them must differ from their semantic value. As Frege emphasized, "Tully is Cicero" is informative whereas "Tully is Tully" is not, for the cognitive value associated with 'Tully' and 'Cicero' differs. Thus a Millian must distinguish, *pace* Frege and the traditional view, between the bearer of truth-value and the bearer of cognitive value. The second problem concerns empty terms. Empty terms, as the name itself suggests, do not have a semantic value at all, yet we successfully interact using empty names. Moreover, we do not associate the same cognitive value to 'Hamlet' and 'Holmes', nor to 'Superman' and 'Clark Kent' even if in the *Superman* stories the latter are assumed to be coreferential. Why, though, should we not welcome the divorce between the bearer of semantic value and the bearer of cognitive value? What reasons do we have for supposing that the very same entity (either a Fregean thought or a Russellian proposition) should carry all the relevant information? I suspect that, in not recognizing this divorce, philosophers have tried to salvage a marriage made in hell in that they either (i) postulate the existence of Fregean senses *qua* thought constituents, or (ii) claim (like Russell) that ordinary proper names are not (logically) proper names.

A Millian should be happy with the idea that a name's cognitive significance is not encapsulated in its semantic value. Questions about semantic value and questions about cognitive value must be kept aside. As we saw, following Kripke, one can competently use 'Feynman' and 'Gellman' without knowing who they were, or without associating any description with either, or even without knowing that they were famous physicists. One competently uses these names insofar as one knows that they are names. In Wittgensteinian fashion, we could say that one is competent in using names insofar as one masters language-games involving proper names, i.e. inasmuch as one manipulates them in accordance with syntactic combinatorial rules and insofar as one knows that they are names. As I claimed, a name's proper function is to name. Names, so conceived, are the tools we use to single out objects of discourse and to keep track of them; they are also the labels we use to cumulate information, acting like labels put on mental folders. Indeed, one need not know anything about an individual in order to use a name, for one can label an empty folder, but one must know that it is a name and that a name is usually used to refer to an individual. One must know that there is a *convention* relating the name with its bearer. This (tacit) knowledge can be spelled out as follows.[43] When a competent speaker hears an utterance like:

(8) Maradona snorted cocaine

she comes to understand at least that:

(8) a. There is an individual x and a convention C such that
    (i) C is exploited by (8)
    (ii) C permits one to designate x with 'Maradona'
    (iii) x snorted cocaine

---

[43] The analysis I propose is taken from Perry (2001). Perry characterizes (8a) as the pure truth-conditions of (8). The latter should be understood as propositions created by an utterance of (8). On top of the pure truth-conditions, Perry recognizes incremental truth-conditions (or official content). The latter is what is said in an utterance and in our example corresponds to the (singular) proposition that Maradona snorted cocaine. Maradona himself is the constituent of this proposition. The constituent of the pure truth-condition, on the other hand, is the name 'Maradona'.

Our competent speaker understands this whether or not she also knows that Maradona was a famous Argentinian football player, that within the British community he is best known as the hand of God, or whether or not she is able to single out Maradona among others. By the simple fact that one knows that 'Maradona' is a proper name, one comes to understand (8a). Of course, one may not be able to spell out one's understanding this way, for one could say (following Wittgenstein) that this competence or knowledge is *manifested* in the accurate way one uses proper names, in mastering the language-games involving proper names. This competence is also what helps us to explain the cognitive significance we associate with names. When one hears and accepts an identity utterance like (6) which I repeat here:

(6) Tully is Cicero,

one comes to understand that:

(6) a. Tere is an individual x, an individual y, and conventions C and C^* such that
   (i) C and C^* are exploited by (6)
   (ii) C permits one to designate x with 'Tully' and C^* permits one to designate y with 'Cicero'
   (iii) $x = y$

(6a) aims to capture and spell out in a more detailed way the platitude that, when one comes to understand and accept as true an identity statement involving proper names, what one comes to understand is that the names stand for the same thing, i.e. that they corefer or codesignate.

The cognitive significance problem is thus explained without resorting to Frege's notion of sense; all we need to appeal to are the speakers' linguistic competencies, the very same capacities that should help explain why one correctly uses proper names.[44]

One could think that the story I just told contrasts with the view of proper names I suggested in Section 4. In particular, with the idea that there is no gap to be bridged between a name and its bearer and that the alleged relation should be viewed as an internal relation. What about, for instance, empty names? One may be competent in using empty names. Yet there cannot be an internal relation between the name and its bearer for the simple reason that there is no bearer. Following the analysis proposed, an identity statement like:

(9) Clark Kent is Superman

---

[44] One could claim that these are precisely the Fregean senses. If this is the case I am happy to characterize the position I am putting forward as Fregean. I am not sure, though, that Frege would welcome the divorce between the bearer of cognitive value and the bearer of truth-value I proposed.

could then be analyzed as:

(9) a. There is an individual x, an individual y, and conventions C and $C^\star$ such that:
   (i) C and $C^\star$ are exploited by (9)
   (ii) C permits one to designate x with 'Clark Kent' and $C^\star$ permits one to designate y with 'Superman'
   (iii) $x = y$

The tension, however, is only apparent, for in claiming that there is a convention permitting one to designate an individual, we do not commit ourselves to the view that the individual *must* exist. In other words, (9a) need not be true. In particular, if we follow Perry and take (9a) to be a proposition, it is a false proposition; the only thing that must exist is the convention itself. To use Donnellan's (1974) happy terminology, a convention can exist even if it ends in a block. This is, for instance, the case with 'Vulcan'; the convention bridging the gap between 'Vulcan' and the individual it supposedly stands for ends in a block, corresponding to LeVerrier's introduction of the name into the language. Two conventions can end in the same block, as in the case of coreferential empty names such as 'Clark Kent' and 'Superman'. The block corresponds to the novel or fiction.

Mill's friends can be, and should be, happy with the picture I am proposing, for I maintain that the *semantic* contribution of a name is exhausted by the object it refers to. Yet a name's cognitive contribution *must* differ from its semantic contribution, for it is the latter which helps us handle the cognitive significance problem and thus which helps explain how people can competently use empty names. One may also (competently) use an empty name even if one does not know that it is empty: think, for instance, of a child's use of 'Santa Claus'. Would we say that they are not competent with 'Santa Claus' because they are not aware that the alleged individual, who supposedly comes down the chimney with presents, does not exist?

More should be said about empty terms and what they contribute to the proposition expressed. The view I favor is that when an empty term is involved, no proposition is expressed and the utterance containing an empty term lacks a truth-value.[45]

7. Indexicals and Cognitive Significance

A similar story can be told about indexical expressions. When a competent speaker uses or comes to understand an utterance like:

(10) I can play football [said by Henry]

---

[45] For more on a similar position see Perry (2001). For a discussion on the way in which indexicals behave within fictional discourse, see Corazza and Whitsey (2003).

she comes to understand at least that:

(10) a. There is an *x* such that:
   (i) *x* is the agent of (10)
   (ii) *x* can play football

If one, for instance, reads this sentence on a postcard or as a graffito without knowing who produced it, i.e. without knowing who is the referent of the 'I', a competent speaker would come to understand (10a). Perry characterizes (9a) and (10a) as the *reflexive truth-conditions* of respectively (9) and (10). These should be distinguished, Perry argues, from the *incremental truth-conditions*. The latter correspond to the intuitive notion of what is said or, to adopt Kaplan's terminology, the proposition expressed. They correspond to what I characterized as the minimal proposition in the Introduction. While (9) will not have an incremental truth-condition because 'Clark Kent' is an empty name, in the case of (10) the incremental truth-condition or proposition expressed will be *that Henry can play football*. Since the incremental truth-condition (10) corresponds to the (singular) proposition *that Henry can play football*, it is not suited to deal with the difference in cognitive significance problem. For (10) would express the very same proposition as an utterance of "Henry can play football". Yet we recognize that the cognitive significance of "I can play football," said by Henry, and "Henry can play football" differs. The latter is dealt with by the reflexive truth-conditions. Roughly, an utterance's reflexive truth-conditions can be understood as the utterance's linguistic meaning or character. The condition "x is the agent of (10)" of (10a) is directly given by the character or linguistic meaning of 'I'. In the case of proper names, though, we do not have characters. For this very reason the reflexive truth-conditions of an utterance containing a proper name are spelled out, as in (9a), by appealing to a *convention*. In other words, while with utterances containing indexicals the reflexive truth-conditions are spelled out in appealing to the indexicals' character, in the case of utterances containing proper names they are spelled out in appealing to the convention which, as we saw, happens to be a logical, a grammatical, or an internal relation. We are thus in a position to capture the difference between indexicals and proper names at the level of linguistic meaning (or reflexive truth-condition). This also helps us to understand and capture the different competencies involved when using proper names and indexicals. In this sense it helps us characterize their cognitive significance.

The distinction between the reflexive truth-conditions and the incremental truth-conditions (or the proposition expressed) seems to bring us back to Frege's *Begriffsschrift* meta-linguistic theory, i.e. to the very theory Frege criticizes in his "Sinn und Bedeutung" paper. Before introducing the sense/reference distinction, Frege held that an identity statement like "$a = b$" could be analyzed as: the sign "a"

and the sign "*b*" designate the same thing. But as we saw, Frege states that this cannot be the case. For if this were the case, "the sentence $a = b$ would no longer refer to the subject matter, but only to its mode of designation; we would express no proper knowledge by its means" (Frege [1892] 1952: 57). An utterance's reflexive truth-condition is a proposition about words. It is not a proposition about the subject matter. Frege is quite right. Perry's picture avoids the Fregean objection insofar as it conforms to what I characterize *the multiple propositions view*.[46] That is the view that a single utterance does not merely convey its reflexive truth-conditions. It also expresses its incremental truth-condition. It is the latter, the *official* content, which is the subject matter (what is said) of the utterance. Frege's meta-linguistic account faces difficulties insofar as it does not distinguish between the incremental truth-conditions and the reflexive truth-conditions; it takes the latter to be the subject matter of the utterance. That is, Frege's meta-linguistic account faces difficulties because Frege recognized only one level of content, a unique proposition, and asks it to deliver all the relevant information, i.e. both the information relative to the cognitive significance and the subject matter of the utterance. In a nutshell, Frege's meta-linguistic account cannot succeed because Frege commits the fallacy of misplaced information, i.e. he asks a single entity to deliver all the information. Frege is right in arguing that an identity statement is not about words but about things and thus rejects his meta-linguistic account. He is wrong, though, in claiming that the meta-linguistic account must be supplanted by the sense/reference distinction and that the propositional constituents are the senses expressed by words. Were Frege (and the neo-Fregeans for that matter) to accept the view that a single utterance expresses or conveys several propositions, then Frege and his followers would be happy to accommodate the view that a sentence conveys a proposition about words and yet this proposition is not the subject matter, for the latter is a proposition having the referents themselves as constituents and not the words used to designate them. In other words, since, following Perry, I did not claim that an identity statement, for instance, is about the signs themselves, Frege's criticism does not apply. And it does not apply insofar as, contrary to Frege and his followers, I distinguish between the bearer of truth-value (the proposition expressed, the official content) and the bearer of cognitive value, the reflexive truth-conditions. I can thus maintain that the subject matter of an identity statement is the proposition expressed, while the cognitive significance is carried by the words used in expressing this proposition.

Let us take stock. In this chapter we have seen that the use of linguistic expressions, and in particular of singular terms, relies on context. The picture which has

---

[46] See Ch. 3, below, for a detailed discussion of the multiple-proposition view.

emerged is that context enters the scene in various guises. This is also due to the fact that we are, as I claimed in the Introduction, contextually bound agents. In the next chapter I shall develop this idea further and show how our thoughts are context-bound as well. In other words I shall defend the view that both our linguistic activity and our cognitive activity cannot be accounted for without taking on board the context in which they occur.

2

Thought and Context

"Isn't it very odd that I should be unable—even *without* the institution of language and all its surroundings—to think that it will soon stop raining?"— Do you want to say that it is queer that you should be unable to say these words and *mean* them without those surroundings?

(Wittgenstein *PI*: §540)

It would be natural to treat Z-landers' uses of the sentence *It is raining* as having Z-land as an unarticulated constituent. But what secures Z-land, rather than, say, San Francisco, as the unarticulated constituent of their discourse about rain? It is simply that the perception that gives rise to the beliefs that *It is raining* expresses are perceptions of the weather in Z-land. Z-land is a constituent of the practice, or language game, in which the sentence *It is raining* plays a role. There is no need to postulate a concept or idea of Z-land as a component of their thought, to secure the connection to Z-land. The connection is secured by the role of the whole belief in their lives.

(Perry [1986] 2000: 177)

In this chapter, I concentrate on the way in which our cognitive activity is context-dependent. In developing an idea put forward by Perry (1986), I discuss how we can succeed in thinking about something without having to represent this very thing. To achieve my goal, i.e. to show that the aboutness of our thought may not be represented, I focus on the phenomenon of tacit reference and show how context may bridge the gap between a thought and the event or situation that it represents.

Here is the way in which I proceed. In Section 1, I discuss different ways relevant information can be implicitly conveyed and in Section 2 I show how implicit information relies on the variegated ways in which context is exploited. In Section 3, I focus on meteorological verbs as a case study and show how a two-place predicate can correspond to a one-place representation. Our thought that it is raining, for instance, must be about a determinate location insofar as 'to rain' is a two-place relation, taking a time and a location as values, yet our thought may not represent the relevant location. In Section 4, it is argued that this phenomenon is possible insofar as certain implicit arguments (the argument for a location, for instance)

68   *Thought and Context*

which play a role in selecting the relevant referent, need not be represented by the agent entertaining the thought. In Section 5, the notion of context is used to explain the different kinds of understanding involved when using and/or hearing proper names and indexicals. Lastly, it will be argued, in Section 6, that two kinds of singular thought should be recognized, i.e. acquaintance-based and deference-based thoughts, depending on whether one entertains a thought one would express using an indexical expression or not.

1. Varieties of Implicitness

In "Thoughts without Representation" (1986), Perry argues that one can think about an item without having to represent it. One can entertain thoughts without representation insofar as the *aboutness* of someone's thought need not be articulated. As paradigmatic examples, Perry invites us to consider utterances like:

(1) a. It rains
    b. It's 3 p.m.
    c. Events ξ and φ are simultaneous

Imagine that they are uttered by a 5-year-old child—it is unlikely that a 5-year-old child would utter (1c) though; our child is more likely to utter something like: "This and that happens at the same time". It is a safe claim that (i) our child speaks about a relevant location without designating it, (ii) our child picks out a time relative to a time zone without thinking of the latter, (iii) our child can characterize two events as simultaneous without being aware of Einstein's theory and, thus, without knowing that simultaneity is relative to a frame of reference. By the same token one can argue that our child's thought, i.e. the thoughts s/he entertains while uttering these sentences are, in a way we should specify, related to the items tacitly referred to or presupposed. In what follows, I investigate the different ways a thought can be related to and be about a given item without representing it.

To begin with, let us contrast sentences (2a–e) and sentences (3a–e):

(2) a. It is raining
    b. Jane is not strong enough
    c. Jon is late
    d. Joe is too tall
    e. It is 5 p.m.
(3) a. * Jane devours
    b. * Jeff gave
    c. * Mary manages

d. * Joe founded
  e. * Sue opens[1]

Sentences (2a–e), unlike sentences (3a–e), are syntactically complete and, as such, they are well formed. In order to become well-formed sentences, (3a–e) must be completed; (2a) should become "Jane devours *a hamburger/all her cookies/* . . .", (3b) "Jeff gave *up his job/a hand to Mary/away his car/Mary a kiss/* . . .", etc.

Sentences (2a–e), though syntactically complete, are *conceptually incomplete*. To understand an utterance of (2a), one needs to know *where* it is raining, while to understand an utterance of (2b) one needs to know *for what* Jane is not strong enough. Insofar as these sentences are usually used to talk about things not mentioned, i.e. things merely presupposed or taken for granted, one may suppose that these sentences are also semantically underdetermined. The story, as I understand it, goes as follows. When one understands an utterance of a sentence like (2a–e), one grasps a proposition. What one grasps, however, *transcends* what the words uttered mean, it transcends the minimal proposition expressed, i.e. what is said, strictly speaking. Hence, an utterance of a conceptually underdetermined sentence expresses a minimal proposition. The latter must be *completed* or *enriched* in order for the transmitted message to be grasped. As we saw in the Introduction, however, the completion or enrichment need not be conceptualized in a specific way.

I distinguish between conceptually underdetermined sentences and semantically underdetermined ones, and claim that a semantically underdetermined sentence entails a conceptually underdetermined or incomplete sentence, but not *vice versa*. Thus a conceptually underdetermined sentence can be semantically determined or complete. As a paradigmatic example of a semantically underdetermined sentence, we can quote "It is raining", "It is 5 p.m.", etc. For the utterance of a sentence like "It is raining" to be true/false, a location must be furnished. As a paradigmatic example of a conceptually underdetermined (though a semantically determined) sentence, we can quote "Jane is late", "Joe is too young". Utterances of these sentences are understood insofar as one knows *for what* one is late and too young. It goes without saying that a semantically determined sentence need not be conceptually underdetermined. Utterances like "It's 3 p.m. CET", "Today/Now it is raining in Paris/here", not to mention utterances of eternal sentences like "2 + 2 = 4" or "On Monday, 25 June 2001 AD, it was sunny in Paris", are conceptually determined. To understand an utterance of any one of these sentences (be it context-sensitive or not), one does not have to add further

---

[1] I have been told by baseball and cricket fans that "Sue opens" is an acceptable statement (e.g. "What position does Sue play?" "Sue opens"). I do not have strong intuitions either way on this matter; at first sight, it looks to me that this is either a case of ellipsis and, as such, it goes short for something like "Sue opens the game" or it is an idiomatic use of language, tied to cricket and baseball (-related) games.

information. All the relevant information is conveyed by an element present in the utterance of the relevant sentence.

The situation, as I view it, can be summarized as follows.

- *A propositional constituent may be the value of*:
  (i) a phonetically realized element of an utterance, i.e. a spoken or written element.
  (ii) a phonetically unrealized element of an utterance, i.e. an unspoken or unwritten element, present nonetheless at the level of logical form as an implicit argument.
  (iii) a phonetically unrealized element of an utterance, i.e. an unspoken or unwritten element, not present at the level of logical form as an implicit argument.[2]

The notion of logical form I have in mind comes from the Chomskian school: it is the level of syntactic representation, representing the properties relevant for semantic interpretation. Logical form so understood (or LF, as it is commonly characterized) aims to capture the syntactic structures relevant to a semantic interpretation.[3] As Higginbotham suggests:

Generalizing, it is suggested that the data of the form shown in (13) are to be deduced from the properties of LF as shown in (14):

(13) S can mean that p.
(14) There is an LF-representation Σ for S such that Σ means that p.

And that data of the form shown in (15) are to be explained by formal arguments of the structure (16):

(15) S cannot mean that p.
(16) Every derivation assigning an LF-representation Σ to S such that Σ means that p is ungrammatical.

(Higginbotham 1985: 551)

One of the main tasks this conception faces is to determine how much of the semantic structure of a natural language is manifested in its syntax. Hence, if we apply this notion of logical form to a semantically underdetermined utterance, the main question concerns whether the phonetically unrealized elements are syntactically represented or not. I defend the view that all the semantically relevant elements are represented at the LF level. In other words, I argue that, for the purposes of semantics, all the relevant propositional elements are the value of either a phonetically realized element or an implicit argument. The propositional

---

[2] As I argued in the Introduction, the propositional component does not enter as a constituent of the *minimal* proposition expressed, as it does in (i) and (ii). It merely enters as a constituent of the proposition communicated. Because of the intrinsic underdeterminacy of the utterance the latter need not be specified or even thought about.   [3] For an accurate and well-developed account of LF, see May (1985).

elements not triggered by a phonetically realized element or an implicit argument can be dealt with as either pragmatically imparted or as background presuppositions upon which a given speech act occurs. In this chapter I mainly concentrate on propositional constituents that are semantically triggered, i.e. triggered by, either phonetically realized or unrealized, elements present at the LF level.[4] The following chart should summarize the distinctions I propose:

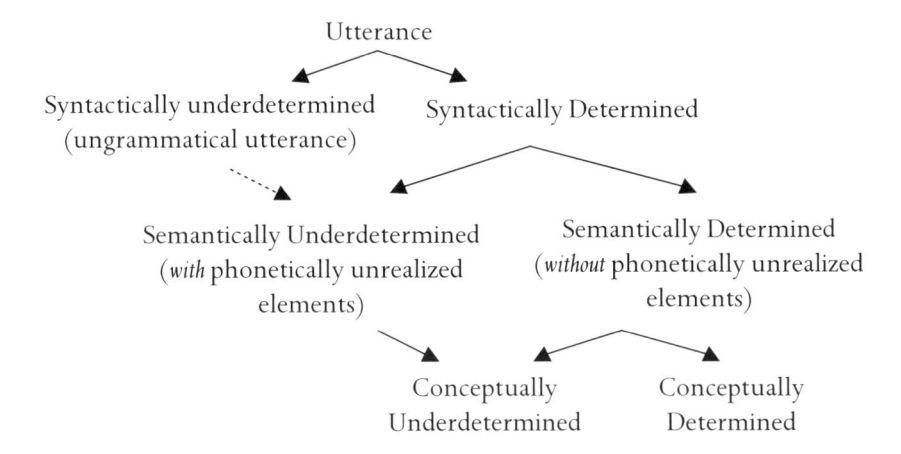

```
                          Utterance
                         /         \
   Syntactically underdetermined    Syntactically Determined
   (ungrammatical utterance)        /                    \
           ⋮                       /                      \
           ↓                      /                        \
   Semantically Underdetermined       Semantically Determined
   (with phonetically unrealized      (without phonetically unrealized
    elements)                          elements)
           ↓                          /        \
                              Conceptually    Conceptually
                              Underdetermined  Determined
```

The truth-conditions of a semantically underdetermined utterance like "It is raining" can be cashed out using the biconditional:

- "It is raining" is true (in English) iff it is raining at time T and location L

where the relevant location is usually given by the location of the utterance (but need not be so given) and the time by the present-tense verb 'is'. For a meteorological utterance like "It is raining" or "It is storming" to express a full and evaluable proposition, *a* location must be supplied. The truth-conditions of a semantically determined, but conceptually underdetermined, utterance like "Jane is late" can be represented by the biconditional:

- "Jane is late" is true (in English) iff Jane is late at time T

To process the truth-condition of an utterance like this we do *not* need to add for what Jane is late.[5] The eventual conceptual enrichment does not affect the truth-value of

---

[4] Roughly, the picture I have in mind is that, in the case of the utterance of a semantically determined (but conceptually underdetermined) sentence, two or more propositions are expressed: the semantically encoded proposition and the pragmatically imparted ones. The latter are the result of a pragmatic enrichment of the semantically encoded proposition operated by the speaker and/or audience. For a more accurate account of this picture, see the Introd., above.

[5] Cf. Jacob (1999) for a similar distinction. These truth-conditions can be spelled out in terms of utterances, as I suggested in the Introd. Moreover, truth must be relativized to a given situation. For the sake of simplicity, I do not go into these details here.

the proposition expressed. The proposition communicated in this case may be richer than the one expressed. In that case, the proposition communicated differs from the one expressed and the enrichment process may be viewed, but may not be so viewed, as a case of pragmatic implicature along Grice's conception. Bach (1994), for instance, argues that when utterances like "It is raining", "Jane is late", and the like occur we do not express a full-fledged proposition, i.e. something that is either true or false.[6] It is, rather, a propositional matrix or schema. As we saw in the Introduction, Bach characterizes such a matrix as a *propositional radical* that must be completed via an "impli*ci*ture" process.[7] This attitude is, no doubt, a pragmatic one inasmuch as it distinguishes between what is said and/or expressed by an utterance (semantics) and what is communicated (pragmatics), for the latter is the result of a pragmatic enrichment process.[8] As should soon become clear, though, I do not follow this path.

This difference between sentences like "It is raining", on the one hand, and sentences like "Jane is late", on the other, seems to suggest that the predicate 'rain' (in English) is a two-place predicate which must be completed by *a location* and *a time* and can *only be so completed*, while the predicate 'late' (in English) need not be semantically completed in a specific way.[9] I take it to be a meaningful fact of English that

---

[6] Kaplan flirts with this thesis: "Thus we think of the temporally neutral 'proposition' as changing its truth-value over time. Note that it is not just the noneternal sentence *S* ["I am writing"] that changes its truth-value over time, but the 'proposition' itself. Since the sentence *S* contains the indexical 'I', it will express different propositions in different contexts. But since *S* contains no *temporal* indexical, the time of the context will not influence the 'proposition' expressed" (Kaplan [1977] 1989: 503–4 n. 28). Kaplan recognizes that his notion of proposition is not the traditional one, so he uses the quotes, in square brackets.

[7] "In implicature one says and communicates one thing and thereby communicates something else in addition. Impliciture, however, is a matter of saying something but communicating something else instead, something closely related to what is said . . . part of what is communicated is only implicit in what is explicitly expressed" (Bach 1994: 126).

[8] The champions of the free enrichment procedure are Sperber and Wilson (1986). See also, among others, Carston (1988; 2002) and Recanati (1993). The enrichment procedure strategy, though, is neutral on whether one distinguishes, like Bach, between what is said and what is communicated. Recanati, for instance, rejects this distinction and claims that what is said *is* what is communicated. For an exhaustive discussion of these positions see Carston (2002: esp. chs. 1 and 2).

[9] Recanati (2002) proposes an example in which a speaker utters "It is raining" on hearing a bell signaling that it is raining *somewhere*. It seems to me that such a sentence would not make much sense within our community. Within our everyday practices, it does not make sense to utter "It rains" when we do not know where it is raining. To be fair, though, Recanati asks us to imagine a scenario in which it rarely rains and, as a consequence, many rain detectors have been placed around the globe. Each detector triggers an alarm bell in the Monitoring Room when it detects rain. Furthermore, Recanati asks us to imagine the presence of a single bell—the location of the triggering detector is indicated by a light on a board in the Monitoring Room. After a few weeks without rain, the bell rings and, upon hearing it, the weatherman on duty in the adjacent room shouts: "It rains!" Following Recanati, the weatherman's utterance is true iff it is raining (at the time of utterance) *in some place or other*. In such a situation, it seems that an utterance such as "It rains" has a *raison d'être*, even if no specific location is considered. My reply is rather simple and straightforward: in such a situation, the verb 'to rain' would not have the same meaning as our own verb. In Wittgensteinian fashion, we could say that, in the scenario imagined by Recanati, the weatherman does not play the same language-game as the one we play when the verb 'to rain' is involved. We would not be speaking the same language. A slightly more controversial example could be the following. In an exam,

'rain' *always* picks up a location, while 'late' does not specify the particular thing or class of things for which one (or something) is late. In other words, from a semantic viewpoint there is not a particular, specific, way verbs and adjectives like 'late', 'eat', 'short', 'strong', must be completed. We can, for instance, say:

(4) a. Jane is *late* and will thus miss the train
 b. The trains in England are often *late*
 c. Jon is always *late* in submitting his scripts
 d. Joe was *late* for the meeting
 e. Each time Sue arrives home *late* at night she calls her parents
 f. This year, the rain season in Zambia is *late*

One of the basic ideas I develop is that semantically underdetermined sentences have an implicit argument operating on some contextual parameters such as time, location, agent, and possible world. As we shall see in Section 3, in the case of the verb "to rain" the contextual parameter is θ-marked as a location by the verb. On the other hand, conceptually underdetermined but semantically determined sentences do not have implicit arguments operating on specific contextual parameters. As I pointed out in the Introduction, one can recognize the presence of a variable at the level of logical form in the case of contextuals without committing oneself to the view that this variable must be satisfied when the (minimal) proposition is expressed. Determining which expressions work this way in a particular language is an open and, I think, an empirical question. While semantic completion is triggered by an implicit argument, the conceptual completion need not be so triggered. The conceptual completion of a semantically determined sentence "is free" and, as such, it is best viewed as *additional* information. The latter may end up in the proposition communicated but it is not, properly speaking, expressed and, most of all, it does not end up in the (minimal) proposition expressed.

In what follows I concentrate on semantically underdetermined utterances and I address the following two questions:

- *Q1*

 How does a semantically underdetermined utterance get completed in order to express a fully determined proposition?

a student is asked what happens when certain meteorological conditions obtain. Her correct reply is: "It rains". In that case the verb 'to rain' seems to be a two-place predicate even if the location is not specified. It seems to me that in this situation we are playing a slightly different language-game than the one we play in ordinary cases. Besides, even if a location and a time is not specified, the predicate may have a place for the time and the location. This example can also be characterized as follows: the questions to which the student replies are about certain conditions for rain, say conditions α and β. If α obtains in the USA and β obtains only in the UK, then it will not rain. So the implicit premiss is that the conditions hold in the same place. Her answer "it rains", therefore, is implicitly saying that it will rain *there*, wherever the conditions hold—either by quantifying over these locations ("It will rain *wherever* conditions α and β hold") or by an anaphoric link "It will rain *there*"). More on this in Sect. 4, below, where I discuss Perry's Z-lander scenario.

74   *Thought and Context*

- Q2

Does one need a mental representation of all the constituents that end up in a fully determined proposition?

As I just said, I claim that a semantically underdetermined utterance expresses a fully determined proposition insofar as: (i) it exploits parameters available from the context and (ii) the context-exploitation is triggered by hidden or implicit arguments present at the level of the logical form. These implicit arguments, however, need not be represented by the speaker and/or hearer. So, one can think about something without having to represent it. One's thought can be about a given time zone, for instance, without representing it.

2. Varieties of Context-Exploitation

Since the studies of Castañeda (1966; 1967), Kaplan (1977), and Perry (1977), it is common knowledge that utterances like:

(5) a. I am busy
    b. *Today* Jane will be *here*
    c. *This book* is rather expensive
    d. *She* is always very well dressed

are context-sensitive. If you utter (5a), you say that *you* are busy while if I utter it I say that *I* am busy. In uttering (5c), one picks out as an object of discourse the relevant book one demonstrates/points at/ . . . In short, if we change the context of utterance, such as the agent, time, or location, we usually end up with different referents and we express different propositions.[10] We can call utterances like these *indexical utterances*. Utterances like:

(6) a. A *local* pub is promoting German beer
    b. Vieira is one of many *foreign* players playing in the Premiership
    c. Jane believes that Jon is an *enemy*
    d. Maria is one of many *immigrants* in the USA

are also context-sensitive: they involve what I termed "contextuals" in the Introduction. The relevant location of the pub in (6a) is provided by the context of the utterance, while Vieira in (6b) is a foreigner *vis-à-vis* English citizens, and so on. The intuitive way to understand these utterances is that the predicate itself is context-sensitive and, thus, that the context-sensitivity of the utterance is triggered by the fact that the predicate is relational. The natural way to understand these predicates is to

---

[10] For a more accurate and detailed discussion of indexical reference see Ch. 1, Sects. 3 and 4, above.

view them as two-places predicates: a location is local *vis-à-vis* someone, *local (p, x)*, a person is an immigrant *vis-à-vis* some country, *immigrant (c, x)*. The dictionary registers that 'local' means "existing in or belonging to the area where you live, or to the area you are talking about", that 'immigrant' means "a person who settles as a permanent resident in a different country", that "a foreigner is someone who belongs to a country which is not your own", etc.[11] Utterances like:

(1) a. It rains
    b. It's 3 p.m.
    c. Events ξ and φ are simultaneous

are also context-sensitive, but unlike (5) and (6) there is no element in the utterance which operates on context to designate a particular item. In (5) the context-sensitivity is triggered by the presence of indexical expressions ('I', 'here', 'today', 'this book') and in (6) by the presence of the relational predicates, i.e. contextuals ('local', 'foreigner', 'enemy'). In (1), though, we do not seem to have elements triggering the context-sensitivity. Where, then, does it come from? How does the relevant location, time zone, and frame of reference get referred to and, thus, end up in the proposition expressed? To borrow Perry's (1986) terminology, we can say that the relevant location, the relevant time zone, and the relevant frame of reference tacitly referred to in (1) are *unarticulated constituents* of the propositions expressed:

The unarticulated constituent is not designated by any part of the statement, but is identified by the statement as a whole. The statement is *about* the unarticulated constituent, as well as the articulated ones. (Perry [1986] 2000: 174)

In this case, I say that the place is an *unarticulated constituent* of the proposition expressed by the utterance. It is a constituent, because, since rain occurs at a time in a place, there is no truth-evaluable proposition unless a place is supplied. It is unarticulated, because there is no morpheme that designates that place. (Perry 2001: 33)

In an utterance of "It is raining here", the relevant location is picked out by the indexical 'here', while in an utterance of "It is raining" it is picked out, following Perry's suggestion, by the utterance as a whole. What does it exactly mean to claim that an utterance *as a whole* can single out a given location? To this specific question I now turn.

3. A Case Study: Meteorological Verbs

I suggested that meteorological predicates like 'rain', 'snow', 'storm', have an implicit argument for a location and that they should thus be treated on a par with relational

[11] See *The New Shorter Oxford English Dictionary* (Clarendon Press, Oxford, 1993).

adjectives like 'local', 'foreigner', 'enemy'. To stress the fact that the latter do have an implicit argument at work, I invite you to consider the following utterances:[12]

(7) a. A local bar is selling cheap beer
b. A reporter for *The Times* got seriously drunk. A local bar was selling cheap beer
c. Every sports fan watched the Superbowl in a local bar

There are different ways in which we can understand how the relevant location is provided. In (7a) it is provided by the location where the utterance occurs; in (7b) it is provided by the previous linguistic discourse, i.e. the location of the reporter for *The Times*; in (7c) it is dependent on the domain of the quantifier. A natural way to understand the different ways in which 'local' works in these utterances, following Condoravdi & Gawron (1996), is to treat them as working like a relational predicate with an implicit argument. The implicit argument triggers the contextual interpretation. In (7a), it works like a free variable and as such it receives an indexical or deictic interpretation; in (7b), it works like an anaphoric pronoun and as such it gets a discourse anaphoric reading; while in (7c) it works like a bound variable and thus receives a bound variable reading.[13]

We can easily see a parallel between these utterances and utterances containing meteorological verbs:

(8) a. It rains
b. Every time Jane goes on vacation, it rains (where she happens to be)

While in (8a) the relevant location is provided by the location where the utterance occurs, in (8b) it depends upon (and varies with) the domain of the quantifier. As in the analysis proposed for 'local', the natural way to understand utterances such as (8a) and (8b) is to posit a hidden argument place for a location, so that the implicit argument place for the verb 'to rain' in (8a) works like a free variable, while in (8b) it works as a variable bound by the quantifier. As far as I know, the first person to suggest that we have to postulate an argument place for the alleged unarticulated constituent when binding is possible is Barbara Partee (1989). For more on the argument from binding and the way it suggests the presence of tacit arguments at the level of LF see Stanley (2000). For a criticism of the argument from binding see Recanati (2002) and Cappelen and Lepore (forthcoming). Recanati's main argument is that it forces unwelcome consequences. In particular, it forces us to postulate the presence of argument places where, intuitively, there are none. Recanati invites us to consider an intransitive verb like 'to eat' which denotes the property of eating. In that case, he argues, the contextually provided constituent results from free

---

[12] I am borrowing this example from Condoravdi and Gawron (1996).
[13] The notion of anaphora will be discussed at some length in Ch. 8, below.

enrichment and not from the semantics of the verb, for in its intransitive reading 'eat' is not a two-place predicate. But in a sentence like "Jon ate" binding can occur:

(9) Jon is anorexic, but whenever his father cooks mushrooms, he eats.

The intuitive way to understand it is that Jon eats *them*, i.e. *the mushrooms his father has cooked*. Examples like this seem to prove that intuitive binding, *per se*, does not entail the presence in the logical form of an argument place and, therefore, that the argument from binding is not compelling. Cappelen & Lepore (forthcoming) propose the following reduction of the argument from binding:

(10) a. Everywhere I go, 2 + 2 = 4

Here is the Binding Argument applied to (10a). Intuitively, (10a) says that, for every place Sally goes, 2 + 2 = 4 at that place. So we should present the logical form of (10a) along the following lines:

(10) b. For all places x, if Sally goes to x, then 2 + 2 = 4 at x.

The quantifier phrase 'Everywhere Sally goes' is binding a place variable in the logical form of "2 + 2 = 4"—otherwise, there would be nothing for the quantifier phrase to bind. This establishes that the logical form of the sentence '2 + 2 = 4' has a freely occurring place variable. As we will soon see, though, my claim that we have to posit an argument place for a location when meteorological verbs are involved does not rest, unlike Stanley, on the argument from binding. I can thus welcome Recanati's and Cappelen & Lepore's argument.

The idea that meteorological verbs present an argument place for a location and time at LF level faces some difficulties. *Every* action or event occurs at a *time* and *location*, so one could go on and argue that every verb should present an argument place for a time and another for a location. Consequently, every verb is at least a two-place predicate. For the time being let us forget the time—the latter being conveyed by the verb tense—and focus on the locational argument-place. To put it in a nutshell, the difficulty runs as follows: if every verb presents an argument place for a location, then the position I am defending is trivial, for then verbs such as 'to sleep', 'to eat', 'to run', 'to kiss', *must* have an argument for a location as well. But then, contrary to our intuition, nothing would differentiate meteorological verbs like 'to rain', 'to storm', 'to snow', from other verbs. To put it slightly differently, if we infer that we have to postulate an argument place for a location in 'to rain' from the fact that it always rains *in some location*, then we should also posit an argument place for a location for 'to sleep', for one always sleeps *in some location*. What is the argument, if any, enabling us to differentiate meteorological verbs from all the other verbs? What is the peculiarity that would make 'to rain' a two-place argument, while making 'to sleep' one-place?

There are two ways in which one can tackle this difficulty. First, one can focus on the competencies required to master the language-games involving meteorological terms. Secondly, one can focus on the metaphysics of locations.

I begin by focusing on the competencies involved when meteorological verbs are at play. It is a peculiarity of these verbs that they convey information about the weather condition *at some given location*. The location where it rains/snows/thunders/ . . . affects our life and actions. If it rains/snows/ . . . where we are located, we act differently to how we would if it had rained/snowed/ . . . miles away from where we are (this is the main reason why weather reports are always linked to a limited location/region). It seems, then, that one is competent with meteorological terms insofar as one acts and reacts to weather reports in an appropriate way, i.e. insofar as one links the weather condition to a given location. On the other hand, the location where one ate dinner last night is not (usually) cognitively relevant. If one asks a visiting friend, "Have you already had dinner?" with the intent to invite her out, the location the addressee ate her dinner is irrelevant. If someone asks about the weather conditions, however, the location *is* relevant and becomes the focus of attention. In a nutshell, while the subject of an utterance like "It is raining" is a location, the subject of an utterance like "Jon slept with Jane last night" is not a location but Jon.

It seems that: (i) with meteorological verbs, the location plays a cognitive role which it does not play with verbs like 'to eat', 'to sleep', and (ii) a competent speaker immediately links a meteorological verb to a given location and understands the message insofar as she can make this link, while she does not (and often need not) do so with other verbs.

This does not prove, however, that it is intrinsic to the lexicon of meteorological verbs that a location needs to be furnished, i.e. that there is an argument place for a location. As a matter of fact, the dictionary does not report that there must be an understood location accompanying 'to rain' and the other meteorological verbs. The competence argument does, though, contribute some evidence in favor of the presence of an argument place for a location in meteorological verbs.

From a metaphysical, or ontological, viewpoint, one can stress the difference between meteorological verbs like 'to rain' and 'to snow', and verbs like 'to run' and 'to eat', in focusing on the property or relation they stand for. It should not be controversial to claim that meteorological properties are properties of locations; this amounts to saying that a location is the "subject" that undergoes meteorological change. If this is the case, then meteorological verbs *do* require an argument for locations inasmuch as the latter are the subjects of these verbs. On the other hand, even if eating and running—like raining and snowing—always take place in a location as well, they cannot be viewed as modifiers of the location. With verbs like 'to rain' and 'to snow', the location can be viewed as the agent/subject undergoing a given modification, while with intransitive verbs like 'to eat' and 'to run' or transitive verbs like 'to kiss' and 'to give' the location of the activity cannot be viewed as the agent/subject undergoing modification. In the latter case, the agents/subjects are not locations. The subject/agent of "... is running" may be Jon, Jane, the train, etc. It cannot be a location. In other words, the noun phrase that completes or saturates open sentences like "x runs", "x kissed y", cannot pick out locations, while the noun phrases that complete utterances of sentences like "It rains ..." *must* stand for locations. In many cases, as we saw, sentences like these can be saturated by 'it'. The latter may be viewed merely as a syntactic filler, taking the place of the subject. We need 'it' because English, unlike Italian and Spanish, for instance, is not a pro-drop language, i.e. it does not allow the subject of a finite clause to remain unexpressed. Since 'it' contributes nothing to the meaning of the sentence in which it appears, its presence is required only for structural reasons. The asymmetry between meteorological verbs and action verbs (e.g. 'to eat', 'to beat', 'to sleep', 'to fall') manifests itself in the fact that the former, unlike the latter, do not take a grammatical subject. Locations enter the picture in very different ways. When a meteorological verb is uttered, locations enter the scene as the subject while, when other verbs are uttered, the location merely enters the picture as the background upon which the subject(s) of the verb either acts or experiences a given event.

The same story can be told using the notion of *Theta-Role (θ-Role)*. It is often said that the lexical information associated with a lexical item must specify the syntactic category by which the thematic roles are realized. A first distinction can be made between the subject arguments and object arguments. While the subject argument does not affect the θ-Role of the object, the choice of the latter does, as is illustrated by:[14]

(11) a. Jeff broke a leg last week
     b. Jeff broke a vase last week

where the choice of the complement determines the θ-Role of the subject. In (11b), Jeff can be considered to be the AGENT while he cannot in (11a) (where he is the subject who undergoes the event)—to be sure, if Jeff were a member of some fascist paramilitary group, or an agent of the mob, he could be the agent doing the action, i.e. breaking someone else's leg. In these cases, it is said that the verb θ-*marks* the subject indirectly, whereas in the latter case, it is θ-marked compositionally, i.e. it is determined by the semantics of the verb and other VP constituents. In some other cases, however, the verb θ-marks the constituent directly. This seems to be the case with meteorological verbs: 'to rain', 'to snow', and the like directly θ-mark the subject. The latter can only take locations as values, *viz.* its thematic

---

[14] For a more accurate discussion, see Haegeman (1994: 71), from whom I am borrowing the example.

role must be a location.[15] On the other hand, the θ-Role of verbs such as 'to kiss', 'to run', 'to sleep', etc. is not θ-marked as a location.

There is, then, an asymmetry between meteorological verbs and other verbs with respect to the way locations enter the picture. The best way to capture this asymmetry is to posit an argument place for a location in the case of meteorological predicates.

4. Implicit Arguments and Representation

I now turn to discuss the second question I asked at the beginning. I defend Perry's idea that one can think about an item without having to represent it. In particular, one can think about an unarticulated constituent without representing it. This thesis seems to contrast with the idea that, at the level of logical form or subsyntactic level, there is an implicit argument that works like a free variable standing for the unarticulated constituent.

As I have already noted, by "logical form" I mean the syntactic structure of a given class of sentences. In *Tractarian* terminology, we can say that this structure reflects the structure of the propositions expressed by utterances of these sentences. Hence, I take propositions to be structured entities whose structure is reflected by the logical form of the sentences expressing them. A sentence of the subject/predicate form Fa reflects the form of the proposition expressed, whose constituents are the object a and the property F. The logical form of a relational sentence like "Jane kisses Jon", $R(a,b)$, reflects the structure of the proposition expressed. This idea is cashed out in the following tree:

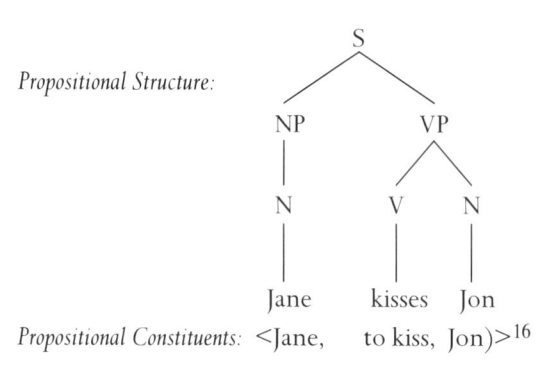

Propositional Structure:

```
                    S
                   / \
                  NP  VP
                  |   / \
                  N  V   N
                  |  |   |
                Jane kisses Jon
```

Propositional Constituents: <Jane, to kiss, Jon>[16]

---

[15] Taylor presents a similar view: "I venture the hypothesis that some unexpressed parameters hide in what we might call the subsyntactic basement of suppressed verbal argument structure. Take the verb 'to rain' as an example. The view which I favor supposes that the verb 'to rain' has a lexically specified argument place which is θ-marked **THEME** and that this argument place takes places [locations] as values. This is a way of saying that the subatomic structure of the verb 'to rain' explicitly marks raining as a kind of change that places [locations] undergo" (Taylor 2001: 53).

[16] The propositional constituents are the individuals Jon and Jane and the property of kissing.

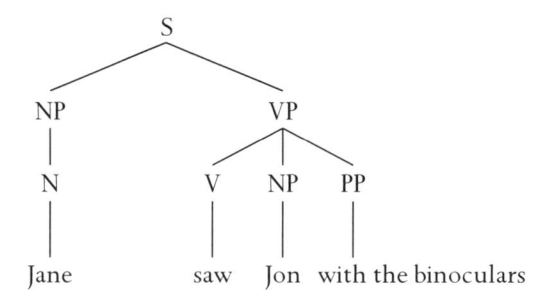

Thought and Context   81

The logical form of a quantified sentence like "Every man smokes"—$\forall x Man(x) \rightarrow Smokes(x)$—can be represented by the tree:

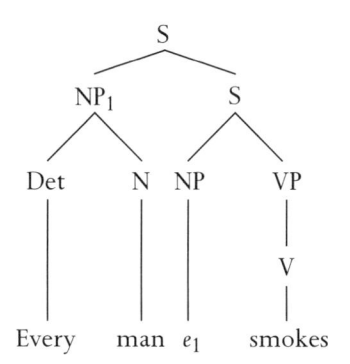

```
                S
              /   \
           NP₁     S
          /|\     / \
        Det N NP  VP
         |  |  |  |
         |  |  |  V
         |  |  |  |
       Every man e₁ smokes
```

An ambiguous sentence like:

(10) a. Jane saw Jon with the binoculars

can be represented either as

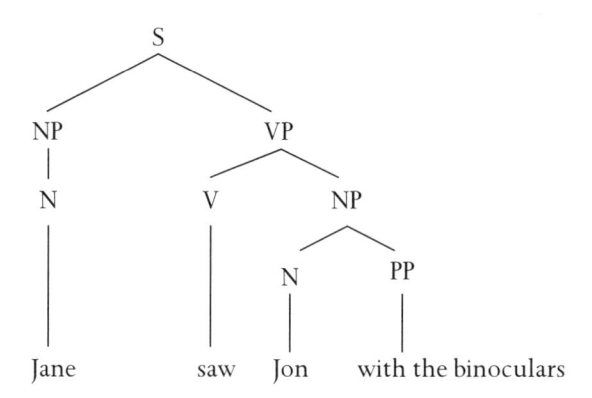

```
              S
            /   \
          NP     VP
          |     /  \
          N    V    NP
          |    |   /  \
        Jane  saw N    PP
                  |    |
                 Jon  with the binoculars
```

or

```
              S
            /   \
          NP     VP
          |     / | \
          N    V  NP PP
          |    |  |   |
        Jane saw Jon with the binoculars
```

What about Perry's idea that one need not have a representation of all the constituents ending up in the proposition expressed? How do we represent the logical form of a sentence like "It is raining"? The notion of logical form I have been assuming is usually committed to the view that LF is a mental representation. Hence, if an argument place is represented at the level of logical form, it is *mentally* represented. The position I am defending, then, seems to contradict Perry's claim that one need not represent the location when one utters, "It is raining".

As far as I can see, there are at least two ways one can accept the position I propose and yet defend Perry's claim. First of all, one could argue that the position which postulates the presence of argument places at the level of logical form is not committed to the assumption, without further argument, that one must represent all the syntactic structure which mirrors the structure of the proposition in order to express the latter. A child can easily express the proposition *that it is raining* without representing either the location where it is raining or the structure of the utterance. Our child merely *exploits* the linguistic resources at her disposal and, in so doing, comes to utter the sentence "It is raining". It is because *in English*, i.e. the language our child uses and exploits, the sentence has such and such a structure and that 'to rain' is a two-place predicate that our child refers to the relevant location and expresses the relevant proposition. Our child can do so without representing either the structure of the proposition or all of its constituents. This can be understood as the phenomenon of *deferentiality*. As Putnam and Kripke told us, one can refer to Gellman and Feynman (or to an elm or a beech) without knowing who Gellman and Feynman are, or even without knowing that they were physicists. One can competently use 'elm' and 'beech' without being able to tell an elm from a beech. By the same token, one can argue that one can refer to a given location without mentioning it or even representing it. In short, one can express a proposition having a given structure and a given location as constituent in virtue of exploiting the linguistic resources at one's disposal. Along this line, the notion of logical form is independent of the mental representation one may have. LF is understood to be the logical form of English *qua* natural, objective and social language. Along this line one could argue that LF is akin to a lot of other mental properties which are, at least in part, dependent on external circumstances. This (externalist) position would, no doubt, be in conflict with the notion of LF *qua* psychological reality, as it is usually conceived within the Chomskian tradition.[17] This position is in accordance with the notion of consumerist semantics I discussed in the previous chapter.

[17] One could argue that the deference involved in the 'Gellman–Feynman' or 'elm'–'beech' cases differs from the deference involved in unarticulated constituents and that, in the case of "It rains *here*", there can be deference just as in the case of "It rains". To begin with, I do not believe that one can defer, as far as

Secondly, the position I am defending is also consonant with the view that logical form *qua* syntactic properties relevant to semantic interpretation *is* a psychological reality and yet can salvage Perry's claim that one's thought may be about something without one having to represent it. Understood this way, LF can be viewed as the mental representation explaining the (grammatical) understanding and capacities of an agent speaking a given language. Even if we understand logical form this way, we do not commit ourselves to the thesis that one cannot refer to (and think about) a given item without representing it. The presence of implicit arguments representing the unarticulated constituents do not commit us to the view that an agent ought to think of the unarticulated constituents of the proposition expressed in order to refer to (and for the thought to be about) them. Logical form, understood along this line, is unconscious:

> [T]he unconsciousness of mental grammar is still more radical than Freud's notion of the unconscious: mental grammar isn't available to consciousness under *any* conditions, therapeutic or otherwise. . . . if at least some other processes in the mind are not open to consciousness, it shouldn't be too distasteful to say that parts of language ability are unconscious too. (Jackendoff 1994: 19)

Unconscious representation is not, properly speaking, representation. One cannot claim that one was unconsciously thinking about something. I can meet someone and tell her "Last night I thought/wondered/talked/ . . . about you", but

---

reference is concerned, when one uses indexical expressions. One cannot say, for instance, "You are kind" and defer to someone else (an expert?) to fix the reference of the pronoun 'you'. The same applies in the case of 'here', 'now', 'today', and the like. One may not know which day it is or what location one is in, but in simply uttering 'now', 'today', or 'here', one immediately picks out and identifies the relevant location/time. Indexical thoughts are *perspectival*, whilst thoughts involving proper names and other terms are not (see also Ch. 4 below). Thus, I do not object to the fact that the kind of deference involved in the Kripke-Putnam example differs from that involved in the case of unarticulated constituents. Like all indexical thoughts, thoughts containing unarticulated constituents are perspectival. The deference involved does not concern the reference-fixing mechanisms. One's thought may be about a given location simply because the thought occurs in that very location, yet one need not represent the latter, i.e. one need not represent the implicit argument at work—Dokic (2002*b*) spells out a theory of situated thoughts which could be adopted to account for the view that a thought can be about something simply by being situated in a given location (see the notion of situated propositions/thoughts that I discuss in the Introd., above). Thus, when one utters "It is raining here", one represents and refers to the relevant location, simply by the act of uttering 'here'. We cannot deny that, in this case, one has a '*here*'-thought, just as one has an 'I'-thought when one uses the first-person pronoun. When one utters "It is raining", on the other hand, one's thought is still about the relevant location, for it too occurs in that very location. Yet one does not represent the latter insofar as one utters no words standing for it; there is no morpheme one entertains standing for the relevant place. Thus, one cannot have a 'here'-thought. The unarticulated constituent at work in these cases need not be represented. It is in this sense that we can say that a child, for instance, can use meteorological verbs in a deferential way, i.e. without realizing that they are two-place predicates. That is to say, one can exploit a two-place predicate without knowing it, or even whilst believing it to be monadic.

I cannot tell her "Last night I *unconsciously* thought/wondered/talked/ . . . about you". The paradox entailed by a sentence like "I am unconsciously thinking about X" should further underline the fact that the unconsciousness of mental grammar and logical form entails that one does not need to represent the items picked out by implicit arguments. It is worth noticing that a third-person attribution like "Jane is unconsciously thinking/dreaming/wondering/ . . . about X" also sounds paradoxical, or at least it would make sense only among some very inspired psychologists and/or cognitive scientists. The awkwardness of attributions like these should further contribute to the point I am making; that is, one can use an *n*-place predicate without having to think of all the predicate's places, i.e. without having a (conscious) representation of each parameter of the corresponding relation. When unarticulated constituents are involved, what gets represented at the level of logical form are *implicit* arguments. An implicit argument is not what comes to mind; when one thinks about a relevant location using a sentence like "It is raining", one need not call to mind the implicit argument for the location. If one were to call to mind the implicit argument, one would make it explicit and hence the relevant location would no longer be an *unarticulated* constituent. It is even possible (and is in fact often the case) that a child, for instance, is unable to recover and articulate all the constituents of a given proposition, i.e. she may not be disposed to articulate the unarticulated constituents. In other words, it is conceivable that a child is unable to go from "It is raining" to "It is raining here" and thus to articulate the unarticulated constituent. On the other hand, someone who goes from the former to the latter would move from an unarticulated to an articulated thought constituent, and thus from a thought without (full) representation (i.e. without a representation of a location) to a thought in which the relevant location is represented. It is in this sense that I claim that the unarticulated constituent becomes represented.[18]

Perry claims that we can even imagine a whole community that is unable to articulate some of the constituents that end up in their propositions. He invites us to imagine an isolated community, living in a location called Z-land. Members of this community never travel or communicate with members of other communities; they do not even have a name for Z-land. After all, they do not need to

---

[18] Perry has suggested a third option to me. LF can be viewed as a combination, reached by accommodation of our linguistic institutions (both individual and community-wide) with the facts about how things work in the world. While the two positions I have described can be viewed as externalist (LF depends on language-*qua*-social-entity) *vs.* internalist (LF depends on language-*qua*-psychological-entity), this third option is a hybrid. As such, it is probably the more plausible, insofar as it recognizes that both internal and external constraints contribute in determining the LF of a relevant class of sentences. Without entering into the details and merits of the three options, it is worth noticing that they are *all* consonant with the view that implicit arguments need not be represented by the speaker and/or audience.

name their own location, insofar as they do not have to distinguish it from other locations. The important thing is that members of this community are unable to say, "It is raining here". If Z-landers desire to report the weather condition when they face rain, all they can say is "It is raining". Perry's moral is:

> It would be natural to treat Z-landers' uses of the sentence *It is raining* as having Z-land as an unarticulated constituent. But what secures Z-land, rather than, say, San Francisco, as the unarticulated constituent of their discourse about rain? It is simply that the perception that gives rise to the beliefs that *It is raining* expresses are perceptions of the weather in Z-land. Z-land is a constituent of the practice, or language game, in which the sentence *It is raining* plays a role. There is no need to postulate a concept or idea of Z-land as a component of their thought, to secure the connection to Z-land. The connection is secured by the role of the whole belief in their lives. . . .
>
> The Z-lander's beliefs have a simple job to do. All of the information (or misinformation) they get about the weather, through observation or reports of others, is about Z-land. All of the actions they perform, in light of their weather beliefs, take place in Z-land. The connection between the place about which they receive weather information, and the place whose weather determines the appropriateness of their action, is guaranteed by their life-style, and need not be coordinated by their beliefs. (Perry [1986] 2000: 177–8)

The first reaction that comes to my mind when considering this scenario is to argue that in Z-landish, unlike in English, 'rain' is a one-place predicate. When (in English) we utter, "It is raining", we express the proposition that it is raining at a given location at the time of utterance, while the Z-landers' utterance of the homophonic sentence "It is raining" expresses the proposition that it is raining at the time of utterance. Hence, the truth-conditions of these homophonic sentences, are cashed out as:

- If u is an utterance of "It is raining", then [u is true (In English) iff it is raining in l_t and u_t]
- If u is an utterance of "It is raining", then [u is true (In Z-landish) iff it is raining *at u_t*]

where 'u_t' and 'l_t' stands for the time and location of the utterance. The English and Z-lander semanticists would thus look at things differently. While we consider 'rain' to be a predicate expressing a two-place relation between times and locations, the Z-lander semanticists would consider it to be a predicate expressing a property of time.

Perry recognizes that there is a distortion in treating the Z-landers' use of "It is raining" on a par with our own use. At the same time, however, Perry insists on the fact that the possibilities the Z-landers fail to recognize are real. Perry seems thus to commit himself to a realist position with respect to properties and relations. That is, rain is a two-place relation regardless of whether we use a two-term predicate while the Z-landers use a one-term predicate.[19] As a consequence, Perry proposes a kind of mixed analysis:

> Suppose we accept the Z-lander semanticist's opinion as to the object of the Z-landers' attitude—what they assert with a use of *It is raining* and what they believe when they hear such a statement from a reliable source—but stick to our view of what those objects are. Then we would say that the Z-landers assert and believe propositional functions, rather than propositions. What would be wrong with this? (Perry [1986] 2000: 178)

Following this suggestion, an utterance of the Z-landish sentence "It is raining" is true if the propositional function it expresses is true relative to Z-land:

> For the Z-landers' discourse about weather, a statement is true if the propositional function it expresses is true relative to Z-land. Z-land comes in not as an unarticulated constituent each Z-landish weather statement is about, but as a global factor that all Z-land discourse about the weather concerns. (Perry [1986] 2000: 179)

To be sure, this characterization allows us to record the difference between the linguistic practice in Z-land and our own. Why, though, does Perry not accept the position I have suggested, i.e. that 'rain' in Z-landish is a one-place predicate and an utterance of "It is raining" in Z-landish expresses the proposition that it is raining at the time of utterance? Succinctly, why does Perry not accept the idea that "It is raining" in English and "It is raining" in Z-landish do not have the same truth-conditions? After all, the Z-landers' meteorological language-games differ from our own. In the Z-landers' language-game, for instance, questions of the form "Where is it raining?", "Where will it snow tomorrow?", etc. do not exist.

As I understand it, Perry's considerations rest on the assumption that, when describing the way members of a given community use their language, we can take an external stance and yet understand how they rationally use and master their own language. The question that springs to mind is whether this is a plausible stance or whether one should instead take an internal stance and describe the community's linguistic activity from inside their own practice. Thus, the question runs as follows: In analyzing the Z-landers' use of "It is raining", can we take our semanticist's viewpoint or are we constrained to take the Z-lander semanticist's one?

Since the kind of knowledge that is at issue when we use sentences like "It is raining" is a sort of implicit knowledge, akin to a practical ability, a kind of knowing-*how*, the best way to capture it seems to be from the Z-landers' viewpoint. Actually, if one's goal is to capture the Z-landers' use of "It is raining" and the way they linguistically

---

[19] If one were to adopt a nominalist stance and assume conceptualism about properties, one would reject Perry's argument insofar as we could not have a non-linguistic access to properties. If so, in Z-landish and in English 'rain' would not have the same meaning. For a defense of conceptualism about properties see Dokic (2001, 2002*a*).

interact with each other and their surroundings, one is constrained to deal with the way *they* understand each other and the way *they master their* language.[20] To do so, however, it seems that we must take the Z-landers' viewpoint.

[O]ne human being can be a complete enigma to another. We learn this when we come into a strange country with entirely strange traditions; and, what is more, even given a mastery of the country's language. We do not *understand* the people. . . . We cannot find our feet with them. . . . If a lion could talk, we could not understand him. (Wittgenstein, *PI*: p. 223)

It may be worth noticing that, if we follow Wittgenstein on this issue, we ultimately ought to accept that our form of life is the non-linguistic context essential to understanding our linguistic activity, for "to imagine a language is to imagine a form of life" (*PI*: §7), for "what has to be accepted, the given, is—so one could say—forms of life" (*PI*: p. 226).

What I have just said does not rule out the fact that our semanticist can describe the Z-landers' linguistic activity and come out with a plausible story, i.e. a story that provides a set of rules that *fit* the Z-landers' linguistic behavior. These rules, though, do not account for the way in which Z-landers *actually* follow rules, for the relation between a rule and the behavior (linguistic or not) it guides is not of the same kind as the relation between a scientific hypothesis and its evidence. The former, unlike the latter, is (to borrow Wittgenstein's terminology) an *internal* relation, i.e. a relation whose *relata* cannot be disentangled. Our semanticist's rules, which "enable" her to explain the Z-landers' linguistic behavior, are merely explanatory hypotheses purporting to describe their linguistic activity.

Since Perry does not take the Z-landers' viewpoint, he does not consider the predicate 'rain' in Z-landish as a one-place predicate. The only alternative Perry can envisage is the one in which Z-land is a context-*in*sensitive unarticulated constituent of the Z-landers' weather condition. This way, whenever a Z-lander utters, "It is raining", she would inevitably express a proposition having Z-land as a constituent. The truth-condition of the Z-landish "It is raining" would thus correspond with:

- If u is an utterance of "It is raining" then [u is true (in Z-landish) iff it is raining *in Z-land at u_t*]

To dismiss this possibility, Perry invites us to imagine a scenario in which Z-landers become nomads and start migrating:

If their use of "It is raining" is keyed to their surroundings, we would have to say its meaning had changed, or that their reports were now false, whenever the weather in their new

---

[20] "This account can only be given in terms of the practical ability which the speaker displays in using sentences of the language; and, in general, the knowledge of which that practical ability is taken as a manifestation may be, and should be, regarded as only implicit knowledge" (Dummett 1993: 101).

environments deviates from that in Z-land. Neither of these steps seems plausible. What we have contemplated is a change in their surroundings, not a change in the meaning of their sentences. (Perry [1986] 2000: 179–80)

Perry's argument rests on the assumption that Z-landish does not change. Why, though, should we accept this assumption? In particular, why cannot we suppose that Z-landish evolves? Why we cannot assume that 'to rain' becomes a two-place predicate when the nomads adapt to their new situations and migrations? Languages do evolve. In a nutshell, why can we not suppose that Z-landish becomes just like English? After all, after their migrations the nomads will come to entertain beliefs that they can express with utterances of sentences like: "It is raining *here*", "It is raining *here* while it may not be raining *where* our relatives are", "It was not raining so much *where* we were before". Z-landers *do* have words like 'here', 'there', i.e. words enabling them to locate objects in space, so it will not be difficult for the nomads to apply these words to their weather conditions as soon as they start moving and realize that the weather condition may change with a change of location. To sum up, unlike Perry, I believe that the Z-landish sentence "It is raining", unlike the English one, *is* semantically determined. If, as I suggested, we take the Z-lander semanticist's viewpoint, we can easily account for this phenomenon.

If I am right, then we can easily recognize the presence of implicit arguments at the level of logical form and, yet, admit that one need not articulate the unarticulated constituents and thus need not have a (conscious) mental representation of all the items that end up in the proposition one expresses using a semantically underdetermined sentence.

The general moral is that we should not be scared by the presence of implicit arguments, i.e. arguments at work when meteorological verbs are used, for implicit arguments do not undermine Perry's thesis that one can have thoughts without representation. The same, or a similar, story can be told about time zones. If we turn the clock back a few centuries, people did not have conceptions of time zones and so the latter were not unarticulated constituents of their utterances involving times. Their language-games involving time probably rested on an absolutist conception of time, i.e. on the view that time statements are not relative to a time zone. Even if this is not historically accurate, we can easily imagine a linguistic community that, like the Z-landers, never travels and does not need to have time statements relative to time zones.

Other cases of unarticulacy, like 'simultaneous', are best understood as a kind of background or presupposed information, which does not need to be implicitly referred to. If so, we do not need to postulate the existence of implicit arguments referring to frames of reference. If one considers (following Wittgenstein) that a linguistic community operates with a plurality of variegated language-games, the fact that not all implicit information can be captured within a single and simple framework should not come as a surprise. In some language-games, the implicit information is confined to the background assumptions or presuppositions upon which the linguistic act occurs. In other language-games, the implicit information is captured in postulating implicit arguments at work during the speech act. In neither case, though, are we forced to assume that the speaker and/or hearer must represent all the constituents that either end up in the proposition expressed or which operate as background assumptions and presuppositions enabling the speech act. The context upon which the speech act occurs bridges the gap and fills in the relevant information in saturating the implicit arguments. It is this contextual phenomenon that makes one's thought *about* something (such as a location or a time zone) and *not* the alleged representation the speaker entertains.

The general moral, so far, is that thoughts are best understood as being situated in a given contextual framework. And it is because of this feature that some of our thoughts need not represent all the constituents they are about. It is also because of this feature that context, as it has been explained and discussed in the previous chapter, can be viewed as the *sine qua non* concerning the aboutness of our thoughts, i.e. as what bridges the gap between our thinking activity and reality. It is, roughly, because we are social agents interacting both with reality and the other members of our community that our words can be viewed as tools enabling us to achieve many different goals and entertain many different thoughts. We thus continue the idea I expressed in the Introduction when I argued in favor of contextual embodiment, i.e. the thesis that we are context-bound agents. In this respect words are best understood as the tools of the mind. I now turn to discuss how two of our different linguistic tools, proper names and indexicals, are different tools of the mind and how our thoughts may differ on whether we entertain a thought we could express using a proper name or a thought expressible using an indexical expression. It should not come as a surprise to hear that, at the end of the day, this rests on the different way indexical thoughts and thoughts entertained using non-indexical expressions rely on context to reach the objects they are about.

5. Understanding Proper Names *vs.* Understanding Indexicals

To begin with, consider that at an FA meeting Sue has been asked to pass an important message to Sir Alex Ferguson. To reach her goal, i.e. to give the message to Ferguson, Sue needs to know who Ferguson is, i.e. Sue needs to know who the referent of the proper name 'Ferguson' is. If at the ceremony she approaches the wrong person and passes the message to, say Arsène Wenger, something went wrong. Sue took Wenger to be Ferguson. Moreover, it may be that Sue has been informed that Ferguson is the manager of Manchester United, that he speaks with a Scottish accent, and so on. In short it may be that Sue has at her disposal some identifying descriptions of Ferguson, i.e. descriptions which apply only to Ferguson. Yet, at the meeting, she is unable to distinguish Ferguson from Wenger. She is unable to form the judgement "*He* is Ferguson". In other words she is unable to indexically anchor her information about Ferguson to Ferguson. Sue may possess lots of relevant information about Ferguson, but her information being of the form "Ferguson is the *F*, the *G*, . . ." may not let her entertain the thought that *he is Ferguson*. Only a thought of this form will enable Sue to pass the message to Ferguson. The moral seems to be that one can competently use a proper name and even attach a lot of information to the relevant name without being able to distinguish the referent. The question which springs to mind is the following: do we need to be able to indexically anchor a proper name to its bearer to understand this very name? If so, the understanding of a proper name does not amount to the possession of an (or some) identifying description(s). This relies on the difference between anchored information and unanchored information I discussed at some length in the previous chapter.

If understanding a name amounts to being able, or at least to being disposed, to entertain a judgement of the form "She/he/this/you . . . is (are) NN" we understand a very small number of names. Besides, it may be that we understand a name only at a certain time. I was able to entertain the thought expressed by "This is Jane Smith" when I was at school while I am unable to entertain this thought nowadays. Moreover, Jane and I kept in touch and I know lots of relevant properties applying only to her. Yet, given that I have not met Jane since we were at school, I am unable to recognize her and entertain a judgement expressible by "This is Jane Smith". I call the knowledge expressible by a sentence of the form "She/he/this/you . . . is (are) NN", *recognitional capacity*.

But, do we need to be able to recognize the referent to understand a given name? Russell thought so:

[W]hen there is anything with which we do not have immediate acquaintance, but only definition by denoting phrases, then the propositions in which this thing is introduced by means of a denoting phrase do not really contain this thing as a constituent . . . Thus in every proposition that we can apprehend . . . all the constituents are really entities with which we have immediate acquaintance. (Russell [1905] 1956: 55–6)

Russell's position has been popularized, by Evans among others, as Russell's Principle. Stated as such, Russell's Principle seems to be defined in a circular way, for what does it mean for someone to be acquainted with something? One could argue that we can be acquainted with the referent in a deferential way. As I take it, though, Russell's Principle, which rests on Russell's way of understanding the notion of acquaintance, requires a discriminating knowledge of the referent. In other words, it requires a *recognitional capacity*. This kind of knowledge is ultimately attained in an indexical way, i.e. expressed by locution of the form "This/that *F*".[21] So a subject *understands* an utterance containing what Evans calls "a Russellian singular term", say "*a* is *F*", if and only if she would be able to form two judgements: "This is *a*" and "This is *F*". As such, Russell's Principle seems to be linked to *demonstrative identification*. It rests on the subject's recognitional capacity.[22]

According to Evans, Russell's Principle requires that the idea (or conception) of the object we have is cognitively grounded in the referent, i.e. it anchors our thought to the referent. For this idea to allow us to discriminate the referent from others, it ought to be a *fundamental idea*. To have a fundamental idea of an object one must think of it as the possessor of the fundamental ground of difference that it in fact possesses. This kind of knowledge rests on our recognitional capacity which, as I have been arguing, requires ultimately an indexical thought of the form *this is NN*.

As I have shown in the previous chapter, proper names are not indexicals and cannot be reduced to them. As we saw, the former, unlike the latter, are needed in order to keep track of objects, in order to speak, think, and communicate, when the referents are not available in our perceptual field. It seems that if we take Russell's Principle at face value, the only names we would be entitled to use ought to rest on our recognitional ability. It may be that this ability is only dispositional and cashed out in counterfactual terms, *viz.* if the referent of the name were in our perceptual field, we would be able to bridge the gap between the name and the referent in an indexical way. This, though, would not capture our everyday practice and in particular the fact that proper names do not reduce to indexicals forces the distinction between two types of singular thoughts.

---

[21] I am abstracting away from the fact that Russell believed that we cannot be acquainted with objects like chairs, frogs, and people and that the only things we can be acquainted with are universals, *sense data*, and, at some point of his career, with the self.

[22] One may be tempted to argue that it is possible to have a discriminating knowledge of, say Aristotle, by simply thinking of Aristotle as the causal origin of this practice of name using. If Russell's Principle is loosened in such a way, though, it would be of no help in accounting for what it was first introduced for, i.e. the requirement that to understand a singular term a speaker need to be acquainted with the referent. In the scenario I have proposed, to understand the name 'Alex Ferguson' one needs to be acquainted with Ferguson and thus able to shake his hand when the situation is presented. In other words, for Russell's Principle to play its role it needs to explain what triggers some action and thus requires a discriminating knowledge of the referent. Hence, if one merely thinks of Ferguson as the causal origin of this practice of name using one is likely to be unable to shake Ferguson's hand.

6. Two Types of Singular Thoughts

The way I understand Russell's Principle may urge the distinction between *understanding* and *communicating*. Consider the following example: I pick up the phone and my interlocutor tells me: "I'm Mary and I'd like to speak with your partner". To which I reply: "S/he isn't here but I'll tell her/him to call back". As it happens, I do not know who Mary is. Nonetheless, I am able to tell my partner that Mary called. My partner, who knows who Mary is, will be able to return the call. Hence, I am able to pass on the relevant information to my partner even if I am not acquainted (and never have been) with Mary: I act, so to speak, like an answering machine. It seems, then, that I did not understand the message I heard while my partner, who knows Mary, understood it. All I know is that someone called "Mary" would like to speak with my partner. But this piece of knowledge seems to be enough for the purpose of communication. To put it slightly differently, the fact that I can grasp the reflexive truth-conditions of a given utterance enables me to pass on the relevant information.

Let us consider another example. Someone I do not know, Sue to give her a name, comes to visit me and says: "I'd like to speak with your partner". I cannot simply tell Sue that I shall pass on the message to my partner. I need further information. To be sure, I could describe the person to my partner and s/he may be able to guess that Sue came. But a more natural procedure would be to ask Sue her name.[23]

In other words, when indexicals are in play, to pass on given information we have to understand the relevant message and Russell's Principle ought to be taken into consideration while, when proper names are in play, Russell's Principle does not need to enter the picture. This, though, should not undermine the picture I am proposing, for indexicals, unlike proper names, are tools usually used to make reference *in praesentia*. As such, a use of an indexical exploits the presence of the referent and this use is acquaintance-based, it rests on a recognitional capacity. To be sure, the recognitional capacity involved when one uses a pure indexical differs from the recognitional capacity involved when using a demonstrative expression. For, from the speaker's or thinker's viewpoint the paradigmatic use of a demonstrative, unlike the use of a pure indexical, is perception-based. While on the one hand the recognitional capacity rests on the perception of the referent, on the other hand it merely rests on the fact that the speaker/thinker occupies a given perceptual field, i.e. that she is egocentrically placed and, thus, has the faculty or

---

[23] The position I am defending bears some similarities with Hintikka's distinction between public identification and perspectival identification: "In perspectival identification, we use an agent's first-hand cognitive relations to persons, objects, places, etc. as the identificatory framework" (Hintikka 1998: 205). Moreover, Hintikka argues that: "What is characteristic of demonstratives is not a special mode of reference but a special mode of identification" (Hintikka 1998: 204).

potential of acting in a given place. As Evans (1982) aptly pointed out, by the simple fact of using a so-called pure indexical one is disposed to gather information from the relevant referent, be it oneself, a time, or a location. In short, to pass an indexical message we can either use an indexical expression and draw our audience's attention to the relevant individual or, if the referent is not in our perceptual field, we need to use another referential tool such as, for instance, a proper name. It could be thought that in the case of answering machines and post-its, i.e. in the cases where one makes what we can characterize as an utterance at a distance, the indexicals involved are used to make reference *in absentia* and the agent of the utterance is not acquainted with the referent.[24] Notice that these cases do not involve demonstratives, namely perception-based indexicals. They involve pure indexicals. It would not make much sense to leave a post-it or a recorded message saying something like "This is a flower" or "She is a wonderful girl".[25] In the case of post-its and answering machines, reference is fixed the very moment, at the very place, the utterance is made, thus it is fixed *in praesentia*.

When proper names are involved the situation is different. When I say to my partner "Mary called" and "Sue came" it seems that I think about Mary and Sue. Besides, my partner can attribute to me thoughts about Mary and Sue. To be sure, in the first case I think about Mary in a deferential way, exploiting the relevant convention, i.e. using Mary's proper name. But deferential thinking is thinking and many if not most of our thoughts are deferential. Indeed there are few names we use which are acquaintance-based. Take 'Aristotle': are we acquainted with Aristotle? If yes, do we go to the past or is it Aristotle who comes to the present? It seems, then, that communication does not rest on Russell's Principle: we can communicate and understand each other without having a discriminating knowledge of the referent. Consider, for instance, Putnam's 'elm-beech' and Kripke's 'Gellman–Feynman' examples. As these examples show, we can use these terms without being able to tell apart a beech from an elm or Gellman from Feynman. As Wettstein nicely puts it:

If one can refer to something without anything like a substantive cognitive fix on the referent, if the use of a name can be virtually blind epistemically, then why should it be the slightest bit surprising that a speaker might be competent with two co-referring names but have no inkling that they co-refer? (Wettstein 1989: 175)

[24] I discuss these cases at some length in Ch. 4, below, where I focus on so-called essential indexicals and how they can be used and understood when answering machines and the like are involved.
[25] Magritte's famous "This is not a pipe" should not undermine what I said, for the token on his painting of a pipe should be understood as meaning something along: "What is reproduced/painted/ . . . on this painting is not a pipe". The same goes for tokens like "This car is rented by XX" printed on cars. These kinds of tokens go short for something like: "The car you are seeing/perceiving/ . . . is rented by XX". Actually to understand these tokens one ought to interpret them this way.

What I said should suggest that to understand a use of an indexical expression, we have to rely on context, while we can understand a use of a proper name without relying on context. Actually, we can easily imagine a language where every individual has a particular name and where it is forbidden to use an already existing name. In this case we would not have to rely on contextual features, to the setting, to refer to someone using a proper name. We cannot, though, imagine a similar language-game involving indexicals.

This picture seems to contrast with our intuitions. Actually, it seems that we should distinguish between at least two kinds of uses of proper names, say the *acquaintance-based* and the *deference-based* uses of proper names. If Sue uses a proper name of someone she is acquainted with (her grandfather or her dog), she is probably in a different position *vis-à-vis* the referent from us. Unlike us, she is able, for instance, to feed her dog, and so on. Unlike us she has a recognitional capacity. Russell's Principle is best understood when we consider the practical abilities of a subject. As such it should not affect our semantics. In particular, it should not undermine the picture I advocate concerning the referential link between a given expression and the item it stands for. The link between the name and its bearer is conventional: it is not bridged by our recognitional capacities.

The general idea is that when we use proper names, our thinking activity is not, and does not need to be, indexically grounded; that is, we do not have to be able to pick out the referent in an indexical way. In such cases our thinking activity may well be deferential and successful communication rests on this very fact, on the fact that we share a common language and exploit common conventions. On the other hand, when indexicals are involved our thinking activity is not deferential: it is indexically grounded. This rests on the very fact that we are using indexical terms. Nonetheless, both deferential thinking and indexical thinking exploit the power of language and, since we use different referential tools, our thoughts are related to the external world in different ways, i.e. either deferentially linked or indexically linked. To argue that all thoughts need to be indexically linked to the external world, as Russell's Principle seems to suggest, amounts to misunderstanding the very difference between the way indexicals and proper names work. Hence, the picture I have in mind differs from Evans's insofar as he seems to require that our thoughts should be indexically grounded in the external world for communication and understanding to be successful:

I think it will be universally acknowledged that understanding a use of a proper name requires one to go beyond the thought that the speaker is referring to *some person known as NN*, and to arrive at a thought in the thinking of which one actually thinks of the object in question. The reason for this is not the one that is usually given, namely that the property of being known as NN is semantical in character, but rather, a consideration of the same sort as I brought to bear in the case of, say, 'you'. One does not understand a remark of the form 'You are F', addressed to oneself, just by knowing that the speaker is saying that the person he is addressing is F; one must go beyond the referential feature and identify the person as oneself. Similarly, if one has a dossier of information associated with the name 'NN', and fails to bring it to bear in understanding 'NN is F', going no further than the thought 'Someone named "NN" is F', one has surely failed to do what it was the point of utterance that one should do. (Evans 1982: 399)

No doubt, when one addresses me using 'you', to understand what she is saying I have to know that I am the addressee. But this is because, as we saw, my interlocutor is using an indexical term. In the case of proper names, on the other hand, no discriminating knowledge is necessary for communication and understanding to succeed. And this difference rests on the very different way proper names and indexicals work within our language, a difference which reflects the way our thoughts are anchored in the external world. To miss this difference is to fail to understand the very way indexicals and proper names are linked to their referents. In short, even if Evans does not claim, like Recanati and Voltolini for instance, that proper names are indexicals, I think that he, like Russell, is in the grip of a confusion. For, when he comes to deal with understanding he seems to conflate indexical reference and reference using proper names. As I mentioned, in order to understand the use of indexical expressions we ought to identify the referent, while we can competently use and understand a proper name without being able to identify the referent. The use of the former, unlike the latter, rests on what I have characterized recognitional capacity. There are different reasons why a speaker can fail to understand an indexical expression: she may be blind, she may misperceive the referent, etc. Such a speaker, though, need not be linguistically incompetent, for she may well know the meaning (or character of the indexical) yet fail to single out the referent. On the other hand, we cannot argue that someone who does not know who the referent of a proper name is, i.e. one who has no recognitional capacity, is incompetent and, as such, unable to use this very name in an appropriate way and hold a singular thought about the bearer of this very name.

So far I hope that I have succeeded in highlighting the importance of context in our linguistic and cognitive activity. I also hope that I have been able to spell out how contextual features manifest themselves in various ways. Actually, in these preliminary chapters, we have seen how singular terms and the thoughts that involve them relate to context in order to gain their value. We have also seen how utterances and thoughts are best viewed as situated. By keeping in mind the importance of context and the way it helps us understand and appreciate linguistic underdeterminacy, we are now in a position to appreciate how contextual features relate to the use of specific terms. In the next two chapters we shall investigate and distinguish various kinds of singular terms. In the next chapter we shall focus on description-names (e.g. 'The Red Devils', 'The Holy Roman Empire') and complex demonstratives (e.g. 'this table', 'that child near the window'). We will see how context affects the use of these singular terms and how a multiple-proposition framework, i.e. the view that a single utterance may express more than one proposition, helps to understand how these NPs work. We shall then be in a position to discuss, in Chapter 4, the way various kinds of indexicals work and how they differ from one another.

3

A Multiple-Proposition Approach

> Almost always, it seems, we connect with the main thoughts expressed by us subsidiary thoughts which, although not expressed, are associated with our words, in accordance with psychological laws, by the hearer. And since the subsidiary thought appears to be connected with our words on our own account, almost like the main thought itself, we want it also to be expressed. The sense of the sentence is thereby enriched, and it may well happen that we have more simple thoughts than clauses. In many cases the sentence must be understood in this way, in others it may be doubtful whether the subsidiary thought belongs to the sense of the sentence or only accompanies it.
>
> (Frege [1892] 1952: 75)

> *If pointing can be taken as a form of describing. Why not take describing as a form of pointing?* Notice that our demonstrative analysis of demonstrations need not, indeed should not, deny or even ignore the fact that demonstrations have both a sense and a demonstratum. It is just that according to the demonstrative analysis the sense of the demonstration does not appear in the proposition. Instead the sense is used only to fix the demonstratum which itself appears directly in the proposition.
>
> (Kaplan [1978] 1990: 24)

In this chapter, I propose a multiple-proposition theory which explains certain linguistic data in a straightforward way. The data I focus on are provided by what I label *description-names*, i.e. proper names like 'The Holy Virgin' and 'The Beatles', and *complex demonstratives*, i.e. NPs of the form 'that table covered in books', 'this pen', 'these horses', etc. The multiple-proposition theory I propose fits within the framework of direct reference that I favored in the previous chapters.

I proceed as follows. In Section 1, I introduce the phenomenon of description-names. In Sections 2 and 3, I discuss the similarities and differences between descriptions and description-names. In Section 4, I propose a logic which helps handle description-names and I show that, contrary to appearances, description-names do conform to Millianism, i.e. the view that proper names are directly referential expressions, referring regardless of whether the relevant individual satisfies the associated description. However, description-names name *and* describe. I will thus be in a position to argue that the best framework within which to accommodate description-names is a multiple-proposition theory, according to which a given utterance may express several propositions. In Section 5, I introduce and discuss personal pronouns and complex demonstratives. I argue that the pronouns 'she' and 'he' are disguised complex demonstratives of the form 'that female/male'. In Sections 6, 7, and 8, three competing theories of complex demonstratives are proposed. I show how they are all committed to the view that the third-person pronoun 's/he' turns out to be an empty term when used to refer to, say, a hermaphrodite. In Section 9, I apply the multiple-proposition theory to complex demonstratives and show how it helps us handle the intuition that complex demonstratives such as 'that female/male' and the pronoun 's/he' can succeed in referring to someone independently of the referent's gender. I argue that an utterance containing a complex demonstrative, like an utterance containing a description-name, expresses two (or more) propositions, the background proposition(s) and the official one. I will thus be in a position to defend the following theses: (i) the referent of a complex demonstrative, like the referent of a description-name, is a constituent of the proposition expressed independently of whether it satisfies the nominal part of the demonstrative expression, (ii) the nominal part of a complex demonstrative only affects the background proposition(s), and (iii) the utterance inherits its truth-value from the official proposition only. In Section 10, I show how Kaplan's 'Dthat' can be amended to represent complex demonstratives and that the multiple-proposition view allows us to deal with utterances containing pronouns anaphorically linked to terms appearing within the nominal part of a complex demonstrative. Finally, in Section 11, I discuss and explain away some objections that the picture I propose faces.

1. A Case Study: Description-Names

There is a category of noun phrases such as 'The Holy Roman Empire', 'The Morning Star', 'The Holy Virgin', 'The Rolling Stones', etc. that has hitherto received little discussion. I call such noun phrases *description-names*: expressions that look like descriptions, but work like proper names. Description-names do not necessarily take the form of a definite description. They may also look like indefinite descriptions: 'Sitting Bull', 'Red Cloud', 'Another Horse' (McManaman and Fowler's thoroughbred), etc. In *written* English, we mark this fact using capital letters. In spoken English, however, the distinction between a description like 'the rolling stones' and the description-name 'The Rolling Stones' is usually contextually marked. In a spoken utterance of "The rolling stones from the hill killed many invaders", the context marks 'the rolling stones' as a description, whilst in a spoken utterance of "The Rolling Stones arrived last night and they'll perform tonight", it is likely to be a description-name.

Description-names should be distinguished from descript*ive* names, which are names introduced into the language *in connection* with some description. They do not usually look like descriptions. A classic example is 'Jack the Ripper', which was introduced to refer to whoever committed the relevant crimes (see Kripke 1980); the same can be said about 'Julius' *qua* name for whoever invented the zip (Evans 1982). With descriptive names, reference is fixed by stipulation; the referent is the individual who happens to satisfy the associated description. The name may turn out to be empty (as was the case with 'Vulcan', introduced by Le Verrier to refer to the alleged planet perturbing the orbit of Mercury).[1]

With description-names, however, the story is rather different, for reference is not fixed by stipulation. Instead, when a description is elected as a proper name, the description-name thus created refers without the mediation of the description, even though the referent may be believed to have some or all of the characteristics attributed to the referent by the description. It may even be the case that the description embodied in the name turns out to be a false description of the referent. Some descriptions have been elected to the role of proper names because the referents were thought to satisfy a certain description, e.g. 'The Evening Star' referring to Venus because it appears in the evening,[2] 'The Holy Virgin' referring to Mary insofar as she gave birth to Jesus whilst a virgin, or so the story goes. Other description-names, e.g. 'The Rolling Stones', 'The Sharks', 'The Yankees', 'The Red Devils', are introduced in electing a description to the role of a proper name due to variegated situations or intents: The Rolling Stones are not stones and Manchester United players are neither red nor devils. Nonetheless, in these cases the description still plays a role, for it *connotes* or purports to connote some information; for example, the descriptive content of 'The Red Devils' is a metaphor for team spirit. Because of the encapsulated description, description-names may be thought to pose a threat to Millianism, i.e. the thesis that a proper name refers *directly* to an object, regardless of the latter possessing determinate characteristics and satisfying determinate descriptions. Following this view, a proper name is like a tag; it is merely a label we use to single out an object of discourse. This particular thesis seems to face difficulties in accommodating

---

[1] In 1846, Le Verrier's calculations indicated the presence of an unknown planet in an orbit outside that of Uranus, leading to the discovery of Neptune. In 1855, Le Verrier also noticed irregularities in the movement of Mercury and predicted the existence of another unknown planet, beyond Uranus, causing the disruption; he named it 'Vulcan'.

[2] For argument's sake, let us forget for the time being that Venus is not a star.

(at least some) description-names. 'The Holy Virgin', for instance, appears to designate its particular referent because of certain properties she satisfies. An attack against Millianism, then, might proceed by citing description-names in favor of an opposing view, i.e. a view that considers proper names to refer by virtue of conditions a referent must satisfy.

In what follows, I shall defend a Millian theory of description-names. This may not sound novel, for Mill himself claimed that 'Dartmouth' would refer to Dartmouth even if the mouth of the Dart changed its location—or even if Dartmouth had never been located near the Dart's mouth. What is novel in my account is the way in which I motivate and justify Millianism regarding description-names, for I vindicate Millianism about description-names focusing on the way definite descriptions work. I distinguish three uses of definite descriptions: on top of Donnellan's now famous distinction between referential and the attributive uses, I recognize description-names. The thesis I defend is, roughly put, that a noun phrase of the form 'the F' can be interpreted either (i) as a quantified expression, (ii) as a complex demonstrative, or (iii) as a proper name.

I shall, then, defend the following naïve view: (i) names name, (ii) descriptions describe, and (iii) description-names name *and* describe, yet the utterances containing them do not necessarily express incompatible truth-conditions.

2. Definite Descriptions

Russell, unlike Frege, championed the view that definite descriptions are not singular terms. Thus, a sentence such as:

(1) a. The present king of France is bald

is not, contrary to appearances, of the subject/predicate form, Fa, but is instead an abbreviation of:

(1) b. At least one thing is King of France, at most one thing is King of France, and everything that is King of France is bald

Using first-order logic, this can be represented as either (1c) or (1d), where 'F' stands for King of France and 'G' for being bald:

(1) c. $\exists x(Fx \,\&\, \forall y(Fy \rightarrow x = y) \,\&\, Gx)$
d. $\exists x(\forall y(Fy \leftrightarrow x = y) \,\&\, Gx)$

Donnellan (1966) challenged the Russellian analysis and argued that sometimes descriptions do not work in the way Russell suggested. Donnellan invites us to consider the following scenario: Sue, on discovering Smith's body, which has been savagely mutilated, claims, "The murderer of Smith is insane". Sue has no specific individual in mind and thus her use of the description works the way Russell told us. Sue's claim is short for: "The murderer of Smith, whoever s/he is, is insane", for she uses the description *attributively*. At the trial, Sue, looking at John (who is alleged to be Smith's murderer and who behaves in a rather strange way), says: "*The* murderer of Smith is insane". Sue's claim is aimed *at John* and the description does not seem to work the way Russell suggested, for Sue's statement goes proxy for "*That* murderer of Smith is insane". If Sue had used the latter sentence, she would have said the same thing and passed to her audience the very same information. In that case, the description is used *referentially* and works like a singular term:

> [T]he description is here [in the referential use] merely a device for getting one's audience to pick out or think of the thing to be spoken about, a device which may serve its function even if the description is incorrect. More importantly, perhaps, in the referential use as opposed to the attributive, there is a right thing to be picked out by the audience, and its being the right thing is not simply a function of its fitting the description. (Donnellan 1966: 303)

Kaplan (1978), like Donnellan, takes a description used referentially to be a singular term and suggests that it works like a demonstrative. Kaplan ([1978] 1990: 23) introduces "a *new* word, 'Dthat' for the demonstrative use of 'that'" and argues that the referential use of the description can be regimented as: Dthat [the murderer of Smith]:

> It would be useful to have a way of converting an arbitrary singular term into one which is directly referential.... we early regarded demonstrations, which are required to "complete" demonstratives, as a kind of description.... why not regard descriptions as a kind of demonstration, and introduce a special demonstrative which requires completion by a description and which is treated as a direct referential term whose referent is the denotation of the associated description? Why not? Why not indeed! I have done so, and I write it thus:
>
> Dthat[α]
>
> Where α is any description, or, more generally, any singular term. 'Dthat' is simply the demonstrative 'that' with the following singular term functioning as its demonstration. (Kaplan [1977] 1989: 521–2)

Kaplan claims that 'Dthat' can be used to make any description *both* a singular term and a rigid designator, i.e. a term referring to the same individual in all possible worlds in which the latter exists.[3] Following Kaplan's suggestion, a sentence of the form "The *F* is *G*", used referentially, can be represented as:

- Dthat [the *F*] is *G*

A word of clarification may be appropriate. In his latest study, Kaplan recognizes that when he first introduced 'Dthat', he confused two distinct uses, namely

---

[3] It may be worth stressing, though, that there are some differences between Kaplan's demonstrative use of 'Dthat' and Donnellan's referential use of descriptions: "my demonstrative use is not quite Donnellan's referential use.... When a speaker uses an expression demonstratively he *usually* has in

'Dthat' as an *operator* with 'Dthat' as a *demonstrative surrogate*. In the former case, 'Dthat' is better understood as a rigidifier and, as such, the 'Dthat'-term becomes a rigid designator without being a directly referential term.[4] In the latter case, however, the 'Dthat'-term is a singular, directly referential, term. In order to capture the referential use of a definite description, 'Dthat' should be understood as a demonstrative surrogate.[5]

A further clarification is needed. While Kaplan seems to hold that the referent of a 'Dthat'-term must satisfy the descriptive content of the description, the position I favor is more liberal. In other words, Kaplan supports the view that the description encapsulated within the demonstrative surrogate 'Dthat' must be understood at the level of character and that the referent is the object satisfying the descriptive conditions of this complex character. The position I favor, on the other hand, considers the descriptive component of a demonstrative to be akin to a demonstration, i.e. merely as a tool used to single out an object of discourse, irrespective of whether the referent satisfies the descriptive condition. Thus, on Kaplan's account, the referent of a 'Dthat'-term like 'Dthat(F)' must be F. If the referent is not F, the 'Dthat'-term is empty. On my account, which is more consonant with Donnellan's views, the 'Dthat'-term can supply an object to the proposition expressed even if the latter is not F.[6] On my account, 'Dthat' works as a demonstrative, referring to a given object independently of the associated description. Thus the referent of a complete 'Dthat'-term, say 'Dthat(F)', need not, *pace* Kaplan, satisfy the predicate 'F'. Yet, as we shall soon see, the descriptive material of a 'D(that)'-term contributes to the expression of the background

---

mind—so to speak—an intended demonstratum, and the demonstration is thus *teleological*. Donnellan and I disagree on how to bring the intended demonstratum into the picture. To put it crudely, Donnellan believes that for most purposes we should take the demonstratum to be the intended demonstratum. I believe that these are different notions that may well involve different objects. . . . we have a case here in which a person can fail to say what he intended to say, and the failure is not a linguistic error (such as using the wrong word) but a factual one. . . . such a situation can arise only in the demonstrative use" (Kaplan [1978] 1990: 29–30). For a discussion of demonstratives and the way their reference gets fixed see Ch. 1, Sect. 3, above, and Ch. 4, Sect. 2, below.

[4] "Complete dthat-terms would be rigid, in fact *obstinately* rigid. In this case the proposition would not carry the individual itself into a possible world but rather would carry instructions to run back home and get the individual who there satisfies certain specifications. The complete dthat-term would then be a rigid description which induces a complex 'representation' of the referent into the content" (Kaplan 1989: 580).

[5] "The operator interpretation is not what I originally intended. The word 'dthat' was intended to be a surrogate for a true demonstrative, and the description which completes it was intended to be a surrogate for the completing demonstration. On this interpretation 'dthat' is a syntactically complete singular term that requires no *syntactical* completion by an operand. (A 'pointing', being extralinguistic, could hardly be a part of syntax.) The description completes the *character* of the associated occurrence of 'dthat', but makes no contribution to content. . . . 'Dthat' is no more an operator than is 'I', though neither has a referent unless semantically 'completed' by a context in the one case and a demonstration in the other" (Kaplan 1989: 581).

[6] I discuss this feature in more detail when discussing complex demonstratives in Sect. 9, below.

proposition. The latter is determined (at least in part) compositionally, i.e. by virtue of the meanings of the terms constituting the descriptive material.

To summarize, the referential use of a definite description goes proxy with the use of a complex demonstrative, i.e. an expression of the form 'that/this F'.

3. Description-Names

As I have already noted, written English has a convention that allows us to make a name out of a description: it suffices to use capital letters. The description 'the rolling stones' became the name of the famous rock group, The Rolling Stones; 'the gunners' became a name for the Arsenal football team, The Gunners; etc. Once a description reaches this status, it simply works like a name;[7] it is a Millian expression referring to an object irrespective of the properties that the latter has or does not have (the Rolling Stones are not stones, Arsenal players are not gunners, the question is still open whether The Holy Virgin was a virgin). As Barcan Marcus aptly stresses:

> Much has been made recently of the fact that a description, even an erroneous one, may serve on occasion to refer (purely) to an object. That may be pragmatically interesting, but such uses are more akin to the use of demonstratives. 'The women over there drinking martini' may serve on a particular occasion to tag a particular man drinking champagne, but if its use is idiosyncratic and transient, it is like a discardable tag, for it does not enter into the common language. Occasionally such ways of referring become entrenched, and a measure of such entrenchment is the conversion of a description fully to a proper name. Ordinary English has a way of marking the change by using capitals. 'The Evening Star' serves as an example. It is curious that so simple a typographical device for separating the proper-name-like use of a description from its predicative use has never been employed in formal analysis. How directly the apparent contradiction in 'The evening star is not a star' is dispelled by 'The Evening Star is not a star'. (Barcan Marcus [1975] 1993: 106–7)

There is nonetheless a feeling of uneasiness in the claim that a description-name works merely as a tag; this is due to the fact that the name encapsulates a description. However, an utterance such as:

(2) a. The Holy Virgin is not a virgin

is not contradictory, for it should be treated on a par with:

(2) b. Mary is not a virgin

---

[7] Just as with proper names, we may find homonym description-names. There are several groups called "The Rolling Stones"; most adopted or borrowed the name of the famous group, just as many places have adopted or borrowed names such as 'Paris', 'Rome', etc.

104 *A Multiple-Proposition Approach*

There is, nonetheless, certain information conveyed by (2a) which is not conveyed in (2b). It is mainly for these reasons that Dummett (1973) dismisses Kripke's criticism of the Fregean conception, arguing that 'St Anne', for instance, could not refer to St Anne if she was not the mother of Mary. This does *not* mean that 'St Anne' could not be used to refer to the relevant woman before she gave birth to Mary, nor that she became St Anne upon giving birth; yet, for 'St Anne' to refer to St Anne, the latter must have mothered Jesus' mother, i.e. Mary.

I do not believe that Dummett's remarks jeopardize Millianism about proper names. 'St Anne' could be used to name St Anne even if Mary turned out to have been adopted, or if St Anne had killed Mary's mother in order to steal her baby. The same can be said of 'The Holy Virgin': it would still refer to Mary if we discovered that she enjoyed a sexual life with Joseph, or even that she had many occasional partners. 'The Holy Virgin' refers to Mary because she is *alleged* to have given birth to Jesus whilst a virgin; whether the story is true or not does not matter for the reference to succeed. There *is* a connotative feature of description-names, which one would like to capture in one's theory without giving up Millianism.[8] In what follows, I attempt to do just that.

I now propose an argument in favor of the thesis that a description-name both names and describes at the same time. That is, I shall show that description-names are directly referential terms, contributing the referent to the truth-conditions, and yet may also convey connotative information of the referent.

Utterances such as:

(3) a. The Holy Virgin mothered Jesus
  b. The Evening Star is Jane's favorite star

can be analyzed as:

(3) c. The Holy Virgin, who was a virgin, mothered Jesus
  d. The Evening Star, which is a star appearing in the evening, is Jane's favorite star

An utterance such as (3c) expresses two distinct propositions: the proposition *that The Holy Virgin/Mary mothered Jesus* and the proposition *that The Holy Virgin/Mary was a virgin*. The theory of description-names I propose mimics a theory of subordinate clauses; I argue that the semantics of a sentence containing a description-name mirrors the semantics of a sentence containing a subordinate clause, which can either be a non-restrictive relative clause, an appositive, a parenthetical, etc. To

---

[8] To be sure, the connotative aspect of description-names like 'The Sharks' and 'The Rolling Stones', is not so striking.

illustrate this point, consider:

(4) a. Louis XIV (the king of France) is bald
b. Louis XIV, who is king of France, is bald

The position I propose is a multiple-proposition view: the utterance of a single sentence can express several propositions,[9] and the truth-conditions on such utterances are independent of their subordinate clauses. In defending this contention, we must accept the following two theses:

- *T1*
Utterances of sentences like (4a) and (4b) do not express a single, conjoint proposition, but instead express two or more distinct propositions. Utterances of (4a) and (4b) express the proposition *that Louis XIV is king of France* and the (distinct) proposition *that Louis XIV is bald*.

- *T2*
The truth-values of utterances of such sentences depend only on one of these propositions, namely the proposition expressed by the main clause.

I characterize the two propositions expressed as *the background proposition* and *the official proposition*, the former being the proposition expressed by the subordinate clause. This distinction should capture the truism that a speaker usually aims to communicate the information expressed by the official proposition. The subordinate clause is often used merely as a tool or support, enabling the speaker to convey information. If one says, for instance, "Aristotle, Jacky Kennedy's husband, is Greek", one adds the description 'Jacky Kennedy's husband' to emphasize that

---

[9] The idea that a single utterance may express/convey/impart/implicate/ . . . more than a single proposition is far from new: it plays a central role in the works of e.g. Grice (1989) and Perry (1988). Perry distinguishes between the proposition expressed and the proposition created, whereas Grice distinguishes between a proposition expressed and a proposition implicated. In more recent works, Perry (see esp. 2001) distinguishes between the incremental (in the sense of additional) truth-conditions and the reflexive truth-conditions, the former being what is said and the latter concerning the utterance itself and the conditions it must satisfy in order to be true. The novelty, if any, is that the position I defend assumes that a singular utterance may *express* several propositions. Bach (1999a) proposes a multiple-proposition view in order to deal with alleged conventional implicature devices such as 'even', 'too', 'despite', 'but', 'therefore', and non-restrictive relative clauses. According to Bach an utterance like "Shaq is huge but agile", e.g., may express, besides the information that Shaq is huge and agile, a proposition to the effect that being huge typically precludes being agile. For a defence of a multiple-proposition view, see also Neale (1999). Neale argues that the second clause in "Bill is a philosopher. He is, therefore, brave" expresses, together with the claim that Bill is brave, the proposition that Bill's being brave follows from his being a philosopher. Bach, like Neale, assumes that all propositions must be taken on a par and, therefore, he is committed to the thesis that sentences do not have a unified truth-value. As will become clear I do not share this view. As we shall see in Sect. 9, below, Dever (2001) applies the multiple-proposition picture to complex demonstratives.

one is using the name of the magnate and not the homonym name of the Greek philosopher.[10]

On the analysis I propose, (3a) is true iff the official proposition is true, i.e. if The Holy Virgin mothered Jesus, regardless of her alleged virginity. The same applies to (3b): whether The Evening Star is a star or not, (3b) is true/false regardless, i.e. independently of the truth-value of the background proposition.

As a further argument in favor of the theory of description-names I propose, I invite you to consider sentences such as:

(5) a. The Evening *Star*$_1$ is Jane's favorite *one*$_1$
 b. Pisa's *Tower*$_1$ is *one*$_1$ of the most famous in Italy
 c. Robin *Hood*$_1$ was so called because he always wore *his*$_1$
 d. Isn't strange that [*The Evening Star*$_1$]$_2$ should be so called since *it*$_2$ is not *one*$_1$?
 e. Little [*Red*$_1$ Riding *Hood*$_2$]$_3$ was so called because *she*$_3$ wore *one*$_2$ of *that color*$_1$

Following the widely accepted convention I introduced in the Introduction, each italicized pronoun in (5) is considered to be an anaphoric pronoun, linked to another italicized term, where the subscripts or indices indicate coreferentiality.[11] Without entering into the details of a theory of anaphora and discussing syntactic constraints,[12] for the sake of my argument it suffices to assume that an anaphoric pronoun *inherits* its reference from its antecedent; the antecedent fixes the semantic value of the pronoun. Note that the anaphoric pronoun does not always go proxy for its antecedent; it is not merely a pronoun of laziness.[13] Anaphoric links may transcend a single sentence, or even transcend utterances spoken by a single speaker, in which case we have an example of *discourse anaphora*.[14] I assume that an *anaphoric chain* is at work when the value of a pronoun is inherited from the value of the head of the chain.[15]

---

[10] When the relative clause is satisfied but the name is not, as is the case with "Socrates, Jackie Kennedy's husband, is a ship owner", the utterance is infelicitous and what is said false, for Socrates does not own a ship.

[11] For a well-developed theory of indices characterizing syntactic and semantic identities, see Fiengo and May (1994). For a more detailed discussion of anaphoric pronouns see Ch. 7, below.

[12] These are particularly evident in the case of so-called *bound-variable anaphora*, where a pronoun is bound by a quantifier. In such cases, the reference of the pronoun varies systematically with the choice of individual determined by the quantifier, e.g. *Every man* loves *his* wife. For a more detailed discussion of this phenomenon see e.g. Larson and Segal (1995: 361 ff.). It is less evident in the case of unbound anaphora and discourse anaphora.

[13] The terminology 'pronoun of laziness' comes from Geach (1962). He does, however, recognize that "not all relative pronouns can ... be treated as pronouns of laziness. ... In (21) [Smith broke the bank at Monte Carlo, and he has recently died a pauper] the pronoun 'he' is apparently one of laziness, but 'he' in (20) [Just one man broke the bank at Monte Carlo, and he has recently died a pauper] is not replaceable by 'just one man' or 'a man' without essentially altering the force of the proposition" (Geach 1962: 125).

[14] In short, I subsume under the label 'anaphora' bound-variable anaphora, bound anaphora, unbound anaphora, and discourse anaphora.

[15] The notion of a chain to characterize anaphoric links is borrowed from Evans (1977).

If description-names were semantically inert, i.e. mere Millian tags, then we would face difficulties accounting for sentences like (5), for how could the anaphoric pronouns inherit their reference from an antecedent if the latter plays no semantic role whatsoever? How could 'one' in (5a) inherit its reference from 'Star' if the latter does not play a semantic role in the name it appears in? The picture of description-names I propose helps us handle this phenomenon with ease, for it allows that 'Star' plays a semantic role insofar as it contributes to the expression of a background proposition.[16]

The same phenomenon, i.e. an anaphoric pronoun bound by an element appearing within the noun phrase, occurs in cases involving complex demonstratives, i.e. expressions of the form 'this/that F'. So, as far as anaphora are concerned, complex demonstratives and description-names present a similar problem. Consider:

(6) a. That woman talking to *Joe*$_1$ is charming *him*$_1$
  b. [*That man drinking* [*white*$_1$ *burgundy*]$_2$]$_3$ is savoring *it*$_2$. *He*$_3$ always drinks wine of *that color*$_1$

Since sentences (6) and (5) are similar (similar anaphoric chains are at work in both), they suggest that complex demonstratives and description-names should be treated, as far as anaphora are concerned, on a par. The picture I propose allows us to do just that, and for this reason I now turn to compare description-names and complex demonstratives in using the functors 'Dname' and 'Dthat'.

4. Dname and Dthat

The theory I propose concerning description-names extends to complex demonstratives. If we adopt Dthat *qua* demonstrative surrogate, as introduced by Kaplan, we can represent a sentence containing a complex demonstrative, i.e. a sentence of the form "That F is G" as:

- Dthat [the F] is G

It should not come as a surprise that the representation we end up with is the same as the one proposed for the referential use of definite descriptions.

It is worth noticing, however, that there is a difference between complex demonstratives and description-names; whilst the former refer in virtue of the demonstrative, proper names do not. This reflects the fact that proper names and

---

[16] It may be worth noticing that, if the argument from anaphora does prove that description-names are not merely semantically inert Millian tags, it does not rule out the Russellian theory that proper names and, *a fortiori* description-names, are disguised definite descriptions.

demonstratives are different tools of reference, the latter referring in virtue of a demonstration or directing intention (Kaplan 1989) to an object made salient in a given context of utterance, the former referring because of a pre-established convention.[17] Proper names *qua* tags stand for their referent in virtue of a convention linking the name to its referent. Description-names, *qua* (proper) names, also refer in virtue of an established convention but, on top of directly referring to their referent, they also convey certain information, i.e. whatever is communicated by the background proposition. To stress the difference between description-names and complex demonstratives, I propose a modification of Kaplan's Dthat device in introducing a new one, Dname, the former being a demonstrative surrogate, the latter a surrogate for proper names. As such, Dname can be used in our formal system to make a description a description-name: roughly, to make a proper name out of a description. Dname should capture the written English convention of using initial capital letters when a proper name is in play. Putting it slightly differently, when a description is used referentially, Dthat *qua* demonstrative surrogate stresses that the description within its scope works like a singular term; in particular, like a complex demonstrative. Dname *qua* proper name surrogate also stresses that the description within its scope works like a singular term; in particular, like a proper name and, more precisely, like a description-name.

There is a further difference worth mentioning: when one uses a complex demonstrative, one *intends* the descriptive material to apply to the referent, even though the success of the reference does not depend on the success of this intention. With most description-names, however, there is no such intention. In a nutshell, when a description is prefixed by Dthat, the latter is transformed into a complex demonstrative and when a description is prefixed by Dname, the latter is transformed into a description-name. Hence when a description is used as a proper name, a sentence like "The F is G" can be represented as:

- Dname [The F] is G

where 'Dname' can be viewed as a functor, which forms directly referential terms (Millian terms) denoting individuals.

Adopting the suggestions I propose, we are in a position to stress, in formal language, the various uses of a definite description: (i) the attributive use, i.e. the use as a quantified term, (ii) the referential use—Dthat is our tool—and (iii) the use as a proper name, where Dname is our tool. We can thus accommodate Barcan Marcus's suggestion that, in formal analysis, we should separate the proper-name-like use of a description from its predicative use. As an illustration of how the distinction can be used in formal analysis, I invite you to consider an

---

[17] I discussed the difference between proper names and indexicals in Ch. 1, above, esp. Sect. 4.

inference of the form:

> The F is G
> The F is H
> So: the F is G & H

This inference can have as many interpretations as the various interpretations we can give of each description. Let us consider the following possible instantiation of this inference:

> (7) The murderer of Smith is insane
> The murderer of Smith is a woman
> So: The murderer of Smith is insane and a woman

This inference is valid insofar as it is represented—where 'F' stands for 'the murderer of Smith', 'G' for 'insane', and 'H' for 'woman'—as:

> (7) a. $\exists x(Fx \& \forall y(Fy \to x = y) \& Gx)$
> $\exists x(Fx \& \forall y(Fy \to x = y) \& Hx)$
> So: $\exists x(Fx \& \forall y(Fy \to x = y) \& Gx \& Hx)$

On the other hand, an inference such as:

> (8) Dthat (The murderer of Smith) is insane
> The murderer of Smith is a woman
> So: The murderer of Smith is insane and a woman

is invalid, for we formalize (8) as:

> (8) a. Ga
> $\exists x(Fx \& \forall y(Fy \to x = y) \& Hx)$
> So: $\exists x(Fx \& \forall y(Fy \to x = y) \& Gx \& Hx)$

For inference (8) to become valid, it should be rephrased as:

> (9) Dthat (The murderer of Smith) is insane [Ga]
> The murderer of Smith is a woman [$\exists x(Fx \& \forall y(Fy \to x = y) \& Hx)$]
> Dthat (The murderer of Smith) = The murder of Smith
> So: Dthat (The murderer of Smith) is insane and a woman [Ga & Ha]

In that case the added premiss "Dthat(The murderer of Smith) = The murder of Smith" captures the content the 'Dthat'-term contributes in the expression of the background proposition.[18] If all the descriptions receive the referential

---

[18] See Sect. 9, below, for a more accurate account on the way the multiple-proposition view deals with inferences.

interpretation, our inference is also valid:

(10) Dthat (The murderer of Smith) is insane [Ga]
Dthat (The murderer of Smith) is a woman [Ha]

So: Dthat (The murderer of Smith) is insane and a woman [Ga & Ha]

The very same exercise, which I leave for the reader, can be done in replacing Dthat with Dname. In our formal system, Dthat and Dname are functors working exactly in the same way, insofar as they form a singular term out of a description.

I now turn to discuss and show how the apparatus proposed for description-names nicely expands to the third-person pronoun 's/he' and complex demonstratives, i.e. NP of the form 'that/this *F*'.

5. Pronouns and Complex Demonstratives

Suppose that, during a fashion show and in awe of the models on the catwalk, Jon utters:

(11) That woman is gorgeous
(12) That man is gorgeous
(13) She is gorgeous
(14) He is gorgeous

Unbeknownst to Jon, however, the model to whom Jon's attention is directed with each utterance is, in each case, the very same individual, Aphrodite, for Aphrodite is a true hermaphrodite.[19] Aphrodite is indeed gorgeous, but does Jon say something true, something false, or neither with each utterance?

My intuitive view of the situation described above is that, with each utterance, Jon says something true. If this is the case, utterances (11)–(14) must succeed in referring to Aphrodite and also in attributing to him/her the property of being gorgeous. I take this to be the datum that a theory of complex demonstratives like 'that *F*' and of pronouns like 's/he' should try to capture. The desideratum can thus be rephrased as follows: our theory of complex demonstratives (and *a fortiori* of personal pronouns) should not exclude hermaphrodites as possible referents. It should be hermaphrodite-friendly.

Before showing how the multiple-proposition theory I proposed satisfies our desideratum, I first describe three prominent theories on the market. I show how

---

[19] According to the scientific tradition, *"hermaphroditism"* is the technical term denoting the presence of both testicular and ovarian tissue. Within the human species, one is a *true hermaphrodite* when one has a DNA chromosome karyotype of 46 XX/XY (mosaic) independently of one's external appearance. Hermaphrodites have two separate chromosome karyotypes, similar to siamese twins sharing one body. This can happen when two fecundated gametes merge.

these theories commit themselves to the thesis that utterances like (11)–(14) always say something false in the hermaphrodite case for, according to these views, hermaphrodites cannot be a referent of the third-person pronouns 'he' or 'she' or of the complex demonstrative 'that woman/man'. These theories are thus hermaphrodite-*un*friendly.

I then develop the theory of complex demonstratives resting on the multiple-proposition view. This theory can be labeled *the naive theory*. For it fits our datum and captures our intuition. The naïve theory is hermaphrodite-friendly insofar as it predicts that in the scenario described, (11)–(14) say something true.

Before going further, however, it is worth mentioning that the personal pronouns 'he' and 'she' have a built-in or hidden sortal. 'She', unlike 'he', refers to a *female*. My *New Shorter Oxford Dictionary*, under the entry 's/he', states: "The, or any, female/male person *who* (or *that*); the female/male person *of*, *with*". Following this suggestion, we can assume that when the third-person singular pronouns are used as demonstratives, they can be treated along the same lines as 'that female/male' or 'that woman/man'.[20] (11) can thus be viewed as synonymous with (13) while (12) as synonymous with (14).

One could challenge my claim and argue that hermaphrodites are *both* male and female and that (11)–(14) are true because Aphrodite satisfies both the predicate of being a male and of being a female. A hermaphrodite is, after all, an organism with both testicular and ovarian tissue. Since Aphrodite's DNA contains both XX and XY chromosome pairs, s/he may qualify as being both male and female. Be that as it may, it does not seem to account for our practice of using the gender distinction when dealing with biological organisms. In our everyday linguistic practice we clearly distinguish between males, females, and hermaphrodites. A biological organism is classed as either male or female or as a hermaphrodite. We would not say, for instance, that a snail is both male and female. We say that it is neither, for it is a hermaphrodite. My objector could argue that we may wish to distinguish between linguistic gender and biological gender. After all, in many languages (such as Italian, Spanish, French, and German, to name but a few) inanimate objects are assigned a gender for linguistic purposes, yet have no biological gender. Aphrodite (and hermaphrodites in general) could thus be said to have both the male and female linguistic gender even if, from a biological viewpoint, a hermaphrodite is neither male nor female.[21] The divide between biological and

---

[20] For the sake of the argument, I do not distinguish between 'that female/male' and 'that woman/man'. We often use the demonstrative 's/he' to refer to pets, however; for this reason, I shall henceforth assimilate 's/he' with 'that male/female', even if it may be more appropriate to assimilate it with 'that woman/man' or 'that female/male person'.

[21] This line of thought could be maintained by noting the fact that in some languages (e.g. German), some things that have biological gender can be referred to with genderless noun phrases (e.g. 'das Kind').

linguistic gender raises the possibility that the pronoun 's/he' and the complex demonstrative 'that female/male' do differ in meaning. From a logical point of view, it is possible that 's/he' can only refer to an object if it possesses the appropriate *linguistic* gender, regardless of its biological gender, while 'that female/male' can only refer to an organism of the appropriate *biological* gender. If this were so, 's/he' and 'that female/male' would differ in meaning and (11) and (12) would be false whilst (13) and (14) would be true. However, my intuitive view is that it sounds implausible, for it does not capture our everyday use of the third-person pronoun. I find it difficult to accept the idea that 's/he' can refer to hermaphrodites whilst 'that female/male' cannot, for it simply does not reflect our linguistic practice. Henceforth, I shall assume that the theory to be defended *should* treat 's/he' and 'that female/male' on a par and I take it to be *non*-negotiable that 's/he' is analogous with 'that female/male (person)'. If, however, you do not agree, then I invite you to assume it for the sake of argument. If you do not like the example I am proposing, you can easily replace it. The aim of this example is merely to put forward a scenario enabling me to stress the virtues of the multiple-proposition theory and how it can accommodate the way complex demonstratives work.

6. Complex Demonstratives *qua* Definite Descriptions

The first theory of complex demonstratives that I would like to consider can be labeled the descriptive theory. According to this theory, 'that' in 'that *F*' can be considered as a determiner, along with 'most', 'some', 'all', 'the', 'no', etc.[22] As far as I know, Lepore and Ludwig (2000) propose one of the most detailed and appealing theories of complex demonstratives *qua* descriptions (for a recent and detailed quantificational account of complex demonstratives see King (2001) as well).[23] Lepore and Ludwig (2000) argue that 'that *F*' should be analyzed as:

(15) the *x*: *x* is that & *x* is *F*

where the description must be understood according to the Russellian theory. An expression such as 'that *F*', therefore, is a quantified term, not a singular term. A sentence like "that *F* is *G*" will be analyzed as:

(16) (the *x*: *x* is that & *x* is *F*) is *G*

[22] Barwise and Cooper (1981), Neale (1993; 1999), King (1999; 2001), and Lepore and Ludwig (2000), among others, defend, modulo some differences, this theory.

[23] I further discuss and criticize King's theory and some problem it allegedly poses to the theory I defend in Sect. 10, below. I discussed King's theory in some detail and defended the view that complex demonstratives are singular terms in Corazza (2003).

If, on the suggestion of my dictionary, I am right in assuming that 's/he' should be analyzed similarly to 'that female/male', then the descriptive theory is committed to the thesis that a sentence like "S/he is *G*" must also be analyzed as:

(17) (the *x*: *x* is that & *x* is *female/male*) is *G*

It should be stressed, however, that while Lepore & Ludwig treat complex demonstratives as disguised definite descriptions, they do not treat simple demonstratives ('this', 'that', etc.) and pronouns ('s/he', 'we', etc.) as disguised descriptions. While the former are semantically complex, the latter are semantically simple; the latter, unlike the former, are singular terms, or so they claim. Hence, Lepore & Ludwig must reject the analogy I propose between 's/he' and 'that female/male'. King (2001), on the other hand, suggests that simple demonstratives and complex demonstratives should be treated on a par: they are *all* quantified expressions. Insofar as King's conception does not distinguish between simple and complex demonstratives, I believe that it is more appealing. It is the more economical option, i.e. it obeys the principle: do not introduce distinctions beyond necessity. In addition, King's theory does not implicitly reject the analogy between 's/he' and 'that female/male' and therefore captures our linguistic practices more accurately.

For the sake of argument, let us imagine a theory similar to Lepore & Ludwig's that treats simple demonstratives and pronouns on a par, i.e. one that accepts the analogy between 's/he' and 'that female/male'. This theory accepts (17) as an accurate representation of "S/he is *G*". On this analysis, utterances such as (11)–(14) turn out to be false, for Aphrodite is neither male nor female. The descriptive theory of complex demonstratives and pronouns is thus hermaphrodite-*un*friendly.[24]

7. The Character Approach to Complex Demonstratives

The second theory of complex demonstratives I would like to consider was proposed in Braun (1994) and Borg (2000). According to this position, a complex demonstrative is a singular term. If the alleged referent does not satisfy the nominal part of a complex demonstrative, however, the latter is an empty term. In order for an utterance of "That *F* is *G*" to be true, the referent must be *F*. If the nominal '*F*' does not apply to the alleged referent, the utterance would be either truth-valueless or false (depending on the theory of empty terms one adopts).[25]

This position elaborates Kaplan's (1977) traditional framework for the logic of indexicals and demonstratives. It focuses on Kaplan's content/character distinction

---

[24] I further discuss and dismiss the thesis that complex demonstratives are quantified expressions in Ch. 4, Sect. 6, below. I will then be in a position to explain away some arguments put forward by King (2001).

[25] "There is an obvious condition for a complex demonstrative's reference in a context. It is this: in every context *c*, *that N* refers in *c* to *x* only if *x* satisfies *N* in *c*" (Braun 1994: 208).

in placing the nominal 'F' at the level of character, which we can understand as a rule enabling us to single out a referent. Such a rule can be captured in descriptive terms, i.e. as a description that gives us constraints that a referent must satisfy. The character of 'I', for instance, can be represented as a rule stating that a use of 'I' refers to the agent of the context. For a given context c, the semantic value of 'I' in c is an individual i iff i is the agent in c. In the same vein, it is argued that the nominal 'F' plays a role in determining the character of 'that F'.

Since this theory appeals to structured characters, it allows for rather fine-grained distinctions in character between different expressions. Braun and Borg could thus argue that the character of 'that female/male' is more structured than the character of 's/he' and, therefore, that they differ in meaning. If this is the case, the character approach to complex demonstratives rejects the analogy I propose between 's/he' and 'that female/male' and the considerations against Lepore & Ludwig's theory apply here as well. A theory that does not implicitly reject the analogy between 's/he' and 'that female/male' should be preferred insofar as it captures our linguistic practices more accurately. For this reason, I assume that the character approach *does* treat 's/he' and 'that female/male' on a par. It is built into the meaning of the third-person pronoun 's/he' that it refers to a male/female and therefore 'That F' is represented at the level of character by a rule of the following kind:

- R1
  an individual i is the semantic value of 'that F' with respect to a context c iff i is the demonstrated item in c and i satisfies the content of F in c.[26]

Following this suggestion, the pronoun 's/he' can be analyzed using the following rule:

- R2
  an individual i is the semantic value of 's/he' with respect to a context c iff i is the demonstrated item in c and i is a female/male in c.[27]

Following these rules, (11)–(14) are all false. Hence, this theory is hermaphrodite-*un*friendly as well.

8. Complex Demonstratives *qua* Articulated Terms

The third theory of complex demonstratives I would like to discuss also assumes that complex demonstratives are singular terms. They are, however, articulated

---

[26] Cf. Braun (1994: 209).
[27] The last proviso 'in c' may sound superfluous. It helps avoiding cases of changes in sex. For i, the demonstrated item in c, may be of a different gender in a context c^* previous or posterior to c.

terms (see Richard 1993a). Unlike the theory discussed in the previous section, this theory does not commit itself to the thesis that 'that *F*' is an empty term whenever the nominal '*F*' does not apply to the alleged referent. Although 'that *F*' may succeed in fixing a reference, the referent must be *F* for "That *F* is *G*" to be true. If the referent is not *F*, "That *F* is *G*" is false. Following this suggestion, a sentence like "That *F* is *G*" is analyzed as:

(18) That$_1$ is *F* and it$_1$ is *G*

The nominal '*F*' and the predicate '*G*' are thus treated at the same level. In terms of propositions, a sentence like (11) expresses the single, conjoint proposition *that Aphrodite is a woman and Aphrodite is gorgeous*.

Like the previous theories I have discussed, this theory maintains that 's/he' and 'that female/male' cannot be treated on a par, for the latter (unlike the former) is an articulated term. Thus the proposition expressed in uttering 'that female/male' (a semantically complex term) could never be the same as the one expressed in uttering 's/he' (a semantically simple term). The former is an articulated proposition, having among its constituents the property of being female/male, while the latter is a singular proposition without this property as a constituent. Again, if the articulated terms strategy rejects the analogy between 's/he' and 'that female/male', it does not capture our linguistic practice. For this reason, I assume that the articulated terms position treats 's/he' and 'that female/male' on a par, i.e. it assumes that the pronoun 's/he' is, contrary to appearances, articulated. It is, after all, built into the meaning of the third-person pronoun that it is gender-sensitive; why should not the articulated terms strategy capture this? Following this suggestion, a sentence like "s/he is *G*" is analyzed as:

(19) That$_1$ is a female/male and it$_1$ is *G*

According to this proposal, a sentence like (13) expresses the false proposition *that Aphrodite is male and Aphrodite is gorgeous*. Since this theory holds that (11)–(14) are false in our scenario it is, like the two theories previously discussed, hermaphrodite-*un*friendly.

9. A Naïve, Politically Correct, Theory of Pronouns

I now argue that the multiple-proposition theory I proposed when discussing description-names nicely generalizes to the case of personal pronouns and complex demonstratives. It is a hermaphrodite-friendly theory. Since the multiple-proposition theory fits our intuitions and captures our datum, I call this theory the *naive theory*.

116   *A Multiple-Proposition Approach*

I defend the view that a theory of complex demonstratives mimics a theory of subordinate clauses; in other words, the semantics of a sentence containing a complex demonstrative mirrors the semantics of a sentence containing a subordinate clause. As we saw, the latter may be a non-restrictive relative clause, an appositive, a parenthetical, or the like. Consider:

(20)   Campbell, the famous supermodel, is gorgeous
(21)   Tim (the man with the hat) is handsome

The theory I have in mind assumes that utterances like (20) and (21) express two distinct propositions. (20) expresses the proposition *that Campbell is a famous supermodel* and the distinct proposition *that Campbell is gorgeous*, while (21) expresses the propositions *that Tim is the man with the hat* and *that Tim is handsome*.[28] I characterized these two propositions as the background proposition and the official proposition respectively. As we saw, this distinction captures the truism that a speaker of utterances like (20) and (21) primarily aims to transmit the information expressed by the official proposition while the subordinate clause is often used merely as a tool to enable the speaker to convey this information. If one says, "Campbell, the famous central defender, is gorgeous", for example, one adds the description 'the famous central defender' to emphasize that one is talking about the Arsenal footballer, Sol Campbell, and not using the homonymous name of the supermodel. This is analogous to saying, "Mary has been to the bank, the financial institution", where the description 'the financial institution' is added merely to disambiguate the noun.

The position I have in mind bears some resemblance to Dever (2001). Dever argues that constructions with appositives, i.e. noun-headed constructions concatenated onto other terms, are the correct models with which to understand complex demonstratives (notice, however, that Dever talks about sentences while I have been talking about utterances. Dever's sentences should be understood as sentences-in-a-context, for a sentence containing a demonstrative is context-sensitive). A sentence with an appositive is, in fact, two sentences expressing two propositions:

The next question, of course, is *why* sentences with appositives express two propositions. The suggestion is that it is because such 'sentences' are in fact *two* sentences. (Dever 2001: 295–6)

When it comes to representing the structure of sentences containing appositives (or complex demonstratives, for that matter), Dever claims (correctly, I believe)

---

[28]   The position I advocate differs from Neale's (1999) in two main aspects. First, I do not assume that the utterance of a sentence containing a complex demonstrative, say "That F is G", expresses a singular and a descriptive proposition. According to the position I have in mind, "That F is G" expresses two singular propositions. Secondly, as we will see, I do not assume that the propositions must be both true or both false for us to feel confident in judging that the utterance expressing them is true or false.

that the syntactic trees can be multi-rooted, i.e. the sentences have a grammar that gives rise to trees where the same noun phrase is shared by both sentences:

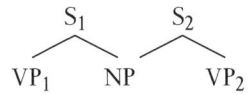

```
      S₁         S₂
     /  \       /  \
   VP₁   NP   VP₂
```

The same noun phrase (NP) (subject) supplies different verb phrases (VP) as components of each sentence. To illustrate this, let us consider the representation of (20):

(20) a.

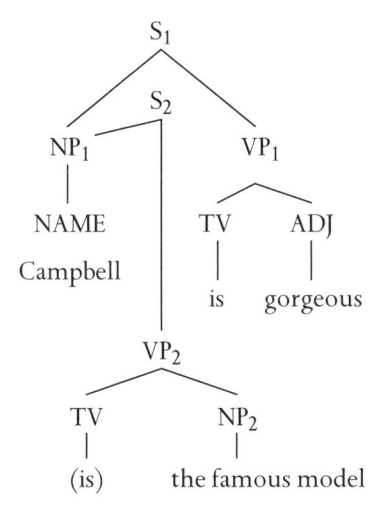

```
              S₁
             /  \
            S₂
           /  \
        NP₁    VP₁
         |     /  \
        NAME  TV   ADJ
         |    |     |
      Campbell is  gorgeous
             VP₂
            /  \
           TV   NP₂
           |     |
          (is)  the famous model
```

where S₁ and S₂ share the same NP, 'Campbell'. This representation stresses the fact that (20) contains two top-level S nodes. One dominates "Campbell is gorgeous" while the other dominates "Campbell is the famous supermodel".[29] An utterance of the former expresses the official proposition while an utterance of the latter expresses the background proposition. To be precise, (20) is a single utterance, but a single utterance can be a token of two distinct sentences, i.e. an utterance can incorporate different sentences. In our example, the subject 'Campbell' performs

[29] For a more detailed discussion of the syntax of appositives and complex demonstratives (and some consequences of the multi-rooted syntax adopted), see Dever (2001). As far as complex demonstratives are concerned, an interesting consequence is that: "The multi-rooted syntax, in essence, solves the difficulties of complex demonstratives by denying that there is any such thing as a complex demonstrative. There is, on this syntactic analysis, no one syntactic unit of the form 'that F'. The simple demonstrative 'that' is a component, but its association with 'F' is a deceptive result of the linearization of an independent sentential tree" (Dever 2001: 316).

a dual role insofar as it contributes *Campbell* to both the official and the background propositions. Thus, an utterance like (20) embodies two sentences. It is for this reason that an utterance can express two distinct propositions and, as we shall now see, be true even if one of these propositions is false.

It is worth mentioning, however, that the theory I propose differs from Dever in one major aspect. While Dever follows Bach and Neale in claiming that both propositions expressed must be true in order for an utterance containing an appositive (or a complex demonstrative) to be judged to be true without hesitation, I argue that the background proposition does not affect the truth-value of the utterance. Unlike Dever, Bach, and Neale, I maintain that an utterance's truth-value is inherited from the official proposition only:

[I]t ["Aristotle, man of the people, was found of dogs"] expresses propositions corresponding to these two sentences ["Aristotle was fond of dogs", and "Aristotle is a man of the people"], and when the two propositions diverge in truth-value, we are left with conflicting intuitions on the truth-value of the whole sentence (as we strive, driven by a mistaken theoretical assumption that there is a one–one correlation between sentences and propositions, to resolve our intuition into a single truth-value). (Dever 2001: 298)

As Neale puts it:

[A] better picture of what is going on will emerge if we say that both a descriptive proposition *and* a singular proposition are expressed. Only when both are true or both false do we feel pulled to judge the utterance to be true or false. (Neale 1999: 66)

Bach shares this view:

In general, intuitions about the truth or falsity of utterances containing ACIDs [alleged conventional implicature devices] tend to ignore the secondary proposition being expressed. This is clearly what happens with utterances containing nonrestrictive relative clauses or appositives (or parentheticals), where the truth-value of the material set off between the commas (or parentheses) tends to be downplayed.... this is possible because such utterances do not express one composite proposition but two separately evaluable ones, one of which is peripheral to the main point of the utterance. When the secondary proposition is false but the primary one is true, intuitions about the truth or falsity of the whole utterance are forced. If we are forced to choose between true and false and we say "true", we do so reluctantly, because we recognize that something isn't right. (Bach 1999*a*: 346–7)

Dever and Neale do not say whether an utterance like (20) can be true when that background proposition is false, although they do seem to indicate that it cannot be *judged* to be true. Bach, however, is more explicit. He maintains that when an utterance expresses more than one proposition (without expressing the conjunction of these propositions), the utterance need not be either true or false:

(27) [Ann's computer, *which she bought in 1992*, crashes frequently] expresses these two propositions, but it does not express their conjunction.... And when the sentence does so without expressing the conjunction of these propositions, and these propositions differ in truth-value, the sentence as a whole is not assessable as simply true or simply false. (Bach 1999*a*: 351)

Bach goes on to argue that:

Although it is arbitrary to assume one sentence, one proposition, the suggestion that a sentence can express more than one proposition might still seem problematic. In fact, it is problematic within the framework of a truth-conditional semantics, because a sentence that expresses more than one proposition, as opposed to a conjunct of propositions, does not have a unitary truth condition. A semantic framework in which meanings of sentences are given not in terms of truth conditions but in terms of things that have truth conditions, namely propositions, is better suited for handling this problem. Then we can speak of the truth or falsity of the different propositions that are expressed by the utterance of one such sentence without having to judge the utterance as a whole as true or false. This would eliminate any temptation to speak of ACIDs as having "non-truth conditional meaning". (Bach 1999*a*: 354–5)

I am sympathetic to Bach's suggestion that the best semantic framework for giving the meaning of an utterance (or a sentence-in-a-context) is the one which focuses on propositions (the content of the utterance) rather than the utterance's truth conditions. Yet, I maintain that the non-unitary truth-condition position (advocated by Dever, Bach, and Neale) does not appear to account for the intuition that a speaker's aim in using an utterance containing a parenthetical, an appositive, or a complex demonstrative is to communicate the official proposition.[30] The background proposition is often used merely as a support, enabling the audience to identify the object of discourse.[31]

One could object that we cannot, from this communicative intuition alone, infer the *semantic* fact that the background and official propositions are not to be treated on

---

[30] Dever, like Bach, distinguishes between the primary proposition and the other proposition(s) expressed by an utterance containing a complex demonstrative or an appositive. But he does not assume that the truth-value of the utterance is inherited by the primary (the official) proposition.

[31] In some cases the subordinate clause can assume a rather important role and extend beyond being a mere support for the expression of the official proposition. In that case, the speaker focuses on the background proposition, for this may be what our speaker aims to convey. Consider e.g. an utterance such as: "Campbell, one of the greatest central defenders of this decade now playing for Arsenal, is British". The background proposition *that Campbell is one of the greatest central defenders of this decade now playing for Arsenal* seems more important than the official proposition *that Campbell is British*. Even in that case (which, one should concede, is far from representing a paradigmatic case), I maintain that our utterance is true insofar as it inherits the truth of the official proposition. It goes without saying that the communicative interchange may focus on (and the topic of discourse may well switch to) the content of the background proposition.

a par. I do not have a knockdown argument against such an objection, just as I do not have a knockdown argument against the non-unitary truth-condition view. In fact, I doubt that knockdown arguments exist in this area. The main question, however, depends on what one expects from semantics and, more precisely, on how one draws the distinction between semantics and pragmatics. I suspect that the objection that the communicative intuitions I am appealing to do not affect or should not be taken into consideration when assessing an utterance's semantic content, rests on a firm distinction between semantic facts and pragmatic facts. As I already stressed in the Introduction, I am skeptical, however, about the possibility of a clear-cut distinction between pragmatics and semantics. Such a distinction would be easier to make within a framework akin to the ones advocated by Frege and Russell, for example. Within this framework, which we may term the *ideal language* school, a theoretician's inquiry should concentrate on the study of an ideal (formal) language, i.e. a language deprived of the imperfections of natural languages. In this study, semantics is confined to truth-conditions, while pragmatics is confined to studying the ways in which speakers use language to attain certain goals and to communicate certain information. Within this framework, the study of communication would mainly be the job of pragmatics. However, the phenomenon of indexicality (and context-sensitivity in general) cannot easily be explained using this semantics/pragmatics divide. Just how much and how far can context affect an utterance's truth-conditions? As far as I know, a firm, clear, and uncontroversial answer has yet to be proposed.[32] On the other hand, if one is more willing to follow the ordinary language school inaugurated by Wittgenstein, one is more likely to take features concerning the way linguistic expressions are *used* into consideration. Within this camp, semantics can be understood as the study of the rules for the correct use of language and the meaning of an expression type is determined by the ways in which it can be correctly used. Semantics, so understood, takes into account the speaker's competencies or, at least, an ideal speaker's linguistic competences. I am not sure that a clear-cut distinction between semantics and pragmatics can be made at all within this framework. I tend to believe that semantics is pragmatically informed and *vice versa*; to paraphrase a famous Kantian dictum, I would say that semantics without pragmatics is empty while pragmatics without semantics is blind. To put it more crudely, I suspect that the semantic/pragmatic divide is neither a welcome nor a healthy distinction. At least, it is unhelpful when one focuses on the study of *natural* or *ordinary* language. For these reasons I believe that the notions of rules and conventions are more promising—or at least more primitive—when trying to analyze the meanings of linguistic expressions.[33]

---

[32] But see Bach (1999*b*) for a different view.
[33] If one accepts these concerns regarding the study of natural language, one should not be surprised by the fact that I appeal to speakers' commitments and aims when trying to spell out an expression's meaning

Against this very idea, viz. the view that the background proposition does not affect the truth-value of the utterance expressing it, one may appeal to inferences of the following sort:

(21) a. Jane (my best student) graduated with a distinction
     b. Therefore Jane is my best student

(22) a. Sue, Paul's wife, is Jon's mistress
     b. Therefore someone is Paul's wife

If these arguments are valid, it is simply not possible for the premisses (21a) and (22a) to be true and the conclusions false. The view I am proposing, however, clearly entails that these inferences are invalid. Since I claim that the truth-conditions on (21a) and (22a) are inherited from the truth-conditions on the official propositions (regardless of the truth-conditions on the background propositions), it would be possible for (21a) and (22a) to be true and yet (21b) and (22b) to be false, for the truth-conditions on the latter depend upon the truth-conditions on the background propositions only.

As I have already said, I do not have a knockdown argument against the view that, for semantics reasons, both background and official propositions must be treated on a par. Having said that, I do not feel comfortable with the idea that arguments (21) and (22), as they stand, are valid. The supposed validity of an argument like (21) mirrors the alleged validity of an argument like:

(23) a. All men are mortal
     b. Therefore Socrates is mortal

In everyday conversation, we encounter utterances like, "If all individuals dislike war, then Mary dislikes war". This conditional is understood insofar as one assumes that Mary is an individual (and not, say, a pet), yet nothing in the utterance itself states that Mary actually is an individual. This information is *implicitly* conveyed, but this does not make that information semantically irrelevant.[34] One need not cognitively process the information, let alone infer it: one simply and automatically takes it for granted. Along this line, (23) must be read as:

(24) a. All men are mortal
     b. *Socrates is a man*
     c. Therefore Socrates is mortal

and semantic potential, i.e. the way it contributes to the expression of a proposition or propositions, and thus in determining the truth-value of the utterance in which it occurs. Along this line, one would also be more likely to appreciate the idea that the background proposition does not affect the truth-value of the utterance and that an utterance's truth-value is inherited from the official proposition alone.

[34] Think e.g. of semantically underdetermined sentences like "It's raining", "It's 3 p.m.", where the relevant location and time zone affect the determination of the truth-condition on the utterance (see Perry 1986). I discussed the phenomenon of tacit reference in Ch. 2, above.

122 A Multiple-Proposition Approach

The same story can be told about arguments (21) and (22). Their alleged validity is suggested by a tacit premiss. For (21) and (22) to be valid, they should read as:

(25) a. Jane graduated with a distinction
b. *Jane is my best student*
c. Therefore Jane is my best student

(26) a. Sue is Jon's mistress
b. *Sue is Paul's wife*
c. Therefore someone is Paul's wife

where the premiss "Jane is my best student" in (25) and the premiss "Sue is Paul's wife" in (26) express the background proposition. One could still object that, in stating the arguments (25a–c) and (26a–c) I should not drop the parenthetical and the relative clause. Thus the arguments should be rephrased as:

(25) d. Jane *(my best student)* graduated with a distinction
e. Jane is my best student
f. Therefore, Jane is my best student

(26) d. Sue, *Paul's wife*, is Jon's mistress
e. Sue is Paul's wife
f. Therefore, someone is Paul's wife

In that case, the premiss (25e) in the argument (25d–f), like the premiss (26e) in the argument (26d–f), sounds redundant and suggests that arguments (25) and (26) are right as they stand, *pace* my claim. I disagree. If I am right in claiming that the truth-value of an utterance with a parenthetical or a non-restrictive relative clause is inherited from the truth-value of the official proposition, regardless of the truth-value of the background proposition, then the sentence expressing the background proposition must come into the formulation of arguments like (25) and (26) and thus the premisses (25e) and (26e) are not superfluous. In other words, if one agrees with the view that an utterance of a sentence with a parenthetical, a non-restrictive relative clause, an appositive, or a complex demonstrative is a token of two sentences (a single utterance can incorporate two or more sentences), then one is forced to accept the way I rephrase the arguments and one must accept that (25a–c) and (26a–c) are the best representations insofar as the two different sentences are *separated* as distinct premisses.

As further support of the thesis that an utterance containing a parenthetical has the same truth-conditions as an utterance just like it but stripped of the parenthetical, we can focus on utterances such as "Snow is white" and "Snow is white, I claim", or "Since it is Jon's birthday he will host a party" and "Since it is

Jon's birthday he will host a party, I suppose". If either pair of utterances is produced in the same context (agent, time, place, and possible world), each utterance would have the same truth-conditions, i.e. that snow is white or that, since it is Jon's birthday, he will host a party. The parenthetical 'I claim', like the parenthetical 'I suppose', does not affect the truth-value of the whole utterance. 'I' and 'claim', however, do not lack a semantic value; their semantic value simply does not affect the truth-value of the utterance. Furthermore, the *force* with which an appositive or a parenthetical is put forward may well differ from the force of the main clause. One can ask, for instance: "Is Jane, the best doctor in town, already married?" The main clause is interrogative, while the subordinate clause is assertoric. Such data should further stress the fact that the subordinate clause cannot and should not be treated on a par with the main clause and, thus, that the official proposition and the background proposition cannot be treated on a par.[35]

Moreover, the fact that the speaker's main goal is to convey the official proposition in an utterance containing a parenthetical, an appositive, or a complex demonstrative can also be stressed in focusing on the natural way one would report such utterances. I shall call this the *reporting test*. The test should capture our intuitive notion of what is said, i.e. what a speaker primarily commits herself to in uttering a given sentence. In reporting what one says with (27) and (28):

(27) Campbell, the famous supermodel, is gorgeous
(28) Tim (the man with the hat) is handsome

one need not mention the background proposition. If (27) and (28) are uttered by Jon, one could correctly report:

(29) Jon said that Campbell is gorgeous
(30) Jon said that Tim is handsome

These are perfectly appropriate reports. These reports relate the attributee, Jon, to the official proposition and are true iff Jon expressed the latter, i.e. he uttered a sentence expressing this official proposition.[36] Since the report's goal is to

---

[35] In support of the thesis that the background proposition does not affect the truth-value of the whole utterance we can further quote utterances like:

(i) a. Jane, as you know, married Ivan
   b. Ivan, as was predictable, got caught by the FBI

(ia) asserts only that Jane married Ivan, while (ib) asserts only that Ivan got caught by the FBI. On top of that (ia) also conveys the proposition that the addressee knows that Jane married Ivan and (ib) conveys the proposition that it was predictable that Ivan got caught by the FBI. The truth-value of (ia–b) depends only on the proposition asserted, i.e. the official proposition.

[36] For simplicity's sake, I intentionally ignore the *de re/de dicto* distinction and assume that these reports are *de re*. Thus they are true iff they relate the attributee to the proposition s/he expresses, regardless of the wording (the *dicta*) the attributee used to express it.

124 *A Multiple-Proposition Approach*

convey the official proposition, the subordinate clause disappears. If the reports were:

(31) Jon said that Campbell, the famous supermodel, is gorgeous
(32) Jon said that Tim (the man with the hat) is handsome

the embedded subordinate clause would not be governed by the psychological prefix 'Jon said that …'. Reports like (22) and (23) do not attribute to Jon the sayings 'the famous supermodel' and 'the man with the hat'. These reports suggest that the subordinate clause is used by the *attributer*, i.e. the subordinate clause is transparent. It is for this reason that the background proposition must be dropped in a report. These reports do not suggest that John *actually uttered* these, or similar, words; they do not relate Jon to the background proposition. To do that job, the reports should be:

(33) Jon said that Campbell *is* the famous supermodel *and that* she is gorgeous
(34) Jon said that Tim *is* the man with the hat *and that* he is handsome

These reports indicate that Jon actually made two distinct utterances.[37,38] So far the moral is that utterances like (27) [Campbell, the famous supermodel, is gorgeous] and (28) [Tim (the man with the hat) is handsome] express two distinct propositions and that the latter cannot be treated on a par.

It may also be worth stressing that the position I am defending is committed to the thesis that utterances such as:

(35) Bush, the President of the USA, will meet Putin, the President of Russia, in Moscow
(36) The President of the USA, Bush, will meet the President of Russia, Putin, in Moscow

may diverge truth-conditionally, for (35) expresses the official proposition, *that Bush will meet Putin in Moscow* while (36) expresses the distinct official proposition *that the President of the USA will meet the President of Russia in Moscow*. This difference reflects the

---

[37] The friend of complex demonstratives *qua* articulated terms (see Sect. 4, above) could hold that "That F is G" is short for "That is F & that is G". If this is the case (24) and (25) are what is said and (26) and (27) are actually the correct reports.

[38] If one adopts a "narrow" view of semantics, one can claim that the speaker's commitments and goals in reporting utterances with parentheticals, non-restrictive relative clauses, and the like can be explained away as pragmatic features. Indeed, if one holds that the official proposition and the background proposition must be treated on a par, one can claim that reports like (29) and (30) are incomplete and that the accurate reports of (27) and (28) should be (33) and (34). Since I do not believe that the speaker's commitments can be explained away merely as pragmatic facts, I hold that (29) and (30) are the accurate reports of (27) and (28) and that the reports (33) and (34) fail to capture Jon's communicative aim. I concede that the reporting test may not constitute a compelling and definitive argument in favor of the picture I propose, but if one accepts, as I do, that semantics should also handle a speaker's commitments and communicative intentions, then the reporting test provides further evidence in favor of the fact that the background proposition and the official propositions should not be treated (semantically) on a par.

difference of stress and the different conversational entailments these utterances carry. (35) can be true even if Bush and/or Putin is not the president of the USA/Russia, while (36) can be true even if the president of the USA/Russia is not Bush/Putin.

As I already anticipated, the theory of subordinate clauses, parentheticals, etc. easily expands to complex demonstratives. Thus, an utterance such as "That F is G" can be analyzed, roughly, as:

(37) That, who is F, is G

(37) is true if the referent is G, regardless of whether it is also F. Following the naïve view, an utterance like "He/she is G" will thus be analyzed as:

(38) That, who is a male/female, is G

(38) can thus be true even if the relevant referent is not a male and/or female. In the Aphrodite scenario I described, utterances (11)–(14) are true. (11) and (13) express, respectively, the background proposition *that Aphrodite is a male* and the official proposition *that Aphrodite is gorgeous*, while (12) and (14) express the background proposition *that Aphrodite is a female* and the official proposition *that Aphrodite is gorgeous*. Since they all express the same official proposition, they all have the same truth-conditions (and the same truth-value when uttered in the same context).

10. Complex Demonstratives *qua* 'Dthat'-Terms and Anaphora

A way to formalize the picture I have in mind is, once again, to adopt Kaplan's 'Dthat' *qua* demonstrative surrogate. As we saw (Section 4), utterances of the form "The F is G." (where the description is used referentially) can be represented as: Dthat [the F] is G. It is worth recalling that I did not follow Kaplan in his suggestion that the referent of a 'Dthat'-term must satisfy the descriptive content of the description. That is to say, I rejected the idea that the description encapsulated in the demonstrative surrogate 'Dthat' should be understood at the level of character and that the referent is the object satisfying the descriptive conditions of the complex character. As far as reference fixing is concerned, I consider the descriptive material of a 'Dthat'-term to be akin to a demonstration. As such, it is best viewed as a contextual tool used to single out an object of discourse, regardless of the referent satisfying the descriptive condition.

If we keep in mind the differences I have just stressed, Kaplan's 'Dthat' (or a similar surrogate) can be adapted to fit the picture of complex demonstratives

I advocate. In other words, Kaplan's suggestion can be made to fit, modulo some minor modifications, into the story of complex demonstratives that I have told. If "That F is G" is represented as "Dthat(F) is G", the fact that the demonstrative's nominal 'F' is not treated on a par with 'G' is more evident (the former does not affect the truth-value of the whole utterance, i.e. is not a constituent of the official proposition). Complex demonstratives should be treated on a par with definite descriptions used referentially; the very same apparatus helps us to handle both cases.[39] As Kaplan claims, when 'Dthat' is a demonstrative surrogate, a 'Dthat'-term contributes only the referent to what is said; it does not contribute the property F. If we adopt the multiple-proposition view, then what is said corresponds to the *official* content or the official proposition. It is this content that affects the truth-value of the utterance. Nothing prevents us, however, from arguing that, in addition to the official content, there is some other pre-official content, i.e. the background content or background proposition. Extending Kaplan's suggestion a little further, it is also natural to claim that reference is secured by 'Dthat', the demonstrative surrogate, whilst the nominal part of the complex demonstrative acts as a help or support. As such, it is like the demonstration or directing intention that accompanies a demonstrative. But, unlike a demonstration or directing intention, it contributes to the expression of the background proposition. This is, after all, the difference between a complex demonstrative and a simple demonstrative: we can hardly ignore the fact that the latter, unlike the former, includes extra-linguistic material. It is for this reason that "That is G" and "That F is G" (when pointing toward X) both express the same official proposition *that X is G* but also that "That F is G", unlike "That is G", expresses the background proposition *that X is F*. Although the linguistic material accompanying a complex demonstrative does not affect its referential success, it nonetheless plays an important semantic role. As I suggested in Section 3, above, pronouns can be anaphorically linked to NPs within a complex demonstrative's descriptive content. In:

(39) That man talking to Jane$_1$ is charming *her*$_1$

the italicized pronoun is anaphoric on 'Jane'. This mirrors the case we encountered when discussing description-names, where an anaphoric pronoun inherits its value from the descriptive aspect of the proper name. In (39), 'her' inherits its semantic value from (and is thus coreferential with) 'Jane'. Thus, the complex demonstrative's nominal part 'man talking to Jane' plays a semantic role.[40]

---

[39] See Sect. 4, above, for a suggestion of the formal apparatus and how Dthat can be used to regiment the referential use of definite descriptions.

[40] If one endorses Larson and Segal's (1995: 362 ff.) position, this criticism may be circumvented, for they assume that the antecedent can contribute to the interpretation of the anaphoric pronoun insofar as it is syntactically related to it and itself has an interpretation. It may be worth mentioning that the friends of

If the traditional anaphoric (coreferential) treatment of 'her' in (39) is correct, 'Jane' must contribute Jane to what is said (the official content) and hence the predicate 'man talking to Jane' seems to be semantically relevant after all. To be precise, what is semantically relevant in the complex demonstrative is the name 'Jane'.

The theory of complex demonstratives I have defended can account for this anaphoric phenomenon. When the nominal of a complex demonstrative is itself compound and a singular term appears within it, the singular term *may* contribute an object to what is said, i.e. the official proposition. It contributes an object *if* the latter is recovered by an anaphoric pronoun. As a first approximation, we can say that, in (39), 'Jane' is truth-conditionally relevant because it is brought to salience or *recovered* by the anaphoric pronoun 'her'. For a term appearing within a compound demonstrative to become truth-conditionally relevant, it needs to be *recovered* by another part of the utterance or discourse.[41] The multiple-proposition theory allows us to capture this idea. To stress this, let us first consider how anaphoric pronouns behave when linked to an element appearing in a subordinate clause:

(40) Jane, pupil of Tim$_1$, admires *him*$_1$
(41) Kripke, the author of *Naming and Necessity*$_1$, cherishes *that book*$_1$
(42) Tim, who is married to Jane$_1$, loves *her*$_1$
(43) Clinton (Hillary$_1$'s husband) cheated on *her*$_1$

The italicized anaphoric pronouns in (40)–(43) are all coreferential with a term appearing within the subordinate clause. (40)–(43), like (20) and (21), each express two distinct propositions. Thus (40) expresses the background proposition *that Jane is a pupil of Tim* and the official proposition *that Jane admires Tim*. The semantic value of 'him' in (40), like the semantic value of 'that book' in (41) and 'her' in (42) and (43), is inherited from an antecedent, which contributes to the expression of a distinct (background) proposition. This phenomenon is known as *cross-sentential anaphora*

the character interpretation of complex demonstrative (e.g. Braun and Borg) can handle this case. To do so, however, they must subscribe to Larson & Segal's (or a similar) theory. Without discussing the merits of this theory of anaphora, I would simply like to stress that the position I am defending is neutral *vis-à-vis* a given theory of anaphora. In particular, it is neutral on whether one should accept or reject the position advocated by Larson & Segal. Moreover, the naïve theory I have in mind also survives arguments invoking discourse anaphora where there is no syntactic link between the head of the chain and the pronoun. To be sure, people may claim that, in these cases, the relevant pronoun is not an anaphora but works more like a demonstrative picking out an object previously made salient. See e.g. Kripke (1977) and Lewis (1979 *a*).

[41] In the example I discuss, the semantic contribution of the demonstrative's description is recovered by an anaphoric pronoun. It can also be recovered by a quantifier binding a pronoun appearing in the demonstrative's description, e.g. "All the French students are disappointed with **that English teacher who insulted *them***", "The secretary, who dislikes **that man who charmed *her***, will report him to the dean", ... Similar examples can be found in Lepore and Ludwig (2000) and King (2001).

and it must be distinguished from *intrasentential anaphora*. The following example stresses this difference:

(44) Jane₁ likes *her*₁ car. *She*₁ also likes music.

In this example, 'her' is an anaphoric pronoun whose antecedent, 'Jane', appears within the same sentence—it is an intrasentential anaphor—while the antecedent of the anaphoric pronoun 'she', i.e. 'Jane', appears in a distinct sentence—thus 'she' is a cross-sentential or intrasentential anaphor. A similar phenomenon occurs with complex demonstratives. If my diagnosis is correct, 'her' in (42) is a cross-sentential anaphor whose antecedent, 'Jane', "belongs" to another sentence.

With this framework in place, the phenomenon of an anaphoric pronoun linked to an antecedent that appears within the nominal part of a complex demonstrative finds a natural place in the theory, for (39) is analyzed as:

(39) a. That, who is a man talking to Jane, is charming her
b. Dthat (man talking to Jane₁) is charming her₁

which can be deconstructed as:

(39) c. That₁ is a man talking to Jane₂
d. That₁ is charming her₂

(39c) expresses the background proposition, while (39d) expresses the official proposition. Both propositions are expressed by an utterance of (39). The merit of this representation is that it stresses the fact that the anaphoric pronouns in (39a) and (39b) are cross-sentential anaphora: 'her' inherits its reference from an antecedent within another sentence. The value of 'her' in (39) can thus be Jane even if her name, 'Jane', does not directly contribute to the truth-condition of the whole utterance. 'Jane' contributes to the expression of the background proposition—so Jane is a constituent of the background proposition—and this is all we need to find a value for the anaphoric pronoun 'she'. Jane is a constituent of the official proposition thanks to the anaphoric pronoun 'she'.

To summarize, the utterances with which I began the discussion of the Aphrodite case can be analyzed and represented as:

(11) a. Dthat(female person) is gorgeous[42]
(12) a. Dthat(male person) is gorgeous
(13) a. Dthat(female person) is gorgeous
(14) a. Dthat(male person) is gorgeous

[42] In this representation, I switch to 'female/male *person*' instead of simply saying 'male/female' to capture the insight that the pronouns 's/he' are used to refer to persons. I think it is uncontroversial that 'woman/man' and 'female/male person' are treated as synonymous; thus, the analogy between (30/31) and (32/33) *qua* representation of (11/12) and (13/14). This representation could also be used to capture an utterance of 'that girl/boy'.

11. Evading Some Objections

The obvious objection faced by the picture I have proposed may be stated as follows: the naïve theory is implausible insofar as it is committed to the thesis that a demonstrative can succeed in singling out an object of discourse, even if the latter does not satisfy the nominal part of the demonstrative. Rather than being a fault of the picture I have proposed, I take this to be a merit. Imagine that, pointing toward an individual drinking martini, one says: "That woman is drinking martini". As it happens, the speaker is not pointing toward a woman but toward a man, Jon (disguised as a woman), or toward a mannequin.[43] If the interlocutor is aware that the supposed referent is not a woman, she can correct the speaker. How is the interlocutor able to rectify the speaker if 'that woman' is considered to be an empty term?[44] One can mention several other examples in favor of my account. For instance, suppose that, whilst pointing towards a red spot on a distant hill, one says: "That tiny red spot is my house" or "I live in that tiny red spot". Would we say that the speaker did not succeed in referring to her house because, literally speaking, one cannot live in a tiny red spot?

The picture I have in mind does *not* commit us to the thesis that a complex demonstrative can never be empty. If one points toward a corner whilst hallucinating (or drugged) and says, "That woman is charming" when no one is there, 'that woman' is empty. All I am committed to is that the *success* of reference does not rest on the referent satisfying the nominal part of a demonstrative. As we saw (Chapter 1, Section 1, above), the proper function of a screwdriver, for instance, is to drive screws. One can nonetheless succeed in driving a screw using a knife, whose proper function is to cut things. We would not say that one did not drive the screw, i.e. that one did not reach one's goal, because one used a knife. A similar story can be told about complex demonstratives. The proper function of 'that F' is to draw the audience's attention to the demonstrated object, (supposedly) satisfying the nominal 'F'. The demonstrative may reach its goal, i.e. pick out an object of discourse, even if the latter is not F. Along this line we can say that complex demonstratives are *conventionally* designed to pick out an object of discourse even if the latter does not satisfy the nominal part of the complex demonstrative. The nominal part is conventionally conceived as an aid used to single out a referent and, as such, it contributes to the expression of the *background* proposition(s).

---

[43] I am thus sympathetic with Donnellan's intuition. When discussing the referential use of descriptions, Donnellan argues: "Using a definite description referentially, a speaker may say something true even though the description correctly applies to nothing" (Donnellan 1966: 243).

[44] This is not a knockdown argument, for one may argue that the intended individual is made *pragmatically* salient, but not *semantically* referred to; so we do have an empty term *and* a (pragmatically specified) individual.

130   *A Multiple-Proposition Approach*

The second obvious criticism that the picture I have in mind faces is inspired by Kripke and rests on the speaker reference/semantic reference distinction.[45] One could argue that, although the complex demonstrative is an empty term, the speaker may succeed in referring to a given item and communicate something about it. If one adopts this line, one commits oneself to the distinction between what is, strictly speaking, said (semantics) and what is communicated (pragmatics).[46] With "It is cold in here", one may say something, i.e. *that it is cold here*, and communicate something else, e.g. *Please close the window*. You may recall that in the Introduction I expressed some skepticism concerning the semantics/pragmatics distinction. Even if one is sympathetic with the Gricean distinction, one may still feel uncomfortable in applying it to complex demonstratives. In other words, one may think that this distinction is not well suited to handle complex demonstratives and the data I discussed. On the other hand, if one were to assume (along with Braun) the character approach to complex demonstratives, one is likely to appeal to the speaker reference/semantic reference distinction in order to capture the intuition that one can successfully communicate something when the speaker reference and the semantic reference differ. In particular, one might appeal to the distinction in order to capture the fact that the speaker can reach her communicative goal, even when the object she directs her attention toward does not satisfy the nominal part of complex demonstrative. If one adopts the position I have put forward, however, one does not need to appeal to the speaker reference/semantic reference distinction and one can embrace the skepticism on this distinction which I expressed in the Introduction. If a given utterance expresses several propositions, then we can appeal both to the background proposition and the official (the communicated) proposition in accounting for a communicative interaction. We can thus capture the fact that if the object demonstrated using 'that *F*' is not *F* then something went wrong, yet the speaker may communicate something true. In that case, the official proposition is true whilst the background proposition is false. In other words, the naïve theory accounts for the intuition guiding the Kripke-inspired criticism, yet does not need to appeal to the speaker reference/semantic reference distinction. The background proposition helps us to capture the fact that a speaker's choice of words is not always the right one (e.g. one may use 'he' to refer to a female). If one embraces the Kripkean criticism, on the other hand, then one is committed to the view that the speaker is forced to use an empty pronoun in the

---

[45] See Kripke's (1977) discussion and criticism of Donnellan's referential/attributive distinction.

[46] Braun e.g. endorses this view: "The above referential rule is concerned with the *semantic* referent of 'that spy', that is, what the term 'that spy' refers to in that context according to the semantic rules of the language. It entails that 'that spy' fails to semantically refer to Barney in the above context. But it is consistent with saying that George (the *speaker*) refers to Barney, and with saying that George (the *speaker*) asserts a proposition about Barney" (Braun 1994: 210).

Aphrodite example, for the referents of 'she' and 'he' ought to be females and males respectively. Aphrodite could not (semantically) be referred to using a third-person pronoun. This by itself is a highly embarrassing and some, mainly in the USA, would say a politically incorrect consequence.

Before ending this chapter it may be worth signaling yet another criticism faced by the view I defend according to which a complex demonstrative is a singular term. King (2001), in his defense of a quantificational account of complex demonstratives, proposes a few challenges to the referentialist position I favor (i.e. the position which takes complex demonstratives to be singular terms). He claims that under the assumption that complex demonstrative are singular terms we face difficulties in handling utterances like:

(45) Every father$_1$ dreads *that moment when **his**$_1$ oldest child leaves home*
(46) Most avid skiers$_1$ remember *that first black diamond run **they**$_1$ attempted to ski*

where the complex demonstrative contains a bound pronoun. King labels this problem the *quantification in* challenge. The problem posed for the referentialist position is that it seems difficult to explain quantification into complex demonstrative terms under the assumption that they are singular referring terms. In this regard, complex demonstratives display important similarities to quantified expressions and should be understood along:

(45) a. Every father dreads *the/some/all/* ... moment(s) when his oldest child leaves home
(46) a. Most avid skiers remember *the/all/few/* ... first black diamond(s) run they attempted to ski

Sentences like these, however, are rather awkward and may be viewed more accurately as idiomatic uses of language. When binding is allowed, such as in (45) and (46), the bound complex demonstrative may often be viewed along a definite description. In that case, 'that' can be understood as a different word—as a pragmatic tool that allows one to emphasize the description. It is something like an emphatic use of the determiner 'the'. (Dever 2001 dismisses the quantifying in case this way.) My *New Shorter Oxford Dictionary* actually suggests this interpretation: "often interchangeable with *the* but usually more emphatic".

My understanding of sentences like these is that they constitute the exception rather than the norm. When translated, sentences like these do not usually come out well formed; the complex demonstrative usually needs to be replaced by a definite description under translation. A literal translation of (45) into French, for example, gives us the ungrammatical:

(45) b. *Chaque père regrette *ce moment* lorsque son fils ainé quitte la maison

132   *A Multiple-Proposition Approach*

For the translation to be appropriate, the complex demonstrative must be translated by a definite description. This seems to prove that these cases are rather unusual and that the bound demonstrative is best understood as an emphatic description. A similar story can be told about the narrow scope reading: it is unusual for a complex demonstrative to have the narrow scope reading. In these cases as well, the complex demonstrative may be best viewed as an emphatic description. Not all cases of quantifying in, however, can be understood along these lines. In some cases, substituting a complex demonstrative with a definite description gives rise to ungrammaticality (see King 2001: 74–6). Consider, for instance:

(47)   Every professor$_1$ cherishes that first publication of hers$_1$

where the substitution of the complex demonstrative 'that first publication of hers' with a definite description gives the ungrammatical sentence:

(47)   a.   *Every professor$_1$ cherishes the first publication of hers$_1$

King's moral (2001: 76, n. 34) is that the "stylistic variant" does not apply here; the fact that the 'that'-phrase in (47) cannot be substituted by a description shows that complex demonstratives and definite descriptions work semantically in very different ways. Notice, however, that all I have said above does not commit me to the view that *every* case where we quantify into a complex demonstrative can be explained as an emphatic description. I have stressed that these cases are best understood as *idiomatic* uses of language. If, for instance, one literally translates (47) into Italian, one obtains the ungrammatical:

(47)   b.   *Ogni professore$_1$ valorizza quella sua$_1$ prima pubblicazione

A correct translation forces us to replace the 'that'-phrase with a description:

(47)   c.   Ogni professore$_1$ valorizza la sua$_1$ prima pubblicazione

Cross-linguistic comparisons show that we cannot derive a *general* moral from examples like these. As soon as we make a cross-linguistic comparison, we realize that we cannot end up with an interesting generalization as far as quantifying into complex demonstratives is concerned. Thus, I maintain that these examples are best viewed as *idiomatic* uses of language. As such, each case may be understood and analyzed in a quite different way.

The very same considerations can be applied to some other arguments King proposes in favor of the quantificational account. In particular, to what he terms *the narrow scope reading*. Like quantified expressions, some uses of complex demonstratives can have both the wide and narrow scope reading:

(48)   *That professor* who brought in the biggest grant in each division will be honored

(49)   *That senator* with most seniority on each committee is to be consulted

If (48), for instance, continues: "In all, ten professors will be honored", the complex demonstrative 'that professor' has a narrow scope reading. Since in this reading the complex demonstrative is not used to refer to a particular individual, it is hard to reconcile with the referentialist position. Under the narrow scope reading, (48) and (49) must be understood along:

(48) a. The/some/few/most/ ... professor(s) who brought in the biggest grant in each division will be honored

(49) a. The/few/many/no/ ... senator(s) with most seniority on each committee is to be consulted

The referentialist position I sketched also allows us to face three other arguments King proposes in favor of the quantificational account of complex demonstratives. The first concerns the so-called Bach–Peters sentences:

(50) Every friend of yours$_1$ who studied for it$_2$ passed some math exam$_2$ she$_1$ was dreading

(51) That friend of yours$_1$ who studied for it$_2$ passed some math exam$_2$ she$_1$ was dreading

where (as the subscripts indicate) each pronoun in each NP is interpreted as anaphoric on the other NP. It seems that these sentences should be treated on a par and, thus, that the complex demonstrative 'that friend of yours who studied for it' must be treated like the uncontroversial quantifier phrase 'every friend of yours who studied for it'.

A further argument set out by King rests on VP deletion, a test for whether a NP is a singular term or a quantifier. Hence the grammaticality of:

(52) a. Tiger birdied every hole Michael did
(52) b. Tiger birdied that hole that Michael did

compared with the ungrammaticality of

(53) *Copp flunked Holmes, who Jubien did

reveals complex demonstratives as akin to quantificational devices rather than singular terms. Another argument rests on the fact that quantified phrases exhibit weak crossover effects whilst referring expressions do not. In:

(54) a. His mother loves some man
    b. His mother loves that man with the goatee

'his' cannot be interpreted as anaphoric on the quantifier 'some man' or the complex demonstrative 'that man with the goatee'. On the other hand, in:

(55) His mother loves John

'his' *can* be interpreted as anaphoric on 'John'. King's moral is that these examples campaign in favor of the quantificational interpretation of complex demonstratives.

It should not come as a surprise to hear that the view I favor would deal with complex demonstratives appearing in Bach–Peters sentences, cases of VP deletion and weak crossover data, by assuming that the 'that' of the complex demonstrative is used in an emphatic way, i.e. it is a way of emphasizing 'the', and that the complex demonstrative is an *emphatic description*.

One could object that the position I end up defending lacks the systematicity of King's theory. For, to salvage direct reference I have ended up arguing that when complex demonstratives do not contribute to the expression of singular propositions they act either as anaphors bound by a quantified expression or constitute idiomatic uses of language. However, systematicity comes at a price. I think that the picture I have proposed has the advantage of recognizing the variegated ways 'that'-phrases can work or, as some would say, the different language-games they can enter. The key point is that the picture I have outlined does not force us to give up the intuition that in the paradigmatic case, i.e. when the speaker and her audience are in presence of, and in a perceptive contact with, the relevant referent (this could be labeled *the demonstration speaker reference* uses to echo King's *no demonstration no speaker reference* uses) the complex demonstrative is used as a singular term enabling the speaker and her audience to single out the relevant object of discourse. I guess that it would be far less appealing to start from these paradigmatic cases and argue that 'that'-phrases are not devices of direct reference. From a methodological viewpoint I would claim that the picture I have proposed focused to begin with on the paradigmatic cases (the demonstration speaker reference use) and then explains away the non-paradigmatic uses as being either anaphoric or idiomatic. By contrast, King's theory focuses on the borderline cases and ends up claiming that *all* uses of 'that'-phrases are akin to the use of quantifiers.[47]

I am now in a position to conclude that complex demonstratives are singular terms and that the multiple-proposition theory, unlike the three theories discussed in Sections 6, 7, and 8, is hermaphrodite-friendly. As we saw in the case of description-names the multiple-proposition framework helps capture the complex demonstrative connotative feature. For this and other reasons we shall discuss in the following chapters, I am quite confident in claiming that the multiple-proposition theory is the most attractive position on the market. In the next chapter I shall concentrate on the distinction between demonstratives and pure indexicals and show how the character of the latter, unlike the character of the former, is complete. We shall also discuss essential indexicals and how they are irreducible to other referential terms. These distinctions will gain further importance in the subsequent chapters when we shall first discuss the first-person pronoun and we shall subsequently see how, from a third-person perspective, we manage to capture and attribute 'I'-thoughts to others.

---

[47] For a more detailed discussion of King's quantificational account of complex demonstratives see Corazza (2003).

4

Demonstratives, Pure Indexicals, and Essential Indexicals

> The word 'this' is, in a sense, a proper name, but it differs from true proper names in the fact that its meaning is continually changing. This does not mean that it is ambiguous, like (say) 'John Jones', which is at all times the proper name of many different men. Unlike 'John Jones', 'this' is at each moment the name of only one object in one person's speech. Given the speaker and the time, the meaning of 'this' is unambiguous, but when the speaker and the time are unknown we cannot tell what object it denotes.
>
> (Russell 1948: 100)

> Philosophers have found indexicals interesting for at least two reasons. First, such words as 'I' and 'now' and 'this' play crucial roles in arguments and paradoxes about such philosophically rich subjects as consciousness, the self, the nature of time, and the nature of perception. Second, although the meaning of these words seems relatively straightforward, it has not been so obvious how to incorporate these meanings into semantical theory.
>
> (Perry 2001: 34)

In this chapter, I concentrate on indexical reference and, after proposing some useful taxonomies, I shall discuss the pure indexicals 'now' and 'here'. I shall explain away the thesis that these indexicals may have different meanings.

I shall proceed as follows. I shall begin, in Section 1, by recapitulating part of the main thesis expressed in Chapter 1 concerning the way we use indexicals in selecting object of discourse. I shall show how indexical reference rests on perspectival identification. In Section 2, I shall distinguish between demonstratives ('this', 'that', 'she', etc.) and pure indexicals ('now', 'today', 'I', etc.). In Section 3, I shall discuss temporal indexicals ('today', 'tomorrow', etc.) and the way they can be coupled with temporal terms ('week', 'year', etc.). I shall defend three main theses: (i) temporal indexicals are pure indexicals, (ii) they must be explained in terms of 'now', i.e. the time at which they are uttered, and (iii) temporal terms are count nouns. As such they can be used as sortal predicates to form either compound indexicals of the form 'last week', 'next year', 'this summer', ... or quantified expressions of the form 'some days', 'every Monday', 'every year', 'all Marchs', ... The former are pure indexicals, while the latter are not singular terms but quantified ones. In Section 4, I shall show how all attempts to reduce temporal indexicals to definite descriptions fail. In Section 5, I shall introduce some data, like the historical present, and show how these data can be accommodated within the framework previously proposed. In so doing I shall criticize Quentin Smith's view that temporal and spatial indexicals may have different linguistic meanings or characters. In Section 6, I shall defend the thesis that temporal indexicals and spatial indexicals do have a single character. The problematic data (e.g. the historical present) will be explained in introducing the notion of presupposition. I shall argue that in these cases the temporal and/or spatial indexical works in an anaphoric way inheriting its value from a previously made reference. The antecedent of the indexical *qua* anaphora may be a tacit initiator, i.e. a noun phrase which has not been uttered but is nonetheless implicit or presupposed. In Section 7, I shall show how the picture I propose is more advantageous than the picture postulating that indexicals may have different characters.

1. The Background: Indexical Identification

As we saw in Chapter 1, indexical expressions play a crucial role in the way humans interact with the external world. Since one of the fundamental types of experience is that of cognizing the world, indexical expressions are the basic mechanisms enabling us to pick up and think about the objects and individuals inhabiting our surroundings:

Indexical reference is personal, ephemeral, confrontational, and executive. Hence it is not reducible to nonindexical reference to what is not confronted. Conversely, nonindexical reference is not reducible to indexical reference. (Castañeda 1989: 70)

Following these considerations we can recognize at least two radically distinct ways one can single out an object of discourse. On the other hand, when one uses an indexical expression the story is rather different. In that case one must bridge the gap between the indexical and the object singled out by this use. The link between the former and the latter is *created* by the very use of the indexical, by the production of the utterance. Thus:

What is characteristic of demonstratives is not a special mode of reference but a special mode of identification. (Hintikka 1998: 204)

For this reason indexicals can also be characterized as *egocentric particulars* (see Russell 1940) inasmuch as they are intrinsically linked with the agent and her spatio-temporal location. In other words, indexicals are used from a point of view. When one makes an assertion, a request, a question, etc. using an indexical one is (usually) anchored to the place and time one produces one's utterance.[1] To put it in a nutshell, since an utterance is an action, i.e. an event produced by an agent, an utterance is strictly tied to an agent, a time, and a place. Hence, the relevant contextual parameters needed to fix an indexical reference are *the agent* (usually the speaker or writer), *the time*, and *the location* of the utterance. For these reasons we can say that indexicals are intrinsically perspectival, for they are tied to an agent's (egocentric) setting. Hintikka (1998) captures the peculiarity of indexical reference in distinguishing between public identification and perspectival identification. In perspectival identification "we use an agent's first-hand cognitive relations to persons, objects, places, etc. as the identificatory framework" (Hintikka 1998: 205). To stress the difference between public and perspectival identification Hintikka invites us to consider the following scenario. In front of the Bodleian Library a tourist asks "What building is that?" while another tourist asks "Where is the Bodleian Library?". In both cases one can answer "That building is the Bodleian Library". The very same answer carries clearly different information, for:

The difference between the two tourists is that the latter starts from a publicly identified object (the world-renowned Library) and tries to find a slot for it among his visual objects, that is, among his visual identified objects. The former takes a visual object ("that building") and tries to place it among his publicly identified objects. (Hintikka 1998: 221)

In Chapter 1 we also saw how Kaplan's content/character distinction, roughly the distinction between referent and linguistic meaning, allows us to accommodate the context-sensitivity of indexical expressions.[2] For the character is represented by a function from context to content. The character of 'I' is thus represented by a function of the form "The agent of this utterance" which takes as argument the context and gives as value the referent, the agent. The character of 'today' is represented by a function like "The day of this utterance" which takes as argument the context and gives as value the relevant day. The character of 'now' is represented by

---

[1] For argument's sake I am here ignoring the case of answering machines, post-its, and other similar devices. In the case of a post-it or a recorded message on an answering machine one makes an utterance at a distance or, to borrow Sidelle's (1991) terminology, a deferred utterance. I shall discuss these cases in Ch. 5, below.

[2] See Kaplan (1977). To be precise, in Kaplan's logical framework the content is a function from circumstances of evaluation to extensions. Henceforth I shall forget these subtleties, for Kaplan's distinctions between context of utterance and circumstance of evaluation and between content and extension do not affect my argument. Besides, I shall characterize the character of an indexical in terms of utterances, for a given token (e.g. a note on a post-it or a recorded message) can be used to make different utterances.

a function like "The time of this utterance", and so on. The way I understand Kaplan's notion of character is to consider it as representing a rule a speaker exploits in fixing the reference of the indexical she uses.

With this framework in place I now turn to discuss the distinction between pure indexicals and demonstratives.

2. Demonstratives and Pure Indexicals

It is often the case that the linguistic meaning of expressions like 'this', 'that', and 'she', together with context (agent, time, and location), is not enough to select a referent. These expressions are often accompanied by a pointing gesture or demonstration and the referent will be what the demonstration demonstrates. Kaplan (1977) distinguishes between *pure indexicals* ('I', 'now', 'today', . . .) and *demonstratives* ('this', 'she', 'they', . . .). The former, unlike the latter, do not need a demonstration to secure the reference.[3] In short, while the reference of a pure indexical is secured by the contextual parameters such as the agent, time, and location of the utterance, the reference of a demonstrative is fixed by these parameters plus something else, such as a pointing gesture, ostension, or demonstration. We can thus propose the following characteristic distinguishing pure indexicals from demonstratives:[4]

- *C1*
  The use of a pure indexical, unlike the use of a demonstrative, never requires a pointing gesture to fix the reference.

Another way to understand the distinction between pure indexicals and demonstratives is to argue that the latter, unlike pure indexicals, are perception-based.[5]

---

[3] "[T]he reference of a type two demonstrative [i.e. what I called demonstratives] is not fixed by the parameters that suffice to specify the occasion in question, that is to say, by a person and his or her spatiotemporal vantage point" (Hintikka 1998: 208).

[4] The characteristics I am mentioning need not be necessary or sufficient conditions distinguishing pure indexicals from demonstratives. It is always possible to find an example of a demonstrative or pure indexical which does not fit within the mentioned characteristics (e.g. 'here' pointing to a map is used as a demonstrative, 'now' in "Millions of years ago the Earth was F, *now* it's G" does not seem to pick out the time it is uttered but rather a long period, . . .). These characteristics should capture, though, the *paradigmatic uses* of pure indexicals and demonstratives. The most prominent counterexamples to C1–C3 I can think of, involve technological devices such as answering machines and videotapes. If Michael Schumacher, watching a videotape of last year's Monte Carlo race, says "Now, is when I lost the race", 'now' does not pick up the time he utters it. These technological devices do not constitute, though, the paradigmatic use of language. Actually, I do not think that language has undergone a radical change to adapt to, and incorporate, these non-paradigmatic uses of indexicals. More on answering machines and "deviant" uses of indexicals in Ch. 5, below.

[5] As Hintikka points out: "there is in any case a close conceptual connection between demonstratives and perspectival identification. It is at its clearest in the case of visual cognition, as usual. Clearly *a* can point to (ostend, demonstrate) *b* if and only if . . . *a* sees *b*" (Hintikka 1998: 206).

When one says 'I', 'today', etc., one does not have to perceive oneself, the relevant day, etc. to be able to use and understand these expressions competently. To use and understand 'this', 'she', etc. competently, one often needs to perceive the referent or demonstratum.[6] In other words, while on the one hand the capacity one has to recognize the referent rests on the perception of the referent, on the other hand it merely rests on the fact that the speaker/thinker occupies a given perceptual field, i.e. that she is egocentrically placed and, thus, has the faculty or potential of acting in a given place. As Evans (1982) aptly points out, by the simple fact of using a so-called pure indexical one is disposed to gather information from the relevant referent, be it oneself, a time, or a place. In short, to pass an indexical message we can either use an indexical expression and draw our audience's attention to the relevant individual or, if the referent is not in our perceptual field, we need to use another referential tool such as, for instance, a proper name.[7] In short, from the speaker or thinker's point of view, perspectival identification can rest on perception or not. C2 should capture this difference.[8]

- C2

  The use of a pure indexical, unlike the use of a demonstrative, is not perception-based.

Moreover, a demonstrative, unlike a pure indexical, can be a vacuous term. 'Today', 'I', etc. never miss the referent. Even if I do not know whether today is Monday or Tuesday and I am amnesic or believe that I am Russell and that today is Wednesday, if, on Friday, 22 December 2000 I say "Today I am tired", I refer to the relevant day (Friday, 22 December 2000) and myself. I do not refer to Russell and Wednesday. By contrast, if hallucinating, one says, "She is funny", or gesturing behind oneself one says "This car is green" when there is nothing, 'she' and 'this car' are vacuous. It could be objected that 'today' can be a vacuous term. For suppose that my utterance "Today is F" is uttered exactly at midnight. Since an utterance

---

[6] In some cases one can refer to something behind one, say a vase, using 'that vase' for the person has been told that the vase is there. Being blind, one can refer to the bottle on the table with 'this bottle' because one has been told that a bottle is on the table. These cases do not constitute, though, the paradigmatic uses of demonstratives, for the speaker is partially "borrowing" someone else's perceptual apparatus. It is also possible that one uses a demonstrative expression without actually perceiving the referent. It would be so for instance in the case, when, pointing to a picture behind me, I say or think "She is F". In this case my use of 'she' is still perception-based. For I used it on the basis of a memory of perception. In all these cases, my audience, if any, would perceive the relevant referents. The demonstrative reference is thus perception-based even in these awkward cases.

[7] For a detailed discussion on the interrelation between language and perception and how it has been developed within the Austro-German tradition, see Mulligan (1997b).

[8] As we shall see in Sect. 6, below, what King (2001) characterizes the *no demonstrative no speaker reference* does not constitute a counterexample of this thesis. I shall claim that in these cases the demonstrative works like an anaphora.

takes some time interval to perform, my uttering of 'today' can start before midnight and finish after midnight. In this case 'today' seems to be empty or, at best, a vague term. Notice, however, that the reference of 'today' is fixed according to the context, day, in which it is uttered. If we fix the context, the day, we fix the reference. The linguistic meaning of 'today' cannot take two contexts, two days. As such 'today' cannot be a vacuous term. In short, in this case 'today' refers either to the day before midnight, say Monday, or the day after midnight, say Tuesday. Since the linguistic meaning of 'today' (i.e. the day of this utterance) *qua* function can have only one day as output, it takes either Monday or Tuesday. As such, it seems that the linguistic meaning is underdetermined. A way out of this problem would be to argue that the relevant context is either the time the uttering of 'today' begins (so 'today' refers to Monday) or the time it finishes (so 'today' refers to Tuesday). If the relevant utterance is "Today I visited London" or "Today I've been busy", the context is the time the utterance starts, while if the relevant utterance is "Today I'll be visiting London" or "Today I'll meet Jane" the context is likely to be the time the utterance finishes. The whole utterance allows us to fix the relevant context, day. Hence, the linguistic meaning of 'today' is not, at least in these cases, underdetermined. It is left to the reader whether we can find cases where the utterance does not allow us to determine the relevant context. In the case of a demonstrative, on the other hand, we can fix the context and, yet, the demonstrative can be vacuous if it is, for instance, based on a hallucination.[9] So:

- *C3*
Pure indexicals, unlike demonstratives, are never vacuous terms.[10]

3. Temporal Indexicals and Temporal Terms

If we consider temporal indexicals we can easily see that they qualify as pure indexicals for they satisfy the distinctive criteria *C1–C3*. Their linguistic meaning (or character) can be, roughly, cashed out as follows.

Now: "the time *of* this utterance"
Today: "the day *of* this utterance"

[9] For argument's sake I am here ignoring cases of deferred reference or ostension such as "He is late today" uttered when pointing at someone's office meaning that the occupier of the office is late or "She is already back" when pointing to someone's car parked in front of her house, etc. I am also ignoring conceptions (like Castañeda's for instance) arguing that the referent of 'I' is not a person/agent but rather a person's stage. In that case, different utterances of 'I' uttered by the same agent refer to different referents.

[10] To be precise, I should distinguish between what may be labeled *basic* pure indexicals ('I', 'now', 'here', 'today') and *derivative* pure indexicals ('tomorrow', 'next Wednesday', 'my car', . . .). For the latter, unlike the former, can be vacuous.

Yesterday:	"the day *before* this utterance"
Tomorrow:	"the day *after* this utterance"
This year:	"the year *of* this utterance"
Next year:	"the year *after* this utterance"
Last year:	"the year *before* this utterance"
This week:	"the week *of* this utterance"
Next week:	"the week *after* this utterance"
Last week:	"the week *before* this utterance"
This Monday:	"the Monday *of* the week of this utterance"[11,12]
Next Monday:	"the first Monday *after* this utterance"
Last Monday:	"the first Monday *before* this utterance"
…	

Before going further, though, two clarifications are needed.

First, an indexical like 'this year' looks like a complex demonstrative. What is the difference, though, between 'this book' and 'this year'? The latter, unlike the former, is coupled with a temporal expression and, when so coupled, it becomes a pure indexical, satisfying criteria C1–C3.

Secondly, 'Monday' looks like a proper name. Like a proper name, say 'Aristotle' or 'Paris', it starts with a capital letter. More importantly, though, 'Monday' like 'Aristotle': (i) may have different referents and (ii) can be used in a predicative way (e.g. "There are four *Mondays* in a month", "There are four *Davids* in this room"). Feature (i) matches the thought that temporal terms are indexicals, for they switch referent according to the context in which they are used. For this very reason some people (e.g. Recanati 1993; Voltolini 1995) have claimed that proper names are indexicals as well.[13] Feature (ii), on the other hand, matches the opposite thought that 'Monday' is a count noun (e.g. "There are four *apples* on the table"). For this very reason some people (e.g. Castañeda 1989) have claimed that proper names are count nouns as well. I am not fully convinced by

---

[11] Another way to characterize the linguistic meaning of 'this Monday' could be: "The first day of the week of this utterance". It is an accident, though, whether Monday is taken to be the first, second, etc. day of the week. On the other hand, the order of the days is not accidental and, as such, cannot be changed. For these reasons when characterizing the meaning of 'Monday' and the like, we have to make reference to the cycle. One knows the meaning of 'Monday' if one knows that it stands for the day following Sunday and preceding Tuesday. For, temporal terms like 'Monday', 'spring', 'January', are defined in a recursive way making reference to the order.

[12] In some cases, though, 'this Monday' does not refer to the Monday of the week in which the utterance occurs. If, on Wednesday, one says "This Monday I'll be visiting Paris", 'this Monday' refers to the Monday of the week following the week in which the utterance occurs. If we accept that a sentence like the latter is grammatical, then it can be viewed to be elliptical of: "This/the *coming* Monday I'll be visiting Paris" or simply "*Next* Monday I'll be visiting Paris". Actually, this is the way one understands our problematic sentence.

[13] I discussed and criticized the indexical interpretation of proper names in Ch. 1, Sect. 4, above.

Castañeda's, Recanati's, and Voltolini's arguments: I believe that proper names are neither count nouns nor indexicals. I addressed this question in Chapter 1. For the present purpose it suffices to say that if we recognize the dual aspect of identification that I have discussed and defended in Section 1 we commit ourselves to the view that indexical and proper names are distinct tools of reference and identification and, more importantly, that they do not reduce to one another. For argument's sake let us assume that we have three kinds of terms: proper names, indexicals, and count nouns and that they do not reduce to each other.[14] My concern here is to see whether temporal terms are count nouns, indexicals, or proper names. We are thus left with a 'trilemma': temporal terms are either indexicals, proper names, or count nouns.

In what follows I shall argue that a temporal expression looks more like a count noun such as 'man', 'lemon', 'alligator', and 'car', than a proper name, i.e. that a temporal term belongs to the category of count nouns. To stress this fact, consider:

(1) Teaching starts on Monday

In this case 'Monday' seems to be short for 'next Monday' and (1) ought to be understood as:

(1) a. Teaching starts next Monday[15]

There are some cases, though, when a temporal expression is not coupled with an indexical to form a pure indexical. A temporal term like 'Monday' can be coupled with an indefinite article to make an indefinite reference:

(2) The teaching starts on *a* Monday.

(2) looks like (3) and (4):

(3) I met *a* man.
(4) I met *a* Paul.

---

[14] My argument, though, is independent of Recanati's, Voltolini's, and Castañeda's arguments. For even if one accepts their viewpoint and ends up assuming that proper names do not form a grammatical category, one would be inclined to accept the thesis I am defending, i.e. that temporal terms are count nouns.

[15] Notice that if we understand (1) as "The teaching starts the Monday of next week" or "The teaching starts the first Monday following today", we would consider 'Monday' to be an abbreviation of a definite description containing temporal indexicals, e.g. 'next week', 'today'. This should not undermine the thesis I am putting forth, i.e. that 'Monday' is a count noun which can be completed by a determiner to form a noun phrase. As we shall see in Sect. 4, though, expressions like 'next Monday' are best understood as singular terms, rather than descriptions. Besides, (1) seems to look like: "The train left on time". The latter, though, seems to be short for: "The train left the time it was scheduled to leave". In this case 'on time' does not seem to work like an indexical but like a definite description. 'Next time' and 'last time' do not seem to work like indexicals either, but like definite descriptions. If translated into French or Italian, for instance, they become definite descriptions '*la prochaine fois*' / '*la dernière fois*' or '*La prossima volta*'/ '*l'ultima volta*'. This suggests, at least to me, that an utterance like "Next time we'll meet . . ." is short for "The next (or first) time we'll meet . . .".

But (4), unlike (3), looks like:

(5) There are several Pauls in England.

As such (4) involves an implicit quotation and is short for:

(4) a. I met someone named 'Paul'

just as (5) is short for:

(5) a. There are several people named 'Paul' in England.

On the other hand, (2), like (3), does not seem to involve implicit quotations. If so, 'Monday' works more like 'man' than like a proper name. As my intuition goes, (2) should be understood as:

(2) a. Teaching starts on one of the Mondays

If (2) were understood as:

(2) b. Teaching starts on one of the days of the week called 'Monday'

something would be lost. To be sure, if teaching starts on Monday it starts on the day called 'Monday'. But when one understands (2) one does not understand it as (2b). If one understands it as (2b) one may have no clue on which day of the week teaching starts. To know that teaching starts on a Monday is to know that it starts on one of the days following Sunday and preceding Tuesday, while to know that teaching starts on one of the days called 'Monday' does not entail the knowledge that teaching starts on one of the days following Sunday. In short, to know that teaching starts on a Monday entails the knowledge of the cycle of the days, while to know that teaching starts on one of the days called 'Monday' does not entail the knowledge of the cycle of the days and, thus, does not entail the mastery of the word 'Monday'.

This difference goes hand in hand with yet another difference distinguishing proper names and temporal terms. The latter, unlike the former, occur in dictionaries. To be sure, some proper names do occur in the dictionary. But you need to be rather famous to get your name into the dictionary. The same for a place: it has to be rather famous to get the same honor. So one can argue that a speaker who does not know that Monday is the day following Sunday, i.e. someone who does not know the order of the days in a week, like someone who does not know that January is the month following December and preceding February, is not fully competent in English. In other words, one does not master the word 'Monday' if one does not know the order of the days and, thus, does not also master the words 'Tuesday', 'Wednesday', etc. On the other hand, we cannot say that someone who does not know the meanings of the thousands designated by a given proper name, say 'Mary Smith', is linguistically incompetent. In short, one can understand a proper name in isolation while one cannot so understand a temporal term. Let us call this the *understanding-competence test*.

As I argued, temporal terms like 'Monday', 'January', etc., unlike proper names, look and behave like count nouns. In favor of this thesis we can also stress that proper names and temporal terms behave in rather different ways when embedded in attitude ascriptions. We can call this the *embedding-substitution test*. I shall argue that temporal terms, unlike proper names, (i) can be substituted *salva veritate* in attitude ascriptions and (ii) in attitude ascription behave like count nouns. To begin with, consider the following inferences:

(1) a. Lois wishes to kiss Superman

(2) a. Superman is Clark Kent

So: (3) a. Lois wishes to kiss Clark Kent

Let us assume, following the Fregean intuition, that this inference is not valid. Actually, as the story goes, Lois wishes to kiss Superman and does not wish to kiss Clark Kent. If in our inference we substitute 'Clark Kent' for 'Superman' we cannot deal with Lois's emotional attitude. To deal with the latter we ought to stress that Lois wishes to kiss Clark Kent *qua* Superman while she does not wish to kiss him *qua* Clark Kent, for she is unaware of the fact that Clark Kent is Superman.[16] A similar reasoning cannot be applied when dealing with temporal terms:

(1) b. Lois wishes to visit us on a Monday

(2) b. Monday is the day after Sunday

So: (3) b. Lois wishes to visit us on the day after a Sunday

This inference, unlike the previous one, is valid even in its *de dicto* reading. For, as I hope to have shown, Lois masters the word 'Monday' if she knows the cycle of the days and, thus, if she knows that Monday is the day after Sunday. Hence, if with (1b) we are assuming that Lois masters the word 'Monday', we are also assuming that she knows (2b) and, therefore, we can substitute 'Monday' with 'the day after Sunday'. If we are reluctant to assume that with (1b) we are attributing to Lois the mastery of the word 'Monday', let us substitute (1b) with "Lois, a perfectly competent speaker of English, wishes to visit us on a Monday". In this case the attribution to Lois of the mastery of 'Monday' is explicitly stated by the clause "a perfectly competent speaker of English". To stress the fact that temporal terms behave like count nouns, let us consider the following inference:

(1) c. Lois wishes to meet a bachelor[17]

(2) c. A bachelor is an unmarried man

So: (3) c. Lois wishes to meet an unmarried man

---

[16] Using the traditional *de re/de dicto* distinction to deal with Lois's emotional attitude, we have to interpret (1b) and (3b) to be *de dicto*. Henceforth I shall interpret all the attributions to be *de dicto*.

[17] For simplicity's sake, I am ignoring the fact that (1c) can have two readings, the *de re* or specific and the *de dicto* or non-specific, and I invite you to understand it in the *de dicto* way, i.e. Lois wishes that there might be a bachelor and that she might meet him.

Like the previous inference this one is valid. For, if Lois has mastered the word 'bachelor', she knows (2c), i.e. that a bachelor is an unmarried man. So we can substitute 'unmarried man' for 'bachelor'. Once again, if we are reluctant to assume that with (1c) we are attributing to Lois the mastery of 'bachelor', we can replace it with "Lois, a perfectly competent speaker of English, wishes to meet a bachelor". It is worth noticing, though, that an inference like:

(1) d. Lois wishes to meet an unmarried man
(2) d. An unmarried man is a bachelor

So: (3) d. Lois wishes to meet a bachelor

does not appear to be valid, for Lois may master the words 'unmarried' and 'man' without mastering the word 'bachelor'. Consider the following scenario. Igor is told to separate the female foxes and the male ones guarded in the zoo. Igor can successfully fulfill the action he has been told to do, for he masters the words 'female', 'male', and 'fox'. If Igor is told to separate the vixens and the non-vixens he may be unable to act, for he may not have mastered the word 'vixen', i.e. he does not know that a vixen is a female fox. This suggests that there is an asymmetry between 'bachelor' and 'vixen', on the one hand, and 'unmarried man' and 'female fox', on the other. For someone who understands the words 'bachelor' and 'vixen' also understands the words 'unmarried man' and 'female fox', while someone who understands the latter may not understand the former. In short, someone who understands and masters a word also understands the definition of this word, while someone who understands a given definition may not master the word this definition stands for.

The embedding substitution test may not furnish a knockdown argument in favor of the fact that temporal terms like 'Monday' are better understood as count nouns than proper names, for it rests on the assumption that synonymous expressions can be substituted *salva veritate* in attitude ascriptions. To be more accurate, the assumption I have endorsed entails that a word can be substituted by its definition while a definition cannot be substituted by the word it defines, an assumption that not all are willing to accept (see Burge 1978a and Mates 1952 for instance). It is worth noticing, though, that in translating a word like "bachelor" or "vixen" into another language we may not find the corresponding word. In French and Italian, for instance, we do not have the corresponding word for "vixen". So we are forced to translate this word's definition. This phenomenon suggests that the definition is more basic than the word it defines and parallels the fact that the knowledge of the definition is more basic than the knowledge of the word it defines. It is for this reason that one can understand 'unmarried man' without understanding 'bachelor' while one cannot understand the latter without understanding the former. To please those who do not accept this assumption, we can take my argument to be a conditional one, i.e. *if* synonymous expressions can be substituted *salva veritate* in attitude ascriptions, *then* temporal terms embedded within attitude ascriptions behave like count nouns.[18] If, we assume, as I suggested, that Lois is perfectly competent with English, then we are assuming that she is aware that bachelors are unmarried men and vixens are female foxes. On the other hand, being perfectly competent with English does not entail that one knows that Superman is Clark Kent, that Bob Dylan is Robert Zimmerman, or that Lenin is Vladimir Ilyich Ulyanov. And this assumption is all we need to show that temporal terms in attitude ascriptions behave like count nouns and not like proper names.

There is another difference between a proper name such as 'Clark Kent', 'Lenin', or 'Superman' and temporal words such as 'Monday', 'summer', 'April', . . . : it is unusual for a given person to bear two distinct names. On the other hand, 'Monday' and 'The day after Sunday' are synonymous. So a person named 'Clark Kent' may not be the same as the one named 'Superman', while the day called 'Monday' ought to be the same as the day following the day called 'Sunday'.

Consider now:

(6) Shops closed on Sunday.

In that case (6) is elliptical for:

(6) a. Shops are closed every Sunday.

'Sunday' is coupled with a quantifier. As such it is not a singular term. Actually, temporal terms, like count nouns, can be coupled with quantifiers and become quantified expressions:

(7) A few years ago Igor married Pauline.
(8) Within a few weeks we will meet again.
(9) In a few days Jane will give us her paper.
(10) Every Monday Ivan has a hangover.

A further, related, consideration in favor of treating temporal terms such as 'Monday' as count nouns comes from the fact that elements of different syntactic categories, unlike elements of the same category, cannot be conjoined when appearing within the scope of a quantifier. To stress this fact consider (11) and (12):

(11) *All the Igors and bachelors are males
(12) All Mondays and vixens are unfriendly

While (11) is agrammatical, (12), even if awkward, is grammatical. The only way to make sense out of (11) would be to interpret it as:

(11) a. All the people named/called/ . . . 'Igor' and bachelors are males

---

[18] For argument's sake, I am ignoring the position of some direct reference theorists (e.g. Salmon and Soames) who argue that proper names can be substituted *salva veritate* in attitude ascriptions as well.

We would then bring in quotation. Hence (11) undergoes the same analysis as (4) and (5). This, once again, proves that count nouns and temporal terms can be treated on a par, while proper names belong to a different syntactic category.

Summing up: there is a difference between pure (temporal) indexicals like 'today', 'now', 'tomorrow', . . . and temporal terms such as 'Monday', 'week', 'year'. The latter, unlike the former, and like count nouns, can behave as temporal sortals becoming pure (temporal) indexicals when coupled with a prefix such as 'this', 'next', 'last', or quantified terms when coupled with a determiner like 'some', 'few', 'many', 'all'.

Moreover, temporal terms such as 'Monday', 'Christmas', 'spring', can be used in dates such as: 'Monday, 2 February 1998', 'On Christmas Day, 1838'. In these cases temporal terms contribute to the building of eternal sentences, i.e. sentences which do not change reference with the change of context. On the one hand, dates seem to work like compound proper names referring to the same time regardless of the context in which they are uttered. Like proper names, dates contribute the referent, the relevant time, to what is said, i.e. the proposition expressed. On the other hand, dates seem to work like definite descriptions in as much as they describe the referent. As such, they contribute a descriptive mode of presentation of the referent, i.e. a description the referent ought to satisfy to be the designatum of the date.

4. Temporal Indexicals *qua* Singular Terms

A question remains to be answered: why are expressions like 'this Monday', 'next week', and the like pure indexicals and not disguised definite descriptions? After all 'next president' is considered to be a definite description—to be sure an incomplete description, for there are several presidents around the world, not to mention the universe. In France we are probably implicitly referring to France and the description goes proxy for 'next president of France', while in the USA it goes proxy for 'next president of the USA' and in England it would quite certainly be used as a metaphor for Tony Blair.

There are two ways one can understand incomplete descriptions: either one follows the Russellian tradition and considers them general terms *or* one follows Russell's critics (the main exponents being Strawson and Donnellan) and tends to consider them singular terms working like complex indexical expressions.[19]

---

[19] Not all incomplete descriptions, though, can be considered to be singular terms, for there are attributive uses of incomplete descriptions. If in front of Smith's savagely mutilated body one claims "The murderer is insane" one need not have a specific murder in mind. The description 'the murderer' is incomplete (unfortunately there is more than one murderer in the universe), yet used attributively in as much as the speaker means that *whoever* committed this specific murder is insane.

If one addresses the first horn of the dilemma one is likely to consider incomplete descriptions to be quantified expressions ranging over restricted domain of discourse, while if one addresses the second horn of the dilemma one is likely to consider the definite article 'the' of an incomplete description, say 'the *G*', to work more or less like a demonstrative like 'that' in 'that *G*'.[20]

Without entering the details of this complex debate I would like to stress that if the thesis that incomplete descriptions are singular terms is embraced, then, as we shall soon see, I would have no objection to considering an expression like 'next Monday' to be an incomplete description of the sort '*the* next/first Monday following today', for the latter would be analyzed/explained using the pure indexical 'today'. On the other hand, if incomplete descriptions are considered to be general, quantified, terms, then I do believe that temporal terms like 'next Monday' are not disguised descriptions. To the defense of this position I now turn. The basic question is: could 'Monday' be understood as an incomplete description, and 'next Monday' as a description of the form '*the* next/first Monday following today' or '*the* first Monday after this utterance'?

This whole issue turns on the way one understands incomplete descriptions. In particular on the question: How could we understand incomplete descriptions if they are not singular terms? As far as I can see we have two possibilities, for context can come onto the scene either in completing the description *or* in restricting the domain of discourse. In the first case an incomplete description would be elliptical for a complete definite description ranging over the whole universe, while in the second case the description would range over a restricted or selected domain. It goes without saying, though, that an incomplete description does not necessarily have to be made into an eternal expression before being understood, for it can be completed by indexical expressions. Whether one addresses the first horn of the dilemma and takes incomplete descriptions to be elliptical of complete expressions (either indexical descriptions or eternal descriptions) *or* takes them to range over restricted domains of discourse, an incomplete description, unlike an indexical expression, does not direct us to some aspect of context and the latter is not part of what is said. Actually, whether one follows the former or the latter proposal one commits oneself to the thought that before an incomplete description gets to work and searches for its referent, i.e. the object satisfying the description's descriptive content, it ought either to be completed or the domain of discourse must be specified.

If what I said comes close to being the right picture, then a definite description is not an indexical that has a meaning that directs us to certain aspects of context.

---

[20] I discussed descriptions and Donnellan's referential/attributive distinction in Ch. 3, Sect. 2, above, where I used Kaplan's 'Dthat' to regiment the referential use of a definite description and of a complex demonstrative.

In other words, in claiming that the meaning of a definite description cannot be equated to the meaning of an indexical, i.e. to a function taking as argument the context and giving as value the referent, I simply mean that such a meaning does not take an aspect of context into what is said. The meaning of an indexical, on the other hand, takes part of the context into what is said. As we saw (Section 1), indexical identification is perspectival.[21] It is for this very reason that an expression like 'this Monday' cannot be equated to an incomplete description understood as a quantified expression. The latter does not involve perspectival identification but public identification. If one understands incomplete descriptions to be short or elliptical for indexical descriptions of the sort 'the person close to *that woman*' or 'the pen on *my left* under *this table*', then the meaning of the description is compound. If one favors this strategy and takes an expression like 'next Monday' to be an incomplete description which will be completed by an indexical expression, then, as I have already anticipated, I have no principled objection. After all, the meaning of an indexical is descriptive. To stress this fact one can focus on the truism that demonstratives like 'this' and 'that' are usually coupled with sortal predicates to form complex demonstratives of the sort 'this *book*', 'that *water*', ... Sortal predicates can be considered to be *universe narrower* which, coupled with other contextual clues, help in fixing the reference. If, pointing to a bottle, one says "This liquid is green", the sortal 'liquid' helps fix the liquid and not the bottle as the referent. Once could argue that this aspect concerning indexical expressions makes them similar to descriptions insofar as they describe the referent. That is to say, the referent picked out by an indexical has to satisfy certain constraints just as the referent of a description must satisfy its descriptive component. Unlike descriptions, though, indexicals are singular terms, for their linguistic meaning is not part of what is said. With a sentence like "*The Queen of England* is visiting France", one says that whoever happens to be Queen of England is visiting France which, as we saw, rests on public identification. On the other hand, with a sentence like "*That lady* [pointing to Queen Elizabeth] is visiting France" or "*She* [pointing to Queen Elizabeth] is visiting France", one says of Queen Elizabeth that she is visiting France. One is not saying that whoever happens to be referred to by 'she' (or whoever happens to be pointed/singled out/ . . . by the utterer when she utters 'she') or whoever happens to be the lady pointed at by the utterer of 'that lady' is visiting France. If an incomplete description is short for an indexical description,

---

[21] Using the well-known Russellian distinction popularized by Kaplan between singular and general proposition, this amounts to saying that with definite descriptions we express general propositions while with indexical expression we express singular propositions. In the latter case the descriptive content (the meaning of the indexical) does not get into the proposition expressed, i.e. what is said). With indexical descriptions we express mixed propositions, i.e. propositions containing both descriptive elements and referents.

150   *Demonstratives and Indexicals*

though, the latter can be assimilated to a complex indexical and thus becomes a singular term involving perspectival identification.[22]

To summarize: if incomplete descriptions are considered to be singular terms then temporal indexicals like 'next Monday' can be assimilated to incomplete descriptions. If, on the other hand, incomplete descriptions are considered to be quantified expressions, then temporal expressions like 'next week' and 'last Wednesday' cannot be assimilated to incomplete descriptions.

Another point in favor of the thesis that a temporal indexical is not a disguised definite description is suggested by the fact that the former, unlike the latter, always takes wide scope with respect to psychological or modal prefixes. In (13) and (14):

(13) Jon believes that *next Monday* it will rain

(14) In some possible worlds *next Monday* it will rain

'next Monday' takes wide scope, i.e. it is not governed by 'Jon believes that' and 'in some possible worlds', while in (15) and (16):

(15) Jon believes that *the next president of the USA* will be a democrat

(16) In some possible worlds *the next president of the USA* will be a democrat

'the next president of the USA' does not necessarily take wide scope.[23] To be sure, this argument shows that if 'next Monday' reduces to a description, the latter turns out to take wide scope as well. Actually, in (17) and (18):

(17) Jon believes that on *the first Monday following today* it will rain[24]

(18) In some possible worlds on *the first Monday following today* it will rain

'the first Monday following today' takes wide scope as well. But this is due to the fact that it contains the pure indexical 'today'. (17) and (18) mirror (19) and (20):

(19) Jon believes that *the agent of this utterance* is rich

(20) In some possible worlds *the agent of this utterance* is rich

'The agent of this utterance' takes wide scope as well because it self-refers to the agent of (19) and (20). For 'the agent of this utterance' to take narrow scope in (19) and (20) it should be rephrased as 'the agent of 'I''. This way, though, we bring in quotations: 'I', unlike 'the agent of this utterance', is not used but mentioned.

---

[22] For an accurate and more exhaustive e.g. discussion of complex demonstratives see Ch. 3, above, where I defended the thesis that they are, *pace* e.g. King (2001), singular terms and that they may succeed in singling out a referent, *pace* Braun (1994) and Borg (2000), even if the latter does not satisfy the demonstrative part of the complex demonstrative.

[23] (15) can have either the wide scope reading rendered adopting Russell's theory of descriptions as follows: $\exists x(x$ is the next president of the USA $\& \forall y(y$ is the next president of the USA $\rightarrow y = x) \&$ Jon believes that x is a democrat), or the narrow scope reading which would be cashed out as follows: Jon believes that $\exists x(x$ is the next president of the USA $\& \forall y(y$ is the next president of the USA $\rightarrow y = x) \& x$ is a democrat).

[24] Notice that if we replace "the first Monday following today" with "the first Monday after this utterance", the latter would take wide scope as well, for it is self-referentially linked to the very utterance.

Actually, consider that Jane utters:

(21) Jon believes that *the agent of 'I'* (whoever he/she happens to be) is rich
(22) Jon believes that *I* am rich
(23) In some possible worlds *the agent of 'I'* (whoever he/she happens to be) is rich
(24) In some possible worlds *I* am rich

(21) and (22), as (23) and (24), do not state the same thing. In (22) and (24) 'I' refers to Jane while in (21) and (23) 'the agent of 'I'' does not necessarily stand for Jane.

The moral I would like to draw from these examples can be stated as follows: 'the first Monday after this utterance' can be understood to be the meaning or character of 'next Monday', just as 'the agent of this utterance' is the character of 'I'. If I am right, 'the first Monday after this utterance' is a function from context to content or referent and, as such, can be viewed as the linguistic meaning or character of 'next Monday'. This goes hand in hand with the thesis that the use of temporal indexicals like 'today', 'next Sunday', 'last year', . . . presupposes perspectival identification. If these terms were to work like proper names or definite descriptions they would rest, like the latter, on public identification. For these reasons expressions like 'next Monday' and 'last week' (like 'I', 'today', 'tomorrow') are not disguised descriptions but singular terms. They are, as I have argued, pure indexicals.

5. The Data and the Multiple Characters Thesis

According to the view I put forward, following the direct reference theory popularized by Kaplan (1977) and Perry (1977), indexicals ('I', 'today', 'this', 'now', etc.) are directly referential expressions. As such, they contribute the referent itself to what is said (i.e. the proposition expressed). This theory has been labeled the direct reference theory. It holds that an indexical expression has a fixed linguistic meaning (character), which can be represented as a function from context of utterance to referent (content). Let us call this the *Fixed Character Thesis*.

The Fixed Character Thesis has been criticized. It has been argued (Q. Smith 1989) that it cannot account for all the relevant data. We use, for instance, present-tense locutions to refer to past or future events. In these cases, a use of 'now' does not pick out the time of utterance. It may be used to refer to a time differing from the time of the utterance. In lecturing about the Nazi invasion of Paris, for example, a teacher can say, "*Now* Hitler takes control of Paris". In that case, 'now' does not refer to the time of the utterance but to the time when the Nazis invaded Paris. We can tell a similar story concerning 'here': 'here' in "It's Monday, 11 September. I'm walking around Yosemite; there are few grizzly bears here", may pick out neither the location where it was written nor where it is read (the writer may have written this note when she arrived back home in San Francisco, or she may simply be in her office writing it as a piece of fiction, for example). 'Here' does not refer to San Francisco or the location where the note is read, however; it refers to the Yosemite national park. If this statement appeared in a novel, 'here' could even refer to an imaginary location, which happens to be called 'Yosemite'.

Examples like this prompt Quentin Smith to claim that indexicals do not have a Fixed Character, for in different situations the same indexical expression may be used in rather different ways. An indexical character does not remain constant across uses. Let us call this the *Multiple Characters Thesis*.

According to the Multiple Characters Thesis, an indexical is an ambiguous expression, for it can have different meanings (i.e. the differing characters).

It is my intention to challenge the Multiple Characters Thesis. To do so, I shall focus on the indexicals 'now' and 'here' and argue that their alleged ambiguity is best dealt with by adopting a framework that assumes the Fixed Character Thesis. In so doing I shall argue that when temporal indexicals like 'now' and 'today', and spatial indexicals like 'here' and 'there', do not refer to the time and location of the utterance, they work as anaphors or bound variables inheriting their value from an antecedent to which they are linked.[25] One may argue that this is a multiple character thesis too, for there are *two* characters: the usual one (the character of 'now' is represented by a function from a context c to the time of c) and the anaphoric one (the character of 'now' is represented by a constant function yielding the semantic value of the antecedent). On this view, however, the supposed indexical ambiguity of 'now' and 'here' reduces to an ambiguity between indexical use/meaning and anaphoric use/meaning. This is similar to the ambiguity of pronouns: 's/he' can be used either as a demonstrative ("S/he [pointing to someone] is my best friend") or as an anaphoric term ("Jane$_1$ thinks that she$_1$ is my best friend"). However, this is not the kind of ambiguity Quentin Smith has in mind, as we shall soon see. To put it slightly differently, while I assume that indexicals are systematically ambiguous, i.e. they can have both an indexical and an anaphoric reading, Smith assumes that they are accidentally ambiguous. The difference between the position I defend and Smith's can also be stated as follows. I claim that indexicals like 'now' and 'here' play different grammatical roles. When they are used as indexicals, they always

---

[25] For the time being it suffices to note that an anaphoric term is referentially defective. The paradigmatic case of anaphors is given by reflexives like the Italian 'se' or the Dutch 'zich' on the one hand and the English 'self' and the Italian 'stesso' on the other hand. The former are characterized as SE anaphors and the latter as SELF anaphors: "Anaphors (of both the SE and the SELF type) are referentially defective NPs, which entails, for example, that they cannot be used as demonstratives, referring to some entity in the world (though it does not entail that they must be bound variables)" (Reinhart and Reuland 1993: 658). I shall further discuss anaphoric terms in Ch. 8, below.

pick out the time/location of the utterance, while when they work as anaphors they inherit their reference from another NP and, as such, they may pick out a time/location different from the time/location of the utterance. On the other hand, Smith assumes that 'now' and 'here' always play the same grammatical role but they are ambiguous regarding their referents.

To begin with, let us consider cases of so-called historical time. It is claimed that in these cases 'now' does not refer to the time of utterance and thus that its character must have changed from that of ordinary uses of 'now'. In an utterance such as:

(25) Last Sunday, Jon visited his mother, *now* a sick old woman

'now' is likely to refer to the time of its utterance, not to the Sunday before, whereas in an utterance like:

(26) In 1834 Jon visited his mother, the once famous actress, *now* a sick old woman

'now' does not pick out the time of the utterance. Instead, it picks out the time (1834) when Jon visited his mother. In this example, the time picked out by 'now' is explicitly stated by the utterance, but in some cases it can simply be presupposed.

The most interesting cases can be found with the historical present. If, during a history class discussing the Nazi invasion of the USSR, the lecturer says:

(27) Now Hitler begins his invasion of the USSR

'now' does not refer to the time of the utterance—it refers to the time of the Nazi invasion. The time picked out, however, is not explicitly stated in the utterance (and it need not even have occurred in previous utterances). If the lecturer assumes that all her students know the period under discussion, she does not need to mention the relevant date, i.e. 22 June 1941. If, whilst watching a recording of one of the last European Champions' League final, one utters:

(28) *Now* Real Madrid are dictating the pace
(29) *Now* you see why Real Madrid won the game

the occurrences of 'now' do not pick out the same time. In (28), 'now' refers to a time during the European Champions' League final, whilst in (29) 'now' refers to the time of the utterance. In other cases, 'now' can also be used to refer to imaginary or fictional times. In watching a movie containing flashbacks, a member of the audience may be confused and ask:

(30) Is this happening *now*?

i.e. is the event happening at the same imaginary time as other represented situations (the time the movie represents as the present) or at a previous imaginary time? One could answer:

(31) No, it happened two years ago

meaning two years before the represented fictional time. In other cases, 'now' can even be used to refer to a nontemporal item. If, in the process of proving a theorem, one states:

(32) *Now* I prove lemma Σ

'now' does not pick out the time of utterance.[26] At this very moment one may stop one's lecture and continue proving the theorem during next week's lecture. In such a case 'now' seems to go proxy for something like 'at this point of the proof'.[27]

On the basis of examples like these, it is claimed that:

> The data regarding these present tense indexicals . . . show these indexicals do not have an invariable character, role or meaning. In some instances they are governed by the reference-fixing rule that they refer to the time of their tokening, in other instances they obey the reference-fixing rule that they refer to an earlier time, in still others to a nontemporal item such as the point in the argument at which they are tokened. (Q. Smith 1989: 176)

The same (or a similar) phenomenon occurs with spatial indexicals such as 'here'. If we consider the following passage from *California: The Ultimate Guidebook* (Riegert 1990, quoted in Predelli 1998*b*):

(33) If an entire neighbourhood could qualify as an outdoor museum, the Mount Washington district would probably charge admission. *Here*, just Northwest of downtown, are several picture-book expressions of desert culture within a few blocks

'here' does not refer to the location of the author, Ray Riegert, when he wrote (33), or to the location where the guidebook is read. It refers without doubt to the Mount Washington district. Similarly, pointing to Paris on a map one can say:

(34) We spent last weekend *here*

and refer to Paris and not the location at which (34) is uttered. 'Here' can also be used to refer to an imaginary location: watching a movie that takes place on an imaginary distant planet, one can say:

(35) The Martians' ancestors first landed *here*

In other uses, 'here' does not even refer or purport to refer to a spatial location, as in:

(36) *Here* Prokofiev always stops playing

---

[26] Whether one takes the time of the utterance to correspond with the time of writing or the time of producing and/or decoding the message does not matter. In this example 'now' picks out none of these times.   [27] Similar examples can be found in Q. Smith (1989).

for one is likely to mean that Prokofiev stops playing at that particular point in the composition. Notice that one could reach the same goal in using 'now' instead of 'here'.

Examples such as these led Quentin Smith to distinguish between the character of an indexical and a metacharacter or metarule. The former (reference-fixing) rule varies with different uses, whereas the latter remains constant:

> These first-order rules are themselves governed by a second-order rule of use, a *rule-fixing rule of use* or a *metarule*. It is not the reference-fixing rule of use that remains constant from use to use, but the metarule. By remaining constant from context to context, the metarule (or 'metacharacter') is able to determine which reference-fixing rule (character) governs the indexical in each context. (Q. Smith 1989: 168)

In short, Quentin Smith assumes that the temporal indexical 'now' and the spatial indexical 'here' are ambiguous. We have a metarule that helps us choose which of the reference-fixing rules (i.e. which character) comes into play in fixing the reference of the indexical in such-and-such a situation. One could ask whether Quentin Smith's position can be extended to account for words like 'bank'. Do all ambiguous expressions have a metarule to decide which word is used in such-and-such a situation? Could the account also be extended to homonyms? Is there a metarule governing all the reference-fixing rules at work with the name 'Aristotle', i.e. selecting the reference-fixing rule for the philosopher or the reference-fixing rule for Onassis?

One could claim that the Multiple Characters Thesis is unmotivated, for it suffices to assume that 'now' and 'here' are abbreviations of 'this time' and 'this location'. Along these lines, one can argue that they have a Fixed Character which is, nonetheless, less restrictive. If 'now' and 'here' mean something like 'this time' and 'this location', then the examples proposed can be dealt with in postulating a single character. The latter, though, would be less limiting than the character of 'now' and 'here'. In particular, the relevant contextual parameters would not be the time and location of the utterance, but *some* time and location picked out by 'this'. According to this suggestion one need not distinguish, *pace* Quentin Smith, between characters (reference-fixing rules) and metacharacters (metarules) either.

This suggestion, though, blurs the traditional distinction between pure indexicals and demonstratives. As we saw, Kaplan (1977) distinguishes between *pure indexicals* ('I', 'now', 'today', ...) and *demonstratives* ('this', 'she', ...). The former, unlike the latter, do not need a demonstration to secure the reference. To put it in a nutshell, while the reference of a pure indexical is secured by the contextual parameters such as the agent, time, and location of the utterance, the reference of a demonstrative is fixed by these parameters plus something else, such as a pointing gesture, ostension, or demonstration. The Multiple Characters Thesis has the merit of fitting into the pure indexicals/demonstratives distinction. As such, it deserves to be taken seriously. If one believes that pure indexicals reduce to (complex) demonstratives, however, one can avoid paying attention to Smith's position. This, though, is not the position I am defending.

Having said that, the Multiple Characters Thesis does not seem to be a very economical position. We should resist positing ambiguity beyond necessity: a position that accounts for these data without positing ambiguity should be preferred. I will now propose a picture that deals with our data and yet does not give up the Fixed Character Thesis, thus avoiding the need to posit ambiguity. In other words, in assuming the Multiple Characters Thesis, Quentin Smith's position turns out to be more complicated that the position I advocate. In particular, in positing metarules, the Multiple Characters Thesis seems to suggest that a competent speaker masters the metarule and in a given context of use she is able to choose the relevant character to fix the reference. The Fixed Character Thesis, on the other hand, simply suggests that a competent speaker masters the character of the indexical and this capacity is all one needs in order to competently use and understand an indexical expression.

6. The Data and the Fixed Character Thesis

I am now going to show how the Fixed Character Thesis can be defended and yet account for the data proposed in favor of the Multiple Characters Thesis. In doing so, I shall defend the following thesis:

- *The Anaphoric Interpretation Thesis*
  When a use of 'now'/'here' does not select the time/location of the utterance as referent, 'now'/'here' works like an anaphoric term inheriting its reference from another noun phrase.

When 'now' and 'here' are not used as indexicals picking out the time and location of the utterance, they do not have referential independence; they work as anaphors inheriting their value from an antecedent to which they are linked and coindexed. This can easily be illustrated if we consider (26) [In 1834, Jon visited his mother the once famous actress, *now* a sick old woman]. As we have seen, 'now' does not pick out the time of the utterance; it refers to 1834. How does it pick out 1834? The most natural answer is to claim that 'now' works like an anaphoric term, inheriting its reference from '1834'. The reference of 'now' in (26) can thus be viewed as depending upon the antecedent to which it is linked and thus coindexed

('1834'). On this view, we can represent (26)—which I repeat here—as (26a):

(26) In 1834 Jon visited his mother, the once famous actress, *now* a sick old woman

(26) a. In 1834_1 Jon visited his mother, the once famous actress, now_1^d a sick old woman

where the subscripts signal coindexation—and in that case coreferentiality—and the superscript '*d*' signals an NP's referential dependency on the antecedent to which it is coindexed.

Before going further, it may be worth emphasizing that, according to the position I have in mind, an NP is always marked as (semantically) independent or dependent, i.e. $NP^{i/d}$. A proper name is always marked as independent, while an indexical is ambiguous between being independent or dependent. If it is independent, then it is used deictically. If it is dependent, then it is an anaphor (or a bound variable). In the latter case, one must look for an antecedent. Within this framework, anaphoricity is not represented by indices (subscripts), but by dependence/independence markers (superscripts). In other words, I take the superscripts, not the subscripts, to represent anaphoricity/non-anaphoricity, i.e. semantic dependence/independence, not coreference. To illustrate how coindexation (and thus coreference) differs from anaphoricity, we can focus on identity statements. In "Tully = Tully", the two occurrences of the proper name must be coindexed. This is constrained by the grammar of '='. Think of mathematical statements such as "2 + 3 = (2 − 1) + 4", where the two occurrences of '2' must be coindexed. Yet they are not anaphoric upon one another. The correct representation should be "$2_1^i + 3_2^i = (2_1^i - 1_3^i) + 4_4^i$". Since proper names are never anaphoric, they are always referentially *independent*; yet they can be coindexed.

Let us now consider (27) which I repeat here:

(27) Now Hitler begins his invasion of the USSR

Since 'now' does not pick out the time of utterance it must, according to the thesis I propose, function as an anaphor; but then where is the antecedent? According to history, Hitler began his war against Russia on 22 June 1941, so this fact should set the value of 'now'; yet since there is no term in our utterance explicitly referring to 22 June 1941, where could the value of 'now' come from? The solution that comes to my mind is that 'now' inherits its reference from a *tacit initiator*, for it is *presupposed* by the discourse situation that the facts described happened on 22 June 1941.[28]

---

[28] If the lecturer believes that the USSR invasion occurred on 22 June 1942, on the account I have in mind we may face two possibilities. If the lecturer utters '1942', 'now' refers to 1942, but if left silent she refers to 1941, since this is the presupposed date. This does not undermine my picture insofar as I am not committed to the thesis that speaker's intention determines reference. More on this later.

The notion of tacit initiator I have in mind can be spelled out as follows. An anaphor inherits its reference from the NP, the antecedent, to which it is linked. The antecedent fixes the reference and initiates the anaphoric chain. For this reason the antecedent can also be characterized as the initiator of the reference. An anaphoric chain too can be initiated by a tacit reference, in which case the antecedent of the anaphor is not expressed. As such, I characterize it as a *tacit initiator*. I could also characterize it as a *tacit antecedent*. I adopt the following notation: if the antecedent is explicit, the indexical has a non-zero number as a subscript, while if the antecedent is implicit the subscript is a *zero* (NP_0^d). So in our syntax we can represent the whole range of indexical NPs as follows:

- *Indexicals, Index, and Dependence*
  Dependence + (non-zero) number index $\Rightarrow$ anaphora with explicit initiator/antecedent (NP_n^d)
  Dependence + zero index $\Rightarrow$ anaphora with tacit initiator/antecedent (NP_0^d)
  Independence + (non-zero) number index $\Rightarrow$ deictic term (NP_n^i)

We can now return to our example (27). If the lecturer does *not* assume that her students are aware of the importance of this date, she might instead say:

(27) a. It is **22 June 1941**$_0$. Now_0^d Hitler begins his invasion of the USSR

where the bold '22 June 1941' can be viewed as the tacit initiator from which 'now' *qua* anaphoric term inherits its value. It is a platitude that during a linguistic interchange a great deal of information is unexpressed and is conveyed tacitly. Without this phenomenon, communication would be extremely difficult and slow, if not impossible, thus the existence of tacit initiators should not come as a complete surprise. These initiators may be understood as what is taken for granted during a speech act. If a cooperative speaker does not believe that her audience is aware of this presupposed information, she would simply express it in her utterance. Presuppositions are usually viewed as the "part of discourse or speech" denoting propositions whose truth is taken for granted. In uttering, for instance, "Jane's hat is red", one conveys two propositions: the proposition *that Jane has a hat* and the proposition *that it is red*. While the former proposition is presupposed, the latter is asserted. In many cases, however, the presupposed propositions are merely taken for granted and nothing in the utterance itself may trigger or bring them to salience.[29] As an approximation of the phenomenon I have in mind, I follow

[29] For a convincing and detailed account of presuppositions, see Stalnaker: "The distinction between presupposition and assertion should be drawn, not in terms of the content of the proposition expressed, but in terms of the situation in which the statement is made—the attitudes and intentions of the speaker and his audience. Presuppositions, on this account, are something like the background beliefs of the speaker—propositions whose truth he takes for granted, or seems to take for granted, in making his statement" (Stalnaker 1974: 48).

Stalnaker when he argues that:

> The notion of common background belief is the first approximation to the notion of pragmatic presupposition... A proposition *P* is a pragmatic presupposition of a speaker in a given context just in case the speaker assumes or believes that *P*, assumes or believes that his addressee assumes or believes that *P*, and assumes or believes that his addressee recognizes that he is making these assumptions, or has these beliefs. (Stalnaker 1974: 49)

If the speaker does not assume that her audience is aware of the presuppositions in place, she can easily express them; thus, the tacit initiator *could* be expressed by the speaker—this accounts for the difference between (27) and (27a). (27) contains a tacit initiator, whilst (27a) contains an explicit initiator, i.e. that which is presupposed in (27) is made explicit in (27a). Both (27) and (27a) express the proposition *that on 22 June 1941 Hitler begins his invasion of the USSR.*[30]

The same analysis applies to (28)—here repeated—which can be analyzed as (28a):

(28) Now Real Madrid are dictating the pace

(28) a. It is **the 2001 Champions' League final**$_0$. *Now*$_0^d$ Real Madrid are dictating the pace.

Before going further, it is worth mentioning that one could object that my claim (that 'now' and 'here' can work in an anaphoric way) does not do justice to the way anaphors have been traditionally conceived, especially within the generative grammar school. Kripke (1977), Lasnik (1976), and Lewis (1979a), to name but a few, could argue that the anaphoric interpretation I am proposing is nothing but a simple variant of the indexical interpretation. For 'now' and 'here' in the example I discuss work like indexicals picking out an object previously made salient. To be precise, the authors mentioned do not make their point regarding 'now' and 'here'.[31] They are concerned with personal pronouns and claim that when the pronoun 's/he' is not bound, as in:

(37) Jon won the lottery. He is now rich

---

[30] One could object that the notion of a tacit initiator *qua* anaphor's antecedent cannot be explained in terms of pragmatic presuppositions, for the notion of the antecedent of an anaphor belongs to semantics, not pragmatics. This objection rests on the idea that we have a clear-cut distinction between semantics and pragmatics. In the previous chapter I dismissed the existence of a clear-cut distinction. In favor of my skepticism *vis-à-vis* a neat distinction between semantics and pragmatics we can further mention (see Huang 2000) that an exhaustive study of anaphora cannot be done in purely semantic or syntactic terms, insofar as an anaphor's antecedent cannot be selected uniquely on the basis of syntactic and semantic considerations. Pragmatics factors often operate in determining the antecedent of an anaphor. This is particularly evident when one concentrates on Asiatic languages, which rely more heavily on pragmatics than English, Italian, French, etc. I shall discuss this issue in more detail in Ch. 8, below.

[31] As we shall soon see, Predelli (1998*b*) can be interpreted as adopting this stance to the case of 'here' and 'now'.

it does not work like an anaphor. It merely works like a demonstrative referring to an object previously made salient. In some cases, the referent of a demonstrative such as 's/he' is made salient by a pointing gesture. In other cases, as in our example, it is made salient by a previous string of the discourse. Yet, in some other cases, the relevant object may be made salient by the setting in which the linguistic episode takes place. Let us imagine, for instance, that Mary and Jane both dislike Jon and that they are both aware of each other's antipathy *vis-à-vis* Jon. During a meeting, after several men (including Jon) have left, Mary can tell Sue that:

(38) We can be relieved now that he has gone.

Given the discourse situation, 'he' refers to Jon even if Jon is not present to be demonstrated or has not been previously raised to salience by the use of an NP.

It should be stressed that if one adopts the Kripke–Lasnik–Lewis attitude to the case of 'now' and 'here', one undermines the distinction between pure indexicals and demonstratives. As we have seen, the character of a demonstrative is incomplete and the demonstrative refers to whatever the act of directing attention directs us toward. A pure indexical, on the other hand, does not need a pointing gesture or an act of directing attention to select a referent. The utterance itself gives us all the relevant contextual parameters (time, location, and agent) needed to secure their reference: reference is automatic. If one claims that 'now' and 'here' refer to a time and location previously raised to salience in the example I proposed, then 'now' and 'here' do not refer to the time and location of the utterance. As such, they do not work like pure indexicals, but instead like demonstratives. The position I am proposing, on the other hand, can handle the examples discussed without giving up the pure indexical/demonstrative distinction.

Before going further, it may be useful to stress that, unlike the third-person pronoun 's/he', 'now' and 'here' cannot act as bound anaphors. They cannot behave as bound variables either. Consider:

(39) a. Jane won the lottery and *she* is rich
     b. Jane thinks that *she* is rich

In (39a) 'she' is not bound by 'Jane', whereas it is in (39b). To stress this point we can replace 'Jane' by a quantifier. We would thus have:

(39) c. Everyone won the lottery and *she* is rich
     d. Everyone thinks that *she* (herself) is rich

In (39c) 'she' is not bound by the quantifier 'everyone': it works like a free variable, while in (39d) it is bound and works as a bound variable.[32] If we consider 'here' and

---

[32] Actually, (39c) and (39d) would be regimented as follows:

(39) e. $\forall x(x$ won the lottery$)$ & y is rich
     f. $\forall x(x$ thinks that x is rich$)$

'now', they are never bound the way 'she' can be in (39b). Thus, if 'here' and 'now' work as anaphoric terms, they are *unbound* anaphors.[33] Some pronouns cannot be bound either. Yet, the intuitive and default interpretation of the plural pronouns 'them' and 'we' in:

(40) a. Jon said that Sue expected *them* to win the competition
b. I told Jane that *we* won the lottery

is the anaphoric one. The natural and default interpretation of 'them' in (40a) is that it is anaphoric on 'Sue' and 'Jon', while the default interpretation of 'we' in (40b) is that it is anaphoric on 'I' and 'Jane'. Yet, they are unbound—pronouns can never be bound by split antecedents.[34] They are unbound anaphors: (40a–b) could be represented as:

(40) c. Jon$_1{}^i$ said that Sue$_2{}^i$ expected *them*$_{1}{}^d{}_{+2}{}^d$ to win the competition
d. I$_1{}^i$ told Jane$_2{}^i$ that *we*$_1{}^d{}_{+2}{}^d$ won the lottery

To be sure, one could still claim that even in this case 'them' does not work in an anaphoric way, but instead works as a demonstrative selecting Jon and Sue as referent because they have previously been raised to salience. The same consideration would apply for 'we' in (40b). In that case, a representation like (40c) and (40d) would not be appropriate, for the superscript 'd' signals that the pronoun is referentially *dependent*, i.e. that it inherits its reference from another/other NP(s).

Needless to say, in the case of unbound anaphora the anaphoric chain is not merely syntactically constrained: semantic and pragmatic considerations also enter the picture.[35] On this issue one can quote recent studies, notably Huang

---

[33] In particular, they do not fall into the category of anaphors according to the principles A, B, and C of Binding Theory. At least as it has been first proposed by Chomsky 1981 (for a clear presentation of Chomsky's Government and Binding Theory see Haegeman 1994):

Principle A: anaphors must be bound in their governing category.
Principle B: pronouns must be free in their governing category.
Principle C: other NPs must be free in all categories.

I shall discuss further these principles in Ch. 8, Sect. 4, below.

[34] "Although pronouns with split antecedents are coindexed with those antecedents, they are never bound by them. This predicts that the distribution of split antecedents will not be limited by Binding Theory" (Fiengo and May 1994: 39).

[35] As an example of a pragmatic constraint on anaphora we can quote *the general pattern of anaphora*, i.e. the fact that "reduced, semantically general anaphoric expressions tend to favour locally coreferential interpretations; full, semantically specific anaphoric expressions tend to favour locally non-coreferential interpretations" (Huang 2000: 214). As examples, consider the following contrasts:

(i) a. Mozart$_1{}^i$ adored his$_{1/2}{}^d$ music
b. He$_1{}^i$ adored Mozart's$_{2/*1}{}^d$ music
(ii) a. The bus$_1{}^i$ came trundling round the bend. The vehicle$_1{}^d$ almost flattened a pedestrian
b. The vehicle$_1{}^i$ came trundling round the bend. The bus$_{2/*1}{}^d$ almost flattened a pedestrian

(2000), which convincingly show that:

(i) syntax, and pragmatics are interconnected to determine many of the processes of anaphora that are thought to fall within the province of grammar, and (ii) the extent to which syntax, semantics, and pragmatics interact varies typologically. (Huang 2000: 205)

There seems to exist a class of languages (such as Chinese, Japanese, and Korean) where pragmatics appears to play a central role which in familiar European languages (such as English, French, and German) has hitherto been alleged to be played by grammar. In these 'pragmatic' languages, many of the constraints on the alleged grammatical processes are in fact primarily due to principles of language use rather than rules of grammatical structure. (Huang 2000: 213)

Be that as it may, if one follows my proposal and accepts the existence of unbound anaphors *inheriting* their reference from other NPs, one can maintain that 'now' and 'here' are systematically ambiguous: they are either pure indexicals or unbound anaphors. On the other hand, one could claim that coreferentiality (and thus coindexation) in the examples I proposed is somewhat accidental, i.e. the relevant NP is coreferential with another NP not by virtue of inheriting its reference but simply because the latter has been previously raised to salience (they are thus referentially *independent*). One is then forced to embrace the thesis that 'now' and 'here' in the example discussed, like all alleged unbound anaphors, actually work like demonstrative expressions selecting as referent a location and time differing from the time and location of the utterance. To summarize, the anaphoric interpretation I proposed, unlike the demonstrative interpretation: (i) maintains that there is a structural difference between unbound anaphora and demonstrative reference (the former is referentially dependent while the latter is referentially independent) and (ii) fits within the distinction between pure indexicals and demonstratives. Besides, as we shall soon see, the position I advocate does not commit itself to the view that 'now' and 'here' are contextually ambiguous. The anaphoric interpretation is thus cheaper than the demonstrative interpretation. Concerning tacit initiators it should also be pointed out that there are many potential initiators that could successfully fulfill the communicative aim. The position I put forward can also be stated as follows: utterances like (27) and (28) are short cuts to utterances like (27a) and (28a). Indeed, there is no one single way in which the former utterances can be successfully completed. (28) could also be successfully completed as:

(28) b. It is **15 May 2001, the Champions' League final match**$_0$. Now_0^d Real Madrid is dictating the pace

Before going further it is worth mentioning that one could claim, along with Predelli, for instance, that the relevant contextual parameter to which the character of 'now' and 'here' is sensitive is not the location and time of the utterance, but an intentional time and/or location. One could thus maintain that the referent of 'now' and 'here' corresponds to the *intended* contextual parameter. In that case, the character takes as argument a relevant contextual aspect and gives as value the relevant (intended) referent. Thus, the contextual parameters to which 'now' and 'here' are sensitive may differ from the time and location of the utterance and so their referent may also differ from the location and/or time where the utterance occurs.[36] Although this position does not distinguish between the indexical and the anaphoric use of 'now' and 'here', like the position I attribute to Kripke, Lasnik and Lewis, it commits itself to the view that a single token of 'now'/'here' may be sensitive, in principle, to infinitely many contexts (times and locations). Since the relevant time and location *qua* parameters of 'now' and 'here' may differ from the time and location of the utterance, they must be contextually furnished. Following this suggestion, 'now' and 'here' can be viewed as contextually ambiguous. The ambiguity of the indexicals is not at the level of character but at the level of context.

The position I propose presents the following advantage over the position advocated by Predelli and the position I attribute to Kripke, Lasnik, and Lewis. On my view 'now', 'here' (and similar indexicals) can be used either as indexicals or as anaphoric terms. As such, they are systematically ambiguous, but their ambiguity rests on their being used either deictically *or* anaphorically. It does not rest on a multiplicity of contexts.[37] Hence, the position I advocate multiplies neither contexts nor characters. It simply rests upon an existing common phenomenon, the phenomenon I characterized as unbound anaphora (sometimes also labeled cross-sentential or discourse anaphora). For instance, "Mary$_1^i$ believes that she$_1^d$ is lucky" contains an intra-sentential anaphora, whilst in "Jon$_1^i$ won a million dollars last night in Monte Carlo. Even though he$_1^d$ won all that money, he$_1^d$ was still not very pleased", we have a case of cross-sentential or intersentential or discourse anaphor, i.e. the anaphor 'he' inherits its value from an antecedent, 'Jon', appearing in another sentence.

Since the picture I defend appeals to existing phenomena, it comes more cheaply than the position claiming that indexicals are contextually ambiguous. Thus, the very same argument I used against Quentin Smith's position (which multiplies characters and thus violates Ockham's razor by positing unnecessary ambiguities) can be used against the Kripke–Lasnik–Lewis–Predelli position. The

---

[36] Predelli (1998*b*) defends a position similar to this. On his account, 'now' and 'here' may not refer to the time and location of utterance, for they can be sensitive to an *intentional context*, which may differ from the context of utterance. Following Predelli's position, the characters of 'now' and 'here', for instance, are sensitive to intentional parameters. He thus rejects the thesis that contextual parameters such as time and location are always identical to the time and location of the utterance.

[37] Insofar as the present tense is interpreted using 'now', we can claim that it can work in an anaphoric way as well. If, watching a video, one claims that "Arsenal are dominating the game", the present tense can be viewed as anaphoric on a tacit initiator referring to the time the game was played. No doubt more should be said on this issue, but time and space prevent me from discussing it any further.

latter views posit ambiguities by multiplying contexts. To be sure, this position accepts the Fixed Character view, but it handles the data in multiplying the contexts that these characters can operate in. The relevant context may thus differ from the context of utterance. The moral is that the Kripke-Lasnik-Lewis-Predelli view also violates a principle of parsimony and Ockham's razor, by multiplying contexts and ambiguities beyond necessity (just as Smith's view multiplies characters and ambiguities beyond necessity). To put it in a nutshell, the conception I propose presents an advantage over the Kripke–Lasnik–Lewis–Predelli position by being more economical and positing less ambiguity (the very same advantage it has *vis-à-vis* Quentin Smith's Multiple Characters view).

As I have already mentioned, if our aim is to understand and explain communicative interaction, we must take into consideration discourse anaphora, which may extend beyond utterances of a single speaker. Hence we should also consider *interpersonal* anaphora, for it is not uncommon that, in everyday communication, anaphors that inherit their reference from an antecedent uttered by someone else are often used. Consider:

(41) Mary: "I'll be in Paris$_1$ on New Year Eve"
Jon: "I'll be there$_1^d$ anxiously waiting for you"

In this case, 'there' *qua* anaphora inherits its reference from a token made by someone else, Mary. If we consider a telephone conversation such as:

(42) Mary (in Paris): "It is still snowing"
Jon (in Lyons): "In that case, I won't be able to be there$_0^d$ before midnight"

we have 'there' inheriting its reference, *Paris*, from another phrase. In that other phrase, though, the reference to Paris is not explicitly made—it is for this reason that the pronoun 'there' has '0' as a subscript. Mary *tacitly* refers to Paris. To borrow Perry's (1986) terminology, *Paris* is an unarticulated constituent of what Mary says. If Mary uttered, "It is still snowing *here*", Paris would be an articulated constituent of what she says and 'there' would be anaphoric and coreferential with 'here'.[38] Cases like this suggest that we do have anaphors inheriting their value from a tacit initiator. I do not see how (42) could be interpreted without taking 'there' to be anaphoric on (and coreferential with) a presupposed tacit term referring to Paris. As we saw in Chapter 3, the best way to understand meteorological terms is to claim that they are two-place predicates, taking as arguments a time and a location, for when it rains/snows/ thunders . . . it must do so at some location and at some time. The location may be viewed as the subject undergoing the meteorological change. If, as I suggested, we adopt the notion of *Theta-Role* (θ-*Role*), the lexical information associated with a lexical item specifies the syntactic category by which the thematic roles are realized. Meteorological verbs θ-mark the subject,

[38] For a more detailed discussion of unarticulated constituents see Ch. 2, above, esp. Sects. 1 and 3.

which must be a location, *viz.* its thematic role must be a location. Given this platitude, a dialogue such as (42) can be represented as follows:

(42) a. Mary (in Paris): "It is still snowing (l_1)"
Jon (in Lyons): "In that case I won't be able to be *there*$_1^d$ before midnight"

where 'l_1' is an argument for a location, in our case Paris, on which 'there' is anaphoric. If one takes into account the phenomenon of tacit reference, tacit initiators should not come as a surprise. Tacit reference and tacit initiators go hand in hand: without tacit reference we would not get tacit initiators. Moreover, we should distinguish between *conceptually* underdetermined and *semantically* underdetermined utterances. A conceptually underdetermined utterance may either be semantically determined, i.e. complete (e.g. "Jon is late" (for what?), "Jane is not strong enough" (for what?), "Mary is too old" (for what?)) or semantically underdetermined (e.g. "It is raining" (where?), "It is 4.15 p.m." (in which time zone?)). For the utterance of a sentence like "It is raining" to be true/false, a location must be furnished; one can claim that, at the level of logical form or underlying grammar, we have implicit arguments that trigger the semantic interpretation and completion.[39] These implicit arguments, like in (35a), can act as tacit initiators. In the case of conceptually underdetermined but semantically determined utterances, the tacit initiator is more likely to be an implicit term standing for the presupposed object of discourse. Cases where anaphors inherit their value from tacit initiators are not confined to spatial and temporal indexicals. In:

(43) Jane is hoping for a baby, whereas *he*$_0^d$ is far from excited by the idea

'he' seems to inherit its value from a tacit initiator ('Jane's partner/husband/...' would suffice), for the speaker of (36) tacitly refers to Jane's partner. 'Jane' is relevant in helping the audience to select Jane's partner/husband/... as the object of discourse and thus in bringing to salience the referent the tacit initiator stands for.

The same analysis applies to cases of reference to an imaginary time, such as (30). Treating the 'now' that picks out an imaginary time as anaphoric on an antecedent referring to an imaginary time, (30)—repeated here—can be analyzed as (30a):

(30) Is this happening *now*?
(30) a. In the play, there is **an imaginary time** t_1. Is this happening *now*$_1^d$?[40]

Notice that the imaginary time need not be specified, for it can be quantified over.

---

[39] In terms of propositions, the situation can be summarized as follows. A propositional constituent may be the value of: (i) a phonetically realized element of an utterance, i.e. a spoken or written element, (ii) a phonetically unrealized element of an utterance, i.e. an unspoken or unwritten element, present nonetheless at the level of logical form as an implicit argument, (iii) a phonetically unrealized element of an utterance, i.e. an unspoken or unwritten element, not present at the level of logical form as an implicit argument.

[40] One could claim that (30a) is unnatural and artificial and that 'now' should be replaced by 'then'. In that case the fact that the original 'now' in (30) works like an anaphora is even more striking.

166 *Demonstratives and Indexicals*

A similar story can be told about 'here'. In (33)—repeated here—'here' is anaphoric on 'the Mount Washington district' and it could thus be represented as:

(33) a. If an entire neighborhood could qualify as an outdoor museum, [the Mount Washington district]$_1$ would probably charge admission. $Here_1^d$, just Northwest of downtown, are several picture-book expressions of desert culture within a few blocks

The same goes for cases like (35), where the speaker refers to an imaginary location. (35) can be interpreted as:

(35) a. This/that is **the imaginary planet XY**$_1$. $Here_1^d$ is where the Martians' ancestors first landed.

To stress this anaphoric interpretation, one can also claim that in such cases 'here' goes proxy for 'there' and that (35a) is equivalent to (35b):

(35) b. This/that is **the imaginary planet XY**$_1$. $There_1^d$ is where the Martians' ancestors first landed.

(35a) and (35b) express the proposition *that the Martians' ancestors first landed on the imaginary planet XY*.

In the case of pointing to a map (say pointing to the spot representing Paris) and saying 'here', one can think of 'here' as going proxy for 'this location' and thus that 'here' is used as a demonstrative picking out the demonstrated location, instead of picking out the location where the utterance occurs. The anaphoric interpretation, however, allows us to reach the very same conclusion without supposing that 'here' works as a demonstrative. For it can be argued that 'here' works as an anaphora, and that an utterance like (10) should be analyzed as:

(34) a. **This/that location**$_1$ is/represents/ . . . Paris. We spent last weekend $here_1^d$

Similarly, we can stress the anaphoric reading, taking (34a) as equivalent to (34b):

(34) b. **This/that location**$_1$ is/represents/ . . . Paris. We spent last weekend $there_1^d$

where 'there' stresses the anaphoric interpretation. (34a) and (34b) express the proposition *that we spent last weekend in Paris*.

When 'now' and 'here' are not used to pick out a time and location, they belong to the idiomatic use of language, i.e. that peculiar use which cannot be captured by a general rule. As such they do not work in their usual, indexical, way to single out the time/location of the utterance. It is for this reason that 'now' and 'here' are often interchangeable without any loss or gain in a communication. My *New Shorter Oxford Dictionary* reads "at this point in an argument, a situation, etc.; at this juncture" under the entry for 'here', while the entry for 'now' reads, "at an important or noteworthy place in an argument or proof or in a series of statements".[41] Again, even in these cases, 'now' and 'here' can be interpreted as anaphors; (32) and (36) can be analyzed as:

(32) a. We are **at this point of the argument/proof/** ...$_1$. Now/here$_0^d$ I am going to prove lemma Σ

(36) b. We are **at this point of the sonata/concert/** ...$_1$. Here/now$_0^d$ Prokofiev always stops playing

It is worth noticing that, if one favors the Multiple Characters Thesis, one must be able to spell out the different characters *qua* reference-fixing rules at play in different examples. Since there is (logically) an infinite number of such examples, one ends up with an infinite number of characters. How can we supply all the characters needed to account for the variegated uses of 'now' and 'here'? It could be objected that the Multiple Characters Thesis does not presuppose a different reference-fixing rule (character) for *each* specific example. Actually, Quentin Smith claims that the metarule delimits *sorts* of contexts in such a way that for each context delimited a corresponding fixing rule is also delimited. As an example, we can quote historical context. In that case a single fixing-rule suffices.[42] Along these lines one can claim that there is only a finite number of fixing-rules. The characters vary according to each different *kind* of example, not with each specific example. The first question that comes to mind is how to group an infinite number of possible examples into kinds. That is to say, how do we group the various examples together? Even in assuming that we have a definite number of kinds and that each specific case can easily be classified as one kind or another, a question remains to be answered. How could one possibly come to master the use of these indexicals? One could, following Quentin Smith, argue that there is a single metarule or metacharacter that must be mastered and that it is this fixed rule that selects, in different occasions of use, the character *qua* reference-fixing rule. A question seems to remain: How does this metacharacter select the reference-fixing character? Quentin Smith's answer should be: by directing the speaker/hearer toward the kind of context which will enable him to select the relevant character. This picture commits itself to the view that a competent speaker must master several

[41] If I am right in considering these examples as idiomatic uses of language, it may be better not to treat them in the same way as the other examples. It is by mere accident that we use spatio-temporal terms to describe non-temporal items. Is it simply because it takes time to run through a proof or a sonata that we adopt the temporal framework. When the proof and sonata are written, we adopt the spatial framework for similar reasons. These phenomena are linked to our cognitive architecture; they are not intrinsic to the semantics of our language. Thanks to Predelli for this suggestion.

[42] In that case the reference-fixing rule for 'now' would be: " 'Now' refers to the historical time the context indicates the speaker/writer wishes to emphasise and take as the chronological point of reference of the event reported in the other relevant portions of the discourse" (Q. Smith 1989: 177).

rules governing the use of indexicals. This may not be a knockdown argument, but a picture suggesting that a competent speaker must master a single rule or character should be preferred insofar as it would be *cognitively* more economical.

Following the Kaplanian picture, an indexical's character can be represented as a function taking as argument the context and giving as value the content or referent. In the case of 'I', for instance, its character will be represented by a rule such as: "The referent of 'I' is the speaker and/or writer". In a more formal way:

- C-'I'

    an individual *i* is the semantic value of 'I' with respect to a context of utterance *c* iff *i* is the *agent* of *c*,[43]

whilst the character of 'now' and 'here' can be represented by the rules:

- C-'now'

    a time *t* is the semantic value of 'now' with respect to a context of utterance *c* iff *t* is the *time* of *c*

- C-'here'

    a location *l* is the semantic value of 'here' with respect to a context of utterance *c* iff *l* is the *location* of *c*

In all other cases, when the referent of 'now' and 'here' is not the time or location of the context of utterance, 'now' and 'here' do *not* work as indexicals, but instead as anaphors. This fact should not come as a surprise, for the pronouns 'he', 'she', 'they', etc. can also work both as indexicals and as anaphoric terms. In:

(44) *She* [pointing toward Jane] is my favorite student

'she' is an indexical, while in:

(45) Jane$_1$ is very bright; she$_1^d$ is my favorite student

'she' acts as an anaphor and is thus coreferential with 'Jane', the antecedent, from which it inherits its semantic value.

Before going further it may be worth mentioning that the solution I suggested enabling us to explain away the Multiple Characters thesis also allows us to deal with

---

[43] It may be worth mentioning that the agent may not be the writer or speaker. In the case of answering machines and similar devices, the agent need not be the writer/speaker of the playback message. One may, for instance, use an answering machine message recorded by someone else, or one can use a post-it note written by someone else. In cases like these, the time and place of the utterance are rarely the time and place the token is produced; one makes an utterance at a distance or, to borrow Sidelle's (1991) terminology, one makes a deferred utterance. In the case of an answering machine, the time of the utterance corresponds with the time the recorded message is played back and the place corresponds to the location it is played, while in the case of post-it notes the place/time of utterance corresponds to the place/time the note is read. In a postcard, on the other hand, the time picked out by the indexical is likely to be the time of the production of the message.

a recent attempt put forward in favor of the thesis that complex demonstratives are quantified expressions (see King 2001). One of King's main arguments in favor of the quantificational account concerns the use of complex demonstratives when the referent is not present in the speaker and/or audience perceptual field. King terms these uses the *non demonstration no speaker reference use*. Paradigmatic examples are:

(46) a. *That hominid* who discovered how to start fire is a genius
b. *That student who scored one hundred in the exam* is a genius

where one uses a complex demonstrative without being or having been in perceptual contact with the referent (and thus without having a specific individual in mind). One way to accommodate such uses without giving up the thesis that complex demonstratives are singular terms contributing the referent into the proposition expressed (the official proposition) would be to treat them as instances of so-called *deferred reference* or deferred demonstration (e.g. when one points to Jane's office door and says "She is not in today" to convey that Jane is not in, or when one points to a Ferrari and says "He must be rich", intending to convey that the owner of that car must be rich, or again when one points to a footprint and says, "He must have been a giant"). In the first case, the speaker has a specific individual in mind, Jane, while in the second and third cases she uses 'he' in an "attributive" way. All these cases, though, involve deferred reference. With the case of deferred reference one may express a singular proposition or a general proposition. In the Sue case one expresses the singular proposition having Sue as constituent while in the Ferrari case one expresses a general proposition. The constituent singled out by 'he' is not an individual but the condition of being the owner of the Ferrari that the alleged referent must satisfy.

The speaker does not refer to the office door or the Ferrari, yet the pronouns 'she' and 'he' do not seem to be used as quantified terms. So, whatever story one may tell about the treatment of deferred reference, the very same story can be told about the no demonstration no speaker reference use. One way to deal with deferred reference is to argue that two distinct propositions are expressed, one of which is entailed or presupposed by the discourse situation. When one points to a footprint, one often intends to talk about the individual who left it (but not always: if a bear hunter says "It is fresh", she probably intends to refer to the footprint itself, not to the bear that left it). In the paradigmatic case, one "expresses" two propositions: the (presupposed) general proposition *that there is a specific individual who left the footprint* and the proposition *that it is a giant*. The value of the pronoun 'it' corresponds to the individual, whoever it happens to be, who left the footprint. In cases like these, the pronoun can be viewed as an anaphor, inheriting its reference from a *tacit* initiator. The same story can be told for (46). An utterance like (46a), for instance, expresses (or presupposes) the proposition *that there is a unique hominid who discovered fire* and expresses the proposition that *that hominid must have been a genius*. The complex demonstrative works like an anaphora, inheriting its value from the tacit initiator 'the hominid who discovered fire'. Since it inherits its value from a definite description it will not contribute to the expression of a singular proposition. The fact that in these cases a complex demonstrative does not contribute to the expression of a singular proposition does not campaign, though, in favor of the thesis that complex demonstratives are quantified expression. All it proves is that when a complex demonstrative *qua* anaphoric term inherits its value from a quantified term, say a definite description, then it contributes to the expression of a general proposition. This parallels the case when a pronoun, say 's/he', inherits its value from a quantified expression, as in the Ferrari example. The main point I am trying to make is that the multiple-propositions view I proposed in the previous chapter enables us to explain how there might be demonstrative uses that do not require perceptual experiences. Such uses should be understood alongside uses of anaphors. Like the latter they may contribute in the expression of singular proposition or general proposition depending on the nature of the antecedent they inherit their value from. In "Jon visited us last night. That charming man almost convinced us to buy his old car", the 'that'-phrase 'that charming man' being anaphoric on 'Jon' contributes to the expression of a singular proposition insofar as it inherits its value from the NP 'Jon'.

You may recall that according to the multiple-propositions view I proposed in Chapter 3, an utterance such as 'That F is G', uttered demonstrating object *o*, expresses two *singular* propositions: *that o is F* and the distinct proposition *that o is G*. In the case of no demonstration no speaker reference, an utterance like 'That F is G' expresses both the *general* proposition *that there is a (unique) F* and the *(general)* proposition *that it is G*. One could thus object that, on the account I propose, complex demonstratives are not singular terms in the case of no demonstration no speaker reference, for such utterances express general propositions. Moreover, since I advocate the view that in one case a complex demonstrative contributes to the expression of a singular proposition (and thus it is a singular term) and in the other it contributes to the expression of a general, quantified, proposition (and thus it is not a singular term), one can also claim that I commit myself to the view that complex demonstratives are ambiguous expressions.

My reaction to the ambiguity objection is that complex demonstratives should be viewed on a par with pronouns. Just as the pronoun 's/he' can have two interpretations, i.e. it can be either a demonstrative or an anaphora, a complex demonstrative can act either as a singular term (expressing a singular proposition) or as an anaphora linked either to a singular term (and thus contributing to the expression of a singular proposition) or linked to a quantified expression (and thus contributing to the expression of a general proposition). The latter, as we have seen, is the interpretation I propose for the no demonstrative no speaker reference use of complex demonstratives. Complex demonstratives, like pronouns, can play two different syntactic roles: they can be referentially independent (i.e. work like demonstratives) or referentially dependent (i.e. work like anaphors).

7. Some Advantages of the Fixed Character Thesis over the Multiple Characters Thesis

We can summarize the competing positions I presented as follows. While the Multiple Characters Thesis distinguishes between character *qua* reference-fixing rule and metacharacter, the Fixed Character position distinguishes between indexical uses and anaphoric uses and further claims that this distinction is not confined to pronouns; it applies to the whole spectrum of indexicals.

A central problem for the Multiple Characters position is to spell out what the metacharacter or metarule of 'now' and 'here' is:

> The fact that each of these rules and the corresponding sort of context are delimited by the metarule implies that the metarule is considerably complex. This need not daunt us, however, for the mastery of this metarule by a language-user does not require the user to be able to explicitly formulate or verbalize this metarule. Clearly we do not "run though in our mind" this metarule on each occasion that 'now' is used. Rather, this metarule is implicitly comprehended and its comprehension is normally evinced by our ability to determine correctly which reference-fixing rule governs 'now' on any particular occasion of use, a determination that is itself evinced by our grasp of the referent of 'now' on that occasion. (Q. Smith 1989: 178)

A competent speaker need not be able to spell out the linguistic rules she follows, for her linguistic capacity or mastery is manifested in the way she actually (successfully) follows these rules. Nonetheless, the semanticist or linguist may wish to spell them out. A story must be told to explain why, on a given occasion, the metarule selects one specific reference-fixing rule and not another. This task, too, may turn out to be more complicated than at first thought, for there are many reference-fixing rules.

If one adopts the Fixed Character picture I proposed, one does not need to posit metarules or multiple reference-fixing rules. A single simple rule, such as those presented in Section 6, suffices. There is only one other way a temporal indexical like 'now', or a spatial indexical like 'here', can work: when 'here' and 'now' do not select as referent the time/location of the utterance, they work as anaphors.

172 *Demonstratives and Indexicals*

It is not difficult, however, to propose grammatical rules governing anaphoric terms, for the very same rules governing anaphoric uses of 'she', 'it', 'they', etc. will also govern anaphoric uses of 'now' and 'here'. In our semantics, we already have all we need.[44] Without entering into detail, we can say that there are simple constraints at work (such as the one I indicated in introducing the superscript '*d*' to signal semantic dependence).

One could object that, while the Multiple Characters supporter posits a complicated metarule and several reference-fixing rules, I posit tacit initiators, for in many utterances there is no expressed NP from which the alleged anaphoric term can inherit a semantic value. This may be seen as the major problem I face; perhaps the Fixed Character Thesis I defend does not come cheaper than the Multiple Characters Thesis defended by Quentin Smith. But is this really an insurmountable difficulty? In particular, would the existence of tacit initiators make the Fixed Character position I present less economical than the Multiple Characters position, which posits a metarule and several reference-fixing rules?

It is worth emphasizing that the Multiple Characters Thesis assumes that, in a specific situation, the speaker and hearer can easily select the reference-fixing rule at work. This capacity is manifested in the way the speaker and her audience succeed in singling out the relevant referent. I have no objection to this assumption; indeed, most of the time the speaker and audience do not face any difficulty individuating the relevant referent and succeeding in their communicative interaction. However, the question remains: do they succeed because they tacitly master a metarule *or* do they succeed simply because the relevant information is presupposed and taken for granted? Is their success due to selection of the right reference-fixing rule *or* because the presence of a tacit initiator, from which 'now' and 'here' *qua* anaphors inherit their reference, is taken for granted? After all, if we ask the speaker and audience to make explicit what they tacitly presupposed, they certainly end up uttering the tacit initiator or a similar, equivalent, term. The analysis I have proposed captures this fact in an elegant way, for the tacit initiator is an NP referring to the object the speaker and her audience intend to talk about.[45] I do not commit myself to the view that there must be a specific tacit initiator. There are and can be many tacit initiators selecting the relevant referent.

The advantage of the Fixed Character position I defend over the Multiple Characters position can be summarized as follows: the Fixed Character Thesis

---

[44] For the sake of my argument I do not need to commit myself to a specific theory of anaphora. A satisfactory theory of cross-sentential anaphora will do the job required.

[45] As we saw, though, the referent may not correspond with the object the speaker and/or audience intend to talk about. If one falsely believes that today is 1 May 2002, in using 'today' or tacitly referring to the day of utterance one picks out the day of the utterance even if the latter differs from the day one intends to talk about.

does not appeal to several reference-fixing rules. All that needs to be spelt out are the reference-fixing rules for 'now' and 'here' and an appeal to a theory of discourse anaphora. We do need the latter for independent reasons; we need a theory of discourse anaphora to handle cases where, in a discourse, people keep track of objects and individuals using anaphors. I have not spelt out the details of a theory of discourse anaphora, for it suffices to say that a correct theory would do the job required. My argument regarding the introduction of tacit initiators to handle the data proposed in favor of the Multiple Characters Thesis does not rest on and does not presuppose a specific theory of discourse anaphora.

Both the rules governing indexicals and those governing anaphors are needed in order to account for the phenomenon of indexicality in general. Since we already have in place the distinction between indexicals and anaphors, we do not have to complicate our semantics by assuming that temporal and spatial indexicals such as 'now' and 'here' force a distinction between metacharacter and character. These indexicals are not, *pace* Quentin Smith, ambiguous expressions. They have a simple and single character. In some cases, however, they work as anaphors. This notion, as we have seen, is all we need to account for the data advanced in favor of the Multiple Characters position.

In the next chapter we shall concentrate on the first-person pronoun 'I', the way we learn to use it and how it functions. By examining the way in which use of the first-person pronoun is mastered, we will bring to light the fact that essential indexicals go hand-in-hand with quasi-indicators. Furthermore, it will help us to put forward ideas in favor of the simulation view which will be explored in Chapter 7. In examining the way one comes to master the use of 'I' and the way it works both in our linguistic and thinking activities, we will also reinforce the thesis that quasi-indexicality plays a prominent role in our cognitive development and linguistic practice. In particular, it will help us to understand how we manage to grasp other people's indexical thoughts and thus how we manage to capture other people's perspectives.

5

The First-Person Pronoun

> Not long ago, after a tiring railway journey by night, when I was very tired, I got into an omnibus, just as another man appeared at the other end. "What a shabby pedagogue that is, that has just entered", thought I. It was myself: opposite me hung a large mirror. The physiognomy of my class, accordingly, was better known to me than my own.
>
> (Mach 1914: n. 4)

> Car Je est un autre. . . . Cela m'est évident: j'assiste à l'éclosion de ma pensée: je la regarde, je l'écoute: je lance un coup d'archet: la symphonie fait son remuement dans les profondeurs, ou vient d'un bond sur la scène.
>
> (Rimbaud [1871] 1972: 250)[1]

In this chapter, I focus on the first-person pronoun and, in particular, on its semantic properties. I will not, however, avoid discussing how it relates to one's psychological states and egocentricity and I will defend the view that someone's self-consciousness is demonstrated in mastering the use of the first-person pronoun.

I proceed as follows. In Section 1, I present arguments in favor of the thesis that one conceives of oneself as a person insofar as one masters the use of 'I' and other personal pronouns. In Section 2, I discuss Kaplan's conception of the meaning of the first-person pronoun. In Section 3, I discuss and explain away a popular attempt to reject the thesis that 'I' is a referring expression. I discuss Anscombe's argument in some detail and show that it fails. In Section 4, I introduce and discuss cases (e.g. answering machines and post-it notes) that seem to jeopardize the Kaplanian framework introduced in Section 2. I focus on Sidelle's answering machine paradox and his *deferred utterance* method of resolving this puzzle. In Section 5, I show how Kaplan's framework needs to be amended to accommodate such cases. It will be shown that the referent of 'I' may not, *pace* Kaplan, be the

---

[1] "For I is someone else. . . . That much is clear to me: I am a spectator at the blossoming of my own thought: I look at it and listen to it: I make a sweep with the bow and down in the depths the symphony begins to stir or comes in one leap upon the stage."

speaker/writer. In this section a novel version of the answering machine paradox, which suggests that, in certain cases, Kaplan's identification of utterer, agent, and referent of 'I' breaks down, will be proposed. In Section 6, I discuss an intentionalist solution and focus on Predelli's revision of the Kaplanian picture, which appeals to the intentions of the utterer. It will be argued that this picture is committed to problematic consequences and, therefore, should be avoided. In Section 7, I propose an anti-intentionalist solution to the allegedly problematic cases. It will be shown that the referent of 'I' is the agent, although the agent may differ from the speaker/writer. The agent is conventionally furnished. The conventionalist picture that emerges fits the considerations about context proposed in Chapter 2. Finally, in Section 8, I show how the conventionalist picture fits within the framework of direct reference and how it helps explain away worries one might have. In doing so, it will also be shown that the conventionalist picture is able to explain the scenario which motivated Predelli's account, without appealing to speaker intentions.

1. The (De)Construction of the Self

It is interesting that an expression such as 'self' has captured so much attention amongst philosophers, psychologists, and linguists. All this attention rests on good and sound reasons.

From a grammatical viewpoint, 'self' is a word which, coupled with possessive pronouns—e.g. 'her', 'your', 'our'—forms *reflexive* pronouns. Consider:

(1) Jane found *her* car

'Her' *qua* possessive pronoun is a relation relating 'Jane' and 'car' and the meaning of 'her' conveys possession, i.e. the fact that Jane is the possessor of the car. When 'her' is coupled with the reflexive 'self', we obtain utterances such as:

(2) Jane found her*self* a car

In this case, 'self' is a relation holding between something and itself. In our example, it is an *identity* relation holding between Jane and herself. But it is a particular relation. In:

(3) Jane found Mark a car

the agent is Jane while the patient is Mark. On the other hand, when 'self' is coupled with a *personal* pronoun, the reflexive relation highlighted by 'self' is a relation holding between an *agent* and her/himself.[2] In our example, Jane is both the *agent* and the *patient* of the action of finding a car.

---

[2] For a detailed analysis of the linguistic properties of reflexive pronouns, see Ch. 9, below.

The word 'self' is not merely a "reflexivizer", i.e. an operator that makes a reflexive pronoun out of a pronoun. In some philosophical circles, 'self' has even emerged as a count noun, 'the self'. Sometimes it is even capitalized and becomes 'The Self', giving it the appearance of a proper name. Whether one takes it to be a count noun or a proper name, one can hardly avoid the ontological commitment; one finds oneself searching for a kind of entity that could count as a Self. The philosophical literature on the subject is extensive. In modern times, it goes at least as far back as Descartes's well-known *cogito* argument. I do not intend to discuss this literature here.

From a psychological viewpoint, the self has been linked to the particular knowledge one has about oneself, or self-consciousness. My aim is to show that this particular knowledge is the knowledge an agent expresses using the first-person pronoun. In other words, one comes to have self-consciousness when one uses 'I' in an appropriate way and, in so doing, one expresses 'I'-thoughts. If I am right, the particular knowledge one has about oneself is in no way mysterious. One does not need to grasp particular (hidden) entities to refer to oneself with 'I'. In the remainder of this section and the next, I concentrate on proving just that.

The question I face can thus be formulated as follows:

- How does one come to master the use of the pronoun 'I'?

Children are not born with mastery of 'I'; it is something that must be learnt. In fact, mastery of the first-person pronoun comes after mastery of other linguistic tools. It is a well-known fact that children usually begin designating themselves using their proper name (for instance, when they wish to draw attention to themselves). Only later do they start using the first-person pronoun to refer to themselves:

> During this early period, then, children might employ their own *names* to refer to their body movements (e.g. sit), their states (e.g. sick), permanent relations of possession (e.g. clothing), and photographs of themselves, but they mainly reserved personal pronouns for settings in which they were participating agents. Only later did the pronouns become referring expressions. Thus at least some of a child's earliest uses of first-person pronouns seemed to occur in contexts of action in relation to (implicit) others, recognized as such. (Hobson 1993: 46)

Some children do not even fully master this pronoun, even if they master numerous other grammatical expressions. It is well documented how autistic children, for instance, face difficulties in using 'I' as an expression with which to refer to themselves. This difficulty forms part of a general difficulty autistics face in using personal pronouns: "personal pronouns are repeated just as heard, with no change to suit the altered situation" (Kanner 1943: 244). This suggests that mastery of the first-person pronoun comes with the mastery of other personal pronouns. In other words, one knows how to use 'I' when one also knows how to use 'you', 'she', etc. In this respect, mastering the use of the first-person pronoun, like mastery of the other pronouns, rests on one's social interaction with the other members of one's linguistic community. If one is deprived, for whatever reason, of this interaction, one will never grow up to learn the use of the first-person pronoun:

> I want to emphasize the close relation between the development of self- and other-awareness, and the earliest developments in conceptualising mental states. I say "earliest" developments . . . The reason is that in normal children, the beginning of personal pronoun comprehension and use occur very soon after the emergence of multiword utterances, toward the end of the second year and into the third year of life. Thus personal pronouns appear at roughly the same time as children begin to make reference to mental states such as feelings.
>
> This is more than a matter of temporal coincidence, however. There is an intrinsic, logical connection between understanding "self", "other", and "psychological attitudes". . . . to conceptualise a mental state is to conceptualise what it is to be a subject of experience, and this is part of what it means to be a "self". A full understanding of self-hood entails that a child understands the range of attitudes (e.g. of embarrassment, acquisitiveness, competitiveness, jealousy, and so on) which selves may experience. (Hobson 1993: 95)

The mastery of the first-person pronoun parallels the "construction" of oneself as a self-conscious individual. From what I said it emerges that for one to know oneself is to know oneself as a person among others. Actually, if I am right in arguing that one's knowledge of oneself is demonstrated in one's mastery of the first-person pronoun and that mastery of the first-person pronoun parallels mastery of other personal pronouns (in particular 'you'), it follows that one's knowledge of oneself is the knowledge of oneself as a *social agent*:

> The unit of personal existence is not the individual, but two persons in personal relation; and . . . we are persons not by individual right, but in virtue of our relation to one another. The personal is constituted by personal relatedness. The unit of the personal is not the "I", but "You and I". (MacMurray 1961: 61)

We are bound to be social agents and it is only insofar as we are social agents that we are capable of using pronouns in the way we do and that we conceive of both ourselves *and* others as persons, i.e. as egocentric and perspectival individuals.[3]

In support of the thesis that someone's self-awareness develops with the development of a mastery of pronouns, we can also mention preverbal children's automatic response to other children's distress (e.g. reactive cry). This shows that

---

[3] "An early and striking manifestation of self-awareness is the two-year-old's ability to comprehend and use personal pronouns such as 'I' and 'you', 'mine' and 'yours', and so on. Peter and Jill de Villiers (1974) point out that 'I' and 'you' are words that can only be understood by non-egocentric individuals who recognise the context of the relationship between the speaker and the addressee, and who have grasped reciprocal roles in discourse" (Hobson 1993: 45).

a preverbal child does not distinguish between her own self and that of another child. At this stage, their self resumes to an experiential, proprioceptive-based self.[4] This notion of self is non-representational. A representational notion of self only develops at around 2 and a half years of age, when infants start recognizing themselves in the mirror, for instance, and start using personal pronouns (see Stern 1985). Before that stage, a child's self-awareness is limited to the continuity of her kinaesthetic sensations and can break down each time she "experiences" (in a sense we shall discuss in the next chapter) another child's distress:

> [T]he infant's sense of continuity may break down anytime the infant "shares" distress with another, as in feeling empathy distress, because the kinesthetic bodily sensations on which the self's continuity is based are mixed with the bodily sensations arising from the infant's feeling empathically distressed (due to mimicry, conditioning, and association). The result is a temporary breakdown of the infant's self boundaries, and a feeling of confusion about where his or her distress comes from. (Hoffman 2000: 69)

With this psychological background in place, I now turn to discuss the semantics of the first-person pronoun.

2. The Meaning of 'I'

Wittgenstein flirted with the thesis that 'I' is not a referring expression and Anscombe explicitly endorsed this thesis. I show that Anscombe's argument rests on a misunderstanding of the way the first-person pronoun works. In so doing I argue that one can endorse most of Wittgenstein's ideas without giving up the thesis that 'I' is a referring expression. This exercise is illuminating insofar as, on the one hand, it helps us highlight the thesis that a mastery of 'I' goes along with the mastery of the other pronouns and, on the other hand, that the referent of 'I', like the referent of 'you' and the other personal pronouns, is nothing but a person. That is, that we do not have, contrary to the tradition, to postulate hidden entities as the referent of the first-person pronoun:

> The word 'I' does not mean the same as 'L.W.' even if I am L.W., nor does it mean the same as the expression 'the person who is now speaking'. But that does not mean that 'L.W.' and 'I' mean different things. All it means is that these words are different instruments in our language. (Wittgenstein, *BB*: 67)

We have to distinguish, Wittgenstein tells us, between the personal pronoun 'I', the proper name 'L.W.', and the description 'the person who is now speaking'. But it has been said that:

- *T1*
 'I' can be explained away in terms of 'the person who is now speaking'.

[4] I discuss a child's emphatic reactions to other children's distress further in Ch. 6, Sect. 2, below.

And even that

- *T2*

'I' is not a referential expression.

Anscombe (1975), for instance, argues in favor of the second thesis while Reichenbach (1947) and Russell (1940) flirt with the first. Indeed, Wittgenstein himself flirts with the second thesis:

[T]he point on which he [Wittgenstein] seemed most anxious to insist was that what we call 'having toothache' is what he called 'a primary experience' . . . ; and he said that "what characterises 'primary experience' is that in its case 'I' does not denote a possessor." . . . He said that 'Just as no (physical) eye is involved in seeing, no Ego is involved in thinking or having toothache'; and he quoted, with apparent approval, Lichtenberg's saying, "Instead of 'I think' we ought to say 'It thinks' " (Moore 1959: 308–9).

The question that springs to mind is: Why have people been tempted by T2? In answering this question, I focus on Anscombe's 1975 influential paper "The First Person".

To begin with we can follow Kaplan ([1977] 1989: 520) and assume that the meaning of 'I' is given by the following rules:

- *M1*

'I' is a (pure) indexical, different utterances of which may have different contents.

- *M2*

'I' is, in each of its utterances, directly referential.

- *M3*

'I' refers, in each of its utterances, to the agent of the utterance.[5]

In M1 it is said that the first-person pronoun is a pure indexical. As we saw in the previous chapter we can distinguish, following Kaplan, between pure indexicals ('I', 'here', 'now', 'today', etc.) and demonstratives ('this', 'that', 'she', etc.). A demonstrative, unlike a pure indexical, is incomplete without a pointing gesture, a demonstration. The pointing gesture is a communicative device which helps the listener to identify the referent. The linguistic meaning which governs a demonstrative's use is insufficient to determine its referent in each context of use for the interlocutor. Moreover, a demonstrative, unlike a pure indexical, can be a vacuous term. In saying, "She is tall", I can be hallucinating, or I can be pointing

---

[5] To be precise, Kaplan says that 'I' refers to the person who utters it. As we shall see in Sect. 4, below, though, 'I' may not refer to the person who utters or writes it. It may not even refer to the one who produced the token. It always refers, though, to the agent of the utterance and the latter (e.g. answering machine cases) may differ from the producer of the token. For a more detailed discussion on the difference between pure indexicals and demonstratives see Ch. 4, Sect. 2, above.

to a disguised man, etc. But one cannot say, "I am here now", and fail to refer. 'I', 'here', and 'now' in each context of use are always referring expressions.[6]

M2 calls for explanation. In saying that an expression is directly referential we mean that in using it we make a reference without the mediation of a Fregean sense; we refer directly to the relevant object or referent.[7] To stress this point, we can borrow Putnam's famous twin-Earth thought experiment. On Earth and twin-Earth everything is qualitatively similar, down to the last molecule. When on Earth I say "I am F", on twin-Earth, my twin, who is qualitatively indistinguishable from me, also says "I am F". Both my twin and I use 'I'. Since we are so similar, we have the same conception of ourselves. We think, if you like, of ourselves in the same way. Imagine now that the way we think of ourselves, i.e. the conception we have of ourselves, constitutes the sense we associate with 'I'. If this is the case, the sense does not help us to determine the referent. For, when my twin uses 'I' he refers to himself, whilst when I use it I refer to myself. And each of us refers to himself because each of us uses the first-person pronoun. Although we have the same self-conception, we do not refer to one another. To bring this point home and down to earth we can use a Castañeda-Perry-inspired example. Someone, Paul, can believe that he is Hume and that he wrote the *Treatise*. When Paul thinks of himself, he thinks of himself, among other things, as the author of the *Treatise*. Hume too thinks of himself as the author of the Treatise. But when Hume says "I wrote the *Treatise*" he says something true whilst when Paul utters this very sentence, he says something false. So far the general moral seems to be that 'I' refers without the mediation of a Fregean sense, for if reference were mediated by a Fregean sense both Hume and Paul would refer to the same person when they used 'I'. This point will be important in the next section where I discuss and criticize Anscombe's defense of T2.

We are now in a position to discuss T2 in some detail.

3. Does 'I' Refer?

Anscombe argues that 'I' is not, contrary to appearances, a referential expression. Her argument is a *reductio*. She starts from the following two theses:

- *A1*
'I' is a referential term.

---

[6] For simplicity's sake, I am ignoring cases where 'here' can be used as a demonstrative. If, for instance, pointing to a map I say, "I will be here tomorrow", 'here' will be a demonstrative and not a pure indexical.

[7] Kaplan argues that a term is directly referential if and only if in using it we express singular (or Russellian) propositions, i.e. propositions whose constituents are the referents themselves.

- *A2*

    A referential term refers *via* the mediation of a Fregean sense or mode of presentation.

Her goal is to refute A1. To do so she seeks to show that A1 entails a contradiction. Anscombe's argument, though, rests heavily on A2. As I have already suggested, A2 is, *pace* Anscombe, a controversial thesis. If one rejects it, Anscombe's argument loses its force. Examining Anscombe's argument in some detail will help us to clarify how the first-person pronoun works both when one uses it in one's thinking episodes, i.e. when one entertains a so-called 'I'-thought, and when one attributes to someone else an 'I'-thought.[8]

Acceptance of A1 commits us to

- *A3*

    'I' has a referent.

Indeed, A1 and A3 are just two sides of the same coin. Now logicians and semanticists take proper names to be the paradigmatic cases of singular terms, i.e. the expressions that get translated in formal language by the constants 'a', 'b', 'c', etc. Expressions such as 'this', 'that', 'today', and the like are singular terms as well. If we focus on natural language, the paradigmatic cases of singular reference turn out to be proper names such as 'Mary', 'Budapest', 'Maradona', and demonstratives such as 'this' and 'that'. Indeed, when singling out an object of discourse we often end up using one of these expressions. The category of singular terms in natural language expands beyond the types of expression which, in everyday speech, we characterize as proper names. It has thus been recognized that in natural language we have at least two categories of singular terms: proper names and demonstratives.[9] Thus we can, following Anscombe, argue that if 'I' is a referential term (A1), then

- *A4*

    'I' is either a name or a demonstrative.

From A4 and A3 Anscombe goes on to infer

- *A5*

    The referent of 'I' is an object or body.

After all, the referent of 'Rome' is a city, while the referent of 'this', pointing to a frog, is the relevant frog and the referent of 'this woman', pointing towards Madonna, is Madonna.

---

[8] I return and explain in full details the attribution of 'I'-thoughts in Ch. 8, below.

[9] As for descriptions Frege, unlike Russell, thought that they are singular terms. Donnellan thought that they could be used either as singular terms or not. For the purposes of this chapter, however, we can ignore this problematic. I discussed definite descriptions and Donnellan's distinction in Ch. 3, above, esp. Sect. 2.

Before going further it may be worth noting that one can object, rightly I think, that the referent of a singular term, whether a proper name or a demonstrative, is not necessarily an object or body. Logicians often speak of individual constants and assume that their referents are individuals. Since we can subsume under this notion objects, bodies, persons, agents, etc., it is less shocking, or at least more natural, to claim that the referent of 'I' is a person or agent rather than claiming that it is a body or object. The same is true for some proper names. It does not sound right to say that the referent of 'Bill Clinton' is a body or object. It sounds more appropriate to claim that it is a person. One can also argue that the concept of a person is irreducible and primitive. In particular, it cannot be explained away using the (more primitive) concept of a body, etc. without implicitly or explicitly endorsing a kind of Cartesian dualism, i.e. without committing oneself to the claim that a person is a body *plus* a soul or ego. I suspect that Anscombe's argument rests on this implicit assumption.

For simplicity's sake and for the sake of argument, though, let us follow Anscombe and assume that the referent of a singular term is either an object or a body. From A5 and A2, we get:

- *A6*
  'I' is associated with an egocentric and unsharable mode of presentation.

Since an object is given *via* a mode of presentation, it is the latter that determines which object the relevant term stands for. In other words, if 'I' refers to an object or body (A5), and the gulf between the pronoun and the referent is bridged by a Fregean sense (A2), the only plausible candidate for being the mode of presentation associated with 'I' seems to be a Cartesian ego. For as Frege told us, we cannot go from reference to sense as it is the latter which determines the former. In short, the mode of presentation which picks out me when I use 'I' ought to differ from the one picking out you or my twin (on twin-Earth) when using the same pronoun. Thus, Frege was led to claim:

Now, everyone is presented to himself in a particular and primitive way, in which he is presented to no one else. So, when Dr. Lauben has the thought that he has been wounded, he will probably be basing it on this primitive way in which he is presented to himself. And only Dr. Lauben himself can grasp thoughts specified in this way. (Frege [1918] 1988: 333)

The task we face, then, is to figure out what this egocentric mode of presentation is or could be if it is not a Cartesian ego. What we have done so far is to characterize this mode of presentation in a functional way: the egocentric mode of presentation associated with 'I' is *whatever plays the role* of selecting its referent. Anscombe is well aware of the problem we are facing:

If 'I' expresses a way its object is reached by him, what Frege called an 'Art des Gegebenseins', we want to know what that way is and how it comes about that the only object reached in that way by anyone is identical with himself. (Anscombe [1975] 1990: 137)

Driven by her Fregeanism, i.e. A2, Anscombe goes on to argue:

The use of a name for an object is connected with a conception of that object. And so we are driven to look for something that, for each 'I'-user, will be the conception related to the supposed name 'I', as the conception of a city is to the names 'London' and 'Chicago', that of a river to 'Thames' and 'Nile', that of a man to 'John' and 'Pat'. Such a conception is requisite if 'I' is a name, and there is no conception that can claim to do the job except one suggested by 'self-consciousness'. (Anscombe [1975] 1990: 141)

Hence we had better figure out which entity, if any, plays such a peculiar role. We are getting into deep water: "To say all this is to treat 'I' as a sort of proper name. That is what gets us into this jam" (Anscombe [1975] 1990: 138).

What about treating 'I' as a demonstrative? After all in A4 it is claimed that 'I' is either a name or a demonstrative. If we take 'I' to be a demonstrative we may be able to get out of the difficulty. But this move will not help us if, as Anscombe does, we subscribe to A2:

Assimilation to a demonstrative will not . . . do away with the demand for a conception of the object indicated. For, even though someone may say just 'this' or 'that', we need to know the answer to the question 'this what?' if we are to understand him; and he needs to know the answer if he is to be meaning anything . . . And the answer to the question 'this what?' might be taken to be 'this self', if it can be shown that there are selves and that they are apparently what is spoken of by all these people saying 'I'. (Anscombe [1975] 1990: 142–3)

The problems, though, do not end here. For, from A4 we can also infer,

- A7

'I' can be an empty term.

For, if 'I' is a name, then like any other name (e.g. 'Robin Hood', 'Santa Claus', 'Vulcan') it can miss the referent. If, on the other hand, 'I' is a demonstrative, it can also fail to refer—as when we use 'this' when gesticulating toward a hallucinated object, or 'that man' when pointing to a car:

It used to be thought that a singular demonstrative, 'this' or 'that', if used correctly, could not lack a referent. But this is not so, as comes out if we consider the requirement for the answer to 'this what?'. Someone comes with a box and says 'This is all that is left of poor Juryes.' The answer to 'this what?' is 'this parcel of ashes'; but unknown to the speaker the box is empty. (Anscombe [1975] 1990: 143)

'I', though, never misses the referent. We cannot imagine a situation when someone using the first-person pronoun does not pick out herself as the referent:

Just thinking 'I . . .' guarantees not only the existence but the presence of its referent. It guarantees the existence because it guarantees the presence, which is presence to consciousness. But note that here 'presence to consciousness' means physical or real presence, not just that one is thinking of the thing. For if the thing did not guarantee the presence, the existence of the referent cannot be doubted. For the same reason, if 'I' is a name it cannot be an empty name. I's existence is existence in the thinking of the thought expressed by 'I . . . '(Anscombe [1975] 1990: 143–4)

A4, then drives us to the problematic thesis A7. But 'I' is never an empty term. Whatever one believes, thinks, etc. when one utters 'I' one refers to oneself. This also holds for 'now' and 'here'. Waking after having been drugged and kidnapped, I still refer to myself and the relevant place and time when I say "Now I am getting cold here". Since names and demonstratives can be empty terms we can infer:

- *A8*
'I' is neither a name, nor a demonstrative.

A8 contradicts A4. So, by *reductio*, Anscombe goes on to reject A1 and to propose T2 as her conclusion. But this is not very convincing. First of all, why does she not give up A2 instead of A1? Moreover, A8 would not be problematic if, following Kaplan, we distinguish between pure indexicals and demonstratives. 'I' is a pure indexical. Hence, we can give up A4 without having to claim that 'I' is not a referring expression. Anscombe, though, fails to appreciate this distinction and jumps to the conclusion that 'I' is not a referring expression.

There are other reasons driving Anscombe to the conclusion that 'I' is not a referential term. I believe that Anscombe is driven to this conclusion because she endorses A2. That is to say, because she assumes that to be a referential term 'I' ought to express a conception that the speaker ought to satisfy and grasp when she uses the first-person pronoun. Since we cannot find such a conception Anscombe concludes that 'I' cannot be a referential term.

If you are a speaker who says 'I' you do not find out what is saying 'I'. You do not for example look to see what apparatus the noise comes out of and assume that that is the sayer; or frame the hypothesis of something connected with it that is the sayer. If that were in question, you could doubt whether anything was saying 'I'. (Anscombe [1975] 1990: 144)

Certainly, if I say 'I', I do not have to look for who says it. If I hear 'I', though, I have to look for who utters it if I am interested in identifying the referent. The simple fact of using 'I' picks me out as the referent. I do not have to associate with my use of 'I' a representation of myself to refer to myself. This is somewhat analogous to the case when we tacitly refer to a place. If I say "It is sunny", I tacitly refer to the relevant place, i.e. the place I am in when I use this sentence. In saying "It is sunny" I do not have to represent to myself the relevant place to refer to it. I think of the relevant place because I am located in the relevant place, because I occupy it. To put it slightly differently, I identify the relevant place because my utterance occurs at the relevant place.[10] The same story can be told about the present tense: the speaker refers to the relevant time because of the time of her utterance. She does not pick out the relevant time because she grasps a specific conception of the time in question. Notice that in order to fulfill the role of a Fregean sense such an (imaginary) conception should change with the change in time and reference.

It seems that Anscombe cannot appreciate this phenomenon because she is driven by A2 and thinks that reference ought to be determined and mediated by a conception of the referent: "[T]he 'I'-user must intend to refer to something, if 'I' is a referring expression" (Anscombe [1975] 1990: 145).

If we give up this Fregean requirement—as we should—nothing prevents us from arguing that 'I' is a referential term referring directly, i.e. without the mediation of a Fregean sense, to the person using it or, as we shall see in Sections 4 and 5, to the agent of the utterance. Certainly, the gap between 'I' and its user is not magically bridged. There is a rule each competent speaker applies when using the first-person pronoun. If one looks in the dictionary one can read that 'I' is "a pronoun used by the speaker or writer referring to himself or herself". This is all one needs to know. To be sure, to be a competent speaker one does not need to be able to spell out the rule the way the dictionary or the semanticist does. As Wittgenstein would say, one manifests one's competence with the rule in following it. In our particular case one manifests one's competence with the relevant rule by using 'I' in an appropriate way. The rule, or character of 'I' (which is, as we saw, a function from context to content or referent) is no more mysterious than the other rules we follow in our everyday linguistic practice. When using 'I' we all follow and apply the same rule. As such the rule cannot be equated with a Fregean sense, i.e. it cannot be the conception Anscombe is looking for. For the rule does not single out a referent in a context-free way.

It goes without saying that the rule, i.e. the linguistic meaning, governing the use of the first-person pronoun cannot, and should not, be equated with a Cartesian ego or mode of presentation. Such a rule is what helps fix the reference. It is not something which gets in between 'I' and its referent.

As a first corollary it is interesting to note that in recognizing that the linguistic meaning of the first-person pronoun is a rule, we commit ourselves, *pace* Anscombe, to the thesis that 'I' refers to a person or agent. It does not refer to a body. For persons follow rules, bodies do not. For exactly the same reason 'I' does not refer to an ego either. The latter does not follow rules. We can say "L.W./this person/ . . . follows such-and-such a rule". It does not make sense to say "L.W.'s body/L.W.'s ego follows such-and-such a rule". What I have been saying

---

[10] I discussed meteorological verbs and the way we can succeed in referring to and thinking of a given place without mentioning it in Ch. 2, Sects. 2 and 3, above.

goes hand-in-hand with the thesis proposed earlier, that the concept of a person is primitive and irreducible.

As a second corollary we can say that in recognizing that the linguistic meaning of the first-person pronoun is a rule taking as argument the context, the agent, and giving as value the referent, we must also recognize that the meaning of 'I' cannot be its referent. It cannot play a dual role. We can thus dismiss Anscombe's suggestion that if 'I' is a referential expression, we are committed to a Cartesian ego which is both what one ought to grasp and that to which one refers. In short, in giving up the Fregean requirement, T2, we are no longer committed to the controversial thesis that an egocentric mode of presentation is both the sense associated with 'I' and its referent.

We can thus conclude that, *pace* Anscombe, 'I' is, after all, a referential term. Its linguistic meaning ought to be understood as a rule dictating or guiding our use of 'I'. This rule does not give us the meaning of the first-person pronoun. All it does is to tell us *how to use* 'I'. And this should come as the natural conclusion to those, like Anscombe, are familiar with and keen on Wittgenstein's later philosophy.

This should not be surprising if, following Wittgenstein, we recognize that the word 'I' does not mean the same as 'L.W.' even if I am L.W., nor does it mean the same as the expression 'the person who is now speaking'. As we saw in Chapter 1, if we look in a dictionary under 'Budapest' we find out that it is the capital of Hungary. We do not find a rule telling us how to use this proper name. Moreover, we do not find in the dictionary proper names of common mortals: we do not find the list of the thousands of John Smiths.

What I said goes hand in hand with Wittgenstein's claim that 'L.W.' and 'I' can mean the same thing. All I am committed to is that these words are different instruments in our language. We can thus happily agree with Wittgenstein:

> One has been tempted to say 'now' is the name of an instant of time, and this, of course, would be like saying that 'here' is the name of a place, 'this' the name of a thing, and 'I' the name of a man [or woman] . . . But nothing is more unlike than the use of the word 'this' and the use of a proper name—I mean the games played with these words, not the phrases in which they are used. For we do say 'This is short' and 'Jack is short'; but remember that 'This is short' without the pointing gesture and without the thing we are pointing to would be meaningless.— . . . Nothing is more characteristic of a proper name A than we can use it in such a phrase as 'This is A'; and it makes no sense to say 'This is this' or 'Now is now' or 'Here is here'. (Wittgenstein, *BB*: 108–9)

We are now in a position to understand why Wittgenstein flirted with T2. Recall that in the *Blue Book* Wittgenstein distinguishes between two uses of the first-person pronoun: the use as subject and the use as object. As examples of the second kind Wittgenstein proposes "My arm is broken", "I have grown six inches", "I have a bump on my forehead", etc., while as examples of the first kind he suggests "I see so-and-so", "I hear so-and-so", "I try to lift my arm", "I have toothache", etc.

[I]n the case in which 'I' is used as subject, we don't use it because we recognize a particular person by his bodily characteristics; and this creates the illusion that we use this word to refer to something bodiless, which, however has its seat in our body. (Wittgenstein, *BB*: 69)

If we understand Wittgenstein's claims as depending on the distinction between pure indexicals and demonstratives, we can easily accommodate both uses of 'I' that Wittgenstein recognizes, without appealing to mysterious referents or conceptions one ought to grasp or entertain in order to competently use the first-person pronoun. We thus resist the temptation of arguing, *pace* Anscombe and Wittgenstein, that 'I' is not a referential term.

If the position I have proposed is coherent, we can conclude with the same quote with which I began when discussing Wittgenstein's position. But let us change it a little, to accommodate the various things that 'meaning' can mean:

The word 'I' does not mean the same as [have the same linguistic meaning as] 'L.W.' even if I am L.W., nor does it mean the same as [have the same linguistic meaning as] the expression 'the person who is now speaking'. But that does not mean that 'L.W.' and 'I' mean [refer to] different things. All it means is that these words are different instruments in our language. (Wittgenstein, *BB*: 67)

If Wittgenstein had had such distinctions at his disposal he would not have been tempted by T2.

4. Answering Machines and Other Devices[11]

When we consider the use of the first-person pronoun as it appears in an answering machine or written on a post-it note, Rimbaud's claim that 'I' is another may not sound so awkward or poetic. In these cases, the question as to whom 'I' refers is legitimate. This does not seem to fit well with Kaplan's idea that the character of 'I' takes the agent as argument and gives the referent as value. Well, it does not seem to fit with Kaplan's idea that the agent/referent is always the speaker and/or writer:

It ['I'] refers to the speaker or writer of the relevant *occurrence* of the word 'I', that is, the agent of the context. (Kaplan [1977] 1989: 505)

In each of its utterances, 'I' refers to the person who utters it. (Kaplan [1977] 1989: 520)

---

[11] This section and Sects. 5–8, below, rest heavily on a co-written paper. (See Corazza, Fish and Gorvett 2002.)

This may be seen as a slip on Kaplan's part. For on his logic of demonstratives he argues that the logic of indexical terms forces the distinction between the utterer, the contextual parameters (agent, time, place, and possible world), and the referents (contents). Kaplan also claims that the logic of demonstratives cannot deal with utterances since they are worldly entities which occur in time. It is, therefore, impossible to provide a semantic evaluation of utterances.

> Utterances take time, and utterances of distinct sentences cannot be simultaneous (i.e., in the same context). But in order to develop a logic of demonstratives we must be able to evaluate several premises and a conclusion all in the same context. We do not want arguments involving indexicals to become valid simply because there is no possible context in which all the premises are uttered, and thus no possible context in which all are uttered truthfully. (Kaplan [1977] 1989: 522)

> Utterances take time, and are produced one at a time; this will not do for the analysis of validity. By the time an agent finished uttering a very, very long true premise and began uttering the conclusion, the premise may have gone false. Thus even the most trivial of inferences, *P* therefore *P*, may appear invalid. (Kaplan 1989: 584)

To overcome this, we need instead to assess the abstract notion of a sentence-in-a-context, and to do this we need to endorse the notion of a context.[12] The *agent* is, therefore, an essentially logical notion, a contextual parameter filling the argument of the character (*qua* function), and giving us the referent of the indexical, and, as such, is logically distinct from the notion of an utterer. Whether Kaplan's argument against the possibility of a logic of utterances is compelling or not is not an issue I intend to deal with.[13] For the sake of argument let us assume that Kaplan is right. On his account, thus, we should distinguish between the utterer and the agent. While the former is a worldly entity, the latter is a logical entity, a contextual parameter needed in the logic of demonstratives. However, given Kaplan's claim that the referent of 'I' is always the utterer or speaker and given his claim that the character of 'I' takes as argument the agent and gives as value the referent, Kaplan is committed to the following identity statements:

- *Kaplan's commitment*
  (i) the agent = the referent
  (ii) the agent = the utterer
  (iii) the referent = the utterer

To be precise, Kaplan is committed to these identities in the case of utterances (i.e. wherever there is an utterer). Kaplan's logical framework allows certain

---

[12] "[Context] is a package of whatever parameters are needed to determine the referent . . . the context supplies the time and place parameters that determine content for the indexicals 'now' and 'here'" (Kaplan 1989: 591).

[13] For a plausible criticism of Kaplan's view on this very issue, see García-Carpintero (1998).

sentences to express a truth only in contexts provided they are not uttered, e.g. "I say nothing" (see Kaplan 1989: 584). The character of the other indexicals, 'here' and 'now', can also be represented in the same way. In each case, the character of the indexical is a function from a contextual parameter (location in the former case and time in the latter) to the referent of the expression. An intuitively plausible model of these indexicals would also include a parallel of the agent-utterer identity we found in the case of 'I'. For 'here' we might identify the (contextual parameter of) location with the place of utterance, and for 'now', the (contextual parameter of) time with the time of utterance. In this way we can ensure that the character of these indexicals will always yield, as referent, the place and time of utterance.

In a number of recent papers, the Kaplanian framework for the indexicals 'here' and 'now' has been criticized. Its critics argue that the framework as it stands is unable to deal with a number of common cases. These include such examples as the outgoing messages on answering machines, messages written on post-it notes, and the like.

Sidelle (1991)[14] introduces us to what he calls the Answering Machine Paradox and asks how, given the linguistic meaning of the indexicals, it is possible that utterances of the form "I am not here now", which wear the form of a contradiction, can nevertheless be true. Statements of this type might be found on a telephone answering machine—hence the answering machine paradox—and written on a post-it note and stuck on an office door when its incumbent is not in residence. The feelings of paradox arise because it seems to demonstrate that Kaplan is wrong when he says that an utterance of "I am here now" is

[U]niversally true. One need only understand the meaning of ["I am here now"] to know that it cannot be uttered falsely. (Kaplan [1977] 1989: 509)

When played on an answering machine, however, it is apparent that such an utterance might well turn out to be false.

A productive way of approaching this so-called "paradox" is to view it as a puzzle concerning the referent of 'now'. The problem arises from a tension between the pre-theoretic intuition that the utterance of an answering machine message occurs when the person records the message, Kaplan's dictum that the referent of 'now' is the time of the utterance, and the fact that, for the answering machine to serve any purpose, 'now' must refer to the time at which the message is heard. Sidelle solves this with the proposal that an utterance can be *deferred*.[15] On this account, the utterance

---

[14] Although Sidelle is considered to be the *locus classicus* of this problem, precursors of this problem can also be seen in Kaplan([1977] 1989: 491 ff.) and Vision (1985).

[15] See Sidelle (1991). Sidelle was the first to propose the notion of deferred utterances as a way of resolving the answering machine paradox. If Sidelle's solution is satisfactory, it should apply to the puzzle in the post-it-note form as well.

takes place when the message is heard by the listener (the decoding time) *not* when it is recorded (the encoding time). In this way the Kaplanian view that the character of 'now' directs us to the time of the utterance is preserved. The utterance occurs when someone makes a telephone call and the message is played. If the individual who recorded the message (the referent of 'I') is not at the place the machine is located (the referent of 'here') at the time the call is made (the referent of 'now') then that utterance of "I'm not here now" can, *pace* Kaplan, express a truth.

The deferred utterance method of resolving this "paradox" leaves the Kaplanian framework untouched as the characters of the indexicals remain the same. 'I' continues to refer to the agent, and 'here' and 'now' to the contextual parameters of location and time. Kaplan's identities also remain, thereby ensuring that 'I' ultimately refers to the utterer, 'here' to the place of utterance, and 'now' to the time of utterance. However, it is important not to assume that, in *every* situation where there is a delay between the production of the message and its being interpreted, an utterance *always* occurs at the decoding time. For example, if you receive a postcard saying "I'm having fun here now", 'here' and 'now' refer to the location and time where and when the postcard has been written (the encoding time/location), *not* the location and time at which it is read (the decoding time/location). In this case, unlike the answering machine case, the relevant contextual parameters are the time when and location at which the message is produced. The notion of an utterance at a distance or deferred utterance should be taken into account for a satisfactory explanation of indexical reference.

5. On the Referent of 'I'

Sidelle's solution proceeds by leaving scope for a temporal distance between the act of writing a note or recording a message, and the moment at which an utterance is made. However, once it is allowed that utterances can occur at a temporal distance from the encoding act, situations can arise in which there is an intriguing and important question of just how the reference of 'I' is determined.

In the version of the puzzle just sketched, reference seems simple to obtain. 'I' refers to the utterer who, in the post-it-note case, is intuitively seen to be the individual who writes the note and attaches it to her office door. However, there is a variation of the puzzle which brings the problems into focus. Jury is not in his office one day and Sue notices that a number of students keep approaching his door and knocking. They then stand around and look bemused for a while before leaving. To avoid the students wasting their time, Sue decides to attach her "I am not here today" note to Jury's door. The trick works; the students, instead of knocking and waiting, take one look at the note and then leave. This scenario differs from the previous one in that, in this case, Jury has no knowledge of, and has played no role in, deferring these utterances. At the moment one student looks at the note, and an utterance is made, the expressions 'today' and 'here' successfully refer to the day and place the note is read, but to what does 'I' refer?

As everything is working so well it would seem strange to deny that it refers in precisely the same way as it refers in the standard scenario—it refers to Jury. After all, this is certainly what the audience of the utterances, the students, take it to refer to. However, given that the character of 'I' states that it refers to the agent, and, on Kaplan's account, the agent is identical with the utterer, Jury must be the utterer if he is the referent. However, this seems to force the extremely counter-intuitive claim that one can make utterances one has had absolutely no role whatsoever in the production of. Jury did not write the note, he did not place it on his door, and he did not ask for it to be placed on his door. In fact, Jury has absolutely no idea that the note is on his door at all. For these reasons it sounds implausible to suppose that Jury is the utterer in this situation. To highlight the unattractive consequences of this claim, imagine if, as a joke, Sue had instead attached a note that stated, "I think the Chancellor is a fool." Would Jury still be prepared to accept this as his utterance? Note that it is not the fact of being unaware of being a referent which is counter-intuitive—it happens to everyone all the time, even after death. How many times has Aristotle been referred to without him being aware of it? Rather, it is being deemed to be the utterer of utterances that one has had absolutely no role in the production of that is counter-intuitive.

If Jury is not the utterer, the only other candidate for this role would be Sue. So, following Kaplan's identity of agent and utterer, the character of 'I' would therefore yield Sue as the referent. Does 'I' then, in this scenario, refer to Sue, the brains behind the note? It does not seem so. First, the mere fact that Sue wrote the note does not secure that reference. Jury could have, had he thought about it, attached Sue's note to his door himself and thereby used it to make deferred utterances. Secondly, it would be decidedly odd to claim that 'I' refers to Sue merely in virtue of his being the one who intended to use the note. After all Sue's intention was for 'I' to refer, not to herself, but to Jury. To claim that 'I' refers to Sue regardless would force the implausible claim that a voice-over artist, recording pre-recorded messages for answer phones, is the referent every time "I'm not in right now" is played.

Another possibility would be to claim that 'I' fails to refer, but again, working back through Kaplan's account, this would force the claim that there is no contextual agent, and therefore no utterer. But how can there be an utterance if there is no utterer, and if there is no utterance, then how can we make sense of the idea that there is any proposition expressed whatsoever? Moreover, it seems odd to claim that, so long as the note states, "I am not here" the note fails to make any meaningful statement, but if the note were to say, "Jury is not here" it would succeed. Either note would work equally well and hence it seems poorly motivated to be forced to claim that the term does not refer at all.

The only remaining option seems to be to claim that, although 'I' refers to Jury, Jury is nevertheless not the utterer. However, taking this line explicitly contradicts Kaplan's plausible account of the linguistic meaning of 'I' where 'I' always refers to the utterer.[16] Effectively, then, we appear to have four alternatives. If we want to retain Kaplan's intuitively plausible account of the indexical 'I' (in other words, we preserve the identities between on the one hand the agent and the utterer and, on the other, the referent of 'I' and the agent) we must either accept that Jury is the referent and can make utterances that he is unaware of, *or* that Sue is the utterer and therefore the referent. Neither of these options appears at all attractive. Alternatively, if one wants to retain the intuitively plausible claim that, whilst Jury is the referent, he is nevertheless not the utterer, one is forced to reject one of Kaplan's two identity statements. One must, to take this option, either reject Kaplan's account of the character of 'I', a function from agent to referent, or reject the further identity of agent and utterer. I now turn to the discussion of this latter possibility.

6. An Intentionalist Proposal

In two recent papers (1998*a*, *b*), Predelli introduces a further variant of the answering machine case which calls into question Kaplan's account of the indexical 'now'. Predelli proposes to deal with these cases by denying the identity relation between the contextual parameter of time and the time of utterance. In effect, Predelli can be seen as opting, for the case of 'now', for the latter of the four options and for this reason, Predelli's picture may well be applicable to the data highlighted.

---

[16] Quentin Smith introduces a number of other examples which, he suggests, are occasions when 'I' can be used to refer to someone other than the utterer (Q. Smith 1989: 182–6). Whilst not necessarily wanting to endorse Smith's examples, it is instructive to consider his positive proposal. In the light of the notion that 'I' can refer to someone other than the utterer, Smith concludes that there are "varying reference-fixing rules that govern . . . indexicals" (Q. Smith 1989: 170). This position, however, commits one to the thesis that indexicals are ambiguous or, to use the terminology I introduced in Ch. 4, above, to the Multiple Character Thesis. As I have shown (Ch. 4, esp. Sects. 5 and 6), a position avoiding this conclusion should be preferred for it is, if nothing else, more economical. As Kripke reminds us: "It is very much the lazy man's approach in philosophy to posit ambiguity when in trouble. If we face a putative counterexample to our favorite philosophical thesis, it is always open to us to protest that some key term is being used in a special sense, different from its use in the thesis. We may be right, but the ease of the move should counsel a policy of caution; Do not posit ambiguity unless you are really forced to, unless there are really compelling theoretical or intuitive grounds to suppose that an ambiguity really is present" (Kripke 1977: 19).

Predelli asks us to consider the following scenario. Before leaving home at 8 a.m. Jury writes the following note to his partner: "As you can see I am not at home *now*. Please meet me in *six hours* in my office" (where "in six hours" is short for "in six hours from now"). Jury, expecting his partner to return at 5 p.m., intends for her to meet him at 11 p.m. The reason Jury does not express his intent in a more explicit way, i.e. by saying "meet me at 11 p.m.", need not concern us. If 'now' in Jury's note refers to the time at which it is read, then Jury's partner will pick out the time at which she reads the note. If, as expected, Jury's partner comes home at 5 p.m. and reads the note, everything will work as planned as, on Kaplan's picture, 'now' will pick out 5 p.m. and Jury's partner will meet Jury in his office at 11 p.m.

Imagine, however, that Jury's partner is unexpectedly delayed and does not return home until 7 p.m. According to Kaplan's picture, 'now' in Jury's note should pick out the time of utterance—7 p.m. But Predelli argues that Jury's partner, being aware that she was expected home at 5 p.m., will not meet Jury at 1 a.m. the following day, but will meet him, as Jury expects, at 11 p.m. Predelli's moral is that 'now' in Jury's note does not always refer to the time Jury's message is read, it rather picks out the time Jury *intended* to be picked out. Predelli's contention is that, in order to explain this variant of the answering machine "paradox", one has to appeal to the notion of *intentional contexts*. Predelli's contention is that:

[A]n adequate explanation [of indexical reference] ought to take into consideration the co-ordinates *intended* . . . as relevant for the[ir] semantic evaluation. (Predelli 1988a: 112, *italics mine*)

On Predelli's account, therefore, 'now' does not always refer to the time of utterance, for 'now' can be sensitive to an *intentional context* which may well differ from the context of utterance. However, in taking this line, Predelli manages to retain half of Kaplan's account. Predelli rejects the claim that the contextual parameter of time is always identical with the time of utterance, claiming instead that this contextual parameter may well be an intentionally specified parameter, but retains Kaplan's account of the character of 'now'. Even on Predelli's account, the character of 'now' is represented by a function that takes the (now intentionally determined) contextual parameter of time as argument and yields the referent.

When applied to 'I', Predelli's picture promises to solve our puzzle by rejecting the role of the utterer in determining the agent, instead allowing for the context, and hence the contextual agent, to be determined intentionally:

In all these examples, the notion of utterance and the idea of a context of utterance do not play any semantically interesting role, and the correct results are obtained by anchoring indexical expressions to the intended context of interpretation. (Predelli 1998a: 114)

If Sue creates an intentional context with Jury as the agent, the character of 'I' will, as before, yield Jury as the referent. This way, Predelli would be able to retain Kaplan's account of the character of 'I' (a function from agent to referent), claiming that Jury is the (intentionally determined) agent and hence referent. The similarities and differences between Kaplan's and Predelli's accounts are illustrated below:

- Kaplan: the utterer is the agent   Character of 'I'(agent) → referent
- Predelli: intentions determine   Character of 'I'(agent) → referent
  the agent

At first sight Predelli's picture might appear convincing. If one considers some paradigmatic or normal cases, though, Predelli appears to be committed to an implausible consequence. If we allow Predelli's appeal to an intentional agent, we must accept that 'I' refers to Jury solely on the grounds that Sue intends it so to refer. However, if one accepts that Sue, purely in virtue of her having the intention to do so, can use 'I' to refer to Jury, why can one not use 'I' to refer to pretty much anybody? Moreover, if Sue had, instead of affixing his note to Jury's door, simply leant out of his own office and said to the students, "I am not here today" (intending thereby to use 'I' to refer to Jury), surely she would have failed in this intention and merely referred to herself. To claim otherwise is a Humpty Dumpty. A picture one should avoid at any price.

Similar reasoning can be used to weaken any claim of reference being secured by *simulation*, where Sue succeeds in using 'I' to refer to Jury as long as Sue is playing the part of, or pretending to be, Jury. It appears that, for this type of simulation to work, the participation of the audience must bear some of the weight—they would have to be, in some sense, *in the know*. If the audience is not required to be aware of the simulation, the resultant picture appears committed to claiming that all that is required to secure reference is the intention of the speaker (in this case, to be playing a part) and, as such, suffers from the same kind of implausibility as Predelli's picture. However, to go one step further and claim that reference is determined solely by the beliefs/intentions of the audience is, in its own way, as implausible as saying that reference depends purely on Sue's intentions. If Sue refers to herself saying, "I am tired", and her class believes her to be playing the part of Aristotle, 'I' does not thereby refer to Aristotle, but to Sue—the class have just made a mistake. If the only plausible version of a simulation picture requires some level of audience participation, it is of no use in solving our puzzle as, in this case, the audience is entirely unaware of any involvement on Sue's part.

Of course, there may be ways in which Intentionalists such as Predelli may attempt to temper their theory so as to avoid these implausible consequences. I consider (and reject) one such possible move in Section 8, below. For the time being, however, I show instead how to solve the puzzle outlined above *without* relying on a potentially problematic appeal to speaker intentions. In explaining this thesis, I also highlight just *why* Predelli's appeal to intentions in the note-leaving example looks plausible. Finally, it is worth pointing out that, whilst Predelli's theory might be faithful to (some of) the letter of Kaplan's picture, it is disloyal to its general spirit.[17] As we saw in Chapter 1 (Section 4), Kaplan's overall approach to language is *consumerist* whereby words and their meanings are mind-independent. We are consumers of words and therefore of their meanings. We have an intention insofar as we choose which words we use. However, Kaplan does not hold that these intentions determine the meanings of the words, but that the meanings are independent of our intentions.[18] The picture I propose below is not only faithful to the letter but also to the spirit of Kaplan's original proposal. In particular, it fits within the direct reference framework I proposed in Chapters 1 and 2.

7. An Anti-Intentionalist Solution

Taking stock. Kaplan's account of the indexical 'I' has two aspects. The first component is the claim that the character of 'I' can be represented as a function which takes as input the contextual parameter, the agent, and returns as value the referent. The second element is the claim that, for any given utterance of 'I', the contextual agent will be identical with the utterer. As we saw, however, this account is not flexible enough to cope with certain possible uses of 'I'. Kaplan's original account suffers from the rigidity of the claim that, *in every situation*, the agent, and hence the referent, will be identical with the utterer.

Predelli's account offers to solve this problem by denying agent-utterer identity and allowing us to determine the agent intentionally. However, as emerged in Section 6, replacing the agent-utterer identity with an intentionally determined agent yields an overall picture which is not restrictive *enough*. So Predelli goes too far in the opposite direction. In a nutshell, Kaplan's original account is not flexible enough to deal with certain problem cases, whereas Predelli's position is so unrestricted it yields counter-intuitive consequences. What is required is a position which avoids these extremes and is flexible enough to account for the problem cases, but is not so loose that it becomes implausible.

---

[17] "Suppose, without turning and looking I point to the place on my wall which has long been occupied by a picture of Rudolf Carnap and I say, "[T]hat is a picture of one of the greatest philosophers of the twentieth century". But unbeknownst to me someone has replaced my picture of Carnap with one of Spiro Agnew. I think it would simply be wrong to argue an ambiguity in the demonstration, so great that it can be Suet to my intended demonstratum. I have said of a picture of Spiro Agnew that it pictures one of the greatest philosophers of the twentieth century" (Kaplan [1978] 1990: 30).

[18] As we saw in Ch. 1, above, I favor Kaplan's view. For, "Words come to us prepacked with a semantic value. If we are to use *those words*, the words we have received, the words of our linguistic community, then we must defer to *their* meanings" (Kaplan 1989: 602). Needless to say, the picture which emerges here fits with the contextual distinctions I introduced and discussed in Ch. 1, Sect. 5, above.

196 The First-Person Pronoun

The aim is to expand Kaplan's original framework to account for the variegated scenarios in which indexicals can be successfully used. The result is a position similar to Predelli's in as much as it retains Kaplan's account of the character of 'I' as a function from agent to referent, and deals with the problem cases by rejecting the agent-utterer identity. This position differs from Predelli's one, however, in that it rejects Predelli's Intentionalist approach to semantics, and replaces the agent-utterer identity with a more objective method of determining the agent. This way the resulting picture is much closer to the spirit, as well as the letter, of Kaplan's original account.

The proposal is rather simple. For any use of the first-person pronoun, the contextual parameter of the agent is *conventionally given*—given by the *social or conventional setting* in which the utterance takes place.[19] For instance, with 'now', the setting or context in which it is used changes the time that the term refers to: if 'now' is heard on an answering machine, we take the relevant time to be the time at which it is heard, and we arrive at the referent accordingly. In contrast, if we read 'now' on a postcard ("the weather is beautiful now"), the change in context or setting determines that the message refers differently. In the case of a postcard, unlike the case of an answering machine message, we take the relevant time to be the time at which the words were written. Hence we get a different referent in each case.

This notion of a setting is part of the context of the utterance and as such plays a role in determining the contextual parameters of agent, location, and time which are then utilized as argument for the character of the indexicals. The relevant factors which Kaplan allows to influence the contextual parameters of agent, location, and time are very narrow. In determining these parameters he is only concerned with the *who, where*, and *when* of the utterance, and does not allow anything else to influence the issues. In contrast, the notion of a setting of an utterance allows us to cast the net much more widely and include, among other things, the language being spoken, the physical environment, and other factors as relevant to determining the contextual parameters. In the terms of the explanation of Kaplan's conception given above, the account here proposed differs from Kaplan and Predelli as follows:

- Kaplan: the utterer is the agent   Character of 'I'(agent) → referent
- Predelli: intentions determine the agent   Character of 'I'(agent) → referent
- Conventional Account: conventions determine agent   Character of 'I'(agent) → referent

[19] I discussed the notion of setting in Ch. 1, Sect. 5, above. As it emerged the picture I favor might be understood along the lines of something like a Wittgensteinian *language-game*. Our linguistic furniture seems to function in different ways dependent upon the setting of a given linguistic act. This can be interpreted as saying that our linguistic pieces play a different role when we play different language-games with them.

This position can also be illustrated with Perry's distinction between *semantic* and *pre-semantic* uses of context:

> Sometimes we use context to figure out with which meaning a word is being used, or which of several words that look or sound alike is being used, or even which language is being spoken. These are *pre-semantic* uses of context. In the case of indexicals, however, context is used *semantically*. It remains relevant after the language, words and meaning are all known; the meaning directs us to certain aspects of context. (Perry 1997a: 593)

As I spelled out in Chapter 1, Section 5, though, I prefer rather to distinguish between broad and narrow context, for in the case of indexicals, context is used both semantically (narrow context) *and* pre-semantically (broad context).

On this account, it is a matter of the setting and the broad context whether a given word, for instance, is used with such or such a *conventional* meaning. In short, features such as speaking English, belonging to a given community, hearing an answering machine, sarcastically imitating someone, acting in a piece of theater, etc. are not part of what one says and usually aims to communicate. These features are better understood as aspects of the setting upon which the linguistic interchange takes place. As we saw in Chapter 1, the fact that one speaks German, for instance, when one says 'Ich' has no semantic role—it is not part of what one says. Our German speaker merely refers to herself using the first-person pronoun 'Ich'. If she were to speak English she would have used 'I' to refer to herself, for if she had uttered 'Ich' she would probably have expressed disgust. Thus facts about the setting such as these do not determine what the terms used *mean*, more which terms are *used*.

In this example, the mere fact that one speaks German is the setting upon which the linguistic interchange takes place. This setting is conventionally governed. If we consider our initial worries on the back of these suggestions, it emerges that it is our social practice which regulates the way we use answering machines and other similar devices. For the use of answering machines and post-it notes, is *conventionally* ruled in such a way that it allows someone to use a token of the first-person pronoun *produced by someone else* to refer to herself. This convention is illustrated by the fact that we do not face difficulties in coping with someone's pre-recorded answerphone message. It is a part of our conventions determining the use of answerphones that someone can buy a tape of a Woody Allen imitator reading a message and use it on their answerphone to refer to themselves. Without such settings and conventions we would be unable to successfully use and manipulate answering machines and other similar devices.

For reasons such as this, we should see that the context or setting of a linguistic interchange plays a role in determining how the agent is determined. In other words, the agent of 'I', like the relevant contextual parameters such as time and place, is best understood to be the *conventionally determined* agent, and the agent determined by convention may well, as we have seen, be distinct from either the utterer or the producer of the token of 'I'.

This attention to conventions goes so far as to explain how the deferred utterance method of resolving the original answering machine "paradox" gets off the ground. It succeeds because we are aware of the conventions governing the use of answering machines and the fact that the purpose of such devices is to inform the caller of the state of affairs *at the time the call is made*. Paying attention to conventions in this way also enables us to explain why we do not treat other superficially similar examples of utterances at a distance (such as postcards) in the same way. The conventions governing the use of postcards have it that their usual purpose is to inform the recipient of the state of affairs *at the time of writing*. It is only by paying attention to the differing conventional roles of these devices that we are able to get these explanations off the ground.

To explain the initial example in this framework; when Sue sticks her own post-it note saying "I am not here today" to Jury's office door with the intention of informing the eventual readers that the usual occupier of the office is not in, Sue can be seen to be exploiting the conventional setting of using notices in this way. The convention is that 'I' on a notice on someone's office door refers to the office's usual occupier. However, the example formulated illustrates that, on occasions when the office's occupant and the utterer come apart, the power of our linguistic conventions serves to ensure that 'I' nevertheless refers to the inhabitant of the office. Moreover, even if Sue intended the note to refer to herself (say she left in a hurry and attached the note to the wrong door by mistake), the conventions would override the intentions thus ensuring that the note still referred to Jury.

It is worth noting that the position proposed also allows us to dismiss cases such as the ones when a post-it note is found in a dustbin or on a corridor floor. As the *normal* function of a post-it note stating "I'm not in now" is to be put on a door, the setting, (i.e. a post-it note in a dustbin) prevents us from taking the post-it note as meaning something like *the agent is not in the dustbin*.

It is for these simple reasons that it is better to understand the agent *qua* contextual parameter upon which the character of 'I' directs us to be the conventional agent. It goes without saying, of course, that in most of the cases the contextual agent is the writer and/or speaker. In certain situations, however, it may not be the same.

8. Issues Arising

Some issues emerge from the conventionalist picture proposed here and in Chapters 1 and 2. Given that Kaplan's account must be somewhat modified to accommodate some cases, why should one retain any of it? Why not instead just reject the entire picture. There are several reasons one wishes to preserve a Kaplanian framework when dealing with indexical reference. First of all, as also emerged in previous chapters, Kaplan's framework is a powerful account which enables us to explain a number of facets of indexical reference. Secondly, as Kaplan says, the logic of demonstrative expressions requires the introduction of a contextual agent. Thirdly, and most importantly, in retaining the idea that every token of 'I' has the same character, we can respond to the objection that, in different scenarios (*pace* Quentin Smith), we are not using the same terms, but linguistically distinct homonyms. On the contrary, every utterance of 'I', regardless of how employed, is an utterance of the same type: in each case the character of the term remains the same. This third aspect fits well with the considerations expressed in Chapter 4.

Moreover, when extended to 'here' and 'now', this treatment enables us to elegantly explain the fact that these terms seem to have two distinct uses—as pure indexicals and as demonstratives. As I already suggested in Chapter 4, we can give an account of these facts as follows. In *every* use of the word 'here', the character of the indexical is a function from the contextual parameter of location to the referent. It is just that different conventional settings determine the location differently. Most of the time, the location is, as Kaplan suggests, identical with the place of utterance. However, in some of its conventional uses this does not hold. Take indicating places on maps as an example. In this convention-governed use of 'here', the character of the indexical remains the same—it is a function which returns the contextual parameter of location as referent. What changes is the way in which the contextual parameter of location is determined—in this case it is determined by the additional demonstration. In this way we can give a powerful and elegant account of the way in which certain indexicals seem to have these two distinct uses.

It remains to give an account of how the conventionalist picture addresses some of the other problematic cases considered. Since this picture allows for Jury to be the referent of an utterance he did not utter, how should one explain the scenario where the note Sue attaches to Jury's door states "I think the Chancellor is a fool"? One might diffuse any concerns about this case in two ways. The first would be to remember that, although Jury is the referent of 'I', he is not, thereby, the utterer. This response would enable us to claim that this scenario is no different for Jury than if Sue had attached a note saying "*Jury* thinks the Chancellor is a fool". In both cases the proposition expressed is the same, and in neither case does Jury have any responsibility for the expression of that proposition. Alternatively one might respond that joke notes like this constitute a conventional setting all of their own. Just as, if we see someone wearing a sign on their back which states "kiss me" we do not assume that they want to be kissed, we do not, in this case, assume that the purported referent of 'me' is responsible for the sign. Reading such a sign is not akin to hearing someone speak and assuming that they are telling the truth (as in normal communicative interaction), it is more like hearing somebody tell a joke or a tall story—normal interpretations are withheld.

Two related issues which need also to be addressed are the following. First there is the thought, following the rejection of the possibility that 'I' might fail to refer, that if an utterance is made, then there must be an utterer. If this is not Jury then who is it? There is also the related concern of how to cope if the note attached to Jury's door found its way there by random means (say Sue threw it away but a gust of wind picked it up from his bin and deposited it on Jury's door). In response to the first concern, we might follow our intuitions as regards Sue's using a note which states "Jury is not here today". In this scenario, there is no basis for denying that Sue is the utterer and Jury the referent. In the "I am not here today" case, we suggest that the same considerations should apply. Sue is the utterer (but not the referent) and Jury is the referent (but not the utterer).

To cope with the second anxiety we should remember that, in order for a proposition to be expressed, there has to be a communicative intention which is sufficient for utterances to occur. In our original scenario the communicative intention was on Sue's part, whereas in the random variant, there was no communicative intention and hence no utterances occur. It should be noted, however, that asserting the necessity of a communicative intention is not equivalent to the Intentionalism picture proposed by Predelli. Actually one has to recognize two distinct kinds of intention—the communicative (consumer) intention and the intention a speaker has to identify/speak about a given item (the individuative intention).[20] The conventionalist picture rejects, *pace* Predelli, that there is any semantic role for the second type of intention. It accepts, on the other hand, the necessity of the first type of intention. After all, if one is to play a (language-) game, one ought to have the intention of following the rules of that game.

Finally, one needs to explain how the conventionalist position accounts for Predelli's note example where Jury's partner, reading the note at 7 p.m. takes 'now' to refer to 5 p.m. The convention exploited in this case is that of leaving notes in a common context. It is only because Jury's partner is aware that Jury would have expected her to come home at 5 p.m. (either because of prior arrangements or because that is the time she usually comes home) that she is able to grasp

---

[20] This fits hand in glove within the framework advocated in Chs. 1 and 2. In particular, with Kaplan's idea that "To use language as language, to express something, requires an intentional act but the intention that is required involves the typical consumer's attitude of compliance, not the producer's assertiveness" (Kaplan 1989: 602). For a more accurate discussion of this phenomenon see Ch. 1, above.

that Jury must have intended 'now' to refer to 5 p.m. If there were no social convention between the couple regarding the time of her arrival home (either normally, or on that specific occasion), then the convention would decree that some other time be used as the parameter, regardless of the intentions of the note writer. If the usual time of Jury's partner's homecoming is 6 p.m., and if she had stipulated that tonight she would, as usual, be home at 6, then surely 'now' would have referred to 6 p.m. *regardless* of Jury's intentions. The only reason communication successfully takes place is because Jury's partner is aware that she usually returns home at a certain time and that this is the time that Jury would have expected her to return home.

It might be argued that all this shows is that these facts about the situation entail that Jury *could not* have intended to use 'now' to refer to 5 p.m. This proposal would amount to adding a qualification to the Intentionalist proposal such that, whilst the listener is supposed to look for the intended referent, this cannot work unless it is possible (in the context) for the decoder to work out who the referent is. However, once we accept that there is a limit to what we can intend to use a term to refer to, we suggest that the Intentionalist picture comes to *assume* something like the very account proposed here. When faced with this kind of situation we need to establish what it is about a given scenario that makes it the case that it is reasonable, or plausible, to expect the decoder to be able to identify the referent of a given indexical. For example, what makes it the case that Sue's leaving the note on Jury's door makes it plausible to expect the decoder to come up with Jury as the intended referent, whereas leaving it on the toilet door does not? Surely what Sue is doing here is exploiting the very type of convention that the conventionalist picture invokes. So, in as much as Sue's intentions are involved in assigning a referent to 'I' in the problem case, it is her intention to exploit the convention of leaving notes on doors that is important rather than her intention that 'I' should refer to Jury. When seen in this light, however, it is easy to see how the communicative intention to exploit a convention might have been mistaken for an individuative intention to assign a referent.[21]

So, we can see then that it is of no account that Jury *intended* 'now' to refer to 5 p.m., if Jury had intended 'now' to refer to 11 p.m. (for whatever reason) it would still only have referred to 5 p.m. given the context in which the note was left. Jury's intentions only come into the picture inasmuch as he leaves the note with

---

[21] This also explains why one cannot do away with this multiplicity of conventions in favor of a single, underlying interpretive rule which all these conventions are merely instances *of*. The kind of rule which might play this role would be something like the qualified Intentionalist rule above. However, as we have seen, this approach only gets off the ground inasmuch as it assumes the existence of certain constraints which look very much like the conventions it proposes to replace.

a communicative intention to exploit a certain convention. One does not, however, have to appeal to the speaker and/or audience's individuative intention to account for the reference of indexical expressions. All one needs to appeal to are conventionally given contextual parameters.

To sum up, Kaplan's story about the character of 'I' rests on his plausible identification of the utterer, the agent, and the referent. So the character of 'I' takes as argument the agent/utterer/referent and gives as value the agent/utterer/referent. The scenario I proposed, however, shows that we cannot always identify the utterer with the referent in this way. Predelli's account of intentional contexts appears to offer a way of biting the bullet and claiming that the referent/agent of 'I' can be picked out by an utterance that she never dreamed of. Predelli affects this by retaining Kaplan's account of the character of 'I' whilst replacing agent-utterer identity with the claim that the agent is determined intentionally. However, it has been argued that, if this picture is accepted, one must also accept the implausible consequence that one can use 'I' to refer to whatever one wants to. The conventionalist picture, on the other hand, powerfully and elegantly accommodates the data discussed, by introducing the notion of the *conventionally determined* agent. This position rests on the plausible distinction proposed in Chapter 1 (Section 5) between the conventional setting upon which the linguistic act takes place, and narrow context, i.e. the parameters (time, place, and agent) *qua* argument and value of the character of indexicals.

Some of the issues that I have discussed in this chapter will be developed further in Chapter 7. In particular, we shall see how cognitive impairments such as autism prevent people from mastering the use of pronouns, not to mention the attribution of indexical thoughts to others. Before turning to discuss the psychological bases which help us to master the use of indexicals and to capture another's indexical thoughts from a third-person perspective, such as empathy and imagination, I shall deal with more general issues such as psychological generalization and mental causation and show how they are handled by the picture I favor. Hence, in the next chapter we shall see how our thoughts are context-sensitive and situated. The context-sensitivity of our thinking activity will be highlighted by focusing on examples such as the twin-Earth scenario. It will emerge that the notion of context-sensitive thought helps us to understand mental causation and how it can support interesting psychological generalizations.

6

Perspectival Thoughts and Psychological Explanation

When you and I entertain the sense of "A bear is about to attack me", we behave similarly. We both roll up in a ball and try to be as still as possible. Different thoughts apprehended, same sense entertained, same behavior. When you and I both apprehend the thoughts that I am about to be attacked by a bear, we behave differently, I roll up in a ball, you run to get help. Same thought apprehended, different sense entertained, different behavior.

(Perry 1977: 18–9)

We want science to give causal explanations of such things (events, whatever) in nature as can be causally explained. Giving such explanations essentially involves projecting and confirming causal generalizations. And causal generalizations subsume the things they apply to in virtue of the causal properties of the things they apply to.

(Fodor 1987: 34)

In this chapter, I discuss the relation between thoughts and the context in which they are entertained. Following what I said in the Introduction, I argue that thoughts are best viewed as situated. The same thought situated in a different context is likely to be about something different. I introduce the notion of perspectival thoughts and show how they can support psychological generalizations in a straightforward way.

Here is the way in which I shall proceed. In Section 1, I present desiderata that a theory concerning psychological generalization should try to capture. In Section 2, I discuss the object-dependent thought picture (ODT) and I show that it faces difficulties in handling the psychological generalization desideratum. To deal with the latter, ODT has to let object-independent thoughts (OIT) into the picture, but then Ockham's razor cuts out object-dependent thoughts and the OIT story turns into the correct picture. In Section 3, I focus on the distinction and relationship between thoughts and context. ODT and OIT use this relationship in a different way. The OIT picture rests on a firm distinction between thoughts and context. In Section 4, on the basis of the thought/context distinction, I introduce the notion of perspectival (context-sensitive) thoughts. One of the main features of these thoughts is that they may be about something without representing it (as we saw in Chapter 2). ODT, on the other hand, is committed to the thesis that thoughts are fully articulated and this does not seem to obey an economical rule governing thinking episodes. In Section 5, I show how perceptual thoughts are perspectival. I introduce the distinction between perceptual content and perceptual states and argue that the latter are property-based and psychologically relevant. In Section 6, I show how perspectival thoughts (OIT) are causally efficacious and, as such, support psychological generalizations. Finally, in Section 7, I answer an objection put forth by the friends of ODT, according to whom context cannot secure the relation between thoughts and reference.

1. Some Desiderata

Who has not heard the following story? Jane is thirsty. She believes that there is a bottle of Evian in the fridge and desires to have some water. She goes to the fridge and takes the bottle of Evian. Twin-Jane, who is a molecule-for-molecule duplicate of Jane, lives on twin-Earth, which is just the same as Earth down to the last molecule except that on Earth we have H_2O and on twin-Earth our twins have XYZ. Indeed, twin-Jane is thirsty as well and believes that there is some water in the fridge. She walks to the fridge and takes the bottle of Evian.

Jane and twin-Jane did something similar, and this is what matters to psychological generalizations and what is going to matter to us in this chapter. Actually, we want our psychology to be able to generalize over Jane's and twin-Jane's behavior (or actions).[1] This is a general desideratum that each theory tries to accommodate. It seems obvious that, to be useful, psychological laws ought to be systematic. They ought to be general enough to subsume similar behaviors. If Jane's and twin-Jane's behavior is not subsumed under the same law our psychology falls apart, or at best, it becomes a solipsistic psychology. I take it for granted that psychology ought to obey this psychological generalization constraint. It is worth noticing, however, that the psychological generalization desideratum should capture the fact that psychological laws *qua* explanations of behavior subsume organisms with the

---

[1] For simplicity's sake I do not distinguish between action and behavior. It could be argued that, although Jane's and twin-Jane's behavior is the same insofar as they accomplish the same movement, their action is different because Jane takes bottle A and twin-Jane takes twin-A. If this is the case, our psychology ought to subsume similar *behavior* under its laws.

same or similar causal potentials (see Section 5). As such, it does not rule out other types of generalization. Psycho-sociology, for instance, may be interested in the relation between an organism and its environment and, thus, its laws refer to worldly and social facts and so forth. Actually, certain scientific classifications must appeal to relational properties and do not merely concern the intrinsic properties of a given individual. If a classification concerns, for instance, daughters or foreigners, such a classification appeals to relational properties (the property of being a daughter and the property of being a foreigner). These properties may play a relevant role in a given causal explanation. The explanation about needing a visa to enter a certain country, for instance, involves the property of being a foreigner *vis-à-vis* the country one aims to enter. Psychology *qua* explanation of behavior is concerned, however, with dealing in abstractions over agents' mental states and its main concern is the identification of the agents' cognitive contribution to their behavior.[2] For this very reason it is the causal contribution of an agent's mental states that matters most for psychological explanations, classifications, and generalizations. If you disagree you are kindly invited to accept it for the sake of the argument. After all, if Jane and twin-Jane say: "I am thirsty", we cannot deny that there is something common going on within their mind. They both refer to themselves and act, *ceteris paribus*, in a similar way.

The *ceteris paribus* clause should rule out the case where Jane, having collateral beliefs and desires (e.g. strongly desiring to get drunk or believing that the water in the fridge is poisonous), does not reach for the water. The *ceteris paribus* clause should also rule out cases where Jane slides on the wet floor and breaks her left leg when going to the fridge or twin-Jane, having arthritis in her right thigh, cannot move and ought rather to call Tyler to bring her some water.

Everybody tends to agree that behavior is controlled and caused by thoughts. Jane and twin-Jane act under the control of their thoughts. The problem is that people, or at least those involved in philosophy, do not agree on the nature of these thoughts. There are two main competing stories. On the one hand, we are told that it is natural to argue that Jane and twin-Jane act in the same way because they entertain the same thought. So their thought is neutral *vis-à-vis* (or independent of the very nature of) the stuff (H_2O or XYZ) they are acting in respect of. On the other hand, we are told that Jane's and twin-Jane's thoughts are different because they are related to different things (thoughts depend on the nature of the

---

[2] For a book-length discussion of the representational power of mental states and their involvement in causal explanation, see Jacob (1997). Jacob argues in favor of the naturalization of intentionality, i.e. the view that the semantic properties of one's propositional attitudes can be derived from non-semantic properties of one's mind. Furthermore, Jacob shows how the semantic properties of one's mind concur in the explanation of one's intentional behavior. The picture I propose should be neutral regarding the naturalization of intentionality.

thing they are about). The first story is often given the label 'internalism' or 'individualism,' while the second is labeled 'externalism'. Since it is not my intent to address the internalist/externalist or individualism/anti-individualism debate, I am going to refer to the first story as the object-independency of thought, and to the second as the object-dependency of thought.[3]

2. Object-Dependent Thoughts

The ODT story holds that thoughts are *object-dependent* or *Russellian*. These thoughts are often called *de re* thoughts, after McDowell (1984). *De re* thoughts are made up of *de re* senses (object-dependent or Russellian senses/modes of presentation). According to Evans:

[A] thought is Russellian if it is of such a kind that it simply could not exist in the absence of the object or objects which it is about. (Evans 1982: 71)

Evans gives us one of the best and most explicit characterizations of the ODT story I have in mind when he writes:

I hold that there are thoughts we have about particular objects which we simply could not have if those objects did not exist. For example, an internal state of a subject can be ascribed the content that *this table is round* only if there is a particular object it is about, on which it is causally dependent. There is no neutral or 'existence-independent' specification of this content to which we can retreat if the subject is hallucinating. If there is no object (whether or not the subject believes there is), there is no content—no thought. (Evans 1985: 402)

The first ODT's motto can be:

- *ODT's motto 1*
No object, no thought

This, you should concede, sounds rather counterintuitive. For it seems natural to say that Jane's behavior is not affected whether she actually sees a lion coming towards her or if she simply hallucinates one. In both cases she acts, *ceteris paribus*, in the same way. It sounds natural to claim that Jane's thoughts (those relevant to psychological explanation) are the same. The folk psychological explanation should run as follows: in both situations, Jane's behavior is of the same type. Jane behaves in the same way whether she is deluded or not because she is in the same

---

[3] For simplicity's sake, I do not distinguish between objects and stuffs or kinds like water and tigers. Hence, I keep speaking of object-(in)dependent thoughts instead of stuff-(in)dependent or kind-(in)dependent thoughts. For a recent extensive discussion of the individualism/externalism debate in philosophy of mind, see Robert Wilson (1995).

mental state. In other words, Jane behaves the way she does because in both cases she entertains a thought of the same type (and this is what matters in psychological explanation). However, if in both cases Jane can have a thought of the same type, the thoughts relevant to psychological explanation are object-*in*dependent after all and thus OIT ought to be the right picture. The same thought is at play whether or not Jane is deluded. To illustrate this point, imagine that, while Jane is deluded, twin-Jane is not. Both Jane and twin-Jane act in the same way, and both act in a rational way.[4] We want our psychology to subsume both Jane's and twin-Jane's behavior under the same psychological law, so there should be something (a level of thinking) they both share and which supports psychological generalizations. This is our psychological generalization desideratum (in the next section I put forth a notion of perspectival and object-independent thought, which allows us to accommodate these intuitions).[5]

To handle the psychological generalization desideratum, the ODT theorist may argue that in both situations there is an *incomplete thought*. This thought gets completed in the veridical situation and remains incomplete when the agent is deluded.[6] Jane and twin-Jane act in a similar way because they share an incomplete thought, so the thoughts relevant for psychological explanation are incomplete and *object-independent*. But then, why do we need object-dependent thoughts? Why should one not be happy dealing with object-independent thought and accept that OIT is the right picture? Besides, if the only thoughts relevant for psychological explanation are incomplete, then the psychologically spurious object-dependent thoughts are not, properly speaking, thoughts at all. By a principle of economy we can thus dismiss object-dependent thoughts.[7]

It can be argued that Evans's characterization of ODT does not apply to the ODT theorist who denies the existence of senses and takes modes of presentation

---

[4] I am using the label 'rational' in an intuitive way. To block my argument, the ODT theorist could argue that a deluded subject does not act in a rational way. I take this step to be *ad hoc* and rather counterintuitive.

[5] Segal (1989) presents the ODT theorist with the following challenge. Imagine that, whenever I think *a* is *F*, twin-me thinks *a* is *F* as well but, unlike me, my twin is deluded. On twin-Earth, there is no *a*. Hence: If ODT cannot make sense of my twin's behavior (who is deluded), then ODT is in trouble, for twin-me acts in a rational way and we want our psychology to explain this fact. On the other hand, if ODT can make sense of my twin's behavior without appealing to a singular thought, then we do not have to invoke singular thoughts in psychological explanation. For a similar argument against ODT, see Noonan who argues that, "if object-dependent thoughts exist they are redundant in the psychological explanation of intentional actions" (Noonan 1993: 289).

[6] Adams et al. go this way. They argue that "In the vacuous situation . . . she has an *incomplete thought*. She has what would be a complete thought, if it had an object . . . The important thing is that [Jane] doesn't realize it is incomplete" (Adams et al. 1993: 95).

[7] Adams et al. put forth an argument supposed to support the need for object-dependent thoughts in intentional explanation. As I am going to argue in Section 7, below, this argument is *ad hoc* and jeopardizes the ODT's enterprise.

to be syntactic strings going on within one's head (see Adams et al. 1993). On such a view (which I am going to label *the syntactic view*), a thought is object-dependent when the syntactic string gets supplied with a semantics. We can think of syntactic strings as open sentences, which become object-dependent thoughts insofar as the variables of these sentences have an interpretation.

At first, it could be thought that the cognitive activity was supported by modes of presentation *qua* syntax. If this were the case, object-dependent thoughts would be psychologically inert insofar as we could explain *both* the veridical situation and the case from illusion in exactly the same way, i.e. in making reference to modes of presentation (thoughts) *qua* syntactic strings and, therefore, to object-*in*dependent thoughts. In other words, following this suggestion it would be possible to argue that Jane's and twin-Jane's water-thoughts can be grouped together, as well as Jane's thought in the presence of a lion and twin-Jane's thought when she hallucinates a lion. In both cases, they entertain the same modes of presentation *qua* the same syntactic strings. If this were the case we would face difficulties, for we would be unable to subsume Jane's water-thoughts under the same law when she mumbles to herself "This water is cold" and the thought she entertains when mumbling "Cette eau est froide". Since the syntactic strings are different, these thoughts *qua* syntactic strings would not fall into the same basket. One could claim that both the English and French strings are syntactically similar insofar as they can be parsed the same way, i.e. they have the same deep structure or grammar. I am not sure that the syntactic view can be understood this way, for the string "A bottle is in front of me" and "A lion is in front of you" are parsed the same way, i.e. are grammatically equivalent. Yet they do not trigger the same behavior. For the syntactic view to be appealing, it must assume that strings with different symbols are distinct syntactic strings. Syntactic strings are thus best viewed as sentences of Mentalese. Indeed, one could argue that the sentence "This water is cold" and "Cette eau est froide" are instances of the same Mentalese sentence, yet one uttering the French sentence may behave differently from one uttering the English one, for one may not know that 'eau' translates as 'water'. These sentences *qua* syntactic strings do not seem to cut finely enough for psychological explanation.

This, however, is not the end of the story, for it is not what the friends of the syntactic view have in mind—it does not represent, for instance, the viewpoint of Adams et al. Actually, they can argue that a syntactic string by itself explains nothing; it is only when a string is either meaningful (expresses a content) or is associated with other meaningful syntactic strings (thoughts) that it plays a role in psychological explanation. One's behavior will be explained by several syntactic strings in one's brain, so the fact that Jane has an object-dependent thought while twin-Jane has a vacuous thought does not entail that their behavior is not subsumed under the same law. Jane and twin-Jane share all sorts of object-dependent thoughts and their similar behavior is explained *via* these common thoughts. Two questions come to my mind: (i) how do we choose the class of thoughts relevant for psychological explanation? and (ii) why do these thoughts have to be object-dependent? In short, which of these thoughts make twin-Jane run when she hallucinates a lion chasing her? Notice that these thoughts should also explain the similarity between the behavior of twin-Jane, who is deluded, and the behavior of Jane, who is not. In our example, these thoughts cannot (or so it seems to me) be object-dependent, corresponding to strings like "George W. Bush invaded Iraq" or "The gorilla I saw last week is nasty". These thoughts need to be cashed out as strings like "*Something* big and powerful is after me". That is, by strings which are generalizations of the original ones. Let us consider that twin-Jane and Jane both have the string "That lion is after me" in their brain and they both run. Twin-Jane is deluded, so her behavior cannot be under the control of an object-dependent thought represented by the string "That lion is after me". Her behavior is under the control of the string "Something big and powerful is after me". Jane is not deluded and entertains the object-dependent thought represented by "That lion is after me". How do we explain why Jane behaves like twin-Jane? The answer that comes to my mind is that Jane behaves like twin-Jane because of the presence of a more general thought, which is also a generalization of the string "That lion is after me". In short, Jane and twin-Jane behave in the same way and their behavior can be subsumed under the same law because of a general thought of the form "*Something* . . .". In other words, the fact that Jane and twin-Jane share the thought *that if something big and powerful is after you, you should run to avoid danger* will explain why they both run. If this is (or comes close to being) the right picture, then psychological explanation is supported by general thoughts of the form "*Something* . . .". Hence, another motivation ought to be furnished in favor of the need for object-dependent thoughts. Adams et al. answered this challenge in claiming that the fact that there are no laws about a given individual does not demonstrate that one's perception of that particular individual is not partially explanatory of one's behavior:

There are no laws about lion*1* or the perception of lion*1* to be sure. But that hardly demonstrates that Alice's perception of that very lion, lion*1*, is not partially explanatory of her running. Her perception (and ODT thought content that "that lion is after me") would instantiate a psychological law and partially explain Alice's running. (Adams et al. 1999: 49)

Adams et al. concede that ODT are relevant to psychological generalizations inasmuch as they instantiate general thought. They also concede that they play a causal role only in virtue of instantiating general thoughts. Let us grant, for argument's sake, that this is the right picture. If I understand it correctly, then what is relevant to psychological laws are the general thoughts, which trigger one's behavior. The object one's thought is about may help in individuating the general thought, yet it plays no causal role. It merely plays an *individuating* role. To illustrate this difference, let us imagine a given community that, under the dominance of a fascist group, decides that they should eliminate all the fascists. For secret (but obvious) reasons, our community decides to adopt the following convention. Each time they discover a fascist, if they are in the presence of a member of the dominant group (i.e. a fascist) they refer to the fascist with the label 'handsome'. Thus, the members of this community can express the thought that NN is a fascist in uttering either "NN is handsome" or "NN is a fascist" (they individuate the fascist this latter way when no members extraneous to the community are present). Thus, the members of this community have two ways in which they can individuate the thought that someone is a fascist. Yet, the way they individuate the relevant thought does not play a causal role: it merely plays an individuating role. A member of this community acts and tries to kill someone insofar as s/he entertains the thought that the one s/he must kill is a fascist, regardless of whether his/her thought is individuated using 'handsome' or 'fascist'. The very same thought can thus be individuated in rather different ways. The way a thought is individuated is not necessarily what explains someone's action. The fascists may come to believe that every time a member of the community entertains the thought that so-and-so is handsome, she becomes dangerous and kills the alleged handsome subject. Yet the anti-fascist's action is not triggered by the thought that so-and-so is handsome; it is triggered by the thought that s/he is a fascist. Our friend's action is triggered by the thought s/he actually entertains, regardless of the way we individuate it. In short, the fact that we refer to worldly entities when individuating a thought does not prove that the thought itself depends on these entities: all it proves is that we individuate it in appealing to the latter. Whether the individuation is successful and whether we can come out with reliable predictions on the basis of such an individuation is another story. It is a story concerning the way we capture what triggers one's behavior. As we shall see in Chapter 8, this story has to do with our practice of ascribing attitudes and it rests, ultimately, on our practice of using 'that'-clauses as they appear in reports such as "NN believes/wishes/thinks/ . . . that *p*".

I can concede that the criticism I advanced against ODT is not a knockdown argument—to be honest I was not, and have never been, after a knockdown argument. Yet I can still maintain that a picture appealing only to OITs gives us all we need and, therefore, that one need not appeal to ODT in order to tell a story about psychological generalizations. Another argument must be put forward in order to show that we must appeal to ODTs. To this argument I now turn.

The friends of the syntactic view argue that we need object-dependent thoughts to explain intentional behavior in veridical situations. So:

> In the veridical situation, it is not an incomplete thought, but a complete object-dependent thought that is the basis of Alice's inference that *there is a man after me*. The full story about how Alice's thoughts arise in the veridical situation is that her thought that *that man is after me* gives rise to her thought that there is a man after her. Why not just say that there is an incomplete thought in both situations, the only difference being that in the veridical situation *context* provides a man for the thought to refer to? The reason this will not work is that the mere fact that context supplies an object does not determine that reference (or intentional action) is to it (directed toward it). (Adams et al. 1993: 96)

I challenge this reason and argue that context supplies the object and fixes, so to speak, the reference of our thoughts. Actually, unlike Adams et al., I think that there is a difference between ODTs and OITs when we come to explain the veridical situation.[8] As I shall suggest in the next section, this difference rests on two distinct conceptions we can adopt in considering the relationship between thoughts and context. But first, let me concentrate on another point of disagreement between ODT and OIT.

ODT faces yet another commitment. It has to do with the nature of psychological taxonomies insofar as we characterize thoughts by their content. Thoughts about different objects *cannot* be grouped together, for if a thought's identity is also given by the objects it is about, thoughts about different objects have different contents. The ODT's motto can now be:

- *ODT motto 2*:
  Change the object, change the content

Therefore, if we taxonomize thoughts by their content and if the latter is object-dependent, then thoughts about different objects necessarily fall into different baskets.[9] Hence, twin-Jane's water-thought, being about XYZ, and Jane's water-thought, being about H_2O, cannot be grouped together, for their content is necessarily different. This, again, runs against the intuition that twin-Jane and Jane fall under the same psychological explanation because their thoughts are of the same type.

---

[8] "In the veridical situation Alice is causally related to the man in the room. She perceives him and runs from him. If context supplies the man and she stands in the right causal relations to him, then her thoughts are indeed *about him*. Her action is intentionally *fleeing from him*. This is just to say that she has a *complete* thought, part of the content of which is that man" (Adams et al. 1993: 96).

[9] To be sure, thoughts about different objects cannot be grouped together, insofar as we taxonomize thoughts on the basis of an identity relation. Thoughts about different objects could be grouped together on the basis of a similarity relation. The difficulty I see is to figure out the nature of this relation.

212 *Thoughts and Psychological Explanation*

A way out of this difficulty for the ODT theorist would be to appeal to types of *de re* sense (roughly, types of object-dependent modes of presentation) to characterize Jane's and twin-Jane's water-thoughts and claim that they are thoughts of the same type.[10] If we go this way, we are left with the distinction between object-dependent thought and types of object-dependent thought, the latter being relevant to psychological explanation: Jane and twin-Jane behave in the same way because the object-dependent thoughts controlling their actions are of the same type.[11] The difficulty is to find a type that is instantiated by both H_2O-thoughts and XYZ-thoughts. It would appear to be a class with a disjunctive extension. An intuitive way to understand a type is to take it to be an abstraction or a class of equivalences of modes of presentations. In other words, it may be useful to think that the formation of a type is like the formation of a concept. We form, say, the water-concept because we encounter several samples of what we are told is water during our learning period. Suppose that these samples are of H_2O; if twin-me and I share the same concept, our water-concept subsumes both H_2O and XYZ: it has a disjunctive extension. The problem I foresee is that, for our concept to have a disjunctive extension, it cannot be an abstraction of object-dependent modes of presentations (*de re* senses). Rather, it has to be an abstraction of the features common to both H_2O and XYZ, i.e. what have been called the stereotypes (see Putnam 1975). If this comes close to being the correct picture, object-dependent thoughts are not at play during type or concept formation, in which case it is difficult to argue that object-dependent thoughts come into play only after the type/token distinction has been engendered. We can illustrate this point as follows: suppose that a child, at different times of her learning period, encounters different samples of H_2O whilst thinking *that is water* (and in so doing acquiring the water-concept). If she does not entertain an object-dependent thought then, why should she entertain an object-dependent thought once she comes to master the concept of water?

Moreover, from the ODT viewpoint, my 'I'-thoughts are necessarily different from your 'I'-thoughts and my 'now'-thoughts are different from one time to the next. How can psychology be useful if it cannot generalize over these thoughts? Given that they are intrinsically tied to action, a useful psychology should appeal

---

[10] Notice, however, that McDowell (1984) argues against the idea that Jane's and twin-Jane's water-thoughts are of the same type. In other words, ODT cannot assume the type/token distinction in order to deal with twin-Earth cases. As I understand it, the argument runs somewhat as follows: Types on Earth are abstractions from Earthly *de re* senses, while types on twin-Earth are abstractions from twin-Earthly *de re* senses. If the classes of *de re* senses are different insofar as they contain senses dependent on Earthly (respectively twin-Earthly) objects, the abstractions which will give us the type will be different too.

[11] The case from illusion could be dealt with in arguing that twin-Jane's incomplete thought belongs to the same type as Jane's object-dependent thought. Because of this reason, Jane's and twin-Jane's behavior can be subsumed under the same law.

to laws that subsume these thoughts.[12] If the ODT theorist is able (maybe by vindicating McDowell's sort of *de re* senses or in appealing to the type/token distinction) to propose psychological laws that subsume different people's 'I'-thoughts, or different 'now'-thoughts, she ought to introduce a level of thought which is not object-dependent. Thus, object-dependent thoughts turn out to be psychologically spurious.[13]

I now turn to discuss one of the main arguments proposed in favor of ODT, i.e. the thesis that we need object-dependent thoughts to deal with intentionality in veridical situations. In so doing, I am going to concentrate on the way ODT and OIT consider the relationship between thoughts and context. I show, *pace* Adams et al., that we cannot infer from the fact that the context secures a referent (an object of our thought) that this referent is part of our thought (i.e. that the latter is object-dependent). As I said above, an object may come into the picture when we individuate and ascribe a thought, yet it plays no role in triggering one's actions. This last point will become more clear when, in Chapter 8, I deal with attitude ascriptions.

3. Thoughts in Context

The distinct conceptions of thought held by ODT and OIT rest on different conceptions of the relationship between thought and context. I first show that the thought/context relationship is a key feature in understanding the distinction between ODT and OIT. I then argue that ODT's difficulties concerning psychological generalizations rest on the rejection of a particular version of the thought/context distinction. Armed with the thought/context distinction, I introduce the notion of perspectival thought and show how it fits into our psychological generalization desideratum.

As I understand it, ODT rests on the refusal to separate mental content and context. In particular, object-dependent thoughts cannot be context-sensitive. Imagine now that Jane entertains the thought that she would express using the sentence "That lion is after me". According to ODT, Jane's thought is object-dependent. If we change the lion, we change the thought. So if the lion happens to be Igor, Jane's thought is fixed on Igor: the thought's identity would depend on Igor. If the lion were Ivan, her thought would be fixed on Ivan. If Jane were deluded, either she would not have a thought at all or else her thought would remain

---

[12] See Perry (1979) on the way essential indexicals such as 'I', 'here', and 'now' are intrinsically tied to action. I discussed this issue in Ch. 4, Sect. 2. I further discuss this issue in Ch. 9, below.

[13] "Particular *de re* senses, each specific to its *res*, can be grouped into sorts. Different *de re* senses (modes of presentation) can present their different *res* in the same sort of way" (McDowell 1984: 103).

incomplete. The important fact is that Jane's thought changes according to the change in the object it is about. Thoughts, so conceived, cannot be context-sensitive and change their aboutness. On the other hand, the OIT theorist I have in mind would argue that Jane's thought is the same and remains constant across the three situations. The very same thought is context-sensitive. In a different context, it picks out a given referent (or none, if the agent is deluded).

I call the ODT attitude just described *contextophobia*. You are contextophobic if you hold that thoughts cannot be abstracted from the context in which they are entertained and are necessarily dependent on the context. On the other hand, you will be a *contextophiliac* if you accept the picture according to which thoughts are separated from context and, as such, may be context-sensitive. From the ODT's (contextophobic) viewpoint, singular thoughts are understood as relations between agents and objects. As such, thoughts are object-dependent, since a relation cannot be instantiated if the terms of the relation do not exist. McDowell is certainly contextophobic:

[T]his division of content from context is recommended only by a conflation . . . [by the fact that] it is so tempting to conflate mental content with means of representation. (McDowell 1984: 102)

A story may illustrate the contextophobia *vs.* contextophilia debate.

Tim Badguy, a notorious killer, lives in New York and has been hired to kill Jane. He has been given detailed information about her: he even recalls having met her at a Halloween party in San Francisco last year. Tim leaves New York for LA to accomplish his mission. At the airport, Tim gets confused and, instead of going to the Trans-World-Airlines terminal, he goes to the Twin-World-Airlines one. So the TWA Boeing, which Tim supposes will take him to LA, instead arrives in twin-LA (on twin-Earth). Indeed, Tim does not realize his mistake and thinks he is in LA. He recognizes the city and drives around in search of Jane: he even asks the barman in a famous pub on Sunset Boulevard where Jane usually shows up. He is told that she was there last night. He finally finds her, waits in front of her house, and, as soon as she comes out of the door, he shoots, killing twin-Jane. He decides to go back home. At twin-LA airport Tim is not confused. He goes straight to the Trans-World-Airlines terminal, back to twin-New York, and gets paid for his clean job.[14]

There are two ways in which we can interpret this story. When in twin-LA, the mode of presentation Tim has acquired on Earth, let us call it MP_{Jane}, is either (i) related to twin-Jane, or (ii) it is still related to Jane, because of the context of acquisition (learning period, etc.).

---

[14] Notice that this story can be complicated. We can imagine that Tim has a twin who gets confused and flies to LA to kill Jane, and so on. So Tim's and twin-Tim's modes of presentation control their actions *vis-à-vis* Jane and twin-Jane.

We can agree that Tim's MP_{Jane} controls his actions that culminate in killing twin-Jane. Had Tim not been mistaken in New York and gone to the right terminal, he would have caught the plane to LA and killed Jane, instead of flying to twin-LA and killing twin-Jane. An intuitive way to interpret this story is to say that a single mode of presentation is at play and that it controls Tim's action. In one case, it controls Tim's behavior in his killing twin-Jane, whilst in the other it controls his behavior in killing Jane. If so, we can wonder whether Tim's mode of presentation is about Jane or twin-Jane. The ODT friend would probably say that it is about Jane and that the thoughts which guide his acting are Jane-dependent. On the other hand, the OIT friends that I have in mind would say that, on Earth, Tim's mode of presentation is about Jane and on twin-Earth about twin-Jane. These modes of presentation would be situated in different contexts or situations. As such, they can be anchored to different individuals, depending on the situation in which they occur. A promising way to understand what is going on in Tim's case is by postulating mental files: the modes of presentation that one entertains are akin to files, each one of which is labeled. Tim's mode of presentation of Jane is label 'Jane'; on Earth 'Jane' refers to Jane, while on twin-Earth 'Jane' refers to twin-Jane. We can further assume that one's modes of presentations *qua* files are labeled with the very same words one uses in one's everyday linguistic and cognitive activity. On Earth, one uses the words 'Jane' and 'water', which stand for Jane and H_2O. On twin-Earth, one uses the words 'Jane' and 'water', which refer to twin-Jane and XYZ. This goes hand-in-hand with the ideas I discussed in Chapters 1 and 2, i.e. that reference is socially secured and that mental representations rest on a deference principle. In our story, Tim asks other people to help him to individuate Jane when he is in doubt. On twin-LA, these people help him to individuate twin-Jane. They help him to anchor his mode of presentation to twin-Jane. This seems to suggest that a mode of presentation implicitly contains an argument place for a context or, more simply, the mere fact that a mode of presentation is entertained in a given context suggests that it is about a given object. In other words, it is because modes of presentation are *situated* in a context that they are about certain individuals. The aboutness is secured by context, broadly conceived. The language one speaks (whether English or twin-English, for instance) will contribute in determining the extension of the words one uses and, therefore, the aboutness of one's modes of presentations.[15] Hence, if we change the social context, we may change the reference. We defer to society to secure reference.

[15] This goes hand in hand with the notion of context I introduced and discussed in Ch. 1, Sect. 5, where I distinguished between the broad notion and the narrow notion of context and how it helps in understanding the difference between proper names and indexicals. The fact that one uses a given language is explained using the broad notion of context. This helps in characterizing which words one uses. The notion of narrow context, on the other hand, enters the scene in order to explain how indexical reference gets fixed.

If so, then modes of presentation are object-independent and the contextophilia attitude seems to be the right one.[16]

For Tim's story to make sense, it seems that a mode of presentation ought to be divorced from the object it happens to be about. We have to let context secure its semantics. In different contexts, the same mode of presentation may be about different individuals, such as Jane and twin-Jane.

The ODT friend could argue that the relevant context in our story is the *context of acquisition* and claim that Tim's mode of presentation is about Jane (regardless of whether he is on Earth or twin-Earth) because he acquired it on Earth. Tim's thoughts are Jane-dependent. But when we come to explain Tim's actions on twin-Earth, it sounds rather counterintuitive, at least to me, to claim that his Jane-dependent thoughts control his action *vis-à-vis* twin-Jane. Why not assume that the relevant context is the *context of use* and say that, on Earth, Tim's thoughts are aimed at Jane and on twin-Earth at twin-Jane? Reference seems to be neutral *vis-à-vis* the context of acquisition and secured by the context of use. Indeed, in normal life, the context of acquisition and the context of use do not differ. In my linguistic community, I learn the name 'NN' and, with the help of the members of my community, I can refer to NN. If I change community, as in Tim's case, the context of use is different from the context of acquisition. In that case I borrow, so to speak, the knowledge of the new community, which will help me to anchor 'NN' to twin-NN. We can summarize the contextophilia attitude with a motto:

- *Context of Acquisition* vs. *Context of Use*
  When the context of acquisition and the context of use come into competition, the context of use wins.

Before going further, let me discuss one of the main intuitions in favor of object-dependent thoughts. It has to do with the possibility of error; we should be able to say that Tim, in his twin-Earth thoughts, is mistaken. Imagine that Tim sees twin-Jane and says: "This is Jane, I remember her from last year's Halloween party".

---

[16] It seems to me that my way of understanding what is going on is somewhat consonant with Loar's (1991) idea that many of the predicates we are using rest on our semantic deference. Like Loar, I am inclined to think that many of the central concepts we use do not work like so-called demonstratives ('this' and 'that', . . .) insofar as they do not entail a discriminative capacity of the user (see Ch. 1, esp. Sects. 2 and 4). With 'this liquid', I pick out the liquid which happens to be in front of me, say H_2O, while with 'water' in the language I am using I pick out the relevant liquid. It is independent of my conceptual apparatus whether 'water' refers to H_2O or to XYZ in my linguistic community. An agent using a deferential concept nonetheless possesses some recognitional capacities: in the relevant context, I can pick out water, tell a lion apart from a tiger, etc. This mirrors the linguistic difference between demonstratives and other terms. As we saw (Ch. 1, Sect. 4), the former are generally used to make reference *in praesentia* while the latter are used *in absentia*. Thus, it does not make sense to appeal to a deferential principle when we pick out an object using a demonstrative, while it is a useful principle to appeal to when we use other terms (e.g. proper names and stuff terms). For a more detailed discussion of this issue, see Ch. 1, above.

One way to interpret Tim's mistake would be to claim that he mistakenly considers twin-Jane to be Jane because the mode of presentation he activates in that situation is about Jane, not twin-Jane. If it were about twin-Jane, Tim would not have made a mistake. A slightly different way to describe the intuition goes like this: the mode of presentation Tim associates with 'this' is about twin-Jane (for Tim is currently perceiving twin-Jane), while the mode of presentation he associates with 'Jane' is about Jane, not twin-Jane. This is the source of Tim's mistake. It also helps us to understand why Tim falsely believes that he killed Jane and so ought to be paid (for he was hired to kill her). Let us stop for a moment and reflect on *why* Tim makes this mistake and subsequently holds a false belief. It seems to me that the source of his mistake relies on the fact that Tim has *no* cognitive faculties with which to discriminate Jane from twin-Jane. He is unable to discriminate them because his mode of presentation put him in relation with different individuals in different contexts. If you prefer, the actions triggered by this mode of presentation are aimed at different objects. Tim's mode of presentation seems to be object-independent: he activates it whether he is in the presence of Jane or twin-Jane. It is because Tim activates his mode of presentation in the "wrong" context (twin-Earth) that he mistakenly takes twin-Jane to be Jane. That is, it is because his mode of presentation is situated in a different situation, i.e. it is because of the situation switch, which is unknown to Tim, that he mistakenly takes twin-Jane to be Jane. It is not because his mode of presentation is Jane-dependent. Tim's mode of presentation is *causally* related to Jane, to be sure, but saying that a mode of presentation is causally related to an object does not mean that it is dependent on that object. What makes a mode of presentation causally related to an object is the context, not the information it conveys.[17]

I suspect that ODT theorists do not take the distinction between the information a mode of presentation can convey (and thus the behaviors it can trigger) and the object causing this information seriously enough. The picture I have in mind is as follows: Tim's mode of presentation is caused (created) by certain properties of Jane. The same mode of presentation could have been caused by twin-Jane's properties, if twin-Jane had occupied the place that Jane occupied when Tim acquired his mode of presentation. Had that been the case, Tim's mode of presentation would have been caused by a different object. In other words, Tim's mode of presentation is causally related to Jane because Jane happened to instantiate the properties that

---

[17] So I agree with Kent Bach (1987: ch. 1) when he argues that the object of a singular thought is determined relationally, not satisfactionally. As we shall see (Sect. 4), this entails that these thoughts are context-sensitive and work somewhat like indexicals. As Bach puts it: "*De re* modes of presentation function as mental indexicals. They determine the contextual relation that something must bear to a thought to be the object of that very thought" (Bach 1987: 13).

caused it. If these properties had been instantiated by twin-Jane (or anyone else), Tim's mode of presentation would be causally related to twin-Jane (or whoever instantiated the relevant properties). Moreover, it is because twin-Jane instantiates the same properties as Jane that Tim mistakenly takes her to be Jane.

The moral I would like to draw is that the very same mode of presentation can be activated in another context and control an action *vis-à-vis* another object. Notice that, in telling the story this way, we can account for Tim's mistake without having to endorse object-dependent modes of presentation (or thoughts). To explain his mistake, we have to trace the history concerning his mode of presentation of Jane and yet, in tracing this history back to its origin, we do not need to appeal to object-dependent thoughts; we only appeal to objects instantiating properties. Modes of presentation are directly dependent on these properties and only indirectly dependent on the objects that instantiate them. Which object instantiates the relevant properties is a matter of context; this information is not conveyed by the mode of presentation. It may be worth mentioning that the picture I am putting forward allows us to account for the case in which, in the presence of two qualitatively undistinguishable twins, we are unable to tell them apart. The perceptual mode of presentation we associate with their names does not help us to distinguish them. We can tell them apart in a demonstrative way (we can, for instance, say, "She is not she"), but in so doing we directly relate to contextual features, which are not represented in our mind—more on this in the following sections.

I now turn to discuss a notion of *perspectival thoughts*, which, unlike ODT, can handle the intuitions concerning the psychological generalization desideratum in a more perspicuous way.

4. Perspectival Thoughts

Perspectival thoughts are thoughts *from a point of view*. They are intrinsically linked to the agent's point of view. Moreover, perspectival thoughts are context-sensitive: their singularity is contextually furnished.[18] This kind of context-sensitivity can be *articulated* or *unarticulated* in our thought, it may either be represented or not. Roughly, our thought can have an explicit or an implicit indexical component, but context-sensitivity extends far beyond indexicality. I am going to show that this move, *viz.* to assume that our thinking activity can have unarticulated constituents, is not open to ODT because it rests on the distinction between thoughts

---

[18] Your point of view is different from mine because it is linked to you, whilst mine is linked to me. What makes two points of view different is that they belong to different agents.

and propositions, a distinction that ODT (see, for instance, McDowell) rejects. Thus, ODT closes the door on what I call the principle of economical thinking.

We can recognize (roughly) two ways in which an utterance can supply a propositional constituent. It can explicitly specify it, or it can convey it in an implicit or tacit way. As we saw in Chapter 2, if I say, for instance, "It is raining *here*", I specify the location where I claim it is raining. This place corresponds to the place picked out by the indexical 'here'. On the other hand, if I simply say, "It is raining", there is no explicit reference to my location, i.e. the place where my utterance occurs. I nonetheless implicitly make reference to the relevant place. If we take what is said to be a proposition, we can say that both utterances, when uttered in the same context (at the same time and location), express the same proposition, having the relevant location amongst its constituents. In "It is raining here," the location is an *articulated* constituent of the proposition, while in "It is raining" it is an *unarticulated* constituent (see Chapter 2, Section 4, above). This mirrors a common feature of natural language, i.e. the principle of economy. We do not have to articulate what can be implicitly conveyed.[19]

This feature of natural language may be said to apply to thoughts as well. Why not assume that a mental representation does not need to represent (articulate) what may be implicitly conveyed or thought? That is, the aboutness of my thought need not be represented. In saying, "It is raining", of course, my thought is also about the location I am occupying, but I do not have to represent it for my thought to be about it. In my thought, I do not have to have a 'here'-counterpart. Why not assume that this is an economical principle governing our thinking and that our thoughts are context-sensitive? If one likes the notion of Mentalese, one is then likely to endorse the idea that sentences in Mentalese can be context-sensitive, just like ordinary sentences. I do not have to think of here when I say "It is raining", just as I do not have to think of the time zone when I say that it is 3.15 p.m. I do not, that is to say, have to represent the location I am occupying, or the time zone I am in, in my thought. The moral that emerged from our previous discussion of this phenomenon (Chapter 2) is that mental representations may be linked to worldly entities without having to represent them. That is, mental representations may be linked to the external world without having to represent all their truth-conditions. My thought that it is raining is *about*, say, Paris, even if I do not, strictly speaking, think about Paris. We do not need to have a mental representation (an image or cognitive fix, as someone might say) for our thoughts to be about something.

[19] Notice that, in some cases, syntax may require an unarticulated constituent. Think of: "Jane has finished" and "Jane has completed". The former is syntactically appropriate, but requires a complement whereas the latter is agrammatical. See Bach (1994). I discussed this difference in Ch. 2, Sect. 1, above.

My aim is to generalize Perry's strategy, as developed in Chapter 2, and claim that our thoughts are *perspectival*.[20] Hence, unlike ODT, we can assume that the very same thought can be about different items, depending on the context(s) to which it is anchored, i.e. the situation in which it appears. My thought that it is raining is about Paris because I am in Paris and yet, if I were in London, the very same thought would be about London.[21]

If we accept the contextophobic picture, we are committed to the thesis that thoughts are *fully articulated* and that our mental representations are fully specified. In specifying them, we have to appeal to relational properties that hold between what goes on in the skull and outside (worldly) items. Why is ODT committed to the existence of fully articulated thoughts (and thus cannot assume the existence of perspectival thoughts)? Here is a sketchy argument: (i) If thoughts are object-dependent, (ii) then the objects from which our thoughts derive their existence necessarily enter into the individuation of the thoughts. So (iii) if the object(s) that the thought is about contributes in determining the identity conditions of the thought, the latter ought to be fully articulated. We cannot say that the very same thought can be individuated *via* different objects.[22]

Let me tell the same story in a slightly different way. Thoughts conceived from the ODT viewpoint have to be fine-grained enough to accommodate both (i) Frege's constraint (which, roughly, concerns how to deal with the cognitive value that the agent associates with her thought) and (ii) the truth-condition of the thought, namely the state of affairs or proposition.[23] Within the OIT viewpoint I have in mind, Frege's constraint is dealt with by perspectival thoughts and

---

[20] Eternal thoughts, if there really are any, may be fully articulated and, as such, context-insensitive. The thought that $2 + 2 = 4$, or that bachelors are unmarried men, for instance, could be good candidates. For more on skepticism about the existence of eternal sentences and the intrinsic underdeterminacy of natural language, see the Introduction, above.

[21] It goes without saying that if the ODT friend makes the syntactic move, she can then argue that syntactic strings are context-sensitive. The same syntax may yield different object-dependent thoughts. The string "This is F" yields different thoughts according to the object referred to by 'this'. As we saw, however, either psychological explanation is dealt with by thoughts *qua* syntax, and thus object-dependent thoughts are psychologically inert, or syntactic strings by themselves explain nothing and need to be meaningful. As such, they ought to be supplied with their semantic value (and thus become object-dependent thoughts); they cannot then be context-sensitive insofar as they could not have a different referent from the one they actually have. In short, the syntactic string "This is F" becomes an object-dependent thought as soon as 'this' is anchored to an object and, once anchored, it cannot change referent. We cannot say that *this* thought could have another referent, for it would then be another thought. This is what I mean in saying that object-dependent thoughts cannot be context-sensitive. The ODT's underlying idea is that you cannot freeze the thought and change the object.

[22] If thoughts are conceived as syntactic strings, mental representations may not be fully articulated insofar as they do not have a place in the syntax for every item of content. For the time being, I hope to have shown that the syntactic move is not very fruitful. In particular, it does not support ODT.

[23] I discussed Frege's constraint and the notion of cognitive significance in Ch. 1, above, esp. Sects. 6 and 7.

the truth-conditions are furnished by the objects and properties that these thoughts are about. A thought in a context represents (stands for) a proposition. If you reject the thought/proposition distinction, your thought has to convey both its cognitive value and its truth-condition. This kind of thought is made up of *de re* (or object-dependent) modes of presentation (senses). In this thought, you do *not* (and cannot) have implicit arguments filled in by a context, as you cannot have unarticulated constituents. Recall Perry's example. In uttering "It is raining", the place where the utterance occurs is implicitly furnished; it is the unarticulated constituent of what is said. The corresponding perspectival thought is about this place without having to represent it. If our thought, though, is object-dependent, the place where this thought occurs is a *necessary* constituent of the individuation of our thought and it contributes in determining its identity. This thought is made up, amongst other things, of a *de re* mode of presentation of the place it occurs in. This thought cannot have an unarticulated constituent:

There is no reason to accept that contextual factors are extraneous to the content-determining power of a conceptual repertoire than there is to accept . . . that what is expressed by a context-sensitive utterance cannot be partly determined by the context in which it is made . . . [A] conceptual repertoire can include the ability to think of objects under modes of presentation whose functioning depends essentially on (say) the perceived presence of the objects. Such *de re* modes of presentation would be part or aspects of content, not vehicles for it; no means of mental representation could determine the content in question by itself, without benefit of context, but that does not establish any good sense in which the content is not fully conceptualized. (McDowell 1984: 102)

In short, the thought that the tomato I perceive is red is represented as a relation between my perceptual apparatus and the tomato. Thoughts so conceived are intrinsically relational.

This characterization seems to entail the thesis that, if Jane were to perceive two qualitatively indistinguishable bottles of water in succession, the thoughts she would thus entertain would differ. Each bottle of water is an essential feature in the identification of Jane's thought. Moreover, if Jane were to hallucinate a bottle of water, she would not entertain a thought.

The OIT friend would claim that Jane's thought would be the same whether she perceives bottle A or bottle B, assuming that they are bottles of the same kind. The context does not affect the thought, or at least, it does not affect its identity, for the OIT view I have in mind claims that Jane's thought is not fully specified. That is to say, Jane's mental representation can be context-sensitive and have an argument place for what I call an anchoring condition, or can simply be about something because it is entertained in a given context. In different contexts the same representation may be anchored to distinct items.[24] I now turn to discuss the nature of these perspectival representations. To state my point, I am going to concentrate on perceptual thoughts because they are usually considered to be a paradigmatic case of object-dependent thoughts.[25]

5. Perceptual Thoughts

How can perceptual thoughts be perspectival? How is it possible that the thought I have when perceiving a red tomato could, in another context, pick out another item? That is, how is it possible that I could entertain the same thought if I were facing another tomato (maybe in another context)? This thought could not pick out a pineapple or a bottle of water, for example, unless some contextual tricks were played, but my thought cannot pick out a pineapple *ceteris paribus*, i.e. if the perceptual conditions remain unaltered. What are these perceptual conditions? Imagine that, instead of tomato A, I perceive tomato B, which is qualitatively indistinguishable from A, and that I perceive it from the same perspective. In this case, we could say that my thought would be the same. If so, perceptual thoughts may be perspectival. The common intuition in favor of this characterization is that, from the agent's viewpoint, there is no difference whatsoever whether she perceives tomato A or a qualitatively indistinguishable one. A word of clarification concerning the nature of the truth or falsity of the thought may be appropriate. Suppose that the tomato that Jane sees was grown in Sicily and she entertains the thought expressed by "This tomato was grown in Sicily". Her thought is true. Imagine now that she perceives a qualitatively identical tomato that was grown in Morocco, but mistakenly thinks that it was grown in Sicily. While Jane's former thought is true, the latter is false. On the view I propose, Jane's thought is the same in both cases. You may remember that I claimed that thoughts are *situated* (see the Introduction): the very same thought may have different truth-values in different situations. This is the case in our example. A given situation can be identified in referring to the object(s) perceived. In saying that an object helps identify a situation, I do not commit myself to the view that the

---

[24] See Ch. 2, above, for an exhaustive discussion of the distinct ways in which a given mental representation can be about something. I argued that we do not always have to postulate hidden indexicals for a representation to be about something and that the simple fact that a representation is situated in a given context may suffice to make a representation about a given object.

[25] As I tried to suggest in discussing Tim Badguy's story and his mode of presentation of Jane, the picture I am putting forth applies also to thoughts involving natural kind terms and proper names. These thoughts are perspectival as well, although I do not have the time and space to discuss and defend this thesis in more detail.

object enters the thought, i.e. that it is a thought-constituent. I do not, therefore, commit myself to the view that the thought is object-dependent. All I am committed to is the view that the situation may be object-dependent. In short, Jane's thought is true relative to the situation in which she perceives the Sicilian tomato and false relative to the situation in which she perceives the Moroccan tomato. That is to say, the very same thought is instantiated in different situations and so may change in truth-value.

Indeed, a detailed story concerning the nature of perception needs to be told. For my purposes, I hope that the following rough picture will do the job. I distinguish between *perceptual content* (the object or state of affairs our perception is about)[26] and *perceptual state* (the thought or mental state one is in whilst perceiving things). I take perceptual states to be *property-based*. More precisely, they are based on perceptually accessible properties, which are phenomenological properties. Our perceptual states are not based on such properties as the property of being XYZ or H_2O, the property of having such and such atomic number, such and such a DNA chain, or the like. According to this picture, perceptual thoughts are perspectival. Actually, if perceptual states (thoughts) are property-based, then our perceptual thoughts are perspectival insofar as the same phenomenological property can be instantiated in different objects. Two phenomenologically indistinguishable bottles of water instantiate the same perceptually relevant properties, the shape, color, etc. So, here is my motto:

- *Perception is property-based*
  Same phenomenological properties, same perceptual apparatus, same perceptual state (*ceteris paribus*).

In another context, the same thought could be anchored to a different object, insofar as the latter instantiates the same perceptual properties.[27] To be sure, my thought could be about another (phenomenologically indistinguishable) object. My perceptual thought can be perspectival in different ways. First, in the same context (say the same room, same table, same light, etc.) I perceive the tomato.

---

[26] Our perceptual experience may be about an object or about a state of affairs; this should reflect the well-known distinction between perceiving an object and perceiving a fact, e.g. The distinction between seeing a brown lion and seeing that the lion is brown. On this distinction, see Dretske (1969).

[27] It may be misleading to speak of *thoughts* when so-called cases of non-epistemic perception are at play. We can differentiate an object from its immediate environment without applying concepts. As Dretske puts it: "[V]isual differentiation . . . is a pre-intellectual, pre-discursive sort of capacity which a wide variety of beings possess. It is an endowment which is largely immune to the caprice of our intellectual life" (Dretske 1969: 29). Our perceptual experience need not be conceptual. My point is that the same non-conceptual experience (non-conceptual content some would say) could be at play in another phenomenologically indistinguishable context and thus relate the perceiver to a distinct object. For simplicity's sake, I am going to ignore the epistemic/non-epistemic distinction in what follows.

If, instead of tomato A I perceived tomato B (which, you may recall, is phenomenologically indistinguishable from A), my thought would be the same and yet occur in different situations. It would thus be anchored to a different item. We can also change the contextual parameters (and thus have a different situation) and yet have the same perceptual thought. We could be in a different (but similar) room, perceive another tomato, and yet entertain the same thought. This is what underlies twin-Earth thought-experiments. On twin-Earth, everything is the same except that we have H_2O and twin-Earth has XYZ. H_2O and XYZ are phenomenologically indistinguishable, so, according to my characterization, twin-me's thoughts are the same as mine, though differently situated. If I were to move to twin-Earth and perceive a phenomenologically indistinguishable bottle of water, my thought would be the same, although differently situated and anchored to a different kind of stuff. Needless to say, my thought could be differently situated and yet anchored to the same object/stuff. If I move into a similar room (or one on twin-Earth) and the relevant tomato moves with me, the thought I express with "That tomato is from Sicily" is anchored to the very same object in both cases.

To avoid confusion, let me stress that the picture I have in mind does not go against the idea that we perceive objects. It does not reject the thesis that what we see, for instance, are chairs, alligators, tables, and the like. As such, perception can be understood to be a relation between an agent and an object.[28] My story fits the idea that seeing is transparent: from "Jane sees water" and "water = H_2O", it follows that "Jane sees H_2O" (just as from "Jane sees Lenin" and "Lenin = Vladimir Ilyich Ulyanov" it follows that "Jane sees Vladimir Ilyich Ulyanov"). My point is about perceptual states, not about the extrinsic relations holding between a perceiver and the entities she is currently related to: these relations do not enter the content of our thought. Actually, what I am trying to prove is that the same perceptual state can be related to different entities, just as the same properties can be instantiated by different entities. H_2O and XYZ are phenomenologically the same, so phenomenological properties such as being transparent, being liquid, etc. (the stereotypes) can be instantiated in different kinds of stuff.[29]

The picture I have in mind accounts for the idea that perception is intrinsically perspectival (to perceive an object is to perceive it from a point of view). The point

---

[28] The paradigmatic case can be represented as "Jane sees a", which licenses the existential generalization "$\exists x$(Jane sees x)".

[29] Given the distinction I proposed between perceptual states and perceptual content, we can have (i) the same object yet different perceptual states (this is what underlines Frege's case) or (ii) different objects and the same perceptual state (this is what underlines the classic twin-Earth cases). On the one hand, we can perceive the same object from different perspectives, so our perceptual states are different. On the other hand, we can perceive phenomenologically indistinguishable objects, so our perceptual states are the same.

of view from which I perceive a given object need not be represented in my thought. That is, to perceive an object is to perceive it *here* and *now*, yet neither the location nor the time my perceptual experience occurs need to be represented in my thought. So the thought is context-sensitive insofar as, in another location/time, it could be related to a different object. And this is possible insofar as my thought is necessarily situated.

There are many ways in which I can see the cup in front of me and, to each of these different ways, different behavior may be appropriate. So, if we are interested in explaining how behavior is linked to perception, we have to focus on the ways in which the object is apprehended in perception, i.e. on the nature of the perceptual states we entertain when we perceive a given object. My point is that these perceptual states are perspectival. The same perceptual state could be about another object (or about nothing, if we happened to be hallucinating an object). What matters to psychological explanation are mental states—the way we experience the world.

It could be thought that, since the identity of thoughts is object-independent and determined by the perceptual state, we thus make perceptual thoughts too coarse-grained. In particular, I could not keep thinking the same thing as I see an object move and think, "This is moving", for as it moves it changes position relative to me. My perceptual state is constantly changing (the moving object looks slightly different at each moment). I think that this difficulty is only apparent, for nothing within the picture I have in mind prevents us from having *dynamic thoughts*. When I perceive a moving object I entertain a single (dynamic) thought, which is based on a single act of perception. So I cannot change my attitude toward the perceived object insofar as I do not lose track of it. Hence Evans's notion of keeping track (see 1981) is compatible with my account.

To summarize: Since the same (perceptually accessible) properties can be instantiated in different objects, perceptual thoughts are perspectival. On Earth, my perceptual thought is about H_2O because the stuff that looks transparent, is a liquid, and so on is H_2O, i.e. because the properties that activate my perceptual states are instantiated by H_2O. On twin-Earth, the same perceptual state will be anchored to XYZ. A perceptual state is intrinsically perspectival. Hence, it is anchored to the world in a context-dependent way: it does not determine which object it is about by itself. If we take away the context, the perceptual state will not tell us the object it is about. In other words, the singularity of perceptual states is given by the context (the singularity is an unarticulated constituent of the perceptual state), *viz.* it is the context that anchors it to reality, yet the contextual parameters (the perspective) need not be represented. Our perceptual thoughts are object-independent. OIT seems vindicated.

McDowell seems to suggest that direct realism is committed to the object-dependency of content insofar as he argues that OIT is analogous to representative realism in the theory of perception:

> With the framework in place [the separation of content from context], the only Fregean treatment of context-sensitive singular terms is to credit particular uses of them with senses that determine objects in such a way that the senses are expressible whether the objects exist or not. At best this generates a falsification of, for instance, demonstrative thoughts, akin to the falsification of perceptual experience that is induced by representative realism. Representative realism postulates items that are 'before the mind' in experience whether objects are perceived or not, with the effect that even when an object is perceived, it is conceived as 'present to the mind' only by proxy. Analogously, if an object thought of demonstratively is present to the mind only by way of something which could have been deployed in thought even if the object had not existed, the object is before the mind only by proxy. (McDowell 1984: 107)

According to McDowell, what is presented to someone's mind when one perceives an object is not a mental substitute for the object but the object itself. The object is, so to speak, in the mind; so goes the ODT story. I do not see how an OIT theorist can fail to be a direct realist. My mental representation (my perceptual state) is anchored to the relevant object. The anchor need not be present to my mind. To put it in a nutshell, when I perceive an object, I entertain a perspectival thought. This (property-based) thought is object-independent, but it is contextually linked to the perceived object. I do not have to represent the contextual relation as something that would come in between my thought and the object. The same can be said about the situation in which the thought occurs. The situation is the background upon which the thought occurs and as such need not be represented by the thought.

To be precise, the position I defend may be labeled *critical realism*. Unlike representative realism, critical realism does not postulate items that are before the mind, nor does it postulate representations that come in between the perceiver and the perceived object. Like direct realism, critical realism claims that we directly perceive objects. But we perceive them *by being in mental (perceptual) states*. Perceiving something by being in state S does not entail that S gets in the way, so to speak, and thus makes our perception indirect, i.e. mediated by S. Notice that, according to critical realism, the referent can be represented and *still* be contextually determined. My perceptual state of object O might represent O, but the fact that it is O (rather than, say, Z—a similar-looking object) that it represents is not itself represented. That is determined by context, i.e. by the fact that my perceptual state is being caused by O (not Z). Think of a photograph. It can represent, say, George Best even though it is, in a sense, a context, a matter of history (the fact that Best was standing in front of the camera when the film was exposed) that fixes the referent—that makes it a picture of Best.

One of McDowell's arguments in favor of the thesis that direct realism seems committed to object-dependent perceptual thoughts is that, in specifying the latter, we refer to the perceived object. I cannot specify someone's perceptual thought without making reference to the object(s) she perceives. I cannot pick out the singularity of someone's thought without referring to the referent(s):

> [A] demonstrative mode of presentation is not capturable in a specification that someone would understand without exploiting the perceived presence of the man himself. In answering the question how the man is presented in such Thoughts, there is no substitute for saying 'He is presented as *that* man', exploiting his perceived presence to make oneself understood. The condition an object must meet to be what such Thoughts bear on—the condition of being *that* man, as one can put it if one is in the right perceptual circumstances—is not one that could be expressed or entertained even if the man in question did not exist. (McDowell 1991: 218)

I think that McDowell's argument rests on a conflation between the thought itself (its very nature) and the way we, from the third person's point of view, describe it.[30] As I claimed in the previous section, if we describe (or attribute) someone's perceptual thought, we usually make reference to the object(s) it is directed at. Our attribution is *de re*. This does not mean, though, that the object is part of the thought, or that the thought would not exist if the object did not. It means, at best, that we, from the third-person point of view, would have problems in describing it. Think, for instance, of the difficulty we have in ascribing a thought to someone who is hallucinating.

Let us take stock. In arguing that perceptual thoughts are perspectival, I claim that their singularity (the referent(s) they are linked to) need not be articulated. They are contextually furnished. As such, perspectival thoughts do not commit us to representative realism. To be sure, perceptual thoughts would commit us to representative realism if we held that the singularity needs be articulated; then, the object(s) that our thought is about would be selected as the object(s) which *satisfies* our representation. On the other hand, if you are contextophobic (like McDowell) and you assume direct realism, then you are committed to the existence of object-dependent thoughts, for you close the door to perspectival thoughts, i.e. thoughts that do not need to articulate the object(s) they are about. The following chart should summarize this:

- *Contextophobia* vs. *Contextophilia*

Contextophobia + Direct Realism → Object-Dependent Thoughts

Contextophilia + Direct Realism → Object-Independent (Perspectival)
Thought
+
Context → Object
(Propositional Constituent)

---

[30] For a similar criticism of McDowell, see Searle's reply (1991: 239).

It should be clear by now that the OIT conception I am defending accommodates the datum that both Jane and twin-Jane have the same psychological states and behavioral dispositions. The fact that Jane perceives the stuff that happens to be H_2O and twin-Jane the stuff that happens to be XYZ does not affect their psychological state.

McGinn (1989) proposes the following example to illustrate and strengthen this intuition. Imagine, he asks us, that on Earth Jane's psychological state, S, is caused by the distal stimulus of round things. On twin-Earth, because of some contextual trick, twin-Jane's psychological state S is caused by square things. Both Jane's and twin-Jane's behavioral dispositions are of the same kind. They both act in a roundwise way.

Before going further, let me say that my first reaction *vis-à-vis* this kind of thought-experiment is to reject it as implausible.[31] For we are losing what I call the *robust (or folk) sense of reality*, i.e. the sense in which agents in counterfactual situations interact with their environment with the same amount of success and reliability as we do in the *actual* situation. In other words, the robust sense of reality should rule out examples which do not satisfy the following conditions: (i) our twins are as well adapted to twin-Earth as we are to Earth and (ii) they interact with their environment with the same degree of success as we with the actual environment. Do McGinn-like examples satisfy the robust sense of reality? At first sight, I would say *no*. For imagine our twins building bridges, playing football (do they play with a square ball in a round field?), and so on. If my reaction is correct, any appeal to these thought-experiments leaves the world as it is; it does not (and cannot) affect a given theory.[32] But you may not agree with my response. Thus, I am going to show how the picture I put forth survives these thought-experiments as well.

McGinn's thought-experiment presupposes that we freeze the perceiver's intrinsic properties (such as the states of the brain and the body) and behavioral dispositions while we keep fluid the relations between these facts and the environmental properties. Thus, the distal stimulus is not relevant in characterizing Jane's and twin-Jane's psychological state. The ODT theorist, who would appeal to the distal stimulus in characterizing Jane's and twin-Jane's psychological state, ought to break the connection between perceptual thoughts and behavior and, therefore, reject the thesis that behavior is thought-controlled. This sounds like a *reductio ad absurdum* of ODT. Hence, I cannot but agree with McGinn:

Surely it is far more plausible to suppose that [Jane] acts as her experience indicates, thus aligning perceptual content with her behavior, not her environment. (McGinn 1989: 66)

---

[31] As we shall soon see, Davies proposes a similar thought-experiment to criticize the individualist's position.
[32] It seems to me that Segal (1991) shares the same kind of reaction *vis-à-vis* these examples.

McGinn's moral is that, when it comes to a competition between action and environment in the fixation of perceptual states, action wins. So Jane's and twin-Jane's psychological state, S, does not depend on distal stimulus, but rather on how things *look* to them. In both cases we attribute to them the same (square-wise, etc.) perceptual state.

If you agree with the picture I put forth, McGinn's example can be accommodated in an elegant way. On twin-Earth, the same phenomenological property (because of the contextual trick) is instantiated by different objects. So our perspectival thought picks out another object, so goes the story.

Davies confronts the internalist (and thus the OIT theorist) with yet another problem. His strategy is to turn the tables on the internalist by providing an example where the same perceptual input to duplicates gives different behavioral outputs. What are frozen in Davies's example are the distal stimuli (inputs) and the intrinsic properties of the perceiver, while the relations between these facts and the bodily movement are kept fluid. He suggests the following modification of McGinn's example. Imagine that twin-Jane's psychological state (S), like Jane's, is produced by distal round things. But her output behavioral disposition, because of her different evolutionary history, is, unlike Jane's, squarewise. Here is Davies's twist on the example:

What is imagined here is not that walking in a square trajectory is the best way of avoiding a round object. Rather, we suppose that environmental differences have the consequence that the same nerve firing and muscle contractions as in the actual situation result in a quite different bodily trajectory. (Davies 1992: 37)

On Earth, entertaining S, Jane acts appropriately in a squarewise way. On twin-Earth, because of her different evolutionary background, twin-Jane acts in a roundwise way when she entertains S. Hence, we have the same (phenomenological) input, the same psychological state S (the same perceptual state), and yet a different bodily output. Externalism (and, by the way, ODT as well) seems vindicated by this example, for the perceptual states of Jane and twin-Jane *qua* causally efficacious states seem different and this difference comes from outside their skin. Perceptual states need to be individuated by making reference to different bodily behavioral dispositions, i.e. to different extrinsic properties.

Notice that, in Davies's example, Jane and twin-Jane are not duplicates in any interesting way; we want our psychology to stress this fact. Jane and twin-Jane are the same inside their skin, but they have a different etiological background. Hence, if we move twin-Jane to Earth, she would behave in a different way from Jane: in the same room they behave in a different way and we want our psychology to capture this. In short, as I understand Davies's example, the only thing that makes Jane and twin-Jane move in a different way is their differing etiological histories. Actually, if we take Jane and twin-Jane in the same context, they act in a different way and they both act, we would say, in a rational way. To be sure, they act in a rational way from their (or their community's) viewpoint: Jane does not act rationally from the twin-psychologist's viewpoint and *vice versa*. What rationalizes their behavior seems to be their etiological history. Does this jeopardize OIT? To this question I now turn.

Before going further, however, notice that Davies concedes that:

[T]he basis of behavioral dispositions is to be found inside the skin. But, if behavior is itself characterized externalistically, then the production of behavior of a certain type depends both upon what happens inside the skin ... and upon environmental factors. In principle, behavior—externalistically characterized—can be varied even while everything inside the skin remains the same. (Davies 1992: 33)

And this concession, as we are now going to see, is all we need to defend OIT.

6. Psychological Generalizations

Psychological generalizations are generalizations by causal power. Causal explanation is what science is about. So scientific laws are assumed to subsume things with similar causal power. The underlying idea comes from Hume and runs like this: Causes and effects ought to be conceptually distinguished. If *A* causes *B*, it must be possible to specify *A* in a noncircular way, without mentioning that it is the cause of *B*. *A*'s status needs to be cashed out independently of its causing *B*, i.e. in another way than merely 'the cause of *B*'. In other words, *A* must have some natural kind of (law-instantiating) property different from the one of being the cause of *B* and in virtue of which it can nomically cause *B*. As Fodor puts it:

[W]hat you need in order to do science is a taxonomic apparatus that distinguishes between things insofar as they have *different* causal properties, and that groups things together insofar as they have the *same* causal properties. (Fodor 1987: 34)

The fact that Jane is related to H_2O and twin-Jane to XYZ is not a difference in causal power relevant for our psychological purposes. In our initial example, Jane's and twin-Jane's thoughts have the same causal potential insofar as they cause, *ceteris paribus*, similar behaviors (walking to the fridge and taking the water). Hence we want our psychology to subsume Jane's and twin-Jane's behavior under the same law. This is our psychological generalization desideratum.[33]

---

[33] For a detailed discussion of Fodor's position on this very issue, see Cain (2002: ch. 6).

The argument by causal power does not seem to support OIT insofar as we recognize that taxonomies in science may appeal to relational properties.[34] Notice, however, that the argument by causal power does not support ODT either. Relational properties are taxonomically relevant insofar as they affect causal power: if they do not affect causal power, they *do not* affect the psychological generalization. So, from the fact that certain relational properties affect causal powers, we cannot infer that *all* relational properties do so. To support ODT, the causal power argument needs to show that the property of being H_2O/XYZ affects Jane's/twin-Jane's causal powers. Similarly, the ODT friend needs to show that the property (whatever it is) that gives the numerical identity of the lion that Jane perceives affects the causal powers of Jane's behavior in presence of the lion.[35]

How does this picture allow us to handle Davies's story? To answer this question, I am going to borrow the distinction between *triggering causes* and *structuring causes*, as made popular by Dretske (see 1988: 42). This distinction accounts for the difference between what causes the process to occur *now* (triggering cause) and what is responsible for its being *this process* (structuring cause). In Davies's case, the same psychological state—the same triggering cause—may cause different behaviors because this very state has a different etiological background (structuring cause). That is, if you change the structuring cause, you *may* change the behavioral output. Notice that if you change the structuring cause, you do not necessarily change the behavior (output) insofar as different facts may have structured a given process, say Jane acting in a squarewise way. The problem, in Davies's example, is that the same triggering cause (Jane's and twin-Jane's psychological state) causes different behaviors.

Psychological laws are *ceteris paribus* laws. In Davies's story, this everything-being-equal clause is not satisfied. Perspectival thoughts *qua* causally efficacious thoughts are the triggering causes of behavior. They cause, *ceteris paribus*, the same behavior. I consider that the *ceteris paribus* clause should prevent us from subsuming thoughts with different etiologies under the same law when the etiologies affect behavior (as in Davies's example).

In other words, psychological generalizations subsume under the same laws organisms with the same triggering causes. But the generalization is permissible only if the triggering causes cause, *ceteris paribus*, similar behaviors. To use McGinn's terminology, we can say that psychological generalizations ought to preserve the alignment between perceptual states (triggering causes) and output behaviors. This alignment is not preserved between Jane and twin-Jane in Davies's

---

[34] Hence, against Fodor's metaphysical point (1987: 44), we deny that causal powers supervene on local microstructure (and thus deny that, in the case of psychology, it supervenes on local neural structure).

[35] This should capture my understanding of Fodor's methodological *vs.* metaphysical point (cf. 1987: 44).

example, so they cannot be subsumed under the same psychological laws. The moral should be:

- *Action* vs. *Environment*

    When it comes to a competition between action and environment in the fixation of psychological laws, action wins.

The distinction between triggering and structuring causes allows us to accommodate the fact that organisms with the same physical base may fall under different psychological taxonomies. They fall under different psychological taxonomies when they have different structuring causes *and* the latter affect the behavioral outputs. If the structuring causes do not affect the output, organisms with the same physical base and yet different structuring causes nevertheless fall under the same psychological laws. In short, two organisms that manifest different behavior in a similar situation do not fall under the same psychological law. These organisms may differ either in the triggering or the structuring cause. In McGinn's example, our organisms differ in their triggering cause, while in Davies's, they differ in the structuring cause.

If I am right, my story allows us to accommodate yet another example put forth by Egan. A company builds a telephone answering-machine which has been hard-wired to produce the following computer-synthesized message in response to input calls: "I love you. Please leave a message". The same company is asked for a similar machine from the Isle of View Hotel with the message: "Isle of View. Please leave a message". Our company managers are happy to be able to sell the unsealed stock from the previous production. They can do so because both messages have the same underlying acoustic forms. Egan's moral is:

> The two machines are by hypothesis physically identical; they therefore have the same causal power. But does it follow that the machines' 'behavior' (the message produced) must be type-identified? Surely not . . . Linguistic theory would type-distinguish the messages, and physical theory would type-identify the machines. The implicit assumption . . . that linguistic types supervene on the physical states of the device is simply false. (Egan 1991: 184)

In this example, as in McGinn's, our organisms differ in their triggering causes and for this reason they do not fall under the same law. The difference in output can be explained by the differences between the situations in which the two organisms (answering machines) operate.

7. Answering an Objection

I claimed that perspectival thoughts come cheaper than object-dependent thoughts insofar as they license psychological generalizations in a more straightforward way. I argued that the singularity of a perspectival thought is an unarticulated constituent of the thought and, as such, need not be represented. The objects that our thoughts are about are contextually furnished. This picture, however, faces a difficulty in explaining how context secures the reference. Roughly, how is a perspectival thought linked to the object(s) it happens to be about? You may recall that Adams et al. (1993: 96) pose the following challenge to the conception I have in mind: "[T]he mere fact that context supplies an object does not determine that reference (or intentional action) is to it (directed toward it)". Imagine that a subject is deluded, e.g. she hallucinates a lion chasing her. I claimed that her thought would be the same, whether or not there is a lion after her. Now imagine that, by accident, there actually is a lion chasing our deluded agent. According to Adams et al. her thought, understood from the OIT point of view, is not about the lion that actually happens to be in front of her. This criticism is somewhat similar to McDowell's (1986) claim that the internalist picture, which rejects object-dependent thoughts and distinguishes between mental content and propositions, is in the grip of Cartesianism. As such, it faces the old skeptical problem. For, if we disentangle thoughts from the object(s) they are about, we face the classic problem of discovering how mental life relates to the external world. That is, how is it that we are not brains in a vat?[36] As I understand this issue, ODT closes the door to the skeptical question. If thoughts are object-dependent, we cannot doubt their aboutness. It does not make sense to say that thoughts could exist in an empty world.[37] This commits ODT with the motto: no object, no thought. Notice that, if we let incomplete thoughts into the picture, we bring in the skeptical question as well, for we can doubt the aboutness of an incomplete thought. Incomplete thoughts exist in empty worlds. So how can we rule out the doubt that we are living in an empty world, i.e. that all I have are incomplete thoughts and I am living under the illusion of having complete (object-dependent) thoughts?

According to the picture I propose, a subject's thought is *contextually* related to the objects it happens to be about. To state my point, imagine, once again, that Jane is deluded, while twin-Jane is not. Their thoughts are the same. The difference is that in one case, the context secures a reference but does not do so in the other. In one case, Jane is related to a proposition having the relevant lion as constituent, whereas she is not related to a singular proposition in the deluded

---

[36] McDowell claims: "There is no independent justification, from general epistemology, for refusing to allow that there can be illusion of entertaining singular propositions" (McDowell 1986: 141). He goes on to claim: "Within the Cartesian picture there is a serious question about how it can be that experience, conceived from its own point of view, is not blank or blind, but purports to be revelatory of the world we live in" (McDowell 1986: 152).

[37] I am borrowing the notion of empty worlds from Blackburn (1984: ch. 9).

case. In both cases, Jane acts as if there were a lion in front of her; she acts under the control of her thought, which is the same in the veridical and the deluded case.

We can explain the difference between the veridical case and the deluded case in appealing to the proposition the agent is related to. So from *our* point of view, we can describe the case. The difficulty is that, if a lion were in front of the deluded agent, the description would be the same both from the subject's point of view and from ours. We would have no clue, contextual or otherwise, with which to figure out whether the agent is deluded or not. We would mistakenly relate the agent to the lion. I bite the bullet. How, though, can the ODT friend tell whether our agent is deluded or not? I think that she would be in no better position than the OIT theorist would; she would mistakenly attribute an object-dependent thought to Jane. She would attribute to Jane a thought whose identity depends on the lion that happens to be there. If you adopt the distinction between complete and incomplete thoughts, the ODT friend would attribute a complete thought to Jane.

On the other hand, if we take Jane's stance, the ODT friend is placed in a no better situation than the OIT friend. Jane thinks and believes that there is a lion in front of her, whether or not she is deluded (thus if Jane were an ODT theorist, she would argue that she entertains a complete thought). If we ask her to shoot the lion in front of her, she would kill the unlucky lion, which just happens to be there. It seems, so far, that both OIT and ODT friends are in the same boat and thus face exactly the same difficulty. All we are left with are the contextual parameters; it may be that we were mistaken in relating Jane to the unlucky lion. But these kinds of mistake are, I am confident, not too common. So we can keep on enjoying our life, swimming in H_2O, having object-independent thoughts, and believing that context does not play bad jokes on us too often.

It seems to me, *pace* McDowell, that nothing is strange or magical in saying that context secures a reference to our thoughts: it simply matches thoughts to reality. Hence, I must disagree with McDowell when he claims that:

[O]nce we picture subjectivity as self-contained, it is hard to see how its states and episodes can be anything but blind. Magic might seem to help, and magical power requires an occult medium. (McDowell 1986: 153)

Perspectival thoughts are our magical power and context is our medium; so goes my story.

Adams et al. claimed that the worries I have suggested for ODT, although sound, are epistemological, whereas the existence of ODTs is a metaphysical question.

Thus, contrary to what McDowell claims, they do not close the door to skepticism.[38] They argue:

> Our point was not epistemological. Our point was metaphysical. . . . As a matter of fact, whether anyone could know or not, Jane's killing of that particular lion, while she is deluded, is not intentionally done (though her firing of the gun may well have been). She does not even intend to kill it, since it is not an element of her thought (articulated or unarticulated). She has no cognitive contact with that lion. She is not smelling it. She is not hearing it. She is not thinking about it. It is a sheer accident that it happens to get in the way of the bullet she may fire intentionally. . . . context alone does not provide an object to be the content of a thought (or intention). There must be some cognitive contact with that object, in the case of a demonstrative thought ("that lion is after me"). And, once there is such cognitive contact (if say, Jane were to stop hallucinating and perceive the lion directly), we maintain that an ODT is available to the agent. (Adams et al. 1999: 56–7)

I do not know whether the ODT/OIT debate is metaphysical or epistemological. I tend to believe that it is epistemological. After all, it concerns thoughts and psychological generalizations. As I view it, it ought to do with the way people *cognize* the world. As I understand it, psychological laws concern people's behavior; they concern the way people act and react to stimuli and the way, given certain beliefs, they try to fulfill their desires. As I have already said, one can appeal to a given object to characterize or attribute a thought to someone: attributions are, most of the time, *de re*. But a *de re* attribution does not make a thought object-dependent. Besides, as I said in discussing perception, one's perception is based on phenomenologically accessible properties. Whether Jane perceives the lion or merely hallucinates one, she is guided by her perceptual states: she smells it (or at least has the feeling of smelling it), she hears it (or at least has the feeling that she hears it), etc. Her perceptual state is the same and her feelings are the same whether or not there is a lion in front of her. Whether or not Jane's feelings and the properties she perceives are instantiated by an object, is a matter of context. I am thus happy to accept that intentionality is context-sensitive. It is thus a matter of context which object happens to be the object of one's intention. The aboutness of one's thought depends on the context in which it is entertained. It may be worth signaling that the position I have defended with regard to perception, and in particular the idea that perception is property-based, does not commit me to a realist

---

[38] "[W]e do not share Corazza's view that ODTs make skepticism impossible. Descartes may have had his fireplace as an object of his ODT, when he meditated upon whether he was really perceiving the fireplace or merely dreaming. . . . What he was sceptical about was whether his thought was indeed an ODT, as opposed to a completely vacuous thought. So the existence of ODTs is metaphysical matter. It does not preclude epistemological worries nor refute scepticism" (Adams et al. 1999: 57 n. 14).

view about properties and relations. The position I put forward is acceptable to a nominalist view, favoring conceptualism about properties. As such, OIT is compatible with a view according to which one cannot have a non-linguistic access to properties. In the next two chapters, I discuss and propose a picture of attitude ascriptions which is in accord with OIT. I shall show that ODT is yet another manifestation of what I characterized (Chapter 1, Section 8), following Perry, as *the fallacy of misplaced information*, i.e. the view that all the relevant information must come from a single entity. The friends of ODT seem to commit themselves to the view that all relevant information comes from the thoughts one entertains. The picture I defend, in accord with direct reference, welcomes the distinction between the bearer of truth-value (the proposition) and the bearer of cognitive value (the thought, or mental state). Thus, it is consonant with the view that an attribution may relate an agent to a singular proposition (i.e. a proposition having objects as constituents) and yet the thought one entertains when believing this proposition is object-independent. As we shall see, one entertains a proposition by being in a given state. The given state may be attributed in appealing to singular propositions, yet it is independent of the proposition. The relation between a token mental state and a proposition is context-sensitive.

Let us take stock. The advantages of positing perspectival thoughts over object-dependent thoughts are the following: (i) Perspectival thoughts allow us to handle the cases where a subject is deluded in a more natural way, insofar as we do not have to postulate another kind of (possibly incomplete) thought; (ii) they license in a more straightforward way psychological generalizations. In particular, we do not have to postulate the existence of two kinds of thoughts, object-dependent and incomplete (object-independent) thoughts, and argue that the latter support psychological generalizations. We are now in a position to focus on the psychological basis that enables us to use and master indexicals and, more importantly, enables us to understand what is going on, from a psychological point of view, when we come to attribute indexical thoughts and propositional attitudes to someone else. In the next chapter, I shall focus on notions such as empathy and mental simulation which constitute the background upon which our semantic practice of attributing perspectival thoughts rests.

7

Empathy, Imagination, and Reports

> Grief and joy strongly expressed in the look and gesture of anyone at once affect the spectator with some degree of a like painful or agreeable emotion.
>
> (A. Smith [1759] 1976: 260)

> People might exist who never use the expression 'seeing something with the inner eye' or anything like it, and these people might be able to draw and model 'out of imagination' or memory, to mimic the characteristic behavior of others etc. They might also shut their eyes or stare into vacancy as if blind before drawing something from memory. And they might deny that they then see before them what they go on to draw.
>
> (Wittgenstein, *RPP* ii: §66)

In this chapter, I discuss the attribution of attitudes. In attributing to someone an attitude, we usually use constructions like: "Jane believes/desires/wishes/said/ ... that *p*", where the 'that'-clause 'that *p*' should capture what the attributee, Jane, believes/desires/wishes/said/ ... The conception I propose concentrates on the notion of imagination. In particular, it rests on the notion of transference, i.e. the way one imagines oneself to be another.

I shall proceed as follows. In Section 1, I stress how the notion of imagination plays a central role in our cognitive architecture. In Section 2, I discuss what is going on when we attribute states like pain to other people and argue that this activity rests on our empathetic capacity. This will help me to set the psychological basis for the thesis that an attitude ascription is an empathetic exercise resting on our more general imaginative faculty. In Section 3, I discuss the case of autism and claim that it provides further empirical evidence in favor of the idea that empathy plays a central role in our understanding of other minds. In Section 4, I defend the thesis that sentences are the best means we have to classify someone's mental life and activity. I defend the view that, from the third-person perspective, the attributee's mental state can be captured by the sentence a reporter would use to express the relevant mental state if she were in the attributee's shoes. In

Section 5, I discuss how attitude reports allow us to classify the attributee's mental life. In Section 6, I argue, *pace* Crimmins and Perry (1989), that *types* of mental representation suffice to deal with certain doxastic puzzles; we do not need to appeal to cognitive particulars. In Section 7, I deal with some classic ascription puzzles, inspired by Frege and Kripke, while in Section 8 I claim that attitude reports are often bound to be unfaithful; because they have to take into consideration the viewpoint of the audience, they cannot faithfully capture someone's mental life.

1. The Background: Imagination

In *Word and Object*, Quine writes:

[I]n indirect quotation we project ourselves into what, from his remarks and other indications, we *imagine* the speaker's state of mind to have been, and then we say what, *in our language*, is natural and *relevant for us* in the state thus feigned. An indirect quotation we can usually expect to rate only as better or worse, more or less faithful, and we cannot even hope for a strict standard of more and less; what is involved is evaluation, relative to special purposes, of an essentially dramatic act. Correspondingly for other propositional attitudes, for all of them can be thought of as involving something like quotation of one's own imagined verbal response to an imagined situation.

Casting our real selves thus in unreal roles, we do not generally know how much reality to hold constant. Quandaries arise. But despite them we find ourselves attributing beliefs, wishes, and strivings even to creatures lacking the power of speech, such is our dramatic virtuosity. We project ourselves even into what from his behavior we imagine a mouse's state of mind to have been, and dramatize it as a belief, wish, or striving, verbalized as seems relevant and natural to us in the state thus feigned. (Quine 1960: 219, italics mine)

The idea that empathy plays a role when we come to understand other people's mental life has also been suggested by Aristotle:

The people we pity are: those whom we know, if only they are not very closely related to us—in that case *we feel about them as if we were in danger ourselves*. (Aristotle, *Rhetoric*: 1378^{a}31–^{b}2, italics mine)

Recent studies in developmental psychology (cf. Hoffman 2000: 62) proved that the degree of structural similarity—and, by the way, the faculty and tendency to empathize with one another—increases with similarities across cultures. In particular, the tendency to empathize is greater amongst people from the same culture and living under the same conditions. It also increases amongst people who interact frequently. Levenson and Reuf (1997) found that this is not only true of the cognitive system; cultural vicinity and interaction augments empathy at the physiological level as well.

The idea that imagination plays a central role in our cognitive architecture when dealing with other people's feelings and attitudes in general has also been suggested by Smith:

> By the imagination we place ourselves in the other's situation, we conceive ourselves enduring all the same torments, we enter, as it were, into his body, and become in some measure the same person with him, and thence form some idea of his sensation, and even feel something which, though weaker in degree, is not altogether unlike them. (A. Smith [1759] 1976: 261)

Inspired by Aristotle, Smith, and Quine I defend the view that an attitude ascription is an empathetic act. As such, it rests on our more general imaginative faculty. In particular, it rests on our capacity to imagine ourselves in someone else's shoes:

> Many philosophers and psychologists would agree that people often predict what another will do in a given situation by imagining being in such a situation and then *deciding* what to do. In deciding what to do, they call on their own motivational and emotional resources and their own capacity for practical reasoning. But like actors, they modify these resources as needed, on the basis of evidence, especially the other's past and present behavior. A similar story holds for attributing mental states to others and explaining their action. (Gordon 1995*b*: 53)

We shall also see how this imitative capacity is crucial to the development of our empathetic faculties, which ultimately enables us to read other people's minds. It may be worth emphasizing that empirical evidence has been proposed in favor of the idea that our brain is a powerful simulating mechanism designed in such a way that it helps us detect intentions from other people's motion and predict future actions of other animate beings. If our brain was not so designed, i.e. if it was not such a powerful simulating mechanism, it would be difficult to explain how we so easily understand other people's intentions. To support this thesis, I first discuss how we attribute pain and similar sensations to other people and how this faculty plays a crucial role in our psychological makeup and in our psycho-social development.

2. Empathy and the Attribution of Sensations

Descartes presented us with the controversial thesis that animals are mere complex robots or machines.[1] This thesis goes against our common-sense views, for if

---

[1] On occasions, Descartes attributes sensations such as feelings, hope, and joy to animals (see Cottingham 1986: ch. 5). This contrasts with Descartes's official viewpoint that animals are mere automata.

we were to see someone beating her dog, we would imagine feeling the pain and feel sorry for it. If we see someone beating her car or her computer, however, we do not "feel the computer's (or car's) pain" and we feel sorry for neither. We may feel sorry if an expensive car or computer is damaged, but we do not feel sorry because the car or computer is suffering. Our feelings *vis-à-vis* the dog and the computer are of a different nature. How, though, can we explain this difference? Of course, the beaten dog behaves in a certain way, while the computer does not so react. Well, imagine that we face a dog and a robot-dog that behave the same way when beaten. In seeing the dog beaten we "feel her pain", while in seeing the robot-dog beaten we do not "feel its pain" (so long as we know it is only a robot). Though we may feel very uncomfortable if the robot-dog behaves in a human-like way, our response would be encapsulated and governed by our belief.

Before going further, a word of clarification is in order. It seems that simulation mechanisms operate at a pre-conceptual level. Actually, it has been proved that neurons in the human cingulate cortex do "simulate" other people's neurons when one perceives what ordinarily causes pain.[2] If one sees another getting hurt, one's neurons simulate the neurons of the wounded person. Hence, if our robot-dog is sufficiently similar to a real dog, our neurons will react in the same way as they would do in the presence of a real dog. We should thus say that, in seeing a robot-dog beaten, we do not feel its pain *conceptually*. The behavioral manifestations need not be necessary conditions either, for two people undergoing the same torture and pain may behave very differently. While one starts shouting, crying, and writhing, the other may stay perfectly quiet, yet we feel sorry for both. Besides, if we know that someone is cheating and behaving as if she were in pain, we do not "feel her pain": we do not "feel the pain" simulated by two wrestlers.[3] Behavior does not seem to be a good guide in explaining our reaction; at least, it is

---

[2] See Hutchinson et al. (1999). I shall discuss the thesis that some simulation mechanisms are innate further later on. In discussing the imitation of actions, Meltzoff writes: "This same cell fires regardless of whether that act is performed by the monkey or observed in another actor. A cell that discharges in both cases could mean that 'grasping' is an innate act, and that prior to experience the cell is tuned to this category of action whether performed by the self or the actor" (Meltzoff 2002: 21). According to Meltzoff, motor imitation is a foundation for the development of empathy and a theory of mind: "According to this view, empathy, role-taking, and theory of mind depend on the fundamental self-other equivalence first realized in infant imitation. Infants first grasp that others are 'like me' in action; from this they develop the more mature notion that others are 'like me' in abstract ways" (Meltzoff 2002: 21). On this issue it is also worth mentioning Jannerod's study (1994), which claims that one's aptitude to simulate a movement parallels one's ability to perform it. For a recent survey on how we are hard-wired to infer other people's intentions from their actions, see Blakemore and Decety (2001) and the studies they quote.

[3] Indeed, the situation is not so simple. Whilst watching a movie, we may "feel the actor's pain" and may put ourselves in the actor's shoes. In this kind of situation, though, we always have the conceptual capacity (or meta-capacity) to retreat and to tell ourselves that it is only a movie and that the actors are merely mimicking pain-behavior. But still, we may not be able to rid ourselves of feelings of discomfort.

not always reliable. Hence behavioral manifestations are not sufficient conditions to justify and trigger our feelings. This does not amount to saying that pain can only be known by its owner. Only I can feel my headache, to be sure, but it does not follow, from the fact that I cannot feel someone else's pain, that I cannot know whether someone else is in pain or not. Moreover:

[O]ne would not have the concept of, say, being in pain, without having encountered organisms displaying pain-behavior. If I were the only advanced organism in the world, my concept, if any, of pain, of experience, of subjects, and of myself, would be quite different from what it is now. This much, at least, is clear from Wittgenstein's argument against private language. (Vendler 1984: 18)

How, then, do we feel entitled to attribute to someone else the feeling of pain? A commonsensical answer is that we put ourselves in her position or situation and conclude that she is in pain from our being aware that we would be in pain in such a situation: if I were beaten like the dog or tortured, I would feel pain. Imagination seems to be one of the key notions that allow us to attribute pain and the like. These kinds of attribution rest on our faculty to put ourselves in someone's shoes and think what we would do/feel/experience/ . . . in her situation. This is a perspectival activity insofar as it rests on the attributer's capacity to project herself into the attributee's context, i.e. it rests on the capacity one has to adopt someone else's viewpoint. It is because of this faculty that we can succeed in predicting someone's movements, feelings, plans, etc. When playing chess, for instance, I can anticipate my opponent's move because I figure out what I would do in her position.[4]

A plausible answer concerning the way we communicate sensations and emotions *via* bodily movements and reactions can be found in theories of evolution. In particular, it sounds plausible to argue that we transmit and understand sensations, primarily facial expressions, because nature programmed us to do so. We evolved to use this 'body-language' because it is, from an evolutionary viewpoint, a useful ability to possess. This evolutionary explanation concerning our capacity to recognize other people's emotions faces the epistemological worry that it is always possible that one can react/act in a given way and manifest a given bodily

---

[4] The general picture I have in mind bears some resemblance to simulation theory in the philosophy of mind, and in particular to the position that views our simulation activity as belonging to a family of mental faculties such as imitation, pretending, motor imagery, etc. For a defense of this view, see Goldman (1995; 2000), Gordon and Heal (2003) (amongst others). The foundational papers on this issue are by Gordon (1995a; 1995b), Heal and Goldman, reprinted in Davies and Stone (1995a). The basic idea put forward is that one's ability to predict someone else's actions rests upon one's ability to engage in simulation, i.e. one's capacity to put oneself into someone else's shoes, i.e. to simulate being that person: "We are mental simulators, not in the sense that we merely simulate mentation, but in the sense that we understand others by using our own mentation in a process of simulation" (Davies and Stone 1995b: 3). On the relation between simulation and imagination, see Currie and Ravenscroft (2002).

expression even if one is not experiencing the sensation we are attributing. One can always fake a sensation. Moreover, there is also the logical possibility of having never experienced any emotion and yet acting/reacting as if a particular emotion were being experienced. This logical possibility should not bother us too much, insofar as we implicitly presuppose, as part of our common-sense psychology, that others are like us. That is, our attribution of sensations to other people is grounded on the fact that we take the attributees to be individuals.[5] As we saw when discussing the construction of the self and the capacity to master personal pronouns (Chapter 5), one comes to master the use of 'I' when one considers oneself to be an individual amongst others. I also stressed that the concept of person should be taken as primitive.

The way we attribute pain to others, however, does not rest on analogy; i.e. it does not rest on an inference the reporter ought to make before being entitled to attribute pain. One need not project one's own pain onto someone else before making a pain attribution:

If one has to imagine someone else's pain on the model of one's own, this is none too easy a thing to do: for I have to imagine pain which I *do not feel* on the model of pain which I *do feel*. That is, what I have to do is not simply to make a transition in imagination from one place of pain to another. As for pain in the hand to pain in the arm. For I am not to imagine that I feel pain in some region of his body. (Wittgenstein, *PI*: §302)

You say you attend a man who groans because experience has taught you that you yourself groan when you feel such-and-such. But as you don't in fact make any such inference, we can abandon the justification by analogy. (Wittgenstein, *Z*: §537)

One reacts and attributes pain *automatically*, without reflection. There is, we can say, a pre-theoretical and pre-inferential foundation for our knowledge of others having their own feelings and sensations.[6] That is to say, the capacity one has to grasp other people's pains and sensations ultimately rests on one's previous grasping that other people do have feelings, pains, sensations, etc. This does not contradict the idea that imagination and empathy play a crucial role when one comes to learn and master the language-game of pain and sensation attribution. If one lacks these basic faculties, one faces difficulties in understanding other people's pain and the like, let alone attributing these kinds of sensation.

I now try to show how this thesis can be empirically substantiated, i.e. that imagination and empathy play a crucial role when we attribute sensations to other people.

---

[5] For a discussion of how we understand other peoples' emotions along these lines, see Goldie (2000: 182–3). See also Sorensen (1998).

[6] "[T]he basis for infants' growing understanding of other people is their experience of reciprocal personal relations with others, what Hamlyn (1974) called 'natural reaction of person to person'. . . . Another person's state of mind is directly grasped in expressive phenomena" (quoted in Hobson 1990: 116).

A way to define empathy is as follows (see Hoffman 2000: 29):

- Empathy = *the vicarious affective response to another person.*[7]

On this account, one is empathizing insofar as one's feelings match the patient's feelings.[8] The whole of the empathic procedure is psychologically complex inasmuch as several psychological processes are involved. To begin with, we should stress that empathy entails distress and on this we can follow Hoffman in arguing that this kind of distress is a *prosocial* motive, insofar as it is correlated with people's helping and caring behavior. We can thus recognize three features of empathic distress:

- *Empathic distress*
  (i) It is associated with helping
  (ii) It precedes helping
  (iii) The empathizer feels better after helping.

Nonetheless the empathizer's ultimate goal is to alleviate the patient's distress, not her own. Actually, it has been proved (Batson and Shaw 1991) that when an empathizer attempts to alleviate someone's pain but does not succeed because of an external cause (independent of the empathizer), the empathizer continues to feel distress as well:

It seems reasonable to conclude that although empathy-based helping makes people feel good by reducing empathic distress and providing empathic relief, the main objective of empathy-based helping is to alleviate the victim's distress. Empathic distress is, in short, a prosocial motive. (Hoffman 2000: 33)

Blair (1995) argues that there is a cognitive mechanism, the violence inhibiting mechanism (VIM), which can get activated by non-verbal communication of distress such as facial expressions, the sight and sounds of tears, etc. When VIM is activated the patient initiates a withdrawal response and the patient is likely to pull out from attacking. Blair argues that VIM is the *sine qua non* of moral development:

VIM is a prerequisite for the development of three aspects of "morality": the moral emotions (e.g., sympathy, guilt, remorse and empathy), the inhibition of violent action and the moral/conventional distinction. (Blair 1995: 4)

In short, the activation of VIM is considered among the moral emotions. Empathy is viewed as an emotional reaction to the representation of the distressed internal

---

[7] This is also characterized as *affective empathy*. Empathy has also been characterized by psychologists as the cognitive awareness of someone else's mental states such as feelings, thoughts, intentions, perceptions. See e.g. Sober and Wilson (1998).

[8] It is worth mentioning that empathy, rather than repression, also helps in reducing antisocial behavior: "Developmental studies have clearly demonstrated that punishment is not associated with a reduction in antisocial behavior; instead, the use of inductive techniques (e.g., asking the child how the victim of the act feels) is associated with a reduction in antisocial behavior" (Blair 1995: 2).

state of another. Such a reaction helps one to refrain from aggression; it helps to inhibit violent behavior. Furthermore, moral transgressions are judged differently from conventional transgressions:

> VIM is a prerequisite for the development of the moral/conventional distinction.... Since conventional transgressions, by definition, do not result in victims, they are therefore never paired with distress cues and will not therefore become stimuli for activation of VIM. (Blair 1995: 7)

Empathy *qua* prosocial motive rests on different modes. Some of them are involuntary. Among the latter we have *mimicry*.[9] The process of mimicry subdivides into *imitation* and *feedback*. Roughly, when observing someone's expression of feelings, one tends to imitate the patient's expression. The brain then produces a similar feeling to the one the patient is expressing in the observer. The important thing to notice here is that the mimicry process does not rest on conscious inferences or reasoning. It is universal—i.e. it does not change from culture to culture—and seems to be innate:[10]

> [M]imicry is probably a hard-wired neurologically based empathy-arousing mechanism whose two steps, imitation and feedback, are directed by commands from the neural central nervous system. This is important for two reasons. First ... hard-wired mimicry provides a quick-acting mechanism enabling infants to empathize and feel what another feels without previously experiencing that emotion.... A second reason ... is that besides being involuntary and fast, mimicry is the only empathy-arousing mechanism that assures a match between the observer's feeling and an expression of feeling and the victim's feeling and expression of feeling, at least in face-to-face encounters. (Hoffman 2000: 44)

We are wired in such a way that we cannot avoid feeling someone else's distress. As evidence of the innateness of this faculty, we can cite a child's reactive cry. Simner (1971) established that when a newborn infant hears another infant crying, she starts crying as well, while hearing a computer-simulated sound of the same volume or an animal cry does not produce this reaction. Moreover, the infant's intensity of distress caused by a reactive cry and the distress caused by a spontaneous cry do not differ. The more plausible explanation seems to be that this reaction is the fruit of natural selection. The underlying psychological mechanism seems to be a form of mimicry in which infants automatically imitate the sound of another infant and empathize with her (see Hoffman 2000: 65).

---

[9] Smith noticed that empathy rests on imitation: "When we see a stroke aimed, and just ready to fall upon the leg of another person, we naturally shrink and draw back our own arm.... The mob, when they are gazing at a dancer on the slack rope, naturally writhe and twist and balance their own bodies as they see him do" (A. Smith [1759] 1976: 4, 10).

[10] For a recent discussion on how innateness has been conceived within evolutionary biology see Griffiths (2002).

Besides, the mimicry faculty plays a crucial role in our social interaction. It is, we could say, our social glue. In other words, mimicry is the *sine qua non* of an agent *qua* social participant. It would be impossible to imagine a community like ours where the empathic mechanism is not at play. It would be like imagining a "community" of robots (or zombies) interacting amongst themselves and cooperating in doing, more or less, what we do. In Wittgensteinian terms, we can say that the mimicry upon which our empathic faculty is developed is an essential ingredient of our form of life:

> To summarize, mimicry, conditioning, and direct association are important mechanisms of empathic arousal for several reasons: (a) they are automatic, quick-acting, and involuntary; (b) they enable infants and preverbal children, as well as adults, to empathize with others in distress; (c) they produce early pairings of children's empathic distress with other people's actual distress whenever they are exposed to another's distress; (d) they are self-reinforcing to some extent because the helping behavior they foster may produce empathic relief; (e) they contribute an involuntary dimension to children's future empathy experiences. (Hoffman 2000: 48)

With the addition of language, a child then develops the meta-empathic capacity. That is to say, a child's original, innate, empathic capacity acquires a metacognitive dimension. At this stage, our infant becomes aware of the fact that her own empathic distress is caused by someone else's feelings. The acquisition of language helps to build some distance between the empathic process and the patient's feelings. It is at this stage that imagination enters the scene and, as we saw in Chapter 5 (Section 1), it is also at this stage that a child begins to form her self-consciousness and to use the first-person pronoun. When a subject imagines herself in the patient's situation, language plays a crucial role. This empathic mode is probably the most advanced and developed. It is the *sine qua non* of the capacity an agent has to imagine herself in someone else's shoes. It is on the basis of this role-taking exercise, I shall claim (Section 4), that our capacity attributing attitudes to others rests. As we shall see in the next section, if one is impaired in this empathic capacity, one faces serious difficulties and may even be completely incapable of attributing mental states to oneself, let alone to someone else. In other words, without this role-playing capacity one would be unable, or at least would face serious difficulties, in attributing mental states such as thinking, believing, wishing, and the like to someone else. Stotland (1969) showed that imagining oneself in another's situation is more empathic-arousing than focusing one's attention on the other's facial expressions and behavior. If we concentrate on the attribution of pain, for instance, the role-play exercise triggers different distress, depending on whether one focuses on one's self or on the attributee:

> Imagining oneself in the other's place reflects processes generated from within the observer ... in which connections are made between the stimuli impinging on the other

person and similar events in the observer's past. That is, imagining oneself in the other's place produces an empathic response because it has the power to evoke associations with real events in one's own past in which one actually experienced the affect in question. (Hoffman 1978: 180)

It goes without saying, however, that an observer often shifts between self-oriented role-playing imagination and other-focused role-playing. A competent adult speaker, in feeling empathic distress and thus in being capable of attributing pain and other sensations, often informs her role-playing process with experiences drawn from her own life. Memory can thus play an important role.

As a general hypothesis, we can say that, during our evolutionary history, empathy became such an important ingredient of our makeup and capacities that it would be impossible to imagine our social behavior and interaction without it. As such, we can easily infer that empathy evolved through natural selection. It thus does not come as a surprise to hear that empathy has also a hereditary component. Identical twins are more similar than siblings in their empathy measures (see Zahn-Waxler et al. 1992).

3. Further Empirical Evidence: The Case from Autism

The problems faced by autistic people are well documented. Autism can be viewed as mindreading impairment. That is, autistic people face difficulties in understanding, let alone attributing, the mental attitudes of other people. They lack the empathetic faculty I described previously:

His mother remarked: "He would pay no attention to me and show no recognition of me if I enter the room.... The most impressive thing is his detachment and his inaccessibility. He walks as if he is in a shadow, lives in a world of his own where he cannot be reached. No sense of relationship to persons.... He used to speak of himself in the second person, now he uses the third person at times; he would say, "He wants"—never "I want".... When he is with other people, he doesn't look up at them.... He has a wonderful memory for words. Vocabulary is good, except for pronouns". (Kanner 1943; quoted in Hobson 1993: 2–3)

We can borrow the words of Kanner and say that autistic children "have come into the world with innate inability to form the usual, biologically provided affective contact with people" (Kanner 1943: 250).

The case from autism furnishes further evidence in favor of the thesis that imagination in general, and, in particular, the empathic faculty, plays a major role in our attributions of mental states to other people:

I think that autistic children's deficient or aberrant capacity for intersubjective engagement with others is what causes their limitation in understanding minds. (Hobson 1993: 13)

One way in which an individual's subjective experiences are linked in with those of others, is through processes of empathy or "fellow-feeling".... there can be little doubt that the question of empathy is relevant for our theories of autism, and that studies of autism may contribute to our thinking about the nature of empathy and the sources of psychological sharing. (Hobson 1993: 61)

To summarize, because autistics face an empathetic impairment, (i) they do not develop the capacity to attribute sensations to other people, and (ii) on a more general level, they lack the capacity to attribute propositional attitudes. In other words, autistic people never come to master the role-play faculty, i.e. the capacity to imagine themselves in other people's shoes. They cannot, so to speak, imagine other people's experiences and sensations.[11] They lack the mindreading capacity that normal children develop quite early on in their life:

When an adult pretended to be hurt, for example, the autistic children often appeared unconcerned and continued to play with toys. When an adult showed fear toward the robot, autistic children were not only less attentive toward the adult.... but they were also less hesitant in playing with the robot subsequently than were non-autistic mentally retarded control subjects. Here we find evidence emerging that autistic children are relatively "unengaged" not only in one-to-one interpersonal-affective transactions, but also with another person's emotional attitudes towards objects and events in the world. (Hobson 1993: 63)

Because of the mindreading impairment, an autistic individual feels herself, to borrow Temple Grandin's words, like an anthropologist on Mars.[12]

Moreover, because of this empathetic impairment and the lack of the mindreading faculty, autistic children also face difficulties in developing a notion of self. This impairment parallels their impairment in metarepresentation.[13] They have problems in developing a self-reflexive conception, for they are unable to conceive of themselves in a way other people may perceive them. As we saw in Chapter 5 (Section 1) in discussing the notion of self, one comes to develop one's own notion of self insofar as one is capable of relating to other people and the world, i.e. insofar as one is capable of taking someone else's perspective.

---

[11] "A large number of studies have repeatedly demonstrated that children with autism have difficulties in shifting their perspective to judge what someone else might think, instead simply reporting what they themselves know" (Baron-Cohen 2000: 5).

[12] See Oliver Sacks's (1993–4) report on Temple Grandin, who was affected by Asperger's syndrome (a form of autism that does not fully affect the subject's capacity for self-consciousness). People affected by this syndrome have some power to introspect and report.

[13] If one accepts Currie and Ravenscroft's account, one can explain these kinds of impairment by focusing on autistics' impairment in their imaginative faculties and their engagement in pretence: "We propose that autism be regarded as a disorder of imagination, and we think of the imagination as a device which assists us in understanding and solving problems across a range of different domains.... people with autism show poor performance. These domains are pretence and planning" (Currie and Ravenscroft 2002: 139).

This capacity, I argued, is manifested in one's correct use of the pronouns 'I', 'you', and 's/he':

> Autistic children are also limited in their capacities of self-reflective awareness. They are at best only partially aware of themselves in the mind of others.... [They] appear to contrast with normal one-year-olds in having little sense of property, little competition or focused self-defense or counterattack, and they may be delayed in saying "No" and "Yes". This kind of list illustrates how a child's awareness of self is sharpened by awareness of other selves, and *vice versa*; for example, normal possessiveness and competition are experienced in relation to rival possessors and competitors.... [They] do have difficulties in *conceiving* of themselves as "selves", but this cognitive difficulty is closely allied to their lack of engagement not only with other people, but also with themselves *as* "selves". (Hobson 1993: 199)

Gerhard Bosh (1970) showed that pronouns may also be used incorrectly in non-echolalic utterances—i.e. the use of someone else's language is unmodified according to the vantage point of the child in the child's own setting. Sometimes the autistic child makes third-person self-references by naming herself or calling herself 'she'. This suggests that there is something unusual about the child's experience of herself as a self *vis-à-vis* others:

> Instead of relating the other person's utterance to that person's attitude and then identifying with the other person's stance, autistic children tend to adopt speech forms that correspond with *their* experience of the circumstances in which the words are uttered, and therefore to repeat utterances as heard (Charney 1981). (Hobson 1993: 98)

This deficit with pronouns appears to prevent autistic children from recognizing people as centers of subjectivity, as holders of different perspectives and, ultimately, as occupants of reciprocal roles in discourse. What is important to stress for our purpose is that these impairments parallel the difficulties one faces in mastering personal pronouns. As further evidence of this phenomenon, we can also stress that the development of symbolic play corresponds to the earlier usage of self-referential pronouns ('I' and 'me'). A congenitally blind child, Kathie, with language competencies comparable to other children of her age, confused the use of pronouns:

> [She] could not represent herself through a doll or a toy. She could not recreate or invent a situation in play. She could not attend to a story or answer questions regarding a story or tell a story herself. (Fraiberg and Adelson 1977: 256)

The obvious question that springs to mind is: why do blind children of an early age often mirror the symptoms of autistic children (e.g. are echolalic)?

Recall the importance of vision for enabling the sighted child to see, literally to "see", the outer-directness of other people's psychological attitudes. Vision enables children to triangulate their own and others' divergent attitudes toward visually-specified objects and events in the world. Recall, too, the significance of such experience for differentiating the respective and potentially transferable roles of participants in communication. The blind child is therefore deprived of a principal means to achieve psychological co-orientation and co-reference with others. (Hobson 1993: 205)

No doubt, these are serious problems and serious difficulties and impairments faced by autistic children. To handle these situations, some autistic people (the less impaired) may have recourse to *visual* simulation. This is the case with Temple Grandin:

Temple constantly runs "simulations," as she calls them, in her head: "I visualize the animal entering the chute, from different angles, different distances, zooming in or wide-angle, even from a helicopter view—or I turn myself into an animal, and feel what it would feel entering the chute."
   But if one thinks only in pictures, I could not help reflecting, one might not understand what nonvisual thinking was like, and one would miss the richness and ambiguity, the cultural presupposition, the depth, of language. All autistics, Temple has said earlier, were intensely visual thinkers, like her....
   She feels she can have sympathy for what is physical or physiological—for an animal's pain or terror—but lacks empathy for people's states of mind and perspectives. When she was younger she was hardly able to interpret even the simplest expression of emotion; she learned to "decode" them later, without necessarily feeling them. (Sacks 1993–4: 115–16)

If my understanding of what is going on in Grandin's case is correct, we have further empirical evidence in favor of the picture I am putting forward. For, if autistic people face obstacles in reporting other people's pain and the like, it is because they lack the empathetic faculty that I claim lies at the bottom of our pain and sensation reports:

[A]utistic individuals lack something essential for the capacity to relate to other people's psychological relatedness to themselves and to the world. This capacity is *the* defining characteristic of the relatedness triangle. It follows that if a non-autistic child's experience of the relatedness triangle is foundational for a range of subsequent developmental accomplishments, then the autistic child's impoverished experience in this respect should result in corresponding psychological sequelae. (Hobson 1993: 197)[14]

To borrow Wittgenstein's terminology, we can further add that, in order to play the language-game of pain attributions and reports, we need to share a form of life:

[O]ne human being can be a complete enigma to another. We learn this when we come into a strange country with entirely strange traditions; and, what is more, even given a mastery of the country's language. We do not *understand* the people.... We cannot find our feet with them.... If a lion could talk, we could not understand him. (Wittgenstein, *PI* ii: 223)

---

[14] For further discussion on these issues see Nichols (2002*a*, 2002*b*).

It may be worth noticing that, if we follow Wittgenstein on this issue, we ought ultimately to accept that what is essential to the understanding of all our linguistic activity, and *a fortiori* the language-game of pain attribution, is our form of life, for "to imagine a language is to imagine a form of life" (*PI*: §7); "what has to be accepted, the given, is—so one could say—forms of life" (*PI* ii: p. 226). The form of life is the background against which our linguistic practice rests. As is often the case with Wittgenstein, these remarks can be understood in variegated ways. Among the possible understandings, the one I favor assumes that our form of life, *qua* foundation of our linguistic practice, can be given a socio-naturalistic interpretation. As such, it is part of both our biological and anthropological nature insofar as they both concur in determining how we linguistically act and react: "commanding, questioning, recounting, chatting, are as much part of our natural history as walking, eating, drinking, playing" (*PI*: §25).[15] To put it in a nutshell, it is because autistic people do not fully share our form of life that they feel like anthropologists on Mars and, therefore, do not easily master many of our linguistic practices.[16] In particular, they do not find themselves at home with the attribution of mental states, for if one is impaired in one's mindreading capacity, *a fortiori* one is in difficulty when it comes to attributing propositional attitudes:

What is it, then, I pressed her further, that goes on between normal people, from which she feels herself excluded? It has to do, she has inferred, with an implicit knowledge of social conventions and codes, of cultural presuppositions of every sort. This implicit knowledge, which every normal person accumulates and generates throughout life on the basis of experience and encounters with others, Temple seems to be largely devoid of. Lacking it, she has insisted to "compute" others' feelings and intentions and states of mind, to try to make algorithmic, explicit, what for the rest of us is second nature. She herself, she infers, may never have had the normal social experiences from which a normal social knowledge is constructed.

[15] Hence, understanding of someone's language does not merely rest on shared beliefs; it ultimately rests on shared behavioral patterns: "The common behavior of mankind is the system of reference by means of which we interpret an unknown language" (*PI*: §206). For these reasons, we cannot feel at ease with a community that never expresses any feelings of pain: "Imagine that the people of a tribe were brought up from early youth to give no expression of feeling *of any kind*. . . . 'These men would have nothing human about them.' Why?—We could not possibly make ourselves understood to them. Not even as we can to a dog. We could not find our feet with them. And yet there surely could be such beings, who in other respects were human" (*Z*: §385, 390). For: "knowledge and understanding of persons, or to put this differently, a conceptual grasp of the nature of minds, is acquired through an individual's experience of effectively patterns, intersubjectively co-ordinated relations *with* other people. A young child comes to know about people's psychological states through having subjective experiences that are shared with, opposed to, or otherwise articulated with the experience (and not merely the "behavior") of others" (Hobson 1993: 4–5).

[16] Autistic people do "have considerable difficulty with a number of emotion-related concepts, with understanding pretence and imagination, and perhaps especially with concepts of belief and knowledge. For example, they have difficulties in understanding how another person may behave inappropriately on the basis of a false belief about a situation" (Hobson 1993: 200).

And it may be from this, too, that her difficulties with gesture and language stem—difficulties that were devastating when she was a near speech-less child, and also in the early days of speech, when she mixed all her pronouns up, not able to grasp the different meaning of "you" and "I," depending on context....

She remains clearly autistic, but her new power of language and communication now gave her an anchor, some ability to master what had been total chaos before....

With the access of language, the terrible triad of impairments—social, communicative, and imaginative—began to yield somewhat....

At eight, Temple was starting to achieve the "pretend play" that normal children achieve as toddlers but the lower-functioning autistic child never achieves at all....

She is now aware of the existence of these social signals. She can infer them, she says, but she herself cannot perceive them, cannot participate in this magical communication directly, or conceive the many-leveled, kaleidoscopic states of mind behind it. (Sacks 1993–4: 116)

The moral I would like to draw is that we do not perceive someone's pain merely as a bodily movement. Instead, we perceive it as we perceive actions and activities with specific aims and goals.[17] As Strawson (1959) suggests, the essential characteristic of a predicate we apply to a person is that it can be ascribed both in the first-person and in the third-person way. To master these predicates is to master both aspects. Thus, we learn how to ascribe such predicates on the basis of certain behavioral criteria and we self-ascribe them without observation. Both kinds of ascription come together and thus empathy seems to play a key role. In other words, a necessary condition of ascribing states of consciousness to oneself is that one is also capable of ascribing them to someone else, and a necessary condition of ascribing states of consciousness to others is to recognize them as individuals of the same type as oneself:

It is only through episodes of intersubjectively co-ordinated experiences that an infant eventually becomes aware *that* people have minds. It does not require reasoning by analogy for infants to recognise the nature of persons as like themselves in being sources of subjective attitudes, yet unlike themselves in having mental states that at any given time may differ from their own. What it does require is not only primary, biologically-given and perceptually-anchored mechanisms for establishing connectedness of minds between infant and care-giver, but also means by which the minds of "self" and "other" are differentiated and ultimately conceptualised. Or to approach the matter from a different angle, it is not that infants first perceive bodies and subsequently confer minds, but rather that they have direct perception of and natural engagement with person-related meanings that are apprehended *in* the expressions and behaviour of other persons. It is only gradually, and with considerable input from the adults, that they eventually come to conceive of "bodies" on the one hand, and "mind" on the other. (Hobson 1993: 117)

[17] For more on this particularity and for the empirical results, drawn both from humans and primates, to confirm this thesis, see Proust (2000).

It is the inter*subjective* linkage that establishes the basis for infants to ascribe "subjectivity" to others. Infants, like adults, are directly aware when they are emotionally connected with other people. Their developmental task is not to infuse bodies with minds, but rather to acquire an understanding of how different people have their own *separate* subjective perspectives and selves in relation to a common world. (Hobson 1993: 119)

Moreover, as I have already suggested, the concept of *pain* is not confined to behavioral manifestations when one is injured or sick. It is also linked to our capacity to attribute pain and to feel compassion, mercy, pity, commiseration, etc. It is also linked to anxiety, fear, apprehension, cruelty, atrocity, etc.:

The concept of pain is characterized by its particular function in our life. (Wittgenstein, Z: §532)

Pain has *this* position in our life; it has *these* connexions; (That is to say: we only call "pain" what has *this* position, *these* connexions). (Wittgenstein, Z: §533)

Only surrounded by certain normal manifestations of life, is there such a thing as an expression of pain. Only surrounded by an even more far-reaching manifestation of life, such a thing as the expression of sorrow or affection. And so on. (Wittgenstein, Z: §534)

Following these suggestions, it emerges that a fruitful way to spell out the different kinds of abilities required by the use of a word like 'pain' (and in particular the mastery of the language-game of pain attribution) can be given by considering what happens when perceiving someone else's pain. We do not perceive pain in the same way we perceive the computer screen in front of us, or a woman crossing the street. Actually, from the discussion of the previous section and this one, it follows that a psychologically normal individual perceives other people's sensations in a non-inferential way. We saw how empathy is a prosocial faculty, contributing to the recipe that helps us to interact in the way we do with our neighbors. We feel their distress and we react in such a way as to alleviate their pain. Unlike Descartes's model, we can claim that we do not perceive someone's sensation on the analogy model. In other words, we do not infer one's mental states from one's body movement. We are hard-wired and we develop in such a way that we *directly* perceive other's mental states. There is no gap to be filled in:

[T]here is no radical developmental disjunction between the perception of "bodies" or "behaviours", and the apprehension of "mind". *A fortiori*, it is not a matter of the infant beginning with the cool perception of things-like bodies, and only subsequently interpreting or theorising that behind bodily behaviour there might be "mind". On the contrary, aspects of mind are perceived in aspect of expressive behaviour. This is true of adult perceptual experience just as it is of an infantile experience....

There is direct perception of "personal meanings" anchored in people's bodies. This form of perception is not reducible to nor supervenient upon the perception of bodies *as* "bodies". The starting point for the I-Thou developmental line is interpersonal and intersubjective engagement, in its infantile form. This special mode of engagement is necessary if the child is to understand what a person is—a special kind of thing with a body and a mind. (Hobson 1993: 187–8)

The picture that emerges is indeed Wittgensteinian, for Wittgenstein argued that the perception and understanding of other people's mental attitudes and the attribution of pain and the like does not work on an inferential basis. In particular, it does not work on the model of analogy, i.e. on the model that one understands someone else's pain because one relates this pain to one's own:

"We see emotion."—As opposed to what?—We do not see facial contortions and *make the inference* that he is feeling joy, grief, boredom. We describe a face immediately as sad, radiant, bored, even when we are unable to give any other description of the features.—Grief, one would like to say, is personified in face. This is essential to what we call "emotion". (Wittgenstein, *RPP* ii: §570)

The non-inferential view stressed by Wittgenstein regarding the attribution of sensation can also be stressed *vis-à-vis* simulation. It has been argued (see for instance Gordon 1995*b*) that simulation should not be conceived as a logical process from one's mental state to someone else's. In particular, simulation should not be conceived as an inference from one's own mental state to the mental states of others. The simulation process is automatic and it works insofar as we do not have to base it on the asymmetry between the first and third person. In other words, one need not go from first-person attributions to third-person attributions. That is to say, one need not first form a first-person mental state and then transfer this mental state onto someone else. The simulation mechanism does not rest on this inferential process:

To simulate *Mr Tees* in his situation requires an egocentric shift, a recentering of my egocentric map on Mr Tees. He becomes in my imagination the referent of the first person pronoun 'I', and the time and place of his missing the plane become the referent of 'now' and 'here'. And I, RMG, *cease* to be the referent of the first person pronoun: what is imagined is not the truth of the counter identical, "RMG is Mr Tees". Such recentering is the prelude to transforming myself in imagination into Mr Tees much as actors become the characters they play. (Gordon 1995*b*: 55)

Gordon's argument depends on the distinction between two kinds of imaginative projects: imagining oneself in another's situation *vs.* imagining oneself being the relevant agent in that situation. It is only in the second kind on imagining, Gordon claims, that no inferential step is involved. Currie and Ravenscroft (2002: 65–7) reject Gordon's idea that no inference is involved in the second kind of imagining (see also Heal 2003: 137). They claim that when we come to the justification of our beliefs we must rely on an inference insofar as a change from imagining oneself in another situation to imagining being another does nothing to justify one's belief:

> Changing the imaginative project in this way does not make the imagining a more reliable guide to what Smith will do; the reliability of the project depends on whether, in imagination, I am getting my mind to work like Smith's. Adding the stipulation 'I am Smith' does nothing to ensure that my mental processes are more like Smith's than they were before the stipulation—except in the unusual case where the thought 'I am Smith' plays a part in Smith's own decision-making. (Currie and Ravenscroft 2002: 56–7)

Be that as it may, we can adopt the terminology I introduced in the previous chapters, and argue that in cases of transference like these, we have a context shift. This amounts to furnishing new contextuals parameters, from which indexicals gain their value. The agent, location, and time may all be shifted and this seems to be what happens when we engage in imaginative processes. If one adopts this model, one need not assume that self-ascription of mental states logically precedes the ascription of mental states to others, i.e. that there is an asymmetry between the two.

As we shall see in the next chapter, when we come to attribute perspectival mental states to others we can appeal to quasi-indicators. We thus automatically attribute an 'I'-thought using 'she (herself)'. One's mastery of indexical reference rests on one's mastery of quasi-indexical reference. If I am right in thinking that indexicals and quasi-indicators are two sides of the same coin, then we can easily recognize that our linguistic faculty of attributing perspectival thoughts rests on, or at least goes hand in hand with, our capacity to assume someone else's perspective. Before going further, it is worth anticipating that when we come to attribute attitudes to someone else, the belief or thought ascribed is not merely a pretend assertion or pretend thought. To be sure, I argued that the pretence game helps us to capture someone's mental state. I did not, however, argue that it helps us to capture the whole story of the attribution game.[18] As Jacob aptly suggests:

> I do not think that belief-ascriptions are *pretend assertions* or *pretend thoughts*. I think that belief-ascriptions (whether utterances or thoughts) are genuine thoughts and/or full assertions with truth-conditions: they are true or false. But they have a characteristic complexity: to think that someone else thinks that p is more complex than to think that p. It is one thing to engage imaginatively in pretence. It is something else to describe somebody else's state of mind ... when I ascribe to Maria the belief that witches have magical power, I entertain a complex thought one ingredient of which is the concept of belief. This complex thought

---

[18] As Currie and Ravenscroft point out: "My saying to myself or to anyone else 'Smith will Φ' as part of a pretence does not constitute my acquiring a belief about what Smith will actually do, and certainly does not constitute my acquiring any knowledge; that can happen only outside the scope of my role-taking" (Currie and Ravenscroft 2002: 57).

which contains the concept of belief is not a pretend thought: it describes a portion of the actual world which contains Maria and her beliefs. (Jacob 2002: 100)

As we shall see, the 'believe' in 'believe that' is a complex predicate with more structure than its superficial grammar suggests. The capacity of engaging in pretence may be a necessary condition underlying the capacity to ascribe attitudes.[19] It is not, however, a sufficient condition. The ascription of attitudes is a more complex activity, an activity which seems to require a metarepresentational capacity as well, i.e. the ability to entertain thoughts about thoughts or to entertain representations about representations. Furthermore, when we come to report someone's perception of pain and the like we do not, however, do so on the model of direct perception. To stress this point, consider the following:

(1) Jon saw that Mary was in pain
(2) Jon saw Mary in pain
(3) Jon saw Mary's partner
(4) * Jon saw Mary's pain

While (1), (2), and (3) make sense, (4) does not (unless it is understood in a metaphorical way). Following these attributions, it seems that one cannot perceive someone's pain, but one can perceive *that* someone is in pain. To spell out the difference between these kinds of attributions, I borrow Dretske's (1969: ch. 1) distinction between epistemic (seeing *that*) and non-epistemic seeing. We can see a leaf without seeing that the leaf is green. The former, unlike the latter, is non-epistemic: seeing a leaf in the non-epistemic way is like stepping on the leaf without realizing it. Another way to state the difference is to argue that non-epistemic seeing does not entail knowledge. One can see a lion without believing and, thus, without knowing that what one saw was a lion (and even without believing that it was an animal). Moreover, non-epistemic seeing is transparent: from "Sue saw Superman", given that Superman is Clark Kent, we can infer that "Sue saw Clark Kent", just as from "Lois kissed Superman" we can infer that "Lois kissed Clark Kent". Epistemic seeing, on the other hand, does not seem to be transparent.

---

[19] I used the conditional for I am not sure whether the capacity to engage in pretence is a necessary condition either. Jacob (2002), for instance, argues that the capacity to entertain thoughts and desires is not a necessary condition underlying the capacity of attributing beliefs and thoughts to others, for it seems reasonable to assume that a creature may have beliefs and desires about her environment without being able to engage in pretence. The latter is a more complex activity than the former. Be that as it may, I do not think that whether one accepts Jacob's view or the view that pretence is a necessary condition underlying our capacity to attribute attitudes greatly affects the picture I have in mind. I am committed to the view that the attribution of indexical thoughts rests on our capacity to engage in pretence, insofar as it requires the capacity to switch context. For it is the latter, I think, that enables us to put ourselves in someone else's shoes and to grasp her perspectival (indexical) thoughts. Whether other thoughts and beliefs can be attributed without engaging in pretence remains an open question.

From "Sue saw that Superman kissed Lois" we cannot infer that "Sue saw that Clark Kent kissed Lois", as from "Lois wishes to kiss Superman" we cannot infer "Lois wishes to kiss Clark Kent".

The general moral I would like to draw is that pain-reports can be rendered only using locutions of the form 'seeing that'.[20] These kinds of reports entail knowledge of someone's pain and, ultimately, mastery of the word 'pain'. This should not, however, dismiss the thesis that one perceives pain directly, without inference. All it shows is that the attribution of pain is a rather complex exercise, which requires a well-developed conceptual and cognitive architecture. What I have shown is that this complex faculty develops because we are innately capable of empathy and that, on the basis of empathy, we end up developing the more complex role-playing faculty. For these reasons, I think that the exercise at play when we attribute pain to someone is similar to the exercise at play when we attribute beliefs, desires, and the like. In particular, the same imaginative and empathetic faculties are at work. To the discussion of this very idea I now turn.

4. Sentences *qua* Thought Classifiers

If one is asked to report what one said, believes, thinks, wishes, etc. one would propose a self-attribution of the form:

- SA. *I* said/believe/think/wish/ . . . that *S*

where *S* is the sentence one would use to express what one said/believes/thinks/wishes/ . . . This sentence can be viewed as a reliable classifier of one's thought, i.e. the thought that one would express in using that very sentence.

Let me introduce the technical notion of *acceptance* in order to characterize the relation between the subject of an attitude report and the sentence *S* that classifies his/her thought. Accepted sentences are taken to be *thought classifiers*:

One has a belief *by* accepting a sentence. Which belief one thereby has also depends on who the believer is and when the believing takes place—factors that need have no representation in the mind. . . . When we believe we do so by being in belief states. These states have typical effects which we use to classify them. In particular we classify them by the sentences a competent speaker of the language in question would be apt to think or utter in certain circumstances when in that state. To accept a sentence *S* is to be in a belief state that would lead such a speaker to utter or think *S*. (Perry 1980*a*: 45)

---

[20] It is worth noticing that, even if a report like (2) is transparent (as far as Mary is concerned)—if Mary is Jeff's partner we can infer "Jon saw Jeff's partner in pain"—it is not transparent as far as the perception of Mary's pain is concerned. We can only infer "Jon saw *that* someone was in pain" from (2); we cannot infer "Jon saw someone's pain".

Here is the picture I have in mind: in accepting a sentence, an agent has a mental representation or thought of a certain type. An agent has the same type of mental representation whether she is in a belief, desire, saying, etc. relation to a proposition.

Before going further, a world of clarification is needed. It is worth reminding that I am working within the framework of direct reference. I thus assume that singular terms refer directly without the mediation of Fregean senses or modes of presentation. I further assume that the utterance of a sentence containing a singular term expresses a singular or Russellian proposition; that is, a proposition having the referents themselves as constituents. A singular proposition is an abstract, structured entity made up of objects, properties, and relations.

A mental state, on the other hand, is a mental representation plus the attitude relation (belief, desire, etc.) the agent bears to the proposition. I would like to think of mental representations as being embedded within attitude operators. A belief state, for example, is a mental representation embedded within the BELIEF operator, so subjects who accept the same sentence share the same mental representation and may be in the same mental state. If they are in the same mental state they tend to behave in a similar way. We could adopt a metaphor made popular by Schiffer. In our mind we have several boxes: the belief box, the desire box, the thinking box, the doubting box, etc. When in a given mental state, one has a representation in the relevant box. If one is in a wishing state, for example, one has a representation in one's wishing box. The very same representation could be in another box, say the belief box, if one were in a belief state.

Besides, two agents who are in the same mental state (e.g. a belief state) may be related to different propositions. If Sue and Mary both accept the sentence "I am thirsty", they may be in the same mental state, but they are related to different propositions, one having Sue as constituent and the other Mary. It is often the case that, in order to be related to the same proposition, two agents (and even the same agent) have to be in distinct mental states. Let us consider a version of an example made famous by Frege. On Monday, Sue accepts "Today I have to call Dr. Lauben". To be related to the very same proposition after midnight, however, Sue needs to accept "Yesterday I had to call Dr. Lauben". Hence, Sue's mental states differ. If Sue were to accept "Today I have to call Dr. Lauben" on Tuesday, she would be in the same mental state but related to a different proposition.[21]

---

[21] Perry argues (1980b) that the notion of acceptance is inadequate to handle the problem of cognitive dynamics, i.e. to explain what is going on in one's mind when one continues to believe the same thing. To do so, he introduces the notion of internal identity, i.e. identity between mental files. So, one can be said to retain the same belief, say about Sue, when one stores the relevant information acquired on the same file. Although I am sympathetic to Perry's treatment of cognitive dynamics, I do not think that we need to make reference to files to deal with the problem of explaining cognitive significance in attitude ascriptions. Besides, to attribute the same belief to someone across time, we often have to attribute to her the

The notion of acceptance captures the intuitive idea that an agent, if asked to express her attitude, would use the sentence the reporter attributes to her. I take this to be the paradigmatic case—this simple test can be run only in "normal" situations. That is, an agent is disposed to utter the very same sentence whose acceptance the reporter attributes to her if the former speaks the language of the latter, is rational, and so on. It goes without saying that these conditions are not always satisfied: we attribute attitudes to pre-linguistic infants, to foreign speakers, to animals, etc.

I think that attitude ascriptions to non-linguistic organisms mirror the attribution of pain (and the like). As I argued in the previous sections, we learn how to attribute pain on the basis of observable conditions in the presence of external stimuli and behavior. Without doubt I know when I am in pain: we self-attribute pain without hesitation. When we come to attribute pain to others, we lack this kind of certainty or self-evidence. However, we often do not hesitate to say that an infant or an animal is suffering. When one is beating a man with a baseball bat and the latter is contorting, crying, etc. we do not hesitate to attribute pain to him: we do not need to look for evidence allowing us to attribute pain. It may also be that the hesitation one may have rests on the fact that one has learnt that some can fake pain. It may also be that infants would be quicker in attributing pain than an adult, but only because the adult becomes cautious and does not always believe what his senses tell him. In other words, even if the attribution of pain to others is defeasible (whereas self-attribution is not), we often do not hesitate in attributing pain and the like to others. Our assurance and certainty comes from the fact that we automatically and naturally imagine ourselves in their situation. Of course, this does not mean that this exercise is merely unconscious and/or confined to preconceptual activities. This idea mirrors the point I made previously about simulation when I stressed, following Gordon, that we do not act on an inferential model when we grasp someone's mental state and predict her behavior, i.e. we do not first self-attribute a mental state and then transfer that mental state onto the attributee. We rather undergo a context shift. More precisely, our attribution (and the understanding involved in it) rests on an egocentric shift. There is, to borrow Gordon's terminology, an *ascent routine*:

A point that needs emphasis is that, unlike introspection, an ascent routine for identifying beliefs would be as well suited to identify another's beliefs as it is to identifying one's own. Whether in my own person or within a simulation of O, I can settle the question, "Do I believe that *p*?" by asking, within the constraints indicated earlier, whether it is the case

acceptance of different sentences. This is the case, for instance, with the attribution of temporal beliefs like in Frege's 'today'/'yesterday' example. An attribution involving proper names, on the other hand, usually does not need to attribute the acceptance of different sentences to stress that the attributee believes the same thing across time. But see Kripke's (1979) Peter-'Paderewski' puzzle, where Peter wrongly takes this proper name to refer to distinct individuals: this subject will have two files in which to store information about the referent of 'Paderewski'. More on Kripke's puzzle later.

that *p*. But in a simulation of O, remember, 'I' refers exclusively to O, the individual on whom my egocentric map has been recentered. So I settle the question of whether O believes that *p* simply by asking, within the context of simulation of O, whether it is the case that *p*. That is I simply concern myself with *the world*—O's world, the world from O's perspective.... —and, reporting what is there, I am reporting O's beliefs. That is, reporting O's beliefs *is* just reporting what is there.... to ascribe to O a belief that *p* is to assert that *p* within the context of a simulation of O. (Gordon 1995b: 60)

The notion of acceptance I have in mind should capture this simulation process. As such, it is best spelled out on the basis of the following *Transpositional Principle*:

- *Transpositional Principle*

  If the reporter, in the attributee's context were to express what the attributee believes, desires, says, etc., the reporter would utter the relevant sentence, i.e. the sentence whose acceptance the reporter is attributing to the attributee.[22]

When we attribute an attitude to someone, we often imagine ourselves in her situation:

In saying what someone else believes, we describe his belief by relating it to one we ourselves might have. And we indicate this potential belief of our own by uttering the sentence we would use to express it. (Stich 1983: 79)

It is not uncommon for us to make attributions whilst observing another's behavior or on the basis of inferences from other beliefs, desires, etc. that we know the attributee holds. We do so by imagining what *we* would do, think, desire, etc. in these cases. Imagine, for example, that you and your partner are looking at Sue, who is behaving in a strange way. Your partner asks: "What do you think she is thinking?" The answer could be: "I guess she is thinking that her life is in danger. So she acts in that strange way". On what basis are you able to answer your partner's query? It could be that you have spoken to Sue and she told you that she was frightened, but it could also be that you are making an inference of the form: (i) I know that Sue is frightened of the strange man who just arrived, (ii) so she may think that her life is in danger. How, then, are you entitled to infer that Sue is thinking that she is in danger? The natural answer that comes to mind is that we make such inferences by imagining ourselves in the attributee's situation. If I were Sue, given (i) I would be scared. It goes without saying that, when we make this

---

[22] Notice that this principle could be spelled out in a more straightforward way, as follows: if the reporter were the attributee, then in order to express what the latter believes, desires, ... the former would utter the sentence she accepts as expressing her belief, desire, ... That is, the reporter would make a self-attribution of the form "*I* believe/think/wish/ ... that *S*" and in so doing she would express the sentence she accepts. However, as a matter of fact, we cannot be someone else; all we can do is to imagine ourselves in the attributee's context, i.e. to take their place. So this straightforward principle is just a short cut to the transpositional one.

kind of attribution, we are presupposing that the attributee is rational (an assumption that can always be cancelled by a paraphrase).

A word of clarification may be useful. According to the picture I am putting forth, accepting a sentence does not always mean accepting it as true. If a subject is in a belief state, she takes the relevant sentence to be true. But one accepts a sentence when one is in a saying (desiring, thinking, etc.) relation to a proposition, as well. From "*A says S*" we cannot infer that *A* accepts *S as true*. The terminology, I agree, is not very felicitous. The notion of acceptance has been given several technical meanings: it is often assumed that an agent who accepts a sentence takes it to be true; otherwise she does not accept it. This is not the notion I have in mind. To simplify, we can spell out the notion of acceptance this way: imagine that in front of an agent there is a set of indefinitely many sentences and a set of psychological verbs like 'believe', 'desire', 'say', 'doubt'. Each time our agent entertains an attitude she is asked to do two things: (i) pick out a psychological verb and (ii) choose from among the sentences the one she would use to express her attitude. The sentence she picks out or points to is the sentence she accepts. So if our agent points to "Bob Dylan was born in Minnesota" she accepts this sentence whether or not she believes, desires, wishes, etc. that Bob Dylan was born in Minnesota.

The sentence one accepts classifies the mental representation one has. So, when you think that Bob Dylan is American, you have a mental representation classified by the sentence "Bob Dylan is American", i.e. the sentence that you accept. Your mental representation cannot be classified by the sentence "Robert Zimmerman is American" even if Bob Dylan is Robert Zimmerman—in the aforementioned situation you do not point to this sentence. It may also be that, if questioned, you refuse to point to this sentence and, thus, you do not accept it. In short, I take the notion of having a mental representation and being in a given state to be a primitive one; I am not trying to cash out these notions in terms of belief. This way we can deal with attitudes other than belief in a straightforward way. We can also deal with fiction and conscious illusions in an easy way. An agent may be in a given state whilst watching a movie without taking the story to be true. In the Müller-Lyer paradox, one line looks longer than the other, even after we have been told that they are of equal length: we have the same representation even if we no longer believe it to be true. To avoid confusion, it may be worth introducing an artificial term to distinguish the case when an agent accepts a sentence to be true from the case where she does not. Henceforth, I shall use the notion of *neutral acceptance* (*n*-acceptance) to stress the fact that a subject does not need to take the sentence used to classify her mental representation to be true.[23] Moreover, when we

---

[23] When one is in a belief state one accepts the sentence as true. In other words, a sentence may be accepted as true only when it is embedded within the BELIEF operator.

attribute to someone the *n*-acceptance of a sentence (and thus classify her mental state), we are not necessarily presupposing that the attributee is aware of her mental state. One can be in a given mental state—e.g. one may have an unconscious desire—which one is not aware of. Most parents will say that they are often more aware of their child's state than the child herself is.

In short, sentences *n*-accepted are devices we use to classify mental representations. Two agents who *n*-accept the same sentence share the same mental representation type. The state they are in depends on the attribution, i.e. the psychological prefix, for it is the latter that classifies the state the agent is in and not the sentence *n*-accepted. If the attribution is "*A wishes that S*", then *A* is in a "wishing state" whose mental representation is classified by the sentence *S* that *A n*-accepts. If the report were "*A says that S*", the sentence *S* that *A n*-accepts would still classify the same mental representation, but it would not attribute to *A* the same mental state: *A* would be in a "saying state". The state the attributee is in is expressed by the psychological prefix. As I said, a way to think of mental representations is to consider them to be governed by operators like BELIEVE, THINK, SAY, WISH, etc. The operator that governs the agent's representation gives us the agent's mental state.

When in a given mental state, the subject activates a token mental state, which I take to be a cognitive particular which may (but need not) be some neurological activity going on in her brain. In other words, when we attribute the *n*-acceptance of a sentence to someone, we classify the type of mental representation instantiated by the corresponding token or cognitive particular she entertains. When someone is in a given mental state she activates a token mental state (a cognitive particular). The latter is what triggers the agent's behavior. Two agents behave (*ceteris paribus*) the same way insofar as their cognitive particulars are of the same type. I now try to spell out the relation between a type of mental representation, as classified by a sentence, and the corresponding cognitive particular.

The *n*-acceptance relation can be cashed out as follows:

- *Neutral-acceptance*
  $n\text{-}ACC[A, S, t]$ iff

  $(\exists mr)(\exists mr^*)\{mr$ and mr^* are token mental representations of the same type and mr would cause the attributer, in the attributee's context at time t, to utter S & $\textit{In-the-desire/belief}\dots\textit{-box-Has}[A, mr^*, t]\}$

This characterization fits with the transpositional principle. In particular, it should allow us to attribute the *n*-acceptance of sentences even to pre-linguistic infants and animals because the attributer projects herself into the attributee's situation. This does not presuppose that we are entitled to attribute mental states to pre-linguistic infants and/or animals. All I am committed to is the conditional thesis that *if* we feel entitled to attribute mental states to them, *then* we are presupposing a certain similarity between their mental life and ours (more on this in Section 7). The notion of *n*-acceptance is spelled out in counterfactual terms: the attributee's token mental representation (or cognitive particular) is similar to the one that would cause the attributer, in the attributee's context, to utter *S*. As a matter of fact, the attributer and the attributee cannot share the same token mental representation. Nonetheless, token mental representations can be similar and be of the same type: two agents' token representations are of the same type insofar as they *n*-accept the same sentences.[24]

5. Reports and Mental Representations

In (SA), the attributee and the attributer are one and the same person. Most attributions, however, are not self-attributions but attributions from the third-person perspective, where the attributee and the attributer diverge. These attributions would be of the form:

- TA. *A* said/believes/thinks/wishes/ . . . that *S*

In this case as well, the sentence *S* helps to classify the attributee's (*A*'s) thought. If the reporter's aim is to characterize the attributee's mental life or state, it is likely that she chooses, as a 'that'-clause, a sentence that comes as close as possible to being the sentence the attributee would utter in expressing her belief/desire/wish/ . . . .[25]

One could argue that the account I am proposing does not allow us to ascribe beliefs to animals, for the sentences whose *n*-acceptance we attribute to them may classify mental states too finely. Since my cat, Felix, does not speak and, thus, does not belong to a linguistic community, he may not master the concept *Doberman*. So, in saying "Felix thinks that a Doberman is around the corner", we cannot attribute him the *n*-acceptance of the sentence "A Doberman is around the corner". Felix's token mental representation is too different from the one that, in Felix's context, would trigger me to utter "A Doberman is around the corner". So, it cannot be of the same type. I do not deny this fact. But, if we do not think that a cat has the concept *Doberman*, then our

---

[24] It could be thought that the transpositional principle is too weak, insofar as we are unable to classify the attributee's mental state when we attribute the *n*-acceptance of a sentence containing ambiguous expressions or homonyms. To anticipate, I would say that it is often the case that context helps us to disambiguate a given sentence and thus classify the relevant mental state. More on this in Section 7.

[25] It goes without saying that, in reporting indexical thoughts, certain changes and adjustments need to be made. In reporting 'I'-thoughts, for instance, the reporter is likely to use what Castañeda (1966; 1967) called quasi-indicators. An indirect report of "I am happy" is likely to be "*A* said that *s/he (her/himself)* is happy". I shall discuss attributions involving quasi-indicators and how they can fit into a direct-reference framework and into the picture of attitude ascription I am presenting in Chs. 8–9, below.

attribution is inappropriate and we should look for a more accurate one, which fits Felix's cognitive world. In so doing, we attribute to him the *n*-acceptance of a sentence that classifies Felix's state *qua* type of its token representation. I think that, when dealing with a non-linguistic organism, this is the best we can do. In other words, if the attributer assumes that Felix has a token representation that is similar to the one she would have in Felix's context, then she is entitled to attribute to Felix the *n*-acceptance of the sentence that she would use, in Felix's context, to state his attitude. If the attributer is not entitled to assume that Felix's token representation is similar to the one which would trigger her to utter the relevant sentence, then she ought to look for another, more appropriate, token representation. This should be closer to Felix's token representation and would trigger the attributer to utter the relevant sentence in Felix's context.[26]

Since the notion of *n*-acceptance is spelled out in counterfactual terms, it also allows us to accommodate so-called tacit beliefs such as the belief that yesterday there were no pink elephants flying on campus. In attributing this attitude to myself, I would say "Yesterday, I did not believe that there were pink elephants flying on campus" and, in so doing, I attribute myself the *n*-acceptance of the sentence "There are no pink elephants flying on campus". Moreover, since the notion of *n*-acceptance is spelled out in counterfactual terms, there are infinitely many sentences one is disposed to *n*-accept inasmuch as there are infinitely many tacit beliefs one can have. If I were to express this belief yesterday, I would have used this very sentence. The same story can be told about the attribution of tacit beliefs to others. It goes without saying that we have many tacit beliefs that will never become manifest. So, when I attribute a tacit belief, all I am doing is claiming that *if* our agent were to express her belief, she would use the sentence whose *n*-acceptance I am attributing to her. In such a case, she would be in the mental state classified by this sentence. I am not attributing the actual presence of a mental representation corresponding to the tacit belief. Moreover, as I said before, one need not be aware of the mental state one is in.

6. Reports and Types of Mental States

I am now going to argue that types of mental representation are all we need to explain attitude ascriptions. In so doing, I explain away the worry that mental states *qua* universals (or types) give us a classification that is too coarse-grained.

---

[26] An alternative and more drastic way to deal with the attribution of attitudes to non-linguistic organisms would be to argue that, since these organisms are conceptually too different from us, all we can do is to use *de re* locutions and, in so doing, we do not specify the mental state they are in.

Although I am sympathetic to the picture that token mental representations are *concrete* entities in one's mind, I do not think that the success of an attitude report rests on our reference to these underlying entities. My point is that we have to find some purpose that the more specific attributions (attributions that make reference to cognitive particulars) could serve, but that the more general attributions (attributions that make reference to universal mental states) could not. My strategy is to show that we cannot find such a purpose.

Friends of the cognitive particulars view argue that it is possible for a subject to be in a given mental state—and thus *n*-accept a given sentence—and assume different attitudes whilst in this state.[27] Notice that on my view it is possible to *n*-accept a given sentence and have different attitudes depending on whether we are in a belief, saying, etc. state; that is, depending on whether the same mental representation is embedded in a BELIEF, SAY, etc. operator. The problem they see, however, is different, for the same mental representation at a given time can be embedded in the same attitude prefix and yet be instantiated by two distinct cognitive particulars. Someone can be in the same mental state and associate very different cognitive values with it. We can appeal to two well-known examples to prove this fact, one found in Perry (1979) and the other in Kripke (1979). Perry's example rests on indexical sentences, while Kripke's appeals to sentences containing proper names.

To begin with, let us consider indexical sentences. It is quite easy to imagine a case where two tokens of the same indexical refer to the same individual and have different cognitive values (or cognitive significances).[28] Hence an agent can *n*-accept the same sentence and associate with that sentence two different cognitive values. I shall refer to this problem as *the problem of explaining cognitive significance*. A famous example runs as follows: whilst looking at the very same aircraft carrier, an agent might assent to "That's the Enterprise" while pointing to the stern and dissent from the same sentence while pointing to the bow (suppose the middle is obscured by a large building). It can be argued that, in this example, our agent does not *n*-accept the same sentence: she first *n*-accepts "That's the Enterprise" and then "That's *not* the Enterprise". It is not difficult, though, to figure out an example where a subject assents to (and *a fortiori n*-accepts) the same sentence twice and yet this sentence carries different cognitive values for her. In the aforementioned situation, our agent may twice assent to "That is an aircraft carrier", but since she believes that she perceives different aircraft carriers, she associates different cognitive

---

[27] Perry argues this way (personal communication) and Crimmins (1992: 45) proposes a Kripke-like example to stress the need to appeal to cognitive particulars in psychological attributions.

[28] I take cognitive value in its intuitive Fregean interpretation: "$a = b$", unlike "$a = a$", is informative, so the cognitive value of the former is different from the cognitive value of the latter. By compositionality, it follows that the cognitive value of 'a' (as it occurs in the aforementioned identity) is different from that of 'b'. I discussed the notion of cognitive significance and Frege's puzzle in Ch. 1, Sects. 6–8.

values with each sentence. "That aircraft carrier [pointing to the stern] is that aircraft carrier [pointing to the bow]" will be informative to our agent. To use Frege's standard terminology, we can say that the cognitive value is the mode of presentation under which a subject thinks of the referent. According to Frege, a sentence like "$a = b$", unlike "$a = a$", may be informative, because the subject thinks of a and b under distinct modes of presentation. A Fregean could explain how, in our example, a sentence like "That = that" could be informative, for our subject associates two distinct modes of presentation with her uses of 'that'.[29]

I now try to propose a solution, or rather dissolution, of this problem. I shall show that n-accepted sentences classify mental representations finely enough for the purpose of explaining cognitive significance. My point will be that demonstrative sentences leave a place for a perceptual anchor and, as such, do not specify a complete mental representation. On the other hand, we cannot generate the same kind of problem with sentences containing indexicals such as 'I' or 'now', for a subject cannot n-accept a sentence containing 'I' or 'now' and (at the same time) assume distinct attitudes toward it. It does not make sense for a subject to claim, "I am a woman and I am not a woman" (at least, used literally it makes no sense).[30] So sentences containing indexicals like 'I' and 'now' cut finely enough for the purpose of explaining cognitive significance.

As you may recall, I endorse Kaplan's distinction between pure indexicals ('I', 'here', 'now', 'today', . . .) and demonstratives ('this', 'that', 'she', . . .). Following Kaplan (1977), a demonstrative without an associated demonstration is incomplete. As I understand Kaplan's distinction, one of the main differences between demonstrative reference and reference made using a pure indexical is that from the *speaker's point of view* (or that of the thinker's), a demonstrative identification presupposes a perception of the referent which is not required in the case of pure indexicals (I do not have to perceive myself in order to use the first-person pronoun). Indeed, it is possible that the perception does not accompany the use of the demonstrative, as would be the case when, for instance, I say "She is F" whilst pointing to a picture behind me or referring to some salient female who just left the room. In both cases my use of 'she' is still perception-based, for I use it on the basis of my memory of a perception.[31]

---

[29] As we shall see in Ch. 9, Sect. 8, though, there are no natural language sentences of the form $a = a$. For an utterance like "Aristotle is Aristotle" or "That is that" may well be informative inasmuch as the terms on both side of the identity relation may (i) carry different information and (ii) refer to distinct referent. A classical example is Kripke's Peter-'Paderewski' story. More on this example later.

[30] This rests on the distinction between so-called essential indexicals and demonstratives, as spelt out in Ch. 4 and as I shall discuss further in Ch. 8.

[31] In some cases, a speaker can refer to something (such as a vase) behind herself using 'that vase' if she has been told that the vase is there. Blind people can refer to a bottle on the table with 'this bottle' if told that the bottle is there. These cases, however, do not constitute the paradigmatic uses of demonstratives, for the speaker is to some extent "borrowing" someone else's perceptual apparatus.

I am now going to show that the difference between pure indexicals and demonstratives is relevant in dealing with the problem of explaining cognitive significance. The difference in cognitive value between two occurrences of a demonstrative expression comes from the act of perception: we can thus argue in favor of the constancy of linguistic meaning and yet a difference in cognitive value. In the case of pure indexicals, the constancy of linguistic meaning entails the constancy of cognitive significance. This, however, does not jeopardize the picture I have been advocating, insofar as a rational being never doubts the identity of the referent. Frege-inspired puzzles cannot arise with pure indexicals: utterances like "I = I", "Today = today", or "Here = here" (if the occurrences of the indexical are tied to the same time) are always trivial. An utterance of "That = that" may be trivial, to be sure, if it is based on the same act of perception,[32] but consider a subject who perceives the same man from different perspectives. She can refer to the same man twice in saying, "That man is handsome" and believe that she refers to two different entities: she takes him to be a rock star at first and then to be a politician.

It could be thought that the difference in cognitive value associated with each utterance of "That is F" comes from the fact that the utterances are made at different moments. We can, however, disregard the time and still generate the puzzle: imagine that our subject looks through fixed binoculars. Our subject is told that these binoculars are special: the left side does not focus on the same image as the right, but instead it focuses on a qualitatively similar image, so when our agent perceives the relevant image, she does not know whether what she is seeing is the same figure. She may label what she sees with her left eye 'Alf' and what she sees with her right eye 'Ralf' and wonder whether "Alf = Ralf". Hence, she has two different attitudes at the same time, for her use of the demonstrative is based upon two distinct acts of perception—our agent does not connect what she is seeing with her left eye to what she is seeing with her right eye. To give a name to this case, let us call it the *binocular puzzle*.[33] What differentiates the binocular case from ordinary vision is that, in the latter, we perceive a spatial relation between objects. Acts of perception are individuated by fields of perception: in the binocular puzzle, we have two fields of perception and, thus, two acts of perception. It seems, then, that we have a single sentence, say "That is F", which classifies a type of mental representation, but we have two distinct token representations (modes of presentation), and thus distinct

---

[32] The characterization I propose should allow us to accommodate Evans's (1982) notion of keeping track. That is, an agent does not doubt the identity of the perceived object as long as she keeps track of it, for her demonstrative thought is based on the same act of perception.

[33] D. Austin proposes a similar puzzle: "Smith is to look through the tubes simultaneously and to report what he sees as he focuses his eyes independently. He is familiar with the apparatus and knows that he does not know how the tubes are oriented . . . so he wonders, 'Is this = that?' " (Austin 1990: 20–1). If I am right, the theory I am defending can deal with this puzzle.

cognitive values are associated with the same sentence. Hence types of mental representation do not cut sufficiently finely, and to report this situation we ought to make reference to cognitive particulars. It seems, then, that if we refer to universal, or types of, mental states, we are unable to deal with the fact that a subject may have distinct attitudes while *n*-accepting the same sentence. This is what I take to be the difficulty for the picture I am advocating.

We are lucky, for this is not a knockdown argument against the thesis that sentences give us a satisfactory classification for the purpose of explaining cognitive significance. I claim that demonstrative sentences *classify a partial mental representation*. Thus, when coupled with the psychological prefix, they classify a partial mental state. It is trivial that a demonstrative sentence is context-sensitive and, as such, it expresses a proposition relative to the context in which it is uttered. Hence, it is natural to hold that a demonstrative sentence carries the information that it is context-sensitive. Furthermore, as we just saw, a use of a demonstrative is perception-based. A rational being can claim "She [pointing to Sue] is *F* and she [still pointing to Sue] is not *F*", for her uses of 'she' are based on different acts of perception. It is important to notice that the difference in cognitive significance comes from the act of perception; that is, from the fact that the agent's perceptual content is anchored in different contexts and, thus, in two fields of perception. So she has two acts of perception and, therefore, two ways of apprehending the object(s) perceived.[34] Hence, given these facts, we can infer that when a subject *n*-accepts a demonstrative sentence the corresponding representation token she entertains is tied to an act of perception. The relevant sentence specifies the partial mental state the agent *qua* perceiver is in. It may be that the type of mental representation is made up, among other things, of a perceptual mode of presentation type or simply of an argument place for a token act of perception. But a classification of a partial mental representation need not be a bad classification and, in particular, it can be sufficient to deal with what I have characterized as the problem of explaining cognitive significance. It is worth noticing that the characterization I am proposing goes hand in hand with the notion of perspectival thought I proposed in Chapter 6, for the very same thought can be anchored to different objects (e.g. H_2O or XYZ) in different contexts.

[34] This fits in with the idea that perceptual content is general and, therefore, the same perceptual content can be anchored to different objects in different contexts. The binocular puzzle is a dramatic representation of this fact, for we have the same place and time, the same subject, the same perceptual content, but different fields of perception and hence two acts of perception. The singularity, i.e. the object our perception is about, is contextually fixed. It is fixed by the act of perception and not by the content of our perceptual judgement. This goes hand in hand with the view developed in Ch. 6, above, where I defended the thesis that mental states are object-independent and that their aboutness is contextually determined, i.e. the view that our thoughts are situated.

The picture I proposed can be summarized with the following chart:

- Sentence: *classify*→ Type mental representation
  − *determine*→ Cog. value
- Demonstrative *classify*→ Partial type mental representation
  Sentence: +
  Act of perception − *determine*→ Cog. value

What I said fits with the idea that the attribution of a demonstrative reference needs to make reference to or describe the attributee's act of perception. A report attributing a demonstrative reference should be of the form "*A* said that the object she perceived is *F*". With this kind of report, we attribute the *n*-acceptance of a sentence of the form "This/That . . . is *F*" and we thus classify a partial mental representation. Since an agent who perceives an object from different perspectives can hold different attitudes toward it (she may fail to recognize that she is perceiving the same object), I do not see why an attribution of a universal mental state is not sufficient for the purpose of explaining cognitive significance. In other words, the attribution of a partial mental representation carries the information that when the agent is in this mental representation her corresponding token representation is perceptually anchored to the external world and the difference in cognitive value is given by the perceptual anchor.

Taking stock: I suggested that when the sentence *n*-accepted is a demonstrative one, it classifies a partial mental representation. The agent who *n*-accepts that sentence *via* her act of perception when she activates the mental state she is in will anchor it to the world. Hence two subjects (and even the same subject at different times) who *n*-accept the same demonstrative sentence share the same type of representation. The cognitive value they associate with it will depend (also) on the act of perception that anchors their mental representation to the perceived object. It seems that, insofar as perceptual demonstratives are involved, sentences classify finely enough for the purpose of explaining cognitive significance.

As I have already mentioned, we cannot generate a cognitive significance puzzle if we only consider the case of sentences containing pure indexicals. Hence, sentences containing pure indexicals classify finely enough for the purpose of explaining cognitive significance. No rational subject can *n*-accept "I am *F* and I am not *F*", "Today is not today" nor "Here is not here".[35] A minimally rational subject cannot assume distinct attitudes toward a sentence like "I am *F* and I am

---

[35] It goes without saying that our subject cannot assume distinct attitudes when she uses 'here' as a pure indexical, for if she were to use it as a demonstrative, e.g. pointing to a map, she can rationally utter: "Here [pointing to L.A.] is not here [pointing to San Francisco]".

not F".[36] A rational agent cannot simultaneously think of herself *via* 'I', to the place she is in *via* 'here' or a particular moment *via* 'now', and have two attitudes. We cannot generate an analogue of the binocular puzzle for these indexicals. We can then conclude that a classification of mental representations by sentences containing pure indexicals is rich enough to deal with the problem of explaining cognitive significance and, therefore, reference to cognitive particulars in our reports is not needed.

Let us now turn to the case of proper names. If a subject *n*-accepts two sentences like "Bob Dylan is F" and "Robert Zimmerman is F", she will have two mental representations and, *a fortiori* be in two mental states, but what about Kripke's puzzle?

Once again, the problem seems to be that a sentence cannot classify the mental representation of an agent finely enough for the purpose of explaining cognitive significance. In Kripke's puzzle, Peter meets Paderewski in two different contexts (in one he takes him to be a musician and in the other a politician) without realizing that he is the same person. Peter holds two distinct conceptions (two cognitive particulars) of Paderewski: one he associates with the musician and the other with the politician. Peter thinks of Paderewski under two distinct modes of presentation and he thus associates distinct cognitive values to his uses of the name 'Paderewski'. Hence, if we want to deal with the cognitive significance problem, one and the same sentence, "Paderewski is F", should classify two mental representations. When Peter comes to realize that Paderewski is Paderewski he will expand his knowledge. Frege, though, suggests that an utterance like "Paderewski is Paderewski" is analytic, i.e. of the form $a = a$. For an utterance like this to be informative, though, it cannot be of the form $a = a$. The way out of this problem is to argue that for an utterance like "Paderewski is Paderewski" to be informative it must be a short cut of an utterance of the form "Paderewski (*the F*) is Paderewski (*the G*)". An utterance like this, though, is of the form $a = b$. This parallels the form of an utterance like "Vladimir Ilyich Ulyanov is Vladimir Ilyich Lenin". It is because these utterances are of the form $a = b$ that they can be informative. But this is simply how it should be insofar as Peter takes "Paderewski is Paderewski" to be informative because he understands it as "Paderewski *the musician* is Paderewski *the politician*".

Let us assume for a moment that our report makes reference to cognitive particulars. How can we refer to Peter's distinct conceptions in using a single proper name, e.g. 'Paderewski'? Which form does our report have to take to make sense of Peter's puzzling situation? An attribution like "Peter said that Paderewski is F" is at best incomplete, for we have to stress which conception enters Peter's thought. To be successful, our report ought to be, for instance, "Peter said that *Paderewski-the-musician*

---

[36] Indeed, a rational subject at different moments of her life can first assent to "I am F" and then dissent or withhold her judgement from "I am F". Think of "I am a mother": At 10, Sue probably dissents from this sentence, while at 30 she may assent to it.

is *F*". This way, we can refer to Peter's conception of Paderewski, to his conception of Paderewski-*qua*-musician, which is distinct from his conception of Paderewski-*qua*-politician. If this is the case, however, we use two distinct reports and, in so doing, we attribute the *n*-acceptance of two distinct sentences to Peter; therefore, we classify two distinct mental representations.[37] We can thus deal with the problem of explaining cognitive significance without having to make reference to cognitive particulars. So far, the moral is that cognitive particulars are not needed to deal with the problem of explaining cognitive significance. When an agent possesses no discriminating knowledge and still holds two conceptions, she ought to label them in a distinct way. In doing so, she can make reference to the causal origin of her conceptions. She may say Paderewski-the-guy-I-met-last-night is different from Paderewski-the-guy-Sue-told-me-about-last-night. An attribution aimed at classifying our agent's mental representations must articulate these data. In doing so, it classifies two mental representations insofar as it attributes the *n*-acceptance of two different sentences.

On the other hand, it might be thought that, in some cases, two types of mental representation are instantiated by one conception or mode of presentation. Peter, being puzzled, may report, "Tim said that Paderewski-the-musician is *F*" and "Tim said that Paderewski-the-politician is not *F*". Peter attributes to Tim the *n*-acceptance of two different sentences and classifies two mental representations. In this case one of the reports is false, so we do not face a problem. But what about two reports such as, "Tim said that Paderewski-the-musician is *F*" and "Tim said that Paderewski-the-politician is *F*"? Our objector would claim that Peter attributes the *n*-acceptance of different sentences and thus classifies two mental representations. Hence, mental representations and mental states may cut too finely for the purpose of explaining cognitive significance, for "Paderewski-the-musician is *F*" and "Paderewski-the-politician is *F*" classify two mental representations, while Tim does not think of Paderewski under distinct modes of presentation and thus does not associate distinct cognitive significance with the two sentences. It seems to me that, in this case, what went wrong is the report itself. Peter wrongly transfers, so to speak, his puzzle to Tim. The fact is that Peter, being puzzled, is unable to classify Tim's mental representation.[38]

---

[37] It goes without saying that the context of the attribution may suggest which sentence the attributee *n*-accepts and that the reporter need not articulate all the relevant information in her report. During the concert, we may say, "Peter said that Paderewski is *F*" and, being aware that Peter does not know that the musician he is admiring is the politician he met last night, suggest that the sentence Peter *n*-accepts is "Paderewski-the-musician is *F*".

[38] A consequence of the picture I am proposing is that attributions like:

  (1) Sue believes that Paderewski is *F*
  (2) Peter believes that Paderewski-the-musician is *F*
  (3) Peter believes that Paderewski-the-politician is *F*

do not attribute the same belief state to Sue and Peter.

Another advantage I see over the Crimmins-Perry conception has to do with general reports of the sort: "The Romans thought that Tully denounced Catiline". The story I am putting forward allows us to stress that the Romans *n*-accept the sentence "Tully denounced Catiline" and have the mental representation classified by this sentence. If we have cognitive particulars in the picture, we have to quantify over them, for we cannot make reference to the single cognitive particulars of each Roman who thought that Tully denounced Catiline. Hence general reports would not fall into the same basket as singular ones, whereas they do in the picture I propose.

To sum up: the picture I put forth, unlike the Crimmins-Perry theory, does not need to appeal to cognitive particulars to deal with what I characterized as the problem of explaining cognitive significance. And, as we saw in the previous chapter, this supports psychological generalizations in a straightforward way.

7. Some Further Alleged Puzzles

Before going further, I would like to address the following question: in attributing the *n*-acceptance of the English sentence "Man is a rational animal" to Sue, do we ascribe the same mental representation to her as we would in attributing the *n*-acceptance of the French sentence "L'homme est un animal rationnel"? Do these sentences classify the same mental representation? If these sentences are translations of one another, my answer is affirmative. The very same attribution can be made in several languages. The question, as I understand it, amounts to knowing whether (and under which circumstances) two sentences translate each other. We feel comfortable in saying that "Sue believes that Tully is Roman" and "Sue croit que Tullius est romain" translate each other and attribute the same belief to Sue. We feel less comfortable in saying that "Sue believes that Tully is Roman" and "Sue croit que Cicéron est romain" translate each other and attribute to her the same belief. That is, we feel entitled to translate 'Tullius' by 'Tully' and not by 'Cicero', although these names are coreferential. The problem is most acute and arises when we do not face this kind of symmetry across languages as, for instance, when one language has more names for an individual than another. In Hebrew, there are two names for Germany: 'Germaniah' and 'Ashkenaz'. So, if Peter, a competent speaker of German, believes that Germany is his country, which sentence of Hebrew does he accept? This is a general problem, having to do with the practice of translation, and should not undermine the basic idea of the picture I am defending. Besides, as we shall see in the next section, reports cannot always be faithful and fully capture the attributee's mental life, for one of the report's aims is to pass information to the audience and, to do so, a report must be accommodated and adjusted according to the audience's knowledge.[39]

You may recall that in a report, we attribute the disposition to *n*-accept the reporter's sentence to the agent. We do so by means of the transpositional principle. This principle allows us to subsume under the same attribution people belonging to very different cultures. It could be that Sue belongs to a completely different community; it could also be that some of her beliefs are incommensurable with ours. The transpositional principle, though, makes her beliefs accessible to us. This principle stipulates, so to speak, a kind of similarity across cultures. But it is on the basis of this stipulation that attributions to people belonging to very different communities are possible. It is worth mentioning that the analogy I proposed between the attribution of pain to others and the attribution of beliefs may be misleading insofar as we distinguish between biological similarities and cultural ones. We do not hesitate to subsume under the same biological category a Mongolian and a Palestinian and attribute the feeling of pain to them. However, we may not subsume them under the same cultural category. So, when we attribute attitudes involving terms intrinsically tied to their culture to them, we guess what is going on and we look for the sentence in *our* language which comes close to what we think represents their attitude. By virtue of the transpositional principle, we attribute the *n*-acceptance of our sentence to them. This is the best we can do in our everyday practice:

When native belief systems and "form of life" differ radically from our own, there is no shorter way to characterize their cognitive world. The descriptive apparatus of folk psychology is not designed to deal with the beliefs of exotic folks. . . . in those contexts where ideological differences are both important and too great to warrant comfortable use of content sentences drawn from our own language, we are not forced into silence about the native doxastic world. We can opt for an anthropological description, using their labels for their beliefs and detailing how their beliefs fit into their own form of life. (Stich 1983: 102–3)

I argued that someone is disposed to *n*-accept whatever sentence translates the sentence whose *n*-acceptance we actually attribute to her. It then seems that my strategy crumbles under Kripke's (1979) Pierre-'London'/'Londres' puzzle. You may recall that Pierre assents to "Londres est jolie" and dissents from "London is pretty". But, if Pierre *n*-accepts "Londres est jolie" he is disposed to *n*-accept "London is pretty" and, conversely, if he *n*-accepts "London is ugly" he is disposed to *n*-accept "Londres est moche". In virtue of the transpositional principle, if our attribution is in French, we attribute to him the *n*-acceptance of a French sentence

---

[39] I shall discuss further the problem of translation and Church's argument against Carnap's sententialist position in Ch. 8, Sect. 5, below.

while if the attribution is in English we attribute to him the *n*-acceptance of the English sentence. So it turns out that Pierre is disposed to *n*-accept both "London is pretty" and "London is ugly." This is the problem.

The puzzle, as I understand it, includes the fact that Pierre does not know that 'London' translates 'Londres.' Notice that, in stating the puzzle, we make reference to 'London' and 'Londres' and to the fact that Pierre does not know that they are the French and English words for the same thing. In so doing, we stress that Pierre is not disposed to *n*-accept the relevant sentence when translated, i.e. the sentences "London is ugly" and "London is pretty" cannot be successfully used to classify Pierre's mental state. This is precisely the point of Kripke's puzzle. If Pierre knew that 'London' translates 'Londres', he would certainly give up one of his beliefs or, at least, suspend his judgement. In saying that a subject who is disposed to *n*-accept a sentence is in a dispositional relation to each translation of the sentence whose *n*-acceptance we actually attribute to her, I am saying that our subject is disposed to *n*-accept these sentences *ceteris paribus*. That is, modulo the fact that if she knew that they translate each other she would *n*-accept them. Pierre does not know that 'London' translates 'Londres', so the *ceteris paribus* clause is not satisfied. In other words, a subject *n*-accepts a sentence of a foreign language either if: (i) she does not know the language in which the report is formulated, or (ii) she knows the language in which the report is formulated and, unlike Kripke's Pierre, knows that the relevant sentences translate each other. The *ceteris paribus* clause allows us to rule out cases where one of these conditions is not satisfied. As I understand Kripke's puzzle, the reports "Pierre believes that London is pretty" and "Pierre croit que Londres est jolie" mean the same thing, *ceteris paribus*. If either (i) or (ii) does not hold, the reports do not mean the same thing, but in that case further information is needed: in Kripke's story we have to point out that Pierre *does not know* that 'London' translates 'Londres'.

8. Bound to Unfaithfulness

The picture I have presented should capture the rather intuitive and commonsensical view that, when we attribute to someone pain and the like, we automatically and without reflection project ourselves into their skin. The same empathetic exercise is at play when we attribute propositional knowledge as well. The attribution of propositional attitudes rests on the very same capacity, on the fact that we are essentially *dramatic personas*. The case of autism I discussed seems to support this picture, while the transpositional principle allows us to understand attitude reports and explain away some famous problems and puzzles.

There is, though, another important issue I did not address. Attitude reports are *audience-directed*. As in any other linguistic interchange the speaker/attributer must take into consideration the viewpoint of her audience. For this reason, the attributer often needs to alter the report in view of the audience's knowledge of the reported situation. Hence, a report may not and cannot always be faithful in capturing the attributee's mental state. In indirect discourse, for instance, we may need to change the words the attributee used because the audience would be unable to understand the report if the original words were preserved. If we are aware of the fact that our audience does not know that vixens are female foxes, we cannot report Jon's utterance "A vixen made a mess in my garden" as "Jon said that a vixen made a mess in his garden". We would rather say: "Jon said that a female fox made a mess in his garden". For this reason, our report may not be fully *de dicto* and thus may not capture the attributee's mental state in its entirety.[40] *Because* a report is audience-directed, it often needs to be (at least partly) *de re*. Besides, it is often difficult, if not impossible, to detect whether a given report is *de dicto* or *de re* or a mixture of both. Thanks to the transpositional principle, the picture I put forward explains the mechanics at play when we try to capture someone's mental life. It does not presuppose, however, that in each report we shall (and are even able to) capture them. Without doubt more should be said about the relationship and the tension between a report *qua* faithful attribution of someone's mental state and a report *qua* audience-directed communicative act. I shall say more on this aspect in the next chapter where I shall discuss *de se* attributions and when I shall introduce the idea that many reports are mixed and that there are degrees of faithfulness, i.e. that some reports, like some men, are more faithful than others. In the next chapter we shall see how multiple embedded attributions involving quasi-indicators are constrained to be unfaithful as well. In "Jane claimed that Ivan believes that she herself is rich," the quasi-indicator 'she herself' attributes an 'I'-thought to Jane. If Jane were to express the claim, she would most probably say "Ivan believes that *I* am rich". However, the original attribution is silent on the way in which Ivan referred to (and thought about) Jane. Igor could have expressed his thought in several ways: "You [addressing Jane] are rich", "Jane is rich", "That woman [pointing toward Jane] is rich", etc. The same phenomenon occurs when plurals are involved. In "Igor thinks that *we* are rich", the pronoun 'we' does not reveal the way in which Igor thought about the reporter. It suggests that Igor entertains an 'I'-thought, i.e. a thought he would express by saying "I am rich", but it does not reveal how he thought about the attributer.

---

[40] For further examples concerning reports which do not, and sometimes cannot, capture what one said, see Cappelen and Lepore (1997).

8

Anaphora, Logophoricity, and Quasi-Indexicality

> Anyone at any time can have access to any proposition. But not in any way. Anyone can believe of John Perry that he is making a mess. And anyone can be in the belief state classified by the sentence "I am making a mess". But only I can have that belief by being in that state.
>
> (Perry 1979: 41)

> The most revealing way of *attributing* indexical references to others is by means of our making *quasi-indexical references*. These are NOT indexical references, but depictions of others' indexical references. This is a type of vicarious presentational way of referring to objects not necessarily present to us through a representation of their presence to others. Quasi-indexical reference, thus, discharges also an *executive* function of putting before one's eyes a *replica* of the others' indexical references. Quasi-indicators are, thus, the most extraordinary and important mechanism of reference in natural language.
>
> (Castañeda 1989: 5)

In this chapter, I focus on 'I'-thoughts and the way we attribute them. I defend the thesis that the only way one can capture an 'I'-thought in an attribution is *via* the quasi-indicator 's/he (her/himself)' which, following Castañeda, will be abbreviated as 's/he*'.

Here is the way I shall proceed. In Section 1, I discuss 'I'-thoughts and the fact that they are irreducible to other thoughts. This goes hand in hand with the thesis defended in Chapter 3 when discussing essential indexicals and, in particular, with the view that the indexicals 'I', 'here', and 'now' are intrinsically perspectival and, as such, cannot be replaced by a coreferring term without failing to capture their cognitive impact. I show that the only way we can attribute an 'I'-thought from the third-person perspective is by means of a quasi-indicator. In Section 2, I show that, contrary to what has often been claimed, quasi-indicators do exist in natural language and that, in English, the unspoken subject of an infinitive clause (which linguists characterize as PRO) must often be understood along the lines of a quasi-indicator. In Section 3, I propose a grammatical analysis of quasi-indicators and focus on their anaphoric features. I show how quasi-indicators linked to a referring NP, like anaphors, inherit their semantic value from the antecedent to which they are linked (and thus coindexed with). In Section 4, I compare quasi-indicators, anaphoric pronouns, and logophoric pronouns (from the Greek 'logos' meaning discourse and 'phoros' meaning bearing or transporting). I claim that the best way to characterize quasi-indicators is to understand them along the lines of logophoric pronouns, i.e. the particular pronouns that, in certain languages (the so-called logophoric languages), are specifically used to attribute a perspective to an agent. Cross-linguistic data in favor of this thesis will then be presented. I will thus be in a position, in Section 5, to defend the thesis that in a non-logophoric language like English quasi-indicators are a unique mechanism allowing the attribution of an indexical reference and thus allowing us to capture someone's psychological perspective. It will emerge that quasi-indicators and logophoric pronouns play the same role. In Section 6, I discuss Castañeda's Unanalyzability Thesis, i.e. the view that a quasi-indicator is a primitive mechanism of reference. In focusing on the quasi-indicator 'she*' I show how it should be understood and I argue that it is best viewed as a compound NP. That is, an NP consisting of the pronoun 'her/him' and the reflexive 'self', where 'self' is a relational noun. Finally, in Section 7, I argue that quasi-indicators cannot be explained away as merely pragmatic tools. I claim that they should be understood as attributive anaphors, i.e. pronouns which are both anaphoric and attributive insofar as they attribute an indexical thought to the referent of the NP from which they inherit their value.

1. *De Se* Thoughts

Uses of the first-person pronoun seem to have a special, privileged, and primitive function. When you use it you refer to yourself, while when I use it I refer to myself. The same story can be told about (paradigmatic) uses of 'now' and 'here'.[1] Their use is intrinsically tied to the time/place when/in which the agent uses them. They are

[1] I said *paradigmatic* uses insofar as, to adopt Kaplan's (1977; 1989) pure indexical *vs.* demonstrative distinction, 'here' and 'now' can also be used to pick out a location/time different from the location/time of the utterance. If, when pointing to a map, one says: "I'll go on vacation here", 'here' does not pick out the place of the utterance but the place pointed to. The same applies to 'now'. When watching a video, if one says, "Now we visit the Mausoleum", 'now' is used to pick out the time when the video was recorded and not the time of the utterance. See Ch. 4 (esp. Sect. 6) for a more detailed discussion of these uses where I claimed that in such cases 'here' and 'now' work in an anaphoric way.

tied, one could say, to the agent's egocentric setting or coordinates. In what follows, I concentrate on the first-person pronoun. What I say about 'I', though, can easily be generalized to the paradigmatic uses of 'now' and 'here'.

An individual, Jon, could believe that someone is making a mess without realizing that he himself is making a mess and thus without adjusting his behavior and acting accordingly. One can look into a mirror and say "His zip is open" without realizing that one's own zip is open and, thus, without bothering to close the zip. Only when one comes to entertain the thought expressed by "My zip is open" is one likely to feel embarrassed and close it. Examples such as these have led people (Castañeda, Chisholm, Lewis, and Perry, to name only a few) to claim that the first-person pronoun is irreducible to other mechanisms of reference. It is, to adopt Perry's happy expression, an *essential indexical*:

> When we replace it ['I'] with other designations of me, we no longer have an explanation of my behavior and so, it seems, no longer an attribution of the same belief. It seems to be an *essential* indexical. (Perry 1979: 27)

The way I understand Castañeda's and Perry's central thesis is as follows: the first-person pronoun has a *cognitive impact*, for it triggers self-centered behavior. A similar story can be told about the indexicals 'now' and 'here'; they trigger self-centered behaviors as well.[2] This phenomenon has been popularized under the label *The Irreducibility Thesis* and can be summarized as follows:

- *Irreducibility Thesis (oratio recta)*
  The first-person pronoun cannot be explained away or replaced by a coreferring term without destroying the cognitive impact its use conveys.

The question that springs to mind is: how do we attribute, from a third-person perspective, a use of the first-person pronoun? Castañeda (1966; 1967; 1968) created an artificial pronoun, 'she*/he*/it*', to represent the use (possibly an implicit use) of the first-person pronoun in an attitude ascription. "Sue says that she* is rich" represents Sue as saying "I am rich". These artificial pronouns are called 'quasi-indicators' and, Castañeda claims, are the only mechanism enabling the attribution of indexical reference from the third-person perspective. They are, therefore, the only tools that allow us to capture the cognitive impact conveyed by the essential indexicals—'she*' captures the cognitive impact conveyed by 'I', 'then*' the cognitive impact conveyed by 'now', and 'there*' the impact conveyed by 'here'. It is an accident of English that a single pronoun 'she/he/it' can be used to perform very different speech acts. In an *oratio recta* construction it works as a

---

[2] "So replacing the indexical 'I' with another term designating the same person really does, as claimed, destroy the force of explanation" (Perry 1979: 29).

demonstrative, while in an *oratio obliqua* construction it can work either as a bound variable, an anaphoric pronoun, or a quasi-indicator:

It is a mere accident of grammar that the same physical objects are used in different logical roles. The underlying rationale is this: indicators are a primary means of referring to particulars, but the references made with them are personal and ephemeral; quasi-indicators are the derivative means of making an indexical reference both interpersonal and enduring, yet preserving it intact. (Castañeda 1967: 207)

Following this suggestion, we can say that the Irreducibility Thesis presents itself under two distinct guises, the *oratio recta* guise and the *oratio obliqua* guise:

- *Irreducibility Thesis (oratio obliqua)*
  In an *oratio obliqua* construction, the cognitive impact conveyed by a use of the first-person pronoun can only be captured by the quasi-indicator 'she*/he*/it*'.

Castañeda claims that the proposition expressed by an utterance containing the first-person pronoun is different from any proposition expressed by an utterance in which the first-person pronoun is replaced by a coreferring expression. Thus Jon's utterance of "I am making a mess" and my utterance of "Jon is making a mess" would never express the same proposition. More recently, Castañeda also claimed that an 'I'-utterance and the corresponding quasi-indexical utterance cannot express the same proposition either (see his correspondence with Adams in Castañeda 1983*a*):

(A) The first-person pronoun used indexically is not reducible to other mechanisms of reference

... A consequence of (A) is this: Sentences with an indexical first-person pronoun express different propositions, different truths, or falsehoods, from those expressed by sentences with third-person expressions ... thesis (A) is immediately complemented with this other thesis:

(B) Quasi-indicators depicting attributions to others of first-person reference are not strictly reducible to nonquasi-indicators. (Castañeda 1989: 80)

I am not convinced by the idea that an utterance containing the first-person pronoun cannot express the same proposition as an utterance containing a coreferential term. I also believe that one's utterance of, say, "I am rich" and the report "S/he said that s/he* is rich", insofar as 'I' and 's/he*' are coreferential, do relate both the attributee and the attributer to the very same proposition, having the attributee her/himself as a constituent. In other words, I sit with Perry when he claims that:

We have here a metaphysical benign form of limited accessibility. Anyone at any time can have access to any proposition. But not in any way. Anyone can believe of John Perry that he is making a mess. And anyone can be in the belief state classified by the sentence "I am making a mess". But only I can have that belief by being in that state. (Perry 1979: 41)

Unlike Perry (1983) and many others, however, I do not believe that quasi-indicators can be explained away merely as a pragmatic phenomenon.[3] I now turn to the discussion of the existence of quasi-indicators in natural language and their semantic relevance.

2. In Search of Quasi-Indicators

Chierchia (1989) proposes two arguments that can be viewed as suggesting that quasi-indicators exist in natural language. In other words, Chierchia's arguments, as I understand them, prove that Castañeda's artificial pronouns 'she*/he*/it*' and the like do represent, after all, an existing phenomenon. Chierchia's first argument concerns unpronounced subjects of infinitive clauses, which linguists call PRO. PRO represents the null pronominal element acting as the syntactic subject of infinitives and gerunds. In other words, PRO is viewed as the null analogue of lexical pronouns.

- *PRO qua de se pronoun*
  The unpronounced subject of an infinitive clause is generally used to report an 'I' or *de se* thought.[4]

Imagine that, after spending a night drinking plenty of wine, Agassi turns on the television and watches a tennis match to cure his hangover. The game he ends up watching features the match he played two days ago, but he does not realize that the bald tennis player is he himself. Agassi finds the bald player utterly annoying and comes to hope that he loses the tournament. In this situation, a self-ascription like (1a) will be appropriate, while a self-ascription like (1b) would not:

(1) a. I hope that he will lose the tournament
    b. I hope to lose the tournament

From a third-person perspective, (1a) and (1b) could be reported as:

(1) c. Agassi hopes that he will lose the tournament
    d. Agassi hopes to lose the tournament

---

[3] I further discuss the attempt to explain away quasi-indicators as a mere pragmatic phenomenon in Ch. 9, Sect. 1, below.

[4] An attribution like "Pavarotti very much wants to get help" entails "Pavarotti very much wants for Pavarotti to get help" but not conversely. That is, a *de se* attribution entails a *de re* one, but a *de re* ascription does not necessarily entail a *de se* one. "This explains why PRO, the subject of infinitives, will in general be interpreted *de se*, and unambiguously so" (Chierchia 1989: 16).

While (1c) captures Agassi's mental state, (1d) does not.

The unpronounced subject (PRO) in (1b) and (1d) can only be understood as attributing an 'I'-thought.[5] On the other hand, (1a) and (1c) must be understood *de re*. I shall represent this peculiarity of PRO by adopting Castañeda's notation and add a '*' to form 'PRO*'. The star simply signals that the report is *de se*. If I am right, (1d) can be represented as:

(1) e. Agassi$_1$ hopes [PRO_1^* to lose the tournament][6]

One could object that "Jon wants a beer" also means that Jon wants a beer for himself. So, why should we posit quasi-indicators in the case of infinitival clauses? Of course, there may be circumstances in which one means that Jon wants a beer for someone else, say Jane, with an utterance like "Jon wants a beer". If Jon is a waiter and Jane is a customer, "Jon wants a beer" is likely to mean that Jon wants a beer for Jane. The difference between an utterance like "Jon wants a beer" and "Jon wants a beer *for himself*" can be traced to the fact that 'for himself' in the latter puts the stress on Jon, i.e. on the fact that Jon does not want a beer for Jane, say. The moral seems to be that we *never* posit the existence of quasi-indicators. In particular, in the case of infinitival clauses we do *not* posit quasi-indicators.[7] I claimed only that PRO in (1e) should be understood as a quasi-indicator. We do not posit PRO, for it is required by syntax. Thus, while we do not have to posit hidden quasi-indicators to capture the fact that in many circumstances "Jon wants a beer" means that Jon wants a beer for himself, we should understand PRO in many infinitival clauses, i.e. the clauses which must be understood to be *de se*, along the lines of quasi-indicators. With the same token I can claim that we do not posit quasi-indicators when dealing with attitude ascriptions of the form "Mary believes that she (herself) is rich". I only claim that the pronoun 'she (herself)' must be understood as a quasi-indicator

---

[5] Schlenker (2003), in discussing Chierchia's datum, makes a similar point. Schlenker proposes a sophisticated treatment of *de se* ascriptions, resting on the notion of context-shifting. On this account, a quasi-indicator picks out an object directly from a context. Given that 'she*' can only be used in a reportive context and since, in general, the reported context is distinct from the context in which the report is uttered, a token of 'she*' will pick out an individual directly from a context quantified over by an attitude verb. As will become clear, however, the picture I suggest does not appeal to context-shifting; it exploits the anaphoric feature of quasi-indicators. For an extensive discussion and criticism of Schlenker's theory, see Whitsey (2003).

[6] Chierchia (1989: 15) interprets PRO as a property-abstractor. An infinitive clause like "PRO to eat cheese" will thus be interpreted as "λx[x eats cheese]." As will become clear in Sect. 7, I do not follow Chierchia on this interpretation.

[7] A way to understand this kind of emphatic use of the reflexive would be in a similar way to the use of particles like 'exactly', 'precisely', and 'just' in utterances like "Ivan is just/exactly/precisely the student Jane was looking for". As König suggests: "[these particles] are primarily used emphatically to assert the identity of one argument in a proposition with an argument in a different, contextually given proposition. Such an identification may be achieved via exclusion. This is probably the right analysis for G. *genau* and E. *exactly, precisely*, and *just*" (König 1991: 127).

and that ascriptions of the form "Jane hopes to win the lottery" and "Jane hopes that she (herself) wins the lottery" must be understood on a par as *de se* attributions. They can be represented, respectively, as "Jane hopes PRO* to win the lottery" and "Jane hopes that she* wins the lottery".

Before going further it is worth stressing how quasi-indicators, *de se* pronouns, and PRO relate to one another. As far as I can see, the main difference between PRO and a quasi-indicator like 's/he*' rests on the fact that, in some cases, PRO is not used as a *de se* pronoun. In:

(2) a. George W. Bush obliged/forced/... Tony Blair PRO to invade Iraq
    b. Italy has been persuaded/convinced/... by the USA PRO to support an illegal invasion of Iraq

PRO does not attribute to Blair or Italy an 'I'-thought; as such it is not a *de se* pronoun. In short PRO, like the pronoun 's/he', can have two interpretations, one *de re* and one *de se*. For this very reason, we can adopt Castañeda's notation and distinguish between PRO and PRO*. This distinction parallels the distinction between 's/he' and 's/he*'. Unlike the pronoun 's/he', though, the *de se* interpretation of PRO is grammatically forced. In:

(3) George W. Bush wants PRO to steal Iraq's oil

PRO *must* be understood as PRO*, while in

(4) Tony Blair said that he wants to steal Iraq's oil

'he' can be understood either as 'he' or 'he*'. In short, grammar alone tells us whether we have PRO or PRO*, while in the case of 's/he' in an *oratio obliqua* construction we have to appeal to extra-grammatical features before the interpretation (either as 's/he' or as 's/he*').

Further evidence in favor of the *de se* interpretation proposed by Chierchia is given by Italian sentences like:

(5) a. Maria ha detto che ha vinto la lotteria
       [Maria said that won the lottery]
       Maria$_1$ ha detto che [PRO$_1$* ha vinto la lotteria]
    b. Maria pensa che ha visto Mario
       [Maria thinks that saw Mario]
       Maria$_1$ pensa che [PRO$_1$* ha visto Mario]

These attributions can only be understood *de se*. Hence, the unspoken subject in (5a) and (5b) can only be understood using the quasi-indicator 'she*'. The appropriate translation of (5a) and (5b) would be:

(6) a. Maria said that she herself (she*) won the lottery
    b. Maria thinks that she herself (she*) saw Mario

It would thus be strange to argue that in Italian, a pro-drop language,[8] the unspoken pronoun in an attitude ascription like (5) works as a quasi-indicator whilst claiming that in their English counterpart (6) (where the pronoun must be present) it does not. This seems to be cross-linguistic evidence campaigning in favor of quasi-indicators.

The second argument in favor of the *de se* interpretation proposed by Chierchia focuses on the different ways we can understand inferences like:

(7) a. Jane believes she is a millionaire
    b. Sue believes whatever Jane believes

So: c. Sue believes she is a millionaire

Assuming that there is coreference between 'Jane' and 'she' in the first premiss (and thus that they are coindexed), the conclusion can be understood in different ways, meaning either that Sue believes that Jane is a millionaire (*strict inference*) or that Sue believes that she herself is a millionaire (*sloppy inference*):

(8) a. Jane$_1$ believes she$_1$ is a millionaire
    b. Sue believes whatever Jane believes

So: c. Sue$_2$ believes she$_1$ is a millionaire

(9) a. Jane$_1$ believes she$_1$ is a millionaire
    b. Sue believes whatever Jane believes

So: c. Sue$_2$ believes she$_2$ is a millionaire

Chierchia (1989) claims that with the strict inference the belief attribution to Sue is understood *de re* while, with the sloppy inference, it must be *de se*. As I understand this, the pronoun 'she' in a sloppy inference must be understood as a quasi-indicator attributing an 'I'-thought to Sue. As a first approximation we can say that, in English, a pronoun like 'she' is multiply ambiguous in an attitude ascription. It can either be: (i) a demonstrative referring to the individual indicated by the reporter (e.g. "Jane$_1$ believes that she$_2$ [pointing to Mary] is rich", (ii) a simple anaphor (e.g. "Jane$_1$ believes that she$_1$ is rich, but she$_1$ (herself)/she$_1$* does not realize that she$_1$ (herself)/she$_1$* is rich"), or (iii) a quasi-indicator (e.g. "Jane$_1$ believes that she$_1$* is rich"). It should be noted, however, that this does not constitute an exhaustive classification of pronouns. For, possessive pronouns exhibit the very same ambiguity, yet they need not appear in an *oratio obliqua* construction (e.g. "Today Jane is wearing *her new hat*" can mean either that Jane is wearing her own hat or someone

---

[8] In so-called pro-drop or null-subject languages like Italian, Spanish, and many others, the subject need not be pronounced. One can say "Mangio [I eat]", "Mangia [s/he eats]", etc. In these languages, *pro* (as opposed to PRO) can be understood as the null analogue of a pronoun. The difference between *pro* and PRO, is that the latter, unlike *pro*, is anaphoric. That is to say, PRO is characterized as +Anaphor and +Pronominal, and *pro* as −Anaphor and +Pronominal.

else's, say Mary's, hat, while "Jane said that *her hat* was new" can mean (i) that Jane said that her own hat was new, (ii) that someone else's hat was new, and (iii) that Jane said of her hat that it is new without knowing that it is her own).

It may be instructive to mention that Bosch's distinction between referential uses and non-referential, syntactic uses, of pronouns does not help us to distinguish between quasi-indicators and other pronouns either:

> If we say that *he* in (33) [Fred thinks *he* is sick] occurs purely syntactically (is an SP), we mean that there is a purely syntactic relation that links the pronoun to the syntactic position of its antecedent. This relation is a relation of congruence or agreement and is independent of whether or not the antecedent occurs referentially. It depends solely on syntactic properties of the antecedent (gender, number, syntactic position) and thus parallels the relation between the person-suffix in the verb (the *–s* of *thinks*) and the subject.
>
> If we say that *he* in (34) [*John* looks pale, and Fred thinks *he* is sick] occurs referentially (as an RP), we mean that the pronoun refers to some referent or other in the domain of reference. If there is an anaphoric relation between *John* and *he* in (34), then *John* must also occur referentially, i.e. must refer to a referent in the domain of reference, and the referent of *he* and *John* must be one and the same. (Bosch 1983: 41)

According to Bosch in the case of syntactic pronouns the relationship between the anaphoric pronoun and its antecedent is syntactically constrained and it is not influenced by contextual or other features pertaining to the discourse situation. Only in the case of referential anaphora can contextual features enter the scene in determining the anaphoric link.[9] It emerges that, although Bosch's notion of syntactic pronouns covers some uses of quasi-indicators, it also covers the use of other pronouns (e.g. certain possessive occurrences). More importantly, it does not recognize so-called intersentential anaphora. In "Jon$_1$ played poker. He$_1$ lost a lot of money" and "Jon: Will you be here$_1$ tonight? Jane: I believe that I am unable to be *there*$_1$* before midnight"), the pronoun 'he' and the quasi-indicator 'there*' work as intersentential anaphors. As such, their resolution cannot be determined by syntax alone. In particular, intersentential anaphora do not obey principle A of Government and Binding Theory whichever way one spells it out.[10] Hence, some

---

[9] "According to our considerations of 'anaphora' and context dependence . . . there should not be any constraints of a syntactic nature on the interpretation of properly anaphoric (and hence referential) pronoun occurrences. Only SPs can be so constrained, and all other pronouns subject to influence from context and speaker's intentions—factors we assume can in principle not be grasped in terms of syntax" (Bosch 1983: 163).

[10] A way to state Principle A is as follows (see Pollard and Sag 1992: 263):

> Every anaphor must be coindexed with an NP in an appropriately defined command relation, within an appropriately defined minimal syntactic domain.

The main questions (and disagreements) focus on how the command relation and the minimal syntactic domain should be specified. This debate, however, transcends the scope of this chapter. I shall further discuss the Government and Binding Theory later.

uses of quasi-indicators cannot be subsumed under the category of syntactic pronouns.[11]

As further evidence in favor of the existence of quasi-indicators, we can quote the behavior of the Italian reflexive 'proprio' [self]. In an ascription like (the example comes from Chierchia 1989: 24):

(10) a. Pavarotti crede che i *propri* pantaloni siano in fiamme
[Pavarotti believes that his own [*self*] pants are on fire]

'proprio' forces the *de se* reading. If, instead of the reflexive 'proprio' we had the non-reflexive pronoun 'suoi' [his], we could have both the *de re* and the *de se* interpretation:

(10) b. Pavarotti crede che i *suoi* pantaloni siano in fiamme[12]
[Pavarotti believes that *his* pants are on fire]

Furthermore, (10c) is not contradictory, while (10d) is. (10d) mirrors the contradictoriness of (10e) (the examples come from Bonomi, quoted in Chierchia 1989):

(10) c. Pavarotti crede che i *suoi* pantaloni siano in fiamme. Ma non si è accorto che i pantaloni sono i propri
[Pavarotti believes that his pants are on fire. But he has not realized that the pants are his own]

d. * Pavarotti crede che i *propri* pantaloni siano in fiamme. Ma non si è accorto che i pantaloni sono i propri
[Pavarotti believes that his own [*self*] pants are on fire. But he has not realized that the pants are his own]

e. * Pavarotti crede di avere i pantaloni in fiamme. Ma non si è accorto che i pantaloni sono i propri

---

[11] Besides, if I am right in understanding quasi-indicators along the lines of logophoric pronouns we gain further evidence in favor of the view that some uses of quasi-indicators cannot be subsumed under the category of syntactic pronouns: "The logophoric use of anaphoric pronouns with concomitant long-distance binding effects is not a restricted phenomenon. It is also possible in languages which otherwise only allow local binding. . . . The essence of the claim that a certain type of binding relation involves logophoricity is that discourse factors enter into it. That is, syntactic conditions are not sufficient. This does not entail that discourse properties yield sufficient conditions, or that the element involved need not be syntactically bound as well" (Reuland and Koster 1991: 22). This phenomenon is stressed by considering sentences such as:

(i) Max's eyes watched eagerly a new picture of himself in the paper
(ii) Bismark's impulsiveness had, as so often, rebounded against himself

As Reinhard and Reuland point out that "these contexts are, indeed, logophoric and should not fall under the binding theory is witnessed also by the fact that the anaphor in these environments is permitted even when not bound (c-commanded)" (Reinhart and Reuland 1991: 289). I shall further discuss sentences like (i) and (ii) later on.

[12] Other languages also mark this difference. e.g. in Norwegian, (7a) would translate as "Pavarotti tror at *sine* bokser brenner" while (7b) would translate as "Pavarotti at *haus* bokser brenner".

[Pavarotti believes [PRO to have burning pants]. But he has not realized that the pants are his own]

It seems then that 'proprio' in Italian works like PRO. As such, it provides a way to single out *de se* ascriptions. The Italian 'proprio' comes close to the quasi-indicator 's/he*' and may provide further evidence of the existence of quasi-indicators in natural language. This shows, at the very least, that quasi-indicators exist in Italian. If we recognize that they exist in Italian, why not welcome them in English as well? In other words, we have further cross-linguistic evidence that quasi-indicators exist in natural language.[13] We can thus verify Castañeda's claim that it is a mere accident of (English) grammar that the same physical objects ('she' and the like) are used in different logical roles. It is an open question why English, unlike other languages, did not evolve in such a way as to grammatically stress or morphologically mark quasi-indicators.[14]

To stress the need for quasi-indicators, we can focus on Castañeda's data: imagine that Privatus, an amnesiac, has forgotten his name. In reading an article reporting that Privatus is the lucky winner of last night's lottery, Privatus comes to entertain the belief that Privatus is a millionaire. Given this situation, the following three attributions can be true together:

(11) a. Privatus believes that Privatus is a millionaire
b. Privatus believes that he is a millionaire
c. I do not believe that I am a millionaire [said by Privatus]

For these reports to capture Privatus' attitudes, (11b) must be *de re*. As such, the pronoun 'he' does not attribute to Privatus a particular way of thinking about himself. Actually, (11b) could continue as:

(11) d. Privatus believes that he is a millionaire but he does not realize (he does not believe) that he himself (he*) is a millionaire

On the other hand, a self-attribution like (11c) specifies the way in which Privatus thinks about himself, i.e. it specifies that he thinks in the first-person way and thus that he entertains an 'I'-thought. From a third-person perspective, Privatus' self-ascription (11c) should be rendered as:

(11) e. Privatus does not believe that he himself (he*) is a millionaire

If 'he' in (11b) were understood as a quasi-indicator, (11e) would contradict (11b).

---

[13] It is also worth mentioning the etymological similarities between English and Italian. It is thus unlikely that they have any major logical differences, so we should assume indicators exist in any sufficiently similar language.

[14] In some African languages (mainly of the Eastern branches of Niger-Congo) such as Dogon, Ewe, Tupuri, etc., quasi-indicators (which, as we shall see in Sect. 5, below, should be viewed along the lines of logophoric pronouns) are morphologically marked and morphologically distinct from personal and reflexive pronouns. On how logophoric pronouns appear and are marked in these languages see e.g. Hagège (1974), Clements (1975), Culy (1994a; 1997). The term 'logophoric pronoun' was introduced by Hagège (1974).

3. Quasi-Indicators, Coindexation, and Dependence

It is worth noticing that Fiengo and May's (1994) dependency theory does not allow us to capture Castañeda's datum. Actually, a *de re* report like (11b) can be represented either as (11f) or (11g):

(11) f. Privatus$_1{}^i$ believes that he$_1{}^i$ is a millionaire
    g. Privatus$_1{}^i$ believes that he$_1{}^d$ is a millionaire

where the subscripts signal coreference.[15] The superscript '*i*' signals independence—if the NP is a singular (referential) term its reference does not depend on the reference of another noun phrase. The superscript '*d*' signals that the pronoun's value is dependent—i.e. it is inherited from the value of the noun phrase it is coindexed with. When a pronoun is coindexed with a referential expression, the former is coreferential with the latter. Before going further it is worth stressing that the picture I have in mind does not commit us to a particular theory of anaphora. In particular, it does not commit us to the view that anaphoric pronouns must be bound. Under the label 'anaphora' I am happy to subsume all NPs which are *referentially defective*, regardless of whether they are bound or not. An NP is referentially defective when its value is (at least partly) determined by another NP which can be recovered in the stretch of discourse. Hence, when an expression bears a '*d*'-occurrence I simply mean that its semantic value is *mediated* by a relation to some other referential expression. This mediation can be of varying natures; it can be syntactic or partly pragmatic (as in the case of so-called unbound anaphors) and, as such, governed by discourse considerations. In particular, according to the picture I have in mind (which differs from Fiengo & May's dependency theory in this respect), '*d*'-occurrences are not limited to intrasentential anaphor but can be found in intersentential contexts.[16] This will become particularly evident when we consider logophoric pronouns in the next section.

---

[15] It should be stressed, though, that while coindexed referring NPs are coreferential, non-coindexation does not mean non-coreference. If, in answering the question "Who left?" one says:

(i) He$_1$ put Jon$_2$'s coat on

what is said may well be consistent with 'he' and 'Jon' being coreferential (see Fiengo and May 1994: 3). This example comes from Higginbotham (1985: 570) who acknowledges Nancy Browman. As Reinhart writes: "Since pronouns can select their reference outside the sentence (either deictically or from an antecedent in previous discourse), the mere fact that a pronoun is not coindexed with a given NP in the sentence is not sufficient to prevent it from receiving the same referential interpretation from an extra-sentential source" (Reinhart 1983: 48).

[16] "Two important properties of Dependence theory can be noted immediately. First, β-occurrences are limited to the domain of dependencies; that is, to phrase markers. Hence, pronouns anaphoric on elements outside their phrase markers must bear independent α-occurrences; β-occurrences cannot resolve outside their structure. It follows, then, that dependencies are a property of intrasentential anaphora; they are not found in intersentential contexts" (Fiengo and May 1994: 54). Fiengo and May use 'β' when I use '*d*' and 'α' when I use '*i*'.

When a pronoun is bound by a quantified expression it works like a bound variable. In that case the antecedent of the pronoun is a variable (e.g. Everyone$_1$[e_1^i wears *his$_1^d$* hat]). As such the pronoun cannot be coreferential with the variable; it is realized as another occurrence of the variable (see Fiengo and May 1994: 75). The subscripts mark the link between the quantifier and the pronouns. It is worth stressing that the anaphoric dependence between an anaphoric pronoun and its antecedent is marked by the superscript, for only a pronoun marked with the superscript '*d*' can be said to be anaphoric on another NP. Two proper names can bear the same subscript (e.g. "Tully$_1$ shaved Tully$_1$", "Tully$_1$ is Tully$_1$"), yet they are not anaphoric on one another, for proper names are always referentially independent and will always bear an '*i*' as superscript.

In short, the pronoun 'he' in (11c) can be understood either as a demonstrative working like a free variable—this is the representation (11f)—or as an anaphor linked with 'Privatus'—representation (11g). A representation like (11g), though, does not attribute a *de se* attitude to the attributee. Only an attribution with the quasi-indicator 'he*/she*' can capture the *de se* nature of an attitude, for an attribution like (11d) would be:

(11) h. Privatus$_1^i$ believes that he$_1^d$ is a millionaire but he$_1^d$ does not realize that he himself is a millionaire

If (11d) were represented as:

(11) l. Privatus$_1^i$ believes that he$_1^d$ is a millionaire but he$_1^d$ does not realize that he$_1^d$ is a millionaire

we would have a contradiction, i.e. we would state that Privatus both believes and does not believe that he is a millionaire. If we aim to capture Privatus' different attitudes *vis-à-vis* himself, we must appeal to the quasi-indicator 'he*'. Hence, in order to capture the nature of *de se* ascriptions, a theory appealing to dependences must be enriched.

A *de se* attribution like (11c) can be rendered, from the third-person perspective, as:

(11) m. Privatus$_1^i$ does not believe that he$_1^{d*}$ is a millionaire

where the '*', following Castañeda's notation, signals that the anaphoric pronoun is a quasi-indicator. Our "formal" language will thus have:

- 'she/he/it$_n^i$' = an independent pronoun, working like a free variable.
- 'he/she/it$_n^d$' = an anaphoric pronoun which can either inherit its value from the noun phrase with which it is coindexed, or else be a bound variable.
- 'he/she/it$_n^{d*}$' = a quasi-indicator which can either inherit its value from the noun phrase with which it is coindexed *and* attribute

an 'I'-thought to the referent of that noun phrase, or else be a bound (quasi-indexical) variable.

The fact that pronouns and reflexives behave in an unusual way when embedded in attitude reports is well known and documented. In Latin indirect discourse, for example, we have reflexive pronouns instead of personal pronouns (see Kuno 1987: 105):

(12) Petiērunt ut   *sibi*   licēret
       begged   so-that   to self   be-allowed
       (They begged that it might be allowed them)

This feature of reflexive pronouns has not been unnoticed. Thus it has been suggested that, when reflexive pronouns are embedded in 'that'-clauses, certain rules should be obeyed:

If the subordinate clause expresses the words or thought of the subject of the main clause, the reflexive is regularly used to refer to the subject ... Sometimes the person or thing to which the reflexive refers is not the grammatical subject of the main clause, though it is in effect the subject of discourse ... If the subordinate clause does not express the words or thought of the main subject, the reflexive is not regularly used, though it is occasionally found. (Allen and Greenough [1883] 1903: 181)

It is also interesting to note that some languages (so-called pure logophoric languages) morphologically mark the distinction between 'he/she/it$_n^d$' and 'he/she/it$_n^{d\star}$'.[17] Logophoric pronouns are used to refer to the person whose attitudes are being reported. Pure logophoric languages are languages in which these pronouns are used *only* as logophors and not as other reflexives or in emphatic uses.[18] Tabury, for instance, distinguishes between the third-person pronoun *qua* anaphoric pronoun, '*à*', and the third-person pronoun *qua* quasi-indicator (logophoric pronoun), '*sé*' (see Hagège 1974: 299):

(13) a. á Dík lí māy mà:gā *à* kó n sú: mònò
      (He$_1^i$ thinks of the young girl that he$_1^d$ saw yesterday)
    b. á Dík lí māy mà:gā *sé* kó n sú: mònò
      (He$_1^i$ thinks of the young girl that he$_1^{d\star}$ saw yesterday)

As a first approximation we could say that, while attributions containing 'she/he/it$_n^i$' and 'she/he/it$_n^d$' represent *de re* attributions, attributions with

---

[17] "[A] pure logophoric language is one that has some morphological and/or syntactic form that is used only in logophoric domains, while a mixed logophoric language is one in which reflexive pronouns have an extended use in logophoric domains to refer back to the logophoric trigger" (Culy 1994a: 1057).

[18] As Culy points out: "In pure logophoric languages, there are always environments in which coreferring with the logophoric trigger can only be done by a logophoric pronoun" (Culy 1994a: 1080). More on logophoric pronouns and how quasi-indicators should be understood as logophoric pronouns in Sect. 5, below.

'she/he/it$_n^{d\star}$' represent *de se* attributions. This classification, though, is far from exhaustive, for we can have mixed cases, i.e. attributions that are partly *de re* and partly *de se*. Overhearing Jon saying: "Sue and I are the only winners of last night's lottery", Sue can report:

(14) a. Jon$_1$ believes that we$_1{}^{d\star}{}_{\oplus 2}{}^i$ are millionaires[19]

It is worth mentioning that the pronoun 'we' is both independent (insofar as it partly picks out its reference independently of the occurrence of another NP) and dependent (insofar as it partly inherits its reference from another NP). This captures the fact that mixed reports like (14a) attribute an 'I'-thought to Jon and, as such, are *de se*. At the same time, though, the pronoun 'we' also works as an independent pronoun picking out the reporter and, as such, it is *de re*. In other words, a report like (14a) is a mixed report insofar at it specifies the attributee Jon's attitude *vis-à-vis* himself, yet it is silent on the way Jon thought about the reporter. To understand this difference we could argue that a report like (14a) is a shortened version of:

(14) b. Jon$_1{}^i$ believes that he$_1{}^{d\star}$ is a millionaire and that I$_2{}^i$ am a millionaire

where 'I' makes it clear that the reporter does not specify the way in which Jon thought about the attributer, i.e. 'I' does not attribute to Jon a specific mechanism of reference. Let us characterize this phenomenon *the attribution indeterminacy*.[20]

Multiple embedded reports bring in indeterminacy as well. Consider:

(14) c. Sue$_1{}^i$ believes that Jon$_2{}^i$ knows that she$_1{}^{d\star}$ is a millionaire

where the quasi-indicator 'she*' attributes an 'I'-thought to Sue and, as such, specifies the way she thought about herself, but is silent on the way Jon thought about Sue. All we can stipulate is that there is *a* way Jon referred/thought about Sue, but that the report does not specify which one. For this reason, the report is indeterminate.[21] Reports can be more or less indeterminate, depending on how much information regarding the attributee is left unspecified. In a multiple

---

[19] Plurals with split antecedents, such as "Jon told Sue that they are millionaires", are represented as:

(i) Jon$_1$ told Sue$_2$ that they$_{1\oplus 2}$ are millionaires

where '1 ⊕ 2' signals that the index of the plural is the fusion of the indices of its antecedents. It is an open question whether in our example the predicate of being a millionaire holds of the antecedents individually or collectively, i.e. whether the plural reference is distributive or collective (see Fiengo and May 1994: 39).

[20] This goes along with the idea I defended in Ch. 7, Sect. 8, where I claimed that, since reports are audience-directed, we are often bound to be unfaithful, i.e. we cannot always capture the attributee's mental state. In cases like (14a), though, the unfaithfulness is syntactically constrained. I further discuss and analyze the case of mixed reports when I introduce (Ch. 9, Sect. 6) the distinction between propositionally opaque and propositionally transparent reports and argue that propositional opacity/transparency proceeds by degrees.

[21] Besides, multiple embedded reports containing quasi-indicators can be ambiguous with regard to the antecedent they are coreferential with. "Jane thought that Mary believes that she* is rich" licenses both readings: (i) "Jane$_1$ thought that Mary$_2$ believes that she$_1$* is rich" and (ii) "Jane$_1$ thought that Mary$_2$

embedded report involving quasi-indicators, whatever is unspecified is easily noticed. It is a matter of grammar that a report like (14c), for instance, is silent on the way in which Jon thought about Sue. Other reports, though, are far more enigmatic, for indeterminate reports do not always present themselves under the (*de re*) guise: "Of *NN*, *A* believes/wishes/ . . . that she/he/it is *F*". A report like "Columbus believed that Santo Domingo was China", for instance, does not specify the way in which Columbus thought about Santo Domingo, insofar as we assume that Columbus did not have the name 'Santo Domingo' at his disposal to refer to the island he landed on. Hence reports that present themselves under the (*de dicto*) guise "*A* believes that *NN* is *F*" may be indeterminate as well.

The indeterminacy problem, however, should not come as a surprise if we remember that, in most cases, reports are *audience-directed*. It is often the case that, in order to pass to the audience a given message, a report needs to be amended and cannot be faithful. If I hear Jon saying "A notorious bachelor charmed my sister" and I intend to report what he said to someone who does not know that bachelors are unmarried men (e.g. to a child or a foreigner with an incomplete mastery of English), I probably end up reporting "Jon said that a notorious unmarried man charmed his sister" and, in so doing, I will not report that Jon used the word 'bachelor'. The success of communication often requires amendments of this type. There is thus a tension between communicating *what* is believed and *how* it is believed, i.e. the *what* and the *how* do not always go hand in hand. I shall return to this specific feature of attitude ascriptions in Section 7.

4. Quasi-Indicators, Logophoric Pronouns, and Anaphora

In this section, I shall discuss how quasi-indicators differ from anaphoric pronouns and how they compare with logophoric pronouns. As a first approximation, we can say that the indexical use of a pronoun refers without contributing any information other than that conveyed by its linguistic meaning (such as the number and gender of the referent, which are dictated by the grammatical features of the pronoun). As for anaphoric pronouns, they may or may not be referential terms. If they are linked (coindexed) to a singular referential term, they contribute its referent to the proposition expressed, whereas if they are bound by a quantifier, they are not referential but instead work like bound variables. As we saw, whether an anaphoric pronoun is referential or not depends on the NP with which it is coindexed: if it is coindexed

---

believes that she$_2$* is rich". Curiously enough, a similar phenomenon occurs with the logophoric pronoun 'yé' in Ewe. "Kofi x⊃-e se be Ama gbl⊃ be yé-ƒu-i" can be translated either as "Kofi$_1$ believes that Ama$_2$ said that he$_1$ beat her$_2$" and "Kofi$_1$ believes that Ama$_2$ said that she$_2$ beat him$_1$" (see Clements 1975: 173).

with a referential expression it is referential while if it is coindexed with a quantified NP it works like a bound variable.[22]

It is instructive to report that first-person and second-person reflexives can occur without an antecedent, contradicting the very idea that a reflexive pronoun must have an antecedent binding it (see Reinhart & Reuland 1991: 311):[23]

(15) a. This paper was written by Ann and *myself*
b. Apart from *myself* only three members protested
c. Physicists like *yourself* are a godsend

Reinhart & Reuland suggest that we cannot explain away these reflexives as being merely deictic expressions. If this were the case, we would be unable to explain the difference between (16) and (17):[24]

(16) a. She ... gave both Brenda and *myself* a dirty look
b. The chairmen invited my wife and *myself* for a drink

---

[22] For argument's sake, I intentionally ignore the case of an anaphoric pronoun coindexed with an empty term, such as 'he' in "Tonight Santa$_1$ will come down the chimney and he$_1$ will bring you a lot of presents".

[23] The idea that a reflexive pronoun must have an antecedent is central to the Government and Binding Theory (GBT) as it has first been proposed. For an introduction to GBT see Haegeman (1994) where the original version of the theory is clearly exposed and explained. It goes without saying, though, that subsequent amendments to this theory have been proposed. These subtleties, though, go behind the scope of my work. The main characters of GBT are:

- *Principle A*
anaphors must be bound in their governing category.
- *Principle B*
pronouns must be free in their governing category.
- *Principle C*
other NPs must be free in all categories.

A governing category (GC) is defined as:

- *Governing Category (GC)*
A is a GC for B if A is the minimal category (i.e. the smallest NP or S) containing B, a governor of B, and a subject accessible to B.

Roughly, the minimal GC is the S or NP node immediately dominating the antecedent and the anaphor. The element that governs is called the *governor* while the element that is governed is the *governee*.

A pronoun is *bound* iff it is c-commanded by a coindexed element, while a pronoun is *free* iff it is not c-commanded by a coindexed element. The notion of c-command is defined as:

- *C-command*
Node A c-commands node B iff:
  (i) A does not dominate B and B does not dominate A; and
  (ii) the first branching node dominating A also dominates B

The notion of dominance characterizes the vertical relation in a tree and can be defined as:

- *Dominance*
Node A dominates node B iff A is higher in the tree than B and if you can trace a line from A to B going only downwards.

[24] Ex. (16a) comes from Roth, quoted in Reinhart and Reuland (1991). The others come from Reinhart and Reuland (1991: 312).

(17) a. *She gave *myself* a dirty look
    b. *The chairman invited *myself* for a drink

If 'myself' were a simply deictic pronoun, then it should be free from grammatical constraints (it would be unbound) and (17a–b) should be well formed. (17a) and (17b) would be treated along the lines of the pronoun 'me' in:

(18) a. She gave *me* a dirty look
    b. The chairman invited *me* for a drink

The general moral seems to be that reflexive pronouns escape strict grammatical rules (in particular some uses do not obey Principle A). Further examples are furnished by picture noun reflexives:

(19) a. The fact that there is a picture of himself$_1$ hanging in the post office is believed (by Mary) to have disturbed Tom$_1$
    b. The picture of herself$_1$ on the front page of *The Times* confirmed the allegations Mary$_1$ had been making for years
    c. John$_1$ was furious. The picture of himself$_1$ in the museum had been mutilated[25]

Pollard and Sag characterize these reflexives *exempt* insofar as Principle A does not apply to them. Furthermore, in (19c) the antecedent of the reflexive does not even appear in the same sentence. We thus have a case of intersentential anaphora. As far as Principle A is concerned, quasi-indicators seem to share some of the feature of exempt anaphors. In particular, they may be coindexed with an antecedent that appears in another sentence:

(20) a. In January 1999$_1$ Igor$_2$ visited Paris$_3$. He$_2$ believed that he$_2$* would find a job there$_3$* and then$_1$*
    b. Next Monday$_1$ Jane$_2$ will be 18. She$_2$ thinks that she$_2$* will inherit a fortune then$_1$*

The moral I would like to draw is that quasi-indicators should be characterized along the lines of logophoric pronouns. As such, they are better characterized as pronouns obeying constraints which must be stated in terms of discourse considerations. As we shall now see, the main notions involved in characterizing these kinds of anaphora are the related ones of *point of view*, *perspective*, and *empathy*. To begin with it is worth quoting Castañeda:

In the sequel we shall be concerned almost exclusively with third-person statements that ascribe self-knowledge to others, like

(3) The Editor of *Soul* knows that he (himself) is a millionaire, and

---

[25] Ex. (18a) comes from Jackendoff (1971; quoted in Pollard and Sag 1992), while Exx. (18b–c) come from Pollard and Sag (1992).

(4) The Editor of *Soul* knows that Mary knows that her niece knows that he (himself) is a millionaire.

In these cases the attribution of self-knowledge is made by means of the third-person pronoun 'he (himself)' to be abbreviated 'he*', which has here the following characteristics:

(i) it does not express an indexical reference made by the speaker;
(ii) it appears in *oratio obliqua*;
(iii) it has an antecedent, namely 'the Editor of *Soul*', to which it refers back;
(iv) its antecedent is outside the *oratio obliqua* containing 'he*';
(v) 'he*' is used to attribute, so to speak, implicit indexical reference to the Editor of *Soul*; that is, if the Editor were to assert what, according to (3) and (4), he knows, he would use the indicator 'I' where we, uttering (3) and (4), have used 'he*': he would assert, respectively,

(3a) I am a millionaire, and
(4a) Mary knows that her niece knows that I am a millionaire.

(Castañeda 1968: 440–1).[26]

Castañeda's characterization of quasi-indicators mirrors Clements's characterization of logophoric pronouns:

Logophoric pronouns can be characterized cross-linguistically in the following way:

(i) logophoric pronouns are restricted to *reportive contexts* transmitting the words or thought of an individual or individuals other than the speaker or narrator;
(ii) the antecedent does not occur in the same reportive context as the logophoric pronoun;
(iii) the antecedent designates the individual or individuals whose words or thoughts are transmitted in the reportive context in which the logophoric pronoun occurs.

(Clements 1975: 171–2)

Logophoric pronouns are thus intrinsically linked to attitude ascriptions.[27] As such, the logophoricity phenomenon is intrinsically linked to the notion of perspective, i.e. the perspective of a protagonist of a sentence and/or discourse (see Huang 2000: 172). In the cases I am interested in, the relevant perspective is the egocentric perspective of the subject of the attitude whose thought is being reported.

The main features worth stressing concerning quasi-indicators and logophoric pronouns linked to referring NP can be summarized as follows:[28]

- *Quasi-indicators and logophoric pronouns*
    (i) appear in *oratio obliqua*,
    (ii) are semantically dependent and as such cannot be used deictically—they are intrinsically syncategorematic terms,

---

[26] For a similar and more specific characterization see Castañeda (1967, rep. in Castañeda 1989: 218 ff.).
[27] "[L]ogophoric pronouns are a type of indirect-discourse pronoun ... logophoric pronouns have a natural place in the typology of indirect discourse" (Culy 1997: 851).
[28] For the simplicity of the argument, I concentrate on quasi-indicators that are linked to singular terms. As we saw, when a pronoun (and thus a quasi-indicator) is coindexed with a quantified expression,

(iii) their reference (or semantic value) depends on the noun phrase they are linked to (coindexed with) and,

(iv) they attribute an indexical reference/thought to the referent of the antecedent that they are coindexed with.

As I have already mentioned, some West African languages have logophoric pronouns that are morphologically marked and thus distinct from other pronouns. In Ewe, for instance, the pronoun 'yé' is used exclusively as a logophoric pronoun and appears exclusively in attitude reports:[29]

(21) a. Kofi be yé-dzo
   [Kofi say LOG-leave]
   (Kofi said that he (himself) left)

b. Kofi be me-dzo
   [Kofi say I-leave]
   (Kofi said that I leave)

c. Kofi be e-dzo
   [Kofi say s/he-leave]
   (Kofi₁ said that she/he₂ leave)

Furthermore, in Ewe the logophoric pronoun 'yé' is also morphologically distinct from the reflexive pronoun 'dokui':

(21) d. Kofi lõ e dokui
   [Kofi self-love]
   (Kofi loves himself)

e. Kofi be yé-lõ yé dokui
   [Kofi say LOG-self LOG love]
   (Kofi₁ said that he₁ loves himself)

One of the main questions, if not the main question, we must now consider concerns how we assign the content necessary for their referential interpretation, i.e. on how they are linked to the NP with which they are coindexed. As we saw, quasi-indicators may not obey Principle A, yet they are anaphoric insofar as their value depends on the noun phrase to which they are linked and coindexed. Furthermore, it has been claimed (see Culy 1997: 851–2) that personal logophoric pronouns,

---

it works like a bound variable and, as such, it is not a referential term; it does not contribute the referent into the proposition expressed. In, e.g. "Every woman will tell a man that *she₁** loves him", the quasi-indicator 'she*' is bound by the quantifier 'every woman' and does not contribute a specific individual into the proposition expressed.

[29] " 'yé' is used exclusively in indirect discourse (and other types of reportive contexts), while it is replaced, in direct discourse, by the appropriate first person singular form" (Clements 1975: 152).

unlike many personal pronouns, cannot be used without a discourse antecedent. Like quasi-indicators, they are syncategorematic terms. Without entering into the details, we can say that when evaluating a sentence containing quasi-indicators *or* logophoric pronouns, the whole discourse must be taken into consideration, for the anaphoricity of a logophoric pronoun and a quasi-indicator may transcend the boundaries of the sentence in which it appears. This mirrors the behavior of exempt picture noun reflexives (see Pollard and Sag 1992: 274). It is often the case that exempt picture noun reflexives inherit their value from an individual whose viewpoint or perspective is reported. Pollard and Sag invite us to consider the following discourse:

(22) John$_1$ was going to get even with Mary. That picture of himself$_1$ in the paper would really annoy her, as would the other stunts he had planned

where the picture noun phrase is naturally interpreted as coreferential with 'John' insofar as the narrator has taken on John's viewpoint. If we compare this discourse with the following, where the narrator takes on Mary's viewpoint, and where the picture name reflexive is coindexed with 'John', we generate ungrammaticality:

(23) * Mary was quite taken aback by the publicity John$_1$ was receiving. That picture of himself$_1$ in the paper had really annoyed her, and there was not much she could do about it

Pollard and Sag's moral is that, when a reflexive is exempt from Principle A, discourse considerations enter the picture: the reflexive must take an NP selecting the agent whose viewpoint is presented in the text as its antecedent. Pollard and Sag (1992: 277–8) also note that psychological verbs such as 'bother' make evident how the notion of viewpoint can be crucial in determining the antecedent of an anaphora. In the case of 'bother', for instance, it is natural to assume that the agent whose viewpoint is being reflected is the direct object of the verb. Thus, the contrast between sentences such as:

(24) a. The picture of himself$_1$ in *Newsweek* bothered John$_1$
   b. * The picture of himself$_1$ in *Newsweek* bothered John$_1$'s father

make clear that the ungrammaticality of (24b) is explained by the fact that the viewpoint represented is that of John's father, rather than John's. This phenomenon is further highlighted if we consider (24c–d) which, though structurally equivalent to the ungrammatical (24b), are grammatical insofar as they reflect John's viewpoint:

(24) c. The picture of himself$_1$ in *Newsweek* dominated John$_1$'s thoughts
   d. The picture of himself$_1$ in *Newsweek* made John$_1$'s day

Similar considerations apply to quasi-indicators and logophoric pronouns. The choice of a logophoric pronoun over an ordinary pronoun rests on considerations pertaining to discourse conditions. People dealing with logophoricity often appeal to notions such as point of view. Reinhart and Reuland (1991: 316–17), for instance, assume that a given utterance is associated with a *center* consisting of the (i) speaker and the hearer, (ii) the time of the utterance, and (iii) the location of the utterance. Pronouns used deictically will operate on the center to fix the reference. Logophoricity is explained as a relation between expressions and centers.[30] The center need not be actual in a report; it is likely to be the center of the attributee. This is particularly evident in the attribution of indexical thoughts to other people. A logophoric pronoun, like a quasi-indicator, depends on a *logocentric trigger*. The latter is the antecedent of the logophoric pronoun/quasi-indicator. Usually the logophoric trigger is an NP, which is the *subject* of the utterance denoting the attributee.[31] Besides, logophoricity is not a phenomenon confined to a single sentence. It can extend across a whole discourse in which the protagonist's egocentric perspective is discussed and reported. We can distinguish, though, between the *sentential logophoric domain* (this is typically constituted by a report of the form "NN believes that she* is F") and the *discourse logophoric domain*. Actually, it is not unusual to find languages (Ewe, Fon, Bwamu, ...) in which logophoric domains also operate across sentences. This is also the case in Donno Sɔ where a logophoric pronoun can occur anywhere in a stretch of indirect discourse. It can also appear embedded within another discourse. In that case the logophoric pronoun may refer to the person whose words, thoughts, etc. are being reported by someone in the higher indirect discourse or to the person doing the reporting (see Culy 1994*b*: 117). This feature parallels the discussion of multiple embedded reports containing quasi-indicators. We saw that a quasi-indicator can appear within a multiple embedded attribution, like 'she*' in "Jane told Igor that Julie believes that *she** is a spy" or 'he*' in "Tim said that Julie thinks that Mary believes that *he** is an intelligent man". This feature, if I am right, also parallels Castañeda's claim that the personal pronoun 'I' can also work as a quasi-indicator:

To complicate things further there is also the dependent quasi-indexical use of the first-person pronoun. Consider:

(6) I believe that I am heading for trouble

[30] "[L]ogophoricity is a relation between expressions and centers (whether actual, or reported). As such it is not strictly a sentence-level phenomenon ... a center-oriented use of third person anaphora does not require an antecedent in the sentence. As with first person anaphors they can find their referent in some center or assumed in previous context" (Reinhart and Reuland 1991: 316–17).

[31] "First, logocentric triggers are generally constrained to be a core-argument of the logocentric predicate of the matrix clause. Secondly, they are typically subjects. In other words, a logophoric pronoun is canonically subject-oriented. Contrariwise, a regular pronoun is not" (Huang 2000: 181).

On *one* interpretation, (6) is simply the first-person instance or filler of the quasi-indexical schema:

(7) X believes that he himself is heading for trouble

Clearly, the variable 'X' is instantiated into 'I' and this, by the agreement of grammatical person ... mandates that the quasi-indicator 'he himself' be replaced with 'I'. Thus, the second, the quasi-indexical 'I' in (6) has a meaning that includes the general meaning of 'he himself'. The role of the quasi-indicator 'he himself' is to depict first-person reference by the speaker. It is, therefore, not entirely vicarious as is the first-person pronoun in (3) [Satan believes of me that I am grouchy]. Yet it is an important difference. The quasi-indicator is a mechanism for the attribution, by depiction, of indexical reference, *not* for making it. Thus, the quasi-indicator 'I' in (6) represents a self-*attribution* of the making of first-person reference. (Castañeda 1983b: 322)

The main idea here can be summarized as follows. In a logophoric domain (whether a sentence or discourse), a logophoric pronoun or a quasi-indicator needs to have an antecedent from which it inherits its semantic value. The logophoric pronoun/quasi-indicator's peculiarity is that it attributes (it *depicts*, as Castañeda says) an indexical reference to the referent of the antecedent. This idea can also be captured using Kuno and Kaburaki's (1977) notion of *empathy*. Empathy corresponds to the speaker's identification (in varying degrees) with the person participating in the event described. Following this suggestion, a quasi-indicator is likely to be used when the reporter is empathizing with the attributee. The fact that one cannot empathize with someone more than one empathizes with oneself explains the difference between reports like:

(25) a. Jane hopes to win the tournament
    [Jane hopes PRO* to win the tournament]
  b. I expect Jane to win the tournament
    [I expect Jane PRO to win the tournament]
  c. (?) No one but herself, Jane expects to win the tournament
    [No one but herself, Jane expects PRO* to win the tournament][32]
  d. * Talking of Jane, I expect herself to win the tournament

The fact that (25a) receives a *de se* interpretation is explained by the fact that the reporter empathizes with the attributee, Jane. The fact that (25b) forces the *de re* reading is explained by the fact that the reporter does not (and cannot) empathize with Jane; the speaker cannot empathize with someone more than she empathizes with herself and this is pointed out by the presence of 'I'. This peculiarity should also explain the ungrammaticality of (25d): the reflexive 'herself' suggests that the speaker empathizes with Jane while the first-person pronoun underlines the

[32] Of the ten natives I questioned about this sentence, six said that it is acceptable, three expressed puzzlement, while one said that it is ungrammatical.

speaker's empathy with herself. This generates a conflict of empathy focus and, thus, ungrammaticality. As I understand it, the notion of empathy helps to explain how one can represent someone else's perspective. There is a kind of perspective switch when one uses a quasi-indicator to report someone else's thoughts. The reporter takes, so to speak, the attributee's perspective. The ungrammaticality of (25d) can thus be explained by the fact that the reporter uses 'I' and, because of this very fact, the reporter cannot take Jane's perspective. On the other hand, the grammaticality of (25a–c) is explained by the fact that the attributer takes Jane's perspective.[33]

A similar explanation can be proposed for Amharic, a language in which the first-person pronoun can work either deictically or as a logophoric pronoun when embedded in an attitude ascription (see Schlenker 2003):

(26) a. John Jägna näNN yt-lall
    [John$_1$ hero I$_1$ am says]
    (John$_1$ said that he$_1$ is a hero)
  b. w ndIme ymmiw dstIn lIJ ag NN
    [my brother whom he likes girl found]
    (My brother$_1$ found a girl he$_1$ likes)
  c. w ndIme ymmIw dstIn lIJ ag NN
    [my brother whom I like girl found]
    (My brother found a girl I like)

It seems that the first-person pronoun in Amharic can behave as a quasi-indicator. This seems to present an instantiation of Castañeda's prediction. In other words, the Amharic 'I' furnishes empirical evidence in favor of the thesis that, at the deep level, or level of logical form, 'I' functions as a quasi-indicator when embedded in a self-ascription such as:

(27) a. I think that I am in danger

and hence it must be understood along the lines of:

(27) b. Jane thinks that she* is in danger.

The correct representation of (27a) should thus be:

(27) c. I$_1$ think that I$_1^{d*}$ am in danger

which mirrors the representation of (27b):

(27) d. Jane$_1$ thinks that she$_1^{d*}$ is danger

This peculiarity can easily be explained in terms of point of view or empathy. In a self-report like (27a), the quasi-indexicality of the embedded 'I' depends on the

---

[33] These ideas go hand in hand with the notion of empathy I introduced and explained in Ch. 7. In particular, they reflect my claim that empathy is a central notion when we come to understand attitude ascription.

fact that it appears in an attitude ascription and that it reflects the viewpoint of the attributee (which happens to be the same as the attributer). In terms of empathy, this amounts to saying that the attributer empathizes with the attributee. Since the attributer and the attributee are the same, the reporter empathizes with herself and, thus, self-ascribes an 'I'-thought. The same pattern applies to multiple embedded self-ascriptions; thus, (28a) and (28b) should be treated on a par as well:

(28) a. I think that Igor believes that I am in danger
b. Jane thinks that Igor believes that she* is in danger

could be represented, respectively, as:

(28) c. I_1 think that Igor believes that $I_1^{d\star}$ am in danger
d. $Jane_1$ thinks that Igor believes that $she_1^{d\star}$ is danger

Once again, the quasi-indexicality of the embedded 'I' is explained by the fact that it reflects the point of view of the attributee, i.e. the subject of the 'that'-clause 'that I am in danger'. As a further example of a situation in which 'I' should be understood as a quasi-indicator, we can present the following situation.

(29) Jane to Ivan: "You are in danger"

In reporting what Jane said, Ivan would probably say:

(29) a. Jane told me that I am in danger

while Jane would say:

(29) b. I told Ivan that he himself is in danger

while a third party would report:

(29) c. Jane told Ivan that he himself is in danger

All these reports present the same underlying structure:

(29) d. X told Y_1 that $s/he_1^{d\star}$ is in danger

This should highlight the parallel between the occurrence of 'I' in (29a) and the quasi-indicator 'he himself' in (29b) and (29c), i.e. it suggests that the second occurrence of 'I' in (29b) is best understood as a quasi-indicator. If 'I' were not understood as a quasi-indicator, (29a) would be an instance of the schema:

(29) e. X told Y that Y is in danger

But a report like

(29) f. Jane told Igor that Igor is in danger

is an instantiation of this schema and yet (29f) does not represent an accurate report. Neither Jane nor Jon or a third party would report (29) in uttering (29f).

To summarize, we can say that quasi-indicators and logophoric pronouns are *oratio obliqua* pronouns which represent the attributee's point of view. As such, they attribute a given perspective to the attributee. Quasi-indicators are the *oratio obliqua* mechanism enabling a reporter to capture the attributee's egocentric setting, i.e. the perspective (agent, time, location) of the latter. As an example we can quote the following exchange between A in San Francisco and B in LA:

    A: Will you be *here* tomorrow?
    B: If it is raining I won't be *there**

where 'here' picks out the place of A's utterance which is, to borrow Reinhart & Reuland's terminology, the center of A's utterance. 'There' is coreferential and it inherits its reference from 'here'. With the quasi-indicator 's/he*' we have a similar phenomenon:

    A to C: (1) I_1^i won the lottery.
    B to C: (2) What did she_1^d say?
    C to B: (3) She_1^d said that she_1^{d*} won the lottery.
    C to D: (4) A_1^i told B_2 that she_1^{d*} won the lottery. She_1^d is now rich.

The center enabling us to fix the reference of 'I' is furnished by A's utterance; the referent is the agent of (1). The very same center, thanks to the anaphoric chain, also allows us to fix the reference of the anaphor 'she' and the quasi-indicator 'she*'. Their reference is inherited from 'I' in (1). The quasi-indicator 'she*' in (3) and (4) also attributes to the utterer of (1) a use of the first-person pronoun and thus an 'I'-thought. To be precise, the quasi-indicator 'she*' in (3) inherits its reference from the anaphoric pronoun 'she' whose initiator is 'I' in (1). The same goes for the quasi-indicator 'she*' in (4); it inherits its semantic value from 'A'. As a general rule governing the third-person quasi-indicator 's/he*', we can thus propose the following:

- *The quasi-indicator's antecedent*
  The antecedent of a third-person quasi-indicator must be an NP referring to, or ranging over, the *agent(s)* whose attitude is/are reported. When a quasi-indicator is linked to a referring NP, the latter need not be the immediate antecedent and can occur in distant clauses.

In the case of multiple embedded ascriptions, a quasi-indicator may not appear in the immediate subjacent clause. In

    (30) $Jane_1$ told Igor that Jon believes that she_1* won the lottery

for instance, the quasi-indicator 'she' is coreferential with 'Jane' and, therefore, it does not appear in the immediate subjacent 'that'-clause. We have cross-linguistic evidence in favor of this fact as well, for the logophoric pronoun of Ewe is not restricted to the immediate subjacent clause but can appear in clauses at *any* depth of embedding (see Clements 1975: 154).

5. Quasi-Indicators and the Unanalyzability Thesis

A quasi-indicator cannot be substituted *salva veritate* by a coreferring term:

There is no individual constant 'a' containing no occurrence of the quasi-indicator 'he*' such that: "The Editor of *Soul* knows that he* is a millionaire" either (i) entails or (ii) is entailed by its corresponding statement of the form "The Editor of *Soul* knows that *a* is a millionaire. (Castañeda 1968: 442)

In the case of multiple embedded sentences such as:

(31) a. Sue said that she* said that Jon said that she* is rich.

Castañeda's position is that, although both occurrences of 'she*' have as their antecedent 'Sue', only the first occurrence depends on it immediately. The second occurrence of 'she*' depends on the preceding occurrence of 'she*' and it is only *via* this first occurrence that it refers back to 'Sue'. Since the first occurrence is separated from its antecedent by only one psychological prefix, Castañeda characterizes it an *occurrence of degree 1*. The second occurrence of 'she*' is separated from its antecedent by two psychological prefixes. It is thus an *occurrence of degree 2*. (31a) can thus be represented as:

(31) b. Sue said that [she* believes that [Jon said that [she* is rich]]]

A report like this is silent on the way in which Jon referred to (and thought about) Sue. Jon may have said "You [addressing Sue] are rich", "Sue is rich", "The woman in this picture [pointing to a picture of Sue] is rich", etc. Castañeda claims that a quasi-indicator occurrence of degree 2 is analyzable *via* an occurrence of degree 1 and the occurrence of an existential quantifier ranging over possible ways of referring. It is important to note that Castañeda claims that occurrences of degree 1 are unanalyzable. I call this the *Unanalyzability Thesis*:

T1. The occurrences of 'he*' of degree 1 are unanalyzable; they constitute a peculiar and irreducible mechanism of reference to persons

T2. Each occurrence of 'he*' of degree greater than 1 is analyzable in terms of both occurrences of 'he*' of degree 1 and occurrences of one existential quantifier per pseudo-antecedent. (Castañeda 1968: 447)

To understand the Unanalyzability Thesis, we can use the notion of indices and dependence previously introduced. Thus the subscript numbers signal coevaluation and the superscripts '*i*' and '*d*' signal referentially independent and referentially dependent terms respectively. The use of these notions can be illustrated by:

(32) a. Sue believes that she is rich but she does not believe that she is rich

One possible consistent reading of (32a) is represented as:

(32) b. Sue$_1'$ believes that she$_1^d$ is rich but she$_1^d$ does not believe that she* is rich

where the reference of both occurrences of 'she' depend on the reference of 'Sue'. The quasi-indicator 'she*' helps to stress that Sue does not believe herself to be rich in the first-person mood, i.e. that Sue is not disposed to express her belief using 'I'. Another possible (and maybe more natural) reading of (32a) would be:

(32) c. Sue$_1'$ believes that she$_1^d$ is rich but she$_1^d$ does not believe that she$_2'$ is rich

where the last occurrence of 'she' is as a demonstrative pronoun; hence it need not be coindexed with 'Sue' and it is referentially independent. If, however, (32a) were represented as:

(32) d. Sue$_1'$ believes that she$_1^d$ is rich but she$_1^d$ does not believe that she$_1^d$ is rich

we would ascribe a contradictory belief to Sue, for we would state that Sue both believes and does not believe that she is rich. The only way Sue can consistently and rationally both believe that she is rich and not believe that she is rich is to entertain the first belief from a third-person point of view and the second from the first-person point of view, or *vice versa*. The quasi-indicator 'she*' in (32b) helps to stress this very fact; if we aim to capture Sue's different attitudes *vis-à-vis* herself, we cannot avoid using the quasi-indicator 'she*'. The reference of the quasi-indicator 'she*' in (32b) also depends on the reference of 'Sue'[34] and (32b) could thus be represented as:

(32) e. Sue$_1'$ believes that she$_1^d$ is rich but she$_1^d$ does not believe that she$_1^{d*}$ is rich

The anaphoric chain at work here could be represented as follows:

(32) f. Sue$_1'$ believes that she$_1^d$ is rich but she$_1^d$ does not believe that she$_1^{d*}$ is rich

6. Analyzing 'Herself'

Reinhart and Reuland (1991) propose an analysis of 'self' of *self*-anaphors as a relational noun rather than a determiner. Hence, the structure of 'self' has two arguments and can be represented as: SELF<x, y>. Semantically, SELF is an

---

[34] To be precise, we should say that the occurrence of the quasi-indicator depends on the second occurrence of 'she', which itself depends on the first occurrence of 'she', which finally depends on the occurrence of 'Sue'.

identity relation (identifying x and y). When SELF combines with a pronoun determiner, we obtain the noun phrase:

- Herself = her₁[SELF <x₁,y>]

This noun phrase contains an unsaturated argument, 'y', which must be saturated in order for the reflexive to have a semantic value: "Under this view, it is this missing argument which is responsible for the defective nature of SELF-NPs, i.e. for their anaphoric status" (Reinhart & Reuland 1991: 286). In other words, following this interpretation the value of a self-anaphor is provided by the unsaturated argument.

In favor of treating SELF as an identity relation, we can appeal to empirical evidence. If we translate 'him/herself' into Italian or French, for instance, we obtain 'lui/lei *stesso/a*' and 'lui/elle-*même*', where the Italian '*stesso/a*' and the French '*même*' translate into English as 'same'; the literal translation of 'lui/lei *stesso/a*' and 'lui/elle-*même*' into English is 'him/her *same*'.

The first question that springs to mind is whether we can adopt Reinhart & Reuland's proposal in analyzing Castañeda's notion of quasi-indicators. In particular, can quasi-indicators be explained away as self-anaphors? Let us consider:

(33) a. Sue believes herself to be rich

which, following Reinhart & Reuland's suggestion, is analyzed as:

(33) b. Sue₁ⁱ believes [her₁ᵈ SELF(x₁ᵈ, y₁ᵈ)]₁ᵈ to be rich

where the anaphoric link (and thus the reference of the reflexive 'herself') is secured by the argument 'y'. This, however, does not capture a report like:

(34) a. Sue believes that she (herself) is rich

for (33a) represents a *de re* attribution. Following the traditional notation, (33a) could be represented as:

(33) c. Of Sue, Sue believes her to be rich
d. ∃x (x = Sue & Sue believes x is rich)

(33a) could continue as:

(33) e. Sue believes herself to be rich but she does not believe that she herself is rich

But (34a) cannot be continued in this way, for it is a *de se* attribution, i.e. an ascription attributing an 'I'-thought. If (34a) were to continue as:

(34) b. Sue believes that she (herself) is rich but she does not believe that she (herself) is rich

we would have a contradiction. This provides further evidence that (33a) is not equivalent to (34a) and, therefore, that unlike (33a), (34a) is not a *de re* ascription.

304   *Anaphora and Quasi-Indexicality*

The moral, so far, is the following: since (33a) does not represent a *de se* ascription and since *de se* ascriptions do not reduce to *de re* ones, (33b) cannot constitute a good analysis of quasi-indicators. (34a) should be analyzed as:

(34) c. Sue$_1{}'$ believes that she$_1{}^d$ [her$_1{}^d$ SELF($x_1{}^d$, $y_1{}^d$)]$_1{}^d$ is rich

where the anaphoric link (and thus the reference) of the quasi-indicator 'she (herself)' is secured by 'she' being anaphoric on 'Sue'. The reference of the reflexive still depends on the argument 'y', but the latter is linked to 'she' which happens to be anaphoric on 'Sue'. Following this analysis, a quasi-indicator can be viewed as an anaphoric pronoun. The anaphoric nature of the quasi-indicator, unlike the anaphoric nature of a self-anaphora, is not secured by the argument 'y' but by the pronoun 'she'. This, as we will see in the next section, turns out to be an important difference between self-anaphors and quasi-indicators: in fact, it is *the* difference.

7. Quasi-Indicators *qua* Attributive Anaphors

To begin with, let us consider:

(35) a. Mary believes that Jane (herself) is the culprit
(36) a. Mary believes that she (herself) is the culprit.

What is the difference between (35a) and (36a)? In particular, what is the difference between 'Jane (herself)' in (35a) and 'she (herself)' in (36a)? The main difference is that in (35a), 'Jane' is a proper name and, as such, it is referentially *independent*. Proper names are not anaphors. Thus, as far as reference-fixing is concerned, they are always independent. On the other hand, (36a) can have two interpretations, depending on whether the pronoun 'she' is a (referentially independent) demonstrative used by the reporter to single out an object of discourse, or an anaphoric (referentially dependent) pronoun inheriting its reference from the antecedent to which it is linked ('Sue', in our example). The presence of the reflexive 'herself', however, strongly suggests the latter interpretation. I do not know whether an utterance like (35a) will allow a demonstrative interpretation of 'she', i.e. whether it allows us to interpret 'she' as an independent NP, or whether the reflexive 'herself' forces the anaphoric reading. However, for argument's sake, let us assume that both readings are allowed. (36a) can be represented, at least in principle, in the following two ways:

(36) b. Mary$_1{}'$ believes that she$_1{}^d$ (herself) is the culprit
     c. Mary$_1{}'$ believes that she$_2{}'$ (herself) is the culprit.

(36b) gives us the quasi-indexical interpretation. The difference between (35a) and (36a), like the difference between (36b) and (36c), does not explain the fact that quasi-indicators are attributive pronouns. It stresses the fact that the quasi-indicator 'she (herself)', unlike the NP 'Jane (herself)', is an anaphoric pronoun. Its reference depends on the antecedent it is coindexed with (and dependent on). The difference between 'she (herself)' in (36a) and 'Sue (herself)' in (35a) does not stress the fact that 'she (herself)' in (36a) also attributes an 'I'-thought to the referent of its antecedent, Mary.

In order to capture the attributive feature of a quasi-indicator, it may be worth focusing on (35a) and, in particular, on the role that the reflexive 'herself' plays when it is coupled with a proper name (or a pronoun used demonstratively), i.e. when it is coupled with an independent NP. The analysis that comes to mind is to treat the reflexive as being used in an *emphatic* way. That is, 'herself' is used to stress the NP it is coupled with and, thus, to stress the fact that the referent of the NP is the focus of attention. Can we tell the same story (or a similar story) when the reflexive 'herself' is coupled with an anaphoric pronoun? Could quasi-indicators be explained as *emphatic anaphors*? If so, where would the emphasis be put? One might be tempted to claim that, from a semantic viewpoint, a quasi-indicator is nothing but an anaphoric pronoun performing an emphatic act. In other words, a quasi-indicator is an anaphoric pronoun that *pragmatically* conveys that the subject of the attitude thought of her/himself in the first-person mode. This information, however, is *not* semantically encoded. Hence, from a semantic viewpoint, quasi-indicators and anaphors should be treated on a par. This is, for instance, Böer and Lycan's strategy:

Of course 'he himself' refers, not just referentially, but in a further special way. Our claim is that it refers in a *pragmatically* special way. There is a pragmatic constraint on the use of 'he himself' to the effect that an occurrence of 'he himself' inside the scope of a verb of propositional attitudes denotes the subject of that verb; there may be further pragmatic constraints on the use of indexical pronouns that will explain why (1a) [John believes that he himself is in danger] implies or suggests that John is willing to assert "I am in danger". (Böer and Lycan 1980: 441)

On this understanding, the reflexive 'herself' does not play any relevant semantic role and the quasi-indicator 'she (herself)' does not differ from the anaphoric pronoun 'she'. In particular, it can be substituted *salva veritate* by its antecedent.[35] Hence (37a–d) would not differ in truth-value:

(37) a. Mary$_1^i$ believes that she$_1^d$ (herself) is the culprit
   b. Mary$_1^i$ believes that she$_1^d$ is the culprit
   c. Mary$_1^i$ believes that she$_1^i$ [pointing to Mary] is the culprit
   d. Mary$_1^i$ believes that Mary$_1^i$ is the culprit

---

[35] Not all anaphoric pronouns, though, can be replaced *salva veritate* by their antecedent. In some cases the grammar itself prevents such replacement. In "Jon bought some wine and Mary drank it", we cannot replace the anaphoric pronoun 'it' with its antecedent 'some wine' to obtain "Jon bought some wine and Mary drank some wine". For an up-to-date discussion of this and related phenomena see e.g. Neale (1990).

Is this a plausible conclusion? Can one be happy with the view that Castañeda's data can be explained away pragmatically?

If the analysis of the 'self' of self-NPs I have proposed (following Reinhart and Reuland) is correct, the pragmatic strategy is not compelling. If 'self' can be viewed as a relational noun (as an identity relation), then the attributive nature of a quasi-indicator cannot be explained away as a mere pragmatic fact. The fact that 'self' is an identity relation is semantically conveyed, for the structure of a compound noun phrase like 'NN (herself)' or 'she (herself)' corresponds to:

- NN/she (her[SELF $<x,y>$]

The argument 'y' of SELF is linked to either the proper name 'NN' or the pronoun 'she'. Because of this (syntactic) link, 'herself' cannot be discharged as a mere pragmatic phenomenon. It is *syntactically* linked to the name or pronoun it is coupled with. Since one of the arguments of the identity relation (of SELF) is saturated by the NP to which the argument 'y' is linked, the self-nature of the compound noun phrase cannot be dismissed. In other words, by virtue of the fact that this (syntactic) link is built into the meaning of 'herself', the emphasis in these cases is part of the meaning of a self-NP; it is, therefore, semantically conveyed. It is for this reason that a quasi-indicator cannot, *pace* Böer and Lycan, be explained away as a pragmatic phenomenon. For this very reason, quasi-indicators are best viewed as attributive anaphors, i.e. they present the feature "+ anaphor, + attributive".

I can tentatively conclude this chapter by proposing the following two considerations, which should help us to understand the difference between a self-anaphor and a quasi-indicator:

- *Self-anaphors*

When the argument 'y' of the relational noun SELF of a self-NP is saturated by an independent noun phrase (e.g. a proper name: 'Jon (himself)', a demonstrative: 'you (yourself)', a description: 'the girl (herself)'), reference is fixed/selected by the independent NP and the self-NP is used in an emphatic way, i.e. to put the stress on the NP that 'y' is linked to.[36] e.g.

(38) a. In last night's accident, *Jane*[i] injured *herself*[d]
b. *That politician*[i] takes *himself*[d] very seriously

---

[36] A way to understand this kind of emphatic use of the reflexive would be along the use of particles like 'exactly', 'precisely', and 'just' in utterances like "Ivan is just/exactly/precisely the student Jane was looking for". As König suggests: "[these particles] are primarily used emphatically to assert the identity of one argument in a proposition with an argument in a different, contextually given proposition. Such an identification may be achieved via exclusion. This is probably the right analysis for G. *genau* and E. *exactly, precisely,* and *just*" (König 1991: 127). It may be worth mentioning that this account goes hand in hand with the multiple proposition view I defended in Ch. 3, above.

c. I believe that *Jon^i himself^d* ate all the cookies
   d. *The woman^i* you just saw considers *herself^d* to be very intelligent

- *Quasi-indicators*

When the argument 'y' of the relational noun SELF of a self-NP is saturated by an anaphoric pronoun, we have a quasi-indicator. Reference is fixed/selected by the antecedent of the anaphoric pronoun and the self-NP plays an attributive role; it attributes to the semantic value of the anaphoric pronoun an 'I'-thought. e.g.

(39) a. *Mary* believes that *she^d (herself)^d* is a queen
   b. *Jon* thinks that Jane believes that *he^d (himself)^d* is handsome
   c. *Jeff* did not think that *he^d (himself)^d* was the culprit[37]

To put it in a nutshell, when '(him/herself)' is linked to a *dependent* pronoun (an anaphora), the whole noun phrase is a quasi-indicator and thus a kind of attributive anaphora. When it is linked to an *independent* noun phrase, we merely have a self-NP.

Last, but not least: a third-person quasi-indicator always takes as its antecedent an NP referring to the *subject* of an attitude, while the value of a self-NP need not be the subject of an attitude. As the examples I have given above show, quasi-indicators like 'she (herself)' attribute an egological perspective to the protagonist, the subject, of an attitude ascription.

---

[37] It goes without saying that, when a quasi-indicator appears in the scope of a negation, it is used to deny that an 'I'-thought was entertained by the referent of its antecedent.

Quasi-Indexicality and Puzzling Reports

9

> If we could recover our pre-Fregean semantic innocence, I think it would seem to us plainly incredible that the words 'The earth moves', uttered after the words 'Galileo said that', mean anything different, or refer to anything else, than is their wont when they come in different environments.
>
> (Davidson 1968: 108)

> If a strict Millian view is correct, and the linguistic function of a proper name is completely exhausted by the fact that it names its bearer, it would appear that proper names of the same thing are everywhere interchangeable not only *salva veritate* but even *salva significatione*: the proposition expressed by a sentence should remain the same no matter what name of the object it uses. Of course this will not be true if names are 'mentioned' rather than 'used'.
>
> (Kripke 1979: 104)

In this chapter, I propose a picture of attitude ascriptions that goes hand in hand with the conception of quasi-indicators I formulated in the previous chapter. The picture I propose also matches the notion of *n*-acceptance of a sentence I discussed in Chapter 7. I defend the following general idea: in an attitude ascription, we relate the attributee to a proposition *and* a sentence. The latter is the sentence the reporter uses to classify the attributee's mental state. This classification can be more or less accurate and often is; a classification can often only be partial.

I proceed as follows. In Section 1, I claim, *pace* Boër and Lycan, that quasi-indexicality cannot be explained away as a mere pragmatic phenomenon. The presence of a quasi-indicator in an attitude ascription affects the truth-condition of the attribution. In Section 2, I focus on attribution of 'I'-thoughts and I show that they can be accounted for only by assuming the presence of quasi-indicators, which in turn should be understood along logophoric pronouns. I show how conceptions that assume that a *de se* attribution relates the attributee to a property (like Chisholm's and Lewis's, for example) do not succeed in explaining away quasi-indicators.

In Section 3, I argue that 'that'-clauses play a dual role and that they are best understood in a similar way to Quine's 'Giorgione'-sentence: just as 'Giorgione' in "Giorgione was so-called because of his size" is both used and mentioned, an expression embedded within a 'that'-clause can be both used and mentioned. This feature is also supported by the fact that quasi-indicators should be understood as attributive anaphors. Thus, because they display the features +anaphora and +attributive, quasi-indicators contribute the attributee into the proposition expressed by the 'that'-clause and, at the same time, also attribute a thought to (or contribute to specifying the mental state of) the attributee. In Section 4, I propose a logical form for attitude ascriptions that enables us to capture the data proposed so far. I show that, when appearing in a construction of the form "*A* believes that *p*", an attitude verb should be understood as a triadic predicate relating the attributee, *A*, to both the proposition *that p* and a sentence that *A* would accept in believing that *p*. In Section 5, I show how this position does not commit itself to the thesis that attributions in different languages cannot have the same truth-conditions, despite the appeal to sentences in cashing out the logical form of ascriptions. In so doing, I explain away Church's translation argument against sententialism. I also show how the proposed picture fits with the idea, defended in Chapter 6, that many of our thoughts are perspectival and thus that the very same ascription can attribute the same mental state on both Earth and twin-Earth, even if it relates the respective attributees to different propositions. In Section 6, I show that the advocated picture helps us to characterize the *de re, de dicto*, and *de se* distinction. I show that some reports (e.g. multiple embedded reports with quasi-indicators) are mixed reports. I then argue, in Section 7, that the *de re, de dicto*, and *de se* distinction must be complemented by the opaque/transparent distinction (with respect to propositions) and that propositional opacity/transparency proceeds by degrees. This helps us to explain in more detail how we are bound to be unfaithful in our ascriptions (see Chapter 7, Section 8 above). Finally, in Section 8, I show how the suggested picture helps us to capture some inferences and to explain away some alleged puzzles concerning attitude ascriptions, especially the ones involving indexical expressions.

1. Quasi-Indicators: Pragmatics or Semantics?

The view I defended in the previous chapter when I proposed to analyze quasi-indicators along logophoric pronouns entails that the presence of a quasi-indicator affects the truth-value of the report in which it appears. One of the main theses has been that reports like:

(1) Privatus believes that he himself (he*) is a millionaire
(2) Privatus believes that Privatus is a millionaire

may differ in truth-value. On top of saying that Privatus believes of himself that he is a millionaire, (1) *also* signals that he thinks of himself in entertaining an 'I'-thought (whereas (2) does not). For this very reason, the quasi-indicator 'he*' cannot be replaced *salva veritate* by a coreferring term (such as 'Privatus', for example).

As I have anticipated (see Chapter 8, Section 8), Böer and Lycan (among others) claim that quasi-indicators can be explained away as a mere pragmatic phenomenon. As such, they do not contribute to the semantics of attitude ascriptions. Hence, attitude ascriptions like (1) and (2) could not differ in truth-value.[1] This amounts to saying that the information that an attribution like (1) attributes to Privatus (i.e. that he entertained an 'I'-thought) is, at best, pragmatically imparted. It is not semantically encoded. Böer and Lycan go as far as dismissing the Irreducibility Thesis—i.e. the thesis that indexicals cannot be explained away without destroying their cognitive impact their use conveys—in all its manifestations:

> [C]ontra Castañeda, Perry, Lewis, and the rest, we need not admit that the content of an attitude *de se* is inexpressible by any nonperspectival, third-person sentence. The content of John's belief in (1a) [John believes that he himself is in danger] is the proposition that John is in danger (we might think of this proposition, *à la* Russell as being a pair consisting of John himself and the property of being in danger)... Thus if one holds that the objects of propositional attitudes are propositions in the traditional sense of that term or something like it, one can hold that the objects of attitudes *de se* are ordinary propositions in just the same sense. . . . there is nothing special about the semantic content of the proposition expressed; all that is distinctive are the pragmatic rules that compute the indexical terms' denotata. (Böer and Lycan 1980: 433)

Furthermore:

> Of course 'he himself' refers, not just referentially, but in a further special way. Our claim is that it refers in a *pragmatically* special way. There is a pragmatic constraint on the use of 'he himself' to the effect that an occurrence of 'he himself' inside the scope of a verb of propositional attitudes denotes the subject of that verb; there may be further pragmatic constraints on the use of indexical pronouns that will explain why (1a) [John believes that he himself is in danger] implies or suggests that John is willing to assert "I am in danger." (Böer and Lycan 1980: 441)

Böer and Lycan's objection rests on the plausible thesis that a singular term, whether appearing in an *oratio recta* or *oratio obliqua* construction, is used by the speaker and/or writer.[2] To be precise, we should say that it is used by the agent of

---

[1] The idea that sentences like these do not differ in truth-value and that Frege-inspired puzzles must be explained away using the Gricean apparatus of pragmatic implicature has been more recently championed, among others, by Salmon (1986).

[2] "When a purely referential designator occurs transparently, even within the scope of an operator that is capable of creating opacity, the designator is in the mouth of the utterer of the whole sentence, and *in no way* in the mouth of any subject to whom the utterer may be ascribing a propositional attitude" (Böer and Lycan 1980: 438).

the utterance, insofar as one can make utterance using tokens produced by someone else (e.g. post-it notes and answering machines; see Chapter 5, Section 4 for an exhaustive discussion of this phenomenon). One need not reject the thesis that a singular term, whether embedded in an *oratio obliqua* construction or in *oratio recta*, is used by the agent of the utterance to single out a given object. That is, *pace* Frege, one need not give up semantic innocence. In particular, one need not embrace the thesis that embedded terms do not refer to their customary referents. From this, though, it does not follow that *de se* ascriptions are not semantically relevant and thus that quasi-indicators are pragmatic in nature.

The reference of a quasi-indicator is fixed in the very same way as the reference of an anaphoric pronoun. An anaphor is used by the agent of the utterance and if it is linked to a singular term corefers with the term it is linked and coindexed with. Quasi-indicators, like logophoric pronouns, when linked to singular terms refer in a dependent way as well and are also used by the agent of the utterance.

Besides, the pragmatic explanation falls short of explaining the cases in which a *de se* interpretation is forced by grammar, as is the case with silent subjects in infinitival clauses. As we saw (Chapter 8, Section 2), this subject, PRO*, must be understood as a quasi-indicator. PRO* contributes to the semantics of attitude ascriptions. A position which rejects the semantic relevance of *de se* attitudes and, therefore, does not allow us to capture the semantic nature of PRO* should be rejected. To the best of my knowledge, the friends of the pragmatic version claim that *de se* attributions, whether or not they involve PRO*, should be explained away in pragmatic terms. Thus one is not constrained to deny the existence of *de se* attributions; all the friend of the pragmatic explanation denies is the semantic relevance of them. If I was right in arguing that the silent subject of an infinitival clause is often understood as a quasi-indicator and that such understanding is forced by the grammar, i.e. it is syntactically driven, then I am also right in claiming that *de se* attributions of this kind *are* semantically relevant. A given interpretation cannot be syntactically forced and play no semantic role. It would be like claiming that the utterance of a sentence like "It is snowing" does not pick out a location because no morpheme in it stands for a location and, therefore, that the relevant location is at best pragmatically imparted. If, as I believe, an utterance like "It is snowing" tacitly refers to a given location *because* 'to snow' is a two-place relation taking times and locations as arguments, then the place where it is snowing is semantically encoded.[3] In other words, if one accepts that there is an implicit argument for a location at work and that this argument is a syntactic requirement, then the location where it is snowing is semantically relevant and

---

[3] See Ch. 2, Sect. 3, above for a full account and discussion of tacit reference involving meteorological terms. As for the thesis that PRO must be understood as a quasi-indicator, see Ch. 8, Sect. 2, above.

affects the truth-value of the utterance. A similar story can be told about PRO*. If PRO* is syntactically required (and I have argued that it is), then it is semantically relevant. As we saw (Chapter 8, Section 2), the Italian 'proprio' [self] forces a similar *de se* interpretation.

Against the pragmatic explanation we can further quote cases *in English* where a pronoun cannot be replaced by a coreferential NP. Consider:

(3) a. That Ali₁ was the best boxer in the world was claimed by him₁ repeatedly
 b. *That he₁ was the best boxer in the world was claimed by Ali₁ repeatedly

In (3a), the subordinate clause "is the direct discourse representation of what Ali said" (Kuno 1987: 106). Kuno hypothesizes that the derivation of (3a) starts with the following underlying structure:

(3) c. [Ali claimed ["I am the best boxer in the world"]]

With the rule of indirect discourse formation (tense and person agreement), we then have:

(3) d. Ali claimed that *he was* the best boxer in the world

where the first-person pronoun changes to 'he', in agreement with 'Ali'. Kuno claims that there are no transformations that would change 'I' to 'Ali' and, therefore, that it is not possible to use 'Ali' in this position. This explains why (3a) is grammatical while (3b) is not. This seems to bring in further evidence in favor of understanding the pronoun 'he' in (3d) and (3a) to be a quasi-indicator that cannot be replaced by its antecedent, 'Ali'.

2. *De Se* Reports

If we follow Böer & Lycan's proposal and claim that the *de se* interpretation of an infinitive clause is nothing but a case of the *de re* interpretation, then why does a (*de re*) ascription like "Privatus believes that Privatus is rich" lack, i.e. linguistically prevent, the *de se* interpretation? The moral seems to be that the pragmatic explanation does not fit the linguistic facts. As a further example (from Reinhart, quoted in Chierchia 1989: 23), we can also mention:

(4) a. Jon wants to become a doctor but his mother does not want to
 b. Jon wants to become a doctor but his mother does not want that

While (4a) has only the sloppy reading meaning, "his mother does not want to become a doctor", (4b) allows the strict reading, "his mother does not want Jon to become a doctor" as well. If I am right in believing that the sloppy (*de se*) reading in an attribution like (4a), unlike an attribution like (4b), is forced by grammar, then I am also right in claiming that the pragmatic explanation falls short of giving us an account of this phenomenon. If so, we cannot explain away *de se* ascriptions as merely a subclass of *de re* ascriptions, which can be accounted for pragmatically.

Some (e.g. Chierchia) could argue that, in order to capture the perspectival nature of indexical thoughts, we should give up the idea that *de se* ascriptions relate agents to propositions.[4] *De se* attributions relate agents and properties and *de se* attributions can be explained as self-ascriptions of properties. I characterize this position *the property attribution explanation*. It is worth noticing that Lewis and Chisholm claim that they can handle *de se* attributions—and thus explain away quasi-indicators as a mere pragmatic phenomena—within their general account of attitude ascriptions, for the latter is property-based. On their account, attitude ascriptions in general relate an agent to a property, not a proposition:

Believing must be construed as a relation between a believer and *some* other thing; this much is essential to *any* theory of belief ... The simplest conception ... is the one which construes believing as a relation involving a believer and a property—a property which he may be said to attribute to himself. (Chisholm 1981: 27)

An attribution involving quasi-indicators is such that it attributes to the attributee the self-ascription of a given property.[5] A report like (1) attributes to Privatus the self-ascription of the property of being a millionaire. Following Chisholm's proposal, (1) could be analyzed as:

(1) b. The property of being a millionaire is such that Privatus directly attributes it to Privatus.

This proposal, though, is not fine-grained enough to capture some *de se* attitudes. If, for instance, Privatus wrongly believes that vixens are wild dogs, then, after a night of chasing the animal that killed his rabbits, he may say:

(5) a. I believe that I shot a female fox
    b. I do not believe that I shot a vixen

---

[4] The idea that indexical thoughts are intrinsically perspectival rests on the Irreducibility Thesis I discussed in Ch. 8, Sect. 1, above, i.e. on the fact that indexicals are essential and irreducible to other mechanisms of reference. It goes without saying, though, that if one rejects this thesis one is likely to reject the idea that thoughts expressed using indexicals are perspectival.

[5] "*x* believes that he himself is *F* = Df. The property of being *F* is such that *x* directly attributes it to *x*" (Chisholm 1981: 28). Chierchia, unlike Lewis and Chisholm, maintains that only *de se* attributions must be treated as self-ascriptions of properties and that *de re* ascriptions relate the attributee to a proposition. Chierchia argues that we must introduce the self-ascription of properties story in order to capture the nature of *de se* attributions. This story (unlike Chisholm's, for instance) is not independently motivated.

From the third-person perspective these self-ascriptions would be rendered as:

(6) a. Privatus believes that he himself (he*) shot a female fox
    b. Privatus does not believe that he himself (he*) shot a vixen

Following Chisholm's proposal (6a) is analyzed as:

(6) c. The property of shooting a female fox is such that Privatus directly attributes it to Privatus

Given that the property of shooting a female fox is identical to the property of shooting a vixen, (6c) is equivalent to (6d):

(6) d. The property of shooting a vixen is such that Privatus directly attributes it to Privatus

(6d), though, represents the ascription:

(6) e. Privatus believes that he himself (he*) shot a vixen

But (6e) contradicts (6b). The moral seems to be that quasi-indicators cannot be explained away. They are irreducible. The property attribution explanation is thus unsatisfactory.[6]

I now turn to discuss another position, *the hidden indexical* explanation.[7] This position is the one championed by Crimmins and Perry (1989). Following this theory, an attitude ascription relates the attributee to both the proposition expressed by the 'that'-clause and something else. It is the latter which is supposed to capture the mental state of the attributee, i.e. to capture the way the proposition is entertained. The third relatum is a compound cognitive particular. Roughly, this is a token mental state made up by notions (cognitive particulars of individuals) and ideas (cognitive particulars of properties). The ideas and notions under which the attributee grasps the proposition expressed by the 'that'-clause are contextually furnished. They are, to use Crimmins and Perry's terminology, *unarticulated constituents* of the report. It is the context that forces them into the report, but they are not triggered by an indexical present either at the surface or deep level of the report. For this reason this theory could be better labeled the *tacit reference* theory of attitude ascriptions.[8] Nothing in the grammar or logical form of the report stands

---

[6] As we saw (Ch. 8, Sect. 2), Chierchia views PRO as a property-abstractor and argues that the logical form (LF) of "The cat wants to eat the cheese" is "The cat$_1$ wants λ_1 [PRO$_1$ to eat the cheese]." As I just pointed out, though, this representation does not cut finely enough to capture the nature of *de se* ascriptions. Thus the regimentation I proposed, i.e. "The cat$_1$ wants [PRO$_1$* to eat the cheese]", differs from (and cannot be reduced to) Chierchia's. In particular, quasi-indicators cannot be analyzed using a property-abstractor.

[7] The term 'hidden indexical' comes from Schiffer (1992). An early version of The Hidden Indexical Theory can already be found in Schiffer 1977. See also Schiffer 1987a and 1987b for further discussions of it. Schiffer, though, does not endorse this theory.

[8] In characterizing the hidden indexical position, Schiffer (1977; 1992) does not postulate the existence of implicit indexicals as well; he merely argues that within this theory an ascription *tacitly* refers to ways of believing/thinking/... a proposition.

for the notions and ideas that the report tacitly refers to. To put it into a nutshell, a report relates an agent to a proposition and a thought (a token composed of notions and ideas), but nothing in the report or in the report's logical form refers to this thought:

> [T]here is nothing mysterious here, and there is no reason to postulate two different pronouns 'he'. What happens in these cases is simply that the agent is claimed to have a belief about herself *via her self-notion*. The puzzle about indexical belief reports really amounts to just that. (Crimmins 1992: 165)

If I am right in claiming that the unpronounced subject of an infinitival clause must often be understood as a quasi-indicator, then we do have evidence that the *de se* nature of a report is forced into the latter by grammar and, therefore, that quasi-indicators cannot be explained away as unarticulated constituents of the report. Castañeda was thus right in postulating the existence of different uses of the third-person pronoun when it appears in an *oratio obliqua* construal. In the previous chapter I also proposed cross-linguistic evidence in favor of quasi-indicators. Hence, if we recognize that quasi-indicators (*qua* logophoric pronouns) exist in natural language, we may not be so suspicious of recognizing their existence in English.

3. The Dual Feature of 'That'-Clauses

The existence of quasi-indicators and the fact that they are best understood along logophoric pronouns jointly suggest that attitude ascriptions are best understood on the background of the empathetic model I presented in Chapter 7 and, in particular, on the idea that an attitude ascription rests on the capacity one has to imagine oneself in someone else's shoes. As I argued (Chapter 7, Section 4), a report rests on this very capacity. More specifically, it rests on the transpositional principle:

- *Transpositional Principle*

    If the reporter in the attributee's context were to express what the attributee believes, desires, says, etc., the reporter would utter the relevant sentence, i.e. the sentence whose acceptance the reporter is attributing to the attributee.

For these reasons, I suggest that 'that'-clauses should be viewed on the model of Quine's famous Giorgione-sentence, in which there is self-referentiality occurring in a 'that'-clause. That is to say, expressions in *oratio obliqua* may be both used and mentioned; I agree with those who assume that expressions appearing in 'that'-clauses may be used and mentioned at the same time.⁹ To stress this point, I invite you to consider an example that was brought to my attention by David Kaplan. 'Knocked up', 'pregnant', and 'with child' are coextensive, but now consider:

(7) a. It is impolite to tell Sue that she is knocked up, but you have to inform her that she is pregnant.

If we adopt the view that coreferring embedded terms can be replaced *salva veritate* and that the feeling of puzzle can be explained away as a pragmatic fact, we run into problems. For, following this suggestion, (7a) has the same truth-value as:

(7) b. It is impolite to tell Sue that she is with child, but you have to inform her that she is pregnant.

This is implausible. 'Knocked up' in this context affects the truth-value of what is said. A natural interpretation that comes to mind is to say that 'knocked up' in (7a) is both used and mentioned and that it is because of this fact that it cannot be replaced *salva veritate* by 'with child'. The same considerations may apply to attitude ascriptions: within a psychological prefix a proper name, for instance, can play two roles. That is, it can pick out an object of discourse and tell us how the subject thought of this object. If so, a term in an attitude ascription may be both used and mentioned, just as 'Giorgione' in Quine's famous example, "Giorgione was so-called because of his size" is. In short, in (7a) the fact that 'knocked up' is both used and mentioned is suggested by the second clause; in Quine's example the fact that 'Giorgione' is both used and mentioned is suggested by 'so-called' while in an attitude report the fact that a term is both used and mentioned is suggested by the psychological prefix.¹⁰

4. The Logical Form of Reports

In accordance with this idea, I consider the logical form of a belief ascription like "*A* believes that *a* is *F*" (when '*a*' is a singular term), to be:

- *Logical Form of Belief Report (LFB)*
  $BEL(A, <a, F>, "a \text{ is } F")$

[9] See e.g. Burdick (1982), Forbes (1990), Richard (1990), and Recanati (1993; 2000).

[10] One may think that the point I am trying to make is not plausible, for the words 'knock up' and 'with child' do not show how one is thinking about Sue. They merely show the register one is adopting. If so, in cases like (7a) what is at issue is not the way a subject is thinking of the referent but the way one is thinking about the linguistic context. Be this as it may, all I am trying to show is that, in these cases as well as in belief ascriptions, coreferential and co-extensive words may not be substitutable *salva veritate*, for in both contexts they play a dual role; they are both used and mentioned.

Quasi-Indexicality and Puzzling Reports 317

where "*a* is *F*" is a sentence and <*a*, *F*> the proposition expressed by the 'that'-clause. *BEL* is the triadic belief relation and *A* is the believer or attributee. "*a* is *F*" is the sentence *A n-accepts* in her believing that *A* is *F*.[11] In other words, the *BEL* relation holds between an agent, a proposition, and a sentence, where the sentence expresses the proposition and the agent is disposed to *n*-accept that sentence by believing the proposition that she is related to.

You may recall that in Chapter 2, Section 1, I said that the notion of logical form I have in mind aims to represent the level of syntactic representation that displays the properties relevant for semantic interpretation. The purpose of logical form (LF as it is commonly characterized) is to capture the syntactic structures relevant to a semantic interpretation.[12] The LF of an attitude ascription can be represented by the following schema:

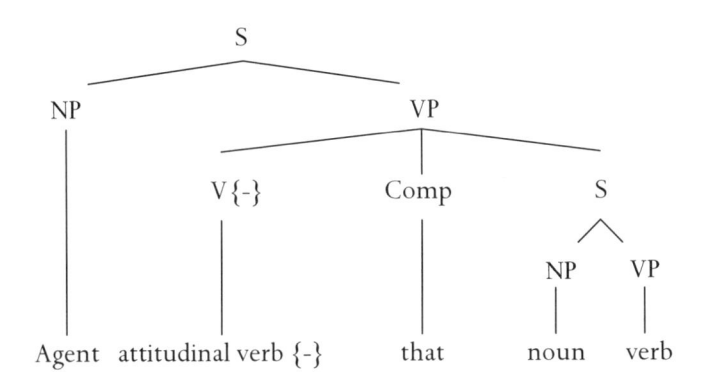

Where 'V {-}' represents the fact that the attitudinal verb is a triadic relation, relating the agent of the attitude, the proposition s/he entertains, and the sentence s/he *n*-accepts. The '{-}' should represent the argument place for the sentence mentioned. In its informal reading an ascription like "Jane said that Tully is Roman" reads as "Jane said that Tully/Cicero is Roman in uttering 'Tully is Roman' ". If I am right in claiming that a 'that'-clause both expresses a proposition and mentions a sentence expressing this very proposition, then at the LF level we must represent somewhat the argument place for the sentence mentioned. If we adopt the terminology I introduced we can say that {-} is the place-holder for the sentence the attributee *n*-accepts in her attitudinal relation with the proposition expressed by the 'that'-clause. This argument place is, indeed, not present at the grammatical level,

[11] It goes without saying that, when a quasi-indicator is embedded within a negation such as 'he*' in "Privatus does not believes that he* is a millionaire" or "Privatus never believed that he* is a millionaire", the report states that the attributee is not disposed to *n*-accept the sentence "I am a millionaire". I discussed the notion of *n*-acceptance in Ch. 7, Sect. 4, above.

[12] For an accurate and well-developed account of LF, see May (1985).

where an attitudinal verb is dyadic, but it must show up at the LF level. The LF of "*A believes that a is F*" can thus be represented as:

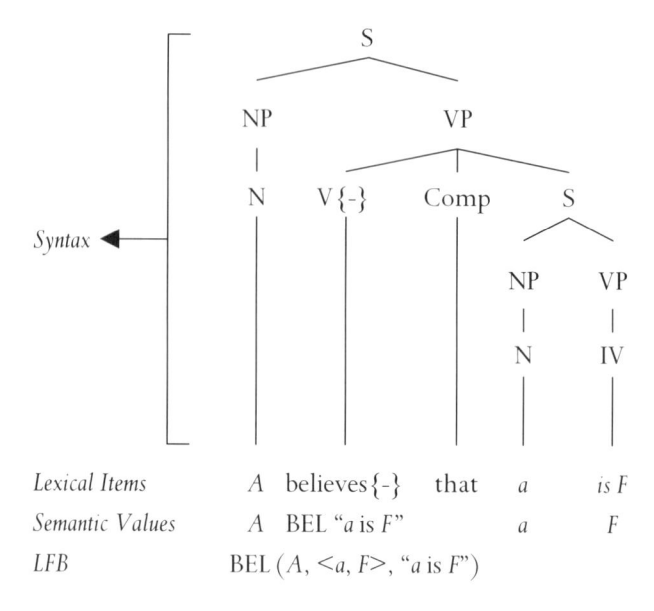

```
                             S
                           /   \
                         NP     VP
                         |     / | \
                         N   V{-} Comp   S
Syntax                                  / \
                                       NP  VP
                                       |   |
                                       N   IV
                                       |   |
Lexical Items        A   believes{-}  that   a   is F
Semantic Values      A   BEL "a is F"         a    F
LFB                  BEL (A, <a, F>, "a is F")
```

This representation makes it clear that 'believes' is a triadic relation, relating the attributee, *A*, to the proposition *that a is F* (<*a, F*>) and the sentence "*a is F*". 'V{-}' should capture the self-referentiality going on in attitude ascriptions, i.e. the fact that a 'that'-clause behaves like a Giorgione-sentence. In short, the meaning of 'believe' requires that both a proposition and a sentence end up in LFB. An attribution like this will be true iff *A* believes the proposition *that a is F* in *n*-accepting the sentence "*a is F*".

The sentence the reporter uses as a 'that'-clause is the one that also classifies the attributee's mental state. However, this *ideal* situation rarely happens. As we saw, the reporter may not be able to fully classify the attributee's mental state. Moreover, when quasi-indicators are involved, the sentence that classifies the attributee's mental state does not correspond to the sentence the attributee *n*-accepts. The presence of a quasi-indicator helps to determine the relevant sentence the attributee *n*-accepts because of its +attributive feature—you may remember that in the previous chapter I argued that quasi-indicators should be understood along logophoric pronouns and, as such, as a kind of attributive anaphors.

The logical form of *de se* ascriptions such as:

(8) Agassi hopes to lose the tournament
(9) Privatus believes that he himself (he*) is a millionaire

would thus be represented respectively as:[13]

    (8) a. *HOPE* (Agassi, *that Agassi loses the tournament*, "I lose the tournament")

    (9) a. *BEL* (Privatus, *that Privatus is a millionaire*, "I am a millionaire")

No doubt more should be said on the way the logical form I am proposing can capture the fact that attitude ascriptions are audience-directed and that some ascriptions, such as "Jon believes that we are millionaires" and "Sue believes that Jon knows that she* is a millionaire", are mixed ascriptions. In particular, more should be said about the *de re*, *de dicto*, and *de se* distinction and how it can incorporate what I characterized as the indeterminacy of attributions. I shall try to tackle this problem in Section 5.

Before going further, it is also worth mentioning that the picture I am providing differs from the picture proposed by Crimmins and Perry in two main respects. First, Crimmins and Perry take the third relatum to be an unarticulated constituent of the report. The third relatum is contextually furnished.[14] In my picture, the third relatum is provided by the 'that'-clause itself, insofar as a 'that'-clause works like a Giorgione-sentence: when the report is *de dicto* there is self-referentiality in the report. Secondly, according to Crimmins and Perry, the third relatum is a compound cognitive particular. Roughly, this is a token mental state made up by notions (cognitive particulars of individuals) and ideas (cognitive particulars of properties), while on my account the third relatum is a sentence classifying a mental state *type*.[15]

The picture I have in mind bears some relation to the interpreted logical form approach: a belief report is a relation between the believer and the interpreted logical form of the 'that'-clause, the latter being made up from couples whose members are linguistic expressions and their values.[16] In other words, the interpreted logical form determined by a node is obtained by replacing every node of the LF with the ordered pair whose first member is the syntactical item and whose second member is the value of that syntactic item. It is thus in virtue of having different ordered couples such as <'Lenin', Lenin>, <'Vladimir Ilyich Ulyanov', Vladimir Ilyich Ulyanov> in the logical form of an ascription that the truth-value of "Sue believes that Lenin is a Bolshevist" may differ from the truth-value of "Sue believes that Vladimir Ilyich Ulyanov is a Bolshevist". The interpreted

---

[13] For the sake of simplicity, I ignore the temporal parameters, i.e. the time at which the attitude is entertained.

[14] As we saw, Schiffer (1992) calls this *The Hidden-Indexical Theory*. Notice that the Hidden-Indexical Theory is neutral on whether the third relatum is a type of mode of presentation (this is Schiffer's version) or a token mode of presentation (this is Crimmins and Perry's version).

[15] I discussed Crimmins and Perry's position in Ch. 7, Sect. 6, above where I showed that the classification of a type of mental state suffices in handling Frege-inspired puzzles.

[16] See e.g. Segal (1989) and Larson and Ludlow (1993).

logical form of an ascription like "*A* believes that Tully is Roman" would be, modulo many simplifications:

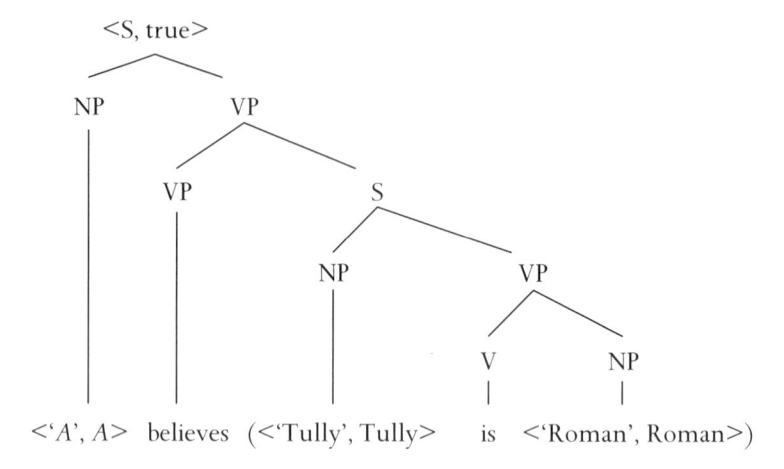

```
                    <S, true>
                   /         \
                  NP          VP
                           /      \
                          VP       S
                          |      /   \
                                NP    VP
                                |    /  \
                                    V    NP
                                    |    |
          <'A', A>  believes  (<'Tully', Tully>  is  <'Roman', Roman>)
```

This representation makes it clear that in the truth-conditions of the ascription, reference is made to the NPs 'Tully' and 'Roman'. Besides, on the interpreted logical form view, an ascription can be viewed as a dyadic relation relating the attributee with an interpreted logical form: "<'Tully', Tully> is <'Roman', Roman>" in our example. In a similar way to this approach, I make reference both to expressions and their value. Unlike the interpreted logical form approach, however, I am not committed to the thesis that reports in different languages cannot be logically equivalent since the interpreted logical form of, say, "Sue believes that Lenin is a Bolshevist" and "Sue croit que Lenin est un chanteur", involve different expressions. Hence, the truth-conditions of these reports would always be logically non-equivalent, for each involves relations to distinct interpreted logical forms.[17] This consequence of the interpreted logical form approach does not fit our pre-theoretical intuitions. Everyday speakers would argue that the French and the English report say the same thing, i.e. are logically equivalent, so a picture that can accommodate this intuition ought to be preferred. As we saw in Chapter 7, Section 4, the notion of acceptance I advocate accommodates this intuition. Actually, the notion of acceptance I developed rests on the Transpositional Principle. Since this

---

[17] See Segal (1989: 88) and Larson and Ludlow (1993: 333–4). Another criticism this position faces has been put forward by Soames: "suppose the person simply said 'Mary believes the interpreted phrase marker whose root node is the pair <'S', truth>, which dominates . . .' Would you understand the person's remark, or know how to determine whether it was true? Surely not. . . . Thus, until we are given an explanation of what it might mean to believe or assert what Larson and Ludlow call interpreted logical forms, accompanied by persuasive empirical evidence that we really do believe and assert these things, we won't have any grip on the right-hand of T-sentences like (10)" (Soames 2002: 151–2).

principle is spelled out in counterfactual terms, it does not prevent one from attributing to someone the acceptance of a sentence of a foreign language. In particular, it does not prevent us from using foreign language sentences to classify a mental state. To this particular question I now turn.

5. *n*-Acceptance, Translation, and Twin-Earth

The underlying question I face is: in attributing the *n*-acceptance of the English sentence, "Man is a rational animal" to Sue, do we ascribe to her the same mental representation as we would in attributing to her the *n*-acceptance of the French sentence "L'homme est un animal rationnel"? Do these sentences classify the same mental representation? If these sentences translate each other, my answer is affirmative: the very same attribution can be made in several languages. The question, as I understand it, amounts to knowing whether (and in which circumstances) two sentences translate each other. We feel comfortable in saying that "Sue believes that Tully is Roman" and "Sue croit que Tullius est romain" translate each other and attribute the same belief to Sue. We feel less comfortable in saying that "Sue believes that Tully is Roman" and "Sue croit que Cicéron est romain" translate each other and attribute to her the same belief.[18] That is, we feel entitled to translate 'Tullius' by 'Tully' and not by 'Cicero' although these names are coreferential. The fact that many of the French and English words have the same etymology certainly helps to explain this. Thus 'Tully' and 'Tullius' translate each other insofar as they have the same origin, while 'Tully' does not translate 'Cicéron' insofar as they do not share the etymology. The problem arises when languages are, from an etymological point of view, very different. The problem also appears when we do not have this kind of symmetry among languages as, for instance, when a language has more names for an individual than another. The example I used (Chapter 7, Section 7) was the Hebrew 'Germaniah' and 'Ashkenaz', both of which are names for Germany. In that case, which sentence of Hebrew does a competent speaker of Hebrew accept when she believes that Germany is her country? We are not, though, forced into silence. For as I have just shown, we are able to state (using English) that in Hebrew there are two names for Germany and that "Germany is *F*" can be translated into two different Hebrew sentences which may be used to classify different representations. To classify one's attitude, we could use a sentence of the form "Germany (translating in Hebrew as

---

[18] On the dyadic view, according to which an ascription relates a subject to a (singular) proposition, reports like "Sue believes that Tully is Roman" and "Sue croit que Cicéron est romain" cannot differ in truth-value.

'Germaniah') is *F*" or "Germany (translating in Hebrew as 'Ashkenaz') is *F*".[19] In this way, we can classify one's mental life finely enough; for the attributer has at her disposal, in her own language, all the tools needed to classify the attributee's mental life. It is often the case that an appropriate attribution needs to mention the very words used by the attributee. In that case, the attributer is not forced to silence and can make what I would call a *meta-linguistic ascent*.

As we saw, the Transpositional Principle makes other people's beliefs (at least partially) accessible to us. This principle stipulates, so to speak, a kind of similarity across cultures. But it is on the basis of this stipulation that attributions to people belonging to very different linguistic communities are possible.

It seems to me that the way I am telling the story allows us to answer Salmon's worry that a theory like the one I am advocating is vulnerable to Church's famous translation argument. Salmon stressed (in a personal communication) that Church's general point is that "Pierre said that London is pretty" and "Pierre a dit que Londres est jolie" end up meaning different things, according to the picture I am defending, which is implausible. Notice, however, that I am arguing that an agent who is disposed to *n*-accept, say, "London is pretty" is also disposed to *n*-accept "Londres est jolie". Both sentences classify the same mental representation and express the same proposition. So the French and English reports mean the same thing. This should mirror the fact that in a usual report, e.g. an English report of an English speaker, the attributer is implicitly assuming that the attributee knows the linguistic meaning of the language used by the attributer. As we shall soon see, this assumption can always be cancelled as, for instance, in Kripke's Pierre-'London'/'Londres' puzzle.

A word of explanation may be useful. Church's argument rests on the fact that, in translating "Sue said, 'Man is a rational animal' " into, for instance, the French sentence "Sue a dit, 'L'homme est un animal rationnel' ", we do not mention the English expression "Man is a rational animal"; Church's point is that we should. In other words, the quoted material should remain unchanged when a sentence containing a quotation is translated: we should not translate what appears within the quotation marks. There are, however, cases of self-reference that require the quoted material to be translated. Consider, for instance:

(10) This sentence begins with a four-letter demonstrative.

---

[19] You may recall that in Ch. 3, above, I claimed that parentheses do not affect the truth-value of the whole utterance containing them. One could thus wonder how and why the parentheses can get into the truth-conditions of a report. These parentheses play a peculiar role. They are like aside information pointing to the fact that the attributee used a specific word. Actually, these parentheses contain some quoted material and, as such, they make reference to the very words used by the attributee. It is simply because they enter into the specification of the mental state of the attributee that they can enter the truth-conditions of a report.

Quasi-Indexicality and Puzzling Reports   323

If we want to preserve the self-reference stressed by 'This very sentence', then in translating (10) into French we would have:

(11) Cette phrase(-ci) commence avec un démonstratif qui comporte cinq lettres.

Self-reference is preserved in (11) without preserving reference. If we want to preserve reference and refer to the English sentence in our translation, we would have:

(12) Cette phrase(-là) commence avec un démonstratif qui comporte quatre lettres.

Reference is preserved in (12) ('quatre' makes it clear that we are referring to the English sentence) but not self-reference.[20] Thus we need the following Translation Principle:

- *Translation Principle*
  An expression that is being used must be translated, while an expression that is being mentioned must not be translated—unless an element of self-reference associated with the sentence that contains the expression requires such translation (see Burge 1978b: 143).

If we analyze Church's argument assuming the Translation Principle, we end up with the following conclusion: in translating "Sue said, 'Man is a rational animal' " we would translate the English expression 'Man is a rational animal' only if it contains an element of self-reference whose preservation is required for good translation. In other words, we have to find out whether this kind of self-reference is preserved in translation. If, in translating "Sue said 'Man is a rational animal' " into French we preserve self-reference, then we can refute Church's argument. It may be worth noticing that in our everyday practice there are several cases that do not satisfy Church's desideratum. In translating, for instance, pieces of literature or historical reports containing dialogues, quoted material is translated too: reference is not preserved. We therefore have cases in which the expression is mentioned (it appears within quotation marks) and yet it is translated. But on what grounds should we assume that translation always requires strict synonymy?

[T]here is no ground for presumption that the practical canons of apt translation always require strict synonymy. In translating, say, a historical narrative, we are accustomed to render into the language of the translation even sentences occurring in *direct* quotation. Church's argument demonstrates, what is in any case obvious, that, in the case of *oratio recta*, such a translation does not preserve strict synonymy with the original text.... What force

---

[20] Burge points out that "an obvious if little-recognized principle of translation is that translation preserves self-reference if and only if it does not preserve reference" (Burge 1978b: 137).

is there in an argument which requires as an axiom that strict synonymy is maintained when we translate, in our accustomed manner, a sentence involving indirect quotation? If belief is an attitude to sentences, then, indeed, we cannot wholly translate a sentence ascribing a belief to someone into another language while preserving strict synonymy: from where does the assumption come that we *must* be able to do so? (Dummett 1981: 90–1)

Our ordinary translation practice seems to suggest the presence of an element of self-reference. Following these intuitive considerations, a sentence like "Sue said 'Man is a rational animal' " is short for:

(13) Sue said, "Man is a rational animal", considered as a sentence of the language of this very sentence

where 'this very sentence' applies self-referentially to the containing sentence "Sue said . . .". We can, then, suggest a convention that recognizes an element of self-reference, which should help us to explain why quoted material must be translated when embedded in a report:

- *The Shift of Reference Principle*
  Uses of a verb under its translatable direct discourse reading presuppose that expressions mentioned in the direct object of the verb are to be understood as they would be if they were used as an embedded clause (rather than merely mentioned) at the time of the use of the verb by the person who uses the relevant token of the containing sentence (see Burge 1978*b*: 146–7).

In accordance with this convention, we have found the required element of self-reference we were looking for. Expressions mentioned within the scope of a direct discourse verb ought to be understood as if they were used (as in a 'that'-clause) and not just mentioned.[21] The Shift of Reference Principle relates the interpretation of the expression mentioned to that of the very sentence in which it occurs.

In short, a sentence *S* whose *n*-acceptance is attributed to the attributee has to be taken as if it were used by the reporter in a 'that'-clause. This sentence is not just mentioned. The sentence whose *n*-acceptance we attribute to the agent of the attitude can be specified only on the basis of the 'that'-clause. Thus, this sentence is related both with the 'that'-clause (which allows us to specify it) and with the sentence embedding the 'that'-clause. In our example, the sentence "Man is a rational animal" is self-referentially related to the 'that'-clause 'man is a rational animal' and 'Sue believes that'. The presence of quasi-indicators, however, shows that 'that'-clauses are not merely translatable, disguised direct discourse.

To put it slightly differently, if the reporter holds that the English sentence "Man is a rational animal" and the French sentence "L'homme est un animal

---

[21] On the other hand, we could say that an expression within the scope of an indirect attitude ascription behaves in a way similar to an expression within translatable direct discourse.

rationnel" are each translatable into the other, she would attribute to Sue the same mental representation whether she attributes to her the *n*-acceptance of the English sentence or the French one. How do we deal, though, with Kripke's famous and well-discussed Pierre-'London'/'Londres' puzzle?

I argued that someone is disposed to *n*-accept whatever sentence translates the sentence whose *n*-acceptance we actually attribute to her. It seems then that my strategy crumbles under Kripke's Pierre-'London'/'Londres' puzzle. You may recall that Pierre assents to "Londres est jolie" and dissents from "London is pretty". But, if Pierre *n*-accepts "Londres est jolie" he is disposed to *n*-accept "London is pretty" and, conversely, if he *n*-accepts "London is ugly" he is disposed to *n*-accept "Londres est moche". In virtue of the transpositional principle, if our attribution is in French we attribute to him the *n*-acceptance of a French sentence and if the attribution is in English, the *n*-acceptance of the English sentence. So it turns out that Pierre is disposed to *n*-accept both "London is pretty" and "London is ugly". This is the problem.

The puzzle, as I understand it, includes the fact that Pierre does not know that 'London' translates 'Londres'. So, in his English mood, Pierre assents to both "Londres is pretty" and "London is ugly" and in his French mood he assents to "Londres est jolie" and "London est moche". It should be stressed that, in stating the puzzle, we make reference to 'London' and 'Londres' and to the fact that Pierre does not know that they are the French and English words for the same thing. In so doing, we stress that Pierre is *not* disposed to *n*-accept the relevant sentence when translated. This is precisely the point of Kripke's puzzle. If Pierre knew that 'London' translates 'Londres', he would certainly give up one of his beliefs. In saying that a subject who is disposed to *n*-accept a sentence is in a dispositional relation to its translations in various languages, am I committed to the thesis that Pierre *n*-accepts both "London is pretty" and "London is ugly"? No, because of the following principle:

- *n-Acceptance and Translation Principle*
  A subject *n*-accepts a sentence of a foreign language either if:
  (i) she does not know the language in which the report is formulated, or
  (ii) she knows the language in which the report is formulated and, unlike Kripke's Pierre, knows that the relevant sentences translate each other.

As I understand Kripke's puzzle, the reports "Pierre believes that London is pretty" and "Pierre croit que Londres est jolie" mean the same thing. If (i) or (ii) do not hold, though, the reports do not mean the same thing, but in that case further information is needed: in Kripke's story we have to point out that Pierre *does not know* that 'London' translates 'Londres'. Once again, we are not forced into silence, for the reporter can cancel what I characterized as the implicit assumption or what could also be characterized as the default interpretation, i.e. that the attributee knows the linguistic meaning of the language used by the attributer.

One could object that the fact that "Pierre believes that London is pretty" and "Pierre croit que Londres est jolie" mean the same thing depending on the languages Pierre knows, is counterintuitive. Thus, the dissolution of Kripke's puzzle I am proposing should be resisted. To this I do not have a knockdown argument. One can hardly argue about intuitions. But whatever solution/dissolution one tries to propose one is likely to face a similar charge. My dissolution of the puzzle may also sound *ad hoc*. I do believe, though, that if one aims to dissolve Kripke's Pierre-'London'/'Londres' puzzle one must, someway or other, make reference to Pierre's mastery of the languages involved, i.e. French and English. Actually, the puzzle arises insofar as Pierre does not know that 'London' translates 'Londres'. Thus an accurate report aiming to capture Pierre's conflicting attitudes *vis-à-vis* London must make reference to this very fact. The *n*-Acceptance and Transpositional Principle stated above aims to capture just this fact. Actually, from "Pierre croit que Londres est jolie" and "Pierre believes that London is ugly" we can infer that Pierre believes of London that it is both ugly and pretty. But he believes it in different ways, *via* the English medium and *via* the French medium. To account for Pierre's mental life (and rationality), we have to stress this fact. The attributer can always articulate the way in which the believer thought about the relevant thing in her ascription. To deal with Kripke's Pierre-'London'/'Londres' puzzle, the attributer can make what I characterized as the meta-linguistic ascent, i.e. she can make reference to the words 'London' and 'Londres'. If the reporter does not make a meta-linguistic ascent the reporter is implicitly assuming the *n*-Acceptance and Transpositional Principle.

If I am right, the story I have been telling allows us to dismiss Loar's claim that 'that'-clauses are the wrong medium to represent how the agent of an attitude ascription personally conceived of things. Loar's moral is that attitude ascriptions do not allow us to explain the attributee's behavior.[22] For, as Kripke's puzzle shows, a 'that'-clause, e.g. "Pierre believes that London is pretty", is incapable of capturing the way Pierre thought about London. It does not tell us which conception of London Pierre held, i.e. whether he thought of London under the French medium 'Londres' or the English one, 'London'. If we must characterize Pierre's mental life using locutions such as "Pierre believes that London is pretty under the French label 'Londres' while he believes that London is ugly under the English label 'London' ", as I claimed, 'that'-clauses turn out to be reliable in characterizing one's psychological attitude. 'That'-clauses reflect, *pace* Loar, how

---

[22] "[P]sychological content is not in general identical with what is captured by that-clauses" (Loar 1988: 102).

the attributee conceives of things.[23] We cannot argue, as Loar seems to suggest, from the fact that a given 'that'-clause does not capture what the attributee has in mind, to the conclusion that 'that'-clauses are the wrong medium to capture the attributee's mental life. Some other 'that'-clause will turn out to be reliable.

It is also worth noticing that the picture I propose allows us to handle the twin-Earth story as well. You may recall that in Chapter 6 I defended the thesis that Sue's 'water'-thoughts and twin-Sue's 'water'-thoughts are the same. These thoughts, I claimed, are perspectival and, as such, may relate to different substances in different contexts (e.g. on Earth or on twin-Earth). Twin-Sue's 'water'-thoughts are about XYZ because 'water' stands for XYZ in her linguistic community, while Sue's 'water'-thoughts are about H_2O because, in her English linguistic community, 'water' stands for H_2O. According to the picture I put forth, I am committed to the thesis that, if both Sue and twin-Sue *n*-accept the English sentence "Water is *F*", they share the same (perspectival) thought. But Sue *n*-accepts the English sentence while twin-Sue *n*-accepts a twin-English sentence. That is, if I attribute the *n*-acceptance of "Water is *F*" to Sue, twin-me attributes the *n*-acceptance of the twin-English sentence "Water is *F*" to twin-Sue. Both sentences classify the same (perspectival) thought or representation. If Sue were to move to twin-Earth, her 'water'-thoughts would be anchored to XYZ. Notice that I am not committed to denying that 'water' means H_2O on Earth; I accept the fact that 'water' has different meanings on Earth and twin-Earth. But meanings, to use Putnam's happy phrase, ain't in the head. All I am committed to is that "Water is *F*" classifies the same representation whether it is an English sentence or a twin-English one. After all, one manifests one's linguistic competence in speaking a language. Sue manifests her competence with the word 'water' in using this word in appropriate circumstances. The same holds for twin-Sue. To use the word 'water' in an appropriate way, one does not need to know that water is H_2O (or XYZ). Ice is H_2O as well, and twin-ice is XYZ. If Sue asks for some water, she would be surprised to receive ice. In this case, the micro-structure of water is not relevant. In the past, our scientists did not know that water was H_2O and their twin-scientists did not know that water was XYZ. These scientists were unable to tell H_2O and XYZ apart; yet, water was H_2O and twin-water was XYZ. 'Water' did not change its meaning with the discovery that its microstructure was H_2O.

Notice also that I am not committed to the thesis that 'water' is ambiguous. To be an ambiguous word (such as 'bank'), 'water' should have two or more meanings in *our* linguistic community, i.e. in English. Earth English and twin-Earth English (twin-English) are different, though homophonic, languages. Ambiguity

---

[23] So I agree with Biro when he claims that "we have principled ways of deciding when a given that-clause does and when it does not succeed in capturing psychological content" (Biro 1992: 287).

is not a notion that holds across languages. Besides, I am also not committed to the thesis that 'water' in English and 'water' in twin-English can be translated into each other. If translation must preserve reference, they are not translatable. The fact that they do not translate each other, though, does not undermine my picture, for all I need in order to maintain that Sue and twin-Sue share the same (perspectival) 'water'-thoughts is to claim that, when Sue *n*-accepts "Water is *F*", twin-Sue also *n*-accepts the twin-English sentence "Water is *F*". To be sure, if Sue were to move to twin-Earth she would *n*-accept the sentence that twin-me attributes to her, i.e. a twin-English sentence, and *vice versa*; conversely, if twin-Sue visits us, she would *n*-accept an English sentence. This goes hand in hand with the scenario I described in Chapter 6, when I argued that the perspectival thoughts of an agent would be anchored to different entities if, unbeknown to her, she were transported to twin-Earth. As such, they would trigger actions *vis-à-vis* different, but qualitatively indistinguishable, objects. Our twins would classify twin-Sue's mental life in attributing the *n*-acceptance of twin-English sentences to her.

6. *De Re, De Dicto, De Se*

As a first approximation, we can say that the relation between the 'that'-clause and the sentence *S* as it appears in LFB can be of three main types, depending on whether the report is *de dicto, de se,* or *de re*.[24] In a *de dicto* ascription (like "Sue believes/thinks/ ... that Lenin is a Bolshevist") the 'that'-clause gives us the sentence *S* ("Lenin is a Bolshevist") that *A* is disposed to *n*-accept.[25] In a *de se* ascription (e.g. "Lenin/Vladimir Ilyich Ulyanov believes/thinks/ ... that he (himself) is a Bolshevist"), the 'that'-clause differs from *S*: 'He (himself)' stresses that *S* contains the pronoun 'I' and corresponds to "I am a Bolshevist". Both true *de dicto* and *de se* attributions specify the whole content of one's attitude; each carries both the external information (the object of one's belief/thought/ ..., the proposition believed/thought/ ...) and the internal information (the way this proposition is believed/thought/ ...).

[24] Roughly, a *de se* attribution differs from a *de dicto* one in that it contains quasi-indicators (e.g. 'she herself') and attributes essentials indexicals (e.g. 'I'). For a more precise characterization of *de se* attributions, see Ch. 9, Sect. 2, above.

[25] I am not sure, however, that the considerations I am putting forth apply to the case of synonymy as well. We may not always substitute synonymous expressions (e.g. 'fortnight' and 'fourteen days' or 'fierce' and 'undomesticated') within attitude ascriptions *salva veritate*. If so, synonymous sentences like "Sue will be away for fourteen days" and "Sue will be away for a fortnight" may classify different mental states; see Ch. 4, Sect. 3, above, where I argued that synonyms can be substituted by their definition, whereas the definition may not be replaced *salva veritate* by the definiens. We can thus substitute 'female fox' for 'vixen' and 'adult unmarried man' for 'bachelor' *salva veritate*, but not the converse.

In a *de re* ascription like "Of Vladimir Ilyich Ulyanov, Sue thinks that he is a Bolshevist", the 'that'-clause does not fully specify the sentence Sue *n-accepts*. The 'that'-clause gives us a sentence of the form "α is a Bolshevist" where 'α' is a placeholder for a referring expression for Lenin. This does not mean, of course, that the subject of the attitude *n-accepts* the sentence "α is a Bolshevist". The 'α' stresses that the attributee has at her disposal a referential mechanism which is coreferential with the one used by the reporter. This does *not* mean that a *de re* ascription does not attribute the *n-acceptance* of a sentence to the agent; all it means is that the sentence in question is not specified. After all, *de re* ascriptions are not used with the intention of specifying the whole content of the belief/thought/... They specify only the *external information*; they are silent about the *internal information*, insofar as they do not fully specify the way the proposition is believed/thought/... If I say, for instance:

(14) Sue believes that you [addressing Igor] are in danger

I do not (and perhaps cannot) specify the way in which Sue believes the proposition that Igor is in danger. All I can say is that there is a certain way in which she believes this proposition. So there is a sentence that Sue *n-accepts*. Indeed, the same kind of situation can arise with attributions involving proper names. In fact, if we consider Chisholm's famous example:

(15) Columbus believed that Cuba was China

the proper name 'Cuba' cannot specify the way in which Columbus believed the proposition *that Cuba is China*. The regimentation of this attribution turns out to be:

(15) a. $\exists S\ BEL($Columbus, *that Cuba is China*, $S)$[26]

where the sentence we use to classify Columbus's mental representation is not specified. Under the Assumption that Columbus uses (or was disposed to use) the name 'China', in his referring to Cuba (15) could also be represented as:

(15) b. $\exists \alpha\ (BEL($Columbus, *that Cuba is China*, "α is China"))

where 'α' is a variable standing for a term that Columbus may have used (or been disposed to use) in thinking of Cuba. The sentence that Columbus *n-*accepted is not fully specified. For simplicity's sake, in what follows I would omit the quantification over terms.

A further question needs to be considered. How can we decide, on linguistic grounds alone, whether an attribution involving proper names is *de dicto* or

---

[26] It seems to me that my way of regimenting *de re* and *de dicto* attributions agrees with Castañeda's distinctions (1989: Ch. 5) between internal/external construals and propositional opacity/transparency. I shall discuss the distinction between propositional opacity and transparency in Sect. 6. Moreover, this regimentation fits with the thesis that a *de dicto* report entails a *de re* report in an elegant way: *BEL*(Sue, *that Lenin is a Bolshevist*, "Lenin is a Bolshevist") entails $\exists S\ BEL$(Sue, *that Lenin is a Bolshevist*, S).

de re? What is the linguistic evidence we can invoke for this distinction? The linguistic grounds are far from transparent. In particular, a *de re* attribution does not always present itself in the form "Of NN, Tim believes that she is *F*" or "Tim believes of NN that she is *F*". It is possible (and it is often the case outside philosophers' offices) for a *de re* attribution to be of the form "Tim believes that NN is *F*". If this sentence continues as "but Tim does not know that she is called 'NN' ", we certainly are not attributing to Tim, as in a *de dicto* attribution, the use (or possession) of the proper name 'NN'. Notice that a self-attribution like "I believe of Vladimir Ilyich Ulyanov that he is a Bolshevist" is not *de re*: I specify the sentence I *n-accept*. Attitude ascriptions are not, however, independent of contextual parameters and, in particular, must consider the audience to whom the reports are directed. That is to say, they are not syntactically transparent.[27] In our example, the contextual parameter is made explicit by the clause "but Tim does not know that she is called 'NN' ". In short, whether an ascription is *de dicto* or *de re* depends on distinct factors. In everyday communication, it is not always possible to draw this distinction and often we do not need to do so. But when these factors are fixed and the distinction *is* made, we can represent it at the level of the logical form, as I did above.

The *de re/de dicto/de se* distinction may be viewed as a mere idealization that we use for semantic classifications, i.e. as a useful tool we can use in analyzing natural language. As such, it can be *instrumentally* useful even if it is merely an idealization. It is like a physicist theorizing about frictionless movement and drawing conclusions from idealized situations. Our physicist finds it useful to assume frictionless movement, even if in reality such a thing does not exist, i.e. even if it is empirically impossible. In our approach to propositional reports, we can assume pretty much the same attitude *vis-à-vis* the *de re/de dicto/de se* distinction. As we shall now see, this distinction should be supplemented by a further distinction, which enables us to capture the fact that we often have mixed cases.

7. Propositional Opacity and Propositional Transparency

Another (and possibly more accurate) way to stress the distinction between *de dicto* and *de se* attributions on the one hand and *de re* ascriptions on the other, is to use Castañeda's distinction between propositionally opaque and propositionally

---

[27] Attitude ascriptions involving quasi-indicators (*de se* attributions) are syntactically transparent insofar as the latter attribute a use of an essential indexical and, as such, specify the sentence that the believer *n-accepts*. To be sure, quasi-indicators are syntactically transparent inasmuch as they are embedded within *one* psychological prefix. In an attribution like "Sue believes that Tom believes that she (herself) is *F*", for instance, the quasi-indicator 'she (herself)' is silent on the way in which Tom thinks about Sue and, as such, it is unable to specify the sentence that Tom *n-accepts*.

transparent ascriptions. The intuitive underlying idea may be summarized as follows:

- *Propositionally Transparent*
  An expression is propositionally transparent when its use reveals the way the subject refers or referred to the item the speaker is currently referring to.

- *Propositionally Opaque*
  An expression is propositionally opaque when its use does *not* reveal the way the subject refers or referred to the item that the speaker is currently referring to.[28]

Since quasi-indicators reveal the way the subject made reference, insofar as they reveal the indexical the subject used, they are propositionally transparent, whereas indexicals used deictically in oblique contexts are always propositionally opaque.[29] Castañeda claims that quasi-indicators are propositionally transparent, for they express the attributee's way of referring. However, propositional transparency/opacity proceeds by degrees; this allows us to handle the fact that we, as reporters, are constrained by *our* context and are thus sometimes unfaithful in our reports (see Chapter 7, Section 8). Since reports are audience-directed, we are not always able to specify the way in which one entertains a given attitude. Our unfaithfulness is particularly evident if we consider plurals with split antecedents. Actually, as emerged in Chapter 8 (Section 3), plurals with split antecedents constitute a *grammatical* constraint, which prevents a report from being fully faithful. As an illustration of this phenomenon, consider:

(16) Jane$_1$ believes that we$_1^{d\star}\oplus_2^i$ are millionaires

This report cannot fully capture the attitudes of the attributee, for it attributes an 'I'-thought to Jon and, as such it is propositionally transparent; yet, at the same time, the pronoun 'we' also works as an independent pronoun picking out the reporter and, as such, it is propositionally opaque. In other words, a report like (16) is a mixed report insofar at it specifies Jane's attitude *vis-à-vis* herself, yet is silent on the way in which Jane thought about the reporter. The peculiarity of such reports is stressed if we rephrase it as:

(16) a. Jane$_1{}'$ believes that she$_1^{d\star}$ is a millionaire and that I$_2^i$ am a millionaire

---

[28] It may be worth noticing that Castañeda's propositional opacity/transparency distinction is somewhat the inversion of the more common distinction between referential opacity/transparency. A term is transparent when it is propositionally opaque. But as we are going to see, the former, unlike the latter, proceeds by degree.

[29] Castañeda writes: "Because indicators in indirect speech constructions express nothing but speaker references, they always have external construal and occur propositionally opaquely except when the subject of attribution of mental states, conceived in the first-person way, is at once the speaker him/herself" (Castañeda 1989: 105).

where the presence of 'I' makes it evident that the report does not specify the way in which Jane thought about the attributer. In the previous chapter I characterized this feature as *attribution indeterminacy*.

As a further illustration of the fact that propositional transparency/opacity proceeds by degrees, I invite you to consider multiple embedded reports. If we consider:

(17) Igor believes that Mary discovered that he* is a Communist

the quasi-indicator 'he*' is propositionally transparent with respect to Igor's self-reference. If Igor expressed his belief, he would probably say:

(18) Mary discovered that I am a Communist

In (18), the first-person pronoun 'I' does not reveal how Mary referred to Igor; hence it is propositionally opaque. In (17), too, the quasi-indicator 'he*' does not reveal the way Mary referred to Jon. In this case, we can say that the quasi-indicator is not completely propositionally transparent, for it is propositionally opaque with respect to how Mary referred to Igor.[30] Although quasi-indicators are always propositionally transparent, this kind of transparency admits degrees. As we saw in Chapter 8 (Section 7), following Castañeda, an indicator is fully propositionally transparent just in case it is separated from its antecedent by just one psychological prefix. In (17), 'he*' is separated from its antecedent ('Igor') by two psychological prefixes and for this very reason it cannot be fully propositionally transparent. We can accommodate this idea in using the notion of *n*-acceptance I proposed in Chapter 7 (Section 4). (17) should be represented as follows:

(17) a. Igor$_1{}^i$ believes that Mary$_2{}^i$ discovered that he$_1{}^{d*}$ is a Communist

This representation makes it clear that the quasi-indicator 'he*' is not linked—and thus not coindexed—to 'Mary'. Hence, it does not attribute the *n*-acceptance of an 'I'-sentence to Mary. The quasi-indicator is linked to 'Igor' and thus attributes the *n*-acceptance of an 'I' sentence to him. This obeys the following syntactic rule:

- *Quasi-indicator linking rule*
A quasi-indicator can be linked to only one antecedent.

For this reason, an utterance like:

(19) Jane believes that Mary thinks that she* is in danger

is ambiguous insofar at it can be interpreted either as (19a) or (19b):

(19) a. Jane$_1{}^i$ believes that Mary$_2{}^i$ thinks that she$_2{}^{d*}$ is in danger
      b. Jane$_1{}^i$ believes that Mary$_2{}^i$ thinks that she$_1{}^{d*}$ is in danger

---

[30] By the way, we can say that an expression that is propositionally transparent cannot be replaced, *salva veritate* by a coreferring term, while an expression that is propositionally opaque can be replaced *salva veritate*.

While (19a) attributes the *n*-acceptance of an 'I'-sentence to Mary, (19b) attributes the *n*-acceptance of an 'I'-sentence to Jane. In (19a), 'she*' is propositionally transparent regarding Mary and propositionally opaque regarding Jane, while in (19b) it is the other way around.

According to the regimentation *LFB*, (19a) and (19b) can be represented, respectively, as:

(19) c. BEL(Jane$_1^i$, *that Mary thinks Mary is in danger*, "Mary$_2^i$ thinks that she$_2^{d*}$ is in danger")

(19) d. BEL(Jane$_1^i$, *that Mary thinks that Jane is in danger*, "Mary$_2^i$ thinks that I$_1^i$ am in danger")

Since multiple embedded attributions work like Chinese boxes, (19c) and (19d) should be further analyzed. That is, the embedded attribution "Mary thinks that she* is in danger" in (19c) and "Mary thinks that I am in danger" in (19d) should undergo the same analysis. We thus obtain:

(19) e. BEL[Jane$_1^i$, *that* THINK(Mary$_2^i$, *that Mary is in danger*, "I$_2^i$ am in danger"), "Mary$_2^i$ believes that she$_2^{d*}$ is in danger"]

(19) f. BEL[Jane$_1^i$, *that* THINK(Mary, *that Jane is in danger*, "α_1^i to be in danger"), "Mary$_2^i$ believes that I$_1^i$ am in danger"]

This stresses how the truth-conditions of (19a) and (19b) differ and that this difference comes from the different sentences whose *n*-acceptance is attributed to Jane and Mary.

The information that 'she*' in (19e) is propositionally opaque *vis-à-vis* the way Mary thought of Jane—i.e. it does not tell us how she referred to Jane—is represented by the fact that the sentence whose *n*-acceptance is attributed to Jane is not fully specified. It is an open sentence containing the free variable 'α'. On the other hand, the information that 'she*' in (19f) is propositionally transparent *vis-à-vis* the way Jane thought about herself is stressed by the fact that the sentence she *n*-accepts contains 'I' and is fully specified. To clarify this point, let us consider an ascription like:

(20) Mary believes that you are intelligent

in which case, the reporter uses 'you' to refer to the addressee, say Jon. The second-person pronoun (unlike 'I' and 'she') cannot (at least in English) be used as a quasi-indicator. Thus it cannot be used to specify someone's mental state. Nonetheless, the reporter assumes that Mary had at her disposal *a* referential mechanism, which she used to single out Jon. In a report like this, the sentence used to classify Mary's mental state is not fully specified. Thus the logical form of this report could be represented as:

(20) a. BEL(Mary, *That Jon is intelligent*, "α is intelligent")

where 'α' signals that Mary had at her disposal a referential term referring to Jon but does not signal which one. A report like this can be said to be *de re*. Let us now consider a Castañeda-inspired example. Privatus, a famous war hero, was seriously injured, became an amnesiac, and also lost all his confidence. As a result, he is now a very shy, frightened, and a panicky character. Needless to say, Privatus has forgotten that, during the war, he was nicknamed 'Rambo II' because of his illustrious enterprises. Back home, Privatus becomes interested in the war he happened to fight and, in particular, in the legendary actions of Rambo II. The crucial fact is that Privatus does not realize that he himself is Rambo II, let alone believe that he is a hero. In reading an interview with Rambo II, Privatus comes to believe that he was far from modest and that he often stressed what a hero he is. In this sort of scenario, a report like the following seems appropriate:

(21) Privatus believes that Rambo II$_1$ believes that he$_1$* is a hero

where the subscript signals that the quasi-indicator 'he*' is linked (and thus attributes an 'I'-thought) to Rambo II. The logical form of this report can be represented as:

(21) a. *BEL*[Privatus, that *BEL*(Rambo II, *that Privatus is a hero*, "I am a hero"), *that Rambo II believes that he* is a hero*, "Rambo II believes that he* is a hero"]

But Privatus *is* Rambo II. Thus the question which springs to mind is the following: if we attribute the *n*-acceptance of a sentence to Rambo II, then with the same token we attribute it to Privatus as well (and *vice versa*). If this is the case, I run into deep water, for in our scenario Privatus is far from disposed to *n*-accept the sentence "I am a hero". To escape this problem, I propose the following general rule concerning multiple embedded reports:

- *n-Acceptance and Multiple-Embedded Reports*
  An *n-accepted* sentence attributed to an agent selected by a term embedded within an attitude ascription cannot be attributed to an agent selected by a term not embedded within the same psychological prefix, whether the agents are the same or not.

In short, sentences whose *n-acceptance* is attributed cannot cross the psychological prefix they are embedded within. This should reflect the peculiarity of multiple embedded reports; they work like Chinese boxes. The representation I proposed stresses that Privatus *n*-accepts the sentence "Rambo II believes that he* is a hero". Privatus does not *n*-accept the sentence "I am a hero". The correct representation must thus be:

(21) b. *BEL*[Privatus$_1$, that *BEL*(Rambo II$_2$, *that Privatus is a hero*, "I$_2$ am a hero"), *that Rambo II believes that he* is a hero*, "Rambo II$_2$ believes that he$_2$* is a hero"]

We saw (Chapter 4, Section 6) that when distinct, though coreferential, proper names appear in identity statements they cannot be coindexed. The same happens when they appear in multiple embedded ascriptions. In an identity statement like "Lenin = Vladimir Ilyich Ulyanov", the grammar of '=' forces the fact that the two occurrences of the proper name must be coindexed (this amounts, roughly, to say that it is of the form $a = a$. This parallels mathematical statements such as "$2 + 3 = (2 - 1) + 4$", where the two occurrences of '2' must be coindexed "$2_1^i + 3_2^i = (2_1^i - 1_3^i) + 4_4^i$". But, the occurrences of different (even if coreferential) names in an identity statement cannot be coindexed. The grammar of '=' prevents it. A representation like "Lenin$_1$ = Vladimir Ilyich Ulyanov$_1$" is ungrammatical. (Roughly, this amounts to say that such an identity is not of the form $a = a$, but of the form $a = b$ and, thus, that the correct representation should be "Lenin$_1$ = Vladimir Ilyich Ulyanov$_2$".)

8. Getting the Inferences Right

The triadic view I propose concerning the logical form of attitude ascriptions ought to deal with yet another question. Since the third relatum, the *n-accepted* sentence, is semantically relevant, we have to see whether inferences like

(22) a. *A* thinks that Lenin is *F*
b. *B* thinks whatever *A* does

Thus: c. *B* thinks that Lenin is *F*

turn out to be valid or not. If they turn out to be invalid, the theory I am advocating loses much of its appeal.

According to the framework I have set out, we can interpret premiss (22) in three different ways. That is, *B* thinks whatever *A* does if:

- (i) *A* and *B* are related to the same propositions,
- (ii) *A* and *B* are in the same mental state and
- (iii) both *A* and *B* are related to the same propositions *and A* and *B* are in the same mental state.

I am going to concentrate on the first two possibilities, which I label *logical validity* and *psychological validity*.[31]

---

[31] I think that the third possibility is useless. To be sure, it is possible for two agents to be related to the same proposition whilst being in the same mental state. When indexicals are involved, however, the situation becomes somewhat complicated. When *A* is related to the propositions that *A* is *F* and that *B* is *F* in *n-accepting* "I am *F*" and "You [*B*] are *F*", *B* is related to the propositions that *B* is *F* and that *A* is *F* in *n-accepting* "I am *F*" and "You [*A*] are *F*".

Before going further, it may be useful to explain away some worries. One can think that since the conception I have proposed appeals to utterances, it crumbles under Kaplan's idea that the logic of indexicals cannot appeal to utterances. Actually, Kaplan claims that to handle inferences involving indexicals we must distinguish between an *utterance* and a *sentence-in-a-context*, insofar as the former are events which come into existence and disappear (see Kaplan [1977] 1989: 522). Hence, since utterances of distinct sentences are normally not simultaneous, they cannot occur in the same context. The logic of indexical expressions, however, requires that we evaluate the premisses and the conclusion in the same context:

> My notion of an *occurrence* of an expression in a context—the mere combination of the expression with the context—is not the same as the notion, from the theory of speech acts, of an utterance of an expression by the agent of a context. An occurrence requires no utterances. Utterances take time, and are produced one at a time; this will not do for the analysis of validity. By the time an agent finished uttering a very, very long true premise and began uttering the conclusion, the premise may have gone false. Thus even the most trivial of inferences, P therefore P, may appear invalid. Also, there are sentences which express a truth in certain contexts, but not if uttered. For example, "I say nothing". (Kaplan 1989: 584)

I do not believe that we have to appeal to the utterance/sentence-in-a-context distinction to propose a plausible logic for indexical expressions.[32] To state this point, imagine an utterance of the form "$a = a$". As we saw at the end of the previous section, sentences like:

(23) a. Aristotle is Aristotle
 b. This is this

are analytic. In a situation in which both utterances are informative, as in Kripke's Peter-'Paderewski' and Perry's Enterprise examples where one refers to the same individual using the very same name or the very same demonstrative without realizing it, one associates different cognitive values to the distinct occurrences of the terms. When Peter subsequently comes to realize that the two men named 'Paderewski' he saw are in fact a single person, he comes to accept "Paderewski is Paderewski" or "This is this" (pointing to two images representing Paderewski). The identities are thus informative. If so they can*not* be of the form $a = a$, which is analytic. For an utterance like "Paderewski is Paderewski" to be informative it must be of the form $a = b$. As we saw at the end of the previous section, though, in "Paderewski is Paderewski" the two occurrences of the name 'Paderewski' must be coindexed and thus the identity statement is of the form $a = a$. With the same

---

[32] For a recent discussion of this issue, see Braun (1996) and García-Carpintero (1998). While Braun advocates a Kaplanian position, García-Carpintero is keener to evaluating utterances. If I am right, though, both positions collapse one into the other.

token, we can say that sentences like:

(24) a. Aristotle is not Aristotle
     b. This is not this

are contradictions. This become even more evident if we focus on instances of "$a = a$" and of contradictions like "$a \neq a$" when anaphoric pronouns are at play, i.e. when we have sentences like:

(25) a. Aristotle is identical with himself
     b. Aristotle is not identical with himself.

It is evident that (25a) is analytical while (25b) is contradictory; this is because of grammatical constraints placed on the reflexive 'himself'. To stress this point, let us also consider:

(25) c. Aristotle is not identical with him

which is not contradictory. The best way to capture these features is in using the notion of indices. Thus, the fact that (25a) is analytic while (25b) is contradictory and (25c) is contingent can be represented using indices, as in:

(25) d. Aristotle$_1$ is identical with himself$_1$ $a = a$
     e. Aristotle$_1$ is not identical with himself$_1$ $a \neq a$
     f. Aristotle$_1$ is not identical with him$_2$ $a \neq b$

In these examples, it is evident how the indices are forced by grammar. So far, the moral we can bring home is that we can use coindexation to stress coreference. As I suggested in Chapter 8 (Section 3), however, noncoindexation does not entail noncoreference. The example I gave was proposed by Higginbotham (1985): "He$_1$ put on Jon$_2$'s coat" in answering "Who left?". In this case, it is perfectly conceivable that 'he' and 'Jon', though they bear different indices, are coreferential. With the same token, we can go on and claim that, when distinct proper names appear in an identity relation, they cannot be coindexed. The fact that they are coreferential is suggested by the identity relation itself, i.e. by the meaning of "is identical with". To stress this fact, let us consider an inference like:

(26) a. Some politicians admire Lenin
     b. Lenin is Ulyanov

Thus: c. Some politicians admire Ulyanov

As Fiengo and May stress (1994: 23), if the proper names 'Lenin' and 'Ulyanov' of the premiss were coindexed, we would have an instance of the trivial schema:

(27) a. A admires X
     b. X = X

Thus: c. A admires X

We can thus propose the following rule concerning indexation and identity:

- *Identity-Coindexation Rule*
  NPs appearing in an identity statement cannot be coindexed, unless coindexation is grammatically forced, i.e. unless the two occurrences are either anaphorically linked or two occurrences of the same term.

This fits with the conception of proper names I proposed in Chapter 1 when I claimed that homonyms are distinct names. Thus Peter gets puzzled insofar as he takes the two occurrences of 'Paderewski' to be two distinct homonyms. When Peter comes to realize that the two people he encountered named 'Paderewski' are one and a single person, what he actually comes to entertain is a statement like "Paderewski (*the musician*) is Paderewski (*the politician*)" which is of the form $a = b$. Using the notion of indices it can be rendered as:

- $[\text{Paderewski}_1 \, (\textit{the musician})]_2 = [\text{Paderewski}_1 \, (\textit{the politician})]_3$

where the distinct indices of the compounds names differ.

The general moral we should bring home is that, while coindexation entails coreference, the opposite does not hold. As I suggested in the previous chapter, the notion of indices I have in mind is inspired by the one defended by Fiengo and May. In particular, I subscribe to the following thought:

> The cases of discourse anaphora we have considered serve to show the role of indices in individuating linguistic expressions, is to say when they are the same or different, even when they have the same (superficial) form and the same reference. . . . What has tied together the various matters we have discussed in this section has been two concerns: (i) how indices afford a notion of syntactic identity in sentences and discourse, determining that counts as the same or different expressions; (ii) how this notion of syntactic identity maps onto semantic identity of reference. Our view is that although identity of indices maps onto identity of reference, nonidentity of indices does not necessarily map onto nonidentity of reference. Coreference in virtue of coindexing, then, is a matter of grammar, but coreference or non-coreference in face of noncoindexing is left open by the grammar. (Fiengo & May 1994: 21)

We can follow Fiengo and May and subscribe to the following rules, linking occurrences of indices to their interpretation:

- *Linking Rule*
  The coindexing of NPs in S contributes to the meaning of S that the NPs are covalued

- *Converse of the Linking Rule*
  The noncoindexing of NPs in S does not contribute to the meaning of S that the NPs are covalued.

With the notion of coindexation, we can account for the relevant inferences insofar as we can maintain that different occurrences can be coindexed and thus covalued.

The notion of indices is precisely what allows us to 'abstract away' certain features of an occurrence. And the notion of coindexing is a notion which helps to capture the logical form of an utterance, i.e. it is what helps us grasp the structure of the sentence embodied by the utterance.

Before going further, it may also be useful to stress that in order to deal with inferences containing demonstratives, Kaplan should welcome the notion of indexing. Consider an inference of the form:

(28) a. You are rich and you are poor
b. All the rich will be penalized

Thus: c. You will be penalized

In its natural and obvious interpretation, the two occurrences of the demonstrative 'you' in (28a) are taken to refer to distinct individuals. Thus, even under the assumption that (28a) is a sentence-in-a-context and not an utterance, one must assume a switch of context in the middle of the sentence to capture the noncoreferentiality of the two occurrences of 'you'. Following Kaplan's theory, one must assume that both occurrences are associated with different demonstrations (or directing intentions) and that it is in virtue of the latter that they refer to different individuals. In order to capture this fact, the more natural strategy is to adopt the notion of index I propose.[33] Furthermore, if Kaplan allows switches of context within a single sentence, then there is no reason to prevent switches of contexts from premisses to conclusion. This, of course, does not undermine the logic of indexicals, for the notion of covaluation is not carried by a single, fixed context, but by the indices. To put it into a nutshell, if Kaplan appeals to indices to deal with inferences involving demonstratives—as I think he should, in order to deal with inferences like (28a–c)—then the notion of a sentence-in-a-context and the notion I propose do not differ.[34] The moral then seems to be that the sentence-in-a-context *vs.* utterance issue is a non-issue, for the notion of indices is precisely what we need to explain away the alleged problem. Whether one starts with utterances or with sentences-in-a-context, one ought to appeal to indices. The two perspectives then collapse into each other.

9. Logical Validity and Psychological Validity

If we accept the notion of indices, we can reformulate our initial inference and see that it turns out to be valid, both under the psychological (psychological validity)

---

[33] As Richard claims, however, a switch of context in the middle of a sentence is contrary to Kaplan's conception: "Switching context in the middle of interpreting a sentence is clearly contrary to the spirit, not to speak of the letter, of Kaplan's approach to indexicals" (Richard 1993*b*: 133).

[34] For a criticism of Kaplan's position along these lines, see García-Carpintero (1998). García-Carpintero, though, does not appeal to the notion of indices in the way I do to deal with Kaplan's worries.

and the logical interpretation (logical validity). Here was our initial inference:

(22) a. *A* thinks that Lenin is *F*
b. *B* thinks whatever *A* does

Thus: c. *B* thinks that Lenin is *F*

Let us start with logical validity. Under this reading, we assume that *B* thinks whatever *A* thinks iff she is related to the same proposition as *A* (although she may be related to it in another way, because she may *n-accept* a different sentence). According to this interpretation of 'what *A* thinks', the argument can be formulated as follows:[35]

(29) a. *THINK*(*A*, that Lenin is F, "Lenin is *F*")
b. ∀*p*[∃*S*(*S* expresses *p* & *THINK*(*A*, that *p*, *S*)) → ∃*S**(*S** expresses *p* & *THINK*(*B*, that *p*, *S**))][36]

Thus: c. ∃*S**[*S** expresses the proposition that Lenin is F & *THINK*(*B*, that Lenin is F, *S**)]

Following this interpretation, we are unable to specify the way in which *B* thinks about the proposition *p*. All we can infer is that *B n-accepts* a sentence which expresses the proposition that Lenin is F. The sentence that *B n-accepts* could be "Vladimir Ulyanov is *F*", but it could also be "He [pointing to a picture of Vladimir Ulyanov] is *F*", and so forth. As an example supporting this interpretation of 'what *A* thinks', we can invoke attitude-reports involving indexical reference. If, for instance, *A* expresses her thought using an 'I'-sentence, then *B* cannot relate to that proposition by *n-accepting* an 'I'-sentence. She must *n-accept* a sentence with a term coreferential with *A*'s use of 'I'.

The notion of psychological validity tells us that we should interpret 'what *A* thinks' by assuming that *B* can think whatever *A* thinks iff they share the same way of thinking, without necessarily being related to the same proposition; what matters is only how a proposition is believed. According to this interpretation, Earth-Jon can think whatever twin-Earth-Jon thinks, although Earth-Jon is related to a proposition containing H_2O whereas twin-Earth-Jon is related to a proposition containing XYZ. In twin-Earth cases, the propositions to which *A* and *B* (assuming that *A* lives on Earth and *B* on twin-Earth) are related are, *ex hypothesi*, different. It is possible to give an example without mentioning twin-Earth cases. If we consider that *B* thinks whatever *A* thinks iff she is in the same mental (thinking) state, then two people who use a sentence containing the first-person pronoun think the same thing. Hence, when *A* expresses her thought using 'I', *B* ought to entertain an 'I'-thought in order to think the same thing as *A*. In so doing, though, she *cannot* be related to the same proposition as *A*; it is simply impossible for two people to express the same (singular) proposition using 'I'. If

---

[35] Richard (1990: 149) proposes a similar reconstruction of the inference.
[36] Indeed, *S* could be the same as *S**, but we do not know if this is the case.

we assume that B thinks whatever A thinks iff they are in the same mental state, regardless of the proposition they are related to, the implication turns out to be:

(30) a. $THINK(A,$ that Lenin is F, "Lenin is F")
 b. $\forall S[\exists p(S$ expresses p & $THINK(A,$ that $p, S)) \to \exists p^*(S$ expresses p^* & $THINK(B,$ that $p^*, S))]$[37]

Thus: c. $\exists p^*[THINK(B,$ that $p^*,$ "Lenin is F")]

Notice that Crimmins & Perry must reject this interpretation. In their account of attitude ascriptions, reference is made to cognitive particulars. Hence, if we relate an agent both to a proposition and to a cognitive particular in an attitude ascription, we do not attribute the same way of believing to different agents. Cognitive particulars, unlike mental states, are unsharable, so the information that our agents apprehend the proposition in the same way cannot be conveyed by a 'that'-clause and therefore must come from another place. It seems to me that if we buy Crimmins & Perry's view, we separate 'that'-clauses and psychological generalizations insofar as, in their theory, attitude ascriptions do not license psychological generalizations (at least not in a straightforward way).[38] On the other hand, the picture I proposed allows for interesting psychological generalizations over different agents. Imagine the following folk explanation:

(31) a. Sue believes that there is some beer in the fridge
 b. Sue wants some beer
 c. Sue goes to the fridge and takes the beer (*ceteris paribus*)

and

(32) a. Tim believes that there is some beer in the fridge
 b. Tim wants some beer
 c. Tim goes to the fridge and takes the beer (*ceteris paribus*)

We can deal with psychological generalization here, for in both (31a–b) and (32a–b) the third relatum is a sentence classifying a type of mental representation. So, with an attribution like (31a) and (32a), or (31b) and (32b), we relate Sue and Tim to the same

---

[37] p can be the same as p^* (as our reconstruction suggests) insofar as we take 'Lenin' in (30a) and in (30c) to be the same proper name. On the other hand, if the sentence S that the agent *n-accepts* is "I am F", p and p^* will differ insofar as A and B are distinct agents.

[38] As far as I can see, Crimmins and Perry need to make abstractions from cognitive particulars and open the door to types of cognitive particular in order to allow psychological generalizations. Two agents act in the same way because they relate to the same type of cognitive particular. Hence, if 'that'-clauses license psychological generalizations, they do so insofar as they make reference to types of cognitive particular. To be sure, Crimmins and Perry recognize two kind of reports: (i) reports where cognitive particulars are provided and (ii) reports where they are merely constrained, but they insist that, in usual attributions, cognitive particulars are provided and not just quantified over: "a plausible case can be mounted for the view that, in all successful belief reports, specific notions are provided for the report to be about" (1989: 226).

mental state. Hence, we explain the similarity of their behavior in an elegant way. Sue and Tim act (*ceteris paribus*) in a similar way because they are in the same mental state. Since 'that'-clauses attribute mental states, they turn out to be a good vehicle for psychological explanation. The picture I am proposing nicely accounts for folk psychology, i.e. it allows us to deal with psychological generalizations and explanations in a straightforward way.[39] Hence, as far as psychological explanation is concerned, the triadic view I am proposing comes cheaper than the Crimmins and Perry account.

Let us now consider Richard's puzzle:

Consider *A*—a man stipulated to be intelligent, rational, a competent speaker of English, etc.—who both sees a woman, across the street, in a phone booth, and is speaking to a woman through a phone. He does not realize that the woman to whom he is speaking—*B* to give her a name—is the woman he sees. He perceives her to be in some danger—a runaway steamroller, say, is bearing down upon her phone booth. *A* waves at the woman; he says nothing into the phone. (Richard 1983: 184)

Richard claims that *A* can utter (33) but not (34):

(33) I believe that she [pointing to the woman he is seeing] is in danger
(34) I believe that you [speaking into the phone] are in danger.

The account I gave allows us to explain this fact in an elegant way: *A*'s beliefs are based upon two distinct acts of perception. Suppose now that *B*, seeing a man (who happens to be *A*) in a phone booth across the street waving frantically, reports:

(35) The man watching me believes that I am in danger

A explicitly agrees with *B* and reports:

(36) The man watching you believes that you are in danger.

Crimmins and Perry (1989: 708) hold that report (36) is true while report (34) is false. It may be worth noticing that the puzzle suggests that *A can utter* (33) but *A cannot utter* (34).[40] A friend of the Kaplanian framework concerning the logic of indexicals (i.e. a friend of the sentence-in-a-context approach) can argue that something else is needed to go from the fact that someone cannot utter a sentence to the fact that this sentence is false.[41] Crimmins and Perry argue that (34) and (36) do not make the same ascription to *A*. The difference cannot come from the 'that'-clause, which in both

---

[39] I discussed psychological generalizations and explanations in Ch. 6, above.
[40] To be precise, we should say that *A* can *sincerely assert* (33) but *A cannot sincerely assert* (34), for we can imagine a situation when someone, say John Perry, who wants the inference to be valid, approaches *A* with a machine gun (or a blank check) and asks him to utter (34). In that case, *A* would utter (34) but would not assert it.
[41] Salmon argues that Crimmins & Perry commit the *pragmatic fallacy*. That is, they accept the inference: "Speaker *a*, in using sentence *S* in context *c*, is correct (speaks the truth, says something true). Therefore, *S* is semantically true with respect to *c*" (Salmon 1995: 18 n. 27). In short: "The pragmatic fallacy embodies the idea that if the use of a particular expression fulfills a certain illocutionary purpose of the speaker's, then that purpose must also characterize the expression's semantic function with respect to the speaker's context" (Salmon 1991: 91).

cases is the same ('you are in danger'). It comes from outside, from the way the believer, A, is referred to. And this, as Crimmins and Perry note, is enough. If this is the case, the inference:

(37) a. The man watching you believes that you are in danger
b. I am the man watching you

Thus: c. I believe that you are in danger

is not valid. Crimmins and Perry's (1989: 709) moral is that a "contextual shift can be brought about by a change in wording outside of the embedded sentence in a belief report".[42] If one adopts Kaplan's framework and assumes that there cannot be a switch of context between the premises and the conclusion, then the conclusion "I believe that you are in danger" follows from the truth of the premises. Moreover, if one accepts the story I told about the logical form of attitudes, nothing at the level of the logical form seems to tell us that the inference does not go through, for the logical form of (37c) is:

(37) d. BEL(I, that B is in danger, "You are in danger")

whereas the logical form of (37a) is:

(37) e. BEL(*the man watching you*, that B is in danger, "You are in danger")

The puzzle is that (37a), as its logical form (37d) shows, suggests that I am *actually* self-attributing the *n*-acceptance of the sentence "You are in danger". But this contradicts the datum.

You may remember that in Chapter 7 (Section 6), when discussing the notion of perceptual thoughts and the way we can classify them using the notion of *n*-acceptance, I argued that a demonstrative sentence classifies a partial mental representation. This feature rests on the fact that demonstrative reference is perception-based (Chapter 4, Section 2). To summarize the picture I proposed, we have the following chart:

- Sentence: *classify* → Type mental representation—*determine* → Cog. value
- Demonstrative *classify* → Partial type mental representation
  Sentence: +
                    Act of perception—*determine*→ Cog. value

---

[42] Notice that if we understand the puzzle as follows:

(i) a. The man watching you believes that you are in danger
b. I do not believe that you are in danger
c. I am the man watching you

we cannot then infer a contradiction of the form:

(ii) I believe that you are in danger and I do not believe that you are in danger.

The puzzle so understood is explained away.

Thus, the *n*-acceptance of a demonstrative sentence classifies a partial mental representation, which needs to be completed by an act of perception. The very same partial mental representation can be completed by different acts of perception and thus can classify different cognitive values. This is precisely what we need to account for Richard's puzzle. In the scenario described, *B* perceives *A* in two very different ways. *B* has a visual perception and an auditory perception of *A*, but she does not realize that her distinct acts of perception are of the same individual. The picture I proposed allows us to deal with this scenario, insofar as the attribution of the *n*-acceptance of a demonstrative sentence classifies a partial mental state, which needs to be completed by an act of perception.

On my account, reports like (37a) and (37c) do not necessarily attribute the same mental state to *B*. Actually, the natural reading of an attribution like "*A* believes/think/says ... that you are *F*" is *de re*. That is, 'you' is used by the reporter and it does not specify the sentence that the attributee, *A*, *n*-accepts. A self-attribution like "I believe/think/say ... that you are *F*", on the other hand, is not *de re* insofar as it specifies the sentence that the attributee *n*-accepts (self-ascribes). A self-attribution is *de se*. As we saw, under a *de re* interpretation of the first premiss, Richard's puzzle is explained away, for the attribution is then silent on the way in which the believer thinks of the proposition expressed by "You are in danger". Richard's puzzle, though, does not suggest a *de re* interpretation of the first premiss. Intuitively, the subject term 'the man *watching you*' explicitly refers to the referent's act of perception and, because of this fact, it attributes to him the *n-acceptance* of the sentence "You are in danger", based on her perception of the addressee. If the report were "Sue believes that you are in danger", the *de re* reading would be more natural, insofar as we would not then mention Sue's way of thinking of the referent picked out by the reporter's use of 'you'.

The problem with Richard's puzzle is that we are dealing with self-ascriptions. Self-reference is a peculiar matter. Castañeda convincingly shows that we cannot explain away a quasi-indicator *via* a coreferring term; Perry echoed him in showing that 'I' is an essential indexical which cannot be replaced without destroying the force of explanation: if we replace 'I' with a coreferring term, something is lost.[43] You may recall that one of Castañeda's data is that an agent, say Sue, may believe that she (herself) is *F* without believing that Sue is *F*, having lost track of her name. The story may be told the other way around. Sue may well believe that Sue is *F* without believing that she (herself) is *F*. Hence, "Sue believes *S*" may well

---

[43] See Castañeda (1966; 1967) and Perry (1979). For an exhaustive discussion of the first-person pronoun, see Ch. 5, above. As for the fact that 'I' cannot be replaced by a coreferring term without loosing its cognitive impact, see the discussion of the Irreducibility Thesis in Ch. 8, Sect. 1, above.

differ in truth-value from "I believe S", even if I am Sue (e.g. if I do not know that I am Sue, "I believe that you are in danger" and "Sue believes that you are in danger" may differ in truth-value). The moral seems to be that in a self-ascription, 'I' cannot be substituted *salva veritate* by a coreferring term. An inference like the one described in Richard's puzzle is not valid because the self-attributer may not know that he is the man watching you. This seems to mirror the Fregean datum that, from "Sue believes that Lenin is F", we cannot infer "Sue believes that Vladimir Ulyanov is F", even though Lenin is Vladimir Ulyanov. The invalidity of these inferences does not come, as Crimmins and Perry suggest, from a switch of context from the premisses to the conclusion. In Frege's case it comes from the fact that 'Lenin' is embedded in a psychological prefix; in Richard's puzzle, it comes from the peculiarity of the first-person pronoun, which is reflected in self-ascriptions. The moral is not that a contextual shift is made from the premisses to the conclusion; it is that self-attributions need special treatment.

Having said that, however, the position I am advocating does not rule out a contextual shift from a premiss to the conclusion. As we saw, to deal with inferences containing demonstratives we must appeal to contextual shifts. But this can easily be captured by the notion of indices I suggested. Two occurrences of the very same indexical in an inference may well be assigned different indices even if they are coreferential. The linking and the converse linking rules allow for just that. An inference like (37) can thus be rephrased as:

(38) a. [The man watching you$_2$]$_1$ believes that you$_2$ are in danger
b. I$_3$ am [the man watching you$_2$]$_1$

Thus: c. I$_3$ believe that you$_4$ are in danger

The fact that in (38b) 'I' and 'the man watching you' cannot be coindexed comes from the Identity-Coindexation Rule. In virtue of the Conversion-Linking-Rule, 'I' and 'the man watching you' may well be coreferential. Stated in this way, Richard's puzzle turns out to be an instantiation of Frege's puzzle. As such, it is an instance of the schema:

(39) a. W believes that Y is in danger
b. X = W

Thus: c. X believes that Z is in danger

This inference is clearly invalid. One could ask why 'you' in (38a) and 'you' in (38c) are not coindexed. My answer is straightforward: they constitute two distinct occurrences of the demonstrative 'you' and, as such, they rest on different acts of perception and thus can have different cognitive values. If they were coindexed, this would suggest, contrary to the scenario, that B is aware of the identity between herself and 'the man watching you'. But, for the puzzle to obtain, this cannot be the case and both occurrences of 'you' cannot be coindexed.[44] This does not prevent them from being coreferential though. If they were coindexed, the inference would be an instance of the schema:

(40) a. W believes that W is in danger
b. X = W

Thus: c. X believes that W is in danger

This inference is indeed valid, but it fails to capture the situation described.

I can end this chapter in claiming that the logical form of attitude ascriptions I proposed allows us to deal with the sloppy identity/strict identity distinction in an elegant way. Consider the following dialogue:

(41) *A*: I think that I am F.
B: I think the same thing.

B's assertion can have two readings: the strict identity reading,

(42) I think that you are F

and the sloppy identity reading,

(43) I think that I am F.

In (42), *B* thinks the same proposition as *A*, but in another way, *n-accepting* another sentence ("You are F"). In (43), *B* thinks a different proposition from *A*, but she shares the same belief state, i.e. *A* and *B n-accept* the same sentence ("I am F").

---

[44] In (38a), the two occurrences of 'you' are coindexed. This captures the fact that *B*'s demonstrative reference does not rest on two distinct acts of perception. Using the notion of dependence I introduced in Ch. 8 (Sect. 3), above, this can be rendered either in claiming that both uses are independent (in which case they rest on a single act of perception and there is a dynamic thought at work), or we could claim that the second occurrence is dependent and thus anaphoric on the first occurrence. In that case, (38a) could be represented as:

[The man watching you$_2'$]$_1$ believes that you$_2^d$ are in danger.

Conclusion

> But isn't clear that the two 'this's' have different meanings, since they can be replaced by different proper names?—Replaced? "This" just doesn't now mean "A", now "B".—Of course not by itself, but together with the pointing gesture.—Very well; that is only to say that a sign consisting of the word "this" and a gesture has a different meaning from a sign consisting of "this" and another gesture.
>
> But this is of course mere juggling with words. What you are saying is that your sentence "This is beautiful and this is not beautiful" is not a complete sentence, because these words have to have gestures going with them.—But that is not a complete sentence in that case? It is a sentence of a different kind from, say "The sun is rising"; it has a very different employment. But such are the differences that there are, this is the profusion that there is in the realm of sentences.
>
> (Wittgenstein, *RPP* i: §39)

In the Introduction, I promised to propose a picture concerning indexicality and quasi-indexicality. The indexical landscape has been depicted from a broad perspective, yet I have tried to include some of the details as well. Thus, notions pertaining to the philosophy of language, to linguistics, and to psychology have all entered the scene. The picture which materialized has turned out to be more complicated than I first imagined. Nonetheless, I hope that it is coherent. One of the main theses has been that the mastery of indexicals presupposes specific cognitive capacities. Some psychological studies have been made to investigate the cognitive base upon which the use of indexicals lies. It emerged that the phenomenon of indexicality plays a key role when we come to explain both linguistic interaction and thoughtful episodes. Indexicality also helps to explain how human beings successfully interact with the external world and anchor their thoughts to reality. In particular, it helps to underline how we constantly exploit contextual features. Thus, the phenomenon of indexicality brings to center stage the fact that we are context-bound agents. For this very reason, notions such as perspective, point of view, and egocentricity, played an important role in characterizing the complexity underlying the phenomenon of indexicality in particular and of context-sensitivity in general.

I hope that in depicting indexicality I have been able to show that it cannot be conceived fruitfully without appealing to the phenomenon of quasi-indexicality. In short, I hope that my reader is now convinced that indexicality and quasi-indexicality go hand in hand. In fact, I maintained the thesis that one cannot be said to master the use of indexicals if one does not also master the use of quasi-indicators. It appeared that we learn how to use indexicals, and in particular the first-person pronoun, insofar as we interact with other people. We evolved the way we did, and talk and think the way we do, because we are social agents. One cannot conceive of oneself *as* oneself without also conceiving others as self-directed, egocentric agents. Thus one does not master 'I' unless one also masters its quasi-indexical counterpart 's/he (her/himself)', one does not master 'now' if one does not also master 'then', and one does not master 'here' if one does not also master 'there'. Psychological pathologies such as autism, for instance, seem to sustain this claim, or so I argued. A promising way to describe how we capture other people's perspectives, i.e. how one grasps someone else's perspectival thought, is in assuming that we are capable of putting ourselves into that person's shoes and, in so doing, grasping their perspective. During this imaginative activity, this act of transference, we take someone else's point of view. In imagination we invoke a context shift. New contextual parameters become crucial in the determination of the value of any indexical expressions we may employ in this imaginative process. In other words, the agent, location, and time may all be shifted in an imaginative process, so that 'I', 'now', 'here', etc. can stand for the imagined subject, time, location, etc. In that case, the indexical expressions are somewhat governed by an imagination operator akin to an operator like "in the fiction" governing fictional discourse. Transference turned out to play a key role when we came to explain the process of attributing propositional attitudes, for this imaginative act, this simulation mechanism, is what underlies our mindreading faculty and, therefore, the way we can capture, in our 'that'-clauses, someone's mental life. Thus, insofar as quasi-indicators appear only in reportive contexts, our capacity to simulate other people's mental life and activity also lies beneath the phenomenon of quasi-indexicality. Upon this model of attitude ascriptions I attempted to deal with some traditional, Frege-inspired, puzzles. To do so I relied on the notion of neutral acceptance and argued that accepted sentences are the best candidates with which to characterize someone's mental life. Along this line, I characterized *de se* ascriptions by focusing on the acceptance of an 'I'-sentence classifying an 'I'-thought. Thus, insofar as the quasi-indicator 's/he (her/himself)' is the only mechanism enabling the attribution of an 'I'-thought, it performs a dual role: it is coreferential with the antecedent it is linked with and it attributes to the referent of the antecedent, the subject of the 'that'-clause, an 'I'-thought.

There is one thing I am sure of. Many readers will still be unconvinced by the picture proposed here. This is often the rule of the game in philosophical inquiries. I am also sure that further work on the topics mentioned in this book needs to be done. If nothing else, I hope that my reader is now convinced of at least two related things, one historical and one programmatic. First, the phenomenon of quasi-indexicality—which was brought into the philosophical forum almost forty years ago by Castañeda—has not been fully recognized and appreciated by the philosophical community.[1] For this very reason it seems to me that quasi-indexicality did not play the role it deserves within the philosophical community. Secondly, I hope that some readers may be convinced that further studies and developments of quasi-indexicality should be proposed. In short, I hope that others will join this venture and may be tempted to reinvigorate quasi-indexicality in their further investigations.

---

[1] To my knowledge few studies focusing on Castañeda's notion of quasi-indicators have been proposed. Among them we have Kapitain (1998) and Rapaport, Shapiro and Wiebe (1998). Unlike the direct reference approach I favor, Kapitain attempts to capture quasi-indexicality within a Fregean framework. As for Rapaport et al., they argue that quasi-indicators should be represented in artificial knowledge-representation systems.

Bibliography

Adams, F. and Fuller, G. (1992), 'Names, Contents, and Causes', *Mind and Language*, 7: 205–21.
—— —— and Stecker, R. (1993), 'Thoughts without Objects', *Mind and Language*, 8: 90–104.
—— —— —— (1999), 'Object Dependent Thoughts, Perspectival Thoughts, and Psychological Generalization', *Dialectica*, 53: 47–59.
Adams, R. M. (1983), 'Knowledge and Self: A Correspondence between R. M. Adams and H. N. Castañeda', in J. Tomberlin (ed.), *Agent, Language, and the Structure of the World*, (Indianapolis: Hackett Publishing Company), 293–309.
Allen, J. H. and Greenough, J. B. (1883/1903), *New Latin Grammar* (New York: Ginn & Co.).
Almog, J. (1981), 'Dthis and Dthat: Indexicality Goes Beyond That', *Philosophical Studies*, 39: 347–81.
—— Perry, J., and Wettstein, H. (eds.) (1989), *Themes from Kaplan* (Oxford: Oxford University Press).
Anscombe, E. (1975), 'The First Person', in Yourgrau (ed.) (1990: 135–53).
Austin, D. (1990), *What's the Meaning of 'This'?* (Ithaca, NY: Cornell University Press).
Bach, K. (1987), *Thought and Reference* (Oxford: Clarendon Press).
—— (1994), 'Conversational Implicitures', *Mind and Language*, 9: 124–62.
—— (1999*a*), 'The Myth of Conventional Implicature', *Linguistics and Philosophy*, 22: 327–66.
—— (1999*b*), 'The Semantics-Pragmatics Distinction: What it is and Why it Matters', in K. Turner (ed.), *The Semantics-Pragmatics Interface from Different Points of View* (Oxford: Elsevier), 65–84.
—— (2000), 'Quantification, Qualification, and Context: A Reply to Stanley and Szabo', *Mind and Language*, 15: 262–83.
—— (2001), 'You Don't Say?', *Synthese*, 128: 15–44.
Barcan Marcus R. (1975), 'Does the Principle of Substitutivity Rest on a Mistake', in A. R. Anderson, R. M. Martin, R. B. Marcus (eds.), *The Logical Enterprise* (New Haven: Yale University Press) 31–8; repr. in R. Marcus (1993), *Modalities* (Oxford: Oxford University Press), 101–9.
—— (1985/6), 'Possibilia and Possible Worlds', *Grazer Philosophishe Studien*, 25/6: 107–33; repr. in R. Marcus (1993), *Modalities* (Oxford: Oxford University Press), 189–232.
Baron-Cohen, S. (1989), 'Are Autistic Children Behaviorists? An Examination of their Mental-Physical and Appearance-Reality Distinction', *Journal of Autism and Developmental Disorders*, 19: 579–600.
—— (1995), *Mindblindness: An Essay on Autism and Theory of Mind* (Cambridge Mass.: MIT Press).
—— (2000), 'Theory of Mind and Autism: A Fifteen Years Review', in S. Baron-Cohen, H. Tager-Flusberg, and D. Cohen (eds.), *Understanding Other Minds: Perspectives From Developmental Cognitive Neuroscience* (Oxford: Oxford University Press), 3–20.

Barwise, J. and Cooper, R. (1981), 'Generalized Quantifiers and Natural Language', *Linguistics and Philosophy*, 4: 159–219.

—— and Etchemendy, J. (1987), *The Liar: An Essay on Truth and Circularity* (Oxford: Oxford University Press).

Batson, C. D. and Shaw, L. L. (1991), 'Evidence for Altruism: Toward a Pluralism of Prosocial Motives', *Psychological Inquiry*, 2: 107–22.

Biro, J. (1992), 'In Defence of Social Content', *Philosophical Studies*, 67: 277–93.

Blackburn, S. (1984), *Spreading the World* (Oxford: Oxford University Press).

Blair, R. J. R. (1995), 'A Cognitive Developmental Approach to Morality: Investigating the Psychopath', *Cognition*, 57: 1–29.

Blakemore, S. J. and Decety, J. (2001), 'From the Perception of Action to the Understanding of Intention', *Nature Reviews: Neuroscience*, 2: 561–7.

Boër, S. E. and Lycan, W. G. (1980), 'Who, Me?', *Philosophical Review*, 89: 427–66.

Borg, E. (2000), 'Complex Demonstratives', *Philosophical Studies*, 97: 229–49.

Bosch, P. (1983), *Agreement and Anaphora: A Study of the Role of Pronouns in Discourse and Syntax* (London/New York: Academic Press).

Bosh, G. (1970), *Infantile Autism* (New York: Springer-Verlag).

Braun, D. (1994), 'Structured Character and Complex Demonstratives', *Philosophical Studies*, 74: 193–219.

—— (1996), 'Demonstratives and their Linguistic Meanings', *Noûs*, 30: 145–73.

Bühler, K. (1934), *Sprachtheorie* (Iena/Stuttgard: Gustav Fisher Verlag); Eng. trans. (1990) *Theory of Language* (Amsterdam: John Benjamins).

Burdick, H. (1982), 'A Logical Form for the Propositional Attitudes', *Synthese*, 52: 185–230.

Burge, T. (1973), 'Reference and Proper Names', *Journal of Philosophy*, 70: 425–39.

—— (1978a), 'Belief and Synonymy', *Journal of Philosophy*, 75: 119–38.

—— (1978b), 'Self-Reference and Translation', in J. F. Guenthner & M. Guenthner-Rutter (eds.), *Meaning and Translation* (London: Duckworth), 137–53.

Cain, M. (2002), *Fodor: Language, Mind and Philosophy* (Cambridge: Polity Press).

Cappelen, H. and Lepore, E. (1997), 'On the Alleged Connection between Indirect Quotation and Semantic Theory', *Mind and Language*, 12: 278–96.

—— —— (forthcoming), 'Unarticulated Constituents and Hidden Indexicals: An Abuse of Context in Semantics', in M. O'Rourke and C. Washington (eds.), *Situating Semantics: Essays on the Philosophy of John Perry* (Cambridge Mass.: MIT Publications).

Carston, R. (1988), 'Implicature, Explicature and Truth Theoretic Semantics', in R. Kempson (ed.), *Mental Representations: The Interface between Language and Reality* (Cambridge: Cambridge University Press), 155–81.

—— (2002), *Thoughts and Utterances: The Pragmatics of Explicit Communication* (Oxford: Blackwell).

Castañeda, H.-N. (1966), ' "He": A Study in the Logic of Self-Consciousness', *Ratio*, 8: 130–57.

—— (1967), 'Indicators and Quasi-Indicators', *American Philosophical Quarterly*, 4: 85–100; repr. in Castañeda (1989: 206–31).

—— (1968), 'On the Logic of Attributions of Self-Knowledge to Others', *Journal of Philosophy*, 65: 439–56.

—— (1983a), 'Knowledge and Self: A Correspondence between R. M. Adams and H.-N. Castañeda', in Tomberlin (ed.), (1983: 293–309).

—— (1983b), 'Reply to Perry', in Tomberlin (ed.), (1983: 313–27).
—— (1989), *Thinking, Language, and Experience* (Minneapolis: University of Minnesota Press).
Charney, R. (1981), 'Pronoun Errors in Autistic Children: Support for a Social Explanation', *British Journal of Disorders of Communication*, 15: 39–43.
Chierchia, G. (1989), 'Anaphora and Attitudes *De Se*', in R. Bartsch, J. Van Bentham, J. and P. van Emde (eds.), *Language in Context* (Dordrecht: Doris).
Chisholm, R. (1981), *The First Person* (Minneapolis: University of Minnesota Press).
—— (1989), 'Why Singular Propositions?', in Almog et al. (eds.), (1989: 145–50).
Chomsky, N. (1981), *Lectures on Government and Binding* (Dordrecht: Foris).
—— (1992), *What Uncle Sam Really Wants* (Monroes, Me.: Odonian Press).
—— (2000), *New Horizons in the Study of Language and Mind* (Cambridge: Cambridge University Press).
Clements, G. (1975), 'The Logophoric Pronoun in EWE: Its Role in Discourse', *Journal of West African Languages*, 10: 141–77.
Cohen, L. J. (1971), 'Some Remarks on Grice's View about the Logical Particles of Natural Language', in Y. Bar-Hillel (ed.), *Pragmtics of Natural Language* (Dordrecht: Reidel), 50–68.
Condoravdi, C. and Gawron, M. (1996), 'The Context Dependency of Implicit Arguments', in K. Makoto, C. Piñon, and H. de Swart (eds.), *Quantifiers, Deduction and Context* (Standord, Calif.: CSLI Publication), 1–32.
Corazza, E. (1994), 'Perspectival Thoughts and Psychological Generalizations', *Dialectica*, 48: 307–36.
—— (1995), *Référence, contexte, et attitude* (Paris/Montréal: Vrin/Bellarmin).
—— (1998), ' "She*": Pragmatically Imparted or Semantically Encoded?', in F. Orilia and W. Rapaport (eds.), *Thought, Language, and Ontology: Essays in Memory of Hector-Neri Castañeda* (Dordrecht: Kluwer Academic Publisher), 217–34.
—— (1999a), 'Washing Away Original *Sinn*', *Dialogue*, 38: 743–63.
—— (1999b), 'Indexicals and Demonstratives', in F. C. Keil & R. A. Wilson (eds.), *MIT Encyclopedia of the Cognitive Sciences* (Cambridge, Mass.: MIT Press), 393–5.
—— (2001), 'Understanding "I": A Wittgensteinian Perspective', *Wittgenstein Studies*, 2: 23–33.
—— (2002a), 'Temporal Indexicals and Temporal Terms', *Synthese*, 130: 441–60.
—— (2002b), 'Reports and Imagination', *Protosociology: Semantic Theory and Reported Speech*, 17: 76–96.
—— (2002c), 'Description-Names', *Journal of Philosophical Logic*, 31: 313–26.
—— (2002d), ' "She" and "He": Politically Correct Pronouns', *Philosophical Studies*, 111: 173–96.
—— (2003), 'Complex Demonstratives *qua* Singular Terms', *Erkenntnis*, 59: 263–83.
—— (2004a), 'Kinds of Context: A Wittgensteinian Approach to Proper Names and Indexicals', *Philosophical Investigations*, 27: 158–88.
—— (2004b), 'On the Alleged Ambiguity of "Now" and "Here" ', *Synthese*, 138: 289–313.
Corazza, E. (forthcoming), 'Thinking the Unthinkable: An Excursion into Z-land', in M. O'Rourke and C. Washington (eds.), *Situating Semantics: Essays on the Philosophy of John Perry* (Cambridge, Mass.: MIT Publications).

—— (forthcoming), 'Essential Indexicals and Quasi-Indicators,' *Journal of Semantics*.
—— and Dokic, J. (1995), 'Why is Frege's Puzzle Still Puzzling?', in J. Biro and P. Kotatko (eds.), *Sense and Reference One Hundred Years Later* (Dordrecht: Kluver Academic Publisher), 151–68.
—— Fish, W., and Gorvett, J. (2002), 'Who is I?', *Philosophical Studies*, 107: 1–21.
—— and Whitsey, M. (2003), 'Indexical, Fiction, and *Ficta*', *Dialectica*, 57: 121–36.
Corblin, F. (1995), *Les Formes de reprise dans le discours: Anaphores et chaînes de référence* (Rennes: Presses Universitaires de Rennes).
Cottingham, J. (1986), *Descartes* (Oxford: Blackwell).
Crimmins, M. (1992), *Talk about Beliefs* (Cambridge Mass.: MIT Press).
—— and Perry, J. (1989), 'The Prince and the Phone Booth: Reporting Puzzling Beliefs', *Journal of Philosophy*, 86: 685–711; repr. in J. Perry (2000: 207–32).
Culy, C. (1994a), 'Aspects of Logophoric Marking', *Linguistics*, 32: 1055–94.
—— (1994b), 'A Note on Logophoricity in Dogon', *Journal of African Languages and Linguistics*, 15: 113–25.
—— (1997), 'Logophoric Pronouns and Points of View', *Linguistics*, 35: 845–59.
Currie, G. and Ravenscroft, I. (2002), *Recreative Minds* (Oxford: Oxford University Press).
Davidson, D. (1968), 'On Saying That'; repr. in D. Davidson (1984), *Inquiries Into Truth and Interpretation* (Oxford: Oxford University Press), 93–108.
Davies, M. (1992), 'Perceptual Content and Local Supervenience', *Proceeding of the Aristotelian Society*, 92: 21–45.
—— and Stone, T. (eds.) (1995a), *Folk Psychology: The Theory of Mind Debate* (Oxford: Blackwell).
—— —— (eds.) (1995b), *Mental Simulation: Evaluations and Applications* (Oxford: Blackwell).
Dever, J. (2001), 'Complex Demonstratives', *Linguistics and Philosophy*, 24: 271–330.
Devlin, K. (1991), *Logic and Information* (Cambridge: Cambridge University Press).
Dokic, J. (2001), 'Conceptualism about Properties: A Defense', MS.
—— (2002a), 'L'invisibilite des propriétés: Defénse d'un conceptualiame post-frigien,' *Cahiers de Philosophie de l'Université de Caen*, 38–39: 53–80.
—— (2002b), 'Steps toward a Theory of Situated Representations', MS.
—— and Proust, J. (eds.) (2002), *Simulation and Knowledge of Action* (Amsterdam: John Benjamins Publishing Company).
Donnellan, K. (1966), 'Reference and Definite Descriptions', *Philosophical Review*, 75: 281–304.
—— (1974), 'Speaking of Nothing', *Philosophical Review*, 83: 3–31.
Dretske, F. (1969), *Seeing and Knowing* (Chicago: University of Chicago Press).
—— (1988), *Explaining Behavior: Reasons in a World of Causes* (Cambridge Mass.: MIT Press).
Dummett, M. (1973), *Frege: Philosophy of Language*, 2nd edn. (1981) (Oxford: Duckworth).
—— (1981), *The Interpretation of Frege's Philosophy* (Oxford: Duckworth).
—— (1991), *The Logical Basis of Metaphysics* (Cambridge, Mass.: Harvard University Press).
—— (1993), *Origins of Analytical Philosophy* (Cambridge, Mass.: Harvard University Press).
Egan, F. (1991), 'Must Psychology be Individualistic?', *Philosophical Review*, 100: 179–203.
Evans, G. (1977), 'Pronouns, Quantifiers, and Relative Clauses (I)', *Canadian Journal of Philosophy*, 7: 467–536; repr. in G. Evans (1985), *Collected Papers* (Oxford: Oxford University Press), 76–152.

—— (1981), 'Understanding Demonstratives', in G. Evans (1985), *Collected Papers* (Oxford: Oxford University Press), 291–321.

—— (1982), *The Varieties of Reference* (Oxford: Oxford University Press).

—— (1985), 'Appendix I: Commentary on Jerry A. Fodor, "Methodological Solipsism Considered as a Research Strategy in Cognitive Psychology" ', in G. Evans (1985), *Collected Papers* (Oxford: Oxford University Press), 400–4.

Fiengo, R. and May, R. (1994), *Indices and Identity* (Cambridge, Mass.: MIT Press).

Fodor, J. (1987), *Psychosemantics* (Cambridge, Mass.: MIT Press).

Forbes, G. (1990), 'The Indispensability of *Sinn*', *Philosophical Review*, 99: 535–63.

Fraiberg, S. and Adelson, E. (1977), 'Self-Representation in Language and Play', in S. Fraiberg (ed.), *Insight from the Blind* (London: Souvenir), 248–70.

Frege, G. (1892), 'Sinn und Bedeutung'; trans. as 'On Sense and Meaning' by P. Geach and M. Black (1952), *Translations from the Philosophical Writings of Gottlob Frege* (Oxford: Blackwell), 56–78.

—— (1897), 'Logic'; in G. Frege (1979), *Posthumous Writings* (Oxford: Blackwell), 126–51.

—— (1914), 'Logic in Mathematics'; in G. Frege (1979), *Posthumous Writings* (Oxford: Blackwell), 201–50.

—— (1918), 'Thoughts'; in N. Salmon and S. Soames (eds.) (1988), *Propositions and Attitudes* (Oxford: Oxford University Press), 33–55.

García-Carpintero, M. (1998), 'Indexicals as Token-Reflexives', *Mind*, 107: 529–63.

Geach, P. (1962), *Reference and Generality* (Ithaca, NY: Cornell University Press).

Goldie, P. (2000), *The Emotions* (Oxford: Oxford University Press).

Goldman, A. (1995), 'Empathy, Mind, and Morals', in M. Davies and T. Stone (eds.) (1995*b*: 185–208).

—— (2002), 'Simulation Theory and Mental Concepts', in J. Dokic and J. Proust (eds.), *Simulation and Knowledge of Action* (Amsterdam: John Benjamins), 1–19.

Gordon, R. M. (1995*a*), 'Folk Psychology and Simulation', in M. Davies and T. Stone (eds.) (1995*a*: 60–73).

—— (1995*b*), 'Simulation without Introspection or Inference from Me to You', in M. Davies and T. Stone (eds.) (1995*b*: 53–67).

Gorvett, J. (2004), 'Back through the Looking Glass: On the Relationship Between Intentions and Indexicals', *Philosophical Studies*.

Grice, P. (1989), *Studies in the Way of Words* (Cambridge, Mass.: Harvard University Press).

Griffiths, P. (2002), 'What is Innateness', *Monist*, 85: 70–85.

Haegeman, L. (1994), *Government and Binding Theory* (Oxford: Blackwell).

Hagège, G. N. (1974), 'Les Pronoms logophoriques', *Bulletin de la société de linguistique de Paris*, 69: 287–310.

Hamlyn, D. W. (1974), 'Person and Perception and our Understanding of Others,' in T. Mischel (ed.), *Understanding other Persons* (Oxford: Blackwell), 1–36.

Heal, J. (2003), *Mind, Reason and Imagination* (Cambridge: Cambridge University Press).

Higginbotham, J. (1985), 'On Semantics', *Linguistic Inquiry*, 16: 547–94.

—— (1988), 'Contexts, Models, and Meanings: A Note on the Data of Semantics', in K. Kemson (ed.), *Mental Representations: The Interface between Language and Reality* (Cambridge: Cambridge University Press), 29–48.

Hintikka, J. (1998), 'Perspectival Identification, Demonstratives and "Small Worlds"', *Synthese*, 114: 203–32.

—— and Sandu, G. (1995), 'The Fallacies of the New Theory of Reference', *Synthese*, 104: 245–83.

Hobson, R. P. (1990), 'On Acquiring Knowledge about People and the Capacity to Pretend: Response to Leslie (1987)', *Psychological Review*, 97: 114–21.

—— (1993), *The Development of Mind* (Erlbaum: Hove; Psychology Press).

Hoffman, M. L. (1978), 'Empathy, Its Development and Prosocial Implications', in C. B. Keasey (ed.), *Nebraska Symposium on Motivation*, 25: 169–218.

—— (2000), *Empathy and Moral Development* (Cambridge: Cambridge University Press).

Huang, Y. (1994), *The Syntax and Pragmatics of Anaphora: A Study with Special Reference to Chinese* (Cambridge: Cambridge University Press).

—— (2000), *Anaphora: A Cross-Linguistic Study* (Oxford: Oxford University Press).

Hutchinson, W. D., Davids, K. D., Lozano, A. M., Tasker, R. R., and Dostrowsky, J. O. (1999), 'Pain Related Neurons in the Human Cingulate Cortex', *Nature Neuroscience*, 2: 403–5.

Jackendoff, R. (1994), *Patterns in the Mind* (New York: Basic Books Harper Collins Publishers).

Jacob, P. (1997), *What Minds Can Do* (Cambridge: Cambridge University Press).

—— (1999), 'Unarticulated Constituents and Explicit Content', MS.

—— (2002), 'The Scope and Limits of Mental Simulation', in J. Dokic & J. Proust (eds.) (2002: 87–109).

Jannerod, M. (1994), 'The Representing Brain: Neural Correlates of Motor Intention and Imagery', *Behavioral and Brain Sciences*, 17: 187–245.

Jespersen, O. (1924), *The Philosophy of Grammar* (London: George Allen & Unwin Ltd.).

Kanner, L. (1943), 'Autistic Disturbances in Affective Contact', *Nervous Child*, 2: 217–50.

Kapitain, T. (1998), 'On Depicting Indexical Reference', in F. Orilia and W. J. Rapaport (eds.), *Thought, Language, and Ontology: Essays in Memory of Hector-Neri Castañeda* (Dordrecht: Kluver), 183–215.

Kaplan, D. (1977), 'Demonstratives'; in J. Almog et al. (eds.) (1989: 481–563).

—— (1978), 'Dthat', in P. Yourgrau (ed.) (1990: 11–33).

—— (1989), 'Afterthoughts', in J. Almog et al. (ed.) (1989: 565–614).

—— (1990), 'Words', *Proceedings of the Aristotelian Society*, 64: 93–119.

King, J. (1999), 'Are Complex "That" Phrases Devices of Direct Reference?', *Noûs*, 33: 155–82.

—— (2001), *Complex Demonstratives: A Quantificational Account* (Cambridge, Mass.: MIT Press).

König, E. (1991), *The Meaning of Focus Particles: A Comparative Perspective* (London: Routledge).

Kripke, S. (1977), 'Speaker's Reference and Semantic Reference', in A. French, T. E. Ueling, and H. Wettstein (eds.), *Contemporary Perspectives in the Philosophy of Language* (Minneapolis: University of Minnesota Press), 6–27.

—— (1979), 'A Puzzle about Belief', in A. Margalit (ed.), *Meaning and Use* (Boston: Dordrecht), 239–83; repr. in N. Salmon and S. Soames (eds.) (1988), *Propositions and Attitudes* (Oxford: Oxford University Press), 102–48.

—— (1980), *Naming and Necessity* (Oxford: Blackwell).

Kuno, S. (1987), *Functional Syntax: Anaphora, Discourse and Empathy* (Chicago: University of Chicago Press).

—— and Kaburaki, E. (1977), 'Empathy and Syntax', *Linguistic Inquiry*, 8: 627–72.
Larson, R. and Ludlow, P. (1993), 'Interpreted Logical Form', *Synthese*, 95: 305–55.
—— and Segal, G. (1995), *Knowledge of Meaning* (Cambridge, Mass.: MIT Press).
Lasnik, H. (1976), 'Remarks on Coreference', *Linguistic Analysis*, 2: 1–22; repr. in H. Lasnik (1989), *Essays on Anaphora* (Dordrecht: Kluver), 90–109.
Lepore, E. and Ludwig, K. (2000), 'The Semantics and Pragmatics of Complex Demonstratives', *Mind*, 109: 199–240.
Levenson, R. W. and Reuf, A. M. (1997), 'Physiological Aspects of Emotional Knowledge and Rapport', in W. Ickes (ed.), *Empathic Accuracy* (New York: Guilford), 44–72.
Levinson, S. (1987), 'Pragmatics and the Grammar of Anaphora: A Partial Pragmatic Reduction of Binding and Control Phenomena', *Journal of Linguistics*, 23: 379–434.
—— (2001), *Presumptive Meanings: The Theory of Generalized Conversational Implicature* (Cambridge, Mass.: MIT Press).
Lewis, D. (1979a), 'Scorekeeping in a Language Game', *Journal of Philosophical Logic*, 8: 339–59; repr. in D. Lewis (1983), *Philosophical Papers I* (Oxford: Oxford University Press), 233–49.
—— (1979b), 'Attitudes *De Dicto* and *De Se*', *Philosophical Review*, 88: 523–43; repr. in D. Lewis (1983), *Philosophical Papers I* (Oxford: Oxford University Press, 133–59).
Loar, B. (1988), 'Social Content and Psychological Content', in R. H. Grimm and D. D. Merrill (eds.), *Content of Thought* (Tucson, Ariz.: University of Arizona Press), 99–110.
—— (1991), 'Can We Explain Intentionality?', in B. Loewer and G. Rey (eds.), *Meaning in Mind: Fodor and his Critics* (Oxford: Blackwell), 119–35.
Lyons, J. (1977), *Semantics II* (Cambridge: Cambridge University Press).
Mach, E. (1914), *The Analysis of Sensation* (London: Open Court).
McDowell, J. (1984), '*De Re* Senses', in C. Wright (ed.), *Tradition and Influence* (Oxford: Blackwell), 98–109.
—— (1986), 'Singular Thoughts and the Extent of Inner Space', in J. McDowell and P. Pettit (eds.), *Subject, Thought, and Context* (Oxford: Clarendon Press), 137–68.
—— (1991), 'Intentionality *De Re*', in E. Lepore and R. van Gulick (eds.), *John Searle and his Critics* (Oxford: Blackwell), 215–25.
McGinn, C. (1989), *Mental Content* (Oxford: Blackwell).
MacMurray, J. (1961), *Persons in Relation* (London: Faber and Faber).
Marconi, D. (1990), 'Dictionaries and Proper Names', *History of Philosophy Quarterly*, 7: 77–92.
Marti, G. (1995), 'The Essence of Genuine Reference', *Journal of Philosophical Logic*, 24: 275–89.
Mates, B. (1952), 'Synonymity', in L. Linsky (ed.) (1952), *Semantics and the Philosophy of Language* (Urbana, Ill.: University of Illinois Press).
May, R. (1985), *Logical Form: Its Structure and Derivation* (Cambridge Mass.: MIT Press).
Meltzoff, A. N. (2002), 'Elements of a Developmental Theory of Imitation', in A. N. Meltzoff and P. Wolfgang (eds.), *The Imitative Mind* (Cambridge: Cambridge University Press), 19–41.
Mercier, A. (1999), 'On Communication-Based *De Re* Thoughts, Commitments *De Dicto*, and Word Individuation', in K. Murasugi and R. Stainton (eds.), *Philosophy and Linguistics* (Boulder, Colo.: Westview Press), 85–111.
Moore, G. E. (1959), 'Wittgenstein's Lectures in 1930–33', in G. E. Moore, *Philosophical Papers* (London: George Allen and Unwin Ltd), 253–324.

Moore, M. (2003), *Dude, Where's My Country?* (London and New York: Penguin and Allen Lane).

Mulligan, K. (1997a), 'The Essence of Language: Wittgenstein's Builders and Bühler's Bricks', *Revue de métaphysique et morale*, 2: 193–216.

—— (1997b), 'How Perception Fixes Reference', in A. Burri (ed.), *Sprache und Denken/Language and Thought* (Berlin/New York: de Gruyter), 122–38.

Napoli, E. (1997), 'Names, Indexicals, and Identity Statements', in W. Kuenne, A. Newen, and M. Anduschus (eds.), *Direct Reference, Indexicality, and Propositional Attitudes* (Stanford, Calif.: CSLI Publications), 185–211.

Neale, S. (1990), *Descriptions* (Cambridge, Mass.: MIT Press).

—— (1993), 'Terms Limits', *Philosophical Perspectives*, 7: 89–124.

—— (1999), 'Coloring and Composition', in K. Murasugi and R. Stainton (eds.), *Philosophy and Linguistics* (Boulder, Colo.: Westview Press), 35–82.

Nichols, S. (2002a), 'How Psychopaths Threaten Moral Rationalism: Is It Irrational to Be Amoral?', *Monist*, 85: 285–304.

—— (2002b), 'Norms with Feeling: Towards a Psychological Account of Moral Judgment', *Cognition*, 84: 221–36.

Noonan, H. (1993), 'Object-Dependent Thoughts: A Case of Superficial Necessity but Deep Contingency?', in J. Heil and A. Mele (eds.), *Mental Causation* (Oxford: Clarendon), 283–308.

Nunberg, G. (1993), 'Indexicality and Deixis', *Linguistics and Philosophy*, 16: 1–43.

Partee, B. (1989), 'Binding Implicit Variables in Quantified Contexts', *Proceedings of the Chicago Linguistic Society*, 25: 342–65.

Peacocke, C. (1981), 'Demonstrative Thought and Psychological Explanation', *Synthese*, 49: 187–217.

Pelczar, M. and Rainsbury, J. (1998), 'The Indexical Character of Names', *Synthese*, 114: 293–317.

Perry, J. (1977), 'Frege on Demonstratives', *Philosophical Review*, 86: 474–97; repr. in J. Perry (2000: 1–26).

—— (1979), 'The Problems of the Essential Indexical', *Noûs*, 13: 3–21; repr. in J. Perry (2000: 27–44).

—— (1980a), 'Belief and Acceptance', *Midwest Studies in Philosophy*, 5: 533–42; repr. J. Perry (2000: 45–56).

—— (1980b), 'A Problem about Continued Belief', *Pacific Philosophical Quarterly*, 61: 317–32; repr. in J. Perry (2000: 57–75).

—— (1983), 'Castañeda on He and I', in J.E. Tomberlin (ed.) (1983: 15–39).

—— (1986), 'Thoughts without Representation', *Proceedings of the Aristotelian Society*, 60: 137–52; repr. in J. Perry (2000: 171–88).

—— (1988), 'Cognitive Significance and New Theories of Reference', *Noûs*, 22: 1–18; repr. in J. Perry (2000: 189–206).

—— (1997a), 'Indexicals and Demonstratives', in R. Hale and C. Wright (eds.), *Companion to the Philosophy of Language* (Oxford: Blackwell), 586–612.

—— (1997b), 'Reflexivity, Indexicality and Names', in W. Kuenne, A. Newen, and M. Anduschus (eds.), *Direct Reference, Indexicality, and Propositional Attitudes* (Stanford, Calif.: CSLI Publications); repr. in J. Perry (2000: 341–53).

—— (1998), 'Indexicals, Context and Unarticulated Constituents', in A. Aliseda, R. van Gabeek and D. Westerståhl (eds.), *Computing Natural Language* (Stanford, Calif.: CSLI Publications), 1–11.

—— (2000), *The Problem of the Essential Indexical and Other Essays* (Stanford, Calif.: CSLI Publications).

—— (2001), *Reference and Reflexivity* (Stanford, Calif.: CSLI Publications).

Pollard, C. and Sag, I. (1992), 'Anaphors in English and the Scope of Binding Theory', *Linguistic Inquiry*, 23: 261–303.

—— and Xue, P. (2001), 'Syntactic and Nonsyntactic Constraints on Long-Distance Reflexives', in P. Cole, G. Hermon, and C.-T. Huang, *Syntax and Semantics, 33: Long Distance-Reflexives* (San Diego, Calif.: Academic Press), 317–42.

Predelli, S. (1998a), 'I am not Here Now', *Analysis*, 58: 107–15.

—— (1998b), 'Utterance, Interpretation, and the Logic of Indexicals', *Mind and Language*, 13: 400–14.

—— (2001), 'Names and Character', *Philosophical Studies*, 103: 145–63.

Proust, J. (2002), 'Can "Radical" Simulation Theories Explain Psychological Concept Acquisition?', in J. Dokic and J. Proust (eds.), *Simulation and Knowledge of Action* (Amsterdam: John Benjamins), 201–28.

Putnam, H. (1975), 'The Meaning of "Meaning" ', in H. Putnam, *Mind, Language, and Reality: Philosophical Papers 2* (Cambridge: Cambridge University Press), 215–71.

Quine, W. v. O. (1960), *Word and Object* (Cambridge, Mass.: MIT Press).

—— (1995), *From Stimulus to Science* (Cambridge, Mass.: Harvard University Press).

Rapaport, W. J., Shapiro, S. C., and Wiebe, J. M. (1998), 'Quasi-Indexicals and Knowledge Reports', in F. Orilia and W. J. Rapaport (eds.), *Thought, Language, and Ontology: Essays in Memory of Hector-Neri Castañeda* (Dordrecht: Kluver), 235–94.

Recanati, F. (1993), *Direct Reference: From Language to Thought* (Oxford: Blackwell).

—— (2000), *Oratio Obliqua, Oratio Recta: An Essay on Metarepresentation* (Cambridge, Mass.: MIT Press).

—— (2002), 'Unarticulated Constituents', *Linguistics and Philosophy*, 25: 299–345.

Reichenbach, R. (1947), *Elements of Symbolic Logic* (New York: Macmillan).

Reinhart, T. (1983), 'Coreference and Bound Anaphora: A Restatement of the Anaphora Question', *Linguistic and Philosophy*, 6: 47–88.

—— and Reuland, E. (1991), 'Anaphors and Logophors: An Argument Structure Perspective', in J. Koster and E. Reuland (eds.), *Long Distance Anaphora* (Cambridge: Cambridge University Press), 283–321.

—— —— (1993), 'Reflexivity', *Linguistic Inquiry*, 24: 657–720.

Reuland, E. (2001a), 'Primitives of Binding', *Linguistic Inquiry*, 32: 439–92.

—— (2001b), 'Anaphors, Logophors, and Binding', in P. Cole, G. Hermon, and C. T. J. Hung (eds.) *Syntax and Semantics, 33: Long-Distance Reflexives* (San Diego, Calif: Academic Press), 343–70.

Reuland, E. and Koster, J. (1991), 'Long-Distance Anaphora: an Overview', in J. Koster and E. Reuland (eds.), *Long Distance Anaphora* (Cambridge: Cambridge University Press), 1–25.

Richard, M. (1983), 'Direct Reference and Ascription of Belief', *Journal of Philosophical Logic*, 12: 425–52; repr. in N. Salmon and S. Soames (eds.) (1988) *Propositions and Attitudes* (Oxford: Oxford University Press), 169–96.

—— (1990), *Propositional Attitudes* (Cambridge: Cambridge University Press).
—— (1993a), 'Articulated Terms', *Philosophical Perspectives*, 7: 207–30.
—— (1993b), 'Attitudes in Context', *Linguistics and Philosophy*, 16: 123–48.
Riegert, R. (1990), *California: The Ultimate Guidebook* (Berkeley: Ulysse Press).
Rimbaud, A. (1972), *Œuvres complètes* (Paris: Bibliothèque de la pléiade, Gallimard).
Russell, B. (1905), 'On Denoting', in B. Russell (1956), *Logic and Knowledge: Essays (1901–1950)*, ed. R. C. Marsh (London: Allen & Unwin), 39–56.
—— (1940), *An Inquiry into Meaning and Truth* (London: Allen & Unwin).
—— (1948), *Human Knowledge: Its Scope and Limits* (London: Allen & Unwin).
Sacks, O. (1993–4), 'A Neurologist's Notebook: An Anthropologist on Mars', *New Yorker*, 27 Dec.–3 Jan.: 106–25.
Salmon, N. (1986), *Frege's Puzzle* (Cambridge, Mass.: MIT Press).
—— (1991), 'The Pragmatic Fallacy', *Philosophical Studies*, 63: 83–97.
—— (1995), 'Being of Two Minds: Belief without Doubt', *Noûs*, 28: 1–20.
Schiffer, S. (1977), 'Naming and Knowing', *Midwest Studies in Philosophy*, 2: 28–41.
—— (1987a), *Remnants of Meaning* (Cambridge, Mass.: MIT Press).
—— (1987b), 'The "Fido"-Fido Theory of Belief', *Philosophical Perspectives*, 1: 455–80.
—— (1992), 'Beliefs Ascriptions', *Journal of Philosophy*, 89: 499–521.
Schlenker, P. (2003), 'A Plea for Monsters', *Linguistics and Philosophy*, 26: 29–120.
Searle, J. (1978), 'Literal Meaning', *Erkenntnis*, 13: 207–24.
—— (1980), 'The Background of Meaning', in J. Searle, F. Keifer, and M. Bierwish (eds.), *Speech Act Theory and Pragmatics* (Dordrecht: Reidel), 221–32.
—— (1991), 'Replies', in E. Lepore and R. van Gulick (eds.), *John Searle and his Critics* (Oxford: Blackwell).
Segal, G. (1989), 'The Return of the Individual', *Mind*, 98: 39–57.
—— (1991), 'Defence of a Reasonable Individualism', *Mind*, 100: 485–94
Sidelle, A. (1991), 'The Answering Machine Paradox', *Canadian Journal of Philosophy*, 81: 525–39.
Simner, M. L. (1971), 'Newborn's Response to the Cry of Another Infant', *Developmental Psychology*, 5: 136–50.
Smith, A. (1976; 1st pub. 1759), *The Theory of Moral Sentiments* (Oxford: Clarendon Press).
Smith, Q. (1989), 'The Multiple Uses of Indexicals', *Synthese*, 78: 167–91.
Soames, S. (1989), 'Presuppositions', in D. Gabbay and F. Guenthener (eds.), *Handbook of Philosophical Logic IV* (Dordrecht: Reidel Pub.), 553–616.
—— (2002), *Beyond Rigidity: The Unfinished Semantic Agenda of Naming and Necessity* (Oxford: Oxford University Press).
Sober, E. and Wilson, D. S. (1998), *Unto Others* (Cambridge, Mass.: Harvard University Press).
Soldati, G. F. (1998), *The Epistemological Basis of Subjectivity* (Tübingen: Habilitationsschrift, University of Tübingen).
Sorensen, R. (1998), 'Self-Stengthening Empathy', *Philosophical and Phenomenological Research*, 58: 75–98.
Sperber, D. and Wilson, D. (1986), *Relevance: Communication and Cognition* (Oxford: Blackwell).
Stalnaker, R. (1970), 'Pragmatics', *Synthese*, 22; repr. in R. Stalnaker (1998), *Context and Content* (Oxford: Oxford University Press), 31–46.

—— (1974), 'Pragmatic Presuppositions', in M. Munitz and P. Unger (eds.), *Semantics and Philosophy* (New York: New York University Press), rep. in R. Stalnaker (1998), *Context and Content* (Oxford: Oxford University Press), 47–62.

Stanley, J. (2000), 'Context and Logical Form', *Linguistic and Philosophy*, 23: 391–434.

—— and Szabo, Z. (2000), 'On Quantifier Domain Restriction', *Mind & Language*, 15: 219–61.

Stern, D. (1985), *The Interpersonal World of the Infant* (New York: Basic Books).

Stich, S. (1983), *From Folk Psychology to Cognitive Sciences* (Cambridge, Mass.: MIT Press).

Stotland, E. (1969), 'Exploratory Investigations of Empathy', in L. Berkowitz (ed.), *Advances in Experimental Social Psychology 4* (New York: Academic Press), 271–314.

Strawson, P. (1959), *Individuals* (London: Methuen).

Taylor, K. (2001), 'Sex, Breakfast, and Descriptus Interruptus', *Synthese*, 128: 45–61.

Thau, M. and Caplan, B. (2001), 'What's Puzzling Gottlob Frege?', *Canadian Journal of Philosophy*, 31: 159–200.

Tomberlin, J. (ed.) (1983), *Agent, Language, and the Structure of the World* (Indianapolis: Hackett Publishing Company).

Travis, C. (1985), 'On What Is Strictly Speaking True', *Canadian Journal of Philosophy*, 15: 187–229.

—— (1989), *The Uses of Sense: Wittgenstein's Philosophy of Language* (Oxford: Oxford University Press).

—— (1996), 'Meaning Role in Truth', *Mind*, 105: 451–66.

Vendler, Z. (1984), *The Matter of Minds* (Oxford: Oxford University Press).

Vision, G. (1985), 'I am Here Now', *Analysis*, 45: 198–9.

Voltolini, A. (1995), 'Indexinames', in J. Hill and P. Kotatko (eds.), *Karlovy Vary Studies in Reference and Meaning* (Prague: Filosofia-Filosofia Publications), 258–85.

Wettstein, H. (1988), 'Cognitive Significance without Cognitive Content', in H. Wettstein (1991), *Has Semantics Rested on a Mistake? And Other Essays* (Stanford, Calif.: Stanford University Press), 132–58.

—— (1989), 'Turning the Tables on Frege, or How it is that "Hesperus is Hesperus" is Trivial', in H. Wettstein (1991), *Has Semantics Rested on a Mistake? And Other Essays* (Stanford, Calif.: Stanford University Press), 159–77.

Wettstein, H. (1998), 'Revolution in the Philosophy of Language', *Lingua e stile*, 33: 427–43.

—— (2004), *The Magic Prism: An Essay in the Philosophy of Language* (Oxford: Oxford University Press).

Whitsey, M. (2003), 'Putting Monsters into Context', MS.

Wilson, D. (1975), *Presuppositions and Non-Truth-Conditional Semantics* (New York: Academic Press).

Wilson, R. A. (1995), *Cartesian Psychology and Physical Minds: Individuality and the Sciences of the Mind* (Cambridge: Cambridge University Press).

Wittgenstein, L. (1953), *Philosophical Investigations* (Oxford: Blackwell) (referred to as *PI*).

—— (1958), *The Brown and Blue Books* (Oxford: Blackwell) (referred to as *BB*).

—— (1967), *Zettel* (Oxford: Blackwell) (referred to as *Z*).

—— (1980a), *Remarks on the Philosophy of Psychology, Volume I* (Oxford: Blackwell) (referred to as *RPP* i).

—— (1980b), *Remarks on the Philosophy of Psychology, Volume II* (Oxford: Blackwell) (referred to as *RPP* ii).

Yourgrau, P. (ed.) (1990), *Demonstratives* (Oxford: Oxford University Press).

Zahn-Waxler, C., Robinson, J. L., Emde, N. E., and Ploming, R. (1992), 'The Development of Empathy in Twins', *Developmental Psychology*, 28: 1038–47.

Index of Names

Adams, F. vii, 207, 208–11, 233–5, 351
Adams, R. M. 278, 351
Adelson, E. 248, 355
Allen, J. B. 288, 351
Almog, J. vii, 35, 351
Anketell, R. vii
Anscombe, E. 29, 178, 179, 180–6, 351
Aristote 238
Austin, D. 266, 351

Bach, K. vii, 9, 12, 72, 105, 118–9, 120, 217, 219, 351
Barcan Marcus, R. 35, 40, 45, 53, 103, 108, 351
Barker, S. vii
Baron-Cohen, S. 247, 352
Barwise, J. 16, 18, 112, 352
Batson, C. D. 243, 352
Biro, J. vii, 327, 352
Black, R. vii
Blackburn, S. 233, 351
Blakemore, S. J. 240, 352
Blair, R. J. R. 243–4, 352
Bodrozic, D. vii
Boër, S. E. 305–6, 308, 310, 312, 352
Bonomi, A. 284
Bosh, G. 248, 283, 352
Borg, E. vi, 113–14, 126, 150, 352
Bouveresse, J. vi
Braun, D. 113–14, 126, 130, 150, 336, 352
Browman, N. 286
Bryant, R. vii
Bühler, K. 4, 35, 45, 46, 50, 352
Burdick, H. 316, 352
Burge, T. 35, 43, 44, 145, 323–4, 352

Cain, M.. 230, 351
Caplan, B. 59, 361
Cappelen, H. 76–7, 274, 352
Carr, B. vi
Carston, R. vii, 10, 12, 15, 27, 72, 352
Casati, R. vii
Castañeda, H. -N. vi, ix, 30, 35, 74, 136, 141, 142, 180,
    262, 275, 277–8, 285, 292–3, 296–7, 298, 301, 310,
    330–2, 334, 344, 349, 352, 353
Charney, R. 248, 353
Chierchia, G. 279–82, 284, 312–4, 353

Chiesa, C. vi
Chisholm, R. 277, 308, 312, 329, 353
Chomsky, N. 1, 27–8, 42, 161,
Church, A. 309, 322–4
Clark, M. vii
Clements, G. 285, 290, 293–4, 300, 353
Cohen, L. J. 27, 353
Condoravdi, C. 76, 353
Cooper, R. 112, 352
Corblin, F. 7, 354
Correia, F. vii
Cottingham, J. 238, 354
Crimmins, M. 30, 264, 271, 314–15, 319, 341–3, 354
Culy, C. 285, 288, 293–4, 296, 354
Currie, G. vii, 241, 247, 253–4, 354

Davidson, D. 308, 354
Davies, M. 228–32, 241, 354
Decety, J. 240, 351
Descartes, R. 238
Dever, J. 105, 116–9, 131, 354
Devlin, K. 17, 354
Dokic, J. vi, 23, 59, 83, 86, 354
Donnellan, K. vii, 45, 63, 100–2, 129, 147, 181, 354
Dretske, F. vii, 223, 231, 255, 354
Dummett, M. 7, 48, 87, 104, 323–4, 354

Egan, F. 232, 354
Etchemendy, J. 16, 18, 352
Evans, G. 30, 48, 49, 90–1, 93–5, 99, 106, 139,
    206, 266, 354, 355

Fiengo, R. 161, 286–7, 289, 337–8, 355
Fish, W. vii, ix, 187, 354
Fodor, J. 30, 203, 230, 231, 355
Forbes, G. 316, 355
Fraiberg, S. 248, 355
Frege, G. 7, 8, 44, 45, 46, 48, 58–60, 62, 64–5, 97, 100,
    120, 181, 269, 311, 355
Fuller, G. (see Adams F.)

Ganeri, J. vii
García-Carpintero, M. 188, 336, 339, 355
Gawron, M. 76, 353
Geach, P. 106, 355

Glauser, R. vi
Goldie, P. 242, 355
Goldman, A. 241, 355
Gordon, R. M. 238, 239, 241, 253, 258–9, 355
Gorvett, J. vii, ix, 187, 354, 355
Greenough, J. B. 288, 351
Grice, P. 22, 24, 27, 72, 105, 355
Griffiths, P. 244, 355

Haegeman, L. 79, 161, 291, 355
Hagège, G. N. 285, 288, 355
Hamlyn, D. W. 242, 355
Heal, J. 241, 253, 355
Higginbotham, J. 15, 70, 286, 337, 355
Hintikka, J. 49, 92, 136–8, 356
Hobson, R. P. 176, 177, 242, 246–53, 356
Hoffman, M. L. 178, 238, 243–6, 356
Huang, Y. 25–6, 159, 161–2, 293, 296, 356
Hutchinson, W. D. 240, 356

Jackendoff, R. 83, 356
Jacob, P. vi, 71, 205, 254–55, 356
Jannerod, M. 240, 356
Jespersen, O. 35, 356
Jones, N. vii

Kaburaki, E. 297, 357
Kamp, H. 35
Kanner, L. 176, 246, 356
Kapitain, T. 349, 356
Kaplan, D. vii, ix, 3, 18, 28, 29, 33, 34, 35, 36–7, 40, 46, 47, 49, 50, 51, 57, 72, 74, 97, 101–2, 109, 113, 137–8, 148, 149, 151, 155, 174, 179, 180, 187–92, 193, 195–6, 199, 200, 2002, 265, 316, 336, 339, 356
Keller, P. vii
Ketland, J. vii
King, J. vii, 44, 112–13, 127, 131–4, 139, 150, 169, 356
Kirk, R. vii
König, E. 280, 306, 356
Koster, J. 284, 360
Kripke, S. 44, 46, 58, 61, 82, 83, 93, 99, 126, 130, 159–60, 163–4, 192, 264–5, 269, 272, 308, 325–6, 356
Kuno, S. 288, 297, 312, 356, 357

Larson, R. 106, 126, 319–20, 357
Lasnik, H. 159–60, 163–4, 357
Lepore, E. vii, 76–7, 112–13, 127, 274, 357
Levenson, R. W. 238, 357
Levinson, S. 24–5, 26, 357
Leyvraz, J.-P. vi

Lewis, D. 126, 159–60, 163–4, 277, 308, 310, 312, 357
Loar, B. vii, 216, 326–7, 357
Ludlow, P. 319–20, 357
Ludwig, K. 112–3, 127, 357
Lycan, W. G. 305–6, 308, 310, 312
Lyons, J. 5, 357

Mach, E. 174, 357
MacMurray, J. 177, 357
Marco Polo, 42
Marconi, D. vii, 52, 357
Marcus, R. B. (see Barcan Marcus, R.)
Marti, G. vii, 357
Mates, B. 145, 357
May, R. 70, 106, 161, 286–7, 289, 317, 337–8, 355, 357
McDowell, J. 30, 206, 212, 213, 214, 219, 221, 226–7, 233–5, 357
McGinn, C. 228–32, 357
Meltzoff, A. N. 240, 357
Mercier, A. vii, 42, 357
Mill, S. 60, 100,
Momtchiloff, P. vii
Moore, G. E. 179, 358
Moore, M. xiv, 358
Mulligan, K. vi, 4, 139, 358
Mumford, S. vii

Napoli, E. 43, 358
Neale, S. 105, 116, 118–9, 305, 358
Nichols, S. 249, 358
Noonan, H. 207, 358
Noordhof, P. vii

Orilia, F. ix
O'Rourke, M. ix

Pacherie, E. vi
Palma, A. vii
Partee, B. 76, 358
Peirce, 1
Pelczar, M. 35, 39, 51, 358
Pelletier, J. vii
Perry, J. vi, ix, 3, 14, 19, 28, 30, 31, 35, 36, 43, 46, 51, 57, 61, 63, 64, 65, 67, 74, 75, 82, 84–9, 105, 121, 135, 151, 164, 180, 197, 203, 213, 236, 256, 257, 264, 271, 275, 277–9, 310, 314–5, 319, 341–3, 344, 351, 354, 358, 359
Pollard, C. 283, 292, 295, 359
Popa, M. vii
Predelli, S. vi, 51, 154, 159, 162–4, 167, 192–6, 200, 2002, 359
Proust, J. vi, 251, 359

Putnam, H. 46, 82, 83, 93, 327, 359

Quentin Smith (*see* Smith, Q.)
Quine, W. v. O. 42, 238, 239, 308, 315–16, 359

Rainsbury, J. 35, 39, 51, 358
Rapaport, W. J. ix, 348, 359
Ravenscroft, I. 241, 247, 253–4, 354
Recanati, F. vi, 10, 12, 16, 18, 35, 38, 39, 72, 76–7, 95, 141, 142, 316, 359
Reichenback, R. 179, 359
Reinhart, T. 152, 284, 286, 291, 296, 302–3, 305, 312, 339, 340, 359
Reuf, A. M. 238, 357
Reuland, E. 152, 284, 291, 296, 302–3, 305, 359, 360
Richard, M. 115, 316, 342–6, 360
Rimbaud, A. 174, 187, 360
Russell, B. 8, 31, 33, 40, 48, 60, 61, 90, 95, 100, 101, 120, 135, 137, 181–2, 360

Sacks, O. 247, 249, 360
Sag, I. 283, 292, 295, 359
Salmon, N. vii, 146, 310, 322, 342, 360
Sandu, G. (*see* Hintikka, J.)
Schiffer, S. 257, 314, 319, 360
Schlenker, P. 280, 298, 360
Searle, J. 10–11, 227, 360
Segal, G. vii, 106, 126, 207, 228, 319–20, 360
Shapiro, S. C. 349
Shaw, L. L. 243, 351
Sidelle, A. 137, 168, 189–90, 360
Simner, M. L. 244, 360
Smith, A. 237, 238, 244, 360
Smith, Q. 136, 151, 152, 154–6, 167, 171–3, 192, 360
Soames, S. 146, 320, 360, 361

Sober, E. 243, 361
Soldati, G. F. vii, 361
Sorensen, R. 242, 361
Sperber, D. 10, 72, 361
Stalnaker, R. 158, 159, 361
Stanley, J. 11, 20, 77, 361
Stecker, R. (*see* Adams F.)
Stern, D. 178, 361
Stich, S. 259, 272, 361
Stotland, E. 245, 361
Strawson, P. 147, 251, 361
Swain, C. vii
Szabo, Z. 11, 20, 361

Taylor, K. 80, 361
Thau, M. 59, 361
Travis, C. 10–11, 361

Vallée, R. vii,
Vendler, Z. 241, 361
Vision, G. 189, 361
Voltolini, A. vii, 35, 51, 95, 141, 142, 361

Washington, C. ix
Wettstein, H. vi, 32, 48, 63, 93, 351, 361, 362
Whitsey, M. vi, 280, 354, 362
Wiebe, J. M. 348
Wilkerson, T. vii
Wilson, D. 10, 26, 72, 361, 362
Wilson, D. S. 243
Wilson, R. A. 206, 361, 362
Wittgenstein, L. 1, 4, 8, 31, 32, 33, 36, 39, 40, 44, 45, 47, 49–50, 52, 53, 55, 62, 67, 87, 88, 120, 178, 185, 186–7, 237, 242, 249–50, 252–3, 347, 362

Zahn-Waxler, C. 246, 362

Index of Subjects

Acceptance
 and attitude ascriptions 315–21
 of a sentence 256–62, 315–30
 of 'T'-sentences 333, 348
 neutral acceptance 260–1, 263–4, 268–73, 317–8, 321–8, 322, 324–9, 332–4, 340, 446
Acquaintance (*see also* recognition) 40, 45, 53, 54–5, 92, 93–4
 knowledge by acquaintance *vs.* knowledge by description 91
Ambiguity 7–8, 39, 43, 152, 170, 327
Analogy 242, 252
Anaphora 4–7, 25, 106–7, 126–7, 131–3, 152–3, 156–67, 172–3, 283, 286–7, 290–300, 311, 337–9
 attributive 304–5, 318
 intersentential/intrasentential 126–7, 163, 283, 286
 interpersonal 164
 unbound 161–3
 zero 24
Antecedent 25–6, 106, 156–8, 164, 283, 287, 289, 291–7, 300–6, 312, 331–2
 split 289, 331
 tacit (*see* tacit initiator/antecedent)
Autism
 and empathy 246–56
 and mastery of pronouns 176, 248, 348
 and mindreading 246–9, 250

Binding argument 76–7

Ceteris Paribus 205–6, 222, 223, 230–1, 261, 273, 341
Character 14, 35, 51–2, 64, 125, 151–73, 185–6, 189
 and competence 52, 185
 and linguistic meaning 3, 35–6, 51, 185
Cognitive
 fix 48
 significance/value 61, 62–3, 220, 264–71
 significance/value *vs.* truth-value 60, 62, 65, 221, 236
 significance and Frege's puzzle 59–60, 62, 65, 319
 particulars 261, 264, 314, 319, 341
Coindexation 157, 286, 290–1, 332, 335–9, 345
Consumerism 32, 42, 46–7, 82
Content *vs.* character 35, 114, 137–8

Context 8–9, 22, 39–40, 53, 54ff, 215
 acquisition *vs.* use 216–7
 bound 21, 347
 narrow *vs.* broad 51, 54–8
 semantic *vs.* pre-semantic use of 19, 43, 197
 post-semantic use of 18–19
 shift 246–7, 253–4, 258, 280, 324, 343, 345,
Contextual embodiment 21–3, 89
Contextualism
 radical 10, 16–19
 situational 14, 17–20, 23
Contextuals 5, 8, 12, 74–5
 vs. indexicals 3–4, 14
Conventions 28–9, 39, 41, 43–6, 51, 53, 61, 63, 64, 108, 129, 199–203, 210, 250
 and indexical interpretation 53, 195–203
Coreference (*see also* coindexation) 62, 106, 127, 286, 335–9, 345

De Dicto/De Re/De Se 144, 263, 274, 276–7, 279–81, 285, 287, 289–90, 297, 303–4, 318–9, 328–30, 344, 348
Deference 44, 46–9, 53, 93–4, 189–90, 215–16, 311–15
Deferred reference 169
Dependence Theory 286–7, 289, 301–2
Demonstratives 34–8, 92–3, 97, 100–34, 138–40, 155–6, 162, 183, 266, 268, 276
 and demonstration 36, 138, 179, 265, 339
 and directing intention 36–7, 108, 126
 and directing attention 37–8, 43–4, 54, 126, 160, 339
Descriptions 98–100, 147–50
 definite 6, 8, 60, 100, 126, 181
 incomplete 147–50
 description-names (*see also* Dname) 98–100, 107–10
 descriptive names 99, 103–7
Direct reference 32, 46, 53, 99–100, 103, 104, 108, 151, 180, 185, 236, 257
Direct realism 226–8
Distress 177–8, 243–6
Dname 98–100, 107–10
Dthat 101–2, 107–10, 125–6, 128, 148

Index of Subjects

Economy of saying principle 21–3, 25
Empathy 239–56, 315
  and distress 243–6
  and logophoricity/quasi-indexicality 292, 297–8, 305, 315
  meta empathy 245
  qua prosocial faculty 243–4, 252
Essential indexical 36, 93, 173, 277, 344
e-type pronouns 6
Evolution 229, 241, 246

Form of life 55, 87, 245, 250, 272
Folk psychology/explanation 206–7, 242
Frege's puzzle 34, 58–61, 64–5, 144–5, 220, 264–6, 269, 310–11, 319, 345
Function (*see also* character)
  proper 32–3, 61, 129

Generic names 39–41, 43–4, 52
Genuine names 48
Giorgione-sentence 315–16, 318

Hallucination (*see also* illusion) 140, 208–9, 233–5
Historical time 153–4
Homonyms 39, 41, 338
Humpty Dumpty picture 194

Identification 30, 33, 49, 58–9, 91–2, 205, 221, 265, 297
  perspectival 49–50, 58–9, 137, 149–51
Identity (*see also* coindexation) 303, 336–8
  and indices (*see* dependence theory and coreference)
  self-identity 175
  statements/utterances 58–65, 224, 265–6, 269, 335
Illusion 208, 212, 233–5
Imagination 238–56, 348
  and reports 238–9, 246, 259
  and transference 241–6, 259, 348
Indeterminacy 12–13, 289–90, 319, 331–2
Individualism/externalism (*see* object dependent/independent)
Inferences 121–2, 335–46
  and *de se* reading 282
  and attributions 335–46
  strict *vs.* sloppy 282
Information/thought
  anchored *vs.* unanchored 33–5, 47, 58–9, 90, 95
Innateness 244
Internal relation 44–5, 62
Irreducibility Thesis 277–8

Kripke's puzzle 269–70, 272–3, 322, 325–6

Language-game 55–6, 61, 62, 72, 78, 86, 88, 89, 94, 196, 242, 249, 252
Logical form (LF) 70–1, 80, 82–4, 165, 298, 314–15, 316–21, 333–4, 343, 346
  interpreted 319–20
Logophoricity
  logophoric pronouns 2, 285, 288, 290–300, 315
  logophoric pronouns and quasi-indicators 2, 290–300
  logophoric trigger 296
  logophoric center 300

Mental states types *vs.* tokens 257, 261, 263–71
Mentalese 208
Meta-linguistic 64–5, 322, 326
Millianism (*see* direct reference)
Mimicry 244–5
Mindreading 246–7, 348
  impairment (*see* autism)
Mode of presentations (*see also* senses) 182–3, 214–18, 221

Narrow/wide scope 132–3, 150–1

Opacity/Transparence 290, 309–10, 329, 330–3
  propositional 289, 330–3

Perception 221, 222–9, 266–8, 344–5
  and demonstratives 44, 47, 92, 138–9, 169, 264–6, 345
  content *vs.* state 223–4, 226
  of pain 240–6, 251–2
Perspective 92, 137, 177, 218–20, 222–6, 241, 247–8, 267, 292, 298, 327–8, 347, 348
Point of view (*see also* perspective) 137, 218, 224–5, 265, 292, 302, 347
  and logophoric pronouns 295
Pragmatics
  and anaphora 245
  vs. semantics 7–27, 72, 120, 124, 130, 279, 309–11
  presuppositions 158
Presuppositions 56, 71, 89, 157–8
  and communication 54–5
Principle A 161, 283, 291–2, 294
PRO 279–81, 297, 311–12, 314
Pro 282
  pro-drop language 79, 282
Proper names 33–64, 68, 90–5, 181–3, 186
  and contextuals 4–5
  and descriptions 108

368 Index of Subjects

vs. generic names 39–41, 43–4, 52
vs. indexicals 4, 33–58, 68, 89–95, 107–8, 289
Pronouns 110–12, 113, 160, 288
  first person 176–202
  reflexive (see reflexive pronouns)
Pure indexicals 35–8, 138–40, 155–6, 160, 162, 179, 265–6, 268–9, 276

Quasi-Indicators 154, 277–307, 309–12, 331–5, 348
  and essential indexicals 277–8
  and logophoric pronouns 276, 290–300, 311, 315

Reactive cry 177, 244
Realism
  direct 226–7
  critical 226
Recognition (see also acquaintance) 90–1, 92, 95
Referential/attributive distinction 100, 108, 129, 130, 148
Reflexive pronouns 175–6, 280, 284–6, 288–95, 297–8, 303–6, 337
Richard's Puzzle 342–6
Rigid designator 101–2
Russell Principle 48–9, 90–4
Russellian though (see object dependent)

Scope (see narrow/wide scope)
Semantics
  innocence 311
  vs. pragmatics (see pragmatics vs. semantics)
  vs. meta-semantics 57–8
Senses (see also modes of presentation)
  de re 206, 212, 221
  Fregean 60, 61, 62, 180–2, 185, 257
Self
  anaphors 302–4, 306
  attributions 256, 258–9, 313–14, 330, 343–5
  reference 323–4, 344–5
Simulation (see also imagination and transference) 249, 258–9, 348
  theory 239
Singular propositions 3
Sloppy/strict interpretation (see also inferences sloppy/strict) 282, 312–13
Split antecedent 289, 331
Substitution salva veritate 305, 316, 328, 332
Synonymy 323–4, 328

Tacit
  antecedent/initiator 6, 157–8, 164–5, 169
  belief 263
  knowledge 61–2
  reference (see also unarticulated constituents) 68, 164–5, 184–5, 311, 314–15
Temporal
  indexicals 140–1, 153–6
  terms 141–7
Theta role/mark 73, 79–80, 164–5
Thought
  dynamic 225
  object dependent/independent 206–22, 225–30, 231, 233
  singular (see object-dependent)
  situated 17, 83, 89, 95, 222–3
Translation 145, 208, 271–3, 320–8
  and Church's argument 272, 322–4
  and Kripke's puzzle 272–3, 324–5
  and Twin-Earth 321–8, 327–8
Transference 241–55, 348
Transparence 124, 329–30
  propositional 330–3
  vs. opacity 255–6, 329–30
Truth
  and propositions 16–21
  situated 18–19, 71, 222–3
  T-schema 15, 19, 71, 85, 87
Twin-Earth 180, 202, 204–5, 214–18, 224–5, 228–30, 327–8, 340
  and object-dependent thought 211–16, 224–5, 327
  and translation 328

Unanalyzability thesis 301–2
Unarticulated constituents 67, 75, 83–4, 88, 164, 218–19, 225, 314–15
Undeterminacy 21, 69, 71, 73, 165

Validity
  logical vs. psychological 339–46
Violence Inhibiting Mechanism (VIM) 243–4
VP deletion 133–4

What is said 9–12, 16, 19, 22, 24, 38, 49, 56, 61, 64–5, 69, 127, 130, 147, 149, 151, 219
What is believed 290